AF560745

THE MARCH TO PAKISTAN
1937–1947

Pathway to India's Partition

Volume III

The March to Pakistan 1937–1947

BIMAL PRASAD

Issued under the auspices of the
Rajendra Prasad Academy, New Delhi

MANOHAR
2016

First published 2009
Reprinted 2016

© Bimal Prasad, 2009

All rights reserved. No part of this publication may be reproduced or transmitted, in any form or by any means, without prior permission of the author and the publisher

ISBN 81-7304-247-0 (Series)
ISBN 81-7304-250-0 (Vol. III)

Published by
Ajay Kumar Jain *for*
Manohar Publishers & Distributors
4753/23 Ansari Road, Daryaganj
New Delhi 110 002

Typeset at
Digigrafics
New Delhi 110 049

Printed at
Salasar Imaging Systems
Delhi 110 035

Contents

Preface

THIS VOLUME, A CONTINUATION of the earlier two volumes, deals with the final phase of the history of Muslim nationalism in India which witnessed its success in carving out Pakistan, a separate, sovereign State, based on the Muslim majority areas of India. For this, it had to wage a bitter struggle under the dynamic and devoted leadership of Jinnah. The volume shows that Jinnah is deservedly called Father of the Nation in Pakistan and all the recent attempts to show that he was not keen on Partition and that it was really forced upon him by the stupid tactics followed by the Congress leadership are without any basis in facts. The volume also seeks to throw light on the valuable support extended to Jinnah by the British, of course, in their own interest and not for any love for either Jinnah or the Pakistan idea.

In the end I must apologize to the readers for the long delay on my part in completing this volume. This was caused partly by the sudden passing in August 2001 of my wife who had been the main source of inspiration and strength behind all my scholarly endeavours and who had particularly been pushing me to give priority to this work. Occasional bouts of ill health also came in the way of timely completion of this work. Besides, even while working on this volume, I had to pay attention to another labour of love; editing of the *Selected Works of Jayaprakash Narayan*. It is not a mere coincidence that the last (tenth) volume of that publication is going through the press at exactly the same time when the present work is passing through the same state.

In the absence of my wife, our three children—Jayant, Sujata and Sanjay—and their spouses—Bunty, Trips and Sangita—rendered me all possible help and support and went on encouraging me not to be deterred by old age and ill health but continue with my self-imposed assignments. By insisting on my staying with one or other of them, as per convenience, they kept me free from all worries relating to house-keeping and enabled me to concentrate, as before, on study and writing. Sujata went a step further and, in spite of being extremely busy with her own official duties, shared my pains in going through the proofs of this volume. I am grateful to all of them.

I must also thank my friend, Professor Margaret Chatterjee, for constantly nagging me to complete this volume and for valuable advice on aspects of my work.

Srimati Sangita Mallik, Research Officer at the Rajendra Prasad Academy, provided me all necessary assistance and support. I am thankful for to her for this.

At the end, I must thank Ms Laina A. Kumar for attending to all the secretarial work in connection with this volume, with perseverance and devotion.

I shall be failing in my duty if I do not thank my publisher, Sri Ramesh Jain, and his staff, particularly Sri Bansi Ram, for their kindness and patience in dealing with me at every stage during the long period the project lasted.

BIMAL PRASAD

Introduction

AS NOTED IN THE previous volume, the idea of Pakistan had been born by the 1920s in the Punjab and aired fairly widely in the press in the 1930s, particularly after the forceful exposition of it in 1933 by Choudhary Rahmat Ali, a Punjabi Muslim student at Cambridge. It has also been noted that although that idea was not then supported, at least publicly, by any important leader of the Muslim League or of any other party claiming to speak on behalf of the Indian Muslims, the most important among such leaders, M.A. Jinnah, permanent president of the League, had become a convert to it along with Muhammad Iqbal, the greatest poet-philosopher of Muslim nationalism, at least by May–June 1937, if not earlier. The present volume deals with the movement for the fruition of this idea and the creation of Pakistan, by dividing India, in the course of the next ten years.

Again, as already noted, Iqbal was impatient and wanted a conference of north Indian Muslims to be summoned in 1937 itself, presumably as a launching pad for a movement for Pakistan. However, Jinnah, being a shrewd and experienced politician, counselled caution and patience on the ground that Muslims were not by then properly organized and disciplined. He made it his task first to remove this lacuna as far as possible. He apparently thought that the League must emerge as a powerful organization, owning the allegiance of Muslims in all parts of India, particularly in the Muslim-majority areas, before coming out with such an ambitious objective.

The League's position in Indian politics after the elections of 1936–7 was not enviable. It had not done well at all in those elections, winning only 108 out of 482 Muslim seats all over India. Bengal was the only Muslim-majority province where it had won a sizeable number of seats, but even there it had not won the majority of Muslim seats and had to be content with entering into a coalition headed by Fazlul Huq, the leader of the Krishak Proja Party, which had secured a larger number of Muslim seats. In the Punjab, the League had secured only one seat and the ministry there was headed by Sikander Hyat Khan, the leader of the Unionist Party, the majority of whose members were Muslims, with a sprinkling of some Sikhs and Hindu Jats. Sind also had a non-League, though Muslim-dominated, ministry. In the North-West Frontier Province (NWFP), in spite of its overwhelming Muslim population, the Congress, thanks to the leadership of Khan Abdul Ghaffar Khan, had emerged as the largest party in the assembly and was soon able to form a ministry under the leadership of his brother, Dr Khan Sahib, with the cooperation of some non-Congress members. The League had done better in the Muslim-minority provinces. However, it had been able to secure a majority of Muslim seats only in Bombay. In UP, just as in Bengal, it had won a substantial number, but not a majority, of Muslim seats. It was keen to join a coalition headed by the Congress in both Bombay and UP, and thus secure a foothold in the two ministries, but as a result of the then Congress policy, it failed in that endeavour. On the other hand, the Congress, although securing only twenty-six Muslim seats all over India, had secured a majority of seats in six Hindu-majority provinces and emerged as the largest single party in another two, one of them being a Muslim-majority province (NWFP). This enabled it to ultimately form ministries in eight out of eleven provinces of India. Even before the formation of the ministries, the Congress, upset by its abysmal performance in the elections, so far as the Muslim seats were concerned, had launched a programme of Muslim mass contact in order to draw more Muslims to its ranks. This project seemed to be initially succeeding in some provinces. The League leaders in various provinces were worried that if that trend continued, the very existence of their organization would be seriously threatened. This further strengthened the atmosphere of gloom and despondency in the League circles, already unhappy at the emergence of Congress rule in the majority of provinces, which they regarded as pure and simple Hindu rule, something deeply abhorred by them.

In such an atmosphere it was indeed a daunting task to revamp the League, turn it into a really representative organization of Muslims all over the country, particularly in the provinces where they constituted a majority of the population, and thereby enable it to acquire a position from which to credibly demand the partition of India and the carving out of a separate, sovereign

Muslim-majority State. However, Jinnah, the supreme leader of the League, proved equal to this task. He realized that the despondency among Muslim ranks as a result of the Congress' rise to power, constituted not merely a challenge but also an opportunity. For there was only one all-India body, the Muslim League, to which Muslims could turn in order to counter-balance the Congress. Muslim alienation from the Congress, present since long, had further deepened. The main problem was to bring them all under the umbrella of the League. Jinnah realized that this objective could be achieved best by strongly attacking the Congress, painting it as the enemy of Muslims, and intensifying the campaign to inculcate among the latter a strong consciousness of a separate nationhood. Such a policy was by no means new and had been part of the dominant Muslim leadership's stance in Indian politics initiated by Syed Ahmad Khan since before the birth of the League. What was new was the vigour with which it was pursued now and the strength it acquired in the post-1937 years because of the then prevailing political situation in the country and the leadership of Jinnah and his indefatigable exertions for the cause in which he had come to believe. Just past sixty in 1937, and steeled by a series of unhappy experiences in private as well as public life, he now worked in politics with a passion he had never shown before and was determined to succeed in achieving his goal, regardless of the difficulties in the way. No lure of office or power could deflect him from his chosen path. With this passion and steadfastness, he combined a deep understanding of the shifting political situation and a mastery of political strategy, in which he was second to none in Indian politics. His greatest asset was that he gradually came to acquire a firm grip over the pulse of the Muslim intelligentsia and youth, and indeed of a growingly large section of the politically conscious Muslims all over the country. This assured him wide public support in whatever he said or did during the decade 1937–47.

II

Jinnah's presidential address at the Lucknow session of the Muslim League on 15 October 1937 marked the beginning of the implementation of his two-pronged strategy—an attack on the Congress and an intensified appeal to the feeling of Muslim nationhood.

The wild enthusiasm that his address aroused among the delegates showed that it represented their heartfelt sentiments. Mounting a strong attack on the Congress leadership on the alleged ground of its efforts to impose Hindu culture on the Muslims in the shape of the Hindi language and the *Vande Mataram* song, Jinnah declared: 'On the very threshold of what little power and responsibility is given, the majority community have clearly shown their hand: that Hindustan is for Hindus.' As the Punjab premier, Sikander Hyat Khan, reported to his Governor, the feeling of resentment against the Congress among the delegates and leaders present at Lucknow was much stronger than even Jinnah represented it to be. More and more speeches expressing similar feelings followed Jinnah's address. Indeed, it was Sikander's estimate that feelings against the Congress had risen so high that if any Congress leader had appeared at the scene, he would have been in danger of being lynched. Sikander's testimony is quite important for it shows that the war on the Congress, which Jinnah launched at Lucknow, had the strong backing of the thousands of Muslims who were present there. Indeed, strong anti-Congress feelings among the latter must have been present even before they arrived at Lucknow. Another notable event at Lucknow was the announcement by the Muslim premiers of the Punjab, Bengal, and Assam—not till then members of the League—of their decision to join that organization. While the tremendous boost that it gave to the prestige of the League as well as to the morale of its cadres has generally been noted, what needs to be really underlined is that it signifies the widespread feeling of concern among Muslims at the rise of the Congress as also of the urge for solidarity among themselves at the all-India level even before the Lucknow session. For such an important decision as joining the League could not have been made by the premiers on the spur of the moment without any deliberation before hand. Jinnah's address at Lucknow is remarkable not only for expressing the widespread anger and resentment among the Muslims against the Congress, but also for exhorting his followers to organize their strength if they wanted to be treated seriously by the majority community and to achieve their destiny as a nation. Emphasizing that they were at that time facing immense difficulties, he advised them not to be disheartened but to face these difficulties bravely with their true conviction and loyalty. If they did so, he had no doubt that they would give birth to a nation 'worthy of its past glory and history', and with its future history being 'greater and more glorious not only in India, but [also] in the annals of the world'.

The Lucknow session of the League proved to be significant in various other ways too. In order to attract the new generation of Muslims, the League now changed its objective to the achievement of 'full independence', thus using words which reflected its determination to maintain its separate identity by not adopting the words 'complete independence' which had been declared the objective of the Congress in 1929. Besides, showing its concern for the position of Muslims in a new constitutional set-up, its resolution on this subject declared that full independence should be in the form of a federation of free and democratic states in which the rights and interests of the Muslims and other minorities were adequately and effectively safeguarded. It is also significant that Maulana Zafar Ali Khan, while seconding the resolution, declared that India did not comprise a single nation; if that were so, according to the principles of democracy, the Muslims would always be at the mercy of the majority community. In order to strengthen the League's appeal to the masses, the Lucknow session asked the Working Committee to take immediate steps to frame and implement an economic, social, and educational programme with a view to improving the lot of the common people working as labourers and farmers. With the same objective in view, the annual membership fee of the League was reduced from one rupee to one-eighth of its value, i.e. two *annas*. In all these ways, the Lucknow session represented a landmark in the evolution of the League.

There was no turning back for either the League or its supreme leader after Lucknow. Buoyed by the enthusiastic response from his audience at Lucknow, Jinnah soon undertook a tour of northern India, visiting both big and small towns, not merely reiterating what he had said at Lucknow but also reinforcing his message with some new points wherever he went. The basic point, of course, remained the same: the Muslims must organize themselves by coming under the banner of the League if they wanted to save themselves from Hindu tyranny. Thus, while addressing a meeting of Muslims at Patna on 25 October, Jinnah drew attention to the plight of the depressed classes among the

Hindus and warned the Muslims that if they did not systematically build up their own organization, they, too, would be reduced to the same position. Inaugurating a conference convened by the All India Muslim Students Federation at Calcutta on 27 December, he declared that if he was dubbed a communalist for demanding a rightful place for Muslims in government and other spheres, he pleaded guilty to the charge. Proceeding again to Bihar, he observed on 1 January 1938 at a meeting of Muslims at Gaya that the flag of the League was the flag of Islam, for the former could not be separated from the latter. At another meeting at the same place, while explaining why the Muslims must have special safeguards in the constitution to protect themselves, he remarked that there was nothing in common between the Hindus and Muslims. Both at Gaya and a day or two later at Calcutta, he placed before the Muslims for their inspiration the achievements of the Prophet, who had begun his preaching when he was the lone Muslim and exhorted them to learn from that and concentrate on organizing themselves, stressing that unless they did so, they were doomed to a life of serfdom and subjection in India. He spoke in the same vein while addressing meetings at Allahabad, Delhi, and Aligarh in the following weeks.

The subsequent years witnessed a further hardening of both Jinnah's anti-Congress stance and his determination to instil among the Muslims of India a feeling of solidarity and a consciousness of their separate destiny, based on their own strength. This is amply illustrated by the perusal of his opening address to the League sessions at Calcutta (17–18 April 1938), Karachi (Sind Provincial Conference, 8 and 9 October 1938), at Patna (26–29 December 1938). Everywhere, the emphasis was on the grievances of Muslims under Congress rule and the hope that the Muslims, by their united endeavours, would achieve their destiny and secure a position of power for themselves. The League's resolutions adopted by all its sessions echoed the sentiments expressed by Jinnah, and again and again drew attention to the grievances of Muslims under Congress rule. A number of committees were appointed to go into them and their findings invariably affirmed those grievances. Most of the grievances were either fictitious or based on exaggeration. They certainly did not bear close scrutiny by the concerned Governors and the Viceroy, no sympathizers of the Congress. However, all the Muslim grievances were not purely imaginary. Whatever they might have been, the important thing is not the nature of those grievances, but the fact that larger and larger numbers of Muslims, not all of them belonging to the League and some of them holding distinguished positions in public life, went on to believe in their genuineness. The state of their feelings against Congress rule is best testified by the fact that almost all the by-elections to Muslim seats in the Provincial Assemblies between 1937 and 1938 were won by the League candidates. It is not surprising, therefore, that Jinnah asked in the course of his concluding remarks at the Patna session of the League held in December 1938: 'What had happened to the Congress Muslim Contact Programme?' There could, of course, be no other answer to this except that the campaign had miserably failed.

This was fully realized by the Congress leadership and, as mentioned in the previous volume, the cell or department for it in the office of the All India Congress Committee was unceremoniously abolished and ceased to exist. The main factor responsible for this was the lack of a sufficiently large number of Muslims in the ranks of the Congress to carry out that programme at the grass-roots level and the consequent lack of interest in it among the Congress leaders, except perhaps Nehru. The level of the latter's interest is also not clear in view of the fact that although he was its founder, after being informed about its fate during his European tour in 1938 by K.M. Ashraf, in-charge of that programme, Nehru hardly did anything to get it restored or revived. By that time perhaps he, too, had come to realize that the gap between the Congress and the majority of Muslims had become too wide to be bridged by the programme that he had fathered. The efforts of the Congress Working Committee to clarify its stand on various issues of concern to Muslims such as the controversy between Hindi and Urdu, the use of the song *Vande Mataram* at gatherings sponsored by the Congress, and the position of minorities in free India, also did not produce any positive result. Hindu–Muslim tension and riots grew month by month, particularly in the Congress-governed provinces in north India such as Bihar, CP, and UP.

Faced with such a situation, the Congress leadership, in contrast to its earlier stance, came to the conclusion that perhaps a dialogue with the League leadership might provide a solution to the Hindu–

Muslim problem. There were preliminary meetings and correspondence between Gandhi and Jinnah, between Nehru and Jinnah, and between Bose and Jinnah, but they all utterly failed in preparing the ground even for the start of such a dialogue. For Jinnah, with the full backing of his Working Committee, laid down a condition, which the Congress was asked to fulfil before the talks could start and the Congress expressed its unwillingness to do so. The condition was that the Congress must agree that the League was the representative organization of Muslims all over India and that the former represented the bulk of the Hindus. The Congress leadership explained that if their organization accepted the League's condition, it would amount to giving up its claim to be a national organization, representing all sections of the people living in India and would reduce its status to that of a purely Hindu organization. So the talks could not make a start and the communal situation all over the country continued to deteriorate. The only result of the efforts to start the talks was to add to the stature of Jinnah as a Muslim leader at whose doors some of the tallest Congress leaders were repeatedly knocking, in spite of his firm refusal to dilute in any way the condition he had laid down for the start of a Congress–League dialogue.

The basic factor conditioning Jinnah's attitude was the fact that the League was making huge gains among the Muslim community by continuously attacking the Congress as a Hindu organization engaged in oppressing the Muslims, and he saw no advantage to be gained by muting that campaign, which would be a natural concomitant of an agreement with the Congress. There was also the fact that the attitude of the Muslim community regarding the issue of its future role in India was yet to fully crystallize and there was hardly any matter of substance—apart from the language controversy, *Vande Mataram*, and such other items—affecting its interests or ambitions on which meaningful negotiations with the Congress could be carried on. It is not, therefore, surprising that while the Gandhi–Jinnah talks were going on with a view to the starting of a formal dialogue between the two, neither the senior British officials, including the Viceroy, nor such senior leaders of the League as Sikander Hyat Khan in the Punjab and Nazimuddin in Bengal, felt that those talks were likely to lead to any positive result. And so they proved to be.

III

s unrelenting war on the Congress and
by its leadership on the separate nationhood
despread interest among the Muslim elite—
belonging to the League—in the creation of
significantly contributed towards preparing the
e adoption by the League of the demand for Partition.
previous years, the lead in this respect was taken by
ary Rahmat Ali, whose interview carefully elucidating
kistan proposal and forcefully justifying it on the basis of
two-nation theory appeared in the famous Turkish writer,
alide Edib's, *Inside India*, published in 1937. Although that book was published in London, it can be safely assumed that the topic of Ali's interview as also his arguments in favour of the creation of Pakistan became fairly widely known in elite Muslim circles and formed the subject of animated discussions among them, both orally and through the columns of newspapers, some of whose contents have been cited in the second chapter of this volume. Several books also appeared in India on this theme. Even though all of them did not suggest outright partition, they ardently championed the two-nation theory and stressed the urgency of devising a new political structure based on it.

Thus, Syed Abdul Latif in his pamphlet, *The Cultural Future of India* (1938), pleaded for the division of India into fifteen cultural zones, with a central government with limited powers, implying a rejection of the Pakistan idea. However, he supported the two-nation theory in as strong a language as Rahmat Ali and pleaded that the differences between Hindus and Muslims were so deep that there was no basis for the concept of a single nationality. Indeed, Latif had begun with supporting the two-nation theory in his pamphlet and then proceeded to outline a constitutional plan based on a united India, though with a weak central authority. On the other hand, A Punjabi (a pseudonym, actually Kefayat Ali), in his *Confederacy of India* (1939), first outlined a constitutional scheme based on a united though confederal India, consisting of five federal units, and then devoted the major portion of his book to supporting the two-nation theory and emphasizing the necessity of separating the Muslim-majority areas of India from the Hindu-majority ones. Indeed, the kernel of his argument was that Muslims constituted a separate [illegible] by themselves, with hardly anything in common between [illegible] and the Hindus.

There were others who did not make a secret of their u[illegible] dislike of a united India, on however tenuous a basis, and ope[illegible] advocated the setting up of a separate federation based on th[illegible] Muslim-majority provinces in the north-west of India, especially if the Congress-governed provinces did not improve their functioning in matters affecting Muslim interests. Influenced by the persistence of such ideas, as reflected in the writings in the contemporary Muslim press, some British observers of the Indian political scene came to the conclusion by 1938–9 that a free India was not likely to remain a united one and in fact two nations were already struggling within its womb. Such observers were influenced in their thinking by the widespread feeling prevailing among a growing section of the Muslim intelligentsia at that time. The thoughts and yearnings of the latter were given concrete shape by two professors of the Aligarh Muslim University—Syed Zafarul Hasan and Mohammad Afzal Kadri—in their scheme of partition forwarded to Jinnah in the latter half of January 1939. That was based on the clear assumption that the Muslim-majority areas, both in the north-west and in the north-east, must be separated from the rest of India and constituted into sovereign States. While it was not yet clear whether the Muslim intelligentsia as a whole stood for such a scheme, it seems reasonable to assume, on the basis of writings in the press, that the attractiveness of the Pakistan idea was definitely growing among them. The open espousal and elucidation of the two-nation theory by V.D. Savarkar in the course of his presidential addresses to the annual sessions of the Hindu Mahasabha between 1937 and 1939 also helped that process by making the Muslim elite realize that the Hindus were aspiring for freedom on the basis of the strength of their own nationality, leaving no scope for an honourable place for Muslims in an independent India, particularly because the Muslims had been dubbed by Savarkar merely as a community in contrast to the Hindus who were, according to him, a nation. Hindustan, Savarkar asserted, was the land of Hindus and it was the Hindu nation which owned it. The leaders of the Rashtriya Swayamsevak Sangh (RSS) publicized more extremist ideas. Although the following of the RSS was even more limited than that of the Hindu Mahasabha, itself not enjoying the support of a majority or even an appreciable section of the Hindus, the ideas propounded by them must have raised serious doubts in the minds of the Muslim intelligentsia about their safety and well-being in a united India. Such doubts must be counted as another factor in strengthening the already growing attraction for the concept of Pakistan in the minds and hearts of the Muslim elite.

IV

This applied also to the leadership of the Muslim League. While Jinnah had already been converted to the Pakistan idea and was only waiting for a suitable opportunity to plead for it publicly, among other League leaders opinion on the issue seems to have been divided for quite some time. Almost all of them, of course, ardently believed in the two-nation theory and desired a new constitutional framework based on it. However, while some thought that the objective might be secured by endowing the Muslim provinces with substantial powers under a very weak central government, some others looked forward to the partition of India and the carving out of it of a fully sovereign Muslim-dominated State (or States). Sikander Hyat Khan articulated the former view and the Sind leader Yusuf Haroon the latter.

The proceedings of the Sind Provincial Conference of the League held at Karachi in October 1938 is the earliest indication that those who were for outright partition were gaining ground. A motion was formally placed before the conference on behalf of the provincial leadership of Sind, recommending that the All India Muslim League devise a constitution providing for the establishment of a sovereign State consisting of the Muslim-majority areas of India. However, as Jinnah, and presumably other prominent leaders of the League present there, did not consider the time opportune for such a resolution, the motion was modified to a mere mention of the existence of two nations in India and a recommendation to the All-India Muslim League to review and revise the entire conception of a suitable constitution for India in which both of them could have an honourable place.

Action immediately followed on that recommendation. The annual session of the League held at Patna in December 1938 adopted a resolution, jointly drafted by Jinnah and Sikander, reiterating the view expressed by the Lucknow session (1937) that the scheme of Federation embodied in the Act of 1935 was not acceptable and authorizing the President of the League to take steps to explore the possibility of devising a suitable constitutional scheme to replace it. It was a cautious move designed by the League leadership to gain time for deliberation as well as to satisfy the growing clamour of those who wanted an immediate declaration in favour of Partition. That Jinnah was still vacillating between immediately demanding Partition or settling for the time being for some constitutional arrangement under which the League might be able to balance the strength of the Congress is revealed by what he told the Viceroy towards the end of February 1939. While he did not reject the federal idea, observed Jinnah, he wanted a Federation which would ensure 'an equipoise between Muslim and Hindu votes'. At the same time, he kept open the option of Partition by remarking to the Viceroy that his project for 'the carving out of this country was a better one than Sikander's'. Needless to say, while Sikander's plan envisaged the setting up of seven federations of provinces and states under a central government with minimal powers, thereby avoiding Partition, Jinnah was obviously thinking of something beyond it. The issue was formally discussed by the Working Committee of the League at Meerut on 26 March 1939. It was decided to appoint a sub-committee headed by Jinnah to consider all the schemes of Partition then under circulation or any new scheme which might be brought out. These were in due course circulated to the provincial branches, which were asked to submit their suggestions by August 1939, to be considered at the next meeting of the sub-committee scheduled to be held in October 1939. By that time, however, a new situation had emerged in India consequent on the outbreak of World War II in the first week of September and the declaration by the Viceroy that India had become a belligerent in that war on the side of Britain and the other Allied powers.

During the five months or so between the meeting of the League Working Committee at Meerut and the outbreak of World War II, opinion among the League leadership continued to be divided as before. Basically, it involved a difference between those who wanted the substance of Pakistan within an Indian Union with minimal powers of the Centre and those who wanted Partition and the setting up of a sovereign Muslim-majority State. Jinnah, whose opinion, of course, would be most decisive, was keeping silent. He explained his difficulty in supporting or opposing any scheme on the ground that as president of the League it was not proper for him to take sides. There were enough hints, however, to indicate what he really wanted. Thus, he told the Viceroy in the latter half of March 1939 that although in the recent past he had supported the introduction of constitutional reforms on the basis of democratic principles, he had come to the conclusion by that stage that a democratic system of government could not work in India. He reiterated this view, with stress on the two-nation theory, in the course of a speech delivered at a meeting of Muslim students in Bombay in the middle of August 1939.

In the light of the expression of such views by the most powerful League leader, both the British and the Congress circles began to feel that India would soon have to face the issue of Partition. Thus, Linlithgow wrote to the Governor of Bihar in January 1939 that the Pakistan proposition could not be pushed aside as Congress would be inclined to think. Actually, however, G.D. Birla, one of the leading industrialists in India, who was quite close to Gandhi and several other top leaders of the Congress, surprised the Viceroy in February 1939 by his view that the setting up of a federation consisting of Muslim-majority provinces in the north-west of India might ease the communal situation in India. This perhaps represented only the views of some of the leading business and industrial houses in India, but not that of the Congress leadership. Gandhi, for instance, told Linlithgow on 15 March 1939 that, according to him, the creation of Pakistan could never solve the communal problem and he doubted whether it would withstand any detailed examination. Even he, however, felt that the Pakistan movement had wide possibilities and, though having no life in it at that time, might acquire it in certain circumstances.

In spite of such forebodings, Linlithgow continued to believe that there was no way the Muslims could prevent the introduction of the Indian Federation once a sufficient number of rulers, as specified in the Government of India Act of 1935, agreed to join it. Zetland, the Secretary of State for India, however, thought differently. He had long since held the view that Muslim solidarity was a hard fact against which it was futile to strike one's head.

By 1938 he had definitely come to the conclusion that the Muslim opposition to Federation could not be ignored. Linlithgow, however, continued to argue that once a sufficient number of rulers agreed to join the Federation, it would not be possible for the League, however opposed to it, to thwart its inauguration.

V

There was a dramatic shift in Linlithgow's role after the outbreak of World War II in the first week of September 1939, mainly because of the new political situation emerging in India in its wake. The Congress adopted the stand that, while it sympathized with Britain and its allies, India's resources in men and money could not be utilized for British war purposes without the consent of the Indian people. This was accompanied by the clear assertion that such consent could not be forthcoming until the British clarified their war aims and explained how they were to apply to India. If the British were fighting for freedom and democracy, affirmed the statement on the war crisis issued by the Congress Working Committee on 14 September 1939, India would be deeply interested and would like to do what it could to assist Britain and its allies, but it would like to be assured that those principles would also apply to India, and do so not in a distant future but in the immediate present. Neither the Viceroy nor his superiors in Britain were prepared to oblige the Congress. On the contrary, they were determined to stick it out in India as long as they could. In contrast to the Congress standpoint, the Working Committee of the Muslim League in its statement issued on 18 September declared that its sympathies were on the British side, but it could not really offer full cooperation with the war effort until the British provided full protection to the Muslims in the Congress-governed provinces through the exercise of the special powers of the Governors and the Governor-General and agreed to scrap the federal scheme of the Act of 1935 and devise a new constitutional system for India under which Muslim interests could be safeguarded. It did not take much time on the part of the Viceroy to conclude that in the context of the developing political situation in India, the Muslim League could become their invaluable ally in stemming the tide of Indian nationalism spear-headed by the Congress. Such an alliance would be particularly useful in meeting the criticism at the bar of British and American opinion that Britain, though fighting a war in Europe as a champion of democracy and freedom, was denying freedom to India. For the British Government could plausibly affirm that it was keen to transfer power to Indian hands, but in view of the sharp division of opinion between the Congress and the League, representing the two dominant communities in India, it did not know to whom to transfer power. Jinnah on his part at once grasped the nature of the British predicament and realized that the British could be safely relied upon in that situation to further the League's interests. This was the background of the emergence of a virtual Jinnah–Linlithgow Axis within a few months of the outbreak of World War II.

The emergence of such an axis is fully borne out by the Viceroy's record of his talks jointly with the Congress and League leaders on 2 and 3 November 1939, followed immediately by his separate conversation with Jinnah on 4 Novermber. At the tripartite meeting, while the Congress leaders pressed the Viceroy for a firm British declaration in favour of India's freedom with immediate transfer of effective power to Indians, Jinnah flatly refused to support such a demand until the Muslim grievances in the provinces were removed and the Congress agreed to share power with the League at the provincial level. On 4 November, in his exclusive interview with Jinnah, the Viceroy thanked the latter profusely for his strong stand against the Congress during the tripartite talks and unambiguously stated that but for that stand the British would have had to face an extremely tricky situation. Jinnah, forgetting his past as an Indian patriot, gracefully accepted the Viceroy's gesture and emphasized the need for the British and the League to stand together against the Congress, which he described as the common enemy of both. At the same time, he took the opportunity to press for an assurance that the British would not agree to any new constitutional set-up without the consent and approval of the League. The Viceroy, of course, found it difficult to immediately give such an undertaking, for it would amount to giving the League a veto on future constitutional development in India. However, Jinnah persisted on this point and next day (5 November) he sent a letter to Linlithgow asking for a clear British assurance on the following two points: (i) the entire problem of India's constitution would be considered *de novo* after the end of the war or sooner, if possible, and (ii) that no new constitutional arrangement for India would be considered without the approval and consent of its two major communities, implying, of course, a virtual veto for the League on the future constitutional development of India.

In the context of the developing political scenario in India, with the Congress having withdrawn its ministries in the various provinces in protest against the British policy and continuing to press its demand for immediate independence, the Viceroy became more and more convinced that the British must give due importance to the League's stand. Muslims, the Viceroy argued in his long letter running into about eighteen pages to the Secretary of State dated 29 November 1939, had not only a large population in India—80 or 90 million—but also a substantial presence in the Indian armed forces and had, besides, close links with the Muslim countries in West Asia. Their views, therefore, required the most careful consideration as it was essential in the British interest to keep them politically satisfied. The Home Member of the Government of India and the Director of Intelligence, whom the Viceroy had consulted, were both in favour of such an approach. With further such pleadings, the British authorities in London also finally came a round to the Viceroy's views.

The result of these consultations was conveyed by the Viceroy to Jinnah on 23 December 1939, with definite British assurances on the two points raised by the latter on 5 November. With regard to Jinnah's first point, the Viceroy pointed out that the declaration of British policy made by him on 17 October did not 'exclude examination of any part either of the Act of 1935 or of the policy and plans on which it was based'. This meant that the constitutional future of India would be wide open after the end of the war and any plan, including the one that the League might like to promote, could be considered in that connection. On the second point, Linlithgow made it clear that the British Government was fully conscious of the importance of the contentment of the Muslim community to the success and stability of any constitution in India.

In the meanwhile, Jinnah had gone on refusing to cooperate with the Congress leadership in putting up a joint front before the British for the declaration of India's independence, making such a front conditional upon the League's grievances in the provincial field being removed and the way cleared for the formation of Congress–League coalition ministries therein. Gandhi, Nehru, and the then Congress President, Prasad, all knocked at his doors, but in vain. Nehru, getting a hint from a common friend that Jinnah was interested in a Congress–League understanding, again started correspondence with him with a view to finding out the exact nature of the League's grievances and demands, but that, too, did not produce any positive result. On 8 December while Nehru was preparing to write to Jinnah to settle a date for their discussion, he saw an item in the daily press reporting that Jinnah had called upon his followers to celebrate Deliverance Day on 22 December by expressing their happiness at the end of Congress rule in the various provinces. That ended all prospects for the time being of any Congress–League talks and Nehru, with full support from Patel and Prasad, immediately called off his projected meeting with Jinnah. Nehru's attitude could not have worried Jinnah in any way. Indeed, it is quite possible that he had called for the celebration of Deliverance Day precisely in order to underline the League's distance from the Congress for, as Jinnah saw it, the League's interest lay not in forging an understanding with the Congress, which would bring to an end its growing understanding with the Government, but in cementing its relationship with the latter.

The Viceroy's letter of 23 December containing valuable assurances, received on the morrow of the celebration of Deliverance Day, further strengthened the Jinnah–Linlithgow Axis and at the same time gave a further boost to Jinnah's leadership of the League. Although not expressing full satisfaction with the Viceroy's assurances and asking for more clarity on the second point in Jinnah's letter of 5 November the League now proceeded more confidently than ever before towards redefining its objective under Jinnah's leadership. The process already in motion in this regard was now further accelerated and Jinnah encouraged that trend without any hesitation. That the redefinition was going to be in terms of creating a Muslim-majority sovereign State or States had been clear for quite some time. At the same time Linlithgow now became more and more eager to strengthen the League's position in the eyes of the British and American public opinion so as to bolster Britain's position in India, for it could then argue, much more plausibly than ever before, that the British were not opposed to the immediate transfer of power to Indian hands, but in view of the widening gulf between the Congress and the League, did not know how to do it. Linlithgow further realized that the League's position abroad could not improve until it gave up its purely negative approach of just opposing the Congress and the growth of democratic institutions in India and came out with a positive objective of its own. He would have perhaps preferred, as he had confided to Sikander, if such an objective could be somehow defined within the framework of an all-India federation of some sort with limited powers in the hands of the Centre. Even when, however, he realized that Jinnah, backed by a majority of the members of the League's Working Committee, favoured Partition, he persistently kept on emphasizing to Jinnah that the League must come out with its own positive scheme as soon as possible. This prepared an ideal background for the League's adoption of the demand for Partition and Jinnah, always alive to the possibilities in a given situation, confidently went ahead. The timing of the adoption of the famous Lahore Resolution demanding Partition on 24 December (not 23 December as is commonly believed), preceded by Jinnah's forceful exposition of the two-nation theory in his presidential address, was the result of this convergence of interests between the League and the British Government. The history of India now took a different turn, with a grave threat hanging over the prospect for a united India.

The adoption of the Pakistan Resolution was generally greeted with a chorus of disbelief in the seriousness of its promoters to really pursue the objective enshrined in it. This was true of both the critics and admirers of the League as also independent observers of the political scene in India. Nehru, of course, brushed it aside as a mad scheme but at the same time observed that it showed what the League was actually driving for. Others generally believed that Jinnah could not have been serious in pushing through such a resolution. This was partly due to their ignorance of what had been going on in the mind of the Muslim intelligentsia and youth since the late 1920s, and their inclination to stick on, regardless of recent political developments as well as changes in Jinnah's thinking, to their old image of him, cherished over several decades. That was the image of Jinnah as an ardent Indian patriot who, even though following a path different from the Congress and indeed leading an avowedly communal organization, was second to none in his desire to see India free from foreign rule as soon as possible and had also been trying to build bridges between the League and the Congress with that aim in view. A rumour going around in political circles, supposedly based on Jinnah's own remark to some friend in Lahore, that the Pakistan Resolution was merely a bargaining counter, was like the sound of music to such persons, who eagerly lapped it up and continued to believe in it for quite some time. Indeed, some people in both India and Pakistan even now continue to do so. The one person who was not influenced by such thinking in 1940–1 was Tej Bahadur Sapru, an eminent liberal leader and a former member of the Viceroy's Executive Council. After a very short period in the beginning when he, too, believed in the bargaining-counter theory, he came to the conclusion that the achievement of Pakistan had become the new passion in Jinnah's life.

Sapru, being a veteran public man and, even when out of active politics, a shrewd observer of the Indian political scene, was quite right in his prognosis. Regardless of how others considered the Pakistan Resolution, once it was adopted, Jinnah never looked back and applied himself assiduously to imparting credibility and legitimacy to the demand for Partition. All his subsequent statements and activities fully testify to this. In spite of his advanced age (64) and indifferent health, he visited almost all parts of India by turn propagating his new message—freely laced with references to Islam and its legacy—and emphasized wherever he went that the Muslims constituted a nation of their own, separate from Hindus and others in India, and must have their own separate homeland or State. This was, he further emphasized, not an empty dream, but a fully realizable objective if only the Muslims remained true to their glorious legacy, believed in their destiny, and became united under the League's flag. The extremely enthusiastic response he received wherever he went worked as a tonic on him and confirmed him in his view that the goal set by the Lahore Resolution represented the deepest yearnings and aspirations of almost all Muslims in India. Indeed, such was the mass enthusiasm for Jinnah now that he was greeted everywhere as the *Quaid-i-Azam*, the great leader. For the first time, he emerged as a really charismatic leader whose word was like the divine gospel, which had to be followed till the goal of Pakistan was achieved regardless of the difficulties in the way. Those who even now continue to harbour the thought that Jinnah was not serious about the creation of Pakistan may go through the texts of his speeches between 1940 and 1942, which have been liberally cited in this volume, and examine whether they were the words of a clever lawyer preparing the ground for bargaining for some more rights for his community within a united India or those of an inspired leader who had deep faith in the goal that he had set before his people at Lahore.

Jinnah's main purpose behind his post-Lahore endeavours was obviously to end the myth that the Pakistan demand was a mere bargaining counter and to mobilize more and more popular support for it. While in his public speeches he mainly appealed to the sentiments of Muslims, in private conversations with influential persons, whether Indians or foreigners, he generally appealed to reason and cogently argued why it would not be in anyone's interest, whether in matters relating to national defence or peace within the country, to yoke together in one State two peoples as different from each other not only in religion, but also in historical traditions, cultural moorings, and social customs as the Muslims and the Hindus. In the course of his presentations, Jinnah freely admitted that both India and Pakistan would have minorities within their States—mainly Muslims in India and Hindus in Pakistan—but argued that once Pakistan was created this would no longer create insurmountable difficulties. Whatever the nature of Jinnah's arguments, the important point is not their validity or otherwise, but the persistence with which they were carried out, showing that Pakistan had indeed become the passion of his life.

In his efforts to impart credibility and legitimacy to the demand for Partition, Jinnah received valuable help from the British side. His axis with Linlithgow remained operational in full force. Linlithgow had, of course, no love either for the Pakistan Resolution, which he thought could not stand any independent scrutiny, or for the personality and tactics of Jinnah, whose diplomatic skill as well as fastidiousness regarding his dignity while dealing with the former, appeared to Linlithgow as showing arrogance and very much irritated him. However, he remained as convinced as ever before that Jinnah was playing a role in Indian politics which ideally suited British interests at that particular juncture in the context of the worsening war situation and the growing pressure from the Congress side, with sympathetic echoes in Britain and the USA, for a British declaration assuring independence at the end of the war and the immediate transfer of substantial power to Indian hands. So Linlithgow made it his task to ensure that though his higher authorities in Britain disliked both the demand for Partition and the personality and tactics of Jinnah, nothing was publicly said by or on behalf of them that might amount to pouring cold water on either. For in Linlithgow's eyes, the two went together and the credibility of the one was inextricably linked with that of the other.

Linlithgow fully succeeded in his endeavours and indeed was able to see to it that the British authorities took positive steps to bolster up Jinnah's leadership. The task became easier for him after a change in the composition of the British Cabinet in May 1940, with Winston Churchill heading a national coalition government and L.S. Amery as the Secretary of State for India. Since long Churchill had not made a secret of his belief that it was not in British interests to try to bring the Hindus and the Muslims together, who once united would show them the door. Amery, though not as much a hardliner as Churchill in dealing with the Congress, ardently believed, in spite of his scepticism in the soundness of the Pakistan scheme, in the utility of Linlithgow's policy of bolstering up the leadership of Jinnah in British interest. In fact, in this respect, both at the time of the August Declaration of 1940 and the formulation of the Plan that was carried to India by Stafford Cripps, a member of the British Cabinet, in March 1942, becoming famous as the Cripps Plan, Amery went much beyond Linlithgow's advice in satisfying Jinnah. The August Declaration granted a virtual veto to the Muslim League on any constitutional advance in India and the Cripps Plan, through its clause on the provincial option, that is, the option of a province to remain out of the proposed Union of India if it so desired, for the first time accepted India's partition in principle.

Needless to say, such steps gave an invaluable boost to Jinnah's leadership as well as to the legitimacy of the League's demand for Partition with which he was closely identified. In between the two occasions, Linlithgow in 1941 helped strengthen Jinnah's leadership of the League by constantly advising Sikander, either directly or through the Punjab Governor, not to do anything that might weaken Jinnah's leadership or create a split in the League. Linlithgow followed this policy in spite of frequent annoyance at Jinnah's behaviour because of his conviction that the existence of a strong political organization of Muslims was essential in order to counter-balance the Congress and that there was no real substitute for Jinnah so far as the leadership of the League was concerned.

Ironically, the Congress Working Committee, too, contributed significantly to the credibility or legitimacy of the Pakistan demand by its stand on the Cripps Plan. For, while describing the clause relating to the provincial option to keep out of the proposed Indian Union as 'a severe blow to Indian unity', it went on to observe that it could not think 'in terms of compelling the people of any territorial unit to remain in the Indian Union against their declared and established will', subject to the condition that it would not involve the coercion of any group of people to go to Pakistan against their wishes. This was a clear indication that the Congress, in spite of all its rhetoric against Partition, would regretfully accept it if the majority of the people in any area backed the demand for it. Actually, Nehru had in the course of a private conversation indicated to a retiring British civilian, Malcolm Darling, even before this, on 24 April 1940, shortly after the adoption of the Pakistan Resolution by the League, that while he was opposed to Partition, he would accept it if the alternative to it was continuation of British rule.

While the Congress showed its preparedness to agree to Partition if there was no other way to achieve independence, there was at least one prominent non-Muslim leader, B.R. Ambedkar, well known for his deep scholarship as well as his championship of the rights of the depressed classes among Hindus, who pleaded for the acceptance of the demand for Partition. In a fair-sized book on the Pakistan demand published in early 1941, he supported the two-nation theory as eloquently as Rahmat Ali and Jinnah were doing and argued that the acceptance of the demand for Partition was in India's own interest from the point of view of both its national defence and maintenance of peace and order among its inhabitants.

VI

What has been written in the just concluded section should make it clear that the League's demand for Partition had acquired considerable legitimacy by the middle of 1942. However, it had a long way to go before it could actually be achieved. For this the most important factor was going to be sufficiently strong support for it among the overwhelming majority of the politically conscious sections of the Muslim population. By 1942, there were indications of such support in the provinces where the Muslims were in a minority, but the situation was different in the provinces where Muslims were in a majority. The League was neither in a strong position in any one of them nor had the demand for Partition evoked any widespread interest or support therein. This situation drastically changed in the next three years.

Among the factors that brought about this change mention may first be made of the exertions of Jinnah, of course, with due support from the majority of his colleagues in the League. He realized that his dream for the creation of a sovereign Muslim State could not be realized until it had become the dream also of Muslims in those parts of India where they constituted a majority. Without it the Pakistan demand would remain a non-starter. So he continued his marathon tours in various parts of India, particularly in the Muslim-majority areas, addressing large congregations of Muslims, trying to strengthen further their consciousness of separate nationhood and underlining the creation of Pakistan as the only viable solution of their problems. Pakistan, according to Jinnah, represented their destiny as well as deliverance and only through it could they live with honour and dignity. Contrary to what is generally assumed, he did not make any effort to hide the fact that all Muslims could not be accommodated in Pakistan and that most of the Muslims who were living in the Hindu-majority provinces would have to continue to do so, but reminded them of the sacrifices they had made for the Muslim nation in the past and expressed the hope that they would not mind a little more sacrifice in the interest of their brethren in the majority areas acquiring sovereign Statehood. He further reminded them that there would be Hindu and Sikh minorities also in Pakistan and assured them that suitable arrangements for safeguarding the interests of all minorities whether in India or Pakistan would be worked out by the two countries on a reciprocal basis.

Jinnah also continued his war on the Congress without any let-up and indeed fully utilized the situation created by the Quit India call to the British by the Congress, under Gandhi's leadership, the mass arrests of Congress leaders and workers and the popular upheavals which followed in their wake in August 1942, to further intensify that war. He described the Quit India movement as directed not towards freeing India from British rule, but towards establishing Hindu Raj all over India and on this ground asked the Muslims to strictly keep aloof from it—something he had never done earlier at the time of any movement launched by the Congress. Many of his non-League admirers in India, both Hindus and Muslims, were quite puzzled by such a change in Jinnah's attitude. This was, of course, mainly the result of their nostalgia about Jinnah's earlier phase as an Indian patriot, and their refusal to face the reality that Jinnah by 1942 was exclusively engaged in a fight to carve out a separate, sovereign Muslim State out of India and had completely left his past behind. Whatever that may have been, Jinnah's stand towards the Quit India campaign served a double purpose. First, nothing inspired and energized the bulk of Muslims in India more than an attack on the Congress, which they had by then come to regard as a purely Hindu body functioning under the cloak of nationalism. Second, Jinnah's bitter attack on the Quit India movement and his complete silence on the atrocities committed by the British forces in quelling it served the purpose of cementing further the League's unwritten alliance with the British and also raised Jinnah's stature in the latter's eyes.

The marathon Gandhi–Jinnah talks held in September 1944 (shortly after Gandhi's release from detention in Poona) formed a landmark in the League's march to Pakistan. The talks were held intermittently for three weeks (7 to 26 September) during which Gandhi called on Jinnah at his mansion for as many as fourteen times without the latter paying a single return visit to Gandhi, who was staying at the Birla House on the same Malabar Hill Road in Bombay on which Jinnah lived. What was even more significant was that the talks were held on the basis of a formula evolved by C. Rajagopalachari (one of the senior-most Congress leaders and a close confidant of Gandhi), which conceded the creation of Pakistan in principle though with provision for common arrangements for the administration of such subjects as defence, foreign relations and commerce. Although Jinnah rejected that formula, there could be no doubt that the Gandhi–Jinnah talks added considerably to his prestige and also to the legitimacy of the demand for Partition. What could be of a greater value in this respect than the news, widely publicized by almost all Indian newspapers, that the C.R. formula had the open blessings of Gandhi, the top-most Congress leader and revered as a Mahatma by millions and millions of Indian people, who, in spite of his strong opposition to the two-nation theory, had repeatedly gone to Jinnah pleading for that formula on bended knees? This was particularly valuable to Jinnah as he had recently failed to bring the Unionist Ministry in the Punjab headed by Khizr Hayat Khan Tiwana under the control of the League and indeed had suffered a strong rebuff at the latter's hands, causing a severe setback to his prestige.

This was not the end of the efforts by the Congress leaders to somehow make a start with Congress–League cooperation. Where C.R., in spite of his high stature, had failed, a much lesser known person, Bhulabhai Desai, leader of the Congress party in the Central Legislative Assembly, hoped to succeed. In January 1945, he was able to come to an agreement with Liaquat Ali Khan, General Secretary of the All India Muslim League and Deputy Leader of the League Party in the Legislative Assembly (Jinnah himself being the leader), for breaking the political deadlock in the country. The agreement provided that the Congress and the League would cooperate in forming a national government within the existing constitutional framework. Desai had obtained Gandhi's approval for this and had been assured by Khan that the latter, too, had secured the approval of Jinnah. When, however, the Desai–Liaquat Pact, as it came to be called, was featured in the press, Jinnah disclaimed all knowledge about it, and seeing his attitude Khan also firmly disassociated himself from it and even denied, falsely of course, that he had ever signed it. So the Desai–Liaquat Pact was stillborn. It had, however, made its contribution to further strengthening the position of both Jinnah and the League in Indian politics. For it stipulated that the national government would be formed on the basis of parity between the Congress and the League representatives therein. It further stipulated that constitutional government would be restored in the provinces at that time under Governor's rule under Section 93 of the Act of 1935 through the setting up of Congress–League coalitions. Needless to say, both these provisions had constituted the key demands of the League since 1940.

What the Congress could do to satisfy the League, the British could do better. This became clear at the conference of prominent political leaders in India summoned by the Viceroy, Lord Wavell, on 25 June 1945 at Shimla in order to consider the British Government's plan, popularly known as the Wavell Plan, for breaking the Indian political deadlock. The plan envisaged the reconstitution of the Viceroy's Executive Council by having on it only Indian political leaders, except the Commander-in-Chief. The membership of the Council was to be based on parity between the caste Hindus and Muslims. However, Jinnah was not satisfied merely with such parity and insisted on all the Muslim members of the Executive Council belonging to the Muslim League. On the other hand, the Congress was claiming for itself at least one out of the five Muslim seats. The same was the demand of the Unionist Party. The Viceroy had no difficulty in ignoring the Congress claim, but was quite keen to nominate a representative of the Unionist Party. However, Jinnah remained firm till the end on his stand. The Viceroy, acting on behalf of the British Government, did not consider it prudent to go ahead with reconstituting the Executive Council without the League's cooperation, even though at that time it had control over only one ministry in a Muslim-majority province (Sind), and announced the failure of the Simla Conference. Nothing could have been of greater value to the League at that critical juncture when major political changes were in the offing and it was seriously engaged in establishing its dominant position in the Muslim-majority provinces. The proceedings of the Simla Conference gave a clear signal to all concerned not only that no constitutional advance in India was possible without the cooperation of the League but also—even more important—that no Muslim politician could look forward to holding any important position or office in the Government unless he or she belonged to the League or enjoyed its patronage. This gave a powerful momentum to the Pakistan movement in the Muslim-majority provinces, where something like a stampede began among aspiring Muslim politicians to jump on the League's band–wagon. It had the most visible, immediate impact on the situation in the Punjab, where the League was then engaged in a bitter struggle to replace the Unionist Ministry by its own.

The failure of the Unionist Ministry at Shimla, in spite of the full backing of the Punjab Governor, to secure a seat for its representative in the Viceroy's Executive Council showed in bold relief that when matters really came to a crunch no Muslim party other than the League could prove effective at the all-India level—a situation that was bound, sooner or later, to be reflected at the provincial level also. The leading landlords in the province, the mainstay of the Unionist Party, naturally concluded that they could no longer bank on the latter for government patronage on a long-term basis. This was one of the key factors in enabling the League to soon emerge as the dominant political force among the Muslims in the Punjab, a matter of crucial importance in the creation of Pakistan.

Similar was the impact on other Muslim-majority provinces like Sind, the North-West Frontier Province, and Bengal, which—with the largest Muslim population in the whole of India—was second in importance only to the Punjab in the League's scheme of things relating to its struggle for Pakistan. In all these provinces, the Pakistan movement had already been gaining ground since 1942, partly with the Governors' helping hands to the League in forming governments whenever possible. This fact was absent in the Punjab, where not the League but the Unionist Party, because of its major contribution to the war effort, enjoyed the Governor's patronage. In spite of the Governor's patronage of the Unionist Party, however, the growth of the Pakistan movement in the Punjab was as spectacular as in other Muslim-majority provinces. We must take note also of the fact that the League's influence and with it the growth of the Pakistan movement in Bengal and the NWFP took the greatest strides not when the League's Ministries were in office, but when they were not.

It should thus be clear that although the role of the Governors of the Muslim-majority provinces minus Punjab in advancing the cause of the League forms a part of the historical record and cannot be ignored in any account of the period, its contribution to the growth of the League's influence in those provinces was not really significant. The latter was the result primarily of the phenomenal growth of the Pakistan movement in all the Muslim-majority provinces under the leadership of Jinnah, who visited them again and again with the message of Pakistan, representing their deliverance as well as their destiny. This message was carried to almost every Muslim household by the large network of branches of the League covering all parts of the country, including the Muslim-majority provinces. The Muslim students in the seats of higher learning—such as the Aligarh Muslim University—described by Jinnah more than once as 'the arsenal of Muslim India'—the Islamia College at Lahore, and the University of Dhaka—also played a significant part in the growth of the Pakistan movement by visiting the remotest parts of the Muslim-majority provinces as messengers of the Pakistan idea. The shift in the loyalty of the big landlords, consequent on the collapse of the Simla Conference, to the League not merely in the Punjab but also in other Muslim-majority provinces in the north-west, in order to safeguard their interests, played even a more important part in the growth of the Pakistan movement. In Bengal, which did not have many such landlords among Muslims, the dream of Pakistan as the harbinger of the end of all exploitation of the Muslim peasantry, was carried to every nook and corner of the province as a result of the exertions of the dynamic leadership of the League at the middle level in that province headed by Abul Hashim, the new general secretary of the League there.

The massive electoral victory of the League in the elections of 1945–6, ordered by the new Labour Government in Britain, can be understood only against the background of the growth of the Pakistan movement. From the point of view of the League, the results of the elections, as is well-known, were impressive beyond measure. Out of a total of 102 seats in the Central Legislative Assembly, the League won all the 30 seats earmarked for Muslims, securing over 86.6 per cent of the votes cast, with many non-League candidates losing their security deposits. In the provincial elections the League's tally was equally impressive though not exactly identical: in the Punjab, it won an overwhelming majority of Muslim seats—75 out of 86. A little later that figure rose to 79 with some newly elected members changing their party loyalties. In Bengal, the League did even better, securing 113 out of 116 Muslim seats. In Sind, the League's score was 27 out of 35 Muslim seats. The NWFP was the only Muslim-majority province where the League could not win a majority of Muslim seats, but only by a narrow margin and had to be content with 17 to 19 for the Congress. However, even there if the long Congress hegemony under the extraordinary leadership of Khan Abdul Ghaffar Khan is kept in view, the League's performance looks impressive enough. In the Muslim-minority provinces' the League's performance touched the sky, except in Bihar and UP, where its tally was not so high, though it still won a clear majority, indeed two-thirds, of Muslim seats in both of them. Thus, it won 31 out of 34 Muslim seats in Assam, 30 out of 30 in Bombay, 29 out of 29 in Madras, 4 out of 4 in Orissa, 13 out of 14 in CP and Berar, 34 out of 50 in Bihar, and 54 out of 66 in UP.

The significance of the League's tally of Muslim seats cannot be overestimated, especially as Jinnah had emphasized again and again during the election campaign that the elections would mean a referendum among Muslims on the issue of Pakistan and that their outcome would decide its future. The results of the elections showed that the overwhelming majority of the Muslim electorate in all parts of India, with the sole exception of those living in the NWFP, were clearly in favour of Pakistan. The path to Pakistan was now wide open, if only the League remained determined till the end to achieve it. For in that case there was no way to prevent the creation of Pakistan. The British were not prepared to leave India without a Congress–League settlement and if the League remained firm on its demand for Pakistan, the only way open to the Congress to achieve independence would be to reconcile itself to the creation of Pakistan. The League remaining firm, the only question remaining to be settled was whether it would be full Pakistan as the League wanted or Pakistan minus the non-Muslim-majority areas in the Punjab and Bengal, which the Congress was not prepared to allow to be taken to Pakistan against the wishes of the people inhabiting them. The following fifteen months were devoted to wrestling with this problem in some form or the other.

VII

The process began with the arrival, in March 1946, of the Cabinet Mission, dispatched by the British Government in order to work out a solution to the Indian constitutional problem in consultation with the Congress and the League. According to the directive of the British Cabinet, the Mission was to try first for a solution on the basis of a united India. However, if that did not seem possible, a solution might be worked out on the basis of Partition, provided both the main parties in India agreed to it. The members of the Cabinet Mission were Lord Pethick Lawrence (Secretary of State for India), Sir Stafford Cripps (President of the Board of Trade), and A.V. Alexander (First Lord of the Admiralty). After long discussions with the Indian leaders, mainly belonging to the Congress and the League, separately and also together, the Mission came to the conclusion that there was no way out except to give an award themselves and invite the Congress and the League leaders to offer their cooperation. This they did through their statement issued on 16 May 1946.

Here they put forward their considered views regarding the best course to ensure the setting up of a Constituent Assembly, representing all sections of the Indian people, with a view to framing a new constitution based on independence as also the formation of an Interim Government consisting of representatives of the major political parties to carry on the administration while the constitution was being framed. In that connection, the statement pointed out, the Mission and the Viceroy had seriously considered the fundamental issue of the unity or division of India. Their conclusion was that, apart from the supporters of the League, there was a universal desire to maintain the unity of India. On the other hand, the Mission was also impressed by the genuine anxiety of Muslims about the prospect of their being placed under a permanent Hindu-majority rule. It, therefore, considered in depth the possibility of recommending the creation of Pakistan. First, it considered the creation of a full, independent Pakistan as desired by the League, i.e. a Pakistan consisting of all the four Muslim-majority provinces in the north-west and two in the north-east, only one of which (Bengal) had a Muslim majority. It rejected this proposition on two grounds. First, as it would contain within its borders a large non-Muslim population, it would not provide a solution to the communal problem. Second, it could not see any justification for including in a sovereign Pakistan those areas in the Punjab as also in Bengal and Assam where non-Muslims were in a majority. The Mission then considered the possibility of a smaller sovereign Pakistan consisting only of those areas in the north-west and the north-east of India where the Muslims were in a majority. This was, however, turned down by the League on the ground that it would entail the exclusion of large areas from Pakistan. The Mission, too, did not favour the partition of the Punjab and Bengal as each one of them had its own distinctive culture and tradition. It felt, therefore, forced to conclude that neither a larger nor a smaller sovereign State of Pakistan would provide an acceptable solution to the communal problem. The Mission also mentioned various administrative, economic, and strategic considerations that stood in the way of the creation of Pakistan and expressed its inability to recommend the handing over of power to two entirely separate sovereign States.

The Mission, however, went on to emphasise that it was not blind to the very real apprehensions on the part of Muslims that their culture and political and social life might become 'submerged in a purely unitary India', where the Hindus, because of their larger numbers, were bound to be the dominant element. The Mission also did not consider practicable or adequate the suggestion made by the Congress that the Muslims' apprehensions might be taken care of by having compulsory and optional lists of subjects at the Centre in order to enable any province, if it so wished, to enjoy greater autonomy by opting for central jurisdiction over only the compulsory subjects. It, therefore, decided to offer its own recommendations for the basic form of the Indian constitution which, in its opinion, would do justice to the essential views of all parties and would at the same time be most likely to bring about a stable and practical constitution for India.

According to the framework of the new constitution proposed by the Cabinet Mission, there was to be a Union of India with limited powers, i.e. confined to defence, external affairs, and communications, with the power to raise financial resources for managing them. All the other powers were to be vested in the provinces. In addition to the Union and the provinces, there would be another unit of government—a group of provinces. There would be three groups of provinces—one in the north-west, the other in the north-east and a third, including the rest of the provinces. A province would be free to join a group of its choice. While this indicated a preference for provincial autonomy, in the procedure suggested for the Constituent Assembly (which was to be elected by the provincial assemblies and not through adult franchise in order to save time), it was suggested that this body, after disposing of some preliminary business, would be divided into three sections representing the three sets of provinces, one Hindu and two Muslim—one in the north-west and the other in the north-east—grouped on the basis of the communal composition of their populations. The sections would be free to form groups and assign defined powers to the latter. This provision at once became a bone of contention between the Congress and the League. On the one hand, the Congress stuck to the principle of provincial autonomy and contended that compulsorily herding the provinces together, first in sections and then in groups, violated that principle, which had been made an essential part of the framework suggested by the Cabinet Mission. On the other hand, the League insisted on the compulsory grouping of provinces, which apparently gifted it the substance of the full Pakistan desired by it though, of course, without sovereignty. Another major bone of contention related to the formation of the Interim Government consisting of representatives of the major political parties. The League demanded parity between its nominees and those of the Congress and the latter strongly opposed it. In addition, while the League insisted that no Muslim not being a member of the League should be appointed a member of the Interim Government, the Congress insisted on appointing at least one Muslim out of its quota of members of that government.

In spite of these differences, both the Congress and the League accepted the Cabinet Mission's statement of 16 May, with, of course, their own respective reservations and interpretations. While the League had accepted the long-term proposals of the Cabinet Mission as early as 6 June 1946, the Congress delayed its acceptance till 25 June, when it finally conveyed its acceptance purely on tactical considerations. However, the Congress on that day also conveyed its rejection of the short-term plan of the Cabinet Mission relating to the formation of the Interim Government, to consist of fourteen members—six from the Congress, including a representative of the Scheduled Castes, five from the League, and three to represent the small minorities like the Sikhs, Parsis, and Indian Christians. The League was not aware of the Congress decision, and after waiting till the night of 25 June it conveyed to the Viceroy its acceptance of the short-term plan also, hoping that it would be in a position to dominate the Interim Government in the absence of Congress. This hope was based on a recent undertaking by Wavell that if any of the two parties did not accept the Cabinet Mission Plan he would constitute the Interim Government with the representatives of the party which had accepted it. Even after the League was made aware that the Congress, too, had accepted the long-term plan of the Mission, the League did not withdraw its claim, arguing that the Congress resolution on that subject was so hedged about by reservations and its own interpretations that it did not really amount to acceptance. The Viceroy in reply contended that the League's resolution, too, was similarly hedged about and so he could not proceed to constitute the Interim Government without having in it representatives of the Congress.

Thus, failing to gain its short-term objective of emerging as the dominant partner in the Government and utilizing that position to hasten the march to its ultimate goal (Pakistan), the League leadership decided to change its strategy. This is amply borne out by the text of Jinnah's letters to Prime Minister Attlee and the leader of the Opposition in the House of Commons, Churchill, on 6 July 1946, expressing his extreme displeasure at the British policy at that stage and warning that the Muslims would be ready to shed their blood if required to achieve Pakistan.

It is significant that these letters were sent on 6 July a day before the meeting of the All India Congress Committee at Bombay and four days before the press conference in Bombay where Nehru is generally supposed to have made remarks which led the League to withdraw, on 29 July, its earlier acceptance of the Cabinet Mission Plan and to decide on a plan of Direct Action to achieve Pakistan. Actually, in the League's resolution containing the decision regarding the former, the attitude of the British Government in refusing to install a League-dominated Interim Government as per its supposed word given earlier was mentioned first and the attitude of the Congress only after it. However, this was soon forgotten thanks perhaps to the subsequent League propaganda in which, for obvious tactical reasons, the main emphasis was placed on the Congress attitude as allegedly revealed by Nehru's remarks in Bombay and partly to the unfounded observations contained in the supposed memoirs of Azad, published after his death, the impression was created that it was Nehru's performance in Bombay which was the primary cause of the League's withdrawal of its acceptance of the Cabinet Mission Plan. This is indeed a remarkable illustration of how sometimes in history fact is superseded by fiction. Actually, Nehru, even though using rather sharp language, had not said anything that was not contained in the resolutions of the Congress and Azad's own comments on the Cabinet Mission Plan.

The same phenomenon of fiction superseding fact is revealed

by the remarks of those, including Azad, who have criticized Nehru for his utterances in Bombay mainly on the ground that they really put paid to all chances of retaining a united India. This is based on a purely imaginary assumption, namely, that by accepting the Cabinet Mission Plan, with its own interpretations, and agreeing to go into the Constituent Assembly, the League had jettisoned its goal of Pakistan. Even a cursory perusal of the text of the resolution adopted by the League's Council on 6 June, accepting the Cabinet Mission Plan, and of the speech delivered by Jinnah on that occasion—which emphatically affirmed the decision to go ahead determinedly with the struggle for the achievement of full Pakistan without any let or hindrance—will show that there is really no basis for such an assumption except wishful thinking and ignorance of the mainsprings of the League's policies and actions at that time as well as of the unflinching determination of its supreme leader to lead it to its goal adopted in 1940 under his own guidance.

VIII

While the League was planning to chart out a new strategy to achieve its goal, the British authorities were keen to revive their efforts to set up an Interim Government as soon as possible. After a good deal of discussion among themselves, the Viceroy, as authorized, wrote identical letters to Nehru and Jinnah, as presidents respectively of the Congress and the League, on 22 July 1946, seeking their cooperation in the formation of an Interim Government consisting of fourteen members. Out of these, six (including a representative of the Scheduled Castes) were to come from the Congress side, five from the League, and three were to represent the minorities like the Sikhs, Parsis, and Indian Christians. Nehru replied immediately, raising the question of the status of the Interim Government and observing that until this was resolved in such a way as to treat that Government as a Cabinet, there was no chance of the Congress considering the Viceroy's proposal favourably. Jinnah replied on 31 July, two days after his Council had withdrawn its acceptance of the Cabinet Mission Plan and decided upon a plan of Direct Action, asking for strict parity between the Congress and the League and an assurance that all Muslims to be appointed to the Executive

Council would belong to the League. After some time, the British adopted a slightly different approach, transferring the task of dealing with the League to the Congress. On 6 August 1946, Wavell wrote to Nehru as Congress president to submit a panel of names for appointment as members of the Executive Council and suggesting that he might have a discussion with Jinnah before submitting his panel. Perhaps seeing in this procedure a new approach that might have a positive bearing on the status of the Interim Government, Nehru forgot his earlier stand and decided to talk things over with Jinnah. After an exchange of not quite cordial correspondence, Jinnah agreed to see Nehru and they did meet, but without any positive result. Jinnah obviously, as was only to be expected, was not enthusiastic about the League joining the Interim Government at the invitation of the Congress. Besides, Nehru, despite all his sweet, persuasive talk regarding the need for Congress–League cooperation, was not prepared to accommodate Jinnah on his demand that the Congress should not insist on nominating a Muslim, even though out of its own quota, for the membership of the Interim Government. Wavell continued to try to persuade Nehru to accommodate Jinnah somehow, especially after the 'Great Calcutta Killings' in the wake of the celebration of Direct Action Day by the League on 16 August, but Nehru thought that any effort to appease Jinnah was likely to aggravate the situation further.

Under the circumstances the British decided to go ahead with the formation of an Interim Government on the basis of the panel submitted by Nehru without any representatives from the League. The decision to do so was announced by Wavell on 24 August. However, he felt most unhappy at the prospect of dealing with a Congress-dominated government, without the presence of an effective balancing factor in the shape of the League, and was also convinced that the communal situation would go on deteriorating in the absence of any reconciliation between the Congress and the League. He, therefore, went on trying to persuade the Congress to somehow accept the League's terms in order to secure its cooperation. When all his efforts failed to produce the desired result, the Interim Government, with Nehru as vice-president (the Viceroy himself being the president) and several Muslim members in addition to prominent Congress leaders as members, was finally sworn in on 2 September.

This was, however, not the end of the story. The Viceroy remained obsessed with the problem of bringing the League representatives into the Interim Government. While using the danger of growing communal violence as his chief argument in his conversations with Nehru, he more than once conveyed to the Secretary of State for India his great discomfort and distress at having to deal with an Interim Government dominated by the Congress alone. On the other hand, Nehru was quite happy with the then existing situation and conveyed his view more than once to Wavell that there was no urgent need to talk to Jinnah in order to persuade the League to join the Interim Government. As for the growing communal tension, Nehru's view was that the Interim Government was quite capable of dealing with any communal trouble fomented by the League. With Wavell persisting with his entreaties, Nehru one day lost his cool and told the Viceroy that while he himself did not see any need to approach Jinnah at that time, if Wavell wanted to talk to Jinnah about it, no one could prevent him from doing so. Wavell took full advantage of Nehru's remark and immediately invited Jinnah for a discussion. The latter had perhaps already realized that it was not in the interest of the League to remain out of the Interim Government and responded positively. The two men had several rounds of discussions. Wavell's line of argument was that in the interest of the League itself, it was necessary for it to join the Interim Government and not remain out of it. Jinnah, as behoved a tactician of his calibre, even though appreciating Wavell's logic, did not show any eagerness to follow his advice and raised a number of questions. The Viceroy showed his inability to persuade the Congress not to keep a Muslim in the Interim Government out of its own quota, but on all other points, with the full, though grudging, cooperation of Nehru, he accommodated Jinnah. As things were moving towards a conclusion, Gandhi opened a dialogue with Jinnah, which was continued by Nehru. However, it was too late to produce any positive result, especially as both sides were still full of suspicion and distrust of each other. This gave Wavell a chance to regain his initiative. After further haggling for a few days on certain minor points such as the portfolios to be allotted to the new entrants, the League members finally took their seats in the Interim Government on 26 October 1946, not on the basis of any understanding with the Congress, but purely on the basis of the Wavell–Jinnah talks. This did not augur well for any improvement in Congress–League relations.

IX

Actually, there was no chance for such an improvement in relations. Wavell's correspondence with Jinnah and summaries of their talks on the eve of the League's entry into the Interim Government make it clear that this was not the objective on the part of either. Wavell had tried to persuade Jinnah, though the latter being a shrewd tactician had already been convinced without mentioning it to Wavell, that joining the Interim Government was primarily in the interest of the League itself and would help preserve its supreme position in Muslim politics. Out of his keenness to have the League in the Interim Government Wavell did not even insist on the withdrawal of the League Council's resolution of 29 July, of achieving Pakistan through Direct Action, an obvious precondition to be fulfilled before the League could enter into the Interim Government. The League took full advantage of it by ioining the Interim Government and at the same time continuing its programme of Direct Action. The Congress, as was only to be expected, did not want to allow this situation to continue. Wavell had assured Nehru that he had made it clear to Jinnah that the League's entry into the Interim Government was conditional upon the League's Council withdrawing its resolution of 29 July. However, there was no sign of any move on Jinnah's part to even summon a meeting of the League's Council, to say nothing of withdrawing its earlier resolution. In the meanwhile, communal tension in almost all parts of northern India was reaching the boiling point. Ferocious riots soon followed in quick succession in such far-flung areas as Noakhali and Tiperrah districts of eastern Bengal, central and northern Bihar, including the Patna district, and UP, particularly Garh Mukteshwar, a place of Hindu pilgrimage in the Meerut district. The Congress now renewed its insistence that the League formally revoke its decisions taken on 29 July. On the other hand, Jinnah continued to maintain that the League's Council resolution of 29 July could not be rescinded until the Congress accepted compulsory grouping of provinces as provided for in the Cabinet Mission Plan. He also objected to the decision of the

Congress, approved by the British Government, to go ahead with the decision to summon the Constituent Assembly on 9 December 1946, in spite of the League's decision to boycott it.

Faced with such a situation, the British Government made another effort to break the impasse by having a conference with selected Indian leaders in London. The latter included two from the Congress (Nehru and Patel), two from the League (Jinnah and Liaquat Ali Khan), and one from the Sikhs (Sardar Baldev Singh). Patel refused straight way to go to London. Nehru and Jinnah had to be persuaded by Attlee to go, and Khan and Singh followed suit. The London Conference opened on 4 December and concluded on 6th. Both Nehru and Jinnah remaining firm on the stand of their respective parties regarding the grouping issue, no agreement could be reached among them. The conference, however, ended with a statement issued by the British Government on 6 December, which in effect supported the stand of the League. Asserting that the Cabinet Mission's intention from the very beginning had been similar to the stand of the League, the statement hoped that the Congress, too, would accept it, thereby paving the way for the League's joining the Constituent Assembly. The last paragraph of the British Government's statement contained a not so veiled warning to the Congress that if all sections of the Indian people were not represented in the Constituent Assembly, the constitution framed by it could not be made applicable to those areas which were not represented in it. This clearly foreshadowed Partition if there was no agreement between the Congress and the League.

There was, of course, as expected, no agreement between the Congress and the League. The resolution adopted by the All India Congress Committee on 6 January 1947 made a show of accepting the British Government's statement of 6 December 1946, by agreeing to advise action in accordance with the interpretation contained in that statement regarding the procedure to be adopted in the sections, but at the same time it declared that this must not involve any compulsion for a province and that the rights of the Sikhs in the Punjab should not be jeopardized. The League naturally treated this as indicating the determination of the Congress to stick to its old stand on the Cabinet Mission's statement of 16 May 1946. The resolution of the League's Working Committee adopted on 3 January 1947 declared that it was clear that the Congress had destroyed all the fundamentals of the Cabinet Mission Plan and all possibilities of a compromise on the basis of that Plan. At the same time, it took strong objection to the Congress continuing with its plan to start the deliberations of the Constituent Assembly on 6 December and again resuming them, after an adjournment, on 22 January 1947, and called for its dissolution. Finally, it declared that no useful purpose would be served by summoning a meeting of the League's Council. The Congress interpreted this to mean that the League planned to continue its programme of Direct Action while remaining inside the Interim Government. The former was in no mood to tolerate it any more and was supported in this matter by all the non-League members of the Interim Government. On 5 February, all of them wrote to Wavell, asserting that in view of the resolution of the League's Working Committee the League members could not continue to function in the Interim Government as it would be contrary to the assurance given by Wavell at the time of their entry into it. Liaquat Ali Khan, writing to Wavell on behalf of the League, on 8 February, saw no justification for such a demand as, according to him, the Congress had never fully accepted the Cabinet Mission Plan of 16 May, while the League had done so from the very beginning. Thus, the situation again seemed to be coming to the breaking point.

The British policymakers were fully prepared to meet this eventuality. Indeed, whatever public position they might be taking, they had realized from the day the statement of 6 December 1946 was issued that it was not likely to bring about a settlement of the India problem. This is borne out by the fact that shortly after that statement had been issued, the India and Burma Committee of the Cabinet began to apply its mind to the preparation of another statement of policy for India. The shape of things to come had already been indicated by the last paragraph of the statement of 6 December 1946. So it did not take the Committee long to come out with a new statement of British policy, which was issued on 20 February 1947 and became known as Attlee's Declaration. That made it clear that the British had finally decided to transfer power to Indian hands on a date not later than June 1948. If a fully representative Constituent Assembly failed to frame before that date a Constitution that was acceptable to people in all parts of India, the British Government would have to consider 'to whom the powers of the Central Government in British India should be handed over, on the due date, whether as a whole to some form of Central Government for British India or in some areas to the existing Provincial Governments, or in such other way as may seem most reasonable and in the best interests of the Indian people'. It was also announced that Wavell would soon return to Britain and would be succeeded by Lord Louis Mountbatten.

X

The British spokesmen, as on all similar occasions in the past, expressed the hope that Attlee's Declaration, by fixing a final date for the end of British rule in India, would force the Indian leaders to finally face reality and come to some agreement. Actually, the sequel, again as in the past, was just the opposite. As Attlee's Declaration had clearly opened the door to Partition by affirming that all power need not necessarily be transferred to a Central Government for the whole of India, the League naturally concluded that if it established control over the Muslim-majority provinces, it could ensure the creation of Pakistan by insisting that power be transferred to the League's governments in those provinces. So Direct Action was intensified in the Punjab, leading to ever-increasing violence and tension and forcing the Unionist Tiwana, to resign as premier on 2 March 1947. This gave a further fillip to the Direct Action programme in the NWFP. Indeed, although the decision was not implemented because of certain developments in the political field ensuring the emergence of Pakistan, it is illustrative of Jinnah's unflinching determination to achieve Pakistan that he had decided to launch an armed struggle in the shape of a *jihad* in the tribal belt between the NWFP and Afghanistan and had entrusted that task to Iskander Mirza, then a senior civil servant in the Political Department who had earlier served in that area. This has been revealed recently by Iskander Mirza's son, Humayun Mirza, in a book dealing with his father's life. In the meanwhile, the Congress stuck to its earlier decision that if the League continued to ask for Pakistan, it could have it but would not be allowed to carry with it the people in any well-marked area who did not want to belong to Pakistan. Keeping in view the developments in the Punjab, the

Congress Working Committee, through a resolution adopted on 8 March 1947, demanded the division of the Punjab into two parts: a Muslim-majority province and a non-Muslim-majority province. This was a clear signal that the Congress had come to the conclusion that Partition had become unavoidable and that all that it could do under the circumstances was to safeguard as best as possible the interests of the people in the Muslim-majority provinces who were opposed to going over to Pakistan.

Thus, by the time Mountbatten landed on Indian soil on 22 March 1947, things had gone too far in the direction of Pakistan to be reversed. Mountbatten had been instructed by Attlee on the eve of leaving for India that he should first explore the possibility of agreement between the Congress and the League on the basis of the Cabinet Mission Plan, but if that was not found possible, to submit his plan for the transfer of power as per the provisions of Attlee's Declaration. Both Attlee and Mountbatten were, of course, aware that the talk of reviving the Cabinet Mission Plan would be a pure formality and that the real solution to the Indian constitutional problem would have to be based on Partition. This alone can explain the fact that by 31 March 1947, just a week after taking charge as Viceroy (24 July) and without having had detailed discussions with such senior leaders like Gandhi, Jinnah, and Nehru, Mountbatten was ready with a tentative Partition Plan which he placed before his sixth staff meeting held on that day. The detailed discussions with the leaders only confirmed Mountbatten's assumption that under the circumstances then present, Partition was the only practical solution. For he found that, on the one hand, Jinnah was immovable as a rock on having a sovereign Pakistan, even though it might well be a truncated one, which, as Mountbatten explained, was the only possibility if the former continued to insist on Partition. Nehru and Patel, on the other hand, had already realized that Partition was unavoidable if India wanted to achieve independence without any further delay. They did not have one word to say against Partition if it did not involve the transfer to Pakistan of areas having a non-Muslim majority, like western Punjab, eastern Bengal, and the whole of Assam except the Sylhet district. Gandhi was the lone dissenter, with his advise to postpone Partition until the British presence in India had ended. This was something impossible to achieve as the British had made it clear that they would not depart before settling the Hindu–Muslim problem. Even so, in order to facilitate his objective, Gandhi proposed to the Viceroy that the British should appoint Jinnah as Prime Minister. There was no reason to hope that Jinnah would ever be attracted by such a proposal, for under Gandhi's formula the Ministry formed by Jinnah would have to be responsible to the Central Legislative Assembly, where the Congress was in an overwhelming majority. Nor could Jinnah be expected to take any interest in a formula according to which the issue of Partition was to be postponed till the British withdrawal from India. However, the proposal never went to him, as Mountbatten wanted to be sure that it had the support of the Congress Working Committee before he could present it to Jinnah. The Congress leaders like Nehru and Patel did not show any interest in the then existing situation, in handing over power to Jinnah, however circumscribed, and considered Gandhi's plan as highly impractical. The latter thereupon conveyed to Mountbatten that he had failed to win the necessary support in the Congress for his proposal.

So the inexorable process of finalizing the Partition Plan in consultation with the leaders of the Congress and the League continued and it was ready by the end of April to be sent to London for the approval of the British Cabinet. After the Plan came back to India with certain changes made in its drafting, Nehru, having been shown a copy of the revised text at Simla, discovered that the changes had the effect of altering the whole basis of the Plan as he and the rest of the Congress leadership had understood it to be. For they had been given to understand that the Indian Union would remain intact with only the Muslim-majority provinces (subject to their non-Muslim-majority parts being given the option to continue to belong to India) being given a chance to secede from it and to found a State of their own, if they so wished. The Plan, as it came from London, however, gave this freedom to every province, thereby opening the door to endless partitions, then as also in the future. This was totally unacceptable to the Congress. Indeed Nehru reacted so strongly against the revised draft that Mountbatten decided not to proceed with it any further. So the meeting with the top leaders, already scheduled, was postponed and the Plan was revised again to meet Nehru's objections. V.P. Menon, Constitutional Advisor to the

Viceroy, played an important part at this stage, particularly by suggesting that the two parts of India to emerge after Partition should do so on the basis of Dominion Status, thus sugarcoating the bitter pill of Partition for the Congress and ensuring India's continuance in the Commonwealth, along with Pakistan, for which Jinnah had already expressed his keenness. Dominion Status was tantamount to independence in all but name and, besides, could be achieved immediately without waiting till June 1948, the final time for the transfer of power stipulated in Attlee's Declaration. Patel, noted for his practical acumen, jumped at it at once. Nehru followed suit, though, having spent a good part of his life opposing Dominion Status, he took a little time in coming around to that view.

As the Plan was being finalized two issues created some controversy. One was the fate of the NWFP. Although the province had an overwhelming majority of Muslims, because of certain special factors, the chief among which was the support of Khan Abdul Ghaffar Khan and his *Khudai Khidmatgar* (Servants of God) organization, the Congress had been able to secure a majority of Muslim seats and form the ministry there both in 1937 and 1946. However, with the intensification of communal tension and the growth of the Pakistan movement in India as a whole, the political atmosphere began to change in the NWFP, especially after the launching of the campaign of Direct Action by the League, one of whose special targets was the Congress Ministry in that province. By the time Mountbatten arrived in India, many, including some Congress leaders, doubted whether the Congress still commanded the support of the majority of the Muslim electorate there. The senior British officials had, of course, always regarded the existence of a Congress Ministry in a Muslim-dominated province as some kind of an anomaly, and they now felt that a fresh opportunity must be given to the electorate to express its choice between India and Pakistan. When Mountbatten first discussed that issue with Nehru on 8 April 1947, the latter himself suggested that perhaps a fresh election might be necessary to assess the true state of feelings in the NWFP, but pointed out that elections could not be conducted when the political atmosphere was vitiated by the League's campaign of Direct Action. Later on, at the time of the finalization of the Mountbatten Plan, the Viceroy thought that a referendum might be better. Although

Gandhi and Azad opposed it and went on arguing that it was unfair to single out the NWFP for such a treatment, Mountbatten was not prepared to change his view. Khan Abdul Ghaffar Khan and his brother Dr Khan Sahib, the Congress chief minister of the NWFP, were most unhappy at this situation. When they found that a referendum was unavoidable, they wanted that the voters should be given an option not only between India and Pakistan, but also for independence. Nehru, who had made a considerable fuss for only the two options being made available to the provinces, completely excluding the third option of independence, and had got the Mountbatten Plan recast on that basis, could not do anything about it. So the referendum was held as planned. The Khan brothers, feeling disheartened and seeing no chance of victory in the name of India, boycotted the referendum, which, as expected, went in favour of Pakistan.

The other issue that caused some stir while the Mountbatten Plan was being finalized related to the proposal for a united and independent Bengal, floated by a few prominent Congress and League leaders in Bengal, not very close to their respective central leaderships, such as Sarat Chandra Bose of the Congress and H.S. Suhrawardy of the League. However, most of the Congress leaders as well as the overwhelming majority of Hindus were opposed to it as they thought that if Bengal remained united, it would inevitably be placed under Muslim rule. The Hindu Mahasabha leaders who, as the election result in 1946 amply demonstrated, had hardly any significant following in Bengal, also carried on a vigorous campaign against the proposal of having a united Bengal on that ground. At the central level, the League leaders, who had been strongly opposed to the Partition of the Punjab as well as Bengal, thought that, with a clear Muslim-majority, a united and independent Bengal could always be counted upon to be on the side of Pakistan, if not becoming another Pakistan itself. Such a prospect, however, could not be alluring to the Congress leadership, especially as they knew that the proposed united Bengal did not have any significant support among the non-Muslims in Bengal, the overwhelming majority of whom were in favour of Partition. Mountbatten, whose first Plan was officially called Plan Balkans and was based upon the principle that every province in India must be free to decide its own future, was naturally quite sympathetic to the proposal for a united and independent Bengal, but he could not do anything in the absence of any agreement on that issue between the Muslim and Hindu legislators of Bengal. So those legislators, as their counterparts in the Punjab, were given the option to decide between remaining in India or joining Pakistan. Sitting separately, the legislators from West Punjab decided in favour of Pakistan and those from East Punjab decided in favour of India. The same pattern emerged in Bengal, with the legislators from East Bengal deciding in favour of Pakistan and those from West Bengal deciding in favour of India.

Thus, the Partition of India was accompanied by the partition also of Bengal and the Punjab. Jinnah had vehemently argued against the latter partly on the ground that both these provinces had acquired a certain unity of culture and that division would cut them asunder. He was, however, cut short when Mountbatten told him that the same argument also applied to India as a whole and that it was better to work for a united India. Jinnah then took the stand that however small the new sovereign Muslim State might be, the League would be for it rather than for a united India. That settled the issue.

CHAPTER I

Preparing the Ground 1937–1939 (I): War on Congress and Intensified Stress on Muslim Nationhood

AS NOTED IN THE previous volume, the desire for Partition and the creation of a sovereign Muslim State or States, based on the Muslim-majority provinces of India, had been in the air, particularly in the Punjab, since the mid 1920s and had been later forcefully articulated by a Punjabi student in Britain, Choudhary Rahmat Ali. The latter's ideas soon travelled to India and won quite a few adherents among the Muslim intelligentsia and youth, as testified to by the writings in the press, both in the Punjab and Bengal. Even more significant was the fact that by the summer of 1937 Jinnah and Iqbal—one, the tallest Muslim politician in India and the leader of the largest political organization of Indian Muslims, and the other, long since acclaimed as the greatest poet–philosopher of Muslim nationalism and at that time holding the position of the President of the Muslim League in the Punjab had begun, on their own testimony, cherishing the new goal, though not yet proclaiming it publicly, obviously for political reasons, before the beginning of the final phase of negotiations between the leaders of the Congress and the League in 1937 regarding the formation of a popular ministry in UP under the Act of 1935; whose failure is even now considered by many as having been responsible for turning the minds of the League leaders, for the first time, towards Partition. This is proved beyond doubt by Iqbal's letters to Jinnah in May–June 1937, and Jinnah's foreword to the booklet containing Iqbal's letters to him, brought out through Jinnah's own initiative in 1943.[1] As much confusion still persists on this point—so vital to the understanding of the course of developments leading to Partition—

it may be appropriate, even at the cost of repetition, to refer here again to both Iqbal's letter and Jinnah's foreword.

Thus, on 28 May 1937 Iqbal drew Jinnah's attention to the gravity of the situation, from the League's point of view, because of the gathering momentum of the Muslim mass-contact programme of the Congress, emphasizing the importance of the economic problems of the masses, especially the problem of poverty, which equally affected the majority of the members of the two communities. He warned that unless the League showed an interest in the economic problems of the Muslim masses, particularly poverty, the latter were not likely to show any interest in it and pointed out that a solution of the problem of poverty was not difficult to find if the law of Islam was properly enforced and further developed in the light of modern conditions. This would at least ensure the right of subsistence to everyone. This was, however, not possible 'without a free Muslim state or states'. The time had come to make this demand. This would be the best reply that Jinnah could give to 'the atheistic socialism' of Jawaharlal Nehru.[2] In his next letter to Jinnah, dated 21 June 1937, Iqbal again stressed the desirability of separating the Muslim-majority areas from the rest of India. He stressed that a storm was soon coming to the North-West and perhaps to the whole country, which was already in a state of virtual civil war, as illustrated by the recent Hindu–Muslim riots. At the same time, Nehru's emphasis on the importance of economic problems and his description of the communal problem as something unreal and unimportant appeared to Iqbal as amounting to a denial of the separate political existence of Muslims. On the other hand, the stand of the Hindu Mahasabha, which Iqbal regarded as the real representative of the Hindu masses, showed that it did not envisage a united Hindu–Muslim nation in India. In view of all this he felt that 'the only way to a peaceful India' was the 'redistribution of the country on the lines of racial, religious and linguistic affinities'. Describing the move to set up a single all-India Federation as 'completely hopeless' and underlining the necessity of setting up 'a separate federation of Muslim Provinces', he asked: 'Why should not the Muslims of North-West India and Bengal be considered as nations entitled to self-determination just as other nations in India and outside India are?'[3]

Although Jinnah's replies to Iqbal's letters have not been found, the following extract from his foreword to the booklet containing them leaves no doubt that the former had already arrived at the conclusion reached by the latter and did not need any persuasion in this regard:

His views were substantially in consonance with my own and they had finally led me to the same conclusions as a result of careful examination and study of the constitutional problem facing India, and found expression in due course in the united will of Muslim India as adumbrated in the Lahore resolution of the All India Muslim League, popularly known as the 'Pakistan Resolution' passed on 23rd March 1940.[4]

However, Jinnah, being a shrewd strategist, thought that in the then existing state of the Muslim League it was premature for it to publicly air such a view at that time. He must have thought that in the absence of a powerful political organization enjoying mass support, it would seriously affect his credibility as a political leader and would indeed prove counterproductive if he were to immediately announce the goal of Pakistan. The following lines from Iqbal's letter to Jinnah dated 21 June 1937 clearly point to such a calculation:

Some Muslims in the Punjab are already suggesting the holding of a North-West Indian Muslim Conference, and the idea of a separate Muslim State is rapidly spreading. I agree with you, however, that our community is not sufficiently organized and disciplined and perhaps the time for holding such a conference is not yet ripe.[5]

II

Both Jinnah and Iqbal were right in their assessment of the League's strength in 1937. The political situation in India in the aftermath of the elections of 1937 was gloomy in the extreme from the point of view of the League. The League party was conspicuous by its absence in the legislatures of almost all the Muslim-majority provinces, except Bengal. Here, too, it had not been able to win the majority of Muslim seats and had to enter, as a junior partner, into a coalition with the Krishak Proja Party and agree to its leader, A.K. Fazlul Huq, becoming the Premier. In the Punjab the League had won only one seat. The ministry was headed by Sir Sikander Hyat Khan, who had become the leader of the Unionist Party after the demise of Fazl-i-Husain.

While the bulk of that party's members were Muslims, it also had some Sikh and Hindu members. In Sind, too, the Ministry was headed by a non-League Muslim, and the effort to rope in a substantial number of legislators into the Muslim League had failed. In the North-West Frontier Province, with an overwhelming Muslim majority, the Congress, though not in a majority, had won the largest number of seats and was later able to form the Ministry. In the Muslim-minority provinces the situation was better. The League, however, had substantial representation only in Bombay and UP, and its bid to enter the Ministries therein had been spurned by the Congress, which was prepared to take in League members as ministers only if the latter agreed to be subject to Congress discipline and to virtually wind up their parties in the legislatures. In July 1937, the Congress formed ministries in six provinces in which it had secured a majority of seats—Bihar, Bombay, CP, Madras, Orissa, and UP. A little later, it formed ministries also in two more provinces—Assam and the NWFP—where, though not in a majority, it had been returned as the largest single party in the Assemblies. Even before forming Ministries, it had launched a Muslim mass-contact programme, which seemed to be forging ahead in both the Muslim-majority and minority provinces.

In his task of extending the influence of the League and turning it into a powerful political force with a mass base, Jinnah had to face tremendous odds. He, however, proved equal to the task of dealing effectively with those odds. Actually, the odds themselves proved to be his greatest source of support. The spectacle of the Congress in office in eight out of the eleven provinces of India, foreshadowing its dominance also in the central government, once the federal part of the Act of 1935 came into force, had filled the minds of a fair section of the Muslim elite, long since nurtured on a separatist ideology, with anxiety regarding their future political prospects in a self-governing India. Those in the Muslim-minority provinces were already under Congress rule, but the sceptre of that rule now haunted also those who belonged to the Muslim-majority provinces. For the Congress was an all-India body and its presence in the Muslim-majority provinces, although small except in the NWFP, was by no means negligible, and it was considered a potential threat by almost all the non-Congress parties therein. Besides, the establishment of a partially democratic central government, constituted on the basis of responsibility to an elected legislature in certain fields, did not seem too far away. On the other hand, if the Muslim mass-contact programme of the Congress really succeeded, it might jeopardize the very existence of Muslims as a separate, recognizable group in Indian politics. The Muslim elite could not meet this situation without the instrumentality of a powerful political organization of their own. The Muslim League, with its long history and prestigious leadership, was the natural claimant to that position. As the Raja of Mahmudabad, one of Jinnah's loyal followers, recalled later:

> The results of the general elections startled the Muslims into an awareness that the Muslim League's failure to attract more Muslim voters was manifestly the result of Muslim political disunity. When they saw the solid Congress successes in several provinces they realized that in order to win a similar success, at least in the Muslim-majority provinces, two things were essential: a closing of their ranks and a reorganization of the Muslim League. It was widely felt that the time had come to develop the League into a broad-based mass organization which could effectively safeguard Muslim rights and interests.[6]

The Raja of Mahmudabad belonged to UP, but similar urges were noticeable also in other parts of India. Even those Muslim leaders who had fought against each other now felt impelled to unite because of a general Muslim feeling in favour of unity. This had indeed been a major factor behind the quick formation of a coalition ministry in Bengal, headed by Fazlul Huq, leader of the Krishak Proja Party, but containing ministers also from the Muslim League. Even while considering Huq as 'a most uncertain quantity', and apprehending serious efforts by the Congress to drive a wedge into the coalition whenever an opportunity presented itself, the Governor of Bengal was still hopeful about the stability of the ministry because, according to him, the fear of general Muslim indignation against anyone who could be publicly held up as responsible for breaking up 'Muslim unity' was a 'real unifying force'.[7] The desire to have a broad-based Muslim organization went hand in hand with this feeling. In the first week of July 1937, S.H. Suhrawardy, one of the most prominent leaders of the League in Bengal, wrote to Jinnah:

> The necessity for having a Muslim organization is so imperative that I am afraid we shall have to take up the work soon. If you want to run

the League here, i.e., in Bengal, we are prepared to assist, but if you are really lukewarm about it and do not very much care whether we should run the League here or not, please let me know so that we can start our own separate organization. We shall have to do something soon as we cannot allow the position to degenerate.[8]

In his next letter, Suhrawardy informed Jinnah that the Muslim leaders in Bengal were thinking of inviting the All-India Muslim League to hold its next annual session in Calcutta instead of at Lucknow as had been decided earlier.[9] The Muslim leaders in the Punjab were having similar thoughts. In his letter of 21 June 1937, advocating the establishment of a separate Muslim State, Iqbal suggested to Jinnah that it would be better to hold the next session of the League in the Punjab and not in a Muslim-minority province. 'The interest in the All-India Muslim League,' he reported, 'is rapidly growing in the Punjab, and the holding of the coming session in Lahore is likely to give a fresh political awakening to the Punjab Muslims.'[10] The growth of interest in the Muslim League went hand in hand with a hardening of feeling against the Congress. The Governor of the Punjab reported seeing signs of it as early as 8 May 1937.[11] Writing about a fortnight later, he affirmed that this was 'now definitely the case'. According to him, one reason for it was the effort of the Congress to approach the Muslim masses directly, ignoring the Muslim leaders. Another was 'the arrogant spirit' shown generally by Nehru. In this connection he referred to a strong speech delivered a few days earlier by the Punjab premier, Sikander Hyat Khan, leader of the Unionist Party, while replying to an address of the All-India Kshatri Conference. That speech had been delivered entirely on his own initiative, and not at the prompting of the Governor. Indeed, when the draft was shown to the latter, he had advised the toning down of one or two passages (which had been done). Even more significant was the information conveyed by Khan to the Governor that his speech had been made as a result of representations made by Muslim members of the Unionist Party, amongst whom the feeling against the Congress was 'greatly increasing'. The Congress, concluded the Governor in a prophetic tone, might succeed in getting a few adherents among Muslims, but every success in that direction would strengthen the feelings of Muslims as a community against it.[12]

Jinnah was alive to both the challenge and the opportunity

that lay before him and the League after the elections of 1937. Aware that the Muslims by and large were already alienated from the Congress, though divided into various regional groups and subgroups, he made it his main objective to unite them all under the League's leadership. For this he had to forge new sanctions in the shape of mass support. While this process was going on, he was willing to show maximum accommodation to the non-League Muslim leaders, particularly in the Muslim-majority provinces, provided the latter were prepared to proclaim adherence to the League. Once the masses, including the youth, rallied sufficiently strongly to his call, the local leaders were bound to fall more clearly in line and, failing that, be suitably disciplined. Such a call could only be in the name of the Muslim community and its interests, including its separate political identity and adequate share in political power commensurate with its historical traditions as well as number. 'Islam in danger' was the most potent rallying cry for the Muslims, and Jinnah decided to unabashedly adopt it. He did so about the same time that he confided to Iqbal that he did not differ from the latter in the ultimate goal to be pursued, but wanted to move cautiously as the Muslims were not yet 'sufficiently organized and disciplined'. Just as the ultimate goal, so also the main strategy for attaining it was decided upon well before the conclusion of the talks on ministry making in UP. This is clearly brought out by a report of Lord Brabourne, then Governor of Bombay, of a talk he had with Jinnah either at the end of May or the beginning of June 1937:

> Jinnah went on to tell me some of his plans for consolidating the Muslim League throughout India and how he is doing his utmost to awaken the Muhammadans to the necessity of standing on their own feet more than they do now. His policy is to preach communalism morning, noon and night, and to endeavour to get the Muhammadans to found more schools, to open purely Muhammadan hospitals, children's homes, etc., and to teach them generally 'to stand on their own feet and make themselves independent of the Hindus'.[13]

While carrying on his campaign, Jinnah virtually launched a war on the Congress, attacking it as a Hindu body bent upon establishing Hindu Raj all over the country, thereby posing a serious threat to the Muslims. In this connection he made ample use of the widespread feeling of grievance among the Muslim elite in the Congress-ruled provinces and tried to show that the

Congress ministries were subjecting the Muslim minorities to various types of 'atrocities', regardless of whether these were based on facts, hearsay or pure fiction. When the communal situation worsened and the Congress leadership showed interest in starting discussions with him with a view to defusing the situation, he put forward a condition that the Congress could not accept without compromising its position as a national organization claiming to represent all sections of the Indian people. This was the starting point of the campaign that was to lead first to the League's adoption of the demand for Partition (1940) and then to its fulfilment seven years later.

III

Jinnah's presidential address to the twenty-fifth annual session of the League, held at Lucknow on 15–18 October 1937, vividly illustrates the nature of his campaign against the Congress after the failure of the Congress–League talks on ministry making in UP and Bombay. After dilating on the achievements of the League during the preceding one year or so, he ridiculed the Congress for using high-sounding phrases such as 'complete independence' and 'wrecking the Constitution' while actually compromising with the imperial Government at various stages and working with it under the Constitution. Further, he held the then Congress leadership as wholly responsible for alienating the Muslims by pursuing a policy that was 'exclusively Hindu'. Since coming to power in the provinces where they were in a majority in the legislatures, Congressmen, he alleged, had 'by their words, deeds and programmes' shown, more and more, that the Muslims could not expect any justice or fair play at their hands. His major grievance was that wherever the Congress was in a majority it refused to have coalitions with the League and insisted on the Leaguers signing its pledge. However, where the Congress did not have a majority, as for example in the NWFP, it freely entered into a coalition with other groups, forgetting the principle of collective responsibility, the ground on which it had refused to form any coalition with the League. Besides, any individual Muslim member who was prepared to sign the Congress pledge was made a minister even though he did not command the confidence or respect of the overwhelming majority of the Muslim members of the concerned legislature. Turning to the programme being pursued by the Congress Governments in various provinces, Jinnah observed:

Hindi is to be the national language of all India and the *Bande Mataram* is to be the national song, and is to be forced upon all and sundry. On the very threshold of what little power and responsibility is given, the majority community have clearly shown their hand: that Hindustan is for Hindus. Only the Congress masquerades under the name of nationalism, whereas the Hindu Mahasabha does not mince words.[14]

In expressing his deep anger and resentment against the Congress, Jinnah was not alone, but was reflecting the sentiments of the vast majority of the leaders and delegates assembled at the Lucknow session, who felt even more bitter than him about the grievances aired by the latter. This comes out clearly in the summing up of the prevailing mood at that session by the Punjab premier, Sikander Hyat Khan, while talking to his Governor. As the latter reported to the Viceroy:

Although this [resentment against the Congress] was voiced in Jinnah's opening address, the resentment was much stronger than even Jinnah represented it to be. The basis of it is the apprehension felt by Muslims regarding the future. In their view the Congress regime in Congress Provinces has been characterized by the spirit of arrogance and domination. . . . Apparently some of the delegates from other Provinces gave concrete examples of the oppression of Muslims . . . Sikander himself admitted that the complaints were probably very exaggerated, but at the moment Muslims everywhere, except in the North-West Frontier Province, are on the lookout for grievances against the Congress and are in a mood to see nothing good in anything that the Congress Ministries may do. . . . Sikander told me that speech after speech was couched in the most bitter invective, and that feeling ran so high that, if any Congress leader had appeared at the Conference, he would have been in physical danger. The words Sikander himself used were that he would have been in the danger of being lynched.[15]

Jinnah's address at Lucknow is important not only for voicing the then widely prevalent feeling of grievance among Muslims, but also, and indeed even more so, for showing the way to their future destiny. Underlining that the latter could depend neither on the Congress nor the British for the redressal of their grievances, he emphasized that they must concentrate on building up their own power 'to the exclusion of every other consideration' by organizing themselves, if they wanted to secure justice:

No settlement with the majority is possible, as no Hindu leader speaking with any authority shows any concern or genuine desire for it. An honourable settlement can only be achieved between equals; and unless the two parties learn to respect and fear each other, there is no solid ground for any settlement. Offers of peace by the weaker party always mean a confession of weakness, and an invitation to aggression. Appeals to patriotism, justice and fairplay and for goodwill fall flat. It does not require political wisdom to realize that all safeguards and settlements would be a scrap of paper unless they were backed up by power. Politics means power and not relying only on cries of justice or fairplay or goodwill.[16]

At the end came the final exhortation. Speaking like an inspired prophet intent on leading his people to the promised land, Jinnah stated that if only the Muslims remained undeterred by the adverse circumstances surrounding them at that time and developed courage and determination in sufficient measure, all the difficulties and hurdles in their way would melt away and they would emerge as 'a nation' with a most glorious future:

There are forces which may bully you, tyrannize over you and intimidate you, and you may even have to suffer. But it is by going through this crucible of the fire of persecution which may be levelled against you, the tyranny that may be exercised, the threats and intimidations that may unnerve you—it is by resisting, by overcoming, by facing these disadvantages, hardships and suffering, and maintaining your true convictions and loyalty, that a nation will emerge, worthy of its past glory and history, and will live to make its future history greater and more glorious not only in India, but in the annals of the world. Eighty millions of Musalmans in India have nothing to fear. They have their destiny in their hands. . . .[17]

With a view to making the objective of the League radical enough to attract the new generation of Muslims and save it from the charge of being stigmatized as a toady of the British, the object of the League was changed to 'full independence' with suitable wording so as to maintain a distinction from the objective of the Congress and at the same time provide safeguards for the interests and aspirations of Muslims. The resolution adopted in this regard declared that the object of the League would be 'the establishment in India of full independence in the form of *a federation of free and democratic states* in which the rights and interests of the Musalmans and other minorities are adequately and effectively safeguarded in the Constitution'.[18] Maulana Hasrat

Mohani, who moved this resolution, explained that the phrase 'complete independence' (the goal of the Congress) had been 'intentionally kept out as its interpretation by Congress had made it meaningless'. Maulana Zafar Ali Khan, who seconded the resolution, observed that 'India did not comprise a single nation. If that were so, then according to the best principles of democracy, the Muslims would always be at the mercy of the majority community.' One of the supporters of the resolution, Husain Imam, observed that the new creed of the League was 'a message of freedom, not only for Muslims, but for all minorities'.[19]

In order to appeal to the Muslim masses and thereby provide a mass base to the League, the Lucknow session adopted a resolution calling upon the Working Committee of the League to take immediate steps 'to frame and put into effect an economic, social and educational programme'. Such a programme was to aim at fixing minimum wages as well as working hours for factory workers and other labourers; improving the housing and health conditions of the labourers and providing for slum clearance; reducing rural and urban debts and abolishing usury; granting a moratorium on all debts till proper legislation had been enacted in this regard; securing exemption of houses from attachment or sale in execution of decrees on loans; providing security of tenure and fixation of fair rents and revenue; abolition of forced labour; undertaking rural uplift; encouraging cottage industries and small, indigenous industries both in rural and urban areas; encouraging the use of swadeshi articles, especially hand-woven cloth; establishing an industrial board for the development of industries and the prevention of exploitation by middlemen; devising means for the relief of unemployment; promoting compulsory primary education; reorganizing secondary and university education, especially in the field of science and technology; establishing rifle clubs and a military college; enforcing prohibition; abolishing un-Islamic customs and usages from Muslim society; organizing a volunteer corps for social service; and devising measures for the attainment of full independence and inviting the cooperation of all political organizations working to that end.[20] These items of the programme were obviously designed to compete with the Congress in the field of mass contact and to effectively counter the charge levelled by Nehru and other Congress leaders that the League was basically an organization of Muslim landlords and other upper class Muslims who had no interest in the economic problems facing the Muslim masses. In this connection it is remarkable that, in spite of its commitment to make Urdu the universal language of India, the resolution on the economic programme adopted at its Lucknow session used even the pure Hindi word swadeshi (meaning things made in one's country) at one place. With the same end in view, the Lucknow session also included a provision in the new constitution of the League adopted therein, reducing its annual membership fee from one rupee to two annas,[21] half of that charged by the Congress.

Apart from the tone and content of Jinnah's presidential address and the measures adopted to give a new look to the League, the most significant as well as spectacular development associated with the Lucknow session was the declaration made by Sikander Hyat Khan that he was joining the League and also advising all the Muslim members of the Unionist Party in the Punjab to do the same. The importance of this development was highlighted by the fact that only a few months ago Jinnah's repeated entreaties to Sikander as well as his deceased mentor, Fazl-i-Husain, had failed to evoke any positive response, resulting in the pitiable record of the League in the last elections, with only one member elected to the Punjab Assembly. Sikander's lead was also followed by A.K. Fazlul Huq, the leader of the Krishak Proja Party, who was heading a coalition ministry in Bengal (including the members of the League as junior partners) and Sir Muhammad Sadullah Khan, the Premier of Assam. Thus, almost in one stroke, the League acquired a new respectability, with a commanding position in both the major Muslim-majority provinces. 'What would have happened,' writes Khaliquzzaman, then one of the prominent leaders of the League in UP and the leader of its party in the Legislative Assembly, 'if the Punjab and Bengal Premiers had not agreed to come to the rescue of the Muslim League organization in UP, I need not dilate. Briefly, it would have remained merely the Muslim League of the Minority Provinces and in time to come would have had to surrender to the Congress.'[22] The aptness of this observation is borne out by the fact, recorded by Jinnah's long-time secretary and biographer, that, before settling upon Lucknow, Jinnah had tried to hold the League's session in one of the Muslim-majority provinces, as Iqbal had been pressing him to do, but had failed due to lack of positive interest on the part of the Muslim leaders of those provinces in shouldering the responsibility for organizing it.[23]

Jinnah fully realized the value of this accession to the League's strength and for quite some time consistently ignored the repeated complaints made by the old leaders of the League in both Punjab and Bengal. In the former, in particular, the terms of the so-called Jinnah–Sikander Pact, under which Sikander had joined the League, were not clear. Indeed, it is a misnomer to call it a pact, for no document had been signed by either Jinnah or Sikander. All that had happened was that the latter had committed himself to joining the League and also asking the Muslim members of the Unionist Party to do the same. Jinnah, on his part, had promised to reconstitute the League's Parliamentary Board for the Punjab, giving due representation to the new League members therein.[24] When conflicts arose between Sikander and the old leaders of the League in the Punjab, who interpreted the Jinnah–Sikander understanding in divergent ways, and the latter complained to Jinnah, accusing the former of undermining the League and not being sincere,[25] Jinnah asked them to be patient and refused to intercede on their behalf or to recognize any distinction between the new Leaguers and the old veterans. This should be clear from the following extract from his letter to Barkat Ali, the sole member of the Punjab Assembly elected on the League's ticket, working in close collaboration with Muhammad Iqbal, President of the provincial Muslim League:

> May I state one principle, that once the Muslim members of the Unionist Party or any Musalman who becomes a Leaguer and pledges himself to the creed, policy and programme, he is no longer anything else but a Leaguer, and those who have been already in the League are not better than these Leaguers. Perhaps you might say that the others have now realized that the policy and the programme which we initiated are the right ones, and hence they whole-heartedly joined us. After that there is no such thing as this group or that group, or that party and this party, because then it really means various cliques. And I assure you people, have a little patience. These small matters of detail will be adjusted fairly and justly and mainly in the interests of the cause for which we stand.[26]

Taken as a whole, the proceedings of the Lucknow session stand out as a landmark in the evolution of Muslim nationalism and mark a major step in the revitalization of its chief instrument, the Muslim League, on which Jinnah had embarked a couple of years earlier and which he was now pursuing with renewed vigour in the post-election scenario. They also represent the firing of the first major salvo by the latter in his campaign against the Congress, which had rebuffed his offer of cooperation in the formation of Ministries in Bombay as well as UP and whose mass-contact programme among the Muslims seemed to pose a serious threat to the very survival of the League as a major force in Indian politics. The impact those proceedings had on the Muslim mind can be easily imagined from the fact that their reverberations reached even the remote NWFP, where the League was barely known till then and the Congress dominated the political scene. According to the Governor, although only three representatives of the NWFP had attended the Lucknow session, 'very keen interest' had been aroused by its proceedings. 'Old-fashioned Khans,' he remarked, 'who had hardly heard the name of the League six months ago, now refer to it freely as an ordinary topic of conversation.'[27]

Although the reactions of some of the notable contemporary observers varied, all were united in underlining the significance of the Lucknow session. In an interview to the press on 17 October Nehru, for instance, described the Lucknow proceedings as 'the last ditch of political reaction', and remarked: 'The League and its supporters stand clearly and definitely today for the division of India, even on a political and economic plane, into religious groups. Whatever this may be, it is against the thesis of the nationalist idea of the unity of India.'[28] Gandhi described Jinnah's presidential address as 'a declaration of war'.[29] The Punjab Governor agreed with this view. His estimate of the proceedings at Lucknow was that 'the real business which overshadowed everything else was the declaration of war against Congress'.[30] The Governor of UP, too, had the same opinion. According to him, the sense of uncertainty earlier prevailing among Muslims had been removed, at any rate for the time being, and they had been given 'a very strong and definite communal lead', which seemed to have inspired great enthusiasm, and would obviously have 'a most important bearing on political developments in the near future'. He further added: 'War has been declared unmistakably between the Congress and the Muslim League.'[31] The Viceroy fully concurred with such an analysis. In a communication sent to the Secretary of State for India after having detailed discussions with Emerson, the Governor of Punjab, regarding the nature and significance of the deliberations at Lucknow, he remarked:

I have no doubt whatever that his conclusion, that the significance of the meeting of the League, and the attitude adopted in it by the Muslims, are of great importance, is correct; and that its reactions on all-India politics and the general position may, if Muslims can but hold together, and work to a common policy, be considerable.[32]

'The proceedings of the Muslim League Conference at Lucknow,' commented the *Times of India* (Bombay), then an organ of non-official British opinion, on 22 October 'should prompt all to pause and consider whether the gulf separating two great communities is not being widened rather than being bridged.'[33]

IV

There was no looking back for Jinnah after Lucknow. Apparently encouraged by the enthusiastic response from the audience to his address there, he now moved from place to place speaking in the same vein and evoking similar response. Thus, speaking at Patna on 25 October 1937, he declared that in the seven provinces in which the Congress had come to power, it had wounded Muslim feelings and sentiments by singing *Vande Mataram* as the national anthem and forcing Hindi on Muslims as the national language. He also remarked: 'The difference between the Muslim League and the Congress is that I mean what I say while the Congress does not mean what it says.'[34] Addressing another meeting of Muslims two days later in the same town, Jinnah observed: 'When the Hindus blame us, do you know what they mean? They want you to be reduced to a minority in the Punjab, Bengal, Sind and N-W Frontier Province. . . . They know that in the Punjab and Bengal they can swamp the Muslim-majority under the device of joint electorate.' Further, he drew attention to the deplorable condition of the depressed classes among Hindus and remarked: 'If you are not united, if you do not build up your organization, by system and method, you will be submerged by the Hindus in this country and reduced to a class of Shudras and Pariahs of the future.' Turning to the Congress, he declared: 'I am convinced that the more you bully, the more you intimidate, the more you tyrannise, the stronger will be the Muslims.'[35] Moving to Calcutta, he inaugurated a conference convened by the All-India Muslim Students Federation on 27 December and declared: 'If for demanding a rightful place for Muslims in the Government of the country and in other spheres of life, I am dubbed a communalist, I plead guilty to the charge. . . .'[36]

Making a foray again into Bihar, Jinnah reached Gaya on new year's day in 1938. Underlining that the Muslims of Gaya had given him a welcome and presented him an address 'worthy of a king', and expressing appreciation for all the praises showered on him, Jinnah remarked in his speech at the public meeting held there that all this indicated that the Muslims and the Muslim League had become one and that the former had understood the issue for which the League had been fighting. For the first time making an explicit appeal in the name of Islam in order to buttress the call for Muslim solidarity, he observed:

> Today in this large gathering you have honoured me by entrusting the duty to unfurl the flag of the Muslim League, the flag of Islam, for you cannot separate the Muslim League from Islam. Many people misunderstand us when we talk of Islam, particularly our Hindu friends. When we say 'This flag is the flag of Islam' they think we are introducing religion into politics—a fact of which we are proud. Islam gives us a complete code. It is not only a religion but it also contains laws, philosophy and politics. In fact, it contains everything that matters to a man from morning to night. When we talk of Islam we take it as an all-embracing word. We do not mean any ill-will.[37]

At the same time Jinnah took pains to emphasize the separateness of Muslims from Hindus. Speaking in Urdu and trying to explain why Muslims must have safeguards in the constitution to protect them from the majority, which would always be Hindu, he observed:

> There is nothing in common between us [i.e. Hindus and Muslims]. Our old philosophy of life as well as our religion and language are different. 'Hindu water' and 'Muslim water' are common enough cries heard at all railway stations. It shows that we do not drink each other's water. We want that we, being in a minority, should be given safeguards for we know in America self-government means a government of the white people, that is the majority. The Negroes have no right to vote

and are treated as slaves. We know that if we do not wake up in time, we may lose.[38]

Addressing another meeting in Urdu the next day in the Juma mosque in the same town, Jinnah reiterated that the flag of the League was the flag of Islam and remarked: 'This is not a new thing. It is there since the last 1,300 years.' Referring to the fact that Muslims constituted only 25 per cent of the total population of India, he asked his audience not to be disheartened by that fact, but derive inspiration from the example of the Prophet, who was the lone Muslim when he had begun his mission:

Thirteen hundred years ago, our Prophet (peace be upon him) preached his faith when there was no [other] Muslim. In 20 years time our Prophet (peace be upon him) had spread not only his faith in Arabia, Egypt and Europe but also brought them under his suzerainty. If a single Muslim can do all this, what is it which 9 crores of Muslims cannot do? If the Muslims have ever been discomfited, it was by another Muslim. And I say if you stand united there is no power on earth which can suppress or oppress you.[39]

Returning to Calcutta a day or two later, he declared at a public meeting that the Indian Muslim community and Islam, 'to which he was proud to belong', faced the danger of disintegration for want of leadership and organization. He stressed that unless the Muslims secured the power and force of organization, they were doomed to serfdom and subjection in India. Calling for a band of selfless and brave workers who would be ready to suffer and sacrifice for the Muslim cause, he again appealed to the religious faith of the Muslims, placing before them the example of the Prophet:

When the Holy Prophet (peace be upon him) started to preach Islam he was a minority of one in the world. By the force of his faith he challenged the whole universe and wrought the greatest revolution in the shortest time in the world with the help of the Holy Quran. If the Muslims procure the power of that 'faith', organization, discipline and sacrifice, they have no reason to fear the hostile forces of the entire world. Let them shake off their lethargy, defeatism and despondency. Let them regain their faith, recapture their souls and remake their history once more in India. (Cries of 'Allah-o-Akbar' and loud cheers)[40]

Moving on to Allahabad, Jinnah exhorted the Muslims there to keep the flag of Islam flying and clarified that he was not against India achieving freedom, but only wanted to ensure that freedom came not only to Hindus, but also to Muslims. He also stressed that there had been a wonderful Muslim awakening in India and the need of the hour was to properly harness and mobilize it.[41] Replying to an address of welcome in Delhi on 30 January 1938, he again stressed the value of organization, remarking that if Muslims, who were numerically, educationally and economically inferior to Hindus, wanted to have an honourable existence in the country, they must achieve unity and solidarity among themselves.[42] The same message was conveyed to the Muslim students at Aligarh whom Jinnah addressed on 5 February. After describing in detail the long history of the efforts on the part of the League to secure a just settlement of the communal problem, he observed:

> My appeal to you is: come to the platform of the League. If Muslims are united, the settlement [of the Hindu-Muslim problem] will come sooner than you think. You will have established your claim to achieve freedom. After a few months' work the League's name is known in every corner of India. Lakhs of people are joining it. Even those who are against us will realize that they are under a serious delusion and their only course is to join the League and make the Musalmans speak with one voice.[43]

Jinnah's exertions and speeches produced the desired results. The first confidential quarterly survey of political developments in India prepared by an agency of the central government and covering the period upto the end of October 1937, while noting that the declared adherence to the League on the part of the Premiers of the Punjab and Bengal was bound to give it power which it had till then lacked, had found it difficult to forecast the results at that stage. 'Jinnah is not an inspired or inspiring leader,' it added, 'and it is doubtful if he has sufficient personality or authority to weld the members into an efficient organisation.'[44] In the next issue of that survey, however, the editor changed his tone in the face of the developments during the succeeding three months (November 1937 to 31 January 1938). For, thanks to Jinnah's exertions and the widespread Muslim resentment against the Congress that period had witnessed the League's victory in three out of four by-elections in UP, and a considerable extension of its organization and an increase in its membership all over northern India; about one hundred and seventy-four new branches had been formed and lakhs of new members enrolled. Ninety of the new branches belonged to UP, forty to the Punjab, and the rest to other parts of northern India. A lakh of new members had been enrolled in UP alone. Although the survey noted that Jinnah had 'little influence in the predominantly Muslim Punjab' and again expressed doubt whether he had 'the personality required for the leader of a League uniting the Muslims of all-India', it recognized his growing stature among Muslims. According to it, he was 'greeted everywhere with great enthusiasm by Muslims who realise that he is actively trying to bind their forces together and is the spokesman of their dislike and distrust of the Hindu Congress party'.[45]

Jinnah was, of course, fully aware of the rapidly growing influence of the League since the Lucknow session. In his presidential address to the special session of the League held in Calcutta on 17–18 April 1938, he pointed out that during his recent tours in different parts of the country, he had found 'a tremendous political awakening and enthusiasm among the Musalmans, and 'an insatiable desire' among them to come under the banner of the League. He added with pride:

> Within less than six months we have succeeded in organizing Musalmans all over India as they never were at any time during the last century and a half. They have been galvanized and awakened in a manner which has astounded and staggered our opponents. Musalmans have shaken off their torpor and shed the miserable state of despair and demoralization into which they were sunk so deep. They are beginning to realize that they are a power. They possess the strength, the potentialities of which they have not yet realized; and if only they will take their affairs in their own hands and stand together united, there is no power that can resist their will.[46]

Jinnah's pride had a solid basis. Muslim League parties had begun functioning in seven out of the eleven provincial legislatures and the large majority of Muslim members in all the seven legislatures now belonged to the League. A Muslim League party had also begun functioning in both houses of the central legislature.[47] Convinced that one of the most effective ways of further strengthening the Muslim awakening was to go on fostering anti-Congress sentiments among them, Jinnah did not let the opportunity provided by the Calcutta session to pass without strongly attacking the Congress. After mentioning various grievances of Muslims in the Congress-ruled provinces, including encouragement of *Vande Mataram* and Hindi and the alleged placing of difficulties in the way of Muslims enjoying their religious rights freely, Jinnah observed:

The High Command of the Congress has no policy except opportunism and arrogance. They are utilizing their organization, because it happens to be the largest and most powerful, to treat every other party with contempt, and they imagine that they have already become the rulers of India. It is astounding that they believe that they have conquered six provinces absolutely, and in the seventh they have a dominant voice, as the majority in the coalition of the North-West Frontier are Congressmen. They talk of drums beating, and they believe that it will not be very long before the remaining four Provinces fall before the conquering heroes of the High Command of the Congress.[48]

The Calcutta address ended, just as the Lucknow address, with an exhortation to the Muslims to realize their power as 'one solid people' and face all difficulties on the basis of their own united strength:

Don't depend upon anybody. You must depend upon your own inherent strength. The Musalmans have not yet realized what power and strength they would possess if they were properly mobilized as one solid people. We have to go through a great deal of spade work and suffering. Our opponents will use all possible means of suppression. They may practise tyranny and may persecute us; but I am confident that we shall emerge out of that ordeal stronger than we have ever been.[49]

Fazlul Huq as chairman of the Reception Committee also did his bit to rouse anti-Congress passion among Muslims. Being a new convert to the cause espoused by the League and trying to be 'more loyal than the king', he indeed went much beyond Jinnah in this regard. Thus, contrasting the position of Muslims in the Congress-ruled provinces with that of Hindus in non-Congress provinces, he remarked:

In Congress Provinces riots have laid the countryside waste. Muslim life, limb and property have been lost and blood has freely flowed, but here in Bengal not one head has been broken, nor one drop of blood shed. There the Muslims are leading their lives in constant terror, overawed and oppressed, but here the Hindus are perfectly happy, leading peaceful lives. . . . There mosques are being defiled and culprits never found, nor is the Muslim worshipper unmolested; but here worship proceeds unhampered in Hindu temples. . . .

Arguing that Muslims could not count on the safeguards provided for the minorities in the Constitution, Huq stressed that Muslims must stand on their own legs and fight their battles alone. He observed towards the end of his welcome address:

> We must fight the battle of Islam alone and with all our resources. Let us resolve to fight it to the bitter end, relying on the justice of our cause, undaunted by the gathering forces against us. Let us prepare to fight, if need be, on a double front, with our backs to the wall. If Panipat and Thaneswar must repeat themselves, let the Muslims prepare to give as glorious an account of themselves as did their forebears.[50]

Huq's language was so intemperate that even some leaders of the League were not happy with it, though they did not publicly say so. Sikander Hyat Khan, for instance, told the Governor of the Punjab after his return from Calcutta that he found it 'completely irresponsible' and had listened to it 'with increasing embarrassment'. The same applied to Sir Nazimuddin, the senior-most League leader of Bengal and Home Minister in Huq's cabinet. Indeed, the latter told Sikander that Huq's speech offended against about half a dozen sections of the Indian Penal Code.[51]

The next major occasion for the articulation of anti-Congress feelings and calls for Muslim solidarity and assertion of Muslim power was provided by the Sind Muslim League Conference at Karachi on 8 and 9 October 1938. Delivering his presidential address on the opening day, Jinnah declared that the Congress High Command was 'obsessed with one idea and determined to divide the Musalmans and particularly to break the solidarity of the Muslim League no matter how low they may have to stoop'. Clarifying that he was not fighting against the Hindu community and that he had many friends among it, he asserted that the Congress High Command was 'the greatest enemy of India's progress and for the matter of that even of the interest of Hindus'. Jinnah also dilated at length on the Muslim grievances under Congress rule and added the Basic or Wardha system of education to complaints about *Vande Mataram* and Hindi. Besides, he alleged that every available post was being given to Congressmen or to those Muslims who had chosen to cast their lot with the Congress. He also asserted that the average Congressmen were posing as rulers and behaving haughtily towards Muslims. Calling upon Muslims to organize themselves in order to defend their interests, Jinnah remarked: 'It is no use relying on anyone else.

We must stand on our own inherent strength and build up our own power and forge sanctions behind our decisions.' Dilating on the urgent need of all Muslims to rally under the League's flag, he again observed: 'It is no use blaming others. . . . If the Muslims are going to be defeated in their national goal and aspirations, it will only be by the betrayal of the Musalmans among us, as it has happened in the past.'[52]

The campaign against the Congress reached a new height at the twenty-sixth session of the League at Patna in 26–29 December 1938. As at the Calcutta Special Session, this also went hand in hand with elation at the continuing success of the League in rallying more and more Muslims under its banner and calls for Muslim solidarity in order to protect their 'national' interests. The League's recent victories in the by-elections to the Provincial Assemblies further added to the confidence of its leaders. It had secured a victory in CP and then in the NWFP.[53] Though the latter seat had been won by an extremely narrow margin of thirteen votes, it was nevertheless a blow to the Congress which enjoyed a dominant position in that province. The League's victory in a by-election in Bihar was equally significant. For it showed that its call for Muslim solidarity had created a favourable response among the majority of Muslim voters even in a remote area in the Chhotanagpur region (Hazaribagh district) of that province. The Congress workers in the constituency were quite confident that their candidate—a resident of the area who had been active in politics since 1920—would win over the League's candidate—a Khan Bahadur and a zamindar belonging to the far away Patna district. The Congress hope for victory rested also on the fact that 80 per cent of the Muslim voters were Momins, who were generally considered apathetic to the League and sympathetic to the Congress. However, when the result came it became known that the Congress candidate had received only about 800 votes against over 3,000 votes secured by his rival.[54] The state of general Muslim public opinion was also indicated by the fact that the Congress had decided not to put up any candidate in the by-election in UP for the Central Assembly, to fill up the vacancy created by the death of Maulana Shaukat Ali. The battle of Muslim mass contact thus seems to have been decisively won by the League by the end of 1938. Noticeable everywhere, it was particularly marked in UP, the strongest bastion of the Congress

Muslim mass-contact campaign. According to the UP Governor, the League had 'captured practically the whole body of Muslims in the Province'.[55] It is not surprising, therefore, that in the course of his concluding remarks at the Patna session Jinnah jubilantly asked: 'What has happened to the Congress Muslim Contact Campaign?'[56]

Jinnah, of course, continued his anti-Congress campaign as vigorously as ever, attacking it in his presidential address as a mainly Hindu body determined to foist Hindu rule over the whole country:

> One thing has been demonstrated beyond doubt, namely that the Congress High Command wanted the Musalmans to be a mere understudy of the Congress, mere footpages of the Congress leaders, to be used, governed and brought to heel when they had served the purpose of the Congress. The Congress leaders wanted them to submit unconditionally to Hindu Raj. That game has now been fully exposed. We have got ample proof of it.

Denouncing the claim of the Congress to speak for the whole country, Jinnah remarked that the Congress was a Hindu body and further that the Congress leaders were aware of this fact. The presence in it of a few Muslims, some misguided and others who joined it for ulterior motives, could not make it a national body. He further added:

> It is a misfortune of our country, indeed it is a tragedy, that the High Command of the Congress is determined, absolutely determined, to crush all other communities and cultures in this country, and to establish Hindu Raj. They talk of Swaraj, but they mean Hindu Raj. They talk of National Government, but they mean only Hindu Government. But the bubble has been pricked too soon. Intoxicated with power gained under the new Constitution, with their majority in six or seven provinces, the Congress has its game exposed a little too soon.

Trying to show how the Congress was seeking to establish Hindu Raj, Jinnah again mentioned the thrusting of *Vande Mataram* on Muslim children in schools, the flaunting of the Congress flag as the national flag, the stifling of Urdu by promoting the use of 'Hindi-Hindustani', and the introduction of the Wardha scheme of education. Jinnah made Gandhi a special target of attack:

> I have no hesitation in saying that it is Mr Gandhi who is destroying the

ideal with which the Congress was started. He is the one man responsible for turning the Congress into an instrument for the revival of Hinduism. His ideal is to revive the Hindu religion and establish Hindu Raj in this country, and he is utilizing the Congress to further this object.

All this effort to rouse Muslim passion against the Congress as an organization bent upon establishing Hindu Raj was not meant just to give expression to Jinnah's anger, but also to serve a set purpose—the welding of Indian Muslims into a nation by fostering (Muslim) national consciousness among them. After enumerating Muslim grievances against Congress rule, Jinnah dilated upon his main objective:

As regards the Musalmans, I can say that it is a matter of great congratulation to the All-India Muslim League that it has succeeded in awakening a remarkable national consciousness among the Muslims. Muslims, as I said before, were like men who had lost their moral, cultural and political consciousness. You have not yet got to the fringe of acquiring that moral, cultural and political consciousness. You have only reached that stage at which an awakening has come—your political consciousness has been stirred.

Today you find—apart from the fact of whether the Congress claims are right or wrong—that the Hindus have to a very large degree acquired that essential quality—moral, cultural and political consciousness—and it has become the [embodiment of the] national consciousness of the Hindus. This is the force behind them; that is the force I want the Muslims to acquire. When you have acquired that, believe me, I have no doubt in my mind you will realize what you want. The counting of heads may be a very good thing; but it is not the final arbiter of the destiny of nations. You have yet to develop a national self and a national identity.[57]

V

Apart from Jinnah's speeches, the resolutions adopted by the Muslim League sessions also drew attention to Muslim grievances. Thus, the Lucknow session (October 1937) adopted a resolution strongly condemning 'the attitude of the Congress in foisting the *Vande Mataram* as the national anthem upon the country, in callous disregard of the feelings of Muslims', and added that it considered that song 'not merely positively anti-Islamic and idolatrous in its inspiration and ideas, but [also] definitely subversive of the growth of genuine nationalism in India'. Another resolution deprecated and protested against the formation of ministries in certain provinces by the Congress parties 'in flagrant violation of the letter and spirit' of the Act of 1935 and the Instrument of Instructions.[58] It also condemned the Governors of those provinces for 'their failure to enforce the special powers entrusted to them for the safeguard of the interests of the Musalmans and other important minorities'.[59]

The Special League Session at Calcutta (April 1938) similarly adopted a resolution viewing with alarm the large number of communal riots taking place in UP, Bihar, CP, Bombay, and other provinces, 'resulting in the loss of life and property of the Muslims'. It also expressed the opinion that the Congress governments had 'signally failed to discharge their primary duty of protecting the Muslim minorities in their provinces', and declared that if immediate steps were not taken to rectify the situation, the consequences to the country as a whole would be disastrous. It went on to congratulate the Muslims in villages and towns on the patience and forbearance that, according to the League, they had shown during those riots.[60] This, of course, implied that the riots had been started by the Hindus and that Muslims alone had suffered.

The Patna Session (December 1938) went further and adopted a resolution authorizing the League's Working Committee to decide to resort to 'Direct Action' if and when necessary in view of the 'atrocities' that, according to it, had been committed against the Muslims in Bihar, UP and CP, where the elementary rights of the Muslims had been 'trampled upon in a systematic manner' and the governments of those provinces had failed to redress the grievances of Muslims and to protect even their elementary rights.[61]

In the meanwhile, in order to impart greater credibility to the catalogue of Muslim grievances, which the League leaders were publicizing on all possible occasions, the Council of the League at its meeting in Delhi in March 1938 had decided to appoint a 'special committee', consisting of nine members, with Syed Mohammad Mehdi, Nawab of Pirpur, as its chairman, to thoroughly enquire into them. While doing so, the Council mentioned that 'numerous complaints' had reached the League's central office about 'the hardship, ill-treatment and injustice' meted out to Muslims, particularly to those belonging to the

League in various provinces having Congress Governments. The committee submitted its report, which became famous as the Pirpur Report, towards the end of 1938 and fully endorsed, with details drawn from different provinces, all the supposed grievances of Muslims as already adumbrated in the speeches of the League leaders as well as in the resolutions adopted by the various League organs.[62] Soon after the receipt of this report, the League's Council, in December 1938, appointed another committee, again with the Nawab of Pirpur as convenor, to report particularly on Muslim grievances relating to the Wardha scheme of education. The committee was specifically asked to report whether the Wardha scheme would result in preventing or circumscribing the progress of the Urdu language and the Urdu script; whether it would obliterate or weaken the religious traditions and culture of the Muslims, thereby making them lose their 'separate national identity' and be moulded according to the Congress ideals; and whether it was essential for the Muslims to have their own separate organization for education under their own control. On all these points the verdict of the committee, as was to be expected, was in the affirmative.[63] The committee's report, submitted on 8 April 1939, was summed up in a resolution disapproving the Wardha scheme adopted by the League's Working Committee at its meeting in Bombay on 3–4 July. Mentioning the grounds for disapproval, the resolution recorded that the scheme was calculated to destroy the Muslim culture 'gradually but surely', and establish the domination of Hindu culture; impose the Congress ideology, particularly the doctrine of non-violence; and infuse the political creed, policy and programme of the Congress into the minds of the children.[64]

According to contemporary British confidential sources, most of the Muslim grievances ventilated by the League, if not entirely baseless, were highly exaggerated.[65] They were largely the products not of the Congress ministries' disregard of the feelings of Muslims, or of their acts of partiality in favour of Hindus, but of the general Muslim feeling of grievance because of their having to live under Congress rule, which, according to them, was synonymous with Hindu rule. Thus, for instance, referring to the growth of tension in UP during the period of Muharram in March 1938 and some communal disturbances caused by it, the Governor observed: 'The Ministry behaved in a most sensible way over these disturbances. Indeed, the situation was handled in effect just as it would have been under the old conditions.' At the same time, however, he held both the Muslims and the Hindus responsible for the prevalence of communal tension in UP:

As I have mentioned more than once, a position in which practically the whole of the important minority community of Muslims is ranged in the legislature in opposition to the Government is bound to lead to serious communal friction. The minority cannot get their own way in the legislature, and as permanent communal minority have no prospect of ever getting it, and they are tempted inevitably to redress the weakness of their parliamentary position by rousing religious feelings and emphasizing the importance of the community outside the legislature, even at the risk of communal outbreaks. This is the Muslim contribution to the trouble. But the Muslims are not solely responsible for the ill-feeling. There is also a reverse side to the picture. The Hindus have been unduly elated by the establishment of what is in effect a Hindu Government. There is a good deal of popular feeling that this is Hindu raj, and several officers have told me that they think the Hindu attitude towards communal questions has been aggressive lately.[66]

About six months later, the Governor of Bihar explained the tense communal situation in that province in a similar way:

The advent of a Congress Ministry has been regarded by the Muslims as the institution of Hindu—and therefore anti-Muslim Raj—and the time was therefore propitious for the campaign which the Muslim League has launched with great vigour—and, I fear, venom—in order to foster the 'class consciousness' of the Muhammadans. Muslim League activities have ostensibly been political in their aim, but it has been impossible with a comparatively uneducated, and certainly fanatically inclined, following to keep on the purely political plane. The principal manifestation of Muslim class consciousness has been the traditional effort to exalt Muslim religion at the expense of Hinduism by asserting an unrestricted right of cow-slaughter. On the Hindu side, there has been no similar widespread organization against the Muslims. On the contrary, the Hindu Sabha has been strangely quiescent in the face of grave provocation from the Muhammadan side. At the same time, the coming of the Congress Raj was interpreted by the Hindus as it was by the Muslims and they have become individually, and in local informal associations, much more assertive of *their* rights *vis-à-vis* the Muslims. . . . The general result is that in many places throughout the Province the two communities are straining to be at one another's throats and elsewhere are in that state of apprehensiveness which on the slightest provocation may change to positive aggression.[67]

In April 1939, the Viceroy called for comments from the Governors of UP, Bihar and CP on the list of grievances (some of a general nature and others concerning Muslims) against the Congress Governments in those provinces submitted by Ziauddin Ahmed, Vice-Chancellor, Aligarh Muslim University.[68] The replies of the Governors of UP and Bihar were roughly on the same lines as contained in their reports to the Viceroy in 1938. The Governor of UP began by saying that as the complaints made by Ahmed covered a wide field, he first thought that it might be necessary to deal with them at considerable length, but when he looked into them closely he came to the conclusion that they did not 'really merit any very elaborate answer'. There was, in his opinion, nothing specifically Muslim in the complaints under the general category and these were being voiced by all opposition groups whether Hindu or Muslim. After dealing with them as well as the complaints specifically relating to Muslims at some length, the Governor thus summed up his findings:

> In general, I think it is correct to say that the provincial Ministry has done its best to be impartial in communal matters and with very fair success. Their good intentions have not however saved them from ceaseless attacks on communal grounds from both sides and . . . at the present moment the Hindus are exceedingly loud in their complaints against the Government on the ground that they show undue favour to Muslims. The one substantial grievance of the Muslims is that they have no part in the Government. This is true, and it is a serious matter, but administratively they have little to complain of except that they do not have the general political influence, and the pull in petty, local matters, that the supporters of the Ministry have. In essence, the grievance is not a religious one, though it assumes an intensely communal form. It is political, and is due to the fact that the community is in opposition. It would largely cease to exist if the Muslim League had a share in the Government.[69]

The Governor of Bihar came to a somewhat similar conclusion. 'There is no reason to hold', he observed, 'that the Congress Government in this province have taken any action hostile to Muslim interests; they have been more than fair in the matter of appointments, and have shown themselves very nervous of offending the Muslims.' Referring to the several communal riots that had occurred in the province, he pointed out that in nearly all of them the Hindus had been the aggressors and that they had felt encouraged by the belief that the Congress Government, being 'predominantly Hindu', would treat them lightly. However, the Muslims who made this point in discussions with the Governor admitted their inability to bring any charges of anti-Muslim prejudice against the Government. The Governor also added that Muslims were by no means blameless as their press had fanned communal feelings by publishing distorted accounts of various incidents. In any case, pointed out the Governor, the growth of communal tension in the wake of the introduction of provincial autonomy was not totally unexpected: 'Political rivalry between Hindus and Muslims gave rise to communal tension after the reforms of 1919 were introduced; it is hardly surprising that the introduction of far wider reforms created an even more difficult position.'[70]

The Governor of CP, though finding some substance in Ahmed's complaints, unlike his counterparts in UP and Bihar, did not fundamentally differ from their conclusions in his final summing-up:

> Ziauddin has placed his finger on some genuine dangers and in discussing them I have had to admit that there is some truth in his accusations. That is not, however, the whole story. By and large it must, I think, be admitted that our Muslims have hitherto suffered little, if any, serious injustice at the hands of the Congress Ministry. That there are pin-pricks this letter will have made clear but of really serious injustice there is no evidence as yet. It is the galling thought, however, that their communal opponents are apparently to be in a perpetual political domination over them that hurts most. It is this feeling which leads them to make sometimes quite baseless accusations—as they did in the Pirpur Report—and so long as Congress dominates the political field I do not see how in this province, where they constitute such a small minority of the population, Muslims can expect anything but virtual exclusion from the control of affairs.[71]

The findings of the Governors of UP, Bihar and CP on the supposed Muslim grievances submitted by Ziauddin Ahmed were fully endorsed by the Viceroy. While forwarding these findings to the Secretary of State for India, he remarked that they adequately exposed 'the somewhat insubstantial character of a good many of those grievances, not least as regards the Muslim share in appointments'. Analysing the origin of the grievances, the Viceroy observed:

> It is perfectly obvious that in this country, where communal feeling runs

so deep, and where with these enormous populations and the slender administrative framework so much oppression and so much unfairness can take place in minor ways without the higher authorities or even the more exalted of the subordinate authorities being aware of its existence, or being competent to do anything to stop it, any political party which sets itself to work can produce at short notice sufficient instances of unfairness, of maltreatment and of prejudice to inflame feeling and to produce the impression that the general situation is much worse than is in fact the case. The fact that a Muslim minority is not, I suspect, much worse off in a Province in which it is a minority than a Hindu minority in a Muslim Province does not meet our problem, which is at the moment how to assuage the grievances of the Muslims.[72]

Some League leaders also realized in due course that it would be better to talk of 'atrocities committed on Muslims in Congress-governed provinces' rather than of 'atrocities committed by Congress Governments'. This suggestion was made to Jinnah by no less a person than Liaquat Ali Khan, General Secretary of the League, in January 1939 and the former readily accepted it. Indeed, he asserted that he had always been using the right words and that the phrase 'atrocities committed by Congress-governed provinces' was the product of Jawaharlal Nehru's imaginative mind'.[73]

By way of summing up, it would not be wrong to say that while some minor acts of injustice or partiality here and there might have taken place, as is customary in a democratic set-up in an underdeveloped country, there was really nothing that could justify the use of the term 'atrocities'. The problem was really psychological. Congress workers in the localities and at district headquarters moved around as men of influence and power and, thanks to their contacts with Congress ministers and their hangers-on, worked as channels for the redressal of grievances and distribution of patronage among their protégés or supplicants. I myself remember how as a Congress sympathizer, even though merely a boy of fourteen or fifteen studying in a secondary school, I was approached by a shopkeeper in my village (Kudra in the then Shahabad district) in Bihar, with a grievance against a local government functionary and that, as it appeared genuine, I advised the latter to write a detailed letter explaining his problem to the general secretary of the District Congress Committee. I am not able to recollect now after a lapse of sixty-five years or so whether that advice had been followed or not, but that is not important.

What is important is the widely prevalent belief at that time that appeal to a district Congress leader might result in the redressal of a villager's grievances. This must have been found abhorrent or galling by members of the Muslim elite, most of whom had traditionally looked upon themselves as superior in status to the likes of Congress workers and had no desire to become their supplicants.

All this need not lead us to conclude that all the Muslim grievances ventilated by the League were entirely baseless and had their origin only in the hurt pride of the Muslim elite or that the political part of the executive in the Hindu-majority provinces was entirely blameless. At least in CP, the Governor found many instances to the contrary. While asserting that it was 'quite untrue' that Muslims did not get a fair share of government appointments in that province, and pointing out that they had some 22 per cent of such appointments while constituting only some 4 per cent of the population, he underlined the validity of Muslim grievances on several other points. Thus, he remarked that, although the situation was changing for the better, interference with the work of local executive officers was a fair charge against the ministry, particularly where Hindu–Muslim tension was acute or a local Congress organization was in any way involved. The Governor also felt that although the Premier, Ravi Shankar Shukla, had not been able to do much by way of 'forcing a Hindu and non-Muslim culture on Muslims', that was not because of any lack of inclination on his part, but because Muslims were very wide awake in such matters and in fact they frequently cried even before they had received any real hurt. Even so, in the Education Department there was 'a definite tendency to favour Hindu language and culture—nothing very obvious or palpable, but the thing is quite definitely there'—and the Governor had no doubt that the Premier, encouraged it. The Governor also affirmed that enquiries were sometimes instituted on complaints against Muslim officers which, he strongly suspected, would not have been taken up if the officers concerned had been Hindus.[74]

Whatever that might have been, the important question is not whether the Muslim grievances aired by the League were genuine or baseless or grossly exaggerated, but whether the Muslims in general believed in their genuineness. There is no doubt that, barring a few exceptions, comprising largely of Congress Muslims, they did so, regardless of whether they belonged to the League or not. After receiving a number of Muslim leaders in March–April 1939, who had separately called on him, the Viceroy noted 'the extreme bitterness of views' expressed by them. These leaders included not only persons like Jinnah, Mohammad Yaqub and Ziauddin Ahmed, owing allegiance to the League, but also the Nawab of Chhatari, the leader of the National Agriculturist Party of UP, who had to face opposition from the League as well as the Congress, both during and after the elections of 1937. 'Without exception,' remarked the Viceroy, 'they have impressed upon me their feeling of uneasiness and distress at the trend of the situation and at the gloominess of the future as they see it for the Muslim community.'[75]

The Nawab of Chhatari was not the only prominent non-League Muslim leader to feel distressed at the supposed plight of the members of his community under Congress rule. Sir Sultan Ahmad, a former member of the Viceroy's Executive Council and one of the most respected non-party leaders not only in Bihar but also in the whole country, found himself in the same position. He had been made to resign the office of Advocate General of Bihar after a fortnight of the installation of the Congress Ministry there, in contrast to Bombay where an English Advocate General had been allowed to continue. However, it will not be proper to imagine that his opinion had been influenced by that episode. A person known to Vallabhbhai Patel, informed him about Ahmad's highly adverse opinion on the performance of the Congress ministries in Bihar and some other provinces. He also mentioned that Ahmad was 'a very patriotic Musalman' and was 'much trusted' by Rajendra Prasad.[76] When Patel's correspondent wrote to Ahmad in October 1938 telling him that it was 'very high time that somebody intervened between the Congress and the League', Ahmad, sharing the distress of his correspondent at the growing 'bitterness of feeling' between the Congress and the League, remarked:

So far, I had blamed the Musalmans for their hot-headedness, impracticable suggestions and unreasonable demands, but after having seen the working of the Congress Ministries in at least two or three provinces I am veering round to the view that the apprehension of the Muslims is justified. The meanness to which some of the Congress people can stoop when power has been given to them has been an eye opener to me. Their tall talk of nationalism is a perfect humbug and I find that in the chair of authority they are guilty of bias, bigotry, inequities and meanness, which are absolutely astounding. For a man with my mentality and sincerity and anxiety for the good of India, which I hope you know better than many people, the use of such strong expressions as I have done may be surprising, but I am afraid I am being forced to come to these conclusions.[77]

On hearing from Prasad, who had received a copy of this letter from Patel and had expressed his amazement at its tone and content, Ahmad reiterated his position on the performance of the Congress ministries on matters concerning Muslims. Avowing that when the Congress had decided to accept office no one outside the Congress circle was happier than he himself and that he had felt that as the ministries were going to carry a heavy responsibility and had a great opportunity to serve the people, they deserved the best support from persons like him, in spite of differences of opinion, he remarked:

For a long time and even now I feel that those who are opposed to the Congress indulge in exaggerations and tall talks and for a long time I attached no importance to the catalogue of grievances placed before me, but within the last few months I was compelled to study the attitude of the Congress Ministry [in Bihar] towards the Muslim community and other minorities and I have been led to the most depressing conclusions.

The sentence that you have quoted in your letter from my letter is strong, but believe me it pained me more than you can imagine when I used it. At times I wondered if I was swerving from the path of impartiality and getting into that groove of exaggeration in which some of my Muslim friends have been indulging, but I am convinced that it is not so.[78]

Ahmad, of course, failed to provide specific instances of injustice meted out to Muslims, as asked for by Prasad, and promised to do so when they met. In the meanwhile, however, he asked Prasad to consider whether a detailed enquiry was not 'clearly indicated'. Widening the area of attack, he added: 'There is no doubt that the Muslims in general are up in arms against the Ministry, the Bengalis have no good words to speak about them, the Kisans have nothing but abuses, the landlords are dissatisfied, and the services are not happy.' The Governor, who had seen copies of the intercepted letters exchanged between Prasad and Ahmad, pithily commented: 'I do not think the criticisms are justified, but when they are made by a person such as Sultan Ahmad, it must mean that they are widely felt.'[79]

They were indeed widely felt, turning more and more Muslims against the Congress. Most of the top Congress leaders realized this, though they might not say so publicly. 'The Musalmans as a body have been alienated [from the Congress],' wrote Prasad to Patel in October 1938.[80] Patel wholly agreed with this view even while differing from Prasad on the main cause of that alienation.[81] This was admitted even by Jawaharlal Nehru, who had, as president of the Congress, initiated its Muslim mass-contact programme in March 1937. 'It is true,' he observed in the course of a letter to Prasad in July 1939, 'that in spite of our efforts, the situation has so deteriorated that it may be said that there is more general ill-will among the Muslim masses towards the Congress than there has been at any time in the past.' He went on to explain that during the previous two-three years the work of the Congress in UP among Muslims had not been negligible. There were many 'Muslims of position' who had been working with their Hindu colleagues with great enthusiasm, not as Muslims or Hindus but just as Congressmen. The feeling of comradeship generated by it was of great value in those 'dark days of communal reaction'. The Muslim membership of the Congress in UP had considerably expanded and was roughly estimated to be around a hundred thousand. Although it did not mean very much, it did mean something. For it meant that 'in spite of the aggravation of communal feeling among Hindus and Muslims alike and in spite of the intensive activities of the Muslim League in the province', there was 'a solid core of Congress-minded Muslims'. With all this, however, Nehru again ruefully admitted, 'There is no doubt that we have been unable to check the growth of communalism and anti-Congress feelings among the Muslim masses.'[82]

For the Muslim masses, of course, 'Congress' and 'Hindus' had indeed become synonymous terms. As Congress–League differences mounted and the feeling grew among both Muslims and Hindus that the installation of Congress ministries virtually meant the establishment of Hindu Raj, communal clashes between the members of the two communities in the urban areas of northern India became endemic between 1937 and 1939. The situation was particularly bad in some of the Congress-ruled provinces like UP, Bihar and CP. The following extract from a confidential report of the Government of India for the period February to April 1939 throws light on the growth of communal antagonism by that time:

There has been a marked deterioration in communal relations, affecting almost the whole of the north and centre of India. Increasing aggressiveness on the part of both Hindus and Muslims has in many places created such an inflammable situation that only a spark is needed to cause a conflagration; and three important religious festivals during the quarter were the occasion for serious clashes, though there have also been riots unconnected with any festivals.

It is particularly in some of the Congress Provinces that bitterness is growing; and, since the circumstances of the new Constitution are themselves regarded as a cause, the remedy is hard to find. It is difficult to exaggerate the strain and responsibility on magistracy and police by the conditions now prevailing in several Provinces.[83]

The report for the next quarter (May to July 1939) shows that although the communal disturbances in it were not so serious as they had been in the preceding one, relations between the members of the two communities had not improved and this created one of the major problems for many provincial governments. Home Ministers from all parts of the country discussed this matter at a conference held in May 1939 and called for recourse to severe measures in communal cases. These were to include concerted action against propaganda of a communal nature, incitement to violence and the tendency to create communal hatred and bitterness, which were recognized to be increasing. This call had received support from all Home Ministers, including those belonging to the Muslim League, and the Punjab Premier, Sikander Hyat Khan, had taken a prominent part in drafting it. The Working Committee of the League, at its meeting in July 1939, however, adopted a resolution viewing with grave apprehension the call for a campaign against 'propaganda of a communal nature'. This was done on the ground that unless such a phrase was explained more fully, the Congress ministries might utilize it to victimize the League and stifle the expression of Muslim opinion.[84] The League leadership was obviously not prepared to countenance any measure that might come in the way of its vigorous propaganda campaign against the Congress, which was producing the desired result from its point of view.

VI

While the League was vigorously pursuing its propaganda campaign against the Congress, the latter adopted a number of measures to counter that propaganda, but to no avail. The fate of its Muslim Mass Contact Campaign has already been noted. Senior Congress leaders like Patel and Prasad wanted to avoid controversy over hoisting the Congress flag on public buildings and asked Congressmen to desist from it if the move was opposed by any section of the people concerned. However, ordinary Congress workers and sympathizers, particularly the youth and students, seldom listened to such counsel of wisdom and the controversy continued. Similarly, on the language issue the top Congress leadership repeatedly clarified that it remained committed to promoting the use of Hindustani as the common language of India, without wishing any harm to either Hindi or Urdu. Nehru wrote a long article on the language problem in India in 1937 in order to clarify the Congress position. Therein he stressed that while Hindustani was to be promoted as the common language of northern India, the separate growth of both Hindi and Urdu would also be welcomed and there could be no question of providing any hindrance to either.[85] In the same year, thanks to the initiative taken by Zakir Husain, Prasad came to an understanding with Maulvi Abdul Huq, the most prominent champion of Urdu, regarding the nature of Hindustani, making it clear that it was inimical neither to Hindi nor Urdu. The joint statement issued by them on 28 August 1937 contained the following paragraph:

> We are agreed that Hindustani should be the common language of India and should be written in both the Urdu and Nagri characters which should be recognized for all educational and official purposes. By Hindustani we mean the largest common factor of the language spoken in Northern India and we believe that common usage should be the criterion for the selection and inclusion of words in its vocabulary. We are further of the opinion that the fullest opportunity for development should be vouchsafed to both Urdu and Hindi as literary languages.[86]

In spite of such efforts, the Hindi–Urdu controversy continued unabated and Muslims in general were influenced by the League's propaganda that the Congress had no genuine interest in promoting Hindustani and was only using it as a cover for promoting Hindi. On the other hand, Hindus generally thought that in the name of Hindustani an artificial language was being created at the cost of Hindi. In order to clarify the Congress position, K.M. Ashraf, in-charge of the Muslim mass-contact work at the office of the All-India Congress Committee, moved a resolution at a meeting of that body in September 1938. Noting that the Hindi–Urdu controversy had taken 'a very communal turn' and that the position taken by the Congress on the language issue was not properly appreciated, the resolution wanted the AICC to reiterate that the Congress stood for Hindustani written in both the Devanagari and Persian scripts and to direct all Congressmen to desist from taking any part in the Hindi–Urdu controversy. It also proposed the appointment of a 'Hindustani Board' under the chairmanship of Prasad and consisting of eight other persons with power to co-opt, in order to prepare a scheme for the development of Hindustani. Although the Working Committee declared its support for the resolution, minus the provision relating to the formation of a board, it aroused so much controversy that a large number of amendments were moved and the resolution could not get through.[87] In order to limit damage and prevent the spread of confusion regarding the Congress stand on the language issue, the Working Committee then adopted a resolution clarifying that the failure of the AICC to adopt Ashraf's resolution did not affect the position of the Congress on the language issue as defined in Article XIX of its Constitution. According to that Article, the proceedings of the Congress, the AICC and Working Committee would ordinarily be conducted in Hindustani. However, English or any provincial language might be used if the speaker was unable to express himself in Hindustani or when permitted by the President. The meetings of the Provincial Congress Committees were to be ordinarily conducted in the language of the province concerned, but Hindustani might be used, if preferred by some one. The resolution also added that it had been the policy of the Congress more and more to insist on the use of Hindustani at all meetings and proceedings of Congress Committees.[88] This resolution had the full backing of Gandhi, who observed in the course of an article published shortly after its adoption:

It is a great pity that bitter controversy has taken place and still continues regarding the Hindi–Urdu question. So far as the Congress is concerned Hindustani is its recognized official language designed as an all-India language for interprovincial contact. It is not to supplant but to supplement the provincial languages. The recent resolution of the Working Committee should set all doubt at rest. . . . The real competition is not between Hindi and Urdu but between Hindustani and English.[89]

All this, however, failed to stem the tide of the Hindi–Urdu controversy, which went on as before. In the meanwhile, the Congress Working Committee had also made some effort to reassure Muslims about their future in an independent India by adopting a resolution on 'Minority Rights' in October 1937. The resolution affirmed that the Congress considered it its duty to protect the rights of the minorities and to ensure 'the widest possible scope for the development of these minorities and their participation in the fullest measure in the political, economic and cultural life of the nation'. Declaring that the objective of the Congress was to work for an 'independent and united India', where no class or group, whether in majority or minority, might exploit another, it clarified that this did not mean 'the suppression in any way of the rich variety and cultural diversity of Indian life'. In this connection it recalled the contents of the resolution of the Karachi Congress (1931) on Fundamental Rights and underlined that they made it clear that all would be treated as equal regardless of any one's religion; that there would be no interference by the State in matters of conscience, religion or culture; and that a minority would be entitled to keep its personal law without any change in it imposed by the majority. The Working Committee's resolution further assured the Muslims that while the Congress remained opposed to the Communal Award (1932) and considered it both anti-national and anti-democratic, it also remained firmly committed to its position that any change in the Award could be brought about only through an agreement among all the parties concerned.[90]

At the same time, the Working Committee issued a statement clarifying its position regarding the *Vande Mataram* song, which had by that time become a major source of controversy. Conscious that the widespread Muslim opposition to the song, fanned by the League's campaign, was based on two main grounds, namely its location in Bankim Chandra Chatterji's novel, *Anandmath* (1882) which had a pronounced anti-Muslim tone, and the idolatrous content of some of its lines, which gave it the appearance of a prayer to Durga, the Hindu goddess symbolizing female power, the Working Committee dealt with both these points in its statement. First, it pointed out that the song was composed independently of, and much earlier than, the book in which it appeared and hence significance need not be attached to its location. At the same time it drew attention to the fact that since the anti-partition agitation in Bengal the song had become a symbol of India's urge for freedom and many had heavily suffered just for uttering the words *Vande Mataram*, which had become a widely used slogan. As for the second ground for Muslim opposition, the Working Committee recognized its validity, but pointed out that actually only the first two stanzas were in general use at most places; they were free from any religious symbolism and had also become 'a living and inseparable' part of the national movement. Keeping all this in view, the committee recommended that wherever *Vande Mataram* was sung at national gatherings only the first two stanzas should be used.[91]

VII

The Congress leadership soon realized that such statements failed to produce any impact on the general Muslim mind and that in order to improve the then existing Hindu–Muslim relations it was necessary to start a dialogue with the League leadership, whose influence over the Muslim masses as well as the elite was growing by leaps and bounds. This, however, failed to take off, as the League laid down a condition for the start of a dialogue, which the Congress found itself unable to accept.

Ironically, it was the League that had made the first move towards the start of such a dialogue after the elections of 1937, before the installation of Congress ministries in the Hindu-majority provinces. Thus, in May that year Jinnah had sent a message to Gandhi through B.G. Kher, leader of the Congress Legislature Party in Bombay, saying that it was time Gandhi turned his attention towards the solution of the problem of Hindu–Muslim unity. This was an indirect way of suggesting the start of a Congress–League dialogue, with a view perhaps to preparing the ground for the installation of Congress–League coalition ministries wherever possible. At that time, however, the Congress was not interested either in a dialogue with the League or in the installation of coalition ministries, but with going directly to the Muslim masses with a view to drawing them towards itself. Gandhi, therefore, sent a purely negative, though polite, reply to Jinnah:

> Mr Kher has given me your message. I wish I could do something, but I am utterly helpless. My faith in [Hindu–Muslim] unity is as bright as ever; only I see no daylight out of the impenetrable darkness and, in such distress, I cry out to God for light.[92]

This policy continued for some time also after the installation of Congress ministries. When in September 1937 two Congress leaders from the Punjab, Dewan Chaman Lal and Raizada Hansraj, suggested that it might be worthwhile for Gandhi to meet Jinnah and talk things over as the latter seemed interested in a settlement of the communal problem, Nehru deprecated this move and wrote to one of them (Dewan Chaman Lal):

> We are always prepared to discuss with anyone the communal or any other important question and to try to find a solution. But these questions cannot be isolated from the basic political and economic issues. There is little use in discussing them with someone who does not agree with the Congress on these basic issues. Then again the old method of one or two individuals coming to terms has been shown to be pretty useless. We are dealing today with democratic forces and cannot sidetrack [them]. The Congress may or may not represent any considerable body of Muslims but the Muslim League certainly does not represent any but the reactionary elements in the Muslims. Jinnah's attitude during the past year has been to encourage extreme communalism and reaction among the Muslims. . . .
>
> What are the communal issues before us today and what are we going to talk about and with whom? On political and economic matters to treat the Muslims or the Hindus as homogeneous groups is absurd, and yet this is what Jinnah thinks should be done. I am afraid I am wholly unable to think on these lines.[93]

Enclosing a copy of this letter to Gandhi, Nehru told him: 'I am sure that a meeting between you and Jinnah at this stage would not only serve little purpose, but might be actually harmful.'[94] Gandhi, though perhaps himself inclined differently, accepted Nehru's advice. He wrote to Patel in the first or second week of October 1937: 'I don't see any chance of my meeting Jinnah at present, Jawaharlal does not desire it.'[95]

Although Gandhi for the time being gave up the idea of proposing a meeting with Jinnah, he was apparently feeling too disturbed by the growing communal tension to indefinitely postpone opening up any communication with the latter. Jinnah's Lucknow address served both as a provocation and an opportunity in this regard. The Gandhi–Jinnah correspondence began immediately thereafter, with Gandhi describing the Lucknow address as 'a declaration of war' (19 October 1938) and Jinnah remarking in reply that it was 'purely in self-defence' (5 November 1938). It is not necessary here to recall all the complaints, counter-complaints and explanations which then followed. It will suffice for our purpose to note that the correspondence between the two, carried on desultorily over several months, finally led to an agreement between them to meet for a fuller exchange of views with a view to preparing the ground for formal talks between the President of the League and the President of the Congress. The meeting had been proposed by Gandhi after Jinnah offered to cooperate with him if the former was earnest about trying to find a solution to the communal problem.

At the same time, Jinnah had made one point clear: any serious talks between the League and the Congress could only proceed on the basis that the former was the representative body of Muslims and the latter of the Hindus. When Gandhi mentioned that since, with the passing away of Ansari, Azad had been playing the role of his 'guide' on Muslim affairs and suggested that it might be better if the proposed Gandhi–Jinnah meeting was preceded by an Azad–Jinnah meeting (24 February 1938), Jinnah responded with a firm 'no' and, indeed, chided Gandhi for making such a suggestion (3 March 1938). Lest the significance of this response be lost on Gandhi, Jinnah proceeded to observe:

> We have reached a stage when no doubt should be left. You recognize the All India Muslim League as the one authoritative and representative organization of Musalmans in India, and, on the other hand, you represent the Congress and other Hindus throughout the country. It is only on that basis we can proceed further and devise a machinery of approach.

Out of his eagerness to meet Jinnah for an exchange of views, Gandhi for the time being ignored 'the various debatable points' raised in the latter's communication and contented himself with clarifying that he still did not see any light on the communal problem and disclaiming his own representative capacity with regard to the Congress or the Hindus. He did, however, assure Jinnah that he would exert all the moral influence he might have with the Congress in the interest of an honourable settlement (8 March 1938). The meeting between Gandhi and Jinnah was finally fixed for 28 April 1938; the venue was Jinnah's residence in Bombay, after Jinnah's firm refusal to go to Gandhi's *ashram* at Sevagram (Wardha).[96]

Before we come to that meeting and its aftermath, it may be worthwhile to recall that Nehru, in spite of his earlier opposition to Gandhi taking any initiative to meet Jinnah, had followed Gandhi in opening correspondence with Jinnah. Before this he had corresponded with the UP League leader, Nawab Muhammad Ismail Khan, sending his first letter on 10 November 1937 and continuing the exchange till February 1938, each deploring the growth of communal tension and holding the attitudes and activities of the other side mainly responsible for it.[97] While this correspondence was still going on, Nehru started corresponding with Jinnah in January 1938 with a view to finding out what actually were the points in dispute between the Congress and the League that had led to so much bitterness and required consideration. Just like Nehru's correspondence with Ismail Khan, his correspondence with Jinnah also led nowhere and indeed acquired the appearance of a slanging match between the two, with Nehru insisting on clarifying various issues in dispute through correspondence before any serious discussion began on them and Jinnah asserting that discussion of such vital matters through correspondence would lead nowhere. 'You prefer talking at each other,' wrote Jinnah to Nehru on 17 February 1938, 'whereas I prefer talking to each other. Surely you know and you ought to know what are the fundamental points in dispute.' Nehru in his reply, dated 25 February 1938, observed: 'I am afraid I must confess that I do not yet know what the fundamental points in dispute are. It is for this reason that I have been requesting you to clarify them. So far I have not received any help in this direction.' He wrote to Jinnah again on 8 March 1938: 'I have no desire to take up your time and to spend my time in writing long letters. But my mind demands clarity before it can function effectively or think in terms of any action.' In his reply dated 17 March 1938,

Jinnah sent cuttings of some recent articles from the *Statesman* (New Delhi) and *New Times* (Lahore) and referred to some suggestions made by others for bringing about Hindu–Muslim unity and asserted that they should give Nehru enough of an idea of the work that was required to be done in that regard. He then added: 'But if you desire that I should collect all these suggestions and submit to you as a petitioner for you and your colleagues to consider, I am afraid, I can't do it for the purpose of carrying on further correspondence with regard to these various points with you.' Nehru in reply (6 April 1938) analysed all the suggestions emanating from Jinnah and the press-cuttings sent by him and remarked that he was surprised to see that list as some of the points on it were wholly covered by previous decisions of the Congress and some others were 'hardly capable of discussion'. He further added that there was nothing in them that referred to or touched the economic demands of the masses or affected 'the all-important questions of poverty and unemployment'. Analysing most of the points (in fourteen sections) emerging out of Jinnah's own observations as well as the enclosures sent by him, Nehru remarked that he did not understand what was meant by the Congress recognition of the League as 'the one and only organization of Indian Muslims' and observed: 'Obviously the Muslim League is an important communal organization and we deal with it as such. But we have to deal with all organizations and individuals that come within our ken. We do not determine the measure of importance or distinction they possess.' Again, coming to the suggestion regarding the formation of Congress–League coalition ministries made in one of the articles in the press enclosed by Jinnah, Nehru remarked: 'I should like to know what is meant by coalition ministries. A ministry must have a definite political and economic programme and policy. Any other kind of ministry would be a disjointed and ineffective body, with no clear mind or direction.' Jinnah, in his rejoinder (12 April 1938), remarked that Nehru's letter had been 'a most painful reading' and that his tone and language displayed 'the same arrogance and militant spirit' as if the Congress were 'the sovereign power'. 'Having regard to your mentality,' added Jinnah, 'it is really difficult for me to make you understand the position any further.' Nehru (16 April 1938) regretted that Jinnah thought that he wrote in an arrogant and militant spirit, as if he considered the Congress as a sovereign power, and went on to remark: 'I am painfully conscious of the fact that the Congress is not a sovereign power and that it is limited and circumscribed in a hundred ways and further that it may have to go through the wilderness many a time again before it achieves its objective.' This was the last letter of this series. Nehru had already suggested to Jinnah the publication of their correspondence. Jinnah had no objection, but wanted his correspondence with Gandhi also to be published simultaneously. In his last but one letter Nehru had suggested that he would be in Allahabad for most of April and mentioned that they might meet if Jinnah went there. Or, if it was more convenient for Jinnah to visit Lucknow, Nehru might go there and see him. Jinnah in reply said he had no plans to visit either Allahabad or Lucknow, but would be available in Bombay. This did not suit Nehru.[98] So the meeting did not materialize, but seeing the wide gulf dividing them in their correspondence one can confidently say that even if a meeting between them had taken place, nothing significant would have emerged out of it.

Taking a long-term view, nothing significant emerged also out of the Gandhi–Jinnah meeting that took place in Bombay, as scheduled, on 28 April 1938. In the immediate aftermath, however, it generated some hope. At the end of the talks, Gandhi and Jinnah issued a brief joint statement saying that they had 'three hours' friendly conversation over the Hindu–Muslim question' and that the matter would be pursued further and that the public would be informed of further developments.[99] On the same day Gandhi wired a woman disciple or confidante: 'Talks not unhopeful.'[100] Gandhi had jotted down the main points that emerged during the talks, but neither their text nor summary is available anywhere. Sending them on to Nehru on 30 April 1938, he remarked: 'It may be that you and the other members [of the Congress Working Committee] may not like the basis. Personally I see no escape from it.' Mentioning his inability to move around the country and the 'inner despondency' that had enveloped him at that time as serious handicaps preventing him from playing an active role, he urged a dispassionate consideration of the proposals on their merits. He also added: 'I do not suppose the first will present any difficulty. The second is novel, with all its implications. You will not hesitate summarily to reject it if it does not commend itself to you. In this matter you will have to give the lead.' On the next step, however, Gandhi had already given the lead. He had wired Subhas Chandra Bose, who had succeeded Nehru as Congress President in February 1938, to go to Bombay at his earliest convenience and open formal negotiations with Jinnah. Bose had wired back that he would be in Bombay by 10 May 1938.[101]

Jinnah's notes on his talks with Gandhi, jotted on the same day, are available in his papers and throw light on some of the matters discussed:

(1) Communal Award to stand till substitute is agreed upon. (2) There should be a pact between the Congress and Muslim League which will include a solution of all the questions outstanding. (3) There should be a formal meeting between Abul Kalam Azad, myself and Mr Jawahar. This I was not prepared even to consider and the matter was dropped. That Muslim members of the Congress shall not be considered to represent the Muslims—but there should be no bar to their becoming members if any one so desires. That Mr Subhas Bose and I should formally meet and that he would come down to Bombay, and see me as soon as possible for a formal talk. That thereafter to set up a machinery consisting of the representatives of the Congress and Muslim League who should meet to hammer out the solution of all outstanding questions and ways and means of cooperation—between the two—that Mr Gandhi and I should be present at the meeting of the representatives of the Congress and League and assist them in arriving at settlement.[102]

VIII

As settled between Gandhi and Jinnah on 28 April, Bose called on Jinnah on 12 May. Their discussion centred around the basis for the Congress–League talks, a subject on which the two could not come to an agreement. When, after consulting his colleagues on the Congress Working Committee, Bose called again on Jinnah on 14 May he handed over to the latter a note specifying and explaining the Congress decision on Jinnah's demand. The note recorded that Jinnah had started with proposing the following basis for the Congress–League talks:

The All India Muslim League, as the authoritative and representative organization of the Indian Muslims, and the Congress, as the authoritative and representative organization of the solid body of Hindu opinion, have hereby agreed to the following terms by way of a pact between the two major communities and as a settlement of the Hindu–Muslim question.

After some discussion Jinnah suggested a somewhat different wording, as follows:

The Congress and the All India Muslim League, as the authoritative and representative organization of the Musalmans of India, have hereby agreed to the following terms of a Hindu–Muslim settlement by way of a pact.

According to Bose, the second formulation apparently embodied the same idea as the first, namely that 'the Congress should represent the Hindus and the Muslim League the Musalmans'; the Congress could not, therefore, accept this. For it could not 'possibly consider itself or function as if it represented one community only, even though that might be the majority community in India'. On the other hand, although the Muslim League was 'an organization representing a large body of Muslim opinion which must carry weight', the Congress would be bound to consider other existing Muslim organizations which had cooperated with it in the past. When asked to make some constructive proposal in this regard, Bose handed over a note to Jinnah the next day, saying that he had nothing more to add to his note handed over earlier and suggesting that they should proceed to the next stage and appoint their respective committees to carry out the negotiations. Jinnah replied to Bose on 16 May saying that the matter would be placed before the Executive Council of the League, which was likely to meet in the first week of June.[103]

While the matter was thus pending, Gandhi, at Jinnah's instance,[104] called on him again, on 20 May. Again, although the notes on the talks between the two, made by Gandhi are not available, we have Jinnah's notes and these show that he fully stuck to the League's position not merely relating to the recognition of its status but also to the various other matters with which it had been recently concerned:

1. The Congress must recognize the Muslim League on a footing of complete equality as the authoritative and representative organization of the Muslims of India;
2. That Muslim mass contact movement, on behalf of the Congress, should cease.

3. The League cannot recognize any other Muslim organization or individual Musalman as representatives of the Musalmans;
4. *Vande Mataram* should be abandoned in all public institutions;
5. *Vande Mataram* should not be sung in mixed gatherings;
6. Hindi should not be made compulsory;
7. The Congress flag should not be forced on any public institution;
8. The Muslim members of the Congress should not be considered to represent the Muslims;
9. Persecution of the Muslim press and members and workers of the League should stop.

After scribbling some words after noting these points—*Vande Mataram*, flag, Hindi, mass contact, ill-treatment and persecution and suppression of press, separate electorates—Jinnah again wrote: 'That Muslim League should be recognized as the authoritative and representative organization of the Musalmans of India and the Congress representing the Hindus. That if the settlement [is] formed [that] should be between the Congress and the Muslim League.'[105]

Gandhi was aware how difficult it was for the Congress to satisfy Jinnah on that point. After his talk with Jinnah on 28 April, he had been somewhat hopeful that with perseverance a settlement might perhaps be arrived at. This inference is based on his wire to Amrit Kaur and letter to Nehru after the talk with Jinnah. While the Bose–Jinnah talks were proceeding, he wrote again to Kaur: 'Talks with J[innah] are still going on. S[ubhas] is very patient. He is a good listener. He may succeed where others might have failed. I would like him to succeed.'[106] After another meeting with Jinnah on 20 May Gandhi was less hopeful. He wrote about it next day to C. Rajagopalachari: 'I had two hours and a half with friend Jinnah yesterday. The talk was cordial but not hopeful, yet not without hope.'[107] He opened his heart more fully in his letter to Amrit Kaur a day later: 'He [Jinnah] is a tough customer. If the other members of the League are of same type a settlement is an impossibility.'[108] He was, however, not apologetic about having talked to Jinnah again. Apparently replying to Nehru's criticism (Nehru's letter on this point is not available), Gandhi wrote to him within a week of that talk: 'I think my second talk with him was inevitable. I hope it won't do any harm.'[109]

The Executive Council of the League met on 4 June and asked Jinnah to inform Bose about its view that it was not possible for the League to negotiate with the Congress except on the basis that it was 'the authoritative and representative organization of the Musalmans of India'. At the same time, Jinnah also conveyed to Bose another resolution of the Executive Council of the League, which declared that it would not be possible for the Congress to include any Muslim in the Committee which it might appoint to negotiate a settlement with the League. Both these conditions were rejected by the Congress Working Committee at its meeting on 23–24 July and duly conveyed to Jinnah by Bose on the 25th. Jinnah on his part reiterated the League's position of 2 August. This virtually marked the end of the effort to settle the basis for the start of the Congress–League negotiations, though the Bose–Jinnah correspondence lingered on in a desultory way till the middle of December 1938.[110]

At one stage, while the Bose–Jinnah talks were still going on, Zakir Husain, an eminent Muslim educationist, known for his pro-Congress sympathies and chairman of the committee responsible for drawing up the details of the Wardha scheme of education and having an excellent personal rapport with Gandhi,[111] entered the fray, though only behind the scenes. In a letter to Gandhi he made an impassioned plea in favour of the Congress accepting the League's status as defined by the latter. Agreeing with the view that the Congress could not agree to be described as an organization representing only the Hindus, he argued that if Jinnah could be persuaded not to insist on such a description, it 'would not be very improper' to describe the League as he wished it described. He further observed:

The very fact that the Congress is negotiating with the League presupposes that the Congress in fact accepts that position. No other Muslim organization can deliver the goods. The Musalmans in the Congress cannot carry their community with them; if they could, the need for negotiations with a Muslim organization outside the Congress would not have arisen.

I understand the difficulty in which you find yourself. Recognizing the League as the sole representative body of Muslims would appear like giving up the Muslim individuals and organizations that have worked with the Congress. . . . It may not be quite correct to ignore these groups. But in dealing with psychological problems of the magnitude and complexity of the Hindu–Muslim problem, we cannot insist only on being correct. Only a bold, courageous gesture will resolve it. From whom will that gesture ever come if not from you and, at your advice, from the Congress. 'Correct' negotiations any one could conduct. What is wanted is an attitude that would disarm chronic, persistent suspicion.

Husain went on to argue that even if the League was asking 'unnecessarily' for a recognition of its 'absolute representative nature', the Congress would lose nothing by making that recognition. Actually, it would strengthen its position by drawing Muslims closer to it. On the other hand, by refusing to do so, it would weaken its national character, for that would 'estrange the Muslims still more' and make the League 'even more representative of the Musalmans than it ever was'. Elucidating that point, he asserted that the strength of the League at that time was 'directly attributable to that rather unfortunate declaration' of Nehru in his wordy duel with Jinnah that there were only two parties in the country—the British and the Congress. Husain was sure that Nehru had no intention of denying the existence of Muslims. But no amount of explaining had succeeded in convincing the Muslims that it was not so. They had rallied 'almost like one man' by Jinnah's side in order to reassure themselves that they, too, were a party worth considering and to convince others that their existence might not be denied even in an implied manner. Husain further added:

If the Congress now refuses to concede the representative character of the League, it would be accused once again of attempting to annihilate the one representative Muslim organization, of trying to cause dissension in Muslim ranks and of insincerity in beginning the negotiations. I am not concerned here with the rights and wrongs of these accusations, but they will be made and made in all sincerity. Communal tension being essentially a psychological problem, these ideas will greatly accentuate it, with results it is not pleasant to contemplate.[112]

Gandhi's reply to Husain's impassioned plea was sympathetic but cautious. It shows that while the former fully shared the latter's concern regarding the consequences of the breakdown of the Congress–League talks, he was not sure whether it would be right for the Congress Working Committee to adopt the means suggested by Husain for averting that breakdown. Gandhi wrote:

Your letter is having the fullest attention. The problem is most difficult. . . . It would be a tragedy if the negotiations break over a pure matter of definition of status. All I can say is that as far as in me lies the greatest care will be taken not to do anything in a hurry or in anger.[113]

The problem was indeed 'most difficult'. An acceptance of the League's claim as being the sole representative of Muslim opinion would automatically reduce the Congress to the position of being representative only of Hindu opinion, whether or not this was stated in so many words—as Jinnah had at first suggested. The Congress Working Committee could not accept that position however keen it might be to put a stop to the growing communal tension in the country largely as a result of the continuing Congress–League differences. 'That', aptly observes Rajendra Prasad, 'would be denying its own past, falsifying its history and betraying its future.'[114] Gandhi himself must have been fully aware of this. In any case, it is not likely that he would have tried to influence the Working Committee in favour of accepting Husain's proposal, which was identical with Jinnah's modified proposal as communicated to Bose in May 1938. Gandhi had been since long trying to persuade the British to recognize the Congress as representing all sections of the Indian people, including the minorities. As late as 20 January 1938 he had handed over the following confidential note, marked 'For Lord Lothian and responsible statesmen only', to Lord Lothian who had played a key role in the framing of the Government of India Act of 1935 and was at that time touring India to assess the possibility of implementing its provisions relating to the setting up of an all-India federation:

My ambition is to see the Congress recognized as the one and only party that can successfully resist the Government and deliver goods. It is the only party which from its inception has represented all minorities.

If the British Government recognize the unique position of the Congress they will not hesitate to postpone inauguration of Federation till they have satisfied the Congress. . . . Anyway, once the right status of the Congress is fully recognized the rest becomes easy.[115]

Again, towards the end of 1938, in the course of an interview with H.V. Hodson, then editor of the *Round Table* (London), Gandhi observed: 'The Congress does claim to be the one and the only party that can deliver the goods. It is a perfectly valid claim to make. . . . It is the ambition of the Congress to become all-representative of the entire nation, not merely of any particular section.'[116]

Against this background it is not surprising that the Congress Working Committee at its meeting held in the last week of July 1938, even with Nehru absent (he was in Europe), emphatically reiterated its earlier position, explained first in a memorandum drafted by Nehru[117] and handed over to Jinnah by Bose on behalf of the Working Committee on 14 May 1938. The new note sent by Bose to Jinnah, on 25 July 1938, explained at length the difficulties faced by the Congress in accepting the League's demand for its recognition as the representative body of Indian Muslims before setting up a machinery for considering the terms of settlement of the communal question. Bose started by pointing out that although the League's resolution on that point did not mention the adjective 'only', the language used in the resolution meant that the adjective was understood. The Working Committee had already received warnings against recognizing the exclusive status of the League. There were Muslim organizations that had been functioning independently of the League. Some of them were staunch supporters of the Congress. Besides, there were many Muslim individuals who were members of the Congress and some of them had occupied the highest positions in it and exercised considerable influence over it. Then there was the North-West Frontier Province, which had Muslims in an overwhelming majority and was solidly with the Congress. In the face of these facts, it was 'not only impossible but [also] improper' for the Congress to accord recognition to the League as per the latter's demand. Bose went on to remark:

> It is suggested that the status of organizations does not accrue to them by any defining of it. It comes through the service to which a particular organization has dedicated itself. The Working Committee, therefore, hopes that the League Council will not ask the Congress to do the impossible. Is it not enough that the Congress is not only willing but eager to establish the friendliest relations with the League and to come to an honourable understanding over the much vexed Hindu–Muslim question.[118]

This drew an equally spirited reply from the League's Council at its meeting on 30 July 1938, forwarded by Jinnah to Bose on 2 August. It stated that the Council was fully convinced that the Muslim League was 'the only authoritative and representative political organization of the Musalmans of India'. That position, it asserted, was accepted when the Congress–League Pact was signed at Lucknow in 1916 and had not been questioned since then. The Prasad–Jinnah talks held in 1935 had also been conducted on the same basis. The League, therefore, did not require any recognition from the Congress. However, since Nehru, then President of the Congress, had in one of his statements questioned that position—'in fact the very existence of the League'—by asserting that there were only two parties in the country, the British and the Congress, the League's Council had considered it necessary to inform the Congress of 'the basis on which the negotiations between the two parties could proceed'. The League's resolution also pointed out that the very fact that the Congress had approached the League for a settlement of the Hindu–Muslim question 'presupposed the authoritative and representative character of the League and as such its right to come to an agreement on behalf of the Musalmans of India'. It recognized that the Congress had some Muslim members, including those in the NWFP, but pointed out that they could not represent the Muslims 'for the simple reason' that their number was 'very insignificant' and that as members of the Congress they had 'disabled themselves from representing or speaking on behalf of the Muslim community'. As for the other Muslim organizations, which Bose had referred to without mentioning their names, the League's Council opined that 'it would have been more proper if no reference had been made to them'. It further added: 'If they collectively or individually had been in a position to speak on behalf of the Musalmans of India, the negotiations with the Muslim League for a settlement of the Hindu–Muslim question would not have been initiated by the Presidents of the Congress and Mr Gandhi.'[119]

Just as in the Congress Working Committee, so also in the League's Council there was apparently complete unity on the attitude to be adopted on the issue in dispute between the two organizations. As Sikander Hyat Khan communicated to the Punjab Governor, at the meeting of the League's Council in Bombay at the beginning of June 1938, all the members present were agreed that the League must demand from the Congress a recognition of its position as the authoritative and representative organization of the Indian Muslims.[120] The communications sent by some of the prominent members of the League's Council and the Working Committee who were unable to attend their meetings throw further light on the atmosphere then prevailing in the decision-making bodies of the League. Thus in a letter addressed to Liaquat Ali Khan, General Secretary of the Muslim League, in July 1938, Fazlul Huq, the Premier of Bengal, remarked: 'The reply given by the Congress to Mr Jinnah is a direct insult to the League. We cannot for any reason whatsoever take this lying down.'[121] Mohammad Aurangzeb Khan, one of the rising League leaders in the NWFP, wrote in October that the League must stick to its stand on the Congress recognition of its status 'at all costs and under all circumstances'.[122] Similarly, Nawab Ismail Khan, the most powerful League leader in UP, sent a draft resolution on 6 October, which said that so far as the question of the status of the League was concerned, it continued to adhere to the position already stated 'clearly and explicitly'.[123]

IX

With both sides firmly sticking to their stated positions, there never was any chance of any serious negotiations starting between them. The basic fact was that Muslim League leaders were conscious of the fact that they were expanding their influence in all directions on the basis of a tearing campaign against the Congress and had nothing to gain by entering into an agreement with that body at that stage. For such an agreement would necessarily result in considerably muting, if not completely ending, that campaign half-way, leaving a large number of Muslims still to be converted to a fully separatist approach to which the League was increasingly committed. That was the main reason why the demand was raised that before any negotiations could take place the Congress must recognize the League as the authoritative and representative organization of Indian Muslims. Such a demand would immensely benefit the League regardless whether it was conceded by the Congress or not. If conceded, it would at once result in a big blow to the prestige of those Muslim organizations and individuals who were still working with the Congress and a big jump for the League from the position it had acquired after the elections of 1937. On the other hand, the League had nothing to lose but only to gain if its demand was not conceded. For the very fact that the top-most leaders of the Congress had publicly sought talks with Jinnah with a view to solving the Hindu–Muslim question and felt happy and thankful at being received by him at his residence was bound to bolster his position as a great leader in the eyes of the Muslims. Besides, the failure of the Congress to recognize the League's demand could be utilized by the League to show that the Congress was not interested in any serious negotiations at all, but only in keeping the Muslims weak and divided so as to maintain its own hegemony over them. Even though aware of this, the Congress, on its part, could not accept the League's demand, for it would mean a formal acceptance of the fact that the Congress could speak only on behalf of the Hindus and that it had no right to ask any Muslim organization or individual to work by its side. So each side had its own compulsions in adopting the line that it did and each had the full backing of its Working Committee in taking up that line.

It is interesting in this connection to note that the British authorities in India, who were closely watching what was going on between the two sides, were fully confident from the start that the Congress–League interactions were not going to produce any agreement. This was not based on wishful thinking, but on reports reaching them from the most authoritative sources. One such report was the following, received by the Viceroy from the Governor of the Punjab, based on his talks with his Premier after the latter's return from Calcutta, where the Muslim League had its special session in the third week of April 1938, just a few days before Jinnah was to receive Gandhi for talks on the Hindu–Muslim question:

> At the opening session Jinnah's speech was also calculated to keep the communal temperature at a high level [the other such speech was by Fazlul Huq]. Sikander thought the speech a bad one and I rather infer from something he said that he had remonstrated afterwards with Jinnah, but Jinnah explained that he had deliberately adopted this tone, as he thought it might secure him some tactical advantage in his approaching conversations with Gandhi. Incidentally, I may mention that Sikander has very little hope that anything will come out of these conversations.[124]

After another talk with Sikander the Governor reported on 25 May:

> I asked Sikander whether he had any information about the Gandhi–Jinnah conversations [28 April and 20 May 1938] and he said he had

none at all. The reports that have appeared in the Press about Jinnah consulting Sikander on the telephone are entirely untrue and Sikander does not think that Jinnah has in fact consulted anyone so far. He did have some talk with Sikander when they were both at Calcutta in April about his forthcoming conversations with Gandhi, and Jinnah then, I gather, expressed the view that the conversations would lead to no real result. Sikander, speaking to me this morning, told me that his own view was, and still is, identical.[125]

The Governor had another conversation with Sikander Hyat Khan after the latter's return from the meeting of the League's Executive Council in Bombay in the first week of June 1938, held to consider the attitude to be adopted in the on-going conversations between Jinnah and Bose. The report is again quite interesting and revealing of the real nature of the Bose–Jinnah interaction:

I asked Sikander what was the point of summoning the whole Executive Council of the League to Bombay and what was the net result of its meeting. To this his reply was that the meeting merely endorsed the attitude already taken up by Jinnah in the conversations and threw the onus on the Congress for breaking off negotiations.

I then told Sikander I had been rather puzzled by Jinnah's savage attack on Congress at a public meeting in Bombay held (I think) on June the 6th. Sikander was present at this meeting and said that Jinnah's attack was quite deliberate. Jinnah considers Congress is suffering from swollen head and that the only way to deal with it is to adopt a truculent attitude, or, in other words, to treat the Congress as *de haut en bas*. Evidently there is no genuine desire on the part of Muslims to come to terms.[126]

The report from the Governor of Bengal about the same time, based on a conversation with Khwaja Nazimuddin, his Home Minister and a person closer to Jinnah than either Sikander Hyat Khan or Fazlul Huq, is equally enlightening: 'The Home Minister repeated to me again before leaving [for Bombay for the meeting of the League's Executive Council] that he does not anticipate a successful outcome [of the Bose–Jinnah conversations] and he again hinted that he much hoped that nothing would come of the 'Talk'.'[127] As early as 30 April 1938, the day when Gandhi and Jinnah met in Bombay, the Viceroy had noted that he found it difficult to believe that 'any positive result' was likely to emerge from the Gandhi–Jinnah conversations.[128] His comment on the Bengal Governor's report on his talk with Nazimuddin shows that he had been getting similar hints/reports from other sources and also that Jinnah's strategy was paying off:

Nazimuddin's anticipation that nothing much was likely to come out of the unity talks appears to have been amply fulfilled. The impression one gets is that so far from Congress having gained any advantage at this stage, one clear and direct result of the negotiations which are taking place has been further to consolidate the position of the Muslim League, and to increase the probability of a more uncompromising attitude still being adopted by the Muslims on matters such as the flying of the Congress flag, the singing of *Vande Mataram* and the like.[129]

It is also remarkable that apart from such items, which were really parts of the League's list of grievances, being aired from public platforms, particularly since October 1937, Jinnah had no other major demand than that relating to the recognition of the League by the Congress as the authoritative and representative body of the Muslims. The notes kept in the Jinnah Papers on his conversations with Gandhi on 30 April and 20 May, which have been mentioned earlier, also confirm this. So the talks were being used by the League not to arrive at a settlement of the Hindu–Muslim question but to highlight the importance of the League as the sole representative organization of the Muslims in India. Apparently, according to Jinnah's strategy, this was the time not to enunciate the demand of the League, which, as shown by his comment on the historical significance of Iqbal's letters to him in 1937, had already been formulated in his own mind, but only to prepare the ground for its enunciation. Even his colleagues had no idea what he was aiming at. According to the Punjab Governor, when during his visit to Lahore in the latter half of January 1938, Nehru told Sikander that the Congress was prepared to concede everything to Muslims, but it could not make out what Jinnah really wanted, 'Sikander naively admitted that he also did not know.'[130] Khaliquzzaman's comment is equally revealing. Describing the refusal of the Congress to accept the League's condition for starting negotiations on the Hindu–Muslim question as 'a piece of good luck', he writes: 'If Congress had accepted the position at the time when demand was made by the League, I wonder what positive demands we could then have made.'[131] As late as April 1939, the Viceroy remarked:

I continue to be rather distressed by the Muslim attitude. The community are completely puzzled as to the wise course to adopt and they are not particularly well led, for Jinnah, though clever, keeps things too much in his own hands and is too much concerned to run a purely personal policy on a basis of mystery.[132]

Linlithgow was getting unnecessarily worried about Jinnah's leadership role. The latter had a superb sense of timing. As we shall see in due course, the mystery was unravelled within less than a year, when he considered the time ripe for it.

NOTES

1. See Syed Shamsul Hasan, ... *Plain Mr Jinnah* (Karachi, 1976), pp. 66–71.
2. Muhammad Iqbal, *Letters of Iqbal to Jinnah, with a Foreword by M.A. Jinnah* (Lahore, 1974), pp. 17–18.
3. Ibid., pp. 18–23
4. Ibid., pp. 6–7.
5. Ibid., pp. 21–2.
6. Raja of Mahmudabad, 'Some Memories', C.H. Philips and Mary Doreen Wainwright, eds., *The Partition of India: Politics and Perspectives* (London, 1970), p. 386.
7. Anderson to Linlithgow, 9 March 1937, F125/112, Linlithgow Collection, India Office Library.
8. S.H. Suhrawardy to Jinnah, 5 July 1937, Reel 19, File 458, Quaid-i-Azam Papers.
9. Suhrawardy to Jinnah, 23 July 1937, ibid.
10. Iqbal to Jinnah, 21 June 1937, Iqbal, n. 2, pp. 24–5.
11. Sir Herbert Emerson to Linlithgow, 8 May 1937, F125/113, Linlithgow Collection.
12. Emerson to Linlithgow, 22 May 1937, ibid.
13. Lord Brabourne to Lord Linlithgow, 5 June 1937, IOR, F125/113, Linlithgow Collection.
14. Syed Sharifuddin Pirzada, ed., *Foundations of Pakistan: All India Muslim League Documents: 1906–1947* (hereinafter *League Documents*), vol. II (Karachi, 1970), pp. 267–8.
15. Emerson to Linlithgow, 21 October 1937, F125/113, Linlithgow Collection.
16. *League Documents*, n. 14, p. 269.
17. Ibid., p. 273.
18. Ibid., p. 274.
19. Ibid., pp. 274–5.
20. Ibid., pp. 280–1.
21. Hasan, n. 1, p. 328.

22. Choudhry Khaliquzzaman, *Pathway to Pakistan* (London, 1961), p. 171.
23. Matlubul Hasan Saiyid, *Mohammad Ali Jinnah* (Lahore, 1953; 1st published 1945), p. 265.
24. Jamil-ul-Din Ahmad, *Creation of Pakistan* (Lahore, 1976), p. 10.
25. See Sikander Hyat Khan to M.A. Jinnah, 3 November 1937, and Ghulam Rasul to M.A. Jinnah, 4 November 1937, Mukhtar Massood, ed., *Eye Witnesses of History: A Collection of Letters Addressed to Quaid-i-Azam* (Karachi, 1968), pp. 12–18, 37–47.
26. Syed Sharifuddin Pirzada, ed., *Quaid-i-Azam Jinnah's Correspondence* (Karachi, 1977), p. 35.
27. Sir George Cunningham to Lord Linlithgow, 23 October 1937, 23 October 1937, F125/112, Linlithgow Collection.
28. *Selected Works of Jawaharlal Nehru* (hereinafter *SWJN*), S. Gopal, ed., vol. VIII (New Delhi, 1976), pp. 185–6.
29. M.K. Gandhi to M.A. Jinnah, 19 October 1937, *Collected Works of Mahatma Gandhi* (hereinafter *CWMG*), LXVI (New Delhi, 1976), p. 257.
30. Emerson to Linlithgow, n. 15.
31. Sir Harry Haig to Linlithgow, 23 October 1937, F125/13, Linlithgow Collection.
32. Linlithgow to Zetland, 27 October 1937, F125/4, ibid.
33. K.K. Aziz, ed., *Prelude to Pakistan: Documents and Readings illustrating the Growth of the Idea of Pakistan*, vol. I (Lahore, 1992), pp. 440–2.
34. Mohammad Ali Jinnah, *The Nation's Voice: Speeches and Statements, March 1935–March 1940* (hereinafter *Jinnah: Speeches and Statements*) Waheed Ahmad, ed. (Karachi, 1992), p. 186.
35. Ibid., pp. 189, 192–3.
36. Ibid., pp. 202–4.
37. Ibid., pp. 220–1.
38. Ibid., p. 223.
39. Ibid., pp. 227–8.
40. Ibid., pp. 212–14.
41. Ibid., pp. 215–16.
42. Ibid., p. 229.
43. Ibid., pp. 235–6.
44. *Quarterly Survey of the Political and Constitutional Position in British India* (hereinafter *Quarterly Survey*), prepared in the Office of the Secretary to Governor-General, I, F125/142, Linlithgow Collection.
45. Ibid., II.
46. *League Documents*, II, n. 14, pp. 290–1.
47. Ibid., pp. 292–3.
48. Ibid., p. 295.
49. Ibid., pp. 295–6.

50. Ibid., pp. 288–9.
51. Emerson to Linlithgow, 25 April 1938, F125/86, Linlithgow Collection.
52. *Jinnah: Speeches and Statements*, n. 35, pp. 285–6.
53. *Quarterly Survey*, n. 44, nos. 3 and 4.
54. Rajendra Prasad to Vallabhbhai Patel, 10 December 1938, Rajendra Prasad Papers, File 4A/38, National Archives of India, New Delhi.
55. Haig to Linlithgow, 19 December 1938, IOR, MSS Eur. F115/2A, Haig Collection.
56. League Documents, n. 14, p. 130.
57. Ibid., pp. 304–7.
58. This obviously referred to the fact that Muslims appointed as members of the Congress Ministries did not enjoy the confidence of a majority of the Muslim members in the Assemblies, but the Instrument of Instructions issued to the Governors only stipulated that members of the minority communities should be included in the Ministries, which had to function on the basis of collective responsibility without mentioning any other requirement. For the text of the Instrument of Instructions on this point, see K.T. Shah, *Provincial Autonomy* (Bombay, 1937), pp. 112–13.
59. *League Documents*, n. 14, pp. 278–9.
60. Ibid., p. 298.
61. Ibid., p. 312.
62. For the text of the Pirpur Report, see K.K. Aziz, ed., *Muslims under Congress Rule, 1937–39: A Documentary Record*, vol. I (Delhi, 1986), pp. 307–86. A good summary is available in Anita Inder Singh, *The Origins of the Partition of India 1936–1947* (Delhi, 1987), pp. 33–6.
63. Text in Aziz, n. 63, pp. 175–82.
64. Ibid., p. 191.
65. This view has been generally accepted by non-Pakistani scholars. See, for instance, Penderel Moon, *Divide and Quit* (London, 1945), p. 23 and Gowher Rizvi, *Linlithgow and India: A Study of British Policy and the Political Impasse in India, 1936–43* (London, 1978), pp. 98–105.
66. Haig to Linlithgow, 23 March 1938, MSS Eur. F115/2A, Haig Collection. See also Haig to Linlithgow, 10 April 1939, ibid: 'To my mind the root cause of the trouble is that the Muslims look upon the present Government as Hindu Raj and to a very large extent the Hindus also have the same feeling.'
67. Thomas Stewart to Linlithgow, 7 September 1938, F125/45, Linlithgow Collection.
68. Linlithgow to Haig, Halleth and Wylie, 13 April 1939, Enclosure from the Private Secretary to the Viceroy to the Private Secretary to the Secretary of State, 27 April 1939, IOR, L/P & J/8/686.

69. Haig to Linlithgow, 10 May 1939, ibid.
70. M.G. Hallett to Linlithgow, 8 May 1939, ibid.
71. Francis Wylie to Linlithgow, 18 April 1939, ibid.
72. Linlithgow to Zetland, 19 May 1939, F125/7, Linlithgow Collection.
73. See Liaquat Ali Khan to Jinnah, 12 January 1939, and Jinnah to Liaquat Ali Khan, 14 January 1939, Jinnah Papers, Reel 6, File 48, Quaid-i-Azam Academy, Karachi.
74. Wylie to Linlithgow, 18 April 1939, n. 64.
75. Linlithgow to Cunningham, 14 April 1939, F125/74, Linlithgow Collection.
76. Letter to Patel (writer's name withheld), 19 October 1939, enclosure from Patel to Prasad, 3 November 1939, Prasad Papers, n. 55.
77. Sultan Ahmad to a friend, 26 October 1939, ibid.
78. Ahmad to Prasad, 16 November, 1938, ibid.
79. Hallet to Linlithgow, 26 November 1938, F125/45, Linlithgow Collection.
80. Prasad to Patel, 11 October 1938, Prasad Papers, n. 55.
81. Patel to Prasad, 15 October 1938, ibid.
82. Nehru to Prasad, 7 July 1939, *SWJN*, VIII, n. 21, pp. 470–1. For a brief review of the Congress Muslim Mass Contact Programme and the causes of its failure see Bimal Prasad 'Congress and Muslim League, 1935–1937', in Richard Sisson and Stanley Wolpert, eds., *Congress and Indian Nationalism* (Berkeley, 1988), pp. 312–14. For more details and a slightly different perspective on the causes of the failure of the Congress Campaign, see Mushirul Hasan 'The Muslim Mass Contact Campaign: Analysis of a Strategy of Political Mobilisation', ibid., pp. 198–222.
83. *Quarterly Survey*, n. 45, no. 7.
84. Ibid., no. 8.
85. See Jawaharlal Nehru, 'The Question of Languages', *SWJN*, vol. VIII, n. 28, pp. 829–45.
86. 'Joint Statement of Maulvi Abdul Huq and Babu Rajendra Prasad on the question of common language in India', 28 August 1937, Prasad Papers, n. 55, File 2H/38. See also Zakir Husain to Prasad, 24 August 1937, ibid.
87. *Indian Annual Register*, 1938, vol. II, p. 279.
88. A.M. Zaidi and S.G. Zaidi, eds., *The Encyclopaedia of the Indian National Congress, 1936-38* (hereinafter *Congress Encyclopaedia*), vol. XI (New Delhi, 1980), pp. 486–87.
89. M.K. Gandhi, 'Hindustani, Hindi and Urdu', *Harijan*, 29 October 1938, reproduced in *CWMG*, vol. LXVIII (New Delhi, 1977), pp. 23–4.
90. *Congress Encyclopaedia*, vol. XI, n. 85, pp. 295–7.

91. Ibid., pp. 299–300.
92. Gandhi to Jinnah, 22 May 1937, *CWMG*, vol. LXV (New Delhi, 1976), p. 231.
93. Nehru to Dewan Chaman Lal, 30 September 1937, *SWJN*, vol. VIII, n. 21, pp. 180–1.
94. Ibid., p. 182.
95. Gandhi to Patel, before 9 October 1937, *CWMG*, vol. LXVI (New Delhi, 1976), p. 212.
96. For the text of the Gandhi–Jinnah correspondence, 1937–38, see Pirzada, n. 26, pp. 88–95; also Aziz, n. 63, pp. 197–203; For Gandhi's letters above, see *CWMG*, vols. LXV–LXVII.
97. Aziz, n. 63, pp. 204–25.
98. Ibid., pp. 226–55; Pirzada, n. 19, pp. 244–9.
99. Gandhi's Statement to the Press, 28 April 1938, *CWMG*, vol. LXVII (New Delhi, 1976), p. 50.
100. Gandhi to Amrit Kaur, 28 April 1938, Telegram, ibid.
101. Gandhi to Nehru, 30 April 1938, ibid., p. 56.
102. Quaid-i-Azam Papers, F.40/10/12; also reproduced in S.A.I. Tirmizi, ed., *The Paradoxes of Partition*, vol. I, *1937–39* (New Delhi, 1998), p. 397.
103. Ibid., F40/13-18; Tirmizi, p. 401.
104. Ibid.
105. Ibid., F40/20, Tirmizi, pp. 405–6.
106. Gandhi to Amrit Kaur, 16 May 1938, *CWMG*, vol. LXVII, n. 96, p. 84.
107. Gandhi to C. Rajagopalachari, 21 May 1938, ibid., p. 90.
108. Gandhi to Amrit Kaur, 22 May 1938, ibid., p. 92.
109. Gandhi to Nehru, 26 May 1938, ibid., p. 95.
110. For the text of the Bose–Jinnah correspondence, May–December 1938, see *Netaji: Collected Works*, vol. IX, Sisir Kumar Bose and Sugata Bose, eds., pp. 110–22. The Bose–Jinnah correspondence is also available in Aziz, n. 55, pp. 256–64; and Pirzada, n. 19, pp. 46–52. However, they contain certain errors. Aziz fails to mention the date of Bose's last letter and also mentions 10 October instead of 9 October as the date of Jinnah's last letter; Pirzada does not include the last letter of Bose and also commits the same mistake about the date of Jinnah's last letter as Aziz.
111. See Bimal Prasad, 'Zakir Husain's Correspondence with Mahatma Gandhi', in Sayida Saiyidain Hamid, ed., *Zakir Husain: Teacher Who Became President* (New Delhi, 2000), pp. 259–60.
112. Husain to Gandhi, 30 June 1938, ibid., pp. 266–7.
113. Gandhi to Husain, 11 July 1938, ibid., p. 262.
114. Rajendra Prasad, *India Divided* (Bombay, 1946), p. 153.
115. Lord Lothian's Memorandum, 24 January 1938, MSS Eur. D609/25A,

Zetland Collection, India Office Library; also available in *CWMG*, vol. LXVI (New Delhi, 1976), p. 344 and Ghanshyam Das Birla, *Bapu: A Unique Association*, vol. III (Bombay, 1977), pp. 145–6.

116. 'Interview to H.V. Hodson', *CWMG*, vol. LXVIII (New Delhi, 1976), p. 240.
117. The draft memorandum in Nehru's own handwriting is available in his Papers (vol. XXXVI), Nehru Memorial Museum & Library, New Delhi.
118. Bose to Jinnah, 25 June 1938, *Netaji*, n. 112.
119. Jinnah to Bose, 2 August 1938, ibid.
120. Henry Craik to Linlithgow, 10 June 1938, MSS Eur. F125/86, Linlithgow Collection.
121. Fazlul Huq to Liaquat Ali Khan, 27 July 1938, Muslim League Papers, vol. 246, Council Meetings, 1938, Archives of the Freedom Movement, University of Karachi.
122. Mohammad Aurangzeb Khan to Liaquat Ali Khan, 5 October 1938, Muslim League Papers, vol. 122, Working Committee Meetings 1932–38, ibid.
123. Ismail Khan to Liaquat Ali Khan, 6 October 1938, ibid.
124. Henry Craik to Linlithgow, 25 April 1938, MSS Eur. F125/86, Linlithgow Collection.
125. Craik to Linlithgow, 20 May 1938, ibid.
126. Craik to Linlithgow, 10 June 1938, ibid.
127. Brabourne to Linlithgow, 3 June 1938, F125/38, ibid.
128. Linlithgow to Brabourne, 8 June 1938, F125/38, ibid.
129. Linlithgow to Brabourne, 8 June 1938, F125/86, ibid.
130. Emerson to Linlithgow, 27 January 1938, F125/86, ibid.
131. Choudhry Khaliquzzaman, *Pathway to Pakistan* (London, 1961), p. 191.
132. Linlithgow to Zetland, 17 April 1939, MSS Eur. F125/7, Linlithgow Collection.

CHAPTER II

Preparing the Ground 1937–1939 (II): Search for a New Polity Based on the Two-Nation Theory

AMONG THOSE WHO contributed towards preparing the ground for the Muslim League's adoption of the demand for India's partition and the creation of Pakistan mention must also be made of all those, within as well as outside the League, who devoted their energies to the popularization of the Pakistan idea among the Muslim elite and youth and elucidated its various aspects, and, even when not directly pleading for the creation of Pakistan, ardently supported the two-nation theory and sketched the outlines of a new polity based on that theory.

Just as earlier, so also during 1937–9, the lead in this respect was taken by Rahmat Ali. He gave a well-thought-out interview, notable for its clarity as well as its deep emotional content, to the well-known Turkish authoress, Halide Edib, who incorporated it fully in her book on India published in London in 1937. In that interview he reiterated that his scheme was 'a plan for an independent and separate Pakistan composed of the five Muslim Provinces in the North and possessing equality of status with Hindus, as with other civilized nations, in the comity of nations'. Underlining its chief merit from the Muslim point of view, he observed: 'We are as proud of our history as we are confident of our future. We know that within Hindustan we will be a minority community, but outside it, a virile nation of forty-two millions'. Explaining the territorial and demographic bases of the proposed State, he asserted that its Muslim population constituted about one-tenth of the entire Muslim world and would be larger in both population and area than fifty-one out of the fifty-four nations then constituting the League of Nations. He further added:

'Our area is four times that of Italy, three times that of Germany, and twice that of France, and our population seven times that of Australia, four times that of Canada, twice that of Spain, and equal to that of France and Italy, considered individually.'

Speaking in a prophetic vein Rahmat Ali declared: 'I admit that in the present struggle our back is to the wall, but we remember that in this very land our forefathers successfully faced far worse situations than we have to meet today. . . . We know that Pakistan is our destiny.' Again: 'The present may frown upon us, but I have my eyes fixed on the future, which is sure to smile on our sacred cause. Till that moment arrives, we will face the ordeal like true sons of Pakistan.' Asked whether the new State would be economically self-sufficient, Rahmat Ali replied: 'Why not? Pakistan has vast resources—both moral and material—and with the exit of British imperialism and Hindu capitalism we can surely pay our way.' Elucidating this point he observed that Pakistan had a first-class port in Karachi and its five harbours could be built along its coastline. Besides, Pakistan had the most productive soil and its mineral resources were not inconsiderable. Commerce and industry were also developing. To these could be added the revenues derived from customs, posts and telegraph, excise, land revenue, income tax, and railways, which were then going to the Government of India. Pakistan could thus look confidently to its future.

Asked about the impact of the creation of Pakistan on the position of millions of Muslims who would be left in India, Rahmat Ali began with an emotional response: 'The truth is that in this struggle their thought has been more than a wrench to me. They are the flesh of our flesh and the soul of our soul. We can never forget them, nor they us.' He then went on to assert that the creation of Pakistan would not adversely affect the position of Muslims of India. On the basis of population their representation in both legislature and administration would be the same as it was then. As for the future, the only effective guarantee was that of 'reciprocity': 'We solemnly undertake to give all those safeguards to non-Muslim-minorities in Pakistan which will be conceded to our Muslim-minority in Hindustan.' The most important point was that the promoters of Pakistan, whom Rahmat Ali described as protectors of Pakistan, were working in the highest interest of 'the Millet'. That belonged to all Muslims whether they lived in Pakistan or India. Rahmat Ali added: 'While for us it is a national citadel, for them it will ever be a moral anchor. So long as the anchor holds, everything is or can be made safe.'

Finally, asked about the alternative of 'one Indian nationhood' for all, Rahmat Ali replied with an emphatic 'No': 'We are not Indians; we are Pakistanis. We can understand 'one Indian nationhood' for the Indians themselves; but for us, the Pakistanis, it would mean our national death.' Explaining the 'Himalayas of heart and soul', which divided Hindus and Muslims, Rahmat Ali thus concluded his interview:

> Our religion, culture, history, literature, economic system, laws of inheritance, succession and marriage are fundamentally different from those of the Hindus. These differences are not confined to the broad basic principles. Far from it. They extend to the minutest details of our lives. We, Muslims and Hindus, do not interdine, we do not intermarry. Our national customs and calendars, even our diet and dress are different. In the presence of these incontrovertible realities to try to unite us politically and physically by destroying our Pakistani nationhood would be the most grievous of disasters. Like every other nation in the world we have a definite mission for the service of mankind, which we can fulfill only if we protect the purity of the Pakistani soul. Therefore for us to shed our nationhood in the interest of 'One Indian Nationhood' would be a treachery against our posterity, a betrayal of our history, and a crime against humanity for which there could be no salvation.[1]

This was the most passionate exposition of the Pakistan idea ever published, and covered almost all possible questions that could be raised on it. One can safely imagine that its text or gist would have reached a fairly large section of the Muslim elite and influenced their thinking in one form or another. Such influence is clearly discernible on many of the scholars, journalists and politicians who championed the Pakistan idea either in full or in part from 1937 onwards. 'Any one coming after him [Rahmat Ali],' aptly observes K.K. Aziz, the great historian of the Pakistan idea, 'could hardly escape his influence or ignore his arguments and conclusions.'[2] This should become clear from a perusal of the various schemes for the solution of the Hindu–Muslim problem propounded between 1937 and 1939. The authors of all these schemes ardently believed in the two-nation theory on the basis of Hindu–Muslim differences in religion and culture, and argued that because of such differences parliamentary democracy in its undiluted form was not suited to India. While a few suggested the establishment of separate homelands for Muslims and Hindus, without partitioning the country, with a federal government that would have minimum powers and would be so constituted as to ensure that neither Hindus nor Muslims could dominate over it, others suggested outright Partition.

II

Among the former, the most prominent was Syed Abdul Latif, a retired Professor of English at the Osmania University, Hyderabad. In a pamphlet entitled *The Cultural Future of India*, published in 1938, he pleaded for a division of India into fifteen cultural zones—four Muslim and eleven Hindu—with large-scale exchanges of population between one zone and another, in order to ensure cultural homogeneity. Besides the two already existing Muslim zones, the north-west and the north-east of India, the two new Muslim zones were to be the Delhi–Lucknow block and the Deccan block, consisting of Hyderabad and the surrounding areas. At the same time, even while rejecting Partition as a solution for the Hindu–Muslim problem, he supported the two-nation theory as strongly as Rahmat Ali had done. Emphasizing that the main problem in India was cultural rather than political or economic, he asserted that culturally India was not one unit. 'Two great cultures, not to speak of others,' he wrote, 'subsist here side by side, inspired by two separate religions affecting almost every detail of one's life.' There was also no common language uniting them. If any programme based on the concept of a single nationality for India was sought to be implemented, it would amount to 'a wilful attempt to strengthen the Hindu nationality only, on whose sufferance the other nationalities may live'. On these grounds Latif strongly pleaded for the abandonment of the concept of a single Indian nationality:

> The idea of a single nationality, therefore, should be given up altogether. It will not thrive on the Indian soil; and no Act of the British Parliament granting even immediately the Dominion Status to India will promote that end. Suspicions deep and abiding exist between the two nationalities. That nobody dare deny. If India is freed from the British domination, the Hindu 'nationals' fear that there might again be an extension of the

Muslim political influence from the north-west on which side there is a block of Muslim countries extending right upto the Atlantic . . . . On the other hand, the Muslim nationality feels that the acquisition of such power by the Hindu nationality would place the Muslims for ever under its subjection and allow them little chance for an independent existence on their own religious, moral and cultural lines.[3]

In 1939, Latif further refined his scheme and also provided the outlines of a Constitution, which was to take the place of the Government of India Act of 1935. Apart from the maximum possible provincial autonomy and a federal government with extremely limited powers, Latif's Constitution also provided for zonal or regional boards for coordinating the activities of such contiguous units as enjoyed affinities in respect of subjects of cultural and economic importance common to them. The formation of such boards was expected to dispense with the need for having sub-federations in the different regions involving much greater expenditure. Further, in order to avoid the domination of a single party over the executive, Latif suggested the replacement of the parliamentary executive by a 'composite executive', which would have representatives of all parties and groups in the legislature on the basis of an agreed programme.[4] All this was, of course, based on the assumption that India would continue to remain one united country. Sir Abdulla Haroon, President of the Muslim League in Sind, commended these proposals in his Introduction to the book. While doing so, he remarked that Muslims neither wanted to dominate over Hindus or any other community nor to be dominated over by any one. That was why they wanted to have for themselves their 'separate homelands where they might live a life of their own and from where they might be in a position to work with their Hindu brethren, living in similar homelands of their own, for the common good of their country as a whole'.[5]

By way of providing a background to his constitutional scheme, however, Latif supported the two-nation theory even more forcefully and at greater length than he had done in his earlier tract. After dilating upon the cultural differences, based essentially on religion, between the Hindus and the Muslims and arguing that they indeed were two nations living in the same country, he wrote:

The cultural differences of the Hindus and the Muslims remaining what they are, the idea of the two joining to form a single, though composite, nation is too remote a possibility, unless the Muslims give up their culture and identity and become a caste or sub-caste of the Hindu hierarchy, or the Hindus themselves choose to discard their symbolic life and caste exclusiveness and enter in the company of Muslims on a thoroughly democratic, monotheistic life. But is such an effort possible for the present generation of Indians?[6]

Gandhi, after going through his earlier pamphlet, had written to Latif: 'I believe in the possibility of the two cultures blending. The difficulties which you picture don't baffle me.' Commenting on this Latif wrote: 'What blending could be expected between cultures so distinctly different in their attitude towards life?' Such blending, he further emphasized, would call for the blending of Hinduism and Islam and that was just not possible. Anticipating questions regarding the relationship of culture with religion he remarked: 'The truth is that culture is synonymous with life, and life is the expression of one's deepest convictions. It is religion in action.' According to Islam, he further emphasized, life 'is indivisible and there is nothing private which does not react on one's public activity'. Proceeding further, he quoted from Gandhi's writings to show that religion really provided the motive force of the latter's public activities and asked: 'If it is religion which ultimately supplies the motive for lasting socio-political activity, and which is the basis on which a culture rests, how can the Muslim and Hindu cultures blend themselves unless Hinduism blends itself with Islam? Is that possible?' Latif also asserted that Gandhi and, under his leadership, the Congress, had done nothing substantial till then to prepare the ground for the blending of the two cultures. Indeed, according to Latif, Gandhi's one aim in life had been to consolidate Hinduism and for him Hinduism was synonymous with Indian nationalism.[7]

It should not be difficult to imagine why, in the context of the political atmosphere prevailing in the country in 1938–9, Latif's intricate constitutional scheme, devised with a view to retaining the unity of India and given wide publicity in the Indian press, was appreciated by only a few among the Muslim elite, long since steeped in a separatist ideology. In contrast, his ardent support of the two-nation theory and his diatribe against Gandhi and the Congress for advancing the cause of Hinduism in the garb of Indian nationalism, which too received similar publicity, were lapped up by a fairly large section of that elite and further strengthened their separatist predilections.

The same applies to the impact produced by another publication in 1939, entitled *A Confederacy of India*. Its author, not mentioning his name and describing himself as 'A Punjabi', was long supposed to be Nawab Sir Shah Nawaz Khan of Mamdot, then President of the Punjab Provincial Muslim League, who had met the cost of its publication and distributed it free to a large number of persons. It has, however, been conclusively established now by K.K. Aziz that the author was one Mian Kafayat Ali, belonging to Batala in the Gurdaspur district of the Punjab (now in India) and author of several other books, who felt compelled to hide his name as he was then a government servant.[8] Needless to say, the general impression about the authorship of the tract at the time of its publication contributed its much wider circulation than might perhaps have been the case otherwise.

Latif had started with expounding in detail the two-nation theory and ended with a constitutional scheme as the basis of a united India. Punjabi, on the other hand, began by outlining a constitutional scheme based on a confederal but united India and then devoted the rest of his book—the major portion—to lucidly and forcefully elucidating the two-nation theory and emphasizing the urgent necessity of separating the Muslim-majority areas of India from the Hindu-majority ones.[9] According to Punjabi's constitutional scheme, India was to be divided into five federations with their own governments and then re-assembled in a confederation with extremely limited powers. The five federations included the two federations of Muslim-majority areas in the west and the east, the federation of Hindu-majority provinces of British India and two federations of Indian states, namely the Rajputana States and the Deccan States.[10] While sending Punjabi's book to various persons, the Nawab of Mamdot, in his covering letter, strongly commended the constitutional scheme contained therein. 'By such a partition', he wrote, 'the Muslim provinces and the Indian States will become immune from the crushing political influence of the all-powerful Congress at the Centre. Such a confederation will safeguard the interests and rights of all parties without breaking the geographical unity of the Indian subcontinent.'[11]

With the exception of the Introduction, however, the whole book was devoted to showing how the Muslims constituted a separate nation by themselves and there was hardly anything in common between them and the Hindus—the points on the basis of which Rahmat Ali had built up his case for Pakistan. Indeed, initially Punjabi, too, had given 'Pakistan' as the title of his book, but later changed it to 'Confederacy for India' after being made aware of the disapproval of Jinnah, to whom a copy of the manuscript had been sent by the Nawab of Mamdot.[12] The confederal scheme, based on a rejection of the Pakistan idea, seems also to have been included in the Introduction as a result of an afterthought in the wake of the abandonment of the original title. There can be no other explanation for the fact that while the Introduction provided a scheme based on confederation, the bulk of the book, while mentioning the word confederation here and there as a possible solution of the Indian problem, was really full of arguments to build up a case for the separation of the Muslim-majority areas from the rest of India on the basis of the principle of self-determination. Even in the Introduction the espousal of the confederal idea seems half-hearted. For, while avoiding the use of the word Pakistan on the ground that it had 'gathered round itself some unwholesome and alien associations', Punjabi openly asserted that if the Hindus did not accept the confederal idea, there would be left no other alternative for the solution of the Indian constitutional problem except complete separation of the Muslim-majority areas from those of the Hindu-majority areas. As he put it:

> It is open to Hindus to agree or to disagree with the proposal of a confederacy of Hindu India and Muslim India. But certainly they are not entitled to oppose separation of the Muslim regions from Hindu India. Confederation depends upon the will of the parties concerned but in case one of them happens to disagree with the plan of confederation, this does not mean that it is morally within its rights in standing in the way of the other's seeking complete separation of its regions. Self-determination in their own regions is the birthright of the Muslims. Constitutionally as well as morally no power can deprive them of this right.

He again wrote: 'We should be separationists–cum confederationists, and if the Hindus disagree with the idea of a confederacy of Hindu India and Muslim India, then we will be simple separationists, demanding separation of our regions from Hindu India without any link between them.'[13]

The rest of the book is devoted not to an exposition of the

merits of confederation, but to an exposition of the grounds for the separation of the Muslim regions from the Hindu regions. It was certainly an exceptionally forceful and detailed exposition. As Aziz points out, although Rahmat Ali first expounded the two-nation theory as the basis for the demand for Pakistan, 'it is in *Confederacy of India* that we meet the fullest exposition of the theory'.[14] This was achieved by analysing in detail all possible ingredients of modern nationhood and showing that they were fully possessed by Muslims in India. Without going through these ingredients and their relationship to the Muslim position in India in the late 1930s, it will suffice for our purpose here to cite a couple of striking passages from the book in order to give the reader some idea of the flavour of Punjabi's book and the impact that it might have created on the mind of the Muslim elite at the time of its publication. Thus emphasizing that there lived not one but two-nations in India, Punjabi wrote:

However sincerely the Congress may try the impossibility of including the Muslims and Hindus in the same Indian nation, its efforts in this direction cannot succeed. Nowhere in India is the unity of culture, language, traditions and martial [material?] ideals and the community of economic interests present between the Hindus and Muslims. There is not the slightest excuse for calling them a homogeneous people. . . . No doubt Hindus and Muslims can be members of the same State. But even such a political association would not be advisable in view of the cultural, religious and traditional differences which have divided them for centuries.[15]

Stressing that it was futile to expect Muslims to separate their politics from their religion—which constituted the hard core of differences between them and Hindus—Punjabi observed:

Religion and politics are inseparably associated in the minds and thoughts of all Muslims. They cannot be first Indians and then Muslims or *vice versa*. Their religion includes their politics and their politics are a part of their religion. The mosque not only constitutes the place of worship but also the Assembly hall. It is open to Muslims to offer their daily prayers individually but it is preferable if they offer them in congregation. In addition to their daily prayers they are also enjoined to say the weekly Juma prayers and the Id prayers in the mosques in the company of fellow Muslims. The mosque forms the centre of all aspects of their public life, religious, social, economic and political. Consequently, they are not in a position to separate religion from politics, or to prefer one to the other.... Unity between them [the Muslim and Hindu communities] would be impossible because one of the parties to it cannot separate religion from politics and the other is very strict with regard to matters which relate to its social system. Hence, in their own interests, they will have to separate.[16]

The idea of some such separation was no longer confined to stray individuals here and there, but can indeed be legitimately described as representing the dominant urge of the Muslim elite during 1938–9. However, there was one difference: while some thought that the separated Hindu and Muslim areas could join together in a pan-Indian confederacy, with extremely limited powers for the confederal government, others thought in terms of a complete separation without any constitutional link at all between the Hindu and Muslim federations. It is remarkable that even Maulana Abul Ala Mawdudi, an orthodox Muslim thinker who was highly critical of the Muslim League's leadership and policies, came out in the last quarter of 1938 in support of the idea of separation with a confederal government at the apex.[17] Though he stopped short of the idea of Partition, many others openly advocated it as the only possible solution of the Indian or Hindu–Muslim problem.

III

Indeed, as early as 10 July 1937, M.G. Gazdar, a key lieutenant of Jinnah in Sind, conveyed to the latter that the condition of the Muslim masses could not be improved without the setting up of a separate federation of the Muslim-majority provinces of north-west India: Sind, Baluchistan, Punjab, and the NWFP.[18] Some others, even though not advocating Partition, or considering it as an ideal solution, thought that if the communal relations further deteriorated, that might be the only option. Thus, Mian Ahmad Yar Khan Daultana, one of the leaders of the Unionist Party in the Punjab, warned in September 1937 that if the Congress Governments in the Hindu-majority provinces continued with the policy which, according to him, they were then pursuing, in total disregard of the interests of minorities, Muslims might be left with no option but to demand Partition. To use his own words, such a policy might 'very well drive India towards that fatal idea with which certain ultra-communalists on both sides have already made the country familiar—I mean the idea of dividing India into a Muslim India and a Hindu India, a Pakistan in which the Hindus are a subject people and a Hindustan in which Muslims occupy a similar position'.[19]

As 1938 rolled on, more and more members of the Muslim intelligentsia began to be attracted towards the 'fatal idea'. Most of them in their writings in the press confined themselves to reflecting the growing feeling of grievance among the Muslims against the Congress. Because of the intensity and frequency of such writings, however, some discerning British observers of the Indian political scene sensed among the Muslim elite a growing sentiment of nationhood as also a yearning for a State of their own, portending Partition. Thus Edward Thompson remarked through one of the characters in a political novel on India (*An End of the Hours*), published in 1938: 'And it was more certain than ever that in the womb of old India, struggling to be born, were two nations tugging and fighting for mastery even before birth'.[20] By the end of the year the Pakistan idea had won more adherents. A despatch from its correspondent in India published in *The Times* (London) on 5 December remarked: 'Many Muslims in the North are again toying with the idea of creating a 'Pakistan' of those Provinces in which the Muslims are in a majority.'[21] A second despatch published in the same paper on 26 December mentioned that there was a renewed interest among Muslims in 'the old proposal of creating a "Pakistan" of the Muslim provinces, a proposal that did not ignore the possibilities of linking the Muslim Provinces of Northern India with those Islamic areas which form a belt of people of one faith stretching from Saharanpur to Istanbul'.[22] This view was confirmed by Sir Harry Hodgson in his confidential report to the Round Table (London), dated 6 January 1939, based on his tour of India in December 1938 and conversations with a large number of leaders representing different shades of opinion. According to him, while accredited Muslim leaders opposed the Pakistan idea at that time, almost all such leaders were strongly opposed to a Hindu-dominated central government and were determined to fight rather than submit. He, therefore, naturally concluded that 'in the long run the unity of India may prove impossible under domestic conditions and that a Muslim north-west may split off and seek its destiny in association with other Muslim countries rather than with South and Central India'.[23]

The growing popularity of the Pakistan idea among the Muslim intelligentsia by the end of 1938 is best illustrated by a pamphlet written by Jamiluddin Ahmad, a lecturer in English at the Aligarh Muslim University, published in early 1939 under the title *Is India One Nation?* as part of a series called the Muslim University Muslim League publications. After discussing the growing differences between Hindus and Muslims, Ahmad, who three years later edited the speeches and writings of Jinnah, remarked: 'The only way out of the impasse therefore seems to be to divide India into two federations—a federation of Muslim-majority provinces and states and another of Hindu-majority provinces and states.' As for relations between the two federations, he suggested that they ought to be governed by 'a voluntary treaty of alliance as between two sovereign states'.[24] When asked three decades later about the influences working on his mind at the time of writing his pamphlet, he replied: 'I merely echoed the prevailing feeling of the Muslim intelligentsia at that time.'[25]

There were several pointers in 1939 to show that Jamiluddin Ahmad's assessment of the general feeling of the Muslim intelligentsia towards the end of 1938 was not off the mark. Thus 'A Punjabi', in the course of an article published in the *New Times* (Lahore) on 3 February 1939, observed:

> All schemes, however elaborately prepared, to secure a single Hindu–Muslim nation as well as a lesser control by the centre, will ultimately prove a failure and the Muslims will have to seek shelter in separation. That is the only harbour which is open to them. They should better enter it at once instead of wandering into it after a criminal wastage of national time and energy.[26]

On the same date there appeared a long article by 'A Muslim Correspondent' in the *Civil and Military Gazette* (Lahore) asserting that in some parts of India (north-west and north-east) Muslims formed a majority of 60 to 80 per cent and were 'capable of uniting themselves into separate national States far stronger numerically than any existing Muslim State and likely to develop in course of time into first-class powers'.[27] More significant articles were published by the headmaster of a high school in Wazirabad (Punjab), Muhammad Sharif Toosy, who, being a government servant, wrote under the pen-name of 'M.R.T.' We have it from a most reliable source that Jinnah was 'quite impressed by his style of writing and pattern of thinking'.[28] In an article published on

10 February in the *Eastern Times* (Lahore), Toosy asserted that India was populated by diverse races and communities and could not be turned into a single nation state. According to him, the proper solution of the Indian problem was to divide the country into three states: two based on the Muslim-majority areas in the north-west and north-east and the third based on the Hindu-majority areas.[29] In a letter to the *Civil and Military Gazette* (Lahore), published in that paper on 20 April 1939, he remarked: 'If Dr Latif's scheme does not find favour with the political India, there will be no alternative left to the Muslims but to suggest the Partition of India.' After explaining the mechanics of Partition involving the setting up of two Muslim States—one Pakistan in the north-west, as demanded by Rahmat Ali, and another in the north-east comprising Eastern Bengal and Assam—Toosy observed:

> The main points to be borne in mind are (I) that the 8 crore Muslims refuse to accept the position of a minority community, more especially when by a proper partition they can claim a majority of 75 to 80 per cent in the north-west and north-east of India, (II) that Western democracy does not suit India in its present form, as the party in power in every provincial or central government will always reflect the will of the majority community, (III) that the injustice done in 1857 by depriving Muslims of all share in the political control of the country will be perpetuated by handing over the central government to untried hands whose past behaviour towards the so-called Harijans suggest grave doubts as to their competence to do justice to minorities. How can a leopard change his spots?[30]

In the meanwhile, two professors at Aligarh Muslim University—Syed Zafarul Hasan and Mohammad Afzal Qadri—had jointly prepared a scheme for Partition and sent it on to Jinnah on 22 February 1939.[31] The main assumption behind that scheme was that an all-India Federation, whatever its nature, structure or composition, would not materially affect the political condition and fate of Muslims. For they would 'invariably remain a subordinate nation under the perpetual domination of an overwhelming Hindu-majority'. The Aligarh scheme, as the Hasan–Qadri scheme came to be popularly called, was based on the following principles:

1. That the Muslims of India are a nation by themselves . . . they have a distinct national entity [identity?] wholly dif-

ferent from the Hindus and other non-Muslim groups. Indeed, they are more different from the Hindus than the Sudetan Germans were from the Czechs;

2. That the Muslims of India have got a separate national future and their own contribution to make to the betterment of the world;
3. That the future of the Muslims of India lies in complete freedom from the domination of the Hindus, the British, or for the matter of that, any other people;
4. That the Muslim-majority provinces cannot be permitted to be enslaved into a single All-India Federation with an overwhelming Hindu-majority at the Centre; and
5. That the Muslims in the minority provinces shall not be allowed to be deprived of their separate religious, cultural and political identity, and that they shall be given full and effective support by the Muslim-majority provinces.

The two Aligarh professors suggested the partition of British India into three States: North-West India, including the Punjab, the NWFP, Sind and Baluchistan; Bengal, including the adjacent district of Purnea (Bihar) and the Sylhet Division (Assam), but excluding the south-western districts of Howrah and Midnapore (Burdwan) and the north-western district of Darjeeling; and Hindustan, including the rest of British India. It was also stipulated that within Hindustan there must be created two new 'autonomous provinces' consisting of a substantial Muslim population—Delhi (28 per cent) including some districts of western UP and extending up to Aligarh; and Malabar (27 per cent) including the adjoining areas on the Malabar coast. Besides, every town of India with a population of 50,000 and above would have the status of a borough or free city. This was suggested as the Muslim population was generally substantial in towns. As far as Muslims living in rural areas were concerned, they were to give up living in scattered villages in insignificant numbers and form large clusters in selected areas. The Indian states within British India were to be divided on the basis of their geographical location. Thus Kashmir along with some other states in the north-west would belong to the federation in that area, which might well be called Pakistan and form the north-western wing of Muslim India. Similarly, Bengal with some additional areas would become the eastern wing of Muslim India. Hyderabad, with all its old territories restored to it, was to be recognized as a sovereign state, forming the southern wing of Muslim India.

It was also proposed by the Aligarh professors that the three States—Pakistan, Bengal and Hindustan—should enter into a defensive and offensive alliance on the following terms:

1. Mutual recognition and reciprocity.
2. That Pakistan and Bengal would be recognized as the homeland of Muslims and Hindustan as the homeland of Hindus, to which they could migrate respectively, if and when they wanted to do so.
3. In Hindustan, the Muslims were to be recognized as a nation in minority and part of a larger nation inhabiting Pakistan and Bengal.
4. The Muslim-minority in Hindustan and the non-Muslim-minority in Pakistan and Bengal would have (i) representation according to population, and (ii) separate electorates and representation at every stage, together with effective religious, cultural and political safeguards guaranteed by all the three States.
   Note: Separate representation according to population might be granted to all substantial minorities in the three States, e.g. Sikhs, non-caste Hindus, etc.
5. An accredited Muslim organization would be the sole official representative body of the Muslims in Hindustan.

It was also provided in the Aligarh Plan that each of the three independent States—Pakistan, Hindustan and Bengal—would have separate treaties of alliance with Britain and separate Crown Representatives, if any. Further, they would have a joint Court of Arbitration to settle any dispute that might arise between themselves or between them and the Crown.[32]

Much thought had obviously gone into the preparation of this scheme. However, the general Muslim attitude was still not clear on this issue. While some Muslims had begun thinking of Partition, there were other Muslims who felt that the Muslim-majority provinces could be separated from others, but could still continue to live within India under some kind of confederal structure. Thus commenting on the general Muslim attitude towards the Pakistan scheme, one observer remarked in the *Times of India*, dated 5 April 1939, that there was 'little support for the scheme at the moment outside the Muslim League leaders'. He further added: 'It is still in an academic stage, as far as the Muslim leaders are concerned, while others describe it as fantastic, unpatriotic, extra-territorial in outlook and so on.'[33] On the other hand, H.V. Hodson observed in *Fortnightly Review* in its issue of May 1939 that the Muslim League stalwarts looked upon Congress dominance as Hindu Raj and were determined to fight it if it really materialized over India as a whole. While it was not clear what shape that fight might take, it was not 'out of the question that when the Hindu Raj was once established, and British power had melted away from India's internal affairs, the Muslim areas in the north-west might attempt a forcible secession from the federal state. Indeed, some people think this highly probable'.[34]

Many others, however, were unable to clearly see what exactly was going to be the result of the Muslim determination to refuse to live under a Hindu-dominated Centre. This is borne out by what 'Shahid' wrote in the *Statesman* dated 16 June 1939. He was a regular columnist of that paper whose writings generally reflected the dominant trends in Muslim public opinion. In his column on 16 June 1939, he observed that the Muslim League was pledged to work for the fullest protection of the political, cultural and religious rights of the Muslims and was bound to oppose an independence in which those rights might be jeopardized. He did not, however, specify what concrete form was likely to be assumed by such an opposition.[35]

III

Whatever that might be, there is some evidence to indicate that the Partition idea continued to gain ground during the two months or so immediately preceding the outbreak of World War II in the first week of September 1939. Thus in July the Punjab Muslim Students Federation adopted a scheme proposing the establishment of a 'Pakistan Caliphate'. It was to comprise not only Punjab, Sind, the NWFP, Baluchistan and Kashmir, but also parts of UP, CP, and Bihar, apparently with a view to securing a corridor right up to Bengal and Assam. While proposing this scheme, the Muslim students asserted that it was the birthright of Muslims in northern India to have their 'homelands'. They also described themselves as 'arch enemies of geographical nationalism and democracy'. It was made clear that the aim was to establish the sovereignty of the *shariat* and that the proposed State would be headed by a spiritual dictator who would be the shadow of God on earth. The non-Muslims living in it would be treated as *Zimmies* and required to pay the *jizya* in lieu of military service.[36] The adoption of such a scheme by the Punjab Muslim Students Federation is highly significant. For it shows that by July 1939 the activists among the Muslim students of the Punjab were fully converted to the Pakistan idea and indeed gave a deeper Islamic colouring to it than the original scheme propounded by Rahmat Ali, who had obviously been the chief source of their inspiration. Professor Aziz, therefore, is right when he observes that the adoption of the Pakistan Caliphate scheme by the Punjab Muslim Students Federation represents 'a major development' in both the history of the idea of Pakistan and the movement for its realization. He, however, goes too far when he remarks: 'In a way it was the Punjabi students who forced Jinnah to adopt the idea of Pakistan and subscribe it on the League charter as the goal of Muslim India.'[37] Just as Jinnah did not require to be persuaded by Iqbal to adopt the Pakistan idea in 1937, he did not require to be forced by the Punjab Muslim Students Federation to do so in 1939. As shown at the beginning of this chapter, and acknowledged also by Aziz,[38] Jinnah's foreword to the book containing Iqbal's letters to him makes it clear that he had been converted to the Pakistan idea at any rate by the middle of 1937, if not earlier. Indeed, while keeping his view on the final goal of Muslim India to himself, he had been doing all that seemed possible or desirable to him to prepare the ground for the public announcement of that goal. His actions and policies since 1937 can be explained only on the basis of such a hypothesis.

Writings in the press from the middle of July to the first week of September 1939, when the World War II broke out and gave a new turn to Indian politics, indicate a growing swing of Muslim public opinion towards the Pakistan idea. A few no doubt expressed their opposition to it, but the bulk of the authors were clearly supportive. To turn first to the former, mention may be made of a letter by one Abdul Rashid, published in the *Civil and Military Gazette* dated 15 August 1939. Therein he wrote that while it had become 'a custom' to call the Muslims a nation and to demand a national home for them, people who wrote that way were speaking against facts as well as the principles of Islam. In his opinion, Muslims were not a nation as they did not possess the essential feature of a nation, that is 'common descendency'. Besides, the Koran never used the word *Kaum* for Muslims but called them *Millat.* He did concede that the people who lived in the Indus or Pakistan zone in the north-west were socially and culturally different from those living in the rest of India. If they wanted to separate themselves from the latter, Rashid's advice was that they should 'profoundly' consider the solution from the economic and political angles and first convince themselves of the soundness of this idea before going to the people. In the meanwhile, however, they should not befool 'the ignorant masses' by asserting that the Indian Muslims were a nation and therefore they must have a 'national home' of their own. 'Let them not confuse the problem with Islam. Islam is above nations and national homes.'[39] This viewpoint was very much liked by at least one person, Amjad Husain, whose letter to the same paper was published on 18 August 1939. He described Rashid's letter as the best among the letters on the question of Pakistan published till then and as one based on 'a true and genuine interpretation of Islamic teaching'. 'Muslims,' he wrote, 'are out to establish their ascendancy and supremacy on every plot of land of the world. They cannot, and should not, support the vulgar idea of confining themselves to the limited part of India called Pakistan.'[40] In a letter published on 29 August 1939, Fida Husain opposed the Pakistan idea on another ground: the existence of sectarian or 'inner' communal troubles among Muslims. His argument was that under a Muslim regime such troubles were likely to 'augment unprecedentally'.[41]

As against these three pieces, we have a large number of letters and articles written by Muslims, and painstakingly collected by Professor Aziz, that ardently supported both the two-nation theory and the demand for Pakistan based on it. Thus, Avaice Asar, in a letter published in the *Civil and Military Gazette* on 27 July 1939, asserted that the basic requirements of a nation such as common ties of race, religion, and language were 'hopelessly lacking' in India. Hindus and Muslims were 'poles apart' in all these respects and to dream that they could ever be fused together to form one nation was 'to live in a fool's paradise'. In another letter published on 10 August 1939, he declared that the concept of a common nationhood for the whole of India was 'ridiculous'. It was 'inherently unwelcome to Hindus and repugnant to Muslims'.[42]

In the meanwhile, Ahmad Bashir, writing on behalf of the 'Pakistan National Movement', inspired by Rahmat Ali, severely criticized an alternative scheme of an all-India federation with limited powers and based on a grouping of provinces into seven different zones as promoted by Sikander Hyat Khan (which we shall soon discuss). In an article published in the *Civil and Military Gazette* on 5 August he argued that 'judging only from the Pakistan point of view', that scheme was entirely opposed to the interests of the 30 million Muslims living in the Punjab, the NWFP, Kashmir, Sind, and Baluchistan, who were fighting for 'the recognition of their separate national status' through the formation of a separate federation of their own. For the first time bringing the economic argument to buttress the demand for Pakistan, he pointedly asked how the interests of agriculturists in 'the Indus region' would be safeguarded by handing over power over vital economic matters to the central government, which was bound to be dominated by the Hindus and whose decisions were likely to be influenced by the Hindu mill-owners of Bombay and Ahmedabad. 'The greatest factor militating against the prosperity of Pakistan,' he wrote, 'is its connection with India, and unless and until it blatantly revolts against this connection and discards the Indian label outright, it is deemed to sink to a mere serf of industrial India.'[43] Again, in the course of a letter published in the same paper on 15 August 1939, he summed up the arguments of the Pakistan National Movement in favour of the creation of Pakistan, drawing heavily from Rahmat Ali's earlier writings on this theme:

> The Movement maintains that India as it is today is not the name of one country nor the home of a single nation. It is in fact a designation of a State created for the first time in history by the British. It includes people who have never previously formed part of India at any period of its history, but who have from time immemorial till the advent of the British possessed and retained distinct nationalities of their own. A critical study of the history of India would reveal that Pakistan has retained during the whole of its existence i ts own laws, and has cherished its own religious, spiritual and cultural ideals. From the dawn of civil-

ization it has possessed an individuality of its own, and its people have always sought their national salvation along their own lines:

Geographically also the structure of its land, the qualities of its soil, the nature of its climate and the flow of its rivers are all different from the rest of India. Moreover, the culture of Pakistan as well as their customs and traditions are all different from those of Hindustanis. In individual habit as in national life there is a vast dissimilarity between the peoples of these countries. Even the features of Pakistanis are unlike those of Hindustanis.[44]

In the meanwhile, a few days back Professor Gulshan Rai had criticized the Pakistan scheme as a 'physical impossibility and financially suicidal' in the course of an article published in the *Civil and Military Gazette* of 15 August. Contradicting him, 'A Pakistani', through a letter published in the same paper on 16 August sought to show that Rai had miscalculated figures to buttress his argument and that actually the Pakistan scheme was financially quite sound. Rai had argued that Pakistan would have to bear the entire cost of the defence of the NWFP, which was at that time borne by the Government of India, and that this would impose a heavy financial burden that the new State would not be able to bear. Controverting this claim, 'A Pakistani' argued that actually Pakistan would have to spend much less on defence than Rai had calculated. 'The new Muslim State of Northern India,' he wrote, 'would enter into alliance with other Muslims of the Middle and Near East and form along with them a common front against any possible threat of aggression from Japan and Hindu India in the East and Europe in the West. The Frontier question would then lose all importance.'[45] Next day the paper published an emotional rejoinder to Rai by Mir Rafique. Instead of dealing with the budgetary problem of the proposed State, the latter asserted that the Muslim claim to Pakistan was 'a claim of a nation fundamentally different from that living in Hindustan'. He further added: 'Our first aim is to secure the independent existence of our Fatherland. For the moment this question eclipses all others.'[46]

Muhammad Rafiq Toosy joined the debate again through a letter published in the *Gazette* on 20 August 1939, in which he controverted the argument presented by Amjad Husain two days before. As mentioned earlier, Husain had argued that since the objective of Muslims was to establish their ascendancy and supremacy over the entire world, it would be foolish for them to support an idea that would result in their confinement within a small territory. Fully commending Husain's vision of seeing Muslim ascendancy over the whole world, Toosy pointed out that for that goal to be achieved Muslims must start with small beginnings. 'The Pakistanis,' he wrote, 'have no other aim but to add one more powerful Muslim State to the Islamic world and thus to make it possible for the Muslims to attain the ideal of political ascendancy, if not in non-Muslim countries, at least in those where they form a majority.' If Husain's idea, Toosy further argued, was to establish the spiritual domination or influence of Islam over the whole world through missionary effort, it was difficult to see how the creation of Pakistan would work as a barrier. On the contrary, it would 'stimulate and promote missionary effort in an organized form'.[47] On 24 August appeared a letter from Saifullah Khan rebutting Abdul Rashid, who, in his letter published on 15 August had contended that Muslims in India were not a nation as they lacked one of the essential ingredients of a nation—common descent—and also pointed out that Islam was above nations and national homes. Saifullah argued that it was not correct to say that people must have a common descent in order to be a nation and asserted that there were other things like common history, politics, language, etc., which could make a people or a nation. He further pointed out that Muslims in India always had a separate history, politics, language, religion, and culture. They could not be called members of the 'Indian nation', for such a thing did not exist. They could not claim Afghan or Turkish nationality, as no one would allow that. They could only be described as members of 'the Muslim nation in India', and as such were fully justified in demanding 'a national home in India'.[48] Similarly, Abdul Aziz Beg, in his letter published on 25 August, asserted that Amjad Husain had confused the ideal with the actual by contending that Islam's mission was to establish its supremacy over the entire world and that, therefore, it could not be circumscribed by the borders of a single country. According to Beg, before Muslims fancied themselves as masters of the world, it was 'imperatively necessary' to strengthen their position in India. Affirming his loyalty to the Pakistan ideal, he finally declared: 'Pakistan is the sovereign panacea for all our ills, the *sine qua non* of our future progress, and an essential prologue to higher things that we might like to do in accordance with the dictates of our religion.'[49]

On the same day that Aziz Beg's letter appeared in the *Civil and Military Gazette* published from Lahore, the *Star of India*, published from Calcutta and generally considered a representative organ of Muslim public opinion, came out with a long editorial entitled 'The Two Indias Must Part'. It pointed out that the Muslims in India had been able to secure all possible safeguards, including weightage, to protect their interests. However, the situation had not improved from their point of view because of their minority status under a democratic constitution—where the majority was bound to have its way. The general political situation in India had also gone on deteriorating. As he put it:

> Today Hindus and Muslims hate one another all the more. Points of dispute have arisen which had never before been so prominent in the public eye. Riots, affrays, bloodshed have become the order of the day. Culture has set itself to conquer culture, language has raised itself against language, educational systems have come to clash and all this is sought to be justified on the ground of "nationalism". . . . All this bears glaring testimony to the fact that there are two peoples and not one who live in India. . . . As long as Democracy is the basis of the Constitution the minority will ever be fighting a losing battle.

The editorial's conclusion on the basis of these facts was: 'Hindus and Muslims must part company and dwell apart. Only then can they be friends. Hindu India and Muslim India must divide to unite.' On 1 September 1939, the same paper published an article by Sayyid Nazir Ahmad, strongly supporting the view articulated by its editorial a week ago. As Ahmad put it:

> India after all is not one nation. The 80 million Muslims by themselves form a nation, as well elucidated by late Dr Sir Muhammad Iqbal. The Muslims cannot realize their mission unless they form a separate State. The two-nations are now existing in India with their separate tendencies, completely different cultural traditions and with diametrically opposite views regarding their social habits, customs and prayers. To fuse these two nations into one is not only impossible but unnatural also. The bringing up of these two nations side by side under two defined geographical limits is both possible and desirable and it will be to their common interest to be in alliance on equal terms and that is why in the interest of both the communities I plead for a separate Federation for the Muslims.[50]

. All this while (1937–9) the top leadership of the Hindu Mahasabha, represented by an ex-revolutionary, V.D. Savarkar, was assiduously championing the two-nation theory. This is very well illustrated by Savarkar's presidential addresses to successive annual sessions of the Mahasabha from 1937 to 1939. Thus, in 1937 he declared that Hindus were 'marked out as a nation by themselves'. He also described Hindus and Muslims as 'two antagonistic nations living side by side in India' and asserted that their antagonism was not likely to end soon. In any case, his view was that while Hindu–Muslim unity was welcome, it would not serve any purpose to hanker after it except to worsen the situation still further. The only wise course of action was to make it clear that Muslims would have the same rights as other Indians, but no special privileges. If on that basis they were to join the freedom struggle, they would be welcome. However, they were not likely to do so, and the Hindus must steel themselves to carry on the struggle themselves. In 1938, he observed: 'No other nation in the world, excepting perhaps the Chinese, can claim a continuity of life and growth so unbroken as the Hindu Nation does.' Hindustan was the land of Hindus and it was the Hindu Nation which owned it. 'If you call it an Indian Nation it is merely an English synonym for the Hindu Nation'. Just as the Germans were the Nation in Germany and the Jews a community, the Hindus were the Nation in India and the Muslims a community. In 1939, he again stressed that the Hindus 'from Kashmere to Madras and Sindh to Assam' stood forth as a Nation by themselves, in spite of numerous differences among them. This was in contrast to the position of Indian Muslims, who were 'on the whole more inclined to identify themselves with Muslims outside India than Hindus who live next door, like the Jews in Germany.'[51] The Rashtriya Swayamsevak Sangh (RSS), a smaller but more militant Hindu organization founded in 1925 by Keshav Baliram Hedgewar, was engaged in propagating a more extremist ideology. This was succinctly summed up in a small book, *We and Our Nationhood Defined* (1939) by M.S. Golwalker, who succeeded Hedgewar as the chief of the RSS in 1940. Therein the former propounded the theory that Hindustan was 'the land of the Hindus and the *terra firma* for the Hindu nation alone to flourish upon'. As for those who did not belong to the 'Hindu Race, Religion and Culture' but were living in India, there were only two courses open to them: 'either to merge themselves in the national race and adopt its culture, or to live at its mercy so long as the national race may allow them to do so and to quit the country at the sweet will of the national race'.[52]

The RSS was not much known at that time. Although that did not apply to the Hindu Mahasabha, the latter's following among the Hindus was also very limited, as borne out by the election results of 1937. However, members of the Muslim elite generally believed that it was the Mahasabha that really represented the views of the Hindus on the communal problem. According to them, the Hindu leaders of the Congress, too, shared those views, but desisted from openly espousing them because of tactical reasons. Iqbal certainly held that view.[53] Another illustration of the general Muslim estimate of the representative character of the Hindu Mahasabha is provided by 'A Punjabi' (Kafayat Ali), who authored the book *Confederacy of India* (1939), discussed earlier. Therein he remarks: 'The real representative of the Hindus, so far as their relations with the Muslims are concerned, is the Hindu Mahasabha. . . .'[54]

IV

As seen in Volume II of the present work, although the Muslim representatives at the Round Table Conference had agreed in principle to the setting up of an all-India Federation, with a partial introduction of responsible government, they had never been enthusiastic about it and had made it known in unmistakable terms that they would like to first go ahead with responsible government in the provinces before proceeding with it at the Centre. Some of them, including Jinnah, had also made known their strong opposition to the federal scheme as embodied in the Act of 1935. This was not unrelated to the general Muslim lack of enthusiasm for the early setting up of responsible government at the Centre because of the fear of inevitable Hindu domination over it. The introduction of responsible government in the provinces in 1937 made the leaders of the Muslim League much more concerned than ever before with this problem. For the emergence of the Congress as a dominant party in the Hindu-majority provinces clearly presaged its emergence in a similar situation in the federal legislature, if and when established. And the failure of the so-called Congress–League coalition talks did not provide a good augury for the League's prospect of having any power at the centre unless it was prepared to virtually merge itself in the Congress.

Unlike what is generally assumed, the lead in bringing this issue to the fore in the new situation was taken not by the leaders of the League in UP, but by those in the Punjab, who had earlier also taken the lead in pressing for the setting up of responsible government in the provinces rather than at the Centre. According to a secret report of the Government, the consideration of the Muslim attitude to the setting up of an all-India Federation was taken up at a closed meeting of the Council of the League on 16 October 1937 in Lucknow on the eve of its annual session there. Opening the discussion, the Punjab Premier, Sikander Hyat Khan, stated that Federation meant the ruination of Indian Muslims. In British India they were already in a minority, but if the representatives of the princely states joined in, as was envisaged under the Act of 1935, the proportion of Muslim representatives in the federal legislature would be still further reduced. Muslims 'would be nowhere'. Hindus would have a strong Centre, and the Muslim-majority provinces would be placed under the 'perpetual subjection of the Hindu Raj'. Therefore, Muslims must oppose the inauguration of the proposed federation and if they failed in that attempt, they should put forward an alternative scheme of federation. With this introduction he presented an outline of his own alternative scheme, which envisaged the setting up of seven Federal States in the country, each consisting of a group of provinces. This, according to him, would ensure that Muslims where they were in a majority would not be hampered in their effort to raise themselves in various walks of life. In the end he hoped that his outline would be developed into a full scheme with all the necessary details. Maulana Hasrat Mohani and Maulana Zafar Ali Khan spoke in the same vein and warned that the Congress was opposed to federation only in name; in reality it was in their interest to form an alliance with the Indian states and create such an atmosphere as to drive out both the English and the Muslims. Choudhry Khaliquzzaman, Nawab Ismail Khan, and Shahid Suhrawardy pleaded for a moderate line on this issue and suggested that the League at that stage should be content to express its opposition to the federal scheme.[55] This was the background of the resolution adopted by the open session of the Muslim League at Lucknow (Resolution VIII), recording its emphatic disapproval of the federal scheme embodied in the Government of India Act of 1935 and its opposition to its introduction and urging the British Government to refrain from its enforcement as the League considered the scheme 'detrimental to the interest of the people of India generally, and to those of the Muslims of India in particular'.[56]

While the League leaders were clear and fully united in opposition to the federal scheme embodied in the Act of 1935, they were to take quite some time in deciding as to what should take its place. Within a year of the Lucknow session, two broad approaches emerged on this issue. One favoured a scheme that would provide for maximum power to the provinces, reduce the power of the federal government to the minimum required, and arrange its organization in such a way as to reduce the Hindu dominance there as far as possible. The other stood for a complete separation of the Muslim-majority provinces and the formation of a federation of their own, broadly on the lines advocated by Rahmat Ali.

The former line was explained at some length by Sikander in his speech on the issue of federation in the Punjab Legislative Assembly on 8 April 1938. The occasion was provided by a debate on a resolution tabled by a member of the Congress party in the Assembly, in line with the general Congress policy, to record its 'firm resolve' to be no party to the inauguration of the proposed Federation. It also recommended that no money be spent out of Provincial revenues and no further arrangements be made by the Provincial Government in connection with the matter of holding elections to the Federal Legislatures or in any other matter connected with it. Sikander moved an amendment, virtually a separate motion, which declared that the Assembly considered the federal scheme formulated in the Government of India Act, 1935 as unsatisfactory, and in view of the urgency of the problem recommended to the Government that 'the earliest possible steps should be taken radically to revise the scheme in full consultation with all sections of the people concerned'.

In his speech in support of his motion, Sikander expressed his doubt about the genuineness of the Congress opposition to Federation. Recalling the earlier Congress opposition to Provincial

Autonomy and the subsequent decision to form ministries in the provinces, he affirmed that there was a suspicion among a large section of people that the Congress would behave in the same way and, after using its opposition to Federation to extract certain concessions from the Government would again decide to work the federal scheme. Explaining his own attitude to the scheme, he pointed out that it did not come up to the expectations of the Indian people and that it had various shortcomings which must be removed, but he recognized that 'some sort of federal government at the centre' was necessary. However, it must be a federal government that did not interfere in the affairs of the federating units and the latter had full assurance of unfettered functioning. As he put it:

> What we want to avoid is a dominating Central Government, a Central Government which is likely to interfere with the provinces so as to put the provinces in a position where they may eventually find it difficult to take any big action because of the conflict with the centre. . . . I visualize the federation in which the representatives of the various units will constitute the Central Government with a view to see that provincial autonomy is not in any way trampled upon by the central body; and with the safeguarding of the interests of their respective units or provinces, they may also serve the common interests of the country as a whole in the federal sphere.[57]

Sikander explained his thinking on the issue of an all-India federation in more precise terms in his two confidential conversations with the Governor of the Punjab. As reported by the latter to the Viceroy, Sikander's main objections to the federal scheme as embodied in the Act of 1935 were based on the apprehension that it would place the Hindus permanently in power at the Centre. This was likely to take the form of a predominantly Congress ministry under the full control of the Congress High Command, as was the situation in the Hindu-majority provinces. He feared that the party in power at the Centre would have a tendency to interfere in provincial matters. This was likely to be especially directed against the Punjab, it being the one province where the Congress exercised comparatively little influence, and aimed at 'clipping the wings of the Punjab as the dominant partner in the Indian Army'. The fact that under the Act of 1935 Defence was a reserved subject under the direct control of the Governor-General would not be a full safeguard against such interference, for once responsible government was established at the Centre the effort of the Congress would be to ensure that even with regard to the reserved subjects the Viceroy should be guided by the advice of the ministry. Sikander, therefore, pleaded that the British should postpone the introduction of the federal part of the Act and carry on with the existing structure till the former was suitably revised.

As for the ideal scheme, Sikander's view was that the federal government should deal only with five vital central subjects, namely, Defence, Customs, External Affairs, Relations with the States, and Communications. Besides, both the federal legislature and the executive should be really representative of the different federating units with equal share of representation in both the legislature and the ministry. For this purpose he suggested a division of the whole of India, including both British India and the Indian States, into the following seven units, roughly having a population of 50 million each:

1. The Madras Presidency and the South Indian States other than Hyderabad;
2. Bombay, the Central Provinces and the Hyderabad State:
3. Bengal;
4. Bihar, Orissa and the Eastern States;
5. The United Provinces and the States within the border of those Provinces such as Rampur, Tehri-Garhwal and Benares;
6. A Central unit consisting of the Rajputana and Central Indian States;
7. A north-western unit consisting of the Punjab, the NWFP, Sind, Kashmir and the Punjab States. It might be desirable to add to this unit one or two of the Rajputana States adjacent to the Punjab, such as Bikaner and Alwar, in order to avoid the appearance of creating a 'Pakistan' or a too predominantly Muslim unit.

Sikander thought that this political reorganization of India would ensure the emergence of a federal legislature and executive which might not be Congress dominated. As the Governor explained his thinking:

He claimed that an incidental advantage of this system would be that it would tend to blur the line of cleavage between British India and the

States. He also claimed that it would tend to secure a stable Federal Government in as much as the Central and North-Western units would be definitely conservative in their outlook; the Bengal unit would be, from the communal point of view, a stabilizing element, while none of the other four would be of a purely Hindu or Congress complexion, as all of them would include a moderating State element.[58]

The other view, namely, that the Muslim-majority provinces of India should have a completely separate federation of their own, surfaced at the first provincial conference of the Sind Muslim League held at Karachi in the first half of October 1938. That was not a very powerful branch and had indeed come into existence only in that year, but the presence of several all-India leaders of the League, including Jinnah himself, Sikander and the Bengal Premier, Fazlul Huq, imparted to it something more than mere provincial significance. Sir Abdullah Haroon, Chairman of the Reception Committee, in the course of his welcome speech, referred to the deep-rooted suspicion of the minorities that their interests were not safe in the hands of the Hindu majority and declared that unless the former were provided with adequate protection and safeguards, Muslims might be forced 'to seek their salvation in their own way in an independent federation of Muslim States'. Drawing a parallel with recent developments in Czechoslovakia, where the Sudetan Germans had seceded from that country and joined Germany, he further added: 'We have nearly arrived at the parting of the ways and until and unless this problem is solved to the satisfaction of all, it will be impossible to save India from being divided into Hindu India and Muslim India, both placed under separate federations.'[59] This theme was repeated in many other speeches. According to the official report of the conference, the gist of these speeches was as follows:

> If the Congress, which was wholly and solely a Hindu organization, was not prepared to agree to the Muslims occupying an equal position in the scheme of the Indian constitutional reform merely because it aimed at the establishment of Hindu rule in India, somewhat similar to that which is now found in the eight Congress-ruled provinces, let us tell the Congress and the Hindu Community that the Indian subcontinent shall have to be divided into two Indias—the Hindu India and the Muslim India, each grouping separately.[60]

Jinnah in his presidential address did not speak so directly, but more than once hinted that if there was no drastic change in the

Indian political situation in the direction of conciliating the Muslim League something like that mentioned in the other speeches might indeed happen. Thus, mounting a fierce attack on the Congress leadership, he at one point accused it of creating a serious situation which might 'break India vertically and horizontally', and at another point asked it to 'mark, learn and inwardly digest' the lesson of the recent happenings in Czechoslovakia.[61] Jinnah, however, was nothing if not an extremely cautious politician. If these remarks show the direction in which his mind was moving at that stage, his subsequent role at that conference—in getting the resolution demanding the setting up of a separate federation of Muslim States modified into a call to the All-India Muslim League to formulate a suitable alternative to the federal scheme of the Act of 1935—shows that he had not yet made up his mind regarding the advisability of publicly demanding at that moment the setting up of a separate federation of Muslim States.

The proposed Resolution (No. 5) referred to the earlier efforts to reach a Hindu–Muslim settlement, the supposed establishment of Hindu Raj in the Congress-governed provinces, and the threat posed by it to the sway of Muslims in the Muslim-majority provinces, and declared:

> The Sind Provincial Muslim League Conference considers it absolutely essential in the interest of an abiding peace in the vast Indian subcontinent and in the interest of unhampered cultural development, the economic and social betterment and political self-determination of the two nations, known as Hindus and Muslims, that India may be divided into [two] federations, namely, the federation of Muslim States and the federation of non-Muslim States.
>
> This conference therefore recommends to the All-India Muslim League to devise a scheme of Constitution under which Muslim-majority provinces, Muslim Indian States and areas inhabited by a majority of Muslims may attain full independence in the form of a federation of their own with permission to admit any other Muslim State beyond the Indian frontiers to join the Federation and with such safeguards for non-Muslim minorities as may be conceded to the Muslim-minorities in the non-Muslim Federation of India.[62]

If a resolution with such a demand was adopted by a conference, even though provincial, presided over by Jinnah, it was bound to lead to the assumption that he himself was in its favour. Even though he cherished the idea of a separate Muslim State, he did not consider it prudent at that stage to openly associate himself with such a demand. If nothing else, the fact that the Muslim League leadership had not yet discussed it in any depth, to say nothing of having come to a definite conclusion or consensus, militated against such a course. He was not a Sikander or a Haroon and could lend his name only to a consensus in the Muslim League—indeed in Muslim India as a whole—and not to any one-sided opinion. Some such considerations must have been responsible for his getting the last two paragraphs replaced by a single paragraph as follows:

> This conference considers it absolutely essential, in the interest of an abiding peace in the vast Indian sub-continent and in the interest of unhampered cultural development, the economic and social betterment and political self-determination of the two-nations, known as Hindus and Muslims, to recommend to the all-India Muslim League to review and revise the entire conception of what should be the suitable Constitution for India which will secure honourable and legitimate status to them.[63]

Even with this modification, however, Resolution No. 5 of the First Sind Provincial Muslim League Conference has a significance of its own in the evolution of the League's stand on the Pakistan issue. Hindus and Muslims had been referred to as two nations in several speeches and writings before, but this was the first occasion when an official conference of the Muslim League, even though provincial, had come forward with such a formulation and also mentioned the right of political self-determination in that context. Indeed, it is indicative of the mood generated at the Karachi Conference that its official report, regardless of the modified paragraph, asserted that there was no doubt that Resolution No. 5 would be a prelude to the Muslims declaring finally that they would go in for a separate federation of their own.[64] Yet there was no immediate or automatic transition to that final goal. Till the outbreak of World War II on 3 September 1939, the Muslim League leadership as a whole remained undecided on this issue.

Thus, shortly after the Karachi Conference Haroon issued a statement supporting the idea of two federations, 'each reflecting the strength of one of the two major communities', and including the Indian States adjoining them, with perfect freedom in the internal affairs guaranteed to them.[65] According to a confidential report of the Government of India, this statement reflected the terms 'known to have been agreed upon in private session at Karachi'.[66] Perhaps what had happened at that meeting was that Jinnah had permitted Haroon as well as Sikander to air their views in public without committing the League in any way. In November 1938 Haroon sent a letter to the rulers of a number of States, including all the leading ones, drawing their attention to his scheme, especially in the light of the attitude of the Congress towards them. It is interesting to note that the Maharaja of Bikaner was believed to have written back asking for more details and enquiring whether the scheme could be so modified as to enable a Hindu state to join the Muslim Federation and had received the reply that modification of the scheme, which was only tentative, was possible, but not to the extent of converting a Muslim majority into a minority.[67]

Soon the determination of the League leadership to oppose the introduction of an all-India federation, as per the provisions of the Act of 1935, was further strengthened because of Congress championship of democratic movements then going on in various states, including Hyderabad, which had a Muslim ruler with a vast majority of Hindu subjects and the insistence of the Congress that the states' representatives in the proposed federal legislature be elected on the pattern of the provinces instead of being nominated by the rulers. As the popular agitations in the states were generally inspired by the Congress, the League looked upon them as a device on the part of the Congress to strengthen its position in the federal legislature.[68] The growing concern of the League on this issue is reflected by its resolution on states adopted by its annual session held at Patna in the last week of December 1938. The latter declared that if the Congress or other Hindu organizations did not desist forthwith from their 'subversive activities in the states, actuated by ulterior motives', the League would be forced to take such action as it considered necessary 'to safeguard the legitimate interests of Musalmans'.[69] As far as the issue of the all-India federation was concerned, the Patna session reiterated the view, adopted at the Lucknow session (1937), that the scheme of federation as embodied in the Act of 1935 was unacceptable and took the first major step towards the preparation of an alternative scheme by authorizing the President of the League to adopt such a course as might be necessary with a view to exploring the possibility of devising a suitable alternative constitutional scheme which would safeguard the interests of the Musalmans and other minorities in India.[70]

It may not be out of place to mention here that the apparently mild resolution on exploring the possibility of an alternative to the scheme of federation under the Act of 1935, although moved by Zafar Ali Khan, had actually been drafted jointly by Jinnah and Sikander.[71] According to a reliable observer, as reported by the Director of the Intelligence Bureau, read with the resolution on Indian States, it meant that the League 'desired to leave the door open for the British Government to placate Muslim feeling by means of negotiation with the League and to provide moral support to the Provinces'.[72] As per the information received by the Bihar Governor, it was understood that Jinnah would be satisfied if Muslims got one-third of the Federal Cabinet posts, the States did not elect but nominate their representatives, Baluchistan was given reforms and representation, Waziristan was made a separate state also with representation, and only Defence, Foreign Affairs, and Finance remained with the Federation.[73] During his conversation with the Viceroy towards the end of February 1939, Jinnah was queried on the issue of Federation. When asked what suggestions he had to make with regard to Federation, he replied that 'while he did not reject the federal idea, it must be a federation which would ensure an adequate equipoise between Muslim and Hindu votes, and in which there should be an appropriate balance between the communities'. On being asked further as to how this could be secured, be said that it could be done through 'the manipulation of territorial votes and the adjustment of territorial divisions'. He further added that his project for the carving up of this country was a better one than Sikander's.[74]

The Pakistan scheme received 'its first real ventilation' at the meeting of the Muslim League's Working Committee at Meerut on 26 March 1939.[75] No decision was, however, taken except to appoint a sub-committee headed by Jinnah himself and including, among others, both Haroon and Sikander, to consider all the alternative schemes then in circulation as also others which might be freshly formulated.[76] Among the alternatives mentioned in the press about this time were those prepared by Latif and Sikander.[77] As pointed out earlier in this chapter, both these schemes, although differing from each other in various ways, provided for a re-grouping of the provinces and states on a religio-cultural basis, and endowing them with the largest possible measure of autonomy within an all-India federation with the minimum powers. In this respect, the Latif scheme, though considered by many to be a variant of the Pakistan scheme, was actually not fundamentally different from Sikander's. Indeed, Latif himself pointed out that much of the criticism to which his scheme was subjected was 'due to misrepresentation and misunderstanding, particularly to confusing it with the Pakistan scheme'.[78] There was, however, another scheme placed before the meeting at Meerut that was truly patterned on the Pakistan scheme—the scheme drawn up by the two professors at Aligarh, which we have noted earlier in this chapter.[79]

About a week before the Meerut meeting two leaders of the Muslim League, Choudhry Khaliquzzaman and Abdul Rahman Siddiqi, who had gone to London to observe the proceedings of the Palestine Conference being held there at that time, called on Lord Zetland, Secretary of State for India (20 March 1939) and in the course of discussions placed before him their own alternative to the federal scheme of the Act of 1935. Khaliquzzaman has claimed in his memoirs that this was based on the concept of Pakistan and asked for separating the Muslim-majority areas from the rest of India and making them independent.[80] Actually, the supposed confirmation of this obtained from the Commonwealth Relations Office in the form of points from Zetland's recording of the impressions of this discussion, and cited by Khaliquzzaman, gives a different version and shows that what Khaliquzzaman and Siddiqi had suggested was not fundamentally different from what Sikander had been suggesting for quite some time and was not in accord with Rahmat Ali's concept of Pakistan as Khaliquzzaman implies.[81] As Zetland wrote to Linlithgow a few days after this discussion, what they had proposed was 'the establishment of three or four federations of provinces and states which would be coordinated by a small central body of some kind or other. The whole object of the scheme, of course, was to give the Muslims as great a measure of control at the centre as the Hindus.'[82]

In the meanwhile, the sub-committee appointed at Meerut to consider the various alternative schemes of federation, was moving at a leisurely pace, leaving the ground free for the protagonists of the different schools to propound their views. Haroon, the enthusiast for Pakistan, was getting restive. He wrote to Jinnah in the later part of April 1939, suggesting a meeting of the sub-committee 'as early as possible so that at this psychological moment one definite goal is fixed before the Musalmans'. He also informed Jinnah that the idea of separate homelands for Muslims was spreading fast.[83] He sought to give a further push to that idea through an article entitled 'The Federation and the Indian Muslims', published in the *Civil and Military Gazette* on 13 July 1939. In it, he remarked: 'The real and fundamental question now before us is whether we should at all accept the principle of the perpetual rule of a perpetual majority, whose "bona fides" we seriously question?'[84]

Similarly, Afzal Husain Qadri continued to press for the early adoption of the scheme prepared by him in collaboration with Syed Zafrul Hasan. On the eve of the meeting of the Working Committee of the League scheduled to be held in Bombay in the first week of July 1939, he wrote to Jinnah:

> In the name of the future of Muslim India and the call of coming generations of our nation I beseech you to save the destiny of our "Millet" from the staggeringly destructive consequences of the All-India Federation.
>
> The Muslims will never accept anything short of these irreducible demands [embodied in the Aligarh Professors' Scheme]. The Muslim-majority provinces have never been subjected to Hindu rule since the advent of Islam in India; nor can the Muslims of the rest of India allow themselves to be merged in the Hindu nation.
>
> The Muslim youths are looking towards you for a bold and clear lead towards a definite goal of independence and the right of self-preservation and self-determination. We are eager to throw ourselves into a struggle like what our brethren have done in Turkey, Persia, Palestine and Egypt.[85]

On the other hand, those who were equally concerned with the problem of Hindu dominance at the centre, but wanted to resolve it through some mechanism that did not involve a complete separation of the Muslim-majority areas from the rest of India, also remained active. Thus, in the course of his presidential address to the Bombay Provincial Muslim League Conference held at Sholapur in May 1939, Sikander, in the presence of Jinnah, while asserting that the scheme of federation embodied in the Act of 1935 was not suitable for India, emphasized that an All-India Federation in some form or the other was essential for the ordered progress of the country. In this connection, he reiterated his view that a federation in order to suit the conditions in India must be such as guaranteed full protection of the provinces. Towards the end of July 1939, he at last published his alternative scheme of federation.[86]

Surprisingly enough, Malik Barakat Ali, a notable League leader in the Punjab, who was a strong opponent of Sikander in provincial politics, also adopted a somewhat similar line and wanted the League's Working Committee to reiterate its commitment to the ideal of a free and united India. In a letter to Jinnah, he observed:

> I should like specifically to draw your attention to the great need of the Working Committee clarifying its attitude so far as the question of Muslim India and Hindu India is concerned. It appears to me that a great deal of loose talk is being indulged in on this subject and that in some quarters it is regarded as if the League stands committed to the scheme of Cultural Federation [actually Confederation] as developed by Dr Syed Abdul Latif of Hyderabad or as fostered by Seth Haji Abdullah Haroon. The Working Committee should see . . . that the misunderstandings thus caused in regard to the attitude of the League in this matter are completely dissipated and the League idea of a Free and United India is restated beyond any possibility of doubt.[87]

While the Muslim League leadership in the Punjab, in spite of its serious concern with the problem of Hindu domination at the Centre, was thus quite opposed to the idea of complete separation of the Muslim-majority areas from the rest of India, the dominant opinion in the League leadership in UP also had not yet moved beyond the idea of a weak Centre. As shown above, Khaliquzzaman's testimony on this issue, presented in his book written more than a decade after Partition, is unreliable, being vitiated by his desire to show that he had taken the lead in pushing the League's top leadership towards it. Nawab Mohammad Ismail Khan, who was president of the UP Muslim League and occupied a very high position in the All-India Muslim League, particularly because, unlike Khaliquzzaman's, his reputation had remained unscathed through the so-called Congress–League coalition talks in UP in 1937, is a more reliable witness on the trend of opinion among the League leadership in UP.

Fortunately, we have an idea of his thinking in the middle of 1939 through the report of a conversation with him recorded by the then Governor of UP. This clearly shows that some important League leaders in UP were still keen only on reducing the powers of the Centre and not looking forward to Partition. The Governor wrote:

I found that though he used moderate language, he seemed now quite [willing?] to accept the position adopted by the more extreme Muslim Leaguers, that there really was little prospect of any accommodation between Hindus and Muslims, that their culture and ideas were fundamentally different, and that it was difficult for them to unite into a nation so long as the barrier created by the exclusive Hindu social customs remained. He also explained the distrust of Muslims of the Federal scheme. They are afraid that the Federal Centre, which must be under the control of the Hindus, will be able to interfere too much with the Muslim Provinces. Therefore they wish to reduce the power of the Centre as far as possible.[88]

V

In the midst of this developing debate, Jinnah, the one man whose views had the greatest importance, was maintaining a sphinx-like silence. The sub-committee appointed by the League's Working Committee to examine and report on the various alternative constitutional schemes had given the provincial branches of the League time up to the end of August 1939 to submit their suggestions and was to meet in October to consider them. Jinnah took the position that as president of the League it was not proper for him to express himself on this issue and thus pre-empt the decisions of both the sub-committee and the Working Committee. It was on this ground that he refused to command Sikander's scheme.[89] While the ground given by Jinnah for not commending Sikander's scheme was quite valid, there was also another, more substantive, reason behind it, though hardly known to anyone. Already a convert to the Pakistan idea, he had obviously realized that Muslim public opinion as a whole was by then veering towards it and was naturally not interested in saying or doing anything that might in any way curb its further growth. On the contrary, without himself commending Partition, he had begun discreetly encouraging others who were talking about it. The Aligarh professors' scheme, based on the notion of Partition, was presented for consideration to the meeting of the League's Working Committee at Meerut in the last week of March at his own 'personal desire'.[90] The following paragraph from the presidential address to the Meerut Divisional Muslim League Conference delivered on 25 March by Liaquat Ali Khan, General Secretary of the All-India Muslim League and known as the most trusted colleague of Jinnah, also illustrates the same point and indeed can be taken as representing the latter's own views:

> I want an independent India where Muslims have power and freedom, for the Muslims are a nation and not a community. It would be a travesty to dismiss 90 million people with a glorious past as a community. Although Hindus and Muslims live in the same country, they live differently because their religion, culture and civilization are different. Muslims do not favour the pseudo-nationalism that the Hindus have borrowed from Europe. If Hindus and Muslims could not now live together amicably in India—and it had become almost impossible for them to co-exist under the same regime—then they might be able to do so by dividing the country on religious and cultural basis.[91]

Jinnah himself, without yet openly demanding the division of India, began to put forward arguments that would make such a demand sound logical and that were in fact used later to support it. Thus he told the Viceroy in the latter half of March 1939 that he had reluctantly come to the conclusion that the democratic system of government could not work in India. He further added that he had realized that he and others like him who had earlier worked for constitutional reforms on democratic lines had been carried away by their patriotic and nationalist feelings and had failed to appreciate the difficulties involved in working such a system.[92] Another window into the working of Jinnah's mind about that time is provided by his reply to the address of welcome presented by the staff of the Aligarh Muslim University on 12 April, where he affirmed his faith in the two-nation theory and expressed the hope that Muslims were going to live like a nation. To quote his own words:

> I make no secret of the fact that Muslims and Hindus are two nations and the Muslims cannot maintain their status as such unless they acquire national self-consciousness and national self-determination. The Muslim mind suffers from defeatism. . . . But we are now awakening to our duties. We are going to live as a nation and to play our part as a nation.[93]

A more revealing picture of Jinnah's mind is provided by his statement issued on 30 July, warning the British Government not to introduce Federation under the Act of 1935 in the teeth of opposition by almost all political parties in India. Apprehending that the Congress, in spite of its opposition to the federal scheme because of its undemocratic features, might be preparing to accept it out of fear that postponement of federation might facilitate the emergence of Pakistan, about which Muslims were already thinking, Jinnah asked:

Will the Congress be allured into accepting this federal scheme, as it is being urged upon them to do so on the ground that otherwise the Muslims will break away as they are thinking already of Pakistan which will mean the destruction of all-India unity? . . . Is Mr Gandhi going to fall into this trap for the sake of merely having a Congress-majority under this wretched federal scheme and is he going to be frightened to death on the score that the Muslims will break away and it might lead to a Partition of India.[94]

Addressing Muslim students in Bombay in the middle of August, Jinnah again let himself go on the two-nation theory and the unsuitability of a democratic system of government for India. As per the summary of that address published in the *Star of India* on 16 August 1939, Jinnah observed:

Muslims and Hindus were poles apart in faith, education, culture and philosophy. They were two distinct races or nationalities. It was a natural thing that whoever had greater power would influence and undermine the other's culture. He wondered how in a country like this democracy could be worked successfully. . . . They talked of democracy in India because it suited the Hindus. For them it was a matter of counting heads. What they had to consider and ponder over was whether a democratic system of parliamentary government was suited to such a vast country with different nationalities.[95]

VI

In the light of conflicting signals emanating from the Muslim League leaders, it is not surprising that the Viceroy was at a loss to fathom what they really wanted. Thus, Linlithgow remarked in April 1939 that along with 'the growing intensity of communal feeling and growing bitterness between Hindus and Muslims', the other marked feature of the Indian political situation at that time was 'the clear uncertainty of the Muslims and their leaders as to where they stand and what policy they are to pursue'.[96] The Governors of both Punjab and UP concurred with this view. According to the former, the British did not need 'to take too seriously the various forms of the Pakistan project'. He added that while Muslims were clearly opposed to the federal scheme of the Act of 1935, they were by no means united and there was 'a good deal of general uncertainty as to what they really want. Time is required to promote unity among their own ranks and for their objections [objectives?] to take definite shape.'[97] After describing some of the trends in the thinking of the Muslim League leadership on the issue of Federation, the Governor of UP remarked:

I am afraid all these views are very vague but the situation itself seems to me essentially vague. Muslims do not really know their minds. They have not fully faced upto the problem. When they do face up to it, I should doubt whether they would carry their opposition to Federation or to particular forms of Federation to the point of organizing mass resistance. But they may make a strong bid to get certain changes made in the scheme.[98]

In spite of all this, however, the Viceroy had a foreboding that the British might soon be called upon to pay serious attention to the Pakistan issue in some form or the other. This should be clear from the following note from Linlithgow to the Governor of Bihar as early as the middle of January 1939:

I do not think that the Pakistan proposition can be easily put aside as Congress would like to suggest. It seems to me a thoroughly unsound one, but that is neither here nor there. I suspect that we are likely to hear a great deal more of it; and it is no doubt inevitable that a minority so important as the Muslim-minority and so apprehensive that any decline in the degree of our direct control in this country can only be to their disadvantage, should think that the course of wisdom is to develop their own organisation and so endeavour to emulate the central control which the Congress have been able to establish and maintain so far as the Congress provinces and the Hindu electorate are concerned. The possibilities of an increase in communal tension which that type of situation holds out are too obvious to call for any comment. But I see nothing for it at this stage but to watch developments.[99]

Behind such thinking lay the assessment of the trend of Muslim public opinion at that time by some knowledgeable Indians.

Mention may here be made of what Firoz Khan Noon, a prominent Muslim leader of the Punjab, not belonging to the League, told Zetland in the first half of December 1938 about it. Asked whether there was any great force behind the Pakistan movement, Noon replied that he thought that 'there was a good deal'. He also added that he necessarily sympathized with 'the desire of the Muslim community, particularly in the north-west of India, to exercise control over that part of the country'. Again, he replied in the affirmative when asked whether 'the inevitable denouement of the Pakistan policy would be the separation of the north-west from the rest of India'.[100]

There is some evidence to suggest that even in circles close to the Congress Partition had begun to appear as a distinct possibility as early as 1938. Indeed, what G.D. Birla, a leading Hindu industrialist who was quite close to Gandhi and some other top leaders of the Congress belonging to its right wing, told the Viceroy during their meeting on 7 February 1938 shows even his preference for it in the context of the then existing communal situation. During their meeting Linlithgow was arguing against the Congress pushing on with the movement for democracy in the Indian states and making its introduction a necessary condition for supporting Federation. In that connection he made a point that if the introduction of Federation was much delayed, the Pakistan movement might become much stronger, resulting in the separation of the north-west from the rest of India. Birla replied that the communal situation in the country was growing rapidly worse day by day, a fact known to the Congress leaders who were full of apprehensions for the future. 'Might it not take the sting out of the communal poison,' Birla asked calmly, 'if the Muslims were given their Federation of the north-west?' Linlithgow was puzzled beyond measure by that reply. 'For a moment I thought,' he recorded, 'that Mr Birla must be teasing me, but his countenance portrayed no such design and I was convinced that for the time being he meant what he said.'[101]

The record of Linlithgow's interview with Gandhi on 15 March 1939 is even more significant, for it shows that by that time Gandhi was fully aware of the growing Muslim support for the Pakistan idea and its possibilities in the future. The Viceroy noted:

> Before we concluded, I thought it well to mention the Pakistan project to him [Gandhi], and to ask him whether he thought it had any life in it.

He said, he understood not, but thought that that might come. I replied that I had it in my mind to give the idea an airing very soon in my own way and get it out of the way. Mr Gandhi said he was sure that that was the right course; that he doubted if it would stand any detailed examination, though it had no doubt wide possibilities. I asked whether by that he meant that it might represent an urge running back into the depths of the Muslim world. He said that that might indeed be the case in certain circumstances, but that even if Pakistan admitted of realization, it would never settle the communal question in India or represent more than a sharp division which might in due course give rise to a major calamity.[102]

In any case, Linlithgow continued to feel that once a sufficient number of the rulers of Indian states were persuaded to join the proposed Federation, there would be no major obstacle in the way of its introduction. The provinces had no option in this matter under the Act of 1935 and were to automatically become parts of the Federation as soon as it came into existence. However, Zetland thought differently. As he himself recalls in his memoirs, he had long since held the view that the solidarity of Islam was a hard fact against which it was futile to strike one's head.[103] By 1938 he had become quite convinced that 'the dominating factor in determining the future form of government in India would prove to be the All-India Muslim League'.[104] In particular, the proceedings of the Patna session of the League (December 1938) had made him wonder 'whether Muslim opposition to Federation might not prove, when the time came, to be even more embarrassing than that of Congress'.[105] The talk with Khaliquzzaman and Siddiqi in March 1939 further confirmed his view that the British were going to face 'greater difficulty in bringing the Muslims into the Federation than the Congress'. He also felt that with the passage of time the difficulty in brining the Federation into existence seemed to be 'gaining in magnitude'.[106] This thought went on exercising his mind and finally he wrote to the Viceroy in early May: 'The deep-seated dislike and fear of Hindu domination on the part of 90 million Muslims is a thing which we cannot possibly brush aside.' He further added: 'I am becoming steadily confirmed in my view that it will be the Muslims rather than the Congress that will provide the biggest obstacle to the early achievement of Federation.'[107]

Linlithgow thought differently and remained firm in his conviction that the scheme of Federation under the Act of 1935, framed after considerable labour and thorough examination of all aspects of the Indian problem, provided the best next step in India. He was particularly at a loss to understand what more safeguards could be provided to Muslims in an all-India democratic set-up where there could be no escape from the majority getting an upper hand. He, therefore, asserted in his rejoinder to Zetland, sent in the third week of May, that if a sufficient number of Princes agreed to join the Federation, it was beyond the power of the League to stop it from coming. As he put it:

Our difficulty is that the root of these Muslim apprehensions is inherent in any system of responsible government at the centre. It is obvious that distribution of power by count of heads must inevitably be distasteful to a minority. No plan for Federation based upon representative government can be acceptable to those Muslims who contemplate the future course of Indian politics as an unending communal contest. . . . I do not wish to underestimate the difficulties likely to arise as the consequence of Muslim opposition to Federation. But I do not think that the Muslims have it in their power to prevent the attainment of Federation, or to make it unworkable—unless indeed they can discover means to prevent a sufficient number of Rulers from acceding.[108]

Linlithgow persisted in pursuing this line in his subsequent correspondence with Zetland on the subject of Federation.[109] He was, of course, taking a strictly constitutional view of things. For according to the Act of 1935, while the provinces of British India were to automatically become parts of the Federation, it could not be introduced unless a number of Indian states, sufficient to occupy 50 per cent seats out of the total number of seats earmarked for states in the federal legislature, agreed to accede to the Federation. Zetland, however, stuck to his thinking. Even after it became clear that in view of the reluctance of almost all the major states to join the Federation, its introduction was not possible in the near future, he persisted in expressing the view that even if the major states agreed to join, it might not be possible to introduce Federation in case the Muslims decided to keep out. Thus, in his rejoinder to Linlithgow in the last week of June 1939, he remarked: 'It would be difficult to contemplate with satisfaction a Federation which did not include let us say the Punjab and Bengal.' He further added: 'I do not see how we could force the Government of the Punjab, or of Bengal, to enter the Federation if they were determined not to do so'.[110]

All this while, unaware of Zetland's attitude, Jinnah had been assiduously applying himself to renewing the old unwritten Anglo–Muslim understanding. Being a shrewd strategist, he was well aware of the fact that the majority of his colleagues in the higher echelons of the League maintained close contacts with the British officials and would not like to take any stand that might seriously displease or annoy the latter. Even otherwise, the British, being the ruling power in India, their support would be of tremendous value in a situation where the League was pursuing a relentless war against the Congress. Before finally announcing the goal of Pakistan, it obviously seemed wise to probe the British and see how far they were prepared to go to support the League. So Jinnah swallowed his old pride as an Indian patriot and offered the British a deal on the issue of an all-India federation, to which the League was irrevocably opposed but which the British were trying to bring about under the provisions of the Act of 1935. This was done in the middle of August 1938 during a call on Lord Brabourne, then acting Governor-General and Viceroy of India. As Brabourne reported to Zetland, Jinnah, 'even more violent than usual' on the issue of Federation, 'ended up with the suggestion that we should keep the Centre as it is now; that we should make friends with the Muslims by "protecting" them in the Congress Provinces and that, if we did that, the Muslims would "protect" us at the Centre'.[111]

Sikander, who called on Brabourne a little later, was 'of course, much more reasonable and moderate in his language, but just as strongly anti-Federation as Jinnah was and he expressed the same view about the future'. That was that the British were mad to go ahead with Federation, which amounted to playing straight into the hands of the Congress, and that the Muslims, given a fair deal by the British, would stand by them 'through thick and thin'.[112] Zetland was pleased to read about Jinnah's offer regarding mutual cooperation on the issue of Federation and remarked that the latter had 'actually been acting in accordance with his words'. In this connection, Zetland recalled that in the Central Assembly Jinnah had recently supported the British against the Congress over the Zanzibar cloves business and saved the British from resorting to certification on the issue of the Bill dealing with anti-recruiting propaganda. In addition, he had promised, through Zafrulla Khan, to support the Government on the proposed trade agreement. However, Zetland found himself unable, 'due to the general pressure of events', to accept Jinnah's request on the federal issue. 'Moreover', he added, 'were we to do so, I can imagine circumstances in which we should find ourselves leaning on a very broken reed.' Apparently, because of Jinnah's past record as an Indian patriot, Zetland had a low estimate of his character and considered him unreliable. This did not apply to Sikander, who had always been in the good books of the British. 'I am sorry,' Zetland added, 'that Sikander Hyat remains as strongly opposed to Federation as ever, for he is a man of very different character and the Punjab is a unit of the prospective Federation of prime importance.'[113]

Not getting any hint of a positive response from the British, Jinnah chose to follow a different strategy in dealing with them. He now began to emphasize that the Muslims were a power in India and could not be ignored. Thus, delivering his presidential address to the Sind Provincial Muslim League Conference at Karachi in October 1938, he dilated at length on the supposed Muslim sufferings in the provinces under Congress rule and the lack of any help from the Governors. Observing that there was no use relying on anyone else, he pointed out that the only way that the Muslims could save themselves was to build up the power of the League. Referring to the developments in Palestine and the setback suffered by the Arabs, he remarked that Great Britain had 'thrown her friends to the wolves and broken her solemn promises'. He further added: 'Only those succeeded with the British people who possess force and power and who are in a position to bully them.'[114] It was not, of course, part of his strategy to burn his boats with the British. Shortly after the Karachi session of the Sind Muslim League, he made a public declaration that, if it considered it worthwhile to do so, the League might openly ally with the British in order to safeguard Muslim interests. In the course of his presidential address to the Patna session of the League (December 1938), he strongly refuted the allegation that the League was an ally of imperialism, but went on to assert that it would be 'the ally of even the devil' if it suited Muslim interests. He then significantly added: 'It is not because we are in love with imperialism, but in politics one has to play one's game as on the chess board.'[115]

That was, of course, a game over which Jinnah had complete

mastery. The next round was played in the Central Legislative Assembly during the debate on the Finance Bill, on 22 March 1939. Jinnah in his speech first of all pointed to the strategic position occupied by the League in the Assembly, a position that corresponded to its position in the country as a whole. 'Fortunately or unfortunately,' he remarked, 'we hold the balance in the House. If we are supporting the Government then I think the Finance Member can safely pilot this Bill to his satisfaction and he can carry this Bill without a comma of it being altered. . . .' The Muslim League, he observed, had supported the Government when the Government had appeared right, just as it had supported the Congress when the Congress had appeared right. That policy, he warned, would now be altered and the League was going to have nothing to do with the Finance Bill. For when the League was right, no one supported it. Jinnah's main grievance was that the Governors had not used their special powers to protect the rights of Muslims in the Congress-ruled provinces. Addressing both the Government and the Congress benches he thundered:

> But let me tell you—and I tell both of you—that you alone, or this organization alone, or both combined, will never be able to destroy that culture which we have inherited, the Islamic culture, and that spirit will live, is going to live and has lived. You may overpower us; you may oppress us; and you can do your worst. But we have come to the conclusion and we have made a grim resolve that we shall go down, if we have to go down, fighting.[116]

The only purpose behind such rhetoric, lumping the Congress and the British together, could have been to impress upon the latter the power of the League and the damage that might be caused to British interests if it was not given due attention. Within less than six months of Jinnah's speech in the Legislative Assembly came the outbreak of World War II, which created a new situation in India and removed the cause of his grievance.

Thus by 1939 Muslims in India, with a few exceptions here and there, had been totally alienated from the Congress, and looked upon it as an essentially Hindu organization bent upon ushering in Hindu Raj after the end of the British Raj. There had also developed a growing conviction among them that they constituted a nation by themselves and that their future would be secure only when some means were found to ensure that they were left free to shape their lives according to their own ways in those areas of India where they constituted a majority. Opinion had not yet fully crystalized as to the means for achieving this. While some wanted Partition pure and simple, others envisaged the separation of the Muslim-majority areas from the Hindu-majority ones, but the retention of some mechanism of control and coordination at the Centre, with extremely limited powers and ensuring equal share in power to Hindus and Muslims. All that remained to be accomplished by Jinnah was to end this contradiction and make the Muslims unitedly adopt his goal of establishing a fully sovereign Muslim State or States. At the same time, he had also to ensure that the British, who were bound to play an important role in future constitutional developments, did not oppose but extended at least tacit support to the Muslim demand. The outbreak of the war provided an excellent opportunity in both these respects. Jinnah immediately grasped its nature and significance and fully exploited it to achieve his desired end. The stage was thus set for the League's adoption of the demand for Partition.

NOTES

1. Halide Edib, *Inside India* (London, 1937), pp. 352–62. According to K.K. Aziz, Rahmat Ali had actually written the supposed interview himself and persuaded Edib to incorporate it in her book in the form of a conversation between him and her. See K.K. Aziz, *A History of the Idea of Pakistan*, 4 vols. (Lahore, 1987), vol. II, p. 362.
2. Aziz, ibid., p. 612.
3. Syed Abdul Latif, *The Cultural Future of India* (Bombay, 1938); reproduced in Aziz, n. 1, pp. 443–54.
4. Syed Abdul Latif, *The Muslim Problem in India* (Bombay, 1939), pp. 30–50.
5. Ibid., pp. v–viii.
6. Ibid., p. 12.
7. Ibid., pp. 13–16.
8. See Aziz, n. 1, pp. 488–91, 518–19.
9. *Confederacy of India* (Lahore, 1939), fully reproduced in Aziz, n. 1, vol. II, pp. 667–776.
10. Punjabi wrote in *Confederacy in India* that he had originally thought of only three federations, but added two more, covering the Indian states, at the suggestion of the Nawab of Mamdot, ibid., p. 672. Much later, however, he claimed that he had himself made the change from

three to five federations in order to make his proposals acceptable to Jinnah, Aziz, n. 1, p. 534.

11. K.K. Aziz, ed., *Prelude to Pakistan: Documents and Readings Illustrating the Growth of the Idea of Pakistan* (Lahore, 1992), vol. II, pp. 665–6.
12. Aziz, no. 1, pp. 532–4. Jinnah's disapproval of the use of the word Pakistan was apparently the product of tactical considerations, especially in view of the fact that the promoter of the book was an important League leader and Jinnah was determined to come out openly for Pakistan only when he considered the time ripe for it.
13. Aziz, n. 11, vol. II, pp. 675–6.
14. Ibid., p. 685.
15. Ibid., p. 704.
16. See Aziz, n. 1, pp. 419–22.
17. Lawrence Ziring, 'Jinnah, the Burden of Leadership', Ahmad Hasan Dani, ed., *World Scholars on Quaid-i-Azam Mohammad Ali Jinnah* (Islamabad, 1979), p. 406.
18. Mian Ahmad Yar Khan Daultana, 'Congress Communalism and Muslim Minorities', the *Star of India* (Calcutta), 16 September 1937, reproduced in Aziz, n. 11, vol. II, pp. 415–18.
19. Aziz, n. 1, p. 413.
20. Ibid., p. 415.
21. Ibid.
22. Ibid., pp. 416–17. For the full text of the report by Hodgson, see Kanji Dwarkadas, *Ten Years to Freedom, 1938–1947* (Bombay, 1968), pp. 26–40. The remarks cited occur on pp. 32, 36–7.
23. Aziz, n. 1, p. 418; also Jamil-ud-Din Ahmad, *Creation of Pakistan* (Lahore, 1976), p. 39. For the full text of Ahmad's pamphlet, see M.H. Saiyid, ed., *India's Problem of the Future Constitution* (Bombay, n.d.), pp. 128–39.
24. Ahmad to Aziz, 9 December 1939, Aziz, n. 1, p. 418.
25. Aziz, n. 11, vol. II, p. 572.
26. Ibid., p. 568.
27. Syed Shamsul Hasan, ... *Plain Mr Jinnah* (Karachi, 1976), p. 166. Some of Toosy's writings were subsequently included in *India's Problem of the Future Constitution: Nationalism in Conflict in India*, and *Pakistan and Muslim India*, each with an identical Foreword by Jinnah (Bombay, 1942).
28. Aziz, n. 1, p. 484.
29. Ibid., pp. 613–14.
30. Syed Zafarul Hasan and Mohammad Afzal Qadri, *The Problem of Indian Muslims and Its Solution* (Aligarh, n.d.), Dr Afzal Husain Qadri Collection, Archives of Freedom Movement, University of

Karachi. See also Afzal Husain Qadri to Jinnah, 22 February 1939, forwarding the Aligarh Scheme, Quaid-i-Azam Papers, Reel 12, File 135. One of the maps appended to the pamphlet bears the date 14 August 1939. That led K.K. Aziz to place it in August 1939 (see Aziz, n. 1, pp. 591, 620). However, he seems to have realized later that it should be placed earlier. This is clear from its placement (without mentioning any date) in his collection of documents published subsequently, see Aziz, n. 11, vol. II, pp. 546–9. It is possible that the scheme sent to Jinnah along with the letter of 22 February 1939 was merely a typed one (copy not available in the Quaid-i-Azam Papers) and that a printed version appeared only in August 1939.

31. Aziz, n. 1, pp. 479–80.
32. Ibid., p. 480.
33. Ibid., p. 481.
34. Aziz, n. 11, vol. II, pp. 783–4.
35. Aziz, n. 1, pp. 555–6.
36. Ibid., p. 409.
37. Aziz, n. 11, vol. II, p. 820.
38. Ibid., p. 825.
39. Ibid., p. 845.
40. Ibid., pp. 788–9.
41. Ibid., p. 811.
42. Ibid., pp. 800–1.
43. Ibid., pp. 818–19.
44. Ibid., pp. 821–2.
45. Ibid., p. 824.
46. Ibid., pp. 826–7.
47. Ibid., pp. 838–9.
48. Ibid., pp. 836–7.
49. Ibid., pp. 838–40.
50. Ibid., pp. 850–2.
51. For fuller citations and references, see Bimal Prasad, *Pathway to India's Partition*, I: *The Foundations of Muslim Nationalism* (New Delhi, 1999), pp. 229–32.
52. Ibid., pp. 232–3.
53. See *Letters of Iqbal to Jinnah* (Lahore, 1942), p. 21.
54. Aziz, n. 11, vol. II, p. 693.
55. Enclosure, Viceroy to Secretary of State, 27 October 1937, MSS Eur. F125/7 (C) (I), Linlithgow Collection.
56. Syed Sharifuddin Pirzada, ed., *Foundations of Pakistan: All India Muslim League Documents: 1906–1947* (hereinafter *League Documents*), vol. II (Karachi, 1970), p. 179.
57. Punjab Legislative Assembly Debates: Official Report, 8 April 1938, vol. IV, no. 12 (Lahore, 1939), p. 837.

58. Sir Henry Craik (Governor of Punjab) to Linlithgow, 5 June 1938, F125/86, Linlithgow Collection.
59. *Daily Gazette* (Karachi), 9 October 1938, cited in Allen H. Jones, 'Mr Jinnah's Leadership and the Evolution of the Pakistan Idea: The case of the Sind Provincial Muslim League Conference, 1938', in Dani, n. 17, pp. 183–4.
60. Syed Ali Muhammad H. Rashidi, *Report of the General Secretary of the First Sind Provincial Muslim League Conference, 8–12 October 1938*, Freedom Movement Archives (University of Karachi), Muslim League Papers, vol. 242, p. 1.
61. Jones, n. 59, pp. 184–5.
62. Ibid., pp. 186–7.
63. Ibid., p. 187.
64. For a view claimed to be based on the Muslim League Papers, that the resolution moved originally at the Sind Provincial Conference of the League was actually adopted with the removal of only one word 'Federation' from it, see Muhammad Aslam Malik, *The Making of the Pakistan Resolution* (Karachi, 2001), pp. 24–5.
65. Rashidi, n. 213, p. 1.
66. See *Quarterly Survey*, n. 45, no. 5 (1 August to 31 October 1938), p. 35.
67. See 'Extract from Weekly Report of the Director, Intelligence Bureau, Home Department, Government of India', 26 November 1938, L/P&J/8/689. Private Office Papers, IOR.
68. *Quarterly Survey*, n. 145, no. 6 (1 November 1938–1 January 1938), p. 31–2.
69. *League Documents*, n. 56, p. 319.
70. Ibid., p. 321.
71. 'Extract from Weekly Report of the Director, Intelligence Bureau', 31 December 1938, n. 66.
72. Ibid.
73. Sir Maurice Hallett to Linlithgow, 6 January 1939, MSS Eur. F125/46, Linlithgow Collection, IOR.
74. Linlithgow to Zetland, 1 March 1939, MSS Eur. F125/7, L.C.
75. Linlithgow to Zetland, 12 April 1939, ibid.
76. *Quarterly Survey*, n. 45, no. 7 (1 February 1939 to 30 April 1939), p. 29.
77. Ibid.
78. Latif to Jinnah, 29 April 1939, Quaid-i-Azam Papers, Reel 6, File 48.
79. Mohammad Afzal Husain Qadri to Jinnah, 25 June 1939, Quaid-i-Azam Papers, Reel 6, File 49.
80. Choudhry Khaliquzzaman, *Pathway to Pakistan* (London, 1961), pp. 205–6.
81. Ibid., p. 207.

82. Zetland to Linlithgow, 28 March 1939, F125/6.
83. Haroon to Jinnah, 22 April 1939, Quaid-i-Azam Papers.
84. Aziz, n. 11, p. 778.
85. Qadri to Jinnah, 25 June 1939, Quaid-i-Azam Papers, Reel 6, File 49.
86. *Quarterly Survey*, n. 45, no. 8 (1 May to 31 July 1939), p. 31. For the text of Sikander's scheme, see Sikander Hyat Khan, *Outlines of a Scheme of Indian Federation* (Lahore, n.d.); reproduced in M. Gwyer, and A. Appadorai, eds., *Speeches and Documents on the Indian Constitution, 1921–47*, 2 vols. (Delhi, 1957), vol. II, pp. 455–62 and Aziz, n. 11, pp. 539–45.
87. Malik Barkat Ali to Jinnah, 21 June 1939, Quaid-i-Azam Papers, n. 78.
88. Haig to Linlithgow, 25 July 1939, MSS Eur. F115/2B, Haig Collection, IOR.
89. See Sikander to Jinnah, 19 July 1939, and Jinnah to Sikander, 23 July 1939. S. Qaim Hussain Jafri, ed., *Quaid-i-Azam's Correspondence with Punjab Muslim Leaders* (Lahore, 1977), pp. 357-61.
90. See Qadri to Jinnah, 25 June 1939, n. 84.
91. Mohammad Ali Jinnah, *The Nation's Voice: Speeches and Statements, March 1935–March 1940* (hereinafter referred to as *Jinnah: Speeches and Statements*), Waheed Ahmad, ed. (Karachi, 1992), p. 355.
92. Linlithgow to Zetland, 28 March 1939, Linlithgow Collection.
93. *Jinnah: Speeches and Statements*, pp. 368–9.
94. Ibid., p. 381.
95. Ibid., pp. 386–7.
96. Linlithgow to Haig, 17 April 1939, F125/102, Linlithgow Collection.
97. Craik to Linlithgow, 19 June 1939, F125/87, ibid.
98. Haig to Linlithgow, 1 July 1939, MSS Eur. F115/2B, Haig Collection, India Office Library.
99. Linlithgow to Maurice Hallett, 15 January, 1939, F125/46, Linlithgow Collection. Emphasis added.
100. Zetland to Linlithgow, 13 December 1938, F125/6, ibid.
101. Note of an Interview between Linlithgow at Birla House, New Delhi, 7 February 1938, F125/5, ibid.
102. Notes of discussion on general topics between Linlithgow and Gandhi, New Delhi, 15 March 1939, F125/157, ibid.
103. Lord Zetland, *The Memoirs of Lawrence: Second Marquess of Zetland* (London, 1956), p. 119.
104. Ibid., p. 246.
105. Ibid., pp. 246–7.
106. Zetland to Linlithgow, 28 March 1939, F125/7, Linlithgow Collection.
107. Ibid., 9 May 1939.
108. Linlithgow to Zetland, 19 May 1939, ibid.

109. Ibid., 26 May 1939; 2 June 1939; 23 June 1939; and 7 July 1939, Linlithgow Collection.
110. Zetland to Linlithgow, 27 June 1939, ibid.
111. Brabourne to Zetland, 19 August 1938, ibid.
112. Ibid.
113. Zetland to Brabourne, 2 September 1938, ibid.
114. *Jinnah: Speeches and Statements*, n. 91, pp. 284–7.
115. Ibid., p. 332.
116. Waheed Ahmad, ed., *Quaid-i-Azam Mohammad Ali Jinnah: Speeches: Indian Legislative Assembly, 1935-1947* (Karachi, 1991), p. 431.

CHAPTER III

The War Crisis and the Pakistan Resolution 1939–1940

THE OUTBREAK OF World War II on 3 September 1939, consequent on Britain's declaration of war against Germany, in retaliation of the latter's attack on Poland a day earlier, and, following it, the Viceroy's immediate declaration, without any consultation with the representatives of Indian opinion, that India had become a belligerent country on the side of Britain at once gave a new turn to Indian politics. The Congress took it as an affront to the Indian people and launched itself on a path that marked the beginning of the last phase of the old conflict between British imperialism and Indian nationalism, accompanied by that of a similar conflict between the latter and Muslim nationalism. The path chosen by the Congress was not at all surprising. It had foreseen the outbreak of a World War years ago and since as early as 1927, and more particularly since 1936, clearly laid down conditions for the use of Indian resources in such a war. Repeatedly expressing its strong opposition to Fascism and Nazism and sympathizing with its victims such as Abyssinia, Spain, and Czechoslovakia, it had simultaneously declared its equally strong opposition to imperialism and made it clear that it would not countenance the use of Indian resources in any war waged for the defence of imperial possessions and privileges. It is this thinking that shaped the Congress policy in the new context.

The stand of the Congress on the war crisis was adumbrated by its Working Committee, after deliberations lasting over a week, through a long statement issued on 14 September 1939. It recalled the past policy of the Congress and declared that if Britain had gone to war to defend its imperial possessions and privileges, India would have nothing to do with it. If, on the other hand, the issue was democracy and new world order based on it, India would be intensely interested in it. If Britain was really fighting for democracy, she must give up her imperialist possessions and grant self-determination to India. The Working Committee, therefore, invited the British Government to clearly state its war aims with regard to imperialism and democracy and the new order that it envisaged, in particular how these were to be applied to India and be implemented in the immediate present[1].

British official circles in London were totally opposed to making any declaration that would tie their hands after the end of the war. When policy towards India, in the light of the Congress demand for a declaration of British objectives, was first discussed in the War Cabinet on 27 September 1939, the conclusion that emerged was that, while it was certain that the World War II like the first, would see great changes in India, 'it was undesirable' at that early stage for His Majesty's Government to enter into any commitments regarding such changes.[2] As for the Viceroy, while he was keen to associate representatives of political parties and interests in India, including the Congress, the Muslim League and the Princes, with the Central Government in order to strengthen India's war effort, he was not at all interested in doing anything that would hasten India's march towards independence. He explained his viewpoint as late as December 1939 in the course of a confidential letter to the Secretary of State for India:

> After all we framed the Constitution as it stands in the Act of 1935 because we thought that way the best way—given the political position in both countries—of maintaining British influence in India. It is no part of our policy, I take it, to expedite in India constitutional changes for their own sake, or gratuitously to hurry the handing over of the controls to Indian hands at any pace faster than that which we regard as best calculated, on a long view, to hold India to the Empire.[3]

The British determination not to make any firm commitment regarding the future and to hold on to the Empire, including India, as firmly as possible came out in the statement issued by the Viceroy on 17 October 1939. Therein he declared that the British Government had not had the time to precisely define the objectives for which it was fighting the war and added that it was also not wise to do so at so early a stage. There was, however, no doubt about the broad general objectives for which Britain was fighting the war. These were to resist aggression whether directed against itself or against others. It not only wanted victory for itself but also looked forward to laying the foundation of a better international order in which war would not be the inevitable lot of each succeeding generation. As far as the British policy towards India was concerned, the Viceroy observed that its ultimate goal was the attainment of Dominion Status by India as was made clear in 1929 by the then Viceroy, Lord Irwin. So far as the immediate present was concerned, it was not possible to improve upon the scheme of government embodied in the Act of 1935. At the end of the war, the British Government would gladly enter into consultations with the several 'communities, parties and interests in India' and with the Princes with a view to framing such modifications in that Act as might be found desirable. In the meanwhile, steps might be taken to constitute a consultative group, consisting of leaders of various political parties and Princes, under the chairmanship of the Viceroy in order to secure the association of Indian public opinion with the conduct of the war.[4]

The Congress found that declaration wholly unsatisfactory and found itself unable to cooperate with the war effort on its basis. As a first step, it called upon its ministries in all the eight provinces to resign after getting suitable resolutions explaining the Congress stand on the war crisis adopted in the concerned legislatures. The resignations of the ministries, which duly followed, failed to create any visible impact on British policy and by March 1940 the Congress felt compelled to decide to launch a programme of civil disobedience in order to register its protest and force the British Government to see reason.[5]

II

The British, keeping a close watch on Indian political developments, were not at all unprepared for such a reaction on the part of the Congress. On the contrary, while hoping for the best, they had, as in the past, apparently decided to turn to the Muslim League to counterbalance the Congress, if required. This can be the only explanation for the Viceroy's action in, by one stroke, catapulting Jinnah from the sidelines to the centre stage of Indian politics by, for the first time, equating him with Gandhi and inviting them to see him (separately though) on the same date, i.e. 4 September 1939, on the morrow of the declaration of war. This marked the beginning of Linlithgow's practice of always inviting Gandhi and Jinnah simultaneously, thereby projecting the latter as a leader of equal importance with the former. Jinnah was not oblivious of the significance of such an action. About three years later, in the course of an address to a meeting at the Aligarh Muslim University in November 1942, he recalled what had happened on 4 September 1939 and observed:

By September 1939 when the war broke out the Muslim League had built up a sufficiently strong position, so much so that the Government of India and the British Government could not ignore it. For the first time in a crisis like the war, alongwith Mr Gandhi, the President of the all-India Muslim League was also invited to meet the Viceroy. Do you remember any case before this when any recognized leader of Muslim India was invited alongwith the Congress leader? From that day Mr Gandhi tried his best to get rid of the position that the President of the Muslim League on behalf of Muslim India had been given: an equal status with the Congress leaders.[6]

Linlithgow, on his part, was so keen to placate Jinnah that he even put up occasionally with what appeared to him as rude behaviour on Jinnah's part. This is borne out by Linlithgow's reaction to Jinnah's failure to see him towards the end of September on account of another engagement already fixed:

Jinnah has been very tiresome as usual. I telegraphed to him to let him know that Gandhi was coming to see me and ask him to come too. There was some delay in the delivery of the telegram on the day he left Delhi for Bombay; but his reply was to the effect that he had an invitation from the Nizam which would detain him in Hyderabad, to which he proposed to proceed that afternoon, until the 1st October after which date he would be very ready to see me! It has not gone too well with Sikander, Zafrulla and other representative Muslims, but as I have told them both, my business must be to try to keep the Muslims together, just as it is in a wider field to keep the various interests in the country together, and it is no use losing our tempers with Jinnah, irritating as he may be.[7]

Occasional rude behaviour, noticeable also in his dealings with the Congress leaders, was part of Jinnah's strategy and had the double purpose of putting his interlocutors in their place and impressing his followers. There is, however, no mistaking his grasp of the background and significance of the changed stance on Linlithgow's part. He realized fully well that the latter had understood the value of the Muslim League to the British as a counterblast to the Congress and decided to cash on it to the maximum possible extent. This was the basis of the three-pronged strategy, followed by him from 4 September 1939 onwards. On the one hand, he took care, through his and the League's public pronouncements as well as interviews with the Viceroy, to promote the establishment of a relationship of mutual trust and confidence with Linlithgow even though vigorously putting forward the League's point of view and even criticizing or attacking the British in public for their inability in saving the Muslims from alleged Congress atrocities in provinces ruled over by its ministries. On the other hand, he continued with renewed vigour his attacks on the Congress leaders for supposedly working for ushering in Hindu Raj and consistently rebuffed their attempts to drag him into a united front against the British with a view to pressurizing the latter to clarify their war aims. At the same time, he continued, with similar vigour, his recent campaign in support of the Pakistan idea without, of course, using the word Pakistan.

Thus we find Jinnah talking frankly about his vision of the future of Indian Muslims with Linlithgow at their very first meeting (4 September) after the outbreak of the war in a way in which he had not talked to anyone else till then—at least as per the historical record. When Linlithgow asked him to explain what he meant by his recently stated proposition that India was not fit for democratic government and wondered how else was India to attain the goal of self-government, Jinnah replied that 'the escape from the impasse . . . lay in the adoption of Partition'. On the Viceroy observing that Partition appeared the less practical the more one examined it in details, Jinnah remarked: 'What about Burma? They are happy enough.' During that interview Jinnah also indirectly sought Linlithgow's help in dealing with Sikandar, who had been insisting, both inside the League and outside, on a more straightforward position on the part of the League in supporting Britain in the war effort, and not showing appreciation for Jinnah's cautious line. That line was geared towards ensuring that no hindrance was placed in the path of the League-dominated ministries in supporting the war effort but at the same time maintained a posture of grievance and defiance against the Government in order to save the League from appearing as a blind supporter of the British. Jinnah assured Linlithgow that he personally shared Sikander's sentiments of loyalty and readiness to give full support to the war effort, but that he was a public man and had to think of his followers. Sikander alone could not deliver the goods. Assuring the Viceroy that he had no feelings against Sikander and was indeed most anxious to work with him, Jinnah asked Linlithgow to do what he could to strengthen his (Jinnah's) hands and announce as soon as possible that the Constitution would be 'completely overhauled and reshaped'. He also pleaded strongly for the British to take suitable steps to protect Muslims from what he termed as oppression in Congress-ruled provinces. When the Viceroy asked Jinnah whether he wanted the Congress ministries to be turned out, Jinnah replied in the affirmative, phrasing his answer in such a way as to underline the common danger faced by the British and the Muslims from the Congress. 'Yes! Turn them out at once,' he said. 'Nothing else will bring them to their senses. Their object, though you may not believe it, and though I did not believe it till two years ago, is nothing less than to destroy both you British and us Muslims. They will never stand by you.'[8]

The Muslim League's formal stand on the war crisis came out in the shape of a resolution adopted by its Working Committee on 18 September 1939. Just a week before this, the Viceroy in the course of his address to the joint session of the Council of State and the Central Legislative Assembly had announced that although the setting up of an all-India federation continued to remain the Government's objective it had decided to suspend all preparations in this regard in view of the supreme necessity of concentrating all its energies on the successful conduct of the war.[9] The League's Working Committee, recalling its old opposition to federation, appreciated the announcement regarding the suspension of preparations for it, but hoped that the objective, too, would be abandoned without any further delay. Further, it strongly urged the British Government to 'review and revise the entire problem of India's future Constitution *de novo*' in the light of the experience gained till then through the working the Constitution in the provinces and the developments that had taken place since 1935 or might take place thereafter. While affirming that Muslim India stood against the exploitation of the people of India and repeatedly declared itself in favour of 'Free India', the resolution declared that it was 'equally opposed to the domination of Hindu-majority over Musalmans and other minorities and vassalisation of Muslim India' and was 'irrevocably' opposed to any federal objective 'which must necessarily result in a majority community rule under the guise of democracy and parliamentary system of government'. Such a Constitution, it further declared, was 'totally unsuited to the genius of the peoples of the country' who were composed of several nationalities.

Turning to the international situation, the Working Committee condemned unprovoked aggression and the doctrine that might was right and expressed deep sympathy for Poland, Britain, and France. It, however, affirmed that 'real and solid Muslim co-operation and support to Great Britain' at that hour of trial could not be secured successfully if the British Government and the Viceroy were unable to secure to Muslims justice and fair play in the Congress-governed provinces through the exercise of the special powers of the Governors. Finally, the Working Committee asked the British Government for an assurance that no declaration regarding constitutional advance in India would be made without the 'consent and approval' of the League nor any Constitution framed and adopted without such consent and approval.[10]

Against this background came the second meeting (since the outbreak of war) between Linlithgow and Jinnah on 5 October 1939. Both of them utilized it to further advance confidence-building among themselves as well as to put forward their respective points of view. 'I found him [Jinnah],' reported Linlithgow, 'in more friendly mood and readier to cooperate than I have known him, and his attitude throughout the discussion was eminently reasonable.'

Thus obviously referring to Linlithgow's role in moderating Sikander, Jinnah took the opportunity to thank the former 'with much graciousness' for what he had done 'to assist him in keeping his party together and expressed great gratitude for this'. Quite pleased, Linlithgow evinced keen interest in the growth of the Muslim League and remarked that it was clearly unsatisfactory' that of the two great parties of equal importance, one (the Congress) should be well organized and well equipped to pursue its objectives, the other (the League) should be prevented from securing its full expression by its failure to secure an effective mouthpiece. 'It was in public interest,' Linlithgow remarked, 'that the Muslim point of view should be fully and completely expressed.' He was also quite forthcoming on his talks with the Congress leaders, which had just been concluded on 3 October (Prasad and Nehru) and 5 October (Gandhi). While during the last interview, on 4 September, Linlithgow had parried Jinnah's question as to what had passed during his interview with Gandhi, on this occasion, without any question from Jinnah, he voluntereed the information that he had not made much headway in his talks with the Congress leaders.

However, Linlithgow failed to provide any satisfaction to Jinnah when the latter repeated his plea for protection for Muslims in the Congress-ruled provinces. In that connection, Jinnah told Linlithgow that he had received a representation from a group of Aligarh professors to the effect that he should not under any circumstance reach agreement with the Congress or the Viceroy unless the plan to make a united India was abandoned and effective protection was provided to the Muslim-minorities in the provinces. Linlithgow remained unmoved and remarked that he had gone into the position of the Muslim-minorities in the provinces most carefully, but was driven to the conclusion that 'it was extremely difficult to find any positive instance of real oppression or the like by provincial governments . . .'.[11]

Linlithgow also did not convey to Jinnah any concession on the main demand made in the resolution on the war crisis adopted by the League's Working Committee on 18 September as suggested by Sikander a few days back. He had already made up his mind on that issue. As he reported to Zetland in the last week of September, Sikander had conveyed to him through the Punjab Governor that while the League's resolution wanted that no declaration regarding the question of constitutional advance for India should be made without the consent and approval of the League, Jinnah would be prepared to accept mere consultation in place of consent and approval, provided the League was given an assurance that in any future scheme of federation Muslim interests would be amply protected. Sikander had also suggested consideration of the advisability of giving Jinnah an assurance that if the League cooperated fully with the war effort, the Viceroy was convinced that its views would not be overlooked by the

British Government. Linlithgow, however, did not consider it advisable at that stage to offer any such assurance. While telegraphing Sikander's suggestion to the Secretary of State, he remarked: 'Position as regards any assurance to the Muslim League is really the same as position regarding any assurance to Congress. I do not want to tie hands if we can possibly avoid it by accepting contingent liabilities at this stage.'[12]

Linlithgow, as we shall soon see, was to resile from this position because of the exigencies of the political situation in India and the value of the Muslim League's cooperation in safeguarding British imperial interests at the bar of British as well as world public opinion. Aware of the deep British interest in bolstering up the League's position, Jinnah took the partial rebuff from the Viceroy in his stride and continued his interaction with the Congress on the basis of his old strategy—always showing a readiness for dialogue and keenness for Hindu–Muslim unity but never ceasing to attack the Congress and remaining firm on his demands. This went on adding to his prestige among the Muslims as well as keeping the British on tenterhooks and prevent them from taking the League for granted by keeping alive the possibility, however slender, of it joining hands with the Congress.

III

The initiative in beginning the Congress–League interaction after the outbreak of the war was taken by the Congress. While its Working Committee was meeting at Wardha to formulate its stand on the war crisis, Prasad, as President, sent a telegram to Jinnah on 11 September inviting him there for a discussion. Jinnah replied the same day, expressing his inability due to previous commitments (not, it may be noted, on the ground that he did not belong to the Congress and saw no purpose in joining such a discussion) and suggesting a meeting in Delhi on any day after 13 September. Prasad, of course, replied that the purpose of inviting Jinnah to Wardha was to have his assistance in shaping the Working Committee's decision on a critical situation and that could not be served by the former's going over to Delhi.[13]

Notwithstanding that courteous exchange between Prasad and Jinnah, the League's Working Committee, at its meeting on 17–18 September resumed, in strong language, its pre-war denunciation of the Congress ministries for their alleged attacks on the life and liberty, property and honour, and the religious rights and culture, of the Muslims and reiterated its grievance against the Governor-General and Governors for their negligence and indifference, resulting in their failure to use their special powers for the protection of the Muslim minority.[14] The attack on the Congress ministries in the provinces went hand in hand with attacks on the central Congress leadership. Thus in the course of an interview with a correspondent of the *Star of India* on 1 October 1939, Jinnah declared that the Congress was suffering from three maladies and unless it succeeded in curing itself of these, it would not be able to contribute to India's advancement. First, it was unable to face realities and was obsessed by the thought that it alone represented India. Second, while championing the cause of democracy in India and desiring to do away with the 'democratic imperialism' of Britain, it had in the previous two and a half years (i.e. since the advent of Provincial Autonomy) not only virtually declared itself as a fascist and authoritarian body but had actually translated that principle into practice. Third, it was reviving throughout India the Hindu renaissance and domination and supremacy of Hinduism over the entire subcontinent.[15]

Reacting to such charges, particularly those relating to the suffering of Muslims in the Congress-ruled provinces, Prasad wrote to Jinnah on 5 October characterizing them as unfounded and based on misapprehension and one-sided reports and suggesting that, if the latter agreed, they might be referred for enquiry to the highest judicial authority in India, namely Sir Maurice Gwyer, Chief Justice of the Federal Court. In case he was not available, some other person of a similar status and judicial position might be approached. Jinnah, in his reply dated 6 October, did not accept this suggestion on the ground that he had already placed the matter before the Viceroy and Governor-General of India and it was then under the latter's consideration.[16] Faced with criticism of his stand, Jinnah issued a press statement on 27 October describing Prasad's suggestion as 'a travesty of justice' and declaring that it showed that the Congress mentality had 'gone beyond any sense of responsibility'.[17] Still later, on 17 December 1939, he suggested the appointment by the British Government of a Royal Commission consisting of purely judicial personnel to look into the Muslim grievances against the Congress ministries.[18]

In the meanwhile, Jinnah, as usual, was also keen to keep open the channels of communication with the top Congress leadership. On 3 October 1939, he had a long conversation with Nehru in Delhi. 'It was friendly talk,' wrote Nehru in a letter to a friend and colleague three days later, 'and at least it removed a certain tension that existed between us.' However, in their visions for the future they remained as far apart as ever. Nehru thus recorded his assessment of Jinnah's thinking:

> Jinnah is exceedingly backward and reactionary in his opinions and thinks in terms of twenty-five years ago. And yet he is more advanced than many of his colleagues in the Muslim League. As he stands at present, we have to give up every principle of nationalism and democracy in order to meet their wishes. That of course is impossible. I think he has overshot the mark.[19]

Regardless of the wide differences in their views, Nehru as well as Jinnah were quite keen to continue the dialogue and indeed it was their understanding that they would meet again within a short time on a date found mutually convenient. That such a meeting did not take place was due to a minor misunderstanding. While Jinnah thought that Nehru would get in touch with him in Delhi, the latter was under the impression that the former would ring him up. When Nehru learnt from his friend, Raghunandan Saran, about Jinnah's puzzlement on the lack of any initiative on his part about their meeting, he immediately wrote to Jinnah explaining the situation. He further added: 'I was in fact looking forward to meeting you again and waiting for some message from you. . . . Our other conversation, though lengthy, had been general and I wanted to have another opportunity of coming to closer grips with the subject.'[20]

This letter was sent on 18 October 1939. By that time a meeting with Jinnah had acquired a new urgency because of Sikander's public statement published in the newspapers on 13 October advising the Congress to hold consultations with the League regarding the communal question with a view to arriving at a settlement. Prasad immediately wrote to Nehru as well as Azad, drawing their attention to Sikander's statement and seeking their advice.[21]

While drawing Azad's attention to Sikander's statement of 13 October, Prasad had also reminded the former that Jinnah had recently rejected the Congress suggestion for an enquiry into the League's allegations against the Congress Ministries by an impartial judge and thus 'practically barred the door for the present at any rate'. Prasad further mentioned that he had discussed the matter with Gandhi and that the latter had advised him to write to Sikander pointing this out and asking for 'definite suggestions'. However, Gandhi wanted Prasad to first write to Azad and secure his advice. Nehru, who saw a copy of that letter (enclosed with that to himself), immediately wrote to Prasad against taking such a view. He admitted that Jinnah's reply to Prasad's suggestion about a judicial enquiry into the League's complaints had not been helpful, but pointed out that it applied to a particular subject. He also informed Prasad that Azad, who was in UP at that time, also held the same view.[22] Both Nehru and Azad must have guessed that Sikander might not have issued such a public statement without any signal from Jinnah. Such a guess was further strengthened by reports from other sources. For about the same time Liaquat Ali Khan, General Secretary of the All-India Muslim League, told Raghunandan Saran, that since Jinnah had fully explained the League's position to Nehru during their meeting in the first week of October, it was for the latter to make the next move. He added that Jinnah at that time was in a sober and friendly mood and was likely to avoid controversies as far as possible. He also mentioned that of all the people Nehru was most welcome to him for such discussions.[23] Then came Raghunandan Saran's letter mentioning his meeting with Jinnah and conveying the latter's deep distress at the continuance of Hindu–Muslim differences till then as also his keen desire for another meeting with Nehru for their solution. All this made Nehru, for once, forget his past distrust of Jinnah and he wrote to the latter with unusual warmth and humility:

I entirely agree with you that it is a tragedy that the Hindu–Muslim problem has not so far been settled in a friendly way. I feel terribly distressed about it and ashamed of myself, in so far as I have not been able to contribute anything substantial towards its solution. I must confess to you that in this matter I have lost confidence in myself, though I am not usually given that way. . . .

But that does not come in the way of trying my utmost to help find a solution and I shall certainly do so. With your goodwill and commanding position in the Muslim League that should not be so difficult as people imagine. I can assure you with all earnestness that all the members of the Working Committee are keenly desirous of finding a solution.[24]

One of the key members of the Congress Working Committee in matters relating to the Hindu–Muslim problem, if not *the* key member, was Azad. He was so excited by the prospect of a settlement of that problem that he had dashed off a letter to Jinnah two days earlier conveying his deep interest in the solution of the Hindu–Muslim problem as soon as possible and also his lack of interest in sharing the laurels for a settlement when that stage was reached. By the time this letter was sent, it was not even clear what would be the modalities of the Congress–League talks or whether they would be held at all. The main purpose of this letter seems to have been to remove misunderstandings in Jinnah's mind regarding Azad. Its broken English shows that it had not passed through Nehru's eyes before being despatched. To quote Azad:

Please do not misunderstand me regarding the Hindu–Muslim problem. I do not wish for a moment that I should carry the laurels of having attained the communal unity, nor I had any such desire when I met you in 1937–38, and tried for Congress–League settlement. My only wish and attempt is centred round the idea that a decent agreement may be reached between the Congress and the League; as I am sure it is urgently needed for the Muslims and the country. Delay is detrimental to the interest of both. Here I may mention that under no circumstances would I like to bring to the notice of the public any one of my efforts in this connection. I only wish to perform my duty according to my belief. Perhaps an occasion may arise in future which may unveil the reality to you. Then alone you will be able to find out that you have been labouring under misunderstandings about me.[25]

Jinnah was apparently not impressed. For he told Saran a few days later that so far as the dialogue with Nehru was concerned, he had not taken the members of the League Working Committee into confidence, either individually or collectively, and expected Nehru also to do likewise with his own Working Committee. Saran further reported to Nehru:

He [Jinnah] said that he was in direct touch with the person [Nehru] and that you two should be left together to carry on the negotiations. After all, this Hindu–Muslim problem has to be solved some time—

today, tomorrow or on the third day. That is the finality, India cannot progress without it. So the sooner the solution is found, the better for all concerned. And till it is solved it means War.[26]

IV

The words conveying Jinnah's message to Nehru were well chosen and beautifully summed up Jinnah's strategy in dealing with the Congress. Exactly one week before these words were uttered to Saran, the Viceroy's statement (17 October) had come out elucidating British policy in the wake of the declaration of war, as demanded by the Congress, and completed the picture of the Indian political reality in the context of which Jinnah had to pursue his three-pronged strategy explained earlier. While the viceregal statement was found deeply disappointing and wholly unsatisfactory by the Congress and prompted it to ask its ministries in the various provinces to resign, the League found in it several features to its liking. In the beginning of his statement, for instance, the Viceroy mentioned that before issuing it he had separate discussions with no less than fifty-two persons with a view to having a proper idea of the different shades of public opinion in India and then made a special mention of Gandhi and the Congress leaders, on the one hand, and Jinnah and the League leaders, on the other, together with the Chancellor of the Chamber of Princes, thereby underlining the parity in political importance accorded to the Congress and the League. Nothing could have sounded more pleasing to the League leaders. The Viceroy then went on to emphasize the prevalence of a wide variety of opinion and the consequent disunity among the leaders consulted. As Linlithgow remarked:

> As was only to be expected, conversations with representatives of so many different points of view revealed marked differences of outlook, markedly different demands, and markedly different solutions for the problems that lie before us. Again, and that too was what might have been expected at a time such as the present, reservations or demands for special protection on one side have tended to be balanced by proposals for still more marked constitutional changes on another.

The Viceroy reaffirmed that while preparations for the setting up of a federal government had been suspended during the tendency of the war, he considered the constitutional system embodied in the Act of 1935, including the provisions for the setting up of a federal government in the future, as the best under the circumstances. At the same time, he made it clear that when the time came, after the end of the war, to resume consideration of the plan for the future federal government of India, the British Government would be 'very willing to enter into consultation with representatives of the several communities, parties and interests in India, and with the Indian Princes, with a view to securing their aid and cooperation in the framing of such modifications as may seem desirable'. Turning to the demand of the minorities for a clear assurance that full weight would be given to their views and interests while contemplating any modifications in the constitutional system in the future, the Viceroy asserted that that indeed had been the British policy for about a decade since the time of the Round Table Conferences in London. He further added that it would be unthinkable that the policy would not be continued when the time came to 'plan afresh or to modify in any respect any important part of India's future Consitution'.[27]

The Muslim League's satisfaction at these observations included in the Viceroy's statement was evident from the resolution adopted by its Working Committee on 22 October 1939. It took into account not merely the actual words used in the statement, but also the implications thereof and sometimes went even beyond them and took into account the implication also of the Viceroy's action in inviting for consultation the representatives of the Muslim League and treating them at par with those of the Congress. Thus it expressed its appreciation for the fact that the Government had 'emphatically repudiated the unfounded claim of the Congress' that it alone represented all India and noted with satisfaction the fact that the Government recognized 'the fact that the All-India Muslim League alone represents the Musalmans of India and can speak on their behalf; also that the rights and interests of the minorities and other important interests concerned have been duly recognized'. At the same time, however, the League's Working Committee's resolution added that it wanted the Government to make some further pronouncements and clarifications if it desired the full and effective cooperation of the League in the war effort. Further, it made it clear that the opposition of the League was not merely to the details of the federal plan embodied in the Act of 1935 and that it wanted that 'the entire problem of India's future constitution should be wholly examined and revised *de novo*. It also reiterated emphatically that no future plan of India's Constitution would be acceptable to the League unless it met with the latter's 'full approval'.[28]

Thanking the Viceroy for the advance copy, Jinnah remarked in his letter to him dated 23 October: 'I was glad indeed when your Excellency asked me to accept from you that you were fully conscious of the various points which I [had] brought to your notice on behalf of the Muslim community and have given full weight to them.'[29] Although not sure how long the League leadership might be able to continue its favourable approach to the Government in view of the likely spread of (Indian) nationalistic sentiments among its cadres, particularly the youth, the Viceroy was, on the whole, quite satisfied with the Working Committee's resolution. As he wrote to the Secretary of State after going through it:

> The Muslim League resolution, so far as it goes, is very satisfactory. I hope that we shall be able to cover Jinnah's points (I have already telegraphed them to you) in debate and I trust that when the time comes for me to see him I shall not find him too intransigent. I do not at the same time regard the support of the Muslim League as necessarily something which we can hope to depend on in all circumstances. . . . But it is for all that of real value that at this moment a body representing some ninety million people should offer us cooperation and accept as generally satisfactory the declaration which we have made.[30]

Just two days after the adoption of the League's Working Committee's resolution on the Viceroy's statement of British policy in the war crisis, the *Statesman* (Calcutta, 24 October 1939) published the text of Jinnah's interview to the *Manchester Guardian*, given a few days earlier. Therein he had observed that Muslims in India in modern times had always had fears and apprehensions about any kind of representative government. Under a fully democratic government the situation would be much worse from their point of view. Democracy, Jinnah emphasized, 'can only mean Hindu Raj all over India. This is a position to which Muslims will never submit.' Denying that the Muslims were opposed to the freedom of India, he asserted that they wanted freedom and liberty, but the question was whose freedom and liberty? Foreshadowing the demand for Partition, he added: 'Muslim India wants to be free and enjoy liberty to the fullest extent and develop its own political, economic and social and cultural institutions according to its own genius and not to be dominated and crushed, while wishing Hindu India well and giving it fullest scope to do likewise.'[31]

When in the last week of October 1939, the Congress ministries in various provinces, before resigning office, moved resolutions in the Assemblies declaring that it was essential in order to secure the cooperation of the Indian people in the war effort that 'the principle of democracy with effective safeguards for the Muslim and the other minorities be applied to India and her policy be guided by her own people', the Muslim League parties in those Assemblies moved amendments declaring that democratic parliamentary government, 'being utterly unsuited to the condition and genius of the people', had failed in India. On this ground a demand was made that the problem of India's future constitution should be considered *de novo* and that the British should not make any commitment regarding it without the approval and consent of the All-India Muslim League, which alone could speak for the Muslims of India, as also without the consent of all important minorities and interests.[32]

V

While the 'war continued, efforts for peace were also going on. The next round of talks between Jinnah and Nehru, planned quite some time ago, took place in Delhi in the first week of November 1939. On one or two occasions Gandhi and Prasad were also present. Nehru perhaps was carried away by the friendly atmosphere in which the talks were conducted and felt that Jinnah had been satisfied with the assurance of the Congress leaders that the Constituent Assembly being demanded by them would be formed on the basis of the widest possible franchise and agreement on communal representation and would fully safeguard the rights and interests of all minorities. 'And so,' he wrote in an editorial in the *National Herald* dated 6 November 1939, 'the whole fabric of communal dissension as a bar to India's progress, conjured up by the Viceroy, fades away and vanishes at the touch of reason and reality.'[33] In reality, there was no basis for this euphoria. Perhaps the article was written while the talks were still going on and represented an example of wish being father to thought.

While Nehru and Jinnah had been looking forward to these talks since the beginning of October 1939, their immediate context was provided by the Viceroy's invitation to Jinnah, on the one hand, and Gandhi and Prasad, on the other, to see him together on 1 November 1939 for talks on breaking the political deadlock. The Viceroy explained during these talks that the British Government was very keen to associate representatives of the principal parties in India with the Government at the centre in order to promote the war effort to the fullest extent possible. While he realized that all the differences between these parties could not be removed, some working arrangement between them in the provincial sphere was necessary in order to enable their representatives, together with a few representatives of other important groups, to participate in the central government as members of the Viceroy's Executive Council within the framework of the then existing constitution.[34] The Viceroy, therefore, asked them to enter into discussions as soon as possible to discover whether they could reach a basis of agreement in the provincial field consequent to which they could submit proposals to the Viceroy about the participation of the representatives of the two-parties in the central government. This in effect meant that the British were not going to take any step to improve upon the declaration of their policy made by the Viceroy on 17 October and rejected by the Congress as wholly unsatisfactory, but were prepared to take a few of the Congress and League leaders as members of the Viceroy's Executive Council provided they could come to an agreement among themselves regarding the administration of the provinces.

This admirably suited the Muslim League, but not the Congress, for it indicated that no advance at the centre was possible unless the League was satisfied with the situation in the provinces. This could be secured only through Congress–League coalitions in the provinces, on the latter's terms. Even if the Congress were prepared for it, the difficulty regarding the declaration of future British policy remained, and the Congress was not prepared to consider any step until that problem was solved first. It held that the main difficulty had been created by the lack of adequate British response to the Congress demand for a declaration of British policy in

India in terms of freedom and democracy for which the war was supposedly being fought. Instead of dealing with this, the British were now trying to put the communal problem at the centre-stage by insisting on an agreement between the Congress and the Muslim League in the provinces. The Congress position was explained by Prasad in his letter to Linlithgow dated 4 November 1939. Stating that it was impossible for the Congress to consider any step for further cooperation unless the policy of the British Government was made clear through a declaration on the lines suggested by it, he observed:

It has pained us to find the communal question being dragged in this connection. It has clouded the main issue. It has been repeatedly said on behalf of the Congress that it is our earnest desire to settle all points of communal controversy by agreement and we propose to continue our efforts to this end. But I would point out that this question does not in any respect come in the way of a declaration of Indian freedom. . . . Such a declaration applies to the whole of India and not to any particular community, and the constitution will be framed on the widest possible basis of franchise and by agreement in regard to communal representation. We are all agreed that there must be full protection of minority rights and interests and this protection should be by agreement between the parties concerned. The British Government taking and sharing the burden has, in our opinion, made a settlement of the question much more difficult than it should have been.[35]

In contrast, Jinnah was in full agreement with the Viceroy's approach. This is borne out by the latter's summary of Jinnah's observations in course of the discussions of the three leaders with the Viceroy in November. After Gandhi and Prasad had raised their objections to the Viceroy ignoring the most important aspect of the matter and concentrating on non-essentials,

Mr Jinnah then remarked that so far as he and his friends were concerned, the first thing was the provincial settlement; and so far as the provincial settlement was concerned, the matter was entirely in the hands of Congress and entirely for them. They were in a position to run the governments in the provinces in question; and neither the Viceroy nor he, Mr Jinnah, could do anything unless Congress could be persuaded to reach a reasonable settlement. So far as the Centre was concerned, if provincial difficulties could be solved, this would create a fairly good basis on which the Muslim League and the Congress could put their heads together for a scheme for the Centre within the framework of the Act.[36]

Between 1 and 3 November Gandhi, Nehru and Prasad held parleys with Jinnah, trying to persuade him to agree to their approach, but Jinnah remained firm and refused to Join in a common approach until an agreement on the communal issue had been arrived at first between the Congress and the Muslim League.[37] In the middle of December 1939, Jinnah said in a press statement that there had not even been any serious discussion on the terms of such an agreement during his discussion with the Congress leaders in Delhi in the first week of November as the Congress refused to recognize the League as the one representative organization of the Indian Muslims.[38] A month later, however, he confided to the Viceroy that during those discussions he had given five terms for a settlement: coalition ministries in the provinces; so far as provincial legislatures were concerned, no measure to be forced through if two-thirds of the Muslim members of the Assembly objected to it; the Congress flag not to be flown on public institutions; *Vande Mataram* to be abandoned as the national anthem; and the Congress to abandon its wrecking tactics against the Muslim League. Jinnah, according to this version, had also urged the Congress leaders to accept the Viceroy's offer to expand his Executive Council subject to agreement in the provinces; but the Congress leaders had not been willing to even look at it.[39]

From an account of these talks as given by Jinnah to Francis Low, editor of the *Times of India* (Bombay) and reported by the latter to the Governor of Bombay, Roger Lumley, it seems that the Congress proposal for a Constituent Assembly based on adult suffrage as a solution to the communal problem had also come up for discussion between Jinnah and the Congress leaders in the Delhi discussions. Jinnah told Low that he had found it impossible to make any progress and that he and Gandhi were really speaking different languages. Gandhi kept on harping on the need for a Constituent Assembly based on adult suffrage. When Jinnah raised questions about it, Gandhi answered in general terms and argued that if Muslims did not cooperate they would be charged with obstructing the national cause. Jinnah, however, remained 'emphatically opposed to any idea of a Constituent Assembly. Jinnah had further pointed out to Low that he was quite willing to cooperate with Hindus if the Muslim position were safeguarded, but he was convinced that 'the Muslims would be squashed if they agreed to the establishment of a Hindu Raj'. In his opinion, Gandhi was 'the biggest Hindu in India' and had as his main object the domination of India by Hindus.[40]

In contrast to this, Nehru asserted that, although Jinnah began later to oppose the Congress idea of a Constituent Assembly, he had not done so during the Delhi discussions.[41] Jinnah's main effort during the Delhi talks was, according to Nehru, centred on having 'a statutory provision to have Muslim League ministers in every cabinet, that is, his own nominees'. Even if such a cabinet was formed by agreement, Nehru felt that there would arise difficulties and rapid progress would become difficult. For it would mean the existence of two-parties in the Cabinet and that would always bring in the third party, that is, the Governor. Cabinet responsibility would disappear and the Governor would become the real foss. That would be bad enough. But if a coalition cabinet was brought about 'at the point of a bayonet, so to say', the result would be disastrous. It would mean 'the consolidation of the reactionary Muslim League elements and very great dissatisfaction in Congress and other circles'.[42]

VI

In spite of these differences, however, both sides—each for its own reasons—were willing to continue talking. In this respect at any rate the November talks in Delhi had not been entirely barren. For it had been decided that Nehru and Jinnah would meet again and continue the dialogue, though it was not clear which side was expected to take the initiative for fixing a date for its resumption. When weeks passed and nothing happened, Nehru, as perhaps the more eager party, took the initiative and wrote to Jinnah on 1 December 1939, making a mild complaint against the lack of initiative on Jinnah's part:

> When we met last in Delhi, it was agreed that we should meet again to discuss various aspects of the communal problem. You told me that on your return to Bombay you would write to me suggesting some date for such a meeting. I have been looking forward to your letter since then. I hope that whenever it is convenient for you to fix a date you will kindly let me know.[43]

Jinnah, in his reply, chose not to make any comment on Nehru's complaint and just told the latter that he would be in Bombay for the next two or three weeks and would gladly see Nehru on any date convenient to him during that period.[44] Later, when a hitch developed and it was not clear whether they would meet again, Jinnah, in his letter dated 13 December, mentioned his understanding of the background of their projected meeting and recalled that at the end of his talks with Gandhi and Nehru in Delhi in the first week of November Nehru had been good enough to express his wish to meet Jinnah again to which the latter had replied that he would be always glad to see Nehru.[45]

Whatever that might have been, Nehru wrote to Jinnah on 7 December, informing the latter that he was going to Bombay soon and hoped to meet him there. Then on the morning of 8 December, he read in the newspapers that Jinnah had fixed 22 December as a day of deliverance and thanksgiving as a mark of relief that the Congress governments in the provinces had at last ceased to function.[46]

In that statement Jinnah had asked the provincial, district, and primary branches of the Muslim League all over India to hold public meetings on the appointed day and adopt a resolution as per the text given there, expressing their sense of relief at the termination of Congress rule and their deliverance from 'tyranny, oppression and injustice', which they had suffered during the last two and a half years. According to the text of the resolution to be adopted at these public meetings, given in Jinnah's statement, it was to be recorded that the Congress ministries, through their 'decidedly anti-Muslim policy' had 'conclusively demonstrated and proved the falsehood of the Congress claim that it represents all interests justly and fairly'. The three paragraphs that followed elucidated this charge in detail by bringing together almost all the major grievances against the Congress ministries sedulously ventilated by the Muslim League under Jinnah's leadership since 1937:

That the Congress ministries both in the discharge of their duties of the administration and in the legislature have done their best to flout the Muslim opinion, to destroy Muslim culture, and have interfered with their religious and social life and trampled upon their economic and political rights.

That in matters of difference and dispute, the Congress ministries invariably have sided with, supported and advanced the cause of the Hindus in total disregard and to the prejudice of Muslim interests.

The Congress Governments constantly interfered with the legitimate and routine duties of the district officers, even in petty matters, to the serious detriment of the Muslims, and thereby created an atmosphere which spread the belief amongst the Hindu public that there was established a Hindu Raj, and emboldened the Hindus, mostly Congressmen, to ill-treat Muslims at various places and interfere with their elementary rights of freedom.[47]

Many of the Congress leaders were shocked beyond measure by Jinnah's statement, especially as Nehru was preparing for talks with him. 'A more mischievous move,' Patel told Nehru, 'can hardly be imagined.' That, according to him, clearly meant that Jinnah did not want peace with the Congress. He also had a suspicion that the agents of the imperialist power were behind that move.[48] In another letter that soon followed, Patel opined that Congressmen all over India would be irritated when they heard that Nehru was meeting Jinnah after his provocative statement and observed: 'We must end this agonizing situation as soon as possible....'[49] Prasad fully concurred with this view. 'My first reaction,' he wrote to Nehru, 'after reading Mr Jinnah's statement was that we should tell him that we would not have any further negotiation or talk with him.'[50]

Nehru, even before seeing the communications from Patel and Prasad, had reacted in a similar way. Indeed, before Prasad had posted his letter dated 10 December to Nehru he received Nehru's dated 9 December, enclosing a copy of his letter to Jinnah.[51] In that letter (written without consulting Gandhi), Nehru told Jinnah that he had read his statement 'very carefully more than once' and had thought over it for twenty-four hours. After remarking that he had no wish to enter into any controversy with Jinnah about facts or impressions or conclusions, he added:

But what has oppressed me terribly since yesterday is the realisation that our sense of values and objectives in life as well as in politics differ so very greatly. I had hoped, after our conversations [in the first week of November], that this was not so great, but now the gulf appears to be wider than ever. Under these circumstances, I wonder what purpose will be served by our discussing with each other the problems that confront us. There must be some common ground for discussion, some common objective aimed at, for that discussion to yield fruit.[52]

That exactly was the reason, said Jinnah in his rejoinder, why he had insisted during his last conversation with Gandhi and

Nehru in Delhi that so long as the Congress was not prepared to treat the Muslim League as the authoritative and representative organization of the Indian Muslims it would not be possible for him to carry on talks on the settlement of the Hindu–Muslim problem. For that was the basis for such talks laid down by the League's Working Committee. Jinnah reminded Nehru that he had further said on that occasion that the League could not support the Congress demand for a declaration of British war aims until there was settlement of the minority problem.[53]

Nehru did not find it possible to accept the first condition put forward by Jinnah, repeating the same arguments that he had advanced against Jinnah's identical demand in 1938. As far as the second condition was concerned, that, according to Nehru, showed that the Congress and the League had no common ground and that their political objectives were wholly dissimilar. That would make discussion among them difficult and fruitless. 'I feel therefore,' concluded Nehru, 'that it will serve little purpose for us to meet at this stage and under these conditions and with this background.'[54] That meant the end of the efforts to resume the Nehru–Jinnah talks, though there was one more exchange of letters between the two: Jinnah to Nehru on 15 December[55] and Nehru to Jinnah on 16 December.[56]

The deep resentment among the Congress leaders caused by Jinnah's refusal to retrace his steps in calling for the celebration of 'Deliverance Day' on 22 December 1939 came out most forcefully in Nehru's speech at a public meeting in Bombay on 14 December 1939. Referring to Jinnah's allegation against the Congress ministries made in connection with his call for the celebration of 'Deliverance Day', Nehru is reported to have observed:

> To swallow this, and to resume negotiations with Mr Jinnah is an utter impossibility. If I were to open discussions with Mr Jinnah in the face of these baseless allegations, the courses open to me are, either to retire from politics and go to the Himalayas as a *Sanyasi* [hermit], or go out of India to a foreign land for good, never to come back, or commit suicide. I would do none of those three things, even if ordered by Mahatma Gandhi, our great leader.[57]

While non-Congressmen might not have felt so deeply resentful about the call for the celebration of 'Deliverance Day', there was certainly widespread criticism of Jinnah's move even among them.

According to a confidential report of the Government of India, even in Muslim circles Jinnah's move was 'by no means universally approved . . . though open disapproval was rarely expressed'.[58] Always alive to the nuances of public opinion, Jinnah took pains more than once to deal with his critics. His most detailed statement in this connection was issued on 13 December 1939. Therein he admitted that his appeal for the celebration of 'Deliverance Day' had been 'variously described as ill-timed, provocative and anti-national' and proceeded to rebut them one by one. While doing so, he traced the Congress–League differences since the installation of the Congress ministries in the provinces and recalled several occasions in the past when he had ventilated Muslim grievances. He further asserted that his appeal was not intended to sabotage the Congress–League talks, or exacerbate Hindu–Muslim bitterness or gloat over the departure of democratically elected governments, but only to register the general Muslim feeling of relief at the end of Congress rule, which had been the cause of a lot of Muslim suffering. In that connection, he explained that the appeal for the celebration had been planned earlier as soon as it became clear that the Congress ministries were going to resign, but had to be delayed due to developments in Assam where a new ministry was being formed without the Congress. It was a mere coincidence that the appeal appeared in the press on the eve of the projected Nehru–Jinnah talks. Jinnah also took care to appeal to his followers and supporters to celebrate Deliverance Day most peacefully and in a spirit of humility and to desist from hartals, processions, and demonstrations.[59] On 17 December, he again issued a press statement clarifying specifically that the projected celebration was not a move against the Hindu community as such, but only against the Congress. He asserted that his main grievance against the Congress was that it had prevented 'the Hindu and Muslim communities from working in a manner honourable to both' and further that the Muslim League stood for justice and fair play for all, regardless of whether people belonged to the Muslim community or any other community. He took the opportunity to appeal for cooperation from all Indians who realized that the condition of the country needed 'popular, rather than party, governments' which can do justice to all sections of the people rather than to an irremovable majority'.[60]

The celebrations of Deliverance Day on 22 December 1939

did pass off peacefully. Jinnah, while replying to felicitations in Bombay on the occasion of his sixty-fourth birthday, claimed on the basis of press reports as well as personal letters and telegrams that they were held all over India with 'complete success'. He was especially happy to underline that other minorities and their leaders and even non-Congress Hindus had joined them.[61] According to a confidential government report, however, the celebrations were not a success everywhere: 'in some Provinces considerable enthusiasm was displayed, in others it fell rather flat'.[62] In Bombay, for instance, the celebration was supported by B.R. Ambedkar on behalf of the Scheduled Castes and by representatives of the Parsis[63]—certainly a great success. On the other hand, the UP Governor did not think that the celebration, 'of which many reasonable Muslims disapproved, was as great a success as would appear from the newspaper accounts'. Some District Magistrates reported little enthusiasm and in most districts meetings were smaller than might have been expected.[64]

VII

By the time the Nehru–Jinnah talks were called off and Deliverance Day celebrated much water had flown down the Jamuna in Delhi. Even though the Viceroy's offer had failed to be implemented, the very fact of its having been made was highly significant from the point of view of the Muslim League, for it now acquired a virtual veto on any advance at the centre as well as a right to be represented in all Congress-led ministries on its own terms. At the same time, the firm refusal of Jinnah to join the Congress in pressing the British to come forward with a satisfactory declaration regarding India's future, and agreeing to India's emergence as an independent country after the end of the War, had immensely pleased the Viceroy. This was especially so because at one stage during the Congress–League talks, the Viceroy had information that suggested that some impression had been made on Jinnah by the Congress leaders in regard to his claim to be formally accepted as the sole spokesman of Muslims. At any rate, there seemed a possibility of his considering the frequency with which the Congress leaders had to go to him and negotiate with him as adequate recognition in the eyes of India and the world of his special position.[65] As Linlithgow later confessed, he had 'one or two rather anxious moments' at that time.[66] Imagine his relief, therefore, when he learnt that the Congress–League talks had finally failed and that Jinnah had firmly refused to join the Congress in exercising pressure on the British to come forward with a satisfactory declaration regarding India's future status, assuring her freedom in clear terms at the end of the war.[67] This paved the way for the emergence of a virtual Linlithgow–Jinnah axis against the Congress.

Meeting on 4 November 1939 against this background, Linlithgow and Jinnah moved much closer to each other than they had ever been before. The conversation began with Jinnah describing how much pressure he had to withstand from the Congress side. In this connection he mentioned that Gandhi had approached him before the conference with the Viceroy on 1 November and enquired of him whether it was not possible for the Congress and the League to join hands together in pressing the Viceroy for a declaration of British policy regarding the issue of India's freedom. Jinnah further mentioned that that point had been pressed upon him for two or three days. As result of this, Jinnah 'had a most exhausting time and been placed in a most difficult position' as the Congress leaders had particularly used the argument that if he did not support the Congress demand for a declaration in favour of India's freedom, he and his friends would be exposed as the one real obstacle to that freedom. The Viceroy reminded Jinnah that he had avoided the idea of an all-parties conference partly with a view to preventing such an argument from being developed against him and had hoped that in the specific context of the last offer there was not so much risk of it. The Viceroy also fully acknowledged the help that Jinnah had rendered to him by not joining hands with Congress in asking for a British declaration of India's freedom and indeed expressed gratitude for it. He was not, however, satisfied with the League's general stand from its own point of view, for it seemed to be anti-national and anti-democratic and lacked a positive content. To use the Viceroy's own words in summarizing what he told Jinnah:

> . . . I said to Mr Jinnah I hope he would not think me impertinent if I talked for a moment of his own position and that of the Muslim League as developed by him. He had given me very valuable help by standing firm against Congress claim and I was duly grateful. It was clear that

if he, Mr Jinnah, had supported the Congress in their demand for a declaration and confronted me with a joint demand, the strain upon me and upon His Majesty's Government would have been very great indeed. I thought, therefore, I could claim to have a vested interest in his position, and I had been asking myself how far that position was intrinsically sound. But I was bound to confess that I did not like it. . . . The Muslims now had the appearance of being anti-national and anti-democratic. What outlet did he foresee for his young men and what method of dealing with the demands for a stronger policy of nationalism which his younger generation would certainly advocate? Moreover, I did not believe that he could escape from this dilemma by the idea which had been so widely ventilated of having two Indias; or that any real solution was to be found in transferring populations from the humid South to the cold and barren North and by parceling out the Princes.

Jinnah, of course, contradicted the latter part of this statement by describing the concept of an all-India federation as nothing but a dream and remarked that if per chance the British were defeated in the war and driven out of India, the latter would be broken into a hundred pieces within three months and also lie exposed to external invasion. He must, however, have drawn considerable comfort from the Viceroy's open acknowledgement of the help that he had received from the Muslim League and his deep concern with it. Being a shrewd politician Jinnah utilized the opportunity to ask for some valuable assurances from the Viceroy. In the first place, he asked whether the review of the scheme of government in the Act of 1935, which the Viceroy had promised in his declaration of 17 October, would be the scheme as a whole or merely of the details therein. He made the purpose of this query clear by stating that this question arose because the British still seemed to be clinging to the idea of an all-India federation. The Viceroy admitted that the British did still adhere to that idea, but pointed out that the review would not be confined to details, but cover the whole position. Having secured satisfaction on this point, Jinnah immediately dismissed it as of relatively little value and went on to say that the really important thing was to secure an undertaking from the British Government that the Muslim community would not be compelled to accept anything which it did not like. After some discussion, in which the Viceroy expressed difficulty in agreeing to a veto by any one party and Jinnah underlined the importance of such an undertaking in view of the possibility of a future government in Britain losing patience with the minorities and seeking to force them to accept an unwanted scheme, it was decided that Jinnah would send a letter to the Viceroy embodying his demands for consideration by the British Government.[68]

The very next day, i.e. 5 November 1939, Jinnah wrote to Linlithgow asking for consideration, among other things, of the following two points:

1. that so soon as circumstances may permit, or immediately after the war, the entire problem of India's future constitution, apart from the Government of India Act of 1935, shall be examined and reconsidered *de novo*;
2. that no declaration shall, either in principle or otherwise, be made or any constitution be enacted by His Majesty's Government or the Parliament without the approval and consent of the two major communities of India, viz., the Mussalmans and the Hindus.[69]

While forwarding Jinnah's letter of 5 November to the Secretary of State, the Viceroy deferred his detailed comments to a later date, for they involved 'delicate matters' and required 'the most deliberate phrasing'. However, he recorded his 'first and very tentative reactions' immediately. Expressing his sympathy with Jinnah's predicament, underlining the importance of the Muslim community in India and the need for supporting it as far as possible, and emphasizing the cultural cleavage in Indian society. Linlithgow observed:

> ... I do feel increasingly, as I watch the reactions of the Muslims and the other minorities to the democratic experiment in this country, that we may have to go a good deal further than we have gone in giving weight to their point of view, and that the fact that they are a numerical minority cannot be allowed to be a decisive factor in the framing of our policy in relation to them and to the numerical majority. At the same time, ... one has also to give weight to the fact that a constitutional advance on paper which is immediately followed by the most serious difficulties with a community of 90 million and a virile community at that, would be short-sighted to a degree from our point of view as well as from that of India. One thought that has crossed my mind as I read his [Jinnah's] letter this morning was that it might be of value at some forthcoming occasion to admit in the House of Lords, or in a speech in the country, that in considering this problem one did definitely have to give weight not only to the size of the minority—twice the population

of the British Isles and as large as the whole of the present German Reich—but also to the deep cultural division and the fundamental cleavage on the religious issue.[70]

It took the Viceroy more than three weeks to send a detailed note to the Secretary of State, 'The issues raised,' he wrote to the Secretary of State while engaged in preparing that note, 'are very substantial indeed; and we shall have to be extremely careful as to what we say to him and as to the manner and form of any reply.' He added that he, of course, did not want in the least to do anything to discourage the Muslims. He noted with apparent satisfaction that their morale had been strengthened as a result of Jinnah's handling of the recent discussions in Delhi and that the impression that had earlier been gaining ground among them that the British might be prepared to throw them over if it suited their book had been to a large extent dissipated. Above all, such information as he had did not in the least suggest any disposition on Jinnah's part to modify his attitude, though he agreed with the Secretary of State that in dealing with Jinnah one had to be 'always conscious of the possibility of a *volte face* of the most drastic character at the shortest of notice'.[71] This shows the close attention with which Jinnah's moods were being watched by the Viceroy and the great importance he attached to keeping Jinnah away from the Congress and close to the British. In his next letter to the Secretary of State, the Viceroy emphasized that the replies to be sent to the points raised by Jinnah should be brief but of such a nature as would 'so far as possible reassure him' and that efforts should be made 'to give even fuller weight than we may have done in the past to the importance of soothing the Muslims in such public statements as you or I may have to make on Indian policy generally'.[72]

Some of Linlithgow's advisers, whom he consulted while preparing his note for the Secretary of State, further underlined the importance of keeping the Muslims satisfied with British policy. Thus Sir John Ewart, Director of Intelligence, in a note handed over to the Home Member of the Viceroy's Executive Council, Sir Reginald Maxwell, stressed that it was necessary to realize and to announce that the status of Muslims in India depended not so much on their number as on the fact that they were a part of the world Islamic community. As he put it:

The real situation is that the Hindus with all their majority have an exclusively Indian influence, whereas the real importance of the Muslims lies not in their numbers in India, or even in their importance as a community from the purely Indian point of view, but in the fact that they represent the influence in India of the world power of Islam. However much Hindus would dislike a statement on these lines, it cannot be escaped as a fact. There comes a stage when the condition of Muslims in India becomes an important interest of Muslims generally, just as, conversely, the condition of Muslims elsewhere becomes an interest of Muslims in India. No political or constitutional device for allotting spheres and proportions to Hindus and Muslims will remove or alter this fundamental reality. The Hindu conception of their majority status is in fact their answer to this Islamic world homogeneousness.

The Home Member strongly supported this line of argument and observed that while framing the Act of 1935, the British had 'underrated the solidarity and independence of the Muslim Community' and asked them to submit to 'an impossible arrangement' by having them in a position of permanent minority in a number of provinces and in India as a whole. In such a situation, 'a clear declaration on the subject of Muslim status and rights would be of profound importance to India and would possibly have reactions in other Muslim countries'. He also felt that communal rivalry which made it impossible for Muslims to take a national view on any question was likely to disappear if they realized that in the determination of India's constitutional future their status as an independent cultural entity would entitle them to an equal voice with the Hindus. If these premises were valid, he further argued, they amounted to a virtual indictment of the whole scheme of constitutional progress in India which the British had till then pursued. The only remedy lay in 'a very early and fundamental reconstruction' of the British policy and announcement of the conclusions arrived at.[73]

In forwarding these views to the Secretary of State on 28 November 1939 the Viceroy himself did not go so far and observed that the stage had not yet been reached when the British could conclude that the democratic experiment had failed in India and that there was no way in which the specific difficulties revealed in its working could be overcome. The practical course as well as the course of political wisdom lay in going ahead with the democratic experiment rather than in turning back. As for the difficulties revealed in the working of that system, particularly in relation to Muslims, it should be possible to devise suitable legal safeguards to deal with them. The Muslim claim to equality with the Hindus was a far more difficult problem. The majority community could not be turned into a minority; nor had the minority community itself really faced the difficulty involved in a right of veto which would turn the majority into a minority. However, unless the two communities could reach some accommodation among themselves there could be 'no hope of their collaborating to work any form of central responsibility in a country in which there are no party divisions, and in which community is the essential basis of separation'.

Proceeding to discuss in this connection the question of defining the status of the Muslim community in India raised by John Ewart, which the Home Member had quoted and supported, the Viceroy felt that the British could not accept the principle that any one community, whether majority or minority, should have the last word on matters relating to constitutional advance. Indeed, the Muslim community itself had not produced any concrete suggestion for working a system under which they, regardless of their being in a minority, should be regarded at par with the majority community. The Viceroy also pointed out that Pan-Islamism had grave political dangers from the British point of view and that it would not be in British interest to follow a policy that might in effect provide encouragement to it or involve a recognition of the Pan-Islamic factor 'as a consideration of decisive weight when dealing with the Indian Muslim problem'. He went on, however, to emphasize the 'real importance' of the point made by Ewart and Maxwell, namely, that since the Muslim community in India was part of the international Muslim community and was very conscious of its extra-Indian Islamic ties, the Indian Muslim problem might well become a matter of international concern to a degree unlikely in the case of the Hindu community, which was after all essentially an Indian community. The British must take particular care to shape their policy in such a way as to avoid the risk of 'the Indian Muslim question becoming a general Islamic question, of deep concern to the other Islamic countries'. Further, while the Viceroy showed his awareness of the difficulties of accepting the principle of equality between the Hindus and the Muslims as communities and while he hesitated to accept the Pan-Islamic argument in its entirety, he took care to record that he had always felt that it would be essential in any major constitutional advance that might be contemplated that His Majesty's Government should take the Muslim community with them. While surveying the political situation in India in his note, he summed up the important position occupied by the Muslim community in India and drew pointed attention to its main anxiety in the following words:

The Muslim Community, consisting of some 80 or 90 million people, divided [from the majority, Hindu community] by a profound gulf culturally, religiously, and in general outlook, holding the Frontier (I do not attach overmuch importance to the fact that there has been a Congress Ministry in the North-West Frontier Province), the Punjab, Sind and Bengal; making a contribution of the first importance of the defence of India; and above all geographically linked with the Muslim States of Western Central Asia and culturally and religiously linked with Islam wherever it may stand, is deeply apprehensive that Congress may with the assistance of His Majesty's Government succeed in producing a constitutional scheme of such a character as severely to hamper the Muslims in their aim of independence as a community and in the safeguarding of their interests.

Concluding his general observations on the question of the status of the Muslim community, he emphasized that 'the greatest attention must be paid to Muslim apprehensions and Muslim demands', and that even if the position of equality for which they asked could not be conceded to them, it would be an error of the first magnitude to fail to give the greatest possible weight to their representations, feelings and suggestions.

Indeed, the Viceroy was so much obsessed by the necessity of keeping the Muslim League satisfied with British policy that while ending his lengthy letter, running into eighteen closely typed pages, he again reverted to the need of paying due attention to the importance of the Muslim community in India and also of appearing to be doing so. Asserting that there was force in the view expressed by Jinnah in the course of his interview with the Viceroy on 4 November that there was perhaps a certain tendency in parliamentary debate in Britain to think merely in terms of numerical majorities and minorities, he pointed out that if the situation was really so, it did injustice to 'the special position of the Muslim-minority and the difference existing between it and other minorities in empire countries'. The Viceroy went on:

If I develop this point further, it is only because it is in my judgement of great importance in considering future constitutional development, and in particular the position of the minorities, to give full weight to the fact that the Muslim-minority is no ordinary minority, but one of 90 million people, occupying in relation to India as a whole strategic positions of great importance, separated by profound differences, religious historical and cultural, from the majority community, and strongly represented in the Defence Forces. I am certain that matters have now reached a point at which it will be necessary to pay increasing attention to the Muslims and to their importance as community. . . .[74]

Matters had indeed reached a critical stage. Discussing the attitude of the League leadership on the question whether to have an understanding with the Government or the Congress, the UP Governor, though not rating very high the chances of the latter materializing, warned Linlithgow in the first week of December 1939 of the high British stakes involved in the then developing triangular political equation. As he put it:

The Muslims naturally look on this matter entirely from the point of view of their own interests: will it be better for them on the whole to support the British or to make terms with the Congress? That position was put to me quite frankly in a recent conversation by Choudhary Khaliq-uz-Zaman, the leader of the Muslim League in this Province. He said that if Jinnah thinks, as a result of his communications with your Excellency, that when it comes to devising a new Constitution after the war, they can depend on firm protection from the British, then they will reject the Congress overtures. If on the other hand they think that the British will not in fact give them safeguards that they would consider adequate, they will probably make such terms as they can with the Congress.[75]

Thanks to Linlithgow's alertness on this point, that eventuality did not arise. After some further correspondence with Zetland, Linlithgow was finally able to send Jinnah his reply on 23 December 1939 to the latter's two questions raised in his letter of 5 November. Therein he observed, first, that the declaration of British policy that he had made on 18 October last did not 'exclude examination of any part either of the Act of 1935 or of the policy and plans on which it is based'. Second, he assured Jinnah that the British Government was 'not under any misapprehension as to the importance of the contentment of the Muslim community to the stability and success of any constitutional developments in India'. Jinnah, therefore, did not need to have any fear that the weight that his community's position in India gave their views would be underrated. [76]

The importance of this letter as a milestone on the road to the League's adoption of the Pakistan Resolution cannot be exaggerated. For it underlined the fact that the whole constitutional future of India was wide open and would not be constrained by the scheme of an all-India Federation, an essential element of the Act of 1935. That meant that the British would not take it amiss if the League even opted for any scheme involving the repudiation of one common centre for the whole of India and further that the League's view, whatever it might be, would be a major factor in determining British policy with regard to India's constitutional future. This gave Jinnah the assurance for which he had been working since even before the outbreak of the war. He could now shape the League's policy on the question of an alternative to the Act of 1935 according to his own inner wish without any fear of losing British support—an essential ingredient of the League's strategy since its very inception. And his own inner wish had been conveyed to Linlithgow as early as 4 September 1939, when they had met for the first time after the outbreak of the war. He, of course, did not act in haste and took his own time before announcing his wish clearly and categorically in public. However, as we shall soon see, he now indicated the trend of his thought more and more frankly and step by step prepared his constituents for the final announcement.

VIII

The correspondence between Jinnah and Linlithgow was published by the former on 6 February 1940,[77] but even before that the Viceroy and his staff made no effort to hide from the Congress their determination not to make any move in the constitutional field that might go against the wishes of the Muslim League, thereby indicating the depth of their commitment to the latter as well as the value they attached to the use of the communal card in dealing with the Congress. This is borne out by the Viceroy's conversation on 11 November with the industrialist G.D. Birla, whom he had been using both for conveying messages to Gandhi and for understanding the working of Gandhi's mind from time to time. When Birla urged the Viceroy not to give the Muslim

League a veto, the latter bluntly told him that the real veto was not anything given by the British, 'but the existence of 90 million Muslims, admirably strategically placed and with views of their own of increasing vigour as to the essential importance of safeguarding the future from their point of view'.[78] Similarly, when on 29 November 1939, Birla told the Private Secretary to the Viceroy, Sir Gilbert Lathwaithe, that Gandhi had been a good deal disturbed by a recent letter from Carl Heath, Chairman of the India Conciliation Committee in London, to the effect that while the British Government was sincere, it was not possible for it to displease the Muslims in time of War because of the Muslim powers with whom the British had friendly relations. Lathwaithe did not make any effort to deny the working of such a factor in British policy. Lathwaithe's own version of what he told Birla is as follows:

I said that the point was one so important and so dangerous that I thought the less said about it the better; but that there was no question about it that Muslim solidarity was a real point and one of which they were very conscious: that it was not a thing I should like to see discussed publicly; but that it was something to be reckoned with and could not be lightly brushed aside: and if the day came when Turkey and Persia began to take an active interest in the affairs of the Indian Muslims and to bring pressure to bear on behalf of them the position would become more complicated still.[79]

Again during a conversation between the Private Secretary to the Viceroy and Birla on 8 December 1939, the former made it absolutely clear that the British were not at that stage inclined to take any fresh initiative to break the political deadlock in India unless the Congress first went to the Muslim League and succeeded in securing an agreement with it.[80] Thus the veto which Jinnah had demanded was already in operation.

In the meanwhile, both the Secretary of State and the Viceroy began to pay more and more attention to increased publicity for the Muslim League's stand in the British press in order to counter the favourable position of the Congress at the bar of British as well as world public opinion. Thus when the Secretary of State learnt about the plans of the India League of Britain, working under the leadership of V.K. Krishna Menon, to issue a statement on the tripartite talks in New Delhi in the first week of November, with possibly adverse reference to the stand of the Muslim League, he immediately conveyed the news to the Viceroy and advised him to alert Jinnah about it.[81] At that stage, the Viceroy felt that it would be better for him not to deal directly with Jinnah on such a matter 'in view of risk of appearing to take any sides whatever in this business, and desirability of maintaining an attitude of complete detachment from both parties'. He was also partly influenced by 'possible risks of building on Jinnah', about which the Secretary of State and the Viceroy had corresponded earlier. However, he asked Sir Roger Lumley, Governor of Bombay, to convey to Jinnah the information regarding the projected statement of the India League in the hope that this would put Jinnah on guard. If he did issue a counter statement in terms satisfactory to the British, the latter could secure the 'utmost publicity' for it both in Britain and the United States.[82] At the same time, the Viceroy conveyed to the Secretary of State his opinion that the time had come when they should get more material into the British press regarding the problem of defence and the crucial importance of that issue in affecting the future of India. In that connection, he pleaded for the Muslim position being highlighted tactfully in both the British and the American press, especially in view of increased Congress effort to project its viewpoint in the British press. As for the points to be covered in that campaign, Linlithgow observed:

> Substantial proportion of Muslim recruitment, geographical position of Muslims, fact that Punjab and North-West Frontier border on Muslim kingdoms, Muslim solidarity throughout Middle Eastern area and fact that Indian Muslim problem cannot like that of the Congress be regarded as purely an Indian problem, are no doubt points that would call for very tactful and careful handling, but they are relevant to our main problem; and are a most important contributory factor in reluctance of Muslims . . . to allow the vital control of defence at the Centre to pass into the hands of the majority community, and to acquisce in a relinquishment of power by us to the advantage of that community.[83]

When Jinnah issued his appeal to the Muslims for the celebration of Deliverance Day on 22 December 1939 on the resignation of the Congress ministries, the Viceroy got the type of material he was looking for in order to strengthen the British position in the world press. He immediately asked the news agency Reuters to telegraph to London the full text of Jinnah's statement and also telegraphed to the Secretary of State urging him 'to get widest possible publicity for it'. He further added: 'It would be a convincing answer to the India League statement (if text has been published) and would help too to disprove Congress contention that we have manufactured the communal bogey and that is not a live issue.'[84]

Linlithgow's deep interest in securing the widest possible publicity abroad for the Muslim League's standpoint, which made the British position in India so much more defensible at the bar of world public opinion, soon made him shake off his initial shyness in broaching the topic directly with Jinnah. He did so for the first time during his meeting with the latter in Bombay on 13 January 1940. Before they parted the Viceroy complimented Jinnah for having clearly put the Muslim League very much on the map both in India and abroad during the recent weeks and expressed the hope that he would realize the value of publicity 'from his own point of view'. He then proceeded to place before Jinnah an article on Nehru by John Gunther, which had appeared in a recent issue of *Life* magazine, and pointed out that it completely ignored the Muslim and British positions. Jinnah's only comment was that he wished he had the funds to arrange for similar publicity.[85]

Linlithgow next discussed the question of publicity with Sikander in the course of their conversation on 25 January 1940. Here he talked more forcefully and expressed the view that the Muslim position at that time was in his judgement 'quite unhelpful and static to a dangerous degree' and could not be held for long. Sikander agreed with this view and said that he proposed when he saw Jinnah next on 3 February to let him know behind the scenes that it was, in his opinion, essential that the Working Committee of the Muslim League should be ready with a scheme of its own. Sikander also indicated his desire to be allowed to go to Britain to put the case of the Indian minorities before the British public and Parliament on the ground that publicity there was too much dominated by the Congress. The Viceroy pointed out that if he were to go to Britain on the basis of a purely negative platform like resistance to home rule or constitutional advance in India, his visit would be 'worse than useless'. 'Could he not,' asked the Viceroy, 'consider the possibility of picking up again the federal scheme embodied in the Act and making it acceptable to the Muslims by putting to Congress Muslim requirements and securing a charter of security for minorities?' The Viceroy further added that unity was essential and federation was the only easy road towards securing that unity.[86] This was in line with what Linlithgow had told Jinnah on 4 September 1939 and establishes the fact that he would have been happier if the Muslim League had formulated its objective within the framework of Indian unity.

However, the records of subsequent interviews with the leaders of the Muslim League as well as his correspondence with the Secretary of State and the UP Governor make it clear that he was not much bothered by whether the League supported an all-India federation in some form or not. What really mattered to him was that the League ceased to be merely anti-this or that and acquired a positive objective of its own. This became quite an obsession with him and he incessantly worked to bring it about. This was because he was looking at the issue not from the point of view of India's future, but from the point of view of publicity in the British and American press and in projecting the League as an organization with a positive objective of its own which had to be treated at par with the Congress. For the League's opposition to the Congress was the British Government's main shield on the propaganda front against pressures to transfer power to Indian hands. So long as that opposition continued, the British could take the position that they were keen to transfer power, but could not ignore an organization representing 90 million persons who remained opposed to the Congress—which alone was in a position to take power from the British—and refused to agree to live under its domination. Knowing the mental make-up of the British and American peoples, Linlithgow realized that an organization with a purely negative platform would never appeal to them. Hence his obsession with the problem of endowing the League with a positive plank.

Thus in his conversation with Sikander and Fazlul Huq on 3 February 1940 Linlithgow again came to his point about the urgent need for a constructive plan for the League. Commenting on Haig's observation that the Muslim case had not been properly presented, the Viceroy remarked that it was not his fault that it was so. He further pointed out that if Huq and his friends could secure that the Muslim case was better understood, nobody could be better pleased than he himself. However, as long as that case remained purely negative and unconstructive, 'it was very hard indeed . . . to get it across, and to make it understood in Great Britain, the United States, and even in this country'.[87] The Viceroy also took the opportunity to encourage the idea of a Muslim delegation visiting Britain—once the League had a positive plan of its own—in order to put forward the League's point of view before the British public.[88] Justifying his action he later told the UP Governor that although he might not agree with what Jinnah and others were saying those days in pubic, he thought there was 'advantage in their stating their case in public as all these developments would serve to bring home to the British public the complexity of the problem with which we are dealing, and the fact that it is not merely a question of satisfying the Congress'.[89]

During his interview mentioned above, Sikander told the Viceroy that he had seen Jinnah on the previous day and strongly urged on him the need for some constructive approach. He further added that Jinnah was 'now out for complete Partition with safeguards for members of his community in minority provinces'. The Viceroy also saw at about the same time reports in the press that 'a Pakistan Scheme' with safeguards for Muslims outside Pakistan had been strongly pressed by the League's Working Committee. However, that did not bother Linlithgow and he felt, on the whole, satisfied that at last the League's Working Committee was going to 'work out a constructive programme'.[90]

When Jinnah went to see the Viceroy on 6 February the latter, after the usual compliments, again pressed hard his old point about the importance of the Muslim League coming out with a 'a constructive programme' of its own as soon as possible. As he reported to the Secretary of State, at the very outset he thought it well to encourage Jinnah 'to move into a constructive position, and . . . emphasized the propaganda value of a constructive plan, and the weakness on a long sight of the present situation.' Although the principles that formed the basis of the Lahore Resolution had been settled by the League's Working Committee on 4 February that had been kept strictly confidential and, contrary to what has been imagined by some,[91] Jinnah did not tell the Viceroy about it. It seems that he was still not sure about the advisability of announcing the decision of 4 February and wanted to take some time in giving a final shape to the League's resolution on its demand. For he told the Viceroy that he was not yet in a position to present in detail the views of his colleagues and himself on that very important subject, but that he would be ready to do so shortly. He further informed the Viceroy that he and his colleagues were on the whole inclined to the view that it was inadvisable from their standpoint to publish in detail their formulated opinions on the constructive plan for the future as it would expose them to criticism. They would like to rather wait till the British Government had reached a point at which they would ask the League for its views. The League would be ready to come forward with a plan at that stage. How strongly the Viceroy dissented from this view and urged the publication of the League's resolution at the earliest should be clear from this summary of what he said to Jinnah then in his own words:

> I said that was all very well: that I fully understood the tactical convenience from his point of view of a purely negative attitude at this stage as opposed to an attempt to formulate and publish a constructive policy. But if I might say so this plan for postponing any announcement of the constructive programme of the Muslim League until the last moment failed altogether to meet the requirements of propaganda. With his great experience he would not disagree with me when I said that it was impossible to hope to be able to educate public opinion in Great Britain, and more particularly the 600 odd representatives of constituencies in the House of Commons, by the submission of formal memorandum to His Majesty's Government, or by the leading of evidence before some committee on the eve of critical decisions. If he and his friends wanted to secure that the Muslim case should not go by default in the United Kingdom, it was really essential that they should formulate their plan in the near future. At the risk of wearing him I was bound to repeat what I had often said before that I was convinced that it was quite useless to appeal for support in Great Britain for a party whose policy was one of sheer negation.[92]

The Viceroy, however, soon received information about the League deciding in favour of Partition through a letter from the UP Governor dated 16 February giving the details of the latter's conversation with Khaliquzzaman on the same date. According to Khaliquzzaman's 'Constructive proposals'—it was not yet clear to the Governor whether these had been definitely accepted by the League—instead of one all-India Federation there should be three dominions in India, two Muslim (one in the north-west and the other in the north-east) and one Hindu, the relations of the Muslim dominions with the British Government being not unlike those of Northern Ireland. 'Though at our first sight,' the Governor commented, 'this so-called constructive plan, so alien from all our ideas of a united India or Federation, may be regarded as out of the question, we cannot disregard it. It may possibly have in it the germs of a settlement; after all Ireland may be a close parallel.'[93] Writing again the next day, the Governor remarked that the scheme for the formation of three separate dominions 'might well be called the nut-cracker scheme'. He did not attempt to speculate on its chances of success, but it seemed to him at best more practical than the scheme envisaging a transfer of population to create Muslim and Hindu zones. Besides, democracy could still be maintained in the three dominions and this might appeal to the people in Britain. On the other hand, it rendered an all-India federation impossible, the views of Hindus and other minorities were not known, and in any case a scheme of such magnitude could not be considered and decided in a time of war. 'However,' the Governor concluded, 'we cannot stop it from being put forward, and if we still believe in self-determination, it will be foolish to do so.'[94] In his reply, Linlithgow fully agreed with this approach and indeed went beyond it in expressing himself strongly in favour of the ventilation of such schemes, though he did not like their content:

> I agree with you that we must let people continue to speculate on proposals such as those put forward by Khaliquzzaman for three 'dominions', though I have never been able to convince myself that a solution lies in a scheme of that nature. . . . But my criticisms of the three 'dominions' scheme apply equally of course to the scheme . . . for a transfer of population so as to create Muslim and Hindu zones. But I share your view that there is everything to be gained by the ventilation of schemes of this nature, or indeed of any scheme that looks like affording a way out of our difficulties here; and I have myself always encouraged Sikander and others whenever they have come to me for advice to work out their ideas in detail and to put them before the public.[95]

In the light of such thinking it is not surprising that when Jinnah saw Linlithgow on 13 March 1940, at the latter's request, the main topic again was whether the League was ready with its 'constructive proposals'. According to Linlithgow's record of their conversation, Jinnah did not seem very keen on replying too directly to that question, and dilated for some time on the war situation and the role the Muslims were capable of playing in it on the British side. It was only after this that he told Linlithgow that if the British could not improve upon their solution of the Indian problem, 'he and his friends would have no option but to fall back on some form of Partition'. He went on to add that 'they had decided as a result of their discussions first of all that the Muslims were not a minority, but rather a nation; secondly, that democracy for all-India was impossible'.[96]

Jinnah was very reluctant to divulge everything while talking to Linlithgow about the League's plan for the future, even after it had been settled by its Working Committee, apparently with some purpose in mind. That purpose, as revealed by the records of his interviews with Linlithgow between December 1939 and March 1940, was to prevent the latter from feeling that the British could take the League for granted and to extract further assurances from him in its interest. He was particularly keen on assurances on two points. First, as mentioned in his letter to the Viceroy on 5 November 1939, he wanted to be assured that the British would not think of settling any constitutional arrangement for India in the future which would not be acceptable to the League, thus in effect securing a veto for the League on India's constitutional development. Second, he wanted to be assured that the British in the meanwhile would not agree to some settlement with the Congress so as to have them back in the saddle in the provinces without the League's nominees also included in the ministries to be formed by the Congress. The frequent talks between Gandhi and Linlithgow made Jinnah particularly worried on this point.

For Jinnah realized that any understanding between the Viceroy and the Congress, without the League being in the picture, would cut the ground from under his feet. As the Governor of Bombay reported to the Viceroy after a long conversation with Jinnah on 12 January 1940:

> Looking back upon this conversation, it seems to me that what is in Jinnah's mind at the moment is anxiety that we have not yet made up our minds to throw in our lot with the Muslims and that we might be tempted still to come down on the side of Congress: for this reason he is stressing the fact that the Muslim League has not yet decided to give us full support in the war and is anxious to persuade us that a firm hand with Congress is the only means of breaking through the present deadlock.[97]

It may be interesting to not here what Jinnah told the Viceroy the next day when he called on the latter during his sojourn in Bombay. When Linlithgow sounded him out about the Consultative Committee, which had been mooted in the former's statement of 17 October 1939, but which had been in cold storage for some time, Jinnah replied that 'he could not come in until he had made up his mind to give unconditional support, which might be a long time'. Asked for advice as to what the Viceroy should do to break the political deadlock and have democratic governments restored in the provinces, Jinnah replied that the British must go on 'as at present', tell the Congress that 'there was nothing doing! Until they did that 'there was no prospect in his judgement of any headway being made.' It was at this meeting that Jinnah gave Linlithgow an idea of the terms he had conveyed to the Congress for cooperation in ministry making in the provinces in the first week of November 1939 (noted earlier), which the latter had rejected. The conversation between Linlithgow and Jinnah on that occasion had, of course, been quite friendly—indeed 'more friendly almost', noted Linlithgow, 'than any I have had with Mr Jinnah'.[98]

Their next interview took place on 6 February 1940, just a day after the Viceroy had seen Gandhi. Although the talks with Gandhi had failed to produce any result, the Viceroy told Jinnah that he was not happy with the continuance of political deadlock in India and was keen to again return to the normal working of the constitutional machine. Jinnah's reaction to it is best presented in the words used by Linlithgow in his record of that interview:

> Mr Jinnah said that he quite understood. Could I, however, hope to achieve unity, much as I might be anxious to do so? He begged me to realise what he described the dreadful effect of this suspense in India. I had never appeared to break with Gandhi and I always left India with the impression that I was going to see him again before very long and that negotiations were going to be reopened. That in turn, as I would understand, produced throughout the community the fear that Congress governments might return to office at any moment.... How could any healthy reaction against Congress develop in conditions such as these? His advice in such circumstances to me and to his Majesty's Government was to make it clear to Congress without undue delay that there was nothing doing; and that this nonsense had to stop, in the same way as Lord Willingdon had done some years ago.[99]

The other point about the requirement for the League's approval of any future constitutional development in India was dealt with by Jinnah in his letter to Linlithgow on 24 February 1940. Writing on behalf of the League's Working Committee, he thanked the Viceroy for declaring in his letter of 23 December that the review of the provisions of the existing constitution after the end of the war would not 'exclude the examination of any part either of the Act of 1935 or of the policy and plans on which it is based'. However, he made it clear that on the second point raised in his letter to the Viceroy on 5 November 1939 the League's Working Committee was not satisfied with the latter's reply. While the League had urged that no declaration of British policy be made or any constitution enforced by the British Government or enacted by the Parliament without 'the approval and consent' of the Muslims of India, the viceregal letter had only conceded 'consultation and counsel' and vested the final decision in the hands of Britain. The Muslim League could not give an assurance of 'whole-hearted support and active cooperation' in the war effort unless it felt confident that the future of Muslims of India was not left 'in the region of uncertainty or doubtful possibility'. While this was the main topic dealt with in that letter, Jinnah did not fail to utilze the opportunity also to indirectly protest against the attention being then paid by the Viceroy to the Congress. Towards the end of his letter he observed:

> We are constrained to state that your Excellency is unnecessarily over-anxious about the interests of other communities. It has never been our desire to unjustly harm any community. The issues that have been raised by us are due to apprehensions that the British Government may be stampeded by other powerful organizations in the country into adopting a course or agreeing to a settlement in the mater of India's Constitution which may prove not only highly detrimental to the interests of the Mussalmans, but may be disastrous for them.[100]

In his interview with Linlithgow on 13 March 1940 Jinnah again emphasized that 'Muslim leadership could not work with Great Britain save on a basis of confidence and partnership'. Further, again expressing his fear of a deal between the British and the Congress, he wished to impress upon Linlithgow that if the British Government wanted Muslim India to give 'definite and effective help' in the prosecution of the war effort, 'they must not sell the pass behind the backs of Muslims'. Jinnah added that the Muslims were keen not to land themselves in a situation where the British hold over India became weak and they felt obliged to hand over to a Hindu Raj. They were equally worried that at the intermediate stage, while the British might remain in India to maintain law and order and keep the ring, they might have to 'uphold the Hindu Raj with British bayonets and to hold the Muslim down'. That, Jinnah emphasized, 'was an intolerable prospect'.

Apparently in order to soothe Jinnah's mind and free him form undue anxiety regarding the future, the Viceroy explained that there were actually three main possibilities. First, in course of time the operation of the Act of 1935 might result in the complete removal of Hindu–Muslim differences. That was the idea for which Parliament had been striving. Second, the British might ultimately withdraw, leaving the Hindus and Muslims to sort out their differences by themselves; that was likely to lead to perpetual conflict with disastrous consequences. The third alternative was that as a result of a tripartite arrangement the British might continue to remain for quite some time in India with responsibility for Defence and in order to keep the ring. Jinnah apparently felt a bit reassured about the future after hearing Linlithgow and remarked that the third alternative was excellent, but insisted that it did not end the prospect of a Hindu Raj over a wide field with power to oppress and threaten the Muslims. He asserted that Muslim interests could be safeguarded only by demarcating a Muslim area run by Muslims in collaboration with Great Britain'. As Linlithgow explained Jinnah's thinking:

> He was fully aware that that meant poverty; that the lion's share of the wealth would go to others. But the Muslims would retain their self-respect, their culture, and would be able to lead their lives in their own way and bring up their children as desired. That might be out of tune with our conception of the future. But the Muslims could see no escape, and by that means they would have some hope of making the Muslim existence happy within a particular area, in addition to feeling that they could reasonably safeguard, because of their military power, the Muslims who were domiciled in the Hindu area.[101]

IX

Jinnah was to speak even more passionately and forcefully in support of the Pakistan idea in the course of his presidential address to the next session of the League scheduled to begin nine days later at Lahore. However, the words uttered before Linlithgow on 13 March 1940, and quoted above, represented his most passionate and forceful exposition of that idea till that date. This does not mean that while carrying on his conversations and negotiations with the Viceroy in a bid to secure his flanks before taking the plunge regarding the demand for Partition, he had in any way neglected the task of preparing the minds of the Muslim intelligentsia and youth for that demand. On the contrary, while avoiding the use of the word Partition or Pakistan, speaking in a guarded way and occasionally even adopting contrary postures, he had been painstakingly putting before his co-religionists some of the fundamental ideas on which that demand was to be based. Indeed, as should have been clear from a perusal of the previous two chapters, he had been doing so right from the summer of 1937 by which time he had, as per his own testimony, become converted to the Pakistan idea. Sometimes, some of his important colleagues also lent him their hands in this endeavour, speaking more clearly than was perhaps considered appropriate at that stage, for the supreme leader himself. Thus Jinnah remarked in the course of his interview with a representative of the *Manchester Guardian*, which was reproduced in the Indian newspapers on 26 October 1939:

The British public way be misled by certain propaganda that the Muslims are against the freedom of India. We want freedom and liberty, but the question is, whose freedom and liberty? Muslim India wants to be free and enjoy liberty to the fullest extent and develop its own political, economic, social and cultural institutions according to its own genius and not to be dominated and crushed, while wishing Hindu India well and giving it fullest scope to do likewise.[102]

What was implicit here—that Hindus and Muslims were two nations and both needed to develop in their own separate ways—was made explicit by Jinnah in the course of a letter to Gandhi in January 1940. As mentioned earlier, Jinnah had been able to secure the support of some members of the depressed classes led by Ambedkar and some other non-Congress Hindus and Parsis for the celebration of Deliverance Day on 22 December 1939. This had led to speculation in the press that Jinnah might form a party bringing together all non-Congress elements in India's public life. Gandhi welcomed that supposed move as it might transform

Jinnah's opposition to the Congress from a communal to a national character and thus change the contours of Indian politics. He explained his ideas in a short article published in the *Harijan* on 20 January 1940.[103] Forwarding its advance copy to Jinnah, Gandhi remarked that the former's plan to amalgamate all the non-Congress parties at once gave his movement 'a national character'. 'If you succeed,' he wrote further, 'you will free the country from communal incubus and, in my humble opinion, give a lead to the Muslims and others for which you will deserve the gratitude not only of the Muslims but of all the other communities.'[104] Jinnah refused to take the compliment and after thanking Gandhi for his letter and his curtsy in sending an advance copy of his article, bluntly added: 'I however regret to have to say that your premises are wrong as you start with the theory of an Indian nation that does not exist, and naturally, therefore, your conclusions are wrong.' Minimizing the significance of some non-Congress groups joining the Deliverance Day celebrations and describing it merely as a case of 'adversity bringing strange bed-fellows together,' he again underlined: 'India is not nation, nor a country. It is a sub-continent composed of nationalities, Hindus and Muslims being the two major nations.'[105]

Jinnah presented a detailed exposition of this idea in an article entitled 'The Constitutional Future of India' published in a British magazine *Time and Tide* on 19 January 1940. Therein he emphasized that the need of the hour was to evolve a Constitution that recognized that 'there are in India two nations, who both must share the governance of their common motherland.' A look at this sentence, particularly of the words 'their common motherland', can lead a casual reader to conclude that Jinnah was not contemplating Partition when he wrote that article—which must have been in November or December 1939. A close perusal of the article, however, leads to an entirely different conclusion. For the whole effort from the beginning to the end was directed towards proving that because of the diverse character of its people and their different socio-political orientations, India was not at all suited for parliamentary government. Quoting the remark contained in the report of the joint Select Committee on Indian Constitutional Reforms (1934) that Hinduism and Islam represented 'two distinct and separate civilisations' and were 'as distinct from another in origin, tradition and manner of life' as were the nations of Europe, he asserted that they were in fact 'two different nations'. 'Experience has shown,' he further added, 'that, whatever the economic and political programme of any political party, the Hindu, as a general rule, will vote for his caste-fellow, the Muslim for his co-religionist.' In such a situation any democratic system at the all-India level was bound to result in the rule of a permanent Hindu majority. Thus was the justification provided for the League's stand at that time. As Jinnah defined that stand: 'While the Muslim League stands for a free India, it is irrevocably opposed to any Federal objective which must necessarily result in a majority community rule, under the guise of democracy and a parliamentary system of government.'[106] Partition was the only logical conclusion of such an argument. Thus the article in *Time and Tide* was not intended to show Muslims' attachment to the 'common motherland' or their keenness to share its governance, but to secure legitimacy for an entirely different objective and prepare British pubic opinion to respond favourably to the demand for Partition, which was soon to follow, by underlining the reasonableness of Muslims and their desire to cooperate with the Hindus if at all possible to do so with honour.

In the meanwhile, some of Jinnah's close associates, who were most unlikely to express any views if they knew that those would not be appreciated by their Quaid-i-Azam, were busy expounding the Pakistan idea even more forcefully than the latter considered appropriate at the stage to do. Thus the Raja of Mahmudabad, quite close to Jinnah and a member of the League's Working Committee, in his address to the Assam Provincial Muslim League Conference on 27 November 1939 observed:

> India today is assuming a distinct shape—Muslim India and non-Muslim India. The distinction existed before and has not emerged suddenly, but it was not so sharp, not so clear.
>
> The provinces in the North, predominantly Muslim, are instinctively and now actively aspiring for a freer and fuller life. . . .
>
> Here then is the genesis of that idea which is known generally as the Pakistan Movement. India will federate, but not on the lines chalked out for it by the British Parliament, the British nation or the Hindu politicians. There must and will be more than one federation, each independent, but at the time complementary of the other. . . .[107]

Liaquat Ali Khan, General Secretary of the All-India Muslim

League, in the course of his presidential address to the District Muslim League Conference at Darbhanga on 24 November 1939, observed that the unreasonable attitude of the Hindus on the issue of sharing power had given birth to 'the idea of Partitioning India into Hindu and Muslim zones'.[108] In an article published on 5 January 1940, Muhammad Sharif Toosy, who though not one of the leaders of the League was quite closely associated with Jinnah, asserted that as independence was drawing near, Muslims living in the majority provinces had before them the clear choice of either remaining a minority under an Indian Government or forming independent States in the north-west and the north-east.[109]

In the light of the ventilation of such ideas in public by persons closely associated with Jinnah, the supreme leader of the League, it is not surprising that the Foreign Committee of the League, functioning under the chairmanship of Sir Haji Abdullah Haroon and engaged for quite some time in considering the various alternatives to the Act of 1935 suggested by various persons, finally came to a decision on 2 February 1940 on the principles to be recommended as a basis for the new Constitution, calling them 'fundamental rights' and forwarded them for consideration by the League's Working Committee. While doing so, it respectfully asked the latter to 'state its mind in unequivocal language with regard to the future of the Indian Muslim Nation and prepare the latter also for launching [a] struggle' for it. The five principles or rights mentioned were as follows:

(a) The Muslims of India, who constitute 90 million of people are a separate nation entitled to the same right of self-determination which has been conceded in respect of the other nations;

(b) The Muslims of India shall in no case agree to be reduced to a position of minority on the basis of extraneous and foreign considerations, or for the sake of any political conveniences or expedience;

(c) That in order to make the Muslim right of self-determination really effective, the Muslims shall have Separate National Home in the shape of an autonomous State;

(d) That the Muslims living in the rest of India shall be treated as the nationals of the aforesaid Muslim State and their rights and privileges shall be fully safeguarded;

(e) That any scheme of Indian Reforms interfering with these basic principles shall be stoutly resisted by the Indian Muslim Nation till it has achieved the aforesaid objectives.[110]

On the basis of these principles, the League's Working Committee agreed to the following broad outlines regarding the future constitution of India on 4 February 1940.

1. Musalmans are not a minority in the ordinary sense of the word. They are a nation.
2. British system of democratic parliamentary party system of Government is not suited to the genius and condition of the people of India.
3. Those zones which are composed of majority of Musalmans in the physical map of India should be constituted into Independent Dominions in direct relationship with Great Britain.
4. In those zones where Muslims are in minority their interests and those of other minorities must be adequately and effectively safeguarded and similar safeguards shall be provided for the Hindu and other minorities in the Muslim zones.
5. The various units in each zone shall form component parts of the Federation in that zone as autonomous units.[111]

That decision was kept strictly confidential. It was neither given to the press nor talked about by either Jinnah or any other member of the League's Working Committee. Contrary to the usual practice, it was not even placed before the next meeting of the Council held on 25 February 1940. Perhaps this was part of Jinnah's strategy to disclose the decision only to the ensuing session of the League scheduled to begin at Lahore on 22 March 1940 for the maximum impact on the people's minds. It is also possible that as that session was still over a month and a half away, he thought it politic to keep his options open for some time more so that if he thought it prudent he might ask the Working Committee to revise its decision before the League's session. This would not be possible if the decision was publicized.

Whatever that might have been, Jinnah now spoke a little more openly about the League's determination to carve out an independent destiny for the Indian Muslims though still scrupulously avoiding the use of the word Partition or Pakistan and sometimes even talking of a common future for Hindus and Muslims provided the Congress realized the then existing realities in India. An inkling into his strategy is provided by his address to the Council of the League, which met in Delhi on 26 February 1940. Jinnah threw a broad hint about the new proposed goal of the League without spelling it out in so many words:

People ask me what is our goal. If you do not understand even now, then I say you will never understand what our goal is. Great Britain wants to rule India. Mr Gandhi wants to rule India and the Musalmans. We say that we will not let either the British or Mr Gandhi to rule the Musalmans. We want to be free.[112]

Addressing the students of the Aligarh Muslim University on 6 March 1940, Jinnah invoking Islam in support of his call for Muslim freedom recalled that he had said at Simla two years earlier that the democratic system of government was not suited to India and that some had then accused him of doing a disservice to Islam, as Islam stood for democracy. 'So far as I have understood Islam,' he added, 'it does not advocate a democracy which would allow the majority of non-Muslims to decide the fate of the Muslims. We cannot accept a system of government in which the non-Muslims merely by numerical majority would rule and dominate us.'[113] Jinnah's address ended with an impassioned call to the students to work for the new goal:

Stand firm as one solid block of steel, go on organising our people, training them, disciplining them. They are with us. Do not worry about handicaps, organise the Muslims, bring them all together, train them, drill them and make of them the most wonderful political army that India has ever seen and we will soon reach the goal of our freedom. (Prolonged applause)[114]

X

Slightly over a fortnight after this came the fateful day—22 March 1940—when the Muslim League met for its twenty-seventh annual session at Lahore. This was obviously the day Jinnah had been waiting for to announce the new objective of the League in a dramatic fashion, speaking in the meanwhile in a guarded manner, even though the relevant decision had been taken by the League's Working Committee under his guidance as early as 4 February. Arriving at Lahore a day earlier, he had remarked that the session there was going to be 'a landmark in the future history of Muslim India'.[115] And so it did indeed became.

Delivering his presidential address, Jinnah declared that the Hindu–Muslim problem in India was 'not of an intercommunal character, but manifestly of an international one'. If the British were really keen to ensure peace and happiness in the country, the only course open to them was to 'allow the major nations separate homelands by dividing India into autonomous national States'. There was no reason to fear that these States would be antagonistic to each other. On the contrary, the main cause of antagonism would disappear as no scope would be left for mutual rivalry and the effort by the one to dominate over the other in the government of the country. Relations between them would be governed by 'international pacts between them'. This would also ensure a friendly settlement of the problem of minorities through 'reciprocal arrangements and adjustments between Muslim India and Hindu India'. Thus was the demand for Partition voiced without actually mentioning the word. Jinnah based this demand solely on the two-nation theory based on religious affiliation. He mentioned that he found it difficult to appreciate why the Hindus failed to understand the real nature of Hinduism and Islam. According to him, they were not religious in the strict sense of the word, but were 'different and distinct social orders'. It was nothing but a dream that their adherents could ever evolve a common nationality. The 'misconception' of one Indian nation, he warned, had gone on beyond limits and had been the cause of most of the troubles India had been facing and would lead to destruction if not revised in time. Underlining the basic divergences between Hindus and Muslims, Jinnah observed:

> The Hindus and Muslims belong to two different religious philosophies, social customs and literature. They neither intermarry, nor interdine together and, indeed, they belong to two different civilizations which are based mainly on conflicting ideas and conceptions. Their aspects on life and of life are different. It is quite clear that Hindus and Musalmans derive their inspiration from different sources of history. They have different epics, their heroes are different, and different episodes. Very often the hero of one is the foe of the other and, likewise, their victories and defeats overlap.

Citing examples from European history, Jinnah asserted that

artificial unions, covering small territories but consisting of culturally disparate peoples, have never lasted for long and decried the attempt being made in India, in the name of one nation, to put the whole country under one central government in spite of the fact that the country had never enjoyed political unity in the past for any length of time. The 'artificial unity' of India existing at that time had been brought about by British conquest and was maintained by British bayonets; the termination of British rule, which was implicit in the recent declaration of the Viceroy, would herald 'an entire break-up with worse disaster than has ever taken place during the last one thousand years under Muslims'. In any case, Jinnah made it clear that Muslim India could not accept any constitution based on a democratic system that must necessarily result in Hindu-majority rule or Hindu Raj. Finally, he declared:

> Musalmans are not minority as it is commonly known and understood . . . Musalmans are a nation according to any definition of a nation and they must have their homeland, their territory and their State. We wish to live in peace and harmony with our neighbours as a free and independent people. We wish our people to develop to the fullest of spiritual, cultural, economic, social and political life in a way that we think best and in consonance with our own ideals and according to the genius of our people. . . . We must be prepared to face all difficulties and consequences, make all the sacrifices that may be required of us to achieve the goal we have set in front of us.[116]

The ideas propounded by Jinnah formed the basis for the resolution on the constitutional problem, moved by Fazlul Huq and seconded by Choudhry Khaliquzzaman, and adopted by the Lahore session on 24 March 1940. Its central idea was contained in the third paragraph:

> Resolved that it is the considered view of this Session of the All-India Muslim League that no constitutional plan would be workable in this country or acceptable to the Muslims unless it is designed on the following basic principle, *viz.*, that geographically contiguous units are demarcated into regions which should be so constituted, with such territorial readjustments as may be necessary, that the areas in which the Muslims are numerically in a majority, as in the North-Western and Eastern Zones of India, should be grouped to constitute 'Independent States' in which the constituent units shall be autonomous and sovereign.

The resolution went on to suggest that the constitution should contain 'adequate, effective and mandatory safeguards' for the minorities in these units and regions for the protection of their religious, cultural, economic, political, administrative and other rights and interests. Similar safeguards should also be provided for the Muslims and other minorities in other parts of India. The resolution also authorized the League's Working Committee to frame 'a scheme of constitution in accordance with these basic principles, providing for the assumption finally by the respective regions of all powers such as defence, external affairs, communications, customs and such other matters as may be necessary'.[117]

The word Pakistan did not figure in the resolution. Nor did it find mention in the speeches in support of it. However, the word, with its connotation of a separate Muslim State or States based on the Muslim-majority areas of India, had acquired such popularity in India by that time that it immediately began to be called the Pakistan Resolution, both by its supporters and opponents. As is clear from Jinnah's studious avoidance of the word till then in his speeches and statements, even while championing the idea behind it, he was not fond of it, whether for personal or tactical reasons. However, he took no time in grasping its potential in spreading his message among the mass of the people, quickly accepted it without much ado, and himself began to refer to the Lahore Resolution as the Pakistan Resolution. The new name of the Lahore Resolution was quite appropriate and also useful for the League leadership, particularly Jinnah, the suprme leader. For that conveyed the gist or the central idea of the Lahore Resolution in a way in which no other word could have done. Moreover, literally meaning the 'land of the pure', it was ideal for being used as a slogan or a symbol and touched the heart of an average Muslim, again as nothing else could have done. Indeed, it at once became a religious as well as a political slogan for the Muslim masses.

XI

Jinnah must have been the happiest person at the adoption of the Lahore Resolution. As shown earlier, since his conversion to the Pakistan idea in 1937, he had been working incessantly for its spread among the intelligentsia and the youth, thereby preparing the ground for its adoption by the League, though, for tactical reasons, he had not taken his constituents into confidence by telling them of the final goal for which he was working. His extreme caution and determination not to divulge all his plans to the public until he had fully prepared the ground for it has led some scholars to conclude that Jinnah was not really interested in the adoption of the Pakistan Resolution at that stage and was pushed towards it as a result of Linlithgow's pressure. Actually, Jinnah's reticence in publicly expounding the full import of his objective was the result of his tactical calculation. This involved first improving the organization of the League before such a high-sounding objective was mouthed by it and, second, covering his flanks by ensuring that the British did not immediately pour cold water on the new objective. The later consideration was dictated not only by the fact that the British occupied a most strategic position in the Indian political triangle and Jinnah, as behaved a political strategist of his calibre, did not consider it prudent at that stage to simultaneously take on both the British Government and the Congress. Second, he was aware that many, if not most, of his colleagues in the highest echelons of the League still clung to the apron strings of the top British officials in India and it might not be safe at that stage to work totally out of step with the latter if he had to maintain unity in the League and strengthen its organization. His real objective is clearly revealed by his preference for Partition as conveyed to the Viceroy during their interview on 4 September 1939, their first since the outbreak of the war. Though the Viceroy at that time as also on some later occasions indicated his preference for a federal objective, it is a tribute to Jinnah's strategical skill, if also the result of the exigencies of the imperial crisis and the difficult predicament of the British, that within a short while the Viceroy himself became anxious that the League should come out into the open with its positive objective even though fully aware that that objective was Partition. The Viceroy's interest in the early announcement of the League's objective in order to facilitate propaganda on its behalf at the bar of world (mainly British and American) opinion, which would also provide an excellent cover for the British position, should not lead us to the absurd conclusion that the Lahore Resolution was the result of the Viceroy's pressure. Even a rudimentarily familiarity with Jinnah's character and personality should preclude such a view, but there is plenty of documentary evidence also, already cited in this chapter, which points to the same conclusion. Indeed, in the light of the latter, it will not be too much to say that enthusiastic adoption of the Pakistan Resolution by the League at a time of Jinnah's choosing was a personal triumph for him. For he had worked for it most sincerely as well as with due care and calculation for several years past.

To say this is not to imply that Jinnah had been able single-handedly to prepare the ground for the adoption of the Pakistan Resolution by the Lahore session of the League. He was certainly in the forefront and played a leading role as the unchallenged head of that organization. However, he was not working in isolation. The great quality of his leadership—just as Gandhi's in the Congress—was that he managed to work in such a way as to ensure that in whatever he did he had the support of the bulk of his colleagues and followers. And, again just like Gandhi, his success in this regard was due in a large measure to his ability to keep his hand firmly on the pulse of his constituents—in his case the bulk of politically conscious Muslims. There can be no doubt that the decision that he guided the League to adopt had the backing of the overwhelming majority of the latter. Weighing public opinion on any issue at any time is a tricky task. The statistical approach does not help. It has, for instance, been mentioned by an eminent Pakistani historian, that during January to March 1940 out of over a hundred newspaper articles appearing in the Indian press, written by the League's sympathizers or supporters, and emphasizing the separateness of Muslims from Hindus, apart from one single exception none suggested Partition or the creation of Pakistan.[118] Much more pertinent and enlightening, is an estimate provided by an extremely shrewd and able observer of the political scene in India, with a moderate approach to politics, though broadly supporting the general Muslim viewpoint. He was Mohammad Zafrullah Khan, at that time Law Member of the Viceroy's Executive Council and his close confidant on matters relating to the Muslims. In a note on the communal problem obviously prepared in the second half of February for submission to the Viceroy, he clearly stated that Muslim public opinion was 'crystallizing more and more' in support of a solution based on the acceptance of the reality that India was 'not one country, but a collection of countries' and that the population of India did not 'consist of one nation but of at least two nations'. He further observed that the scheme that had received 'the largest measure of support from the Muslims' was what he described as 'the scheme of separation' rather than 'the Pakistan scheme'. He made the distinction between the two schemes largely on the basis of his understanding—which was of course wrong—that an exchange of populations formed 'an essential ingredient' of the Pakistan scheme. Actually, there was no essential difference between the two schemes. This becomes even clearer from Zafrullah's descrpiton of the main features of what he chose to call 'the Separation Scheme':

> Briefly the separation scheme is that there should be a North-Eastern Federation consisting of the present Provinces of Bengal and Assam, and a North-Western Federation consisting of the Punjab, Sind, North-West Frontier Province, Baluchistan and the Frontier tribal areas. The rest of India may constitute itself into one Federation or into more Federations than one, as it suits itself. The North-Eastern and North-Western Federations will be in direct relation with the Crown and so will be the Federation or Federations constituted by the rest of India. If Burma can be constituted into a separate Dominion, apart from India, there should be no inherent impossibility or impracticability in setting up the North-Eastern and North-Western Federations.[119]

Another pointer that Muslim public opinion was clearly supportive of the League's proposed adoption of the Pakistan idea came from the Aga Khan, the senior-most leader of Indian Muslims, having been active since the Simla Deputation and the foundation of the Muslim League (1906). Just a few months earlier he had sought to play a moderating role and asserted that the Congress leadership had adopted quite a reasonable attitude towards the demands of the Muslims and if the League leadership adopted a similar attitude and gave up its insistence on the Congress recognizing the League as the representative organization of Muslims, a settlement of the Hindu–Muslim problem might become possible. In early March 1940, however, he made it clear to the Viceroy that he was no longer prepared to play a similar role. On the other hand, he lent his support to the Pakistan idea by asserting that as Muslims constituted a nation by themselves, separate from Hindus, it would be quite unjust to push them under the rule of a central government that was bound to be Hindu-dominated if formed on the basis of Dominion Status.

As the Viceroy reported to the Secretary of State in the second week of March 1940:

> ... The Aga Khan, who, we had some reason to hope, would act as a moderating influence on Jinnah, had, by the time he reached Delhi and as a result of local Muslim contacts, materially changed his ground: and he is now convinced that the Muslims are still a different nation from the Hindus, as they had been at the beginning of the British occupation, and that it was quite unthinkable that we should now contemplate delivering his co-religionists into bondage.[120]

The general Muslim support to the Pakistan idea was, however, tempered by the realization that even after the setting up of an independent Muslim State or States out of the body politic of India, there would be between them and the rest of India many matters of common interest and that some kind of central agencies would be set up for looking after them. This had also been incorporated in Zafrullah's note. In that connection he had actually mentioned, as examples, a customs convention, a postal and telegraph convention, and also a convention to regulate broadcasting and civil aviation. The question of defence could be regulated by treaties between the different dominions. The same applied to the problem of minorities.[121]

Zafrullah had sent a copy of his note to Jinnah and it was his (Zafrullah's) understanding that it was going to be adopted by the Muslim League 'with a view to its being given the fullest publicity. Under the guidance of Jinnah, however, as noted earlier, the League while adopting the demand for the separation of the Muslim-majority areas in the north-west and the north-east from the rest of India, made no mention at all of any of the agencies mentioned in the Zafrullah Plan for looking after matters of common concern between them and the rest of India. It can, of course, be legitimately inferred that the last paragraph of the Lahore Resolution, by authorizing the Working Committee to frame a scheme of constitution according to the basic principles enunciated in the resolution, 'providing for the assumption *finally*, by the respective regions, of all powers such as defence, external affairs, communications, customs and such other matters as may be necessary', accepted by implication the need for their being managed temporarily for some time by certain common agencies, as envisaged in Zafrullah's scheme. By no stretch of the imagination, however, can this be interpreted to mean the nullification of the main objective envisaged in the Lahore Resolution, i.e. Partition. It could only mean that though temporarily some common arrangements could be made to deal with certain matters of common interest, the final goal of a separate sovereign Muslim State or States would remain intact. Yet it is this very term ('finally') that has been used by a well-known Pakistani historian as a major prop of her thesis that Jinnah was not really interested in the creation of Pakistan. The timing of adopting the Pakistan Resolution was, of course, determined by the British imperial needs. However, this is only half the story: for that timing coincided admirally, with Jinnah's own calculations of the interests of the Pakistan movement. He was no one's stooge and always acted on the basis of his own strategic calculations. The Jinnah–Linlithgow Axis was, of course, fully in operation at that time. But it was based purely on a convergence of interests between the two parties, with neither side playing a subordinate role. The second major prop for this thesis is even more difficult to comprehend. For it has been contended that in eliminating all reference to any central agency in the Pakistan Resolution the idea was to create a situation which would force the Congress and the British to make adequate concessions to the League in order to retain a strong Centre. Thus, says Ayesha Jalal, the Lahore Resolution should be viewed as 'a bargaining counter', which 'provided the best insurance that the League would not be given what it now apparently was asking for, but which Jinnah in fact did not really want'.[122] This is a really original but absurd view, based on pure imagination, without the backing of an iota of evidence and flying in the face of all Jinnah's exertions since June–July 1937, devoted to instilling among Indian Muslims the consciousness of separate nationhood by incessantly depicting the Congress as a Hindu organization, whose sole aim was to usher in Hindu Raj all over India and promising Muslims power to shape their own destiny once they became fully imbued with that consciousness.

Viewed in historical perspective, there can be no escape from the conclusion that the Lahore Resolution was neither prompted by pressure from the Viceroy nor did it represent Jinnah's special contrivance to maintain the unity of India, but was the logical culmination of the evolution of Muslim politics in India in modern times. So long as the British seemed to be firmly in the saddle and the end of their rule not all in sight, the objective of that politics was to secure a constitutional system in which Muslims would be somehow or the other saved from being dominated over by Hindus within the framework of British rule. Once the end of that rule began to appear imminent, the thought of many of Muslim leaders, including the most towering among them, Jinnah, turned towards the creation of a separate Muslim State or States based on the Muslim-majority areas of India. This would not solve the problem of Muslims in the areas in which they were in a minority, but it was expected that their interests could be safeguarded by mutual arrangements between the successor States, for just like Muslim minorities in the rest of India there would also be Hindu minorities in the Muslim State or States. This was in fact stated in so many words in the Lahore Resolution itself. As shall be seen in the succeeding chapters, once the goal of separation from the rest of India was adopted by the League, there was no wavering and no second thoughts and the march began on the road to Pakistan under the banner of the Muslim League and the clear-sighted and determined leadership of Jinnah, with rapidly growing support from the people on whose behalf the League claimed to be working and crucial help from the British side at its various turning points.

NOTES

1. All India Congress Committee, *Congress and the War Crisis* (Allahabad, n.d.), pp. 14–19.
2. CAB65, 1, War Cabinet 29(39), 12 (27 September 1939), p. 228, Public Record Office (London).
3. Linlithgow to Zetland, 21 December 1939, MSS Eur. F125/8, Linlithgow Collection, India Office Records (London).
4. Bimal Prasad, *The Origins of Indian Foreign Policy: The Indian National Congress and World Affairs, 1885–1947* (Calcutta, 1962, 2nd edn.), Ibid., pp. 170–1.
5. Ibid.
6. *Speeches and Writings of Mr Jinnah*, Jamiluddin Ahmad, ed., I (Lahore, 1968), pp. 451–2.
7. Linlithgow to Zetland, 27 September 1939, n. 3, Linlithgow Collection.
8. Note of an interview between Linlithgow and Jinnah on 4 September 1939, enclosure to Linlithgow to Zetland, 4 September 1939, ibid.
9. *Indian Annual Register*, 1939, II, p. 99.
10. Quaid-i-Azam Mohammad Ali Jinnah, *The Nation's Voice: Speeches and Statements, March 1935–March 1940*. Waheed Ahmad, ed.,

(Karachi, 1992; hereinafter referred to as *Jinnah: Speeches and Statements*), Appendix XIX, pp. 644–6.

11. Note of an interview between Linlithgow and Jinnah on 5 October 1939, enclosure 2 to Linlithgow to Zetland, 5 October 1939, ibid.
12. Viceroy to Secretary of State, 28 September 1939, MSS Eur. F125/18, Linlithgow Collection.
13. For the texts of the telegrams exchanged between Prasad and Jinnah, see *Jinnah: Speeches and Statements*, n. 10, p. 389.
14. Ibid., pp. 644–5.
15. Ibid., p. 392.
16. Ibid., pp. 395–6.
17. Ibid., p. 403.
18. Ibid., p. 423.
19. Nehru to V.K. Krishna Menon, 6 October 1939, *Selected Works of Jawaharlal Nehru* (hereinafter referred to as *SWJN*), S. Gopal, ed., X (New Delhi, 1977), p. 176.
20. Nehru to Jinnah, 18 October 1939, ibid., p. 359.
21. Prasad to Nehru and Azad, 13 October 1039, Prasad Papers, File XIV/ 40, National Archives of India; reference to these letters may be seen also in *SWJN*, n. 19, p. 188, fn. 2.
22. Nehru to Prasad, 16 October 1939, *SWJN*, X, n. 19, p. 188.
23. Raghunandan Saran to Nehru, 14 October 1939, Jawaharlal Nehru Papers, vol. 84, Nehru Memorial Museum & Library.
24. Nehru to Jinnah, 18 October 1939, *SWJN*, X, n. 19, pp. 359–60.
25. Azad to Jinnah, 16 October 1939, Jinnah Papers, Reel 15, File 17, Quaid-i-Azam Academy (Karachi).
26. Saran to Nehru, 24 October 1939, Nehru Papers, Nehru Memorial Museum & Library.
27. For the text, see *Indian Annual Register*, 1939, II. Linlithgow's view was that his emphasis on differences among the communities and parities in India was not something contrived as a matter of policy but was the result of his actual experience of interviews with their leaders during the weeks preceding 17 October. He informed the Secretary of State a day before that 'this most exhausting series of interviews' had left him with 'a far stronger impression' than he had previously of the 'reality of divergence among the communities'. He further added: 'I had not, possibly, fully realized till now how greatly the gap between Hindu and Muslim has widened since April 1937, or the extent to which experiences, whether real or imaginary, (but beyond any question sincerely believed and zealously propagated) since then have undermined altogether belief in the possibility of common and united action . . .', Linlithgow to Zetland, 16 October 1939, MSS Eur. F125/8, Linlithgow Collection.
28. *Jinnah: Speeches and Statements*, n. 10, p. 646.

29. Jinnah to Linlithgow, 23 October 1939, MSS Eur. F125/121, Linlithgow Collection.
30. Jinnah to Zetland, 23 October 1939, MSS Eur. F125/8, Linlithgow Collection.
31. Viceroy to Secretary of State, 26 October 1939 (telegram No. 2416-S) MSS. Eur. F125/18, Linlithgow Collection. Jinnah's interview to the *Manchester Guardian* was also published in *Civil and Military Gazette* (Lahore) on 26 October 1939; text reproduced in *Jinnah: Speeches and Statements*, n. 10, pp. 399–400.
32. D.G. Tendulkar, *Mahatma*, V (Bombay, 1962), pp. 193–4; see also *Indian Annual Register*, 1939, II, pp. 69–70.
33. S. Gopal, *Jawaharlal Nehru: A Biography*, I (London, 1975), p. 258.
34. Statement by the Viceroy to Messrs. M.K. Gandhi, Rajendra Prasad and M.A. Jinnah at a meeting at the Viceroy's House, 1 November 1939, enclosure 2 from Linlithgow to Zetland, 2 November 1939, MSS Eur. F125/8. Linlithgow Collection. See also the text of the letter sent by the Viceroy to Gandhi, Prasad and Jinnah on 2 November 1939 in Viceroy to Secretary of State, 2 November 1939, Telegram R, 250-S, 2 November 1939, MSS Eur. F125/18, Linlithgow collection.
35. Full text in Viceroy to Secretary of State, Telegram R.2539-S, 3 November 1939, MSS Eur. F125/18, Linlithgow Collection.
36. Note of Interview between the Viceroy and Messrs. Gandhi and Rajendra Prasad, and Jinnah at the Viceroy's House, New Delhi, on 1 November 1939, enclosure 1, Linlithgow to Zetland, 2 November 1939, MSS Eur. F125/8, Linlithgow Collection.
37. Linlithgow to Zetland, 6 November 1939, ibid.
38. *Jinnah: Speeches and Statements*, n. 10, p. 424.
39. Viceroy to Secretary of State, TXX, 16 January 1940, F125/19, Linlithgow Collection. See also Linlithgow to Zetland, 13 January 1940, F125/9, ibid.
40. Lumley to Linlithgow, 25 November 1939, F125/53, ibid.
41. See Nehru to Krishna Menon, 21 December 1939, *SWJN*, vol. X, n. 19, p. 413.
42. Ibid., p. 414.
43. Nehru to Jinnah, 1 December 1939, *SWJN*, vol. X, n. 19, p. 380.
44. Jinnah to Nehru, 4 December 1939, *Jinnah: Speeches and Writings*, n. 10, p. 434.
45. Ibid., p. 435.
46. Nehru's letter to Jinnah dated 7 December 1939 is not available, but there is reference to it in his next letter to Jinnah dated 9 December 1939. See *SWJN*, vol. X, n. 10, p. 390.
47. *Jinnah: Speeches and Statements*, n. 10, p. 417.
48. Patel to Nehru, 7 December 1939, Jawaharlal Nehru Papers, NMML.
49. Patel to Nehru, 9 December 1939, ibid.

50. Prasad to Nehru, 10 December 1939, Jawaharlal Nehru Papers.
51. See P.S. to above (n. 50), ibid.
52. Nehru to Jinnah, 9 December 1939, *SWJN*, vol. X, n. 19, pp. 390–1.
53. Jinnah to Nehru, 13 December 1939, *Jinnah: Speeches and Statements*, n. 10, p. 435.
54. Nehru to Jinnah, 14 December 1939, *SWJN*, vol. X, n. 19, pp. 399–401.
55. Jinnah to Nehru, 15 December 1938, *Jinnah: Speeches and Statements*, n. 10, p. 437.
56. Nehru to Jinnah, 16 December 1939, *SWJN*, vol. X, n. 19, pp. 410–11.
57. Ibid., p. 403.
58. *Quarterly Survey*, no. 10 (1.11.39-31.1.40), p. 31, MSS Eur. F125/143, Linlithgow Collection. It may be pointed out here that among the League leaders who privately disapproved of Jinnah's appeal for celebration, the most prominent was Sikander, who told the Punjab Governor that he treated it as 'a very grave' tactical error. He also told the Governor that Jinnah had issued the appeal 'entirely on his own'—the only person he took into his confidence was Liaquat Ali Khan, General Secretary of the All-India Muslim League. See Craik to Linlithgow, 15 December 1939, F125/. Linlithgow Collection.
59. *Jinnah: Speeches and Statements*, n. 10, pp. 420–4.
60. Ibid., p. 428.
61. Ibid., p. 431.
62. *Quarterly Survey*, no. 10, n. 58, p. 31.
63. Ibid. Nehru was most unhappy at Ambedkar's support for Jinnah on the issue of Congress misrule in the provinces. 'Ambedkar has lined up with Jinnah,' he wrote to Krishna Menon on 21 December 1939, 'and issued a statement which for its impudence and falsity beats even Jinnah's. If there is one thing that the Congress Governments have concentrated upon, it is in giving relief to the depressed classes.' See *SWJN*, vol. X, n. 19, p. 414.
64. Maurice Hallett to Linlithgow, 1 January 1940, F125/103, Linlithgow Collection.
65. Viceroy to Secretary of State, Telegram XX, no. 2536-S, 3 November 1939, F125/18. ibid.
66. Linlithgow to Zetland, 18 November 1939, F12228/8, ibid.
67. Ibid.
68. Note of an Interview between Linlithgow and Jinnah on 4 November 1939, enclosure to Linlithgow to Zetland, 6 November 1939, F125/ 8, ibid.
69. Ibid.
70. Linlithgow to Zetland, 6 November 1939, ibid.
71. Linlithgow to Zetland, 18 November 1939, ibid.
72. Linlithgow to Zetland, 27 November 1939, ibid.

73. Sir Reginald Maxwell to Sir Gilbert Laithwaite (Private Secretary to the Viceroy), 20 November 1939, reproduced in Linlithgow to Zetland, 28 November 1939, F125/8, ibid.
74. Linlithgow to Zetland, 28 November 1939, ibid.
75. Haig to Linlithgow, 4 December 1939, F125/102, ibid.
76. Linlithgow to Jinnah, 23 December 1939, F125/121, ibid.
77. Viceroy to Secretary of State, Telegram R, no. 195-S, 6 February 1940, F125/20, ibid.
78. Linlithgow to Zetland, 13 November 1939, F125/8 ibid.
79. Note of an Interview between Private Secretary to the Viceroy and G.D. Birla on 29 November 1939, F125/8, ibid.
80. Note of an Interview between Private Secretary to the Viceroy and G.D. Birla on 8 December 1939; IOR, L/P&J/8/506B
81. Secretary of State to Viceroy, Telegrams no. 895 and no. 896, 16 November 1939, F125/18, Linlithgow Collection.
82. Viceroy to Secretary of State, Telegram XX, 18 November 1939, ibid.
83. Viceroy to Secretary of State, Telegram XX, no. 2673-S, 18 November 1939, ibid.
84. Viceroy to Secretary of State, Telegram R., no. 2798-S, 8 December 1939, ibid. See also Gowher Rizvi, *Linlithgow and India: A Study of British Policy and the Political Impasse in India 1936–43* (London, 1978), pp. 114–15.
85. Note of an Interview between Linlithgow and Jinnah on 13 January 1940, enclosure to Linlithgow to Zetland, 13 January 1940, F125/9, Linlithgow Collection.
86. Note of a conversation between Linlithgow and Sikander on 25 January 1940, L/P&J/8/506B, Private Office Papers, India Office Library & Records.
87. Note of a conversation between Linlithgow and Sikander and Fazlul Huq, 3 February 1940, enclosure to Linlithgow to Zetland, 6 February 1940, F125/9, Linlithgow Collection.
88. Choudhary Khaliquzzaman, *Pathway to Pakistan* (London, 1961).
89. Linlithgow to Hallett, 28 February 1940, F125/103, Linlithgow Collection.
90. Viceroy to Secretary of State, Telegram XX, 3 February 1940, L/P&J/506B, Private Office Papers, India Office Library; also F125/19, Linlithgow Collection.
91. For instance, by Khaliquzzaman, n. 88, p. 234.
92. Note of an Interview between Linlithgow and Jinnah on 6 February 1940, enclosure 3, Linlithgow to Zetland, 6 February 1940, F125/9, Linlithgow Collection.
93. Hallett to Linlithgow, 16 February 1940, F125/103, ibid.
94. Hallett to Linlithgow, 17 February 1940, F125/103, ibid.
95. Linlithgow to Hallett, 28 February 1940, ibid.

96. Note of a conversation between Linlithgow and Jinnah on 13 March 1940, enclosure, Linlithgow to Zetland, 16 March 1940, F125/9, ibid. For a summary of this talk, see Viceroy to Secretary of State, Telegram XX, no. 161- SC, 16 March 1940, F125/19, ibid.
97. Note of a conversation between Jinnah and the Governor of Bombay, 12 January 1940, enclosure, Sir Roger Lumley to Linlithgow, 12 January 1940, F125.54, ibid.
98. Note of an Interview between Linlithgow and Jinnah on 13 January 1940, n. 85.
99. Note of an Interview between Linlithgow and Jinnah on 6 January 1940, n. 92. Jinnah obviously did not notice the irony involved in his reference to Willingdon, an ex-Viceroy, as a model to be followed by Linlithgow in dealing with the Congress; it was Jinnah's courage in standing up to Willingdon when he was Governor of Bombay that had won him great renown and turned him into a hero of the patriotic section of the Indian intelligentsia.
100. Jinnah to Linlithgow, 24 February 1940, F125/122, Linlithgow Collection.
101. *Jinnah: Speeches and Statements*, n. 10, pp. 399–400.
102. *Collected Works of Mahatma Gandhi*, LXXI (New Delhi, 1978), pp. 109–10.
103. Gandhi to Jinnah, 16 January 1940, ibid., pp. 117–18.
104. Jinnah to Gandhi, 21 January 1940.
105. For the text of Jinnah's article in *Time and Tide* see *Jinnah: Speeches and Statements*, no. 10, pp. 473–9.
106. K.K. Aziz, ed., *Prelude to Pakistan, 1930–1940: Documents and Readings Illustrating the Growth of the Idea of Pakistan*, vol. II (Lahore, 1992), p. 867.
107. K.K. Aziz, *A History of the Idea of Pakistan*, vol. III (Lahore, 1987), p. 641.
108. Ibid., vol. II, pp. 604–5.
109. Sir Haji Abdullah Haroon to the Honorary Secretary, All-India Muslim League, 2 February 1940, reel 7, file 96, Quaid-i-Azam Papers. Haroon also released the recommendations to the press. See *Jinnah: Speeches and Statements*, no. 10, pp. 449–50.
110. Enclosure, Honorary Secretary, All-India Muslim League, to Sir Sikander Hyat Khan, 13 March 1940, vol. 207 (Annual Session at Lahore, Part III, pp. 19–20), Muslim League Papers, Freedom Movement Archives, University of Karachi. Also reproduced in *Jinnah: Speeches and Statements*, no. 10, Appendix XIX, p. 651.
111. *Jinnah: Speeches and Statements*, no. 10, p. 466.
112. Ibid., p. 470.
113. Ibid., p. 472.
114. Ibid., p. 482.

115. Ibid., pp. 493–5.
116. Although 23 March is currently accepted by almost all scholars in Pakistan, India, and elsewhere as well as the Government of Pakistan (which celebrates Pakistan's National Day on that date), the resolution was actually adopted on 24 March 1940. See Aziz, n. 109, pp. 652–3.
117. For the full text of the resolution see Syed Sharifuddin Pirzada, *The Foundation of Pakistan.*
118. Aziz, no. 109, p. 645.
119. 'Note by Sir Muhammad Zafrullah, analysing the present situation from the extremer Muslim Point of View', Enclosure (1), Laithwaite to M.J. Clauson, 6 March 1940, MSS Eur. F128/35, India Office Library.
120. Viceroy to Secretary of State, Telegram XX, 9 March 1940, F125/19, Linlithgow Collection.
121. Note by Zafrullah, n. 119.
122. Ayesha Jalal, *The Sole Spokesman: Jinnah, the Muslim League and the Demand for Pakistan* (Cambridge, 1985), pp. 56–7.

CHAPTER IV

Legitimation of the Pakistan Demand 1940–1942

THE ADOPTION OF THE Pakistan Resolution by the Lahore session of the League on 24 March 1940, under Jinnah's guidance, marked the beginning of a new era in Indian politics. It is, of course, a fact that the idea of Partition or Pakistan had not burst upon the Indian political scene all of a sudden at Lahore, but had been in the air for quite some time before the Lahore session—indeed, for almost two decades. However, its formal adoption by that session gave an entirely new footing to that idea. For the League was not an ordinary political party, but had for long been generally recognized as the representative organization of Indian Muslims and had in recent years emerged much stronger than ever before, with more and more branches and members in all parts of the country. Besides, Jinnah too had by that time emerged as the most popular and powerful leader of the Muslim community.

Ironically, the very fact that Jinnah had been the prime mover behind the Pakistan Resolution partly accounted for the fact that the resolution was not taken seriously by many of his contemporaries. The old image of Jinnah as an Indian patriot, who even while leading the Muslim League had always seemed keen to build bridges between it and the Congress, had not yet vanished from people's memory and they could not imagine that he really intended to divide the country into two. Besides, the idea of Partition appeared to many as quite impractical, indeed absurd, and they could not imagine that Jinnah, known for his shrewdness and practical wisdom, could be serious about it. It was, therefore, widely assumed that it represented merely a bargaining counter for him to be utilized to secure more concessions for Muslims than might otherwise be possible at the time of framing the new Indian constitution. The not so veiled opposition of Sikander Hyat Khan, the most prominent League leader after Jinnah and holding an extremely important strategic position as the Premier of the Punjab, potentially the key province of the future Pakistan, lent further credence to such a view. Even Jinnah was reported to have told some persons, who expressed shock at the adoption of the Pakistan Resolution by the League's session, that it was just 'a tactical move'.[1] Such reports naturally confirmed the belief of many persons in the 'bargaining counter' theory.

Regardless of the veracity of such reports and the soundness or otherwise of the view based upon them, the fact remains that all contemporary evidence available to an unbiased student of history today leads to only one conclusion, namely, that whatever the beliefs or views of others, Jinnah was dead serious about the Pakistan Resolution and never missed a single opportunity after March 1940 to underline its importance as having set the goal for which, in his opinion, all Indian Muslims were expected to work to the best of their ability and strength. On the way to that goal some compromises could be accepted, but without losing sight of the ultimate objective and certainly not at its cost. The great liberal leader, Tej Bahadur Sapru, generally regarded as a seasoned observer of the Indian political scene and not at all given to hyperbole, recognized Jinnah's strong commitment to the new goal as early as December 1940. Although at first he, too, was influenced by the general view that the Lahore Resolution was merely meant for bargaining purposes,[2] after further reflection he soon changed his estimate, 'So far as Jinnah is concerned,' he wrote to one of his eminent Muslim contemporaries, 'Pakistan is now the ruling passion of his life.'[3]

The accuracy of Sapru's assessment is very well brought out by the fact that in the months and years immediately following the League's adoption of the Pakistan Resolution, Jinnah devoted himself most assiduously to the legitimation of the Pakistan demand. The greatest source of such legitimation was, of course, the growing support for that demand among the Muslim masses as well as intelligentsia as also the growing popularity of Jinnah among them. The two went hand in hand. For Jinnah now emerged as not only the mass leader of Muslims, but also as a symbol of the demand for Pakistan. Indeed, he soon acquired the position of a charismatic leader and began to be called the Quaid-i-Azam or the Great Leader, the key to this denouement being the strong emotional appeal of the Pakistan demand among the Muslim masses as well as intelligentsia. It touched the hearts of most of the members of the Muslim society in a way in which no other demand or slogan had ever done before. For the members of the Muslim middle class it opened up the prospect of unlimited opportunities in government and business free from competition with the more numerous as well as more resourceful Hindus. For the Muslim masses it unfolded the prospect of a State where Islam would hold sway; and for them no sacrifice was too great for the cause of Islam. It can indeed be said that while Jinnah did all he could to make the Pakistan demand popular among the Muslim masses that demand also added immensely to his popularity among those masses and enabled him to strengthen beyond measure his grip over the Muslim League.

Reports from various quarters highlighted this fact even while generally treating the Pakistan demand as highly impractical and merely a bargaining counter. Thus, characterizing the Lahore session of the League as 'a personal triumph for Jinnah', the confidential official survey of political developments in India reported that his popularity and reputation had 'never stood so high as they did after the session'.[4] The Punjab Governor, Sir Henry Craik, expressed a similar view and thought that Jinnah's personal prestige had greatly risen as a result of that session: 'His position as the one all-India Muslim leader is now unchallenged, and in practice he alone is in a position to dictate the League's policy.'[5] Few, however, were disposed at that stage to take the League's demand for Partition seriously. It was, of course, generally recognized that it indicated a considerable widening of the gulf between the Congress and the Muslim League and that the hope of a settlement between them had further eroded, if not completely evaporated. 'The League,' observed Nehru within three weeks of the adoption of the Pakistan Resolution, 'is not interested in the Indian nation, but in something else and there can be no common meeting ground between the Congress and the League.' He indeed welcomed the League's latest stand, for it had removed misunderstandings from many minds and shown up the League leadership 'in its true colours'.[6]

Few regarded Partition as a proposition worthy of any serious consideration. Nehru, of course, described it as a 'mad scheme'.[7] But even those generally well disposed to both Jinnah and the League were inclined to consider it as 'little more than a counter-blast' against the Congress.[8] The Governor of Bihar regarded it as 'unthinkable except in terms of civil war.'[9] Linlithgow, while emphasizing that the rank and file of the Muslim League were being increasingly drawn towards the demand for Partition, acknowledged that he did not take Jinnah's new demand 'too seriously' and thought that this was the result of the latter's anxiety 'to dispose of the suggestion that Muslims had no policy, and to do so by putting forward a claim as extreme and probably in practice as unlikely of realization as that advanced by Congress.'[10] He was, therefore, disposed to regard the demand for Partition as 'very largely in the nature of bargaining'.[11] Even some pro-League Muslims, particularly in the minority provinces were reported to feel the same way. The best that any Muslim had said about it, reported the Governor of Bombay, was that Jinnah could not mean it and was 'using it only as a bargaining weapon'. Indeed, among the Muslims in Bombay the general feeling was one of dismay as they saw little in the Pakistan Resolution that would bring advantage to them.[12] Among the contemporary reports, only one, that by the Chief Secretary of UP, R.F. Mudie, after talking to two Muslim League leaders in UP, hazarded the view that it was 'more than a bargaining move'. Although admitting that it had been adopted at that time because it was necessary to put forward an alternative to the Congress demand, he felt that it was not likely to be lightly dropped and in any case should not be underestimated.[13] There is no doubt that Mudie was nearer the truth than many others. Perhaps his being in touch with the UP League leaders, who were at that stage, apart from Jinnah himself, the most ardent supporters of the demand for Partition, enabled him better to realize the seriousness of the Muslim urge for a separate State.

II

The widespread notion that the demand for Partition was merely a bargaining counter shows the nature of the task faced by Jinnah, who worked for its legitimation with single-minded zeal and devotion. He had been drawn towards this since as early as

1937, if not earlier, and had got it adopted by the League only when he became convinced that changes in Indian politics since 1937, and more particularly since 1939, had brought it within the realm of practical politics. All the leaders of the League, however, were not equally enthusiastic or serious about that objective. When the contents of the resolution to be placed before the Lahore session were under discussion, Sikander had tried to secure the acceptance of a draft that provided for a central government for the whole of India in some form or the other. Even after the Lahore Resolution had been adopted, his heart was not in it and, according to the Punjab Governor, he did not consider Partition a practicable proposition.[14] A senior British official who met him a few weeks after the Lahore session found him 'very perturbed' at the adoption of the Pakistan Resolution.[15] Although Fazlul Huq had actually moved the resolution on Partition at the Lahore session, he was also at heart not very enthusiastic about it. Sikander and Huq—both interested in joining the Viceroy's Executive Council—showed great keenness in openly supporting the war effort and had a tendency to look up to Linlithgow as their guide and mentor. This brought them in to frequent clashes with Jinnah over the tactics to be adopted in dealing with the Government. Sikander was also working off and on for some understanding with the Congress, much to the dislike of Jinnah and often involving his defiance. While the leaders of the League in UP were generally firm in their support to Jinnah on the Pakistan issue, they also chafed under his restrictions on displaying open support to the war effort and, besides, were not disinterested in reaching an understanding with the Congress, if that could lead to a sharing of power. This cleavage in the leadership—not at all a secret—was a major source of embarrassment for Jinnah.

An idea of how serious this cleavage was right on the morrow of the Lahore session can be had from the following picture of the League's leadership drawn up in a confidential official survey of political events during the quarter May to July 1940:

> During the quarter Jinnah's influence and authority, which were at their highest after the Lahore session in March, have somewhat declined; the Premiers of Bengal and the Punjab have been openly impatient of his leadership, and at times a split in the League has appeared imminent. The League may now be described as waiting to see the outcome of the

Viceroy's conversation with the party leaders. Though Jinnah is the League's plenipotentiary for that purpose, he is suspected by the malcontents of playing his hand in a manner more conducive to his own predominance than to the best interests of the League.[16]

As for the state of the Muslim League organization, the situation as late as the end of June 1940 is described in the following extract from a letter to Jinnah written by the person in charge of its central office at that time:

> The activities of the League are at present at the lowest ebb. The central provinces are in suspense [suspension?]. In the UP the state of affairs has been going from bad to worse. The Provincial League is seething with internal dissensions. The districts are entirely neglected. In most of them there is no League at all except on paper. In Bihar, recently there has been a terrible communal riot in which the Musalmans have suffered very heavily. As for the majority provinces there is no appreciable change in their attitude except in case of Sind. The Central Office, which is responsible to keep the subordinate Leagues active, is equally indifferent. It is very ominous that the Secretary (Nawabzada Liaquat Ali Khan) does not know what is going on around him, and even under his very nose.[17]

On the other hand, the Azad Muslim Conference, held in April 1940 on the basis of opposition to Partition, attracted a sizeable crowd, though, of course, not comparable to the attendance (100,000 persons) at the Lahore session of the League. Even if the estimate of attendance in it by the pro-Congress press (75,000) is discarded and that of the Government (25,000)[18] accepted, it was by no means a negligible number. As the confidential official survey of political events put it, 'a Muslim Conference so numerically attended as this is an interesting challenge to the pretensions of the League'.[19]

In such a situation it was not an easy task to impart credibility to the new objective of the League. It was clear to all concerned that it was going to be an uphill task to carve a separate State (or States) out of India on the basis of Muslim nationhood. Although dominant in certain well-marked areas, the Muslims were scattered in almost all parts of India and had developed all kinds of affinities with their surroundings. It was obvious that all of them could not be transplanted to the new State, nor was it so intended by the Pakistan Resolution. On the other hand, the areas where the Muslims were in a majority contained substantial numbers of Hindus and others. If the Muslims would not allow the Hindu majority to decide the fate of the country, how could the Hindus in Muslim-majority areas allow the Muslims to decide their future and that too involving the Partition of the motherland and the separation from their kith and kin. It was also evident that Partition would involve the division also of Muslims living in India. Thus though the appeal of an independent Muslim State was certainly strong due to various historical, cultural, economic, and political factors, the difficulties involved in its creation were also evident. It was also clear that the Congress with all its strength and resources, acquired through decades of struggle and suffering, was determined to oppose it. The British attitude was not so clear, for they had encouraged divisive forces in Indian politics in the past and could be relied upon to do so in the future also, but it was not certain whether they would go to such an extent in that direction as to countenance the division of the country itself which they had, in their own interest, done so much to unify—an achievement in which they had been taking considerable pride. Above all, there was the question of whether the League as an organization was fit enough to face these difficulties. The first thing necessary, therefore, in the struggle for the creation of Pakistan, was the acquisition of legitimacy and credibility, both for the goal and the organization which was to work for the achievement of that goal. It had to be shown that the objective declared at Lahore was seriously meant to be so and had not been put forward as a mere bargaining counter. Further, that it was a practicable proposition and that the League was capable enough to achieve it.

If the League came out successful in this battle for legitimacy and credibility, it was to a great extent due to Jinnah's leadership. There were, of course, several other factors that helped, but it was Jinnah who realized their importance and deftly exploited them in order to achieve the League's new objective. Once the decision to demand Partition was made he never looked back. Since he was fully convinced of the correctness of the decision, he could also impart this conviction to others, particularly to the Muslim youth to whom he appealed more and more. Indeed, he never missed a single opportunity to show that he was deeply committed to and determined to work for Pakistan and for nothing else. All other, smaller objectives had to be supported or opposed primarily from the point of view of their relationship with that supreme objective, the achievement of Pakistan. With the same end in view, the activities of some other prominent League leaders, who were interested in short-term gains of various kinds and not in the achievement of the supreme objective, if they actually did not dislike it, had to be curbed and not allowed to cast doubt on the credibility of the supreme objective. They had, of course, to be handled with care for their presence in the League was a source of strength, but if their activities clearly clashed with the work for the main objective, they had to be shown the door. While not dislodging the old leaders from their positions, Jinnah went on encouraging new, younger leaders to come forward and work for the new objective. They were a great help to him in keeping the old leaders in order or disciplining them when required. Similarly, relations with the British had to be conducted with great delicacy. British policy had been a source of help to the League in the past and could be so in the future also. In any case, the British had considerable influence on large sections of the League's leadership and could create problems for Jinnah if that suited their interests. On the other hand, their cooperation could not merely be a help in consolidating Jinnah's leadership, but also in lending credibility to the League's new objective. At the same time, a certain distance and independence had also to be maintained from them. For the Leagues had to establish its hold over the Muslim masses and the youth in a period when the struggle for India's freedom was well advanced. The Congress was known for its suffering and sacrifice for that cause. In such a situation it would not be helpful for the League to appear as a camp follower of the British, however helpful they might be. The League must appear as patriotic and strong willed in standing up to the British as any other organization and should not appear as an underling.

Thus within a week of the adoption of the Pakistan Resolution Jinnah issued a long statement to the press seeking the support of Hindus as well as Muslims for it. Therein he expressed the hope that at least 'the better mind of the Hindus' would give earnest and serious consideration to it as that would ensure the achievement of India's freedom at the earliest. At the same time, he sought to end the misgivings of Muslims living in provinces where they were a minority. Decrying the propaganda that the latter would have to migrate *en bloc* to the Muslim-majority areas at the time of the creation of Pakistan, he pointed out that once that stage arrived the exchange of population 'to the extent practicable', would have to be considered. However, even if this was not found feasible, Muslims in minority provinces would not be better off in any way without the creation of Pakistan. For they would continue to be a minority whether Pakistan was created or not. Keeping this in mind, they had to consider whether it was in their interest to come in the way of the creation of Pakistan which would ensure that at least two-thirds of the Muslim population in India would be free from Hindu domination and be able to shape their destiny according to their own traditions and interests. As Jinnah put it:

> The question for the Muslim minorities in the Hindu India is whether the entire Muslim India of 9 crore Muslims should be subjected to a Hindu majority *raj*, or whether at least the 6 crore of the Muslims residing in the areas where they form a majority should have their own homeland and thereby have an opportunity to develop their spiritual, cultural, economic and political life in accordance with their own genius and shape their own future destiny, at the same time allowing Hindus and others to do likewise. Similar will be the condition of the Hindus and other minorities in the Muslim homelands.

Jinnah also took the opportunity to assure the members of the Sikh community in the Punjab that they would be much better off in 'the north-west Muslim zone' than within a united India or under one central government for the whole country. 'It is obvious,' he pointed out, 'that whereas in a united India they would be mere nobodies, in the Muslim homeland . . . the Sikhs would always occupy an honoured place and would play an effective and influential role.' He also assured the Indian states that if those of them that lay in the Western Zone—Kashmir, Bahawalpur, Patiala, etc.—willingly agreed to join 'the federation of Muslim homelands', the League would be glad to come to 'a reasonable and honourable settlement' with them.

Turning to the criticism of the Pakistan demand by the Congress leadership, Jinnah observed that the set of criticisms emanating from Congressite Muslims, who were 'speaking in their "master's voice"' need not worry anyone. He also brushed aside the criticisms of some other Congress leaders as 'a parrot-like cry and thoughtless'. The only criticism he took seriously was the one offered by C. Rajagopalachari, a member of the Congress Working Committee and a former Premier of Madras. The latter had in his statement, published in the newspapers on 30 March 1940, drawn attention to the fact that not even such Muslim rulers as Hyder Ali, Tipu Sultan, Akbar, and Aurangzeb, 'all of whom lived during days when differences should have seemed more deep-rooted than now, imagined that India was anything but one and indivisible'. He had also proceeded to describe the plea to Partition India as the product of a 'diseased mentality'. Replying to this Jinnah observed that the old Muslim rulers had adopted the attitude that they did as 'conquerors and paternal rulers' and asked: 'Is this the kind of government Mr Rajagopalacharier does still envisage, and did the Hindus of those days willingly accept the rule of these 'great men'? He further added: 'I may or may not be suffering from a diseased mentality, but the statement of Mr Rajagopalacharier and his criticisms of the Lahore resolution indicate that in him there is no mind at all.'[20]

Exuding similar confidence in the soundness of the Pakistan scheme and faith in the final victory of the League in securing it, regardless of the difficulties visible at that stage, Jinnah observed in the course of his message to the Bombay Presidency Muslim League Conference held at Hubli on 26 and 27 March 1940:

> The All India Muslim League has given the Musalmans of India a correct lead. It has given them a flag, a platform, a policy and a well-considered programme, and finally it has defined the ideal and the true goal for Muslim India by its resolution at Lahore last March to fight for and achieve at any sacrifice, for therein lies their true salvation. I am asked, will the British agree to the basic and fundamental principles of the Lahore resolution, namely, the creation of independent Muslim States in the north-western and eastern zones of India? Whether they agree or whether they do not, we shall fight for it to the last ditch.[21]

Addressing the Delhi Muslim Students Federation on 24 November 1940, Jinnah reiterated his faith in the victory of the League in securing Pakistan and made it clear that the demand for it had not been made as a bargaining counter. This is what he said:

> The Hindus must give up their dream of a Hindu Raj and agree to divide India into Hindu homeland and Muslim homeland. Today we are prepared to take only one-fourth of India and leave three-fourth to them. If they continue to bargain, they may not be able to have this

three-fourth. 'Pakistan' is our goal today for which the Muslims of India will live for and if necessary die for. It is not a counter for bargaining'.[22]

Jinnah also pointed out that the Hindu–Muslim problem could not be solved by offering allurements of office or power to the League leaders. Addressing the students of the Arabic College in New Delhi on 3 December 1940, he observed:

Congress leaders say that they are willing to make Mr Jinnah or any Muslim League nominee the Prime Minister of India. They say: 'Let Muslims have all the power. We do not want power. We are ready to accept Muslim rule rather than British rule.' Can any man with a grain of sense believe this? No, the Musalmans have grown up. They are different, totally, fundamentally, radically different from what they were three years ago, and I am as sure as I am standing here that five years hence they will be more different still.[23]

Further, Jinnah took pains to clarify that there was no difference between the Lahore resolution and the Pakistan demand. Referring to some other speakers who had preceded him at a public meeting in Karachi on 23 December 1940 who had mentioned that the word 'Pakistan' did not occur in the Lahore Resolution, Jinnah observed: 'The Lahore resolution embodies a principle which is popularly known as Pakistan and therefore there is no difference between the two.'[24] Four days later in the course of a speech at Ahmedabad, he observed that Pakistan had existed for ages. The homelands of Muslims were located in the north-western and the eastern parts of India, where Muslims constituted 70 per cent of the total population. The League wanted that those regions should be constituted into independent Muslim States so that Muslims there could lead their lives in consonance with their religion, culture, and laws. 'Let us in the minority provinces,' he added, 'face our fate, but free the Muslim majority provinces to live and form their own governments in independent States in accordance with Islamic laws.'[25] In an interview to a London newspaper on 30 December 1940, Jinnah again emphasized that the Pakistan Resolution was not a bargaining counter, but 'a deliberated and determined demand on behalf of Muslim India' and had become 'an article of faith with 99 per cent of Muslim India'. He added: 'We claim the right of self-determination and are ready and willing to go through any reasonable test to get the verdict by plebiscite.'[26]

In a statement to the press on 18 February 1941, Jinnah again clarified that the Lahore Resolution and Pakistan meant the same thing. 'Some confusion,' he observed, 'prevails in the minds of some individuals in regard to the use of the word "Pakistan". This word has become synonymous with the Lahore resolution owing to the fact that it is a convenient and compendious method of describing the Lahore resolution. . . .'[27] Addressing the meeting of the Council of the All-India Muslim League held in New Delhi on 23 February 1941, Jinnah again asserted that the Lahore Resolution represented the only solution of the constitutional problem in India and its implementation would serve the interests of all concerned. In any case, the League would not accept any concession by the British Government at the cost of any of the fundamental principles on which that resolution was based.[28]

In his presidential address to the special Pakistan session of the Punjab Muslim Students Federation at Lahore on 2 March 1941, Jinnah again went into the fundamentals of the two-nation theory and declared:

> It is now more than a thousand years that the bulk of the Muslims have lived in a different world, in a different society, in a different philosophy and a different faith. Can you possibly compare this with that nonsensical talk that mere change of faith is no ground for a demand for Pakistan? Can't you see the fundamental difference? Now, therefore, I do not think really that any honest man can possibly dispute the fact that the Muslims are a nation by themselves, distinctly separate from the Hindus.

In this speech Jinnah also ridiculed the argument advanced by a section of the Indian nationalist and Hindu press that the creation of Pakistan would pose a threat to India's security. 'My dear friends,' he asked the Hindus, 'you will be at least 200 million Hindus in India, if not more, and the poor Muslims in the northwest zone and the eastern zone will not be more than 70 millions. Are you afraid . . . that these 70 millions will run over the whole of the country?' If this was true, Jinnah further asked, how would India's security be safeguarded in a united India with all the 90 million Muslims remaining inside India?[29]

These ideas were re-echoed by Jinnah in more emphatic terms in the course of his address to the students of the Aligarh Muslim University on 10 March 1941. 'What I have done,' he declared at the outset, with obvious reference to the adoption of the Pakistan Resolution at Lahore, 'is to declare boldly what was stirring in the heart of Muslim India.' Explaining the rationale behind that resolution, he recalled his repeated assertions in the past that the democratic, parliamentary form of government was entirely unsuited to India. For in India Hindus and Muslims differed in everything that was 'fundamental and essential to life' and it was 'no use shutting one's eyes to realities'. It was these considerations that led to the passing of the Lahore Resolution advocating 'the establishment of independent sovereign States in regions of Muslim-majority, namely the north-west and the north-east of India'. According to Jinnah, it did not 'require a great genius or a great constitutionalist to understand the scheme of Partition'. Under it two-thirds of India would pass into the hands of Hindus and one-third to Muslims. The Hindus, Jinnah emphasized, should be content with their share; they could never have the whole of India. Turning to the Hindu argument of the danger of a security threat to India if Pakistan became a reality, Jinnah repeated what he had said at Lahore a few days back. He also drew attention to the fact that contrary to the contention of some Hindus India had not been invaded only by land through the north-west and asked how the European powers had conquered India. Besides, air power had by then emerged as the most important factor in defence. The solution of the subcontinent's security problem, therefore, lay not in the denial of the Pakistan demand, but in Hindus and Muslims living as good neighbours and cooperating with each other in the defence of the subcontinent. In the end came Jinnah's stirring exhortation to the students of Aligarh, in the name of Islam, to play their due role in the struggle for Pakistan:

> Pakistan is not only a practical goal but the only goal if you want to save Islam from complete annihilation in this country. We have yet to go a long way. . . . The realization of Pakistan is in the actual theatre of war but a sort of war is going on even in India. I appeal to you: prepare yourselves and be ready for any emergency which may arise. Aligarh is the arsenal of Muslim India and you are its best soldiers. Go to the countryside. Educate our people and uplift them. Explain to our people what is our goal. There are many who are trying to mislead them. Let them understand things and then they will march on to their destined goal.[30]

The next annual session of the League held at Madras in April 1941 reaffirmed in clear terms the goal adopted by the previous session at Lahore in March 1940. The tone was set by Jinnah in the course of his presidential address on 14 April. Mentioning some of the notable achievements of the League in the recent past, he declared:

> We have established a flag of our own, a national flag of Muslim India. We have established a remarkable platform which displays and demonstrates a complete unity of the entire solid body of Muslim India. We have defined, in the clearest language, our goal about which Muslim India was groping in the dark and the goal is Pakistan.

Elucidating this goal, Jinnah observed that the League wanted 'the establishment of completely independent States in the north-western and eastern zones of India with full control of the defence, foreign affairs, communication, customs, currency, exchange, etc.'. In order apparently to clear all possible confusion on that point, Jinnah further stated that the League did not want a constitution with an all-India character with one government at the centre. He also took the opportunity to reaffirm the ideology of the League. 'And now let me say,' he observed, 'that the ideology of the League is based on the fundamental principle that Muslims of India are an independent nationality, and any attempt to get them to merge their national and political identity and unity will not only be resisted, but in my opinion it will be futile for anyone to attempt it.'[31]

The Madras session of the League further marked a reaffirmation of the Lahore Resolution by amending the League's constitution on the lines of the latter. Through its resolution II, the aims and objective of the League were now amended so as to include the following:

> (1) the establishment of completely Independent States formed by demarcating geographically contiguous units into regions which shall be so constituted, with such territorial readjustments as may be necessary, that the areas in which the Mussalmans are numerically in a majority, as in the North-Western and Eastern zones of India, shall be grouped together to constitute Independent States as Muslim Free National Homelands in which the constituent units shall be autonomous and sovereign.[32]

When confronted by a remark made by one of the top Congress leaders, Rajendra Prasad, that the Congress could consider the Pakistan scheme only after its details had been worked out by the

League, Jinnah took the stand that the principle of Partition, which was the basis of the demand for Pakistan, must be accepted first before the details were worked out. As many critics of the League referred to this stand again and again it may be pertinent to note here that by details Jinnah meant only the 'ways and means' of affecting Partition, apparently assuming that the Lahore Resolution had clearly spelled out what the League wanted. This should become clear from a careful perusal of the actual words used by Jinnah in his rejoinder to Prasad, issued on 17 April 1941:

> Babu Rajendra Prasad with his judicial mind ought to know that first the principle of Partitioning India must be agreed upon, then alone comes the question of what ways and means should be adopted to give effect to that decision. The question of details will arise then and with goodwill, understanding and statesmanship, we shall, let us hope, settle them among ourselves. Where there is a will there is a way.

Jinnah also took care to put forward a reasoned defence of his stand, pointing out that there had been hardly any case of Partition when the procedure suggested by him had not been adopted:

> Has Babu Rajendra Prasad known any example where the details have been discussed before without the principle having been accepted? Even in the case of Partition of joint families, with which Babu Rajendra Prasad is so familiar, there is either an agreement or a decree and then comes the question how best and equitably to divide the property.
>
> The latest example in history is that of Ireland. The constitution of north and south of Ireland was finally agreed upon after the principle and the basis of division was settled. So was the case with Burma. Similarly, the decision to separate Sind was taken first and then the details of the scheme were considered and given effect to.[33]

Ignoring the oft-repeated complaint about the lack of details concerning the Pakistan scheme, Jinnah continued with his blitzkrieg campaign in favour of the Pakistan demand, always combining passion with reason. 'The time is not far distant,' he observed in the course of his address at a public meeting at Ootacamund (Madras) on 3 June 1941, 'when Pakistan will be adopted by every Indian in spite of the false and misleading propaganda against it.' Pointing out that India had never been a single nation or had ever had a national government, he asserted that it was the British bayonet that was then holding it together and that after it was removed India would cease to be even a geographical unit. Elucidating the rationale behind the demand for Partition, he further observed:

So long as the Hindus remain Hindus and Muslims remain Muslims, the Hindu nation, which is in a majority in India, cannot but give expression to its will, faith, culture and social order. Willingly or unwillingly these will be imposed on the Muslims who are of a different nation and civilization. Hence the Muslims ask that where they are in a majority they should be allowed to have their own way of life and that where Hindus are in a majority they should continue to have their own way of life, each nation according to its own philosophy, faith and culture. To describe such a proposal as vivisecting India is to poison the minds of the people.

Without skirting the problems of the minorities, Jinnah pointed out that the minorities, whether Muslims in Hindu zones or Hindus in Muslim zones, were not going to be neglected. In any settlement that might be reached, the League would see to it that Muslim minorities were safeguarded fully and to the same extent as any minority might be safeguarded under any civilized government. This would apply equally to Hindu minorities in Muslim zones.[34]

Addressing a second meeting in the same town on the same date, Jinnah reiterated his main point about the inevitability of Partition:

Let me tell you that it is impossible, having regard to history behind us and [present] conditions and having regard to the fact that Hindus and Muslims are two nations, to have a joint *raj*. You cannot put two lions in one den and therefore the only solution is Partition. Let me live in my den and let the Hindus live in their den and I wish them all happiness, prosperity and Godspeed.

Jinnah went on to stress that Partition need not mean that Hindus and Muslims would not live as friends wherever they might be placed as a consequence thereof. Taking the situation in the Madras Presidency as an example, he said that Muslims constituted 7 per cent of the population therein. There were other minorities, too, like the Christians and the Sikhs. If the people there ever got 'independence and sovereign government', that government could only succeed if the majority dealt with the minorities justly and fairly and created a sense of security and confidence among them. Indeed, he assumed that the majority community was already determined to follow that course: 'Do you, the majority community in this province, wish to do injustice to Muslims? No. Do you not want to give them fair play? Yes. Do you want to be inimical towards them? No.' The situation with regard to minorities in Muslim India, he then solemnly affirmed, was going to be exactly similar:

> I can give you the highest authority of our book in Islam and the authority of our history that Islam has not only treated minorities justly and fairly but generously wherever they had any authority or power. That is almost a sacred injunction upon the Muslims. And I may assure you that whatever false propaganda may be carried on, Islam will treat the Hindu minority, Sikh or any other minorities as citizens of the State and as our brothers though we may not agree in our respective faiths.[35]

Again, commenting on a speech at Lahore by a well-known Congress leader, K.M. Munshi, in which the latter was reported as saying that in Pakistan non-Muslims would be treated as untouchables, Jinnah remarked in the course of his address to the students of the Aligarh Muslim University on 2 November 1941 that untouchability was not known to Islam, which formed the basis for the Pakistan scheme. 'Islam,' he added, 'stands for equality of manhood. It stands for justice and fair play, nay generosity, to non-Muslims who are like brothers to us, and would be the citizens of the State.'[36]

Jinnah's main effort, however, was directed towards rallying the Muslims around the cause of Pakistan rather than assuring the Hindus of fair treatment in that State. Thus addressing a meeting of Muslims at Bangalore on 8 June 1941, he exhorted them not to be led astray by self-seeking leaders, but to always remember that Pakistan was their goal and that it was a goal 'worth living for, worth dying for'.[37] In his message to the first Bengal Muslim Students' Pakistan Conference, which opened in Calcutta on 19 September 1941, he observed:

> Let our motto be faith, unity and discipline. Pakistan is our sacred goal and stands for equality of manhood, justice, freedom and peace. To achieve this ideal we should neither rest nor shirk sacrifice. We should not be deterred by opposition or obstacles. The caravan must march on.[38]

In his message to the Muslims on the occasion of Id-ul-Fitr, issued on 20 October 1941, Jinnah, while complimenting them on the successful completion of a month of fasting and prayer, exhorted them to prepare themselves 'for another duty no less important and make a firm resolve on this great day that we will do our duty by our nation that is struggling for its freedom in this country'.[39] Addressing a public meeting in Delhi on 23 October he observed: 'I want to reaffirm with all the emphasis at my command that we stand for Pakistan and for faith, unity and discipline.'[40] Again, delivering his presidential address at the fifth annual session of the All-India Muslim Students' Federation at Nagpur on 26 December 1941, Jinnah observed: 'The Muslim League has given you a goal which in my judgement is going to lead you to the promised land where we shall establish our Pakistan.'[41]

At the same time, Jinnah took care to warn the British that any new constitutional move in India that militated against the Pakistan demand would be firmly resisted by the Muslim League. This becomes clear from his comment on the plea made by the Chinese leader, Chiang Kai-Shek, during his visit to India in February 1942 that the British should transfer real political power to India without waiting for any demand from 'the people of India'. Reacting to this, Jinnah reiterated the Pakistan demand through a press statement issued on 22 February and remarked: 'There is no difference on the point with regard to freedom of the peoples of India, but we desire that both the Hindu and Muslim nations should be free equally in their respective homelands and zones.'[42]

III

Jinnah's campaign in support of the Pakistan demand during 1940–2 was not confined to his public speeches and statements, but was conducted with equal force also in his private conversations and correspondence with important dignitaries. These clearly show that there was absolutely no ambivalence or ambiguity in his mind about the objective of Pakistan and that he had got it adopted by the League after considerable thinking. Just like his public speeches and statements, they also show that the assertions made by some historians that he deliberately kept the picture of Pakistan vague is not based on facts. For what he said in his interviews and statements left no vagueness about the essential features of the Pakistan scheme.

This is borne out by what Jinnah said to G.S. Bajpai, then a member of the Viceroy's Executive Council, when the latter called on him for tea on 17 April 1940, only three weeks after the adoption of the Pakistan Resolution at Lahore, and spent an hour and three quarters with him 'practically all the time in the role of a listener'. As per the record of Jinnah's talk prepared by Bajpai, the former began by 'emphasising his initial prejudice to the idea of breaking up India into separate Sovereign States, a prejudice which, he added, had lasted for many years and which had only been overcome finally during the last few weeks, as the result of concentrated and detached thinking'. Asserting that what had appeared earlier as a poet's daydream had, with 'improvements that he had introduced', become 'the only logical and practical solution of the India problem'. This is how Jinnah, according to Bajpai, elucidated the rationale behind the Pakistan scheme:

> Muslims, he claimed, represented a distinct religious and social entity and could never tolerate the idea of Hindu domination. Such domination, he continued, must be an essential feature of an All-India Federation. India was more comparable to Europe than to any other political unit. If the political unity of Europe was a mere dream how could it be anything else in the case of India? . . .
>
> It is not a feature of the scheme of separate States as expounded by Mr Jinnah that the Muslim-minorities such as those which exist in Bihar and the United Provinces should migrate to those Provinces where Muslims are in a majority. He concedes that, in the proposed separate Sovereign States there would be Hindu and Muslim minorities. But he has persuaded himself that, so long as there are certain States where the Muslims control not merely internal administration but such matters as Defence, Communications and Commerce, in brief all those subjects which would otherwise be Federal, Muslims will have a consciousness of political power, independent and complete, without which their historical sentiments would never be satisfied.

When Bajpai mentioned to Jinnah that if the Muslim sentiment was as vitally and fiercely opposed to Hindu hegemony as the latter contended, Partition was likely to inaugurate a series of wars between predominantly Hindu and Muslim States, Jinnah admitted that the Hindu–Muslim problem could not be entirely free from risks.[43]

In his conversation with W.H.P. Gardiner, a Major in the British Army and a member of the British Labour Party in December 1940, Jinnah spoke with similar seriousness and clarity. According to a summary of this talk prepared by Jinnah himself with a view to its transmission to the Secretary of the Labour Party, the former had told Gardiner:

You have a parallel situation in Ireland which is a few miles away [from London] which you finally settled by division. There you dealt with one religion. In India you deal with two and fundamentally different in their culture, language, social order, laws and their outlook and expect a different settlement and imagine a unitary constitution for India—a subcontinent of 400 millions of people to say nothing of the Indian Princes who constitute one-third of India.

Let me assure you with all the earnestness at my command that it is an utterly impossible idealism. The sooner it is realised the better that in India at least two major nations exist—Hindus and Mussalmans—with totally different and distinctive civilizations behind them. . . .

Briefly, I feel that the fault of the British Government lies in their failure to realize that the political machine that they have formed and still envisage may be workable in England but cannot work in India. As I put it to you, you cannot wear a fur coat everywhere. India is a communally-minded continent, not a politically-minded country. . . .

Asserting that the British had in 'statement after statement' recognized the right of minorities for self-determination, he pointed out that the only excuse they could advance against the Muslim League was that it was not fully representative of the Muslims. Gardiner was asked to convey to the British that 'no greater failing' existed. If the intelligence service of the Government was functioning properly, it was sure to endorse that claim 'most emphatically'. 'Of the 90 millions of Mussalmans in this country,' Jinnah added, 'I speak for fully 90 per cent and my following is growing regularly. We are willing to submit to any reasonable test with regard to this assertion of mine.' [44] A little later he forwarded the summary of his talks with Gardiner to both Prime Minister Churchill and Secretary of State for India, Amery, reiterating his claim of having the support of 90 per cent of the entire Muslim population of India.[45]

In March 1941, Jinnah wrote to Jamsaheb of Nawanagar, then Chancellor of the Chamber of Princes, forwarding the text of the Lahore Resolution, and explaining its essential features, as well as Pakistan's future policy towards the Indian states. Describing the idea of a strong central government for the whole of India as 'a mere dream' he remarked therein:

You will observe from this [the text of the Lahore Resolution] that it does not contemplate any form of central government or legislature and has for its basic principle that Muslim Zones in the North-West and the East while being vested with full responsible government will continue in direct relationship with the British Parliament, as the Indian States, and the scheme will provide for the assumption finally by the respective regions of all powers such as defence, external affairs, communications, customs and such other matters as may be necessary.

In the light of these proposals, as I have already made it clear in my previous statements, we do not wish to interfere with the Indian States so far as the Muslim Zones are concerned. If an Indian State pertaining to the North-Western Zone or the Eastern Zone desires to come into the Federation of that Zone, we shall be glad to welcome any such State on reasonable and fair terms being agreed upon.[46]

Towards the end of May and the beginning of June 1941, Jinnah had long conversations with the Governor of Madras, himself doing much of the talking and during most of it explaining his ideas regarding the Pakistan scheme and hoping that the south too would separate from India, thereby dividing it into four States. As the Governor reported:

He wishes to divide India into four self-governing Dominions of the pre-Statute of Westminster variety, each Dominion being completely separate from each other, each with a Governor-General responsible to Parliament through the Secretary of State. The Governor-General should have control of Foreign Policy, External Defence, etc., and the amount of self-Government would be limited. . . . The four Dominions would be roughly (I) Dravidistan (approximately the Madras Presidency); (II) Hindustan, i.e., Bombay and Central India; (III) Bengalistan with Assam; and (IV) Punjab (with exceptions). Sind and the North-West Frontier. He reckoned by this that he would get 72 million Muslims into the two Muslim Dominions, and have an over 70 per cent majority. He is now actively supporting the Justice Party here for a Dravidian State. In reply to the accusation that he wants to disrupt India, he says that India has never been a nation and never will be.[47]

Evelyn Wrench, a British author who talked to Jinnah for an hour and a half on 2 December 1941, recorded that the latter was 'most vehement and positive' that the majority of the Muslim population in India, for whom he spoke, would never agree to participate in any scheme that might ensure Hindu domination of all India. Justifying the Pakistan scheme, Jinnah told Wrench again and again that in trying to make the whole of India one Dominion the British were attempting the impossible. 'We have no ill-will against the Hindus,' observed Jinnah, 'but they are fundamentally different from us. Our fundamental way of life, our laws, our jurisprudence differ.' When Wrench suggested that the Muslims were originally Hindus, Jinnah remarked: 'You can't go back a thousand years. We are governed by Mohamedan laws, the law of succession is different, affecting inheritance, the entire economic basis of our life is different. Germany is nearer to you than the Hindu is to the Muslim.'[48] Writing to the British Liberal leader, Sir George Schuster in February 1942, Jinnah emphasized that the demand for Partition 'is not only a political reality, it is our creed and our article of faith. We shall not rest content until we have achieved our goal.'[49]

All this effort on Jinnah's part to popularize the Pakistan demand among the mass of the Muslim population and convince all concerned, including the British, of the growing support for it among the Muslim masses did not prove to have been in vain. This is borne out by the confidential reports of the Governor of Bombay to the Viceroy. Thus writing to the latter about the League's celebration of Pakistan Day on 19 April 1940, the Governor noted:

> There were a few large meetings in the city, but otherwise no great enthusiasm was displayed. The Muslim League, however, appears to be successful in keeping the rank and file behind it on Pakistan resolution, and there are signs that it has succeeded in dispelling the fear that Partition would mean mass migration of Muslims from a Province like this. I do not suppose that the rank and file of Muslims have much idea as to what the Partition resolution means, but having been persuaded that it will not mean their own uprooting, they now seem to be prepared to continue to support the Muslim League as the best chance of securing the best terms for Muslims. Amongst the more educated Muslims in Bombay City there is I think a good deal of opposition to Jinnah and the Partition scheme. But the attempts of Nationalist Muslims to organise counter-demonstrations were not successful, and the few Muslims from this Province who attended the recent Nationalist Muslim Conference in Delhi were all well-known pro-Congress Muslims who have no following among their community here.[50]

Considering that this note was written within hardly a month of the adoption of the Pakistan Resolution, its tone was positive enough so far as the impact of Jinnah's exertions on the Muslim mass mind was concerned. After seven or eight months of Jinnah's vigorous campaign, both public and private, in support of the Pakistan Resolution, the Governor's tone about the impact of his campaign, and also about his seriousness of purpose behind it, became considerably more positive. Thus he wrote to the Viceroy early in January 1941, drawing attention to the fact that Jinnah had been making 'some very emphatic' speeches about Pakistan and appeared to have become 'more deeply interested in it himself' than appeared to have been the case earlier. This assumption was based on the Governor's information that Jinnah had been 'at some pains in private conversations, to persuade his listeners of its merits'.[51]

Linlithgow, of course, did not need to be enlightened about the nature of Jinnah's pleadings on behalf of the Pakistan demand. For he had himself been repeatedly exposed to them. Thus in the course of his conversation with the Viceroy on 27 June 1940, Jinnah made it clear that he was indifferent to the contents of any future declaration to be made on behalf of the British Government so long as 'it did not compromise him over Pakistan'. It was essential that any fresh declaration should not, 'either implicitly or explicitly, exclude the two-nation theory'.[52] During his talk with Linlithgow on 12 August 1940, Jinnah again put up a strong plea on behalf of the Pakistan demand. As Linlithgow summed it up in his telegram to Amery, the then Secretary of State: 'He left on me the very strong impression . . . that this Pakistan business, which I have never myself been disposed to take seriously, may prove a much more important issue politically (to the extent that it is sincerely backed by Jinnah) than one might have hoped. He was most emphatic about the case for a separate Muslim India, and most emphatic too that he was not greatly concerned with considerations of tactics'. When Linlithgow suggested that that exactly was the criticism being made, Jinnah replied that he was aware of that criticism. He added that he was also aware of the criticism that the younger generation among Muslims were doubtful regarding the validity of his case, but remarked that he himself had had '100 per cent support at Aligarh' over the Pakistan issue.[53]

IV

In spite of such assertions by Jinnah, Linlithgow was not sure how far the former was genuinely committed to the Pakistan demand. Replying to a letter from the Governor of Bombay in January 1941, cited earlier, underlining the seriousness with which Jinnah had been pleading the case for Pakistan with his interlocuters, Linlithgow observed that in his view Jinnah had taken it up as 'a political cry' and had realized that it was 'an extremely useful negative slogan'. Remarking that he was not yet satisfied as to the degree of sincerity with which Jinnah had been pushing the Pakistan demand, Linlithgow observed: 'Jinnah might find Pakistan a pretty expensive business before he is finished.'[54]

Yet, in spite of his reservations regarding both the soundness of the Pakistan scheme and Jinnah's sincerity in pushing it, it was Linlithgow who more than any one else on the British side worked as a bulwark of support to Jinnah in the period immediately following the League's adoption of the Pakistan Resolution. His main objective, for which he strove most diligently and consistently, was to ensure that nothing was done or said on behalf of the British Government in London that might be disparaging either to Jinnah or to the League's demand for Pakistan. He followed such a policy out of his realization of the immense value to Britain of the existence of an organization like the Muslim League remaining strong and united under Jinnah's leadership as a counterforce to the Congress, whose challenge to the continuance of British rule in India was becoming day by day more strident in the midst of continuing British reverses in the war. He pursued such a policy even when he felt terribly annoyed by Jinnah's tactics or behaviour.

The policy persued by Linlithgow proved quite helpful to Jinnah in keeping the League united under his leadership. For quite some time he had been facing considerable challenges from such prominent colleagues in the League as Sikander Hyat Khan and Fazlul Huq, who increasingly felt unhappy with Jinnah's ways. Besides, there were many fence-sitters in the higher echelons of the League's leadership. In such a situation any exhibition of British displeasure with the Pakistan Resolution, which was primarily Jinnah's handiwork, would have encouraged his opponents and deprived him of valuable support in the League's Working Committee. The growing adulation for him among the

Muslim masses and intelligentsia was, of course, his greatest source of support. Besides, neither Sikander nor Huq had the force of personality or the required following among the rank and file of the League to pose a really serious challenge to Jinnah. However, this does not negate the value of Linlithgow's help to Jinnah, however limited, in strengthening his grip over the League at a critical point in its history as well as in according legitimacy to the Pakistan demand. Linlithgow's contribution was all the more significant in view of the generally adverse British reactions to the adoption of the Pakistan Resolution by the League. The British had in the past generally encouraged the separatist outlook of the League, but this had been primarily motivated by a desire to encourage a counter force to the Congress, which was spearheading the demand for Indian freedom and they could not feel enthusiastic about a demand which, if fulfilled, would result in cutting India into two. For the political unification of India had for long been considered an important achievement of British rule and British statesmen had taken considerable pride in it. The adoption of the Pakistan Resolution, therefore, generally came as a rude shock to them and they did not hide their dislike for it although at the same time squarely holding the Congress responsible for pushing the League to adopt such a stand.

Thus, among the organs of British opinion in India the *Times of India* described the Pakistan Resolution as vague and far from providing a solution to the Muslim problem in India. At the same time, it took care to warn that if 'the extreme view' then adopted by the League became in due course an article of faith with the Indian Muslims, the Congress leadership would be blamed more than the others.[55] The *Civil and Military Gazette* described the Pakistan demand as unnecessary in view of the fact that there was already a provision for four autonomous Muslim states under the federal plan of the Act of 1935 and there was nothing to prevent them from cooperating among themselves for their common good.[56]

Among the papers in Britain the *Times* published two pieces that were sympathetic to the League, but commented that it could not support the Pakistan demand as it envisaged 'an end to Indian unity'.[57] The *Manchester Guardian* observed that by sponsoring the Pakistan Resolution Jinnah had 'reestablished the reign of chaos in Indian politics'.[58] The *New Statesman* supported the Nehru line by asserting that the real division in India was economic and not communal and that the British Government had encouraged the latter for its own ends.[59] Not all British comments, however, were critical of the Pakistan Resolution. On the contrary, a few were quite sympathetic. Thus the *Economist* commented that differences of race and culture had created divisions all over the world and that it could not be different in India.[60] Such comments in a few places could not, however, hide the fact that while generally sympathetic to the League and critical of the Congress, British opinion as a whole had no liking for the Pakistan Resolution and abhorred the prospect of the break-up of Indian unity.

Linlithgow, therefore, acted promptly to ensure that the Pakistan Resolution did not come in for attack at the hands of British statesmen. From the very beginning, he took the line that although the British must go on stressing the value of maintaining India's unity in a general way while at the same time blaming the Congress for putting it in jeopardy, they should not directly say anything against the objective of Pakistan. Since they had already committed themselves to revising the constitutional scheme in India in its entirety after the end of the war, any observation on their part against the soundness of the Pakistan scheme would be highly improper and also annoying to the Muslims and a source of encouragement to the Congress. Explaining this line in his telegram to Zetland sent on 6 April 1940, Linlithgow remarked:

> There is much that could be said in criticism of Jinnah's Partition ideas and we clearly could not accept or endorse them. But quite apart from the fact that we have left the whole scheme and policy of the Act open for discussion after the war, and that Jinnah's scheme itself has I suspect largely been provoked by unreasonable demands of Congress, any condemnation of Jinnah's scheme will at once irritate Muslim feeling and will be seized on by Congress. In present temper here I would myself, therefore, think it preferable to quote it as illustrating extent to which the gulf has widened between the parties, and to take line that His Majesty's Government attached all the more importance in such circumstances to reaching a solution, with agreement of all parties, which would secure the unity of India.[61]

This was written before Linlithgow received Zetland's telegram dated 4 April wherein the latter announced his intention to use the forthcoming debate on the India policy in the British Parliament on 18 April for, among other things, 'pouring much cold water' on the demand for Partition, 'though not necessarily at this stage conclusively rejecting it'. What Zetland proposed was to 'emphasise that this would be a counsel of despair and wholly at variance with the policy of a united India, which British rule has achieved and which it is our aim to perpetuate after British rule ceases.'[62] This led Linlithgow to reiterate his advice to Zetland on 8 April:

While fully appreciating your feeling with which I entirely sympathise as regards the Muslim Partition plan, I would again emphasise the great importance of saying nothing which will antagonise the Muslims and of avoiding any direct attack on them . . . I am confirmed by enquiries I have made here in my feeling that any over-emphasis on unacceptability and faults of Muslim scheme would be politically unfortunate . . . I think you will . . . feel with me that wise tactics would be to keep our hands free until the critical moment is reached in the future constitutional discussions and we can make clear our true attitude towards it in the light of circumstances then prevailing.[63]

In the meanwhile, Jinnah sought a reply to his letter to the Viceroy dated 24 February 1940, asking for a clear assurance that in future no constitution would be imposed on India without the express approval of the Muslim League.[64] Although the Viceroy felt that the acceptance of this demand would in effect mean 'to deny to His Majesty's Government their responsibility for determining the future constitution of India, and by implication to vest this decision in the Muslim League', he also felt that the British reply should be so worded as to encourage the Muslim League to the extent possible and also have a sobering impact on the Congress:

My advisers express the view, with which I agree, that while we cannot go the whole way to meet Jinnah consistently with our own obligations, it is desirable to do what we reasonably and properly can to give the Muslim League as much encouragement as is safely possible, and that it is important equally to avoid saying anything to Jinnah which would too clearly give Congress to understand that they had nothing to fear from the Muslim League and had no reason for apprehension as regards the attitude of His Majesty's Government towards the Muslim demand for an equal voice in India's future Constitution.[65]

While Zetland stuck to his view that the British should not encourage the Pakistan idea, not much effort was required to convince him that it was sound British policy to meet the League's other demands as far as possible. He had long since been impressed by the strength of Islamic solidarity and was quite sceptical of making Muslims willing partners in an all-India Federation. As he told the War Cabinet, he would not bless the League's demand for India's Partition; if successful, it would annul in a moment the constructive work of many years. Nevertheless, he could not imagine any British Parliament seeking to impose on the Indian Muslim community a form of constitution not acceptable to it.[66] This view found public expression, in a somewhat muted form, in Zetland's speech in the House of Lords on 18 April. 'I am bound to say,' he observed while referring to the Pakistan scheme, 'that while I appreciate fully the grounds on which the proposal is based, I cannot but regard it as constituting not far short of a counsel of despair.' Speaking after Zetland, Lord Snell of the Labour Party also criticized the Pakistan demand. 'I do not myself feel,' he observed, 'that that is a satisfactory way out of the difficulty. It would perpetuate divisions, and might lead to continued internal strife.'[67]

In a similar debate on the same day in the House of Commons, Sir Hugh O'Neill, Under-Secretary of State for India, followed Zetland in describing the Pakistan demand as 'a counsel of despair' and remarked that if that demand was ever to be fulfilled, 'it would shatter completely the whole conception of Indian unity', which had been laboriously built up by the British system of government over a long period of years. Speaking on that occasion on behalf of the Labour Party, Wedgwood Benn, a former Secretary of State for India, complimented O'Neill for his speech and observed:

> At the moment when Europe is considering federation, when even America and the new world have been drawing together, when we find our own Commonwealth drawing together more tenaciously than ever, it is perfectly hopeless to come forward with a proposal to divide India into sovereign States by race and religion, and it is well that it should be said plainly in this House that it will not find any support in this country.[68]

In the middle of May 1940, as a result of a number of serious reverses faced by Britain on the war front in Europe, there was a change of government in Britain. The Chamberlain Government resigned and in its place was installed a national coalition government headed by Winston Churchill and including members of both the Conservative and Labour Parties, with the former, of course, as the dominant partner. L.S. Amery, a Conservative, replaced Zetland, also a Conservative, as the Secretary of State for India. While the former had earlier supported constitutional advance in India and affirmed his intention of continuing Zetland's policy, the installation of Churchill as Prime Minister must have appeared as a great source of encouragement to Linlithgow in the pursuit of his policy of playing off the League against the Congress. For Churchill had been a consistent opponent of constitutional advance in India in a progressive direction and had indeed warned Linlithgow as early as November 1937 against the policy of promoting an all-India federation, and working for Hindu–Muslim unity. As he put it:

I think the main difference between us is that you consider a united All-India an end desirable in itself; whereas I regard it as an abstraction, which in so far as it becomes real will be fundamentally injurious to British interests. I look upon India as on the same scale as Europe with all its divisions and counter-poises, and upon the British function being to preserve the balance between these great masses, and thus maintain our own control for our advantage and their salvation. Following this line of thought I should rather like to see the Muslims of the north joining together as a counter-check upon the anti-British tendencies of the Congress. I hope that the 'Princes' of India will preserve a separate entity and outlook from the rather dismal and bleak manifestations of British India. I should have thought that it was in the preservation of these forms of culture and organization that one of the essentials of British strength rested. I am not at all attracted by the prospect of one united India, which will show us the door. We might not be able to prevent it, but that we should devote our best efforts to producing it, is to my mind distressing and repugnant in the last degree.[69]

Churchill's views had not changed after he had become a member of the Cabinet as First Lord of the Admiralty. This is clear from his observations in the course of a discussion on India at a meeting of the War Cabinet on 2 February 1940. According to the official report of the proceedings, he had said on that occasion that alarming prospects had been held out of what might happen if the Congress ministries resigned, but actually after their resignation India had enjoyed a period of perfect tranquillity and for the first time in several years the Congress provinces had been properly administered. He had then also made it clear that he did not share the anxiety to encourage and promote unity between the Hindu and the Muslim communities. 'Such unity was, in fact, out of the realm of practical politics, while if it were to be brought about, the immediate result would be that the united communities would join in showing us the door. He regarded the Hindu–Muslim feud as a bulwark of British rule in India.'[70] In line with this approach, he had not hidden his happiness at the adoption of the Lahore Resolution by the League. At a meeting of the War Cabinet held shortly after the adoption of that resolution, he expressed the view that 'the awakening of self-reliance and self-assertiveness on the part of the different communities, of which the Muslim League's resolution was a sign, constituted a hopeful development'.[71]

It is not, therefore, surprising that after Churchill became Prime Minister Linlithgow began to be more outspoken in his communications to London regarding the need to bolster the Muslim League and the inadvisability of saying anything against Pakistan. Thus in a telegram to Amery on 10 June 1940, he first conveyed to the latter his assessment that Jinnah retained his ascendancy in the Muslim camp. Relations between him and Sikander were not good. Between the two, Sikander was 'more progressive' and the prospect of an understanding between the League and the Congress would be better if he were in command. However, he was at that stage not strong enough to stand up to Jinnah and the machinery of the League. Then he came to the main point:

> While I have never attached, as you know, much importance to Pakistan as a serious proposition, it is an admirable rallying cry, and there are signs that it is taking roots, particularly among the rank and file. The general Muslim League policy, as was abundantly made clear by the Lahore resolutions of last March, is in flat contradiction to that advocated by Kalam Azad. And it remains as important as ever that the fullest weight should be given to the Muslim position at a time when they alone are working the constitution in the provinces, and when their assistance and support is so essential to us both from the military point of view (they provide at the moment 60 per cent of the Army) and because of possible reactions in other Muslim countries.[72]

Linlithgow also did not forget to remind Amery that any statement which prejudiced, 'in the least degree', a full consideration of the Pakistan solution after the war would be violently resisted by the Muslim League, which would have grounds to complain that this went contrary to the British commitment to overhaul the Act of 1935 after the war.[73] In his letter to the King, sent a day later, the Viceroy went beyond all that he had said until then to prevent any serious criticism of the Partition plan by, for the first time, presenting a rationale or justification for it:

This plan has been adopted by the leaders of the League because it offered the sole means of escape from the dilemma in which the Muslim minority finds itself in face of the introduction of democratic institutions. Thus, Muslims are in favour of self-government. They recognise that self-government can come only by way of popular government. They refuse to contemplate a future in which they would be in constant subordination to the Hindu majority. They are therefore constrained to suggest the constitutional severance of the country in such a manner as to secure to them political control in those areas in which the Muslim population exceeds the Hindus. Holding themselves superior to the Hindus in all martial virtues, they claim that given control over their own area they will be able to protect their fellow Muslims in the Hindu areas from any persecution or unfair treatment.[74]

Against this background Jinnah did not have much difficulty in securing satisfaction on the League's old demand that the British should not impose a Constitution on India that did not have its approval. As mentioned in the earlier chapter, he had raised that demand first in his letter to the Viceroy on 5 November 1939, and not being satisfied with the Viceroy's reply dated 23 December he had raised it again in his letter to the Viceroy on 24 February 1940 and followed it up in his interview with the latter on 13 March 1940. Shortly after the Lahore session, he had again reminded the Viceroy of it.[75] The Viceroy's communications to London regarding the importance of keeping the Muslim League satisfied had produced the desired result and, as mentioned earlier, Zetland, in his speech in the House of Lords on 18 April had said something soothing for Jinnah on this point, though, of course, without any reference to his letter. The Viceroy found it handy and drew Jinnah's attention to it, hoping that this would remove any possible doubts that the latter might still have on that point.

This failed to satisfy Jinnah and the Working Committee of the Muslim League, and through a resolution adopted on 16 June it described it as unsatisfactory. [76] During his meeting with the Viceroy on 27 June Jinnah again pressed this point. Rejecting the

Viceroy's plea that the British had given enough proof of their determination to have full regard for Muslim opinion and for the legitimate rights of so large a minority of the Indian people, he emphasized the need for a firm British declaration on it. While acknowledging that the Secretary of State had said that he could not conceive of any British Government imposing by force upon 80 million Muslims a constitution not liked by them, Jinnah wanted the Secretary of State to say that 'no British Government *would* ever do such a thing'. The speeches of persons like Sir Stafford Cripps and Wedgwood Benn in the House of Commons during the last debate on India on 18 April criticizing the proposal to divide India, had not escaped the attention of the Muslim League leaders. In the absence of a firm British declaration how could the League be sure, Jinnah asked Linlithgow, 'that some future Government at Westminster might not sell them into bondage to the Hindus'.[77] In his memorandum submitted to the Viceroy in July 1940, Jinnah again came to this point and stressed that the British Government 'must give definite and categorical assurance to the Musalmans of India that no interim or final scheme of constitution would be adopted by the British Government without the previous approval and consent of Muslim India'.[78]

The desired assurance did not take long in coming. The next declaration of British policy, which was issued on 8 August 1940 and became famous as the August Offer, contained a clause making it clear that the British 'could not contemplate transfer of their present responsibilities for peace and welfare of India to any system of government whose authority is directly denied by large and powerful elements in India's national life'.[79] This clause had been originally drafted by Amery in consultation with Linlithgow and submitted, along with other proposed clauses, to the War Cabinet on 8 July 1940.[80] Although Churchill, being authorized by the War Cabinet, remodelled that draft,[81] he did not make any change in this clause. As it had been inserted in the August Declaration primarily as the result of pressure from Jinnah and virtually gave him a veto over India's constitutional advance, it amounted to a clear stamp of British recognition of the League as the representative organization of the Muslims of India as also of Jinnah as its supreme leader. It was at the same time a major step in the legitimation of the Pakistan demand. The fact that it came within less than 6 months of the adoption of that demand by the League also marks it out as a great achievement for Jinnah, facilitated, of course, by the common interest that the League shared with the British leaders at that point of time in checkmating the Congress.

V

The August Offer had been primarily intended as a gesture to the Congress, which had decided, at its annual session at Ramgarh (Bihar) held in March 1940, a few days earlier than the Lahore session of the League, to launch a campaign of civil disobedience in protest against the British refusal to declare its war aims and make substantial moves towards the grant of independence to India by agreeing to the setting up after the war of a Constituent Assembly, elected on the basis of adult suffrage, to frame a constitution for India and to the establishment of a provisional national government to carry on administration for the time being. Therefore, before assuring the Muslims regarding their future, the Viceroy, while making the new announcement of British policy on 8 August 1940, expressed sympathy with the view that the future constitution of India should be framed after the war primarily by Indians themselves and promised that after the end of the war the British Government would take early steps to set up a body representative of the principal elements in India's national life to prepare the framework of a new constitution. So far as the immediate present was concerned, the Viceroy mentioned that he had been authorized by His Majesty's Government to invite a certain number of representative Indians to join his Executive Council and also to set up a War Advisory Council in order to closely associate the leaders of Indian public opinion with the conduct of the war.[82]

The Congress was not at all satisfied with the Viceroy's statement and immediately rejected it, the Congress President, Abul Kalam Azad, even declining the Viceroy's invitation to see him in order to discuss it. The League, however, showed interest in joining both the Viceroy's Executive Council and the War Advisory Council provided it was satisfied that it was going to have a major or dominant voice in those bodies. The negotiations with that end in view went on for quite some time without any concrete result. Yet they are important for throwing light on the nature of British policy towards the League, particularly Jinnah, and illustrate how Linlithgow remained firmly committed, in spite of Jinnah's excessive demands and annoying behaviour, to bolstering the latter's leadership of the League and desisting from doing or publicly saying anything that might weaken it in any way or cause a split in the League. This went a long way in further legitimizing the Pakistan demand. For Jinnah's leadership and the Pakistan demand went together.

Jinnah had already shown interest in the Muslim League representatives joining the Viceroy's Executive Council. Indeed, as shown in the earlier chapter, he had been agreeable to it as early as the first week of November 1939 on the occasion of the tripartite talks between the Viceroy, Gandhi, and Prasad, and he himself had reaffirmed his readiness for it again during conversations with the Viceroy in the first week of February 1940. On both occasions nothing had come out of such talks because of the lack of interest on the part of the Congress. In the course of his conversation with the Viceroy on 13 March 1940, Jinnah had again hinted at his readiness to countenance the Muslim League's participation in the central government even though the Congress might not be interested in it. In a statement to the press on 27 May, Jinnah repeated this hint by referring to the League's attitude on the earlier occasions and affirming that if the British Government showed trust in Muslim leadership and sought its cooperation on the basis of a partnership, 'we shall not fail'. He also claimed that though the Congress had been hoping to force the British Government to abandon Muslim India to its tender mercies, the League had shown patience and forbearance and further that it was the resistance of the League to the 'machinations' of the Congress that had forced the latter to make a virtue out of necessity by declaring that it did not want to embarrass the British Government by launching civil disobedience immediately.[83] The Working Committee of the League at its meeting in the middle of June 1940 endorsed Jinnah's statement and authorized him to enter into consultations with the Viceroy with a view to exploring 'the possibility of devising prompt and effective measures to mobilise the country's resources for the purpose of intensifying the war effort and the defence of India'. It also made it clear that a satisfactory basis for cooperation could only be on an all-India basis, and not province-wise, between the Government, on the one hand, and the League and other parties, on the other, willing to take responsibility for the defence of the country. At the same time, it declared that no real purpose would be served by the Muslims joining the war committees at various levels at that time. They should wait for the result of Jinnah's efforts to explore avenues of cooperation with the Government.[84] As Sikander briefed the Private Secretary to the Viceroy a few days later, all this meant that the League was perfectly ready to cooperate, but must be given an opportunity to do so effectively, i.e. by participation in the central government.[85]

This was confirmed by Jinnah in the course of his interview with the Viceroy on 27 June. When asked to explain his Working Committee's resolution regarding the war effort, Jinnah said that it seemed unsatisfactory from the outside. Once the League leaders were taken into confidence and had an opportunity to look at it from the inside, the thing might look quite different. They would then also be in a position to tell the people about what was being done and secure their support and confidence. This could be done by taking the League representatives, along with the representatives of the other parties willing to cooperate, on the Viceroy's Executive Council. If the Congress finally decided against cooperation, the nominees of the parties cooperating at the Centre should be appointed as non-official advisers to the Governors in the Congress provinces then under Governor's rule under Section 93 of the Act of 1935. This, explained Jinnah, would work to destroy the Congress ascendancy by either capturing the support of members of the existing Provincial Legislatures or by preparing the provincial constituencies to support non-Congress candidates at the next general election.[86] The Viceroy thus summed up Jinnah's presentation in his telegram to the Secretary of State: 'What it comes to is briefly that he is anxious above all things to get into the administration.' While the Viceroy wanted some time to make up his mind about the proposal regarding the expansion of his Executive Council, he was, on the whole, inclined to welcome it and felt that it would provide him with much needed support in dealing with the Congress. Above all, he was happy with the general tenure of his conversation with Jinnah and remarked that he was 'much more favourably impressed by Jinnah's general attitude' than he had expected to be.[87]

The Viceroy's happiness proved to be short-lived. On 1 July, Jinnah sent to him a memorandum marked 'Tentative Proposal', specifying the Muslim League's terms for cooperation at the all-India level. The first two items related to the safeguarding of the League's position in future negotiations regarding the shape of India's constitution and would not have appeared jarring to Linlithgow as in his own way he had himself been working for them. Jinnah demanded, first, that no pronouncement or statement on behalf of the British should in any way militate against the Lahore Resolution of the Muslim League calling for Partition and, second, that no future constitution should be adopted without the approval and consent of Muslim India. Proceeding further, Jinnah observed that in view of the grave developments in the war situation that had taken place recently all efforts must be directed towards intensifying the war effort and mobilizing all the resources of India for her defence and for maintaining peace and tranquillity in the country. This could, however, be achieved only if the British Government was willing to associate the Muslim leadership as equal partners in the Government both at the Centre and in all the Provinces. Spelling out his proposal, Jinnah demanded that the Muslim representation in the Viceroy's Executive Council must be equal to that of Hindus if the Congress came in; in case the Congress kept out, the Muslim members must be in a majority among the additional members. The same would apply to the War Council, the setting up of which was suggested by Jinnah as a means of securing greater Indian cooperation with the war effort. The ground for seeking Muslim representation on this scale in both the bodies, as given by Jinnah, was that 'the main burden and the responsibility' would be borne by the Muslims. Similarly, in the provinces which, since the resignation of the Congress Ministries, were being administered directly by the Governors under Section 93 of the Act of 1935, the majority of non-official Advisers should be Muslims. In the end, Jinnah made it clear that all the Muslim representatives in both the Centre and the provinces should be chosen by the Muslim League.[88]

The Viceroy's immediate reaction, as communicated to the Secretary of State, was that many of Jinnah's proposals, if taken literally, were clearly unacceptable. He had no doubt that there was a considerable bargaining element in them. The objections, for instance, to accepting the Muslim claim to complete equality with Hindus over the whole field were obvious. Nor could he accept Jinnah's conditions regarding the enlargement of the Executive Council and the appointment of non-official advisers. The Viceroy, therefore, thought that the best thing for him was to make the position clear to Jinnah without any delay.[89] A few days later, he wired to the Secretary of State that he was inclined to send an immediate reply to Jinnah 'damping him down on his memorandum'. He did not, of course, want to 'frighten him off', but thought that 'it would be a mistake to let him imagine that he is in a position to blackmail us, or make us accept unacceptable terms'.[90] After he had received the views of the Governors, which amounted to a 'chorus of condemnation of Jinnah's excessive demands', he thought he would do well 'to torpedo Jinnah without much further delay . . . if he is not to be allowed to set up a fresh nuisance value which it may be difficult to dispose of later'.[91]

In line with such thinking, Linlithgow sent a somewhat curt though polite reply to Jinnah, telling the latter that there were several parties that would have to be considered for membership of his Executive Council and that none of them was expected to bear any special responsibility. He also made it clear that the new members would not be the nominees of political parties, but would be selected by the Secretary of State in consultation with the Viceroy. As for the provinces under Section 93, the responsibility for them rested wholly with the Governors. The idea of a War Council was welcomed, but it was again made clear that its membership would be determined on the same basis as that of the Viceroy's Executive Council. Further, the Viceroy made it clear that it would be 'constitutionally impossible' to ensure that the choice of Muslim members or advisers rested with the League. He, however, assured Jinnah that he needed to have no fear that any suggestion he might make would not receive full consideration.[92] Jinnah would not have relished Linlithgow's reply, but he did not show any displeasure. On the contrary, with his usual resilience he expressed his appreciation to Linlithgow for clarifying the constitutional and legal position and his gratitude for the assurance that as far as the membership of various bodies from the Muslim side was concerned his suggestion would receive full consideration.[93]

After the announcement of the August Offer, the Viceroy

pursued the matter of the League joining the Government with greater urgency. Jinnah, too, continued to be interested in it provided it could be done on the basis of the terms specified by him in his memorandum to Linlithgow submitted on 1 July 1940. He showed no eagerness to join the Government unless he secured a dominant position for the League in it if the Congress did not join it. At the same time, he utilized the negotiations with Linlithgow to press home to the latter the seriousness that he attached to the objective of Pakistan. This was obviously intended to secure a British commitment to Partition, if at all possible, or at any rate to make them treat it as a serious objective of the League and not merely a bargaining counter. Thus during his conversation with Linlithgow on 12 August, Jinnah, most strongly urged in the first place the Pakistan claim and the case for the recognition of a separate Muslim nation in India. He in fact asserted that this position had already been conceded in the report of the joint Select Committee of the Parliament in 1934. He also showed the Viceroy a letter from the Calcutta branch of the League, which he described as typical of the Muslim attitude, bitterly complaining that the Viceroy's statement (of 8 August) neither contained any direct reference to the Muslims nor did it recognize their claim to be a separate nation; the case for Muslim majority or equality in the Executive Council was also not mentioned. In view of all this, Jinnah pleaded for some reference to the Muslims in the course of the next debate in the British Parliament, and particularly in view of the refusal of the Congress to cooperate, full consideration to the League for its readiness to cooperate.[94] The Viceroy, however, while keen to have the League's representatives on his Executive Council was not prepared to promise them a position of dominance or majority in it.[95] On the other hand, some prominent League leaders like Sikander and Huq were keen for cooperation without any condition or haggling over terms, and indeed had their eyes on membership of the Viceroy's Executive Council; Huq had even formally offered himself for that position just two days after the announcement of the August Offer.[96] Faced with this situation, Jinnah postponed the meeting of the League's Working Committee, originally scheduled to meet on 17 August, keeping the Viceroy guessing and showing to him that Jinnah was not too eager for the League to get into his Executive Council, allowing for time for the

Congress attitude towards cooperation under the terms of the Viceroy's statement being finally clarified (the Congress Working Committee was scheduled to meet on 18 August) and the ardour of some League leaders for joining the Viceroy's Executive Council to cool down. In the meanwhile, the Viceroy fumed and fretted, sometimes inclined to bypass Jinnah and go ahead with the co-operation of Sikander and Huq, and at other times impressed by the continued necessity for a strong Muslim organization and the likely harm to British interests by any serious split in the League. The victory finally lay with Jinnah, who managed to put Sikander and Huq in a situation in which they had no option but to cooperate with him and steered the League's executive to a decision against joining the Viceroy's Executive Council, leaving the Viceroy no option but to manage as best he could without the League's representatives therein.

The Viceroy's predicament and changing moods can be seen in his correspondence with the Secretary of State. Thus on 16 August he informed the latter of his view that it might be necessary for the British to put stronger pressure on Jinnah if he continued to procrastinate. He significantly added: 'I suspect now that his [Jinnah's] real object is to manoeuvre himself into a position in the Expanded Council approximately to that of a Prime Minister, a state of things, I need not say, which I have not the very least intention of allowing him to achieve'.[97] On 22 August he wrote that he hoped that Sikander and Huq would be able to bring sufficient pressure on Jinnah to make him toe the line. If they failed, he would be prepared to go ahead without Jinnah. He already had Huq's application in his pocket and Sikander, too, was not likely to be unwilling to serve on his Executive Council. He had thus little doubt that he could 'get together a pretty effective team and one which Jinnah would be sorry to see operating without his blessing'.[98] Four days later he wrote that he expected Jinnah to bargain still further and added: 'We cannot allow ourselves to be blackmailed by Jinnah any more than we can by the Congress.'[99]

The Working Committee of the League finally met in Bombay from 31 August to 2 September. The situation on the eve of the meeting was that Jinnah, as conveyed by his friend, Cowasji Jehangir, to the Governor of Bombay was still aiming at the League's dominance in the Viceroy's Executive Council: 'What he wanted in return for full cooperation from the Muslims was an alliance between the Muslims and the British who between them would run the country.' According to Cowasji's understanding, Jinnah was likely to try to secure a postponement of the final decision by the Working Committee. On the other hand, Sikander had told another informer of the Governor most definitely that the members from Bengal and the Punjab were determined to force the issue in the Working Committee and that they would not mind even splitting the League to this end.[100] The outcome of the meeting, however, showed a clear victory for Jinnah. The Working Committee adopted a resolution acknowledging that the recent statements of the Viceroy and the Secretary of State announcing the August Offer constituted a considerable advance towards the League's point of view on the future constitution for India and met its demand for a clear assurance that no future constitution should be adopted without its approval and consent. It also welcomed what it described as a recognition of the League's claim to be treated as a partner. However, it found the detailed proposals in this regard, contained in the Viceroy's letter dated 14 August to its president, as most unsatisfactory, pointing out as many as six specific shortcomings in it and authorized the President to seek further information and clarification from the Viceroy on those points. The only concession that the Working Committee made to the enthusiasts for cooperation with the Government was to permit those Muslims who thought that they could 'serve any useful purpose by merely associating themselves with the war committees' to do so.[101]

The confidential official survey of political events ruefully commented: 'The outcome showed once more the power of Jinnah's cold and confident leadership, and his domination over personalities far more generous but less determined than himself.'[102] Among the latter the most prominent was, of course, Sikander. He had opposed further haggling and suggested that the August Offer should be accepted in principle, leaving the details to be settled through personal negotiations. On this he had the support of the majority, only four members supporting Jinnah who was opposed to such a course.[103] However, the latter with his adroit handling of the situation, was able to turn the tables on Sikander. Jinnah said that he was prepared to go along with the majority, but warned the members of the consequences of full cooperation with the Government: the League would have to shoulder the entire burden of responsibility for protecting the Indian Empire, crushing the Congress (then moving towards civil disobedience), suppressing internal strife, supplying men and money, and running the administration. Besides, Jinnah added, the League members of the Viceroy's Executive Council would have to work under the constant fear that the Congress might decide to cooperate with the Viceroy and that the Government might decide not to consider the Pakistan scheme.[104] The Viceroy, too, was suitably impressed by this exhibition of Jinnah's firm grip over the League after so much talk by Sikander and Huq of forcing a division in favour of joining the Viceroy's Executive Council. He informed the Secretary of State for India that Jinnah had apparently maintained his ascendancy in the Bombay discussions. As far as the roles of Sikander and Huq were concerned, they both were very courageous before they went to Bombay, but 'as so often in the past when in the presence of the Master, they both piped very much lower on arrival'. The Viceroy was confirmed in this view by the effort then being made by Sikander to put up a brave front after the meeting and to assert that it went off quite well.[105]

The next meeting of the League's Working Committee was fixed for 28 September, to be followed by that of its Council on the next day. The time in between was to be utilized by Jinnah in seeking further information and clarification from the Viceroy. He, of course, showed no hurry in doing so. The Viceroy suspected that Jinnah was trying to blackmail him, but found himself helpless to do anything. As he wrote to the Secretary of State: 'it is lamentable that we should have to await in this way on Jinnah's vanity, but it cannot of course be helped'. He was clear in his mind that there could be nothing doing on the basis of what the Muslim League had 'had the courage to suggest, namely that it should be taken into full and equal partnership with the British Government in the running of the country and authority shared with it. It was obvious that such a scheme could not be countenanced as it would leave the Hindu community out in the cold and place the Sikhs and the scheduled castes also in the same position.' At the same time, however, Linlithgow thought it 'important to hold the Muslim League together if we can do so, and in these circumstances there is nothing for it but to be patient with Jinnah, though one's patience is beginning definitely to run out'.[106] A fortnight later Linlithgow complained that Jinnah had been 'excessively tiresome' and apprehended trouble from him. He was not sure what the attitude of Sikander and Huq would be if Jinnah decided against the League's representatives joining the Viceroy's Executive Council; the British might have to contemplate what he had been 'throughout anxious to avert—a split in the Muslim League'.[107]

Jinnah, however, managed the situation with extreme finesse. He defied Linlithgow and at the same time held the League together, without any help from the latter, making his hold over that organization and over the Muslims generally firmer than ever before and also making the Viceroy realize this. He was interested in the League joining the Viceroy's Executive Council only if it could acquire real power and an image of a great political force in the country, equal to if not bigger than the Congress. He attached even greater importance to the terms on which the Congress came in later and was apprehensive that these might be better than the ones under which the League was being asked to join at that time. This would place the Congress on a higher pedestal as had happened on the issue of the formation of popular Ministries in 1937. He, therefore, wanted the Viceroy 'either to refuse altogether to let Congress in until the war was on or if they did come in not to let them in on any basis which they could represent as a triumph or on better terms than might have been accepted by the Muslim League'. Linlithgow and Jinnah discussed these matters back and forth for a full three hours on 24 September but could not reach any agreement. The Viceroy refused to discuss either the actual portfolios which would be entrusted to the League representatives, apart from making it clear that Defence would not be one of them, or the exact number of new members to be appointed to the Executive Council. He equally firmly rejected Jinnah's request for taking three League representatives rather than two which he had offered earlier. The only concession of some value he was prepared to make to Jinnah was over the panel of names to be submitted, allowing them to be settled through private discussion on the understanding that the same privilege would be accorded to the leaders of other groups if they showed interest in having it. Still the Viceroy was hopeful of a satisfactory outcome. 'Though extremely obstinate and difficult,' he commented while concluding his detailed note on discussions with Jinnah, 'he was on the whole rather better than I had feared he might be, and though we are still very far from out of the woods, I am slightly more optimistic as to the possibility of Muslim League cooperating'.[108]

The Viceroy's optimism proved to be baseless. The Council of the Muslim League met in Delhi on 29 September and unanimously accepted the resolution proposed a day earlier by the Working Committee, refusing participation in the Executive Council or the War Advisory Council under the terms of the August Offer. The grounds given for this rejection were: (i) that the proposed inclusion of only two members of the League in the Viceroy's Executive Council would not give the League any real or substantial share in the authority of the Government at the Centre; (ii) that no indication had been given as to what would be the position of the League's representation in the event of any other party's representatives joining the Executive Council at a later stage; (iii) that the Viceroy had not accepted the demand of the League for appointment of its members as Advisers in the provinces being administered by Governors under Section 93 of the Government of India Act of 1935; (iv) that the proposal about the War Advisory Council was still in embryo and no information was available regarding its constitution, composition and function; and (v) that out of the various points raised in the League's Working Committee's resolution on 2 September 1940 only one relating to a panel of names had been satisfactorily met.[109]

This was no doubt a milestone in building up the image of the League as a powerful organization, united under Jinnah's leadership and capable of taking a decision contrary to the wishes of the Government as well as of getting over the lure of office while pursuing its objective. Not for the first time, commented Linlithgow, had Jinnah copied Congress in basing his rejection partly on the alleged British refusal to part with power.[110] He added that though Jinnah was undoubtedly well satisfied for the moment to find himself where he was, his tactic was 'essentially negative—he is like the chess-player who waits for the other man's move and devotes himself to protecting his position by a counter-move. But there is nothing constructive and I suspect nothing original about Jinnah.'[111] The confidential official survey of political events in India also commented in the same vein: 'If any one cause is to be named for this barren and disappointing conclusion, it is Jinnah's personality: steeped in suspicion and negation, lacking all administrative experience or desire to acquire it, forceful only through the narrowness of the channel of his interests and aims. . . .'[112] Amery thought Jinnah was 'eaten up with vanity and was only prepared to cooperate if he felt that he was to be the shadow behind the throne in the future—and a very definite and visible shadow at that'.[113] All this was, of course, nothing but venting spleen. In a more sober mood, the Viceroy realized that he had really no option but to put up with Jinnah and that any British move, contrary to the League's interests, would be not only impracticable, but also, in the long term, undesirable, keeping in view the continued opposition of the Congress. In the first place, the League was solidly united behind Jinnah and there was no prospect either of a split in the League or of the Viceroy being able to select a couple of sufficiently representative members of the League for inclusion in his Executive Council. It would not be possible to bring about a split in the League, but even if it were so, it would not be in the British interest to do so. As Linlithgow put it:

> It is I suspect of real importance to keep together some authoritative mouthpiece of general Muslim opinion in this country—and there is nothing that in any way compares with the League for that purpose at the moment—its authority and its cohesion have been consolidated out of all recognition during the last twelve months, more particularly in view of possible post-war constitutional discussions. Nor do we want, at a time when we may have to take the Congress on, unnecessarily to antagonise the main organisation of the second largest party and community in this country.[114]

VI

Linlithgow consistently held on to this position even when under attack from Jinnah, with whom his personal relations deteriorated to a considerable extent after the failure of their negotiations regarding the Viceroy's Executive Council. In his interview with Major Gardiner in December 1940, to which reference has been made earlier, Jinnah charged Linlithgow with adopting an incredibly negative and prevaricating attitude during those negotiations, ascribed the entire responsibility for their failure to him, and was 'most emphatic in demanding that his term of office be expired after the normal period'. This demand was based on the assumption that the British Cabinet was bound to depend for advice on India policy on the man on the spot and so long as Linlithgow remained Viceroy, his 'faulty deductions and advice' would continue to influence the Cabinet and hinder a proper understanding of the Indian situation.[115] Linlithgow saw the text of this interview when the Secretary of State consulted him about the nature of the reply to be sent to Jinnah, who had sent him a letter enclosing it. The Viceroy informed the Secretary of State that the opportunity should not be missed of 'administering a slight cooler' to Jinnah by sending a brief though courteous reply. He, however, stuck to his view about the importance of Jinnah as the one person in India who had the support of the overwhelming majority of the Muslim population. Commenting on Jinnah's interview with Gardiner, Linlithgow remarked that he did not dispute Jinnah's claim to have 90 per cent of Muslim support and went on to add:

> . . . however much there might be to be said against Jinnah, and however difficult and even unreliable he might be in discussion or negotiation, he had continued to get the mass of the Muslim population behind him, and had also, by making his policy communal, and by the cry of Pakistan, created a situation in which it would be most difficult politically for either Sikander or Fazlul Huq, even if they wanted to do so themselves, to come out against him, for they would be in the position of underbidding him and open to very obvious retort of a character calculated to go down well with the ordinary Muslim constituents.[116]

Linlithgow also continued to remain convinced that British interests in India required a strong organization of Muslims, opposed to the Congress, and that organization could only be the Muslim League. He did not like anything to be done which might weaken it in any way or cause a split in it. It was this consideration which led him in March 1941 to ask the Punjab Governor to dissuade Sikander from resigning from the League. Sikander had no sympathy with the Pakistan scheme and, though keen on limiting the powers of the Hindu-majority at the Centre by one device or another, was not in favour of a complete separation of the Muslim-majority provinces from the rest of India. The safeguarding of his position as the head of the Government in the Punjab also required aloofness from the Pakistan movement, for he needed the support of rural Hindu and Sikh members of the Unionist Party in the Assembly and they were becoming more and more restive as the Pakistan demand was gathering momentum. On the other hand, his effort to persuade Jinnah and the League's Working Committee to abandon the slogan of Pakistan proved unavailing and he found himself in the minority of one in the Working Committee. Relations between Jinnah and Sikander deteriorated to such an extent that during the former's visit to Lahore on 1 and 2 March 1941 there was no meeting between the two and none of the Muslim Ministers or Parliamentary Secretaries and very few of the prominent Muslim members of the Unionist Party were present at the public meeting addressed by Jinnah, a fact that became the subject of press comments. Sikander had apparently decided to resign not only from the League's Working Committee, which was known to Jinnah, but also from the primary membership of the League and had thought over all its consequences. He was convinced that even with Jinnah's opposition, he would be able to command a majority in the Punjab Assembly and also retain his majority when the next election was held. The Punjab Governor agreed with this estimate.[117] Linlithgow, however, thought differently. Sikander explained his difficulties to Linlithgow and asked in so many words whether a place could not be available to him in the Viceroy's Executive Council, showing that he was not really as confident as he had communicated to the Governor about retaining his position as the Punjab Premier in the event of an open break with Jinnah and the League. Linlithgow told Sikander clearly that his place was in the Punjab and that he would be able to contribute more to the war effort from that position than from anywhere else. Linlithgow did not think it proper to talk to Sikander more directly in dissuading him from taking any step that would lead to his open rupture with the League, but he sent a telegram to Craik, the Punjab Governor, asking the latter to talk things over with Sikander and dissuade him from a break with Jinnah.[118] As he explained in that telegram and also in his letter to Amery on the same day, that advice was based on the assumption that any step of the type being considered by Sikander might jeopardize his position as head of the government in the Punjab and Linlithgow was convinced that he was, in the circumstances then prevailing, the best man for that job. The stability of the Punjab administration was very important, particularly in the context of the war situation, and nothing should be done that might put that in jeopardy. This was, however, not the only consideration that influenced Linlithgow. He was equally certain that nothing should be done that might affect the strength of the Muslim League and cause a split in that organization and he was convinced that Sikander was contemplating a step that would have that result. As he wrote to Amery:

> But equally this is not the moment at which I want to see any split in the Muslim League, which I still think is very important (tiresome as its activities may be in some ways) to maintain as a solid political entity, able to speak, as it certainly is able to speak at the moment, on behalf of Muslim opinion in this country generally. That is the more desirable since we are moving into the next phase of Gandhi's Satyagraha campaign, and any fissure in the Muslim ranks, more particularly over this vital question of Pakistan, . . . would be a very great encouragement to the Congress and so to the anti-war party, and might well make our position in dealing with the Satyagraha issue much more difficult.[119]

In the event Sikander did not actually resign even from the Working Committee of the League and the only step he took in order to safeguard his position with his Hindu and Sikh supporters in the Punjab Assembly was to make a statement therein on 11 March 1941, making clear his dislike for the Pakistan scheme, a step suggested as a possible way out by Linlithgow to Craik.[120] In that speech Sikander reiterated that he was opposed to an all-powerful Centre, but realized the necessity of some central government or agency to coordinate the work of the units. There was provision for the latter in the resolution drafted by him, but the League's Working Committee had deleted that provision. Proceeding further, he declared: 'We do not ask for freedom that there may be Muslim Raj here and Hindu Raj there. If that is what Pakistan means, unalloyed Muslim Raj in the Punjab, then I will have nothing to do with it' [hear, hear].[121]

In May 1941 when Linlithgow again thought of expanding his Executive Council under the terms of the August Offer, a sitting member, Zafrullah Khan, suggested that he could go ahead and select some Muslim public men of stature, ignoring Jinnah whom he at that time regarded as even more irritating than Gandhi. He was sure that if such men were offered membership in the Council they would accept regardless of Jinnah's wishes. Among the persons he mentioned in this connection were such names as Sikander, Nazimuddin, and Sultan Ahmad, a former member of that Council. They were, however, all members of the Muslim League and the Viceroy, though interested in securing the services of Muslims of stature for his Council, refused to accept Zafrullah's advice as he was not interested in doing anything that might bring about a split in the League or in pushing it in the direction of cooperation with the Congress, which, he thought, was quite possible. As he explained his viewpoint:

> Now this, of course, is a point of policy of cardinal importance. Rightly or wrongly we have hitherto proceeded on the basis that it is not desirable to split the Muslim League, tiresome and indeed maddening as Jinnah and his close collaborators may prove to be. There are very solid arguments which have always carried great weight with me against any split. In the first place the Muslim League is the only organized and regular opposition to the Congress; in the second, I do not in the least want to find Congress and the Muslim League uniting against us; and the possibility, if the situation was loosely handled, of their doing so on lines which I think the left-wing Muslims and Congress adopted in 1920–21 over the Khilafat agitation, is one that cannot be excluded. It is all the more important to give full weight to that consideration with the war moving into the Middle East, the Iraqi and Egyptian position delicate as it is at the present time; and the slight uneasiness of Muslim opinion here over our operations in Iraq.[122]

Finally, Linlithgow settled on three new members of his Council, a Parsi, a Hindu, and a Muslim, the last one being Sir Akbar Hydari. He was seventy-two and the Viceroy had recently noticed some deterioration in his health, but he was, in his view, a person of quite high standing and 'a good Muslim with valuable contacts'. His most important qualification, according to the Viceroy, was, of course, the fact that his appointment was not likely to be interpreted as a challenge to Jinnah and the Muslim League.[123] Sometimes, as for instance when he failed to reply to Zafrullah's letter suggesting the names of the League members of the Central Legislature to serve on the Defence Council, Linlithgow felt rather 'tired of Jinnah' and thought of moving ahead without bothering about him, but on calmer consideration he realized that one had to curb one's natural instincts according to the needs of a situation.[124]

Linlithgow soon got an opportunity to show his tremendous capacity in this regard. After the expansion of his Executive Council, he and the Secretary of State decided that it was time also to constitute the National Defence Council as provided for in the statement of 8 August 1940. Between the two they also decided that while it was futile to expect either the Congress or the Muslim League to be officially represented in it, it would be a good idea if the Premiers of Assam, Bengal, Punjab, and Sind, all Muslims and the first three of them members of the Muslim League, could be included in it. The Viceroy was quite pleased with the thought that if they were invited as heads of provincial administrations, and not as representatives of the Muslims or of the Muslim League, they might gladly come in. 'I cannot help feeling,' he wrote to the Secretary of State, 'that if we are able to get away with this without a major row with Jinnah it may have a slightly deflating effect on the Quaid-i-Azam—and none too soon if so!'[125]

Linlithgow, however, miserably failed in that effort. Halfway through this operation his courage gave way and though he had not consulted Jinnah about offering the membership of the National Defence Council to the four Muslim Prime Ministers, and some other prominent Muslims, he thought that courtesy demanded that Jinnah be suitably informed. Acting on his instruction, the Governor of Bombay, Roger Lumley, sent a letter to Jinnah on 20 July 1941, telling him that the Viceroy regarded it 'as essential' that the great Muslim community should be represented on the National Defence Council by persons of the highest prominence and capacity. He had accordingly invited the Premiers of Assam, Bengal, Punjab, and Sind to serve as members of it, and he had extended the invitation also to certain other prominent Muslims, such as Sir Mahomed Usman.[126]

The letter had been so constructed in order to show to Jinnah that the British 'were not forgetting the Muslims' while expanding the National Defence Council. In the light of subsequent experience, Linlithgow admitted that it would have been better to mention that the Prime Ministers were being invited as Prime Ministers instead of talking about the need for suitable representation of the Muslim community. He himself later conveyed to Jinnah in an interview that the latter was in fact the position.[127] Jinnah was not to be so easily convinced. As the

Viceroy reported to the Governors of the concerned provinces, during his interview with Linlithgow on 16 August 1941, Jinnah was 'exceedingly stiff, non-cooperative and aggrieved, and most insistent that nothing could properly be done by any Muslim in India on any subject save through himself and the Muslim League'.[128] He saw in this move a challenge to his own authority as President of the All-India Muslim League and proceeded dexterously to thwart it, using as his chief instrument Lumley's letter mentioned above. At the next meeting of the League's Working Committee at Bombay in the last week of August, he used it to silence Sikander when the latter pressed his argument that he had been invited as Prime Minister. Though acutely embarrassed, Sikander rightly felt that Lumley's letter to Jinnah gave an 'entirely different complexion' to the basis of his appointment and saw no option except to comply with Jinnah's wishes and refuse to serve any longer on the National Defence Council.[129] Linlithgow blamed him for not arguing that whatever the terms of Lumley's letter, he was serving as Prime Minister only or asking for time to consult his Governor and expressed the view that his 'lack of backbone' had facilitated Jinnah's task.[130]

Actually, on that occasion this epithet applied more appropriately to Linlithgow himself. His attitude during that episode shows that even if Sikander had not immediately capitulated to Jinnah, he would have had to do so subsequently, as was ruefully discovered by Fazlul Huq at a very heavy cost. The latter had not gone to Bombay but came to know of developments there on 25 August through Sikander on the telephone and immediately got in touch with the Viceroy through his Private Secretary, stating that he had taken the position that he required time to consider the situation and could not resign from the National Defence Council without consulting the Viceroy and the Governor. It was clear that with a little encouragement from the Viceroy, Huq might have refused to resign, but Linlithgow was quite cowed down by Jinnah's anger and not merely refused to offer any encouragement himself but also asked the Governor of Bengal to desist from doing so. This is borne out by his telegram to the Governor of Bengal, repeated also to the Governors of Assam, Punjab, and Sind, containing the following:

> ... I am quite clear that it would be the greatest mistake for us to try to split the League or to bring pressure to bear. My conclusion in these

circumstances is that however much we may regret the disappearance of the Prime Ministers we should take the line that this is a decision which it must be for them to take, and that if they, despite the fact that it has been made perfectly clear that they were invited to serve as Prime Ministers and are serving in that capacity, feel unable to assist in the National Defence Council, we must do without them. I think it is desirable, too, to leave the responsibility for the decision entirely to individuals.

The Governor was also asked to convey to Huq that the Viceroy had received his message and was greatly obliged to him for this, but regarded this 'as a matter for the individuals concerned to decide and did not wish to influence this decision in any way. It was a matter which they must settle for themselves.'[131] A few days later, he again telegraphed the Bengal Governor: 'I remain as before very clear that no pain must be spared to avoid any action which could be construed as exercise of pressure by a Governor or Governor-General in a matter which may result in a rift in the Muslim League.'[132]

Sikander saw Linlithgow on 29 August, and mentioned that he had two alternatives before him: (a) he should resign from Prime Ministership and also from membership of the Muslim League; or (b) just resign from the Muslim League. If his idea in posing these alternatives was to get some hint from the Viceroy as to which step the latter might prefer, it did not work. For Linlithgow was 'at special pains to avoid indicating any view' of his own as between these alternatives or on any other solution. The only concession he was prepared to make to Sikander was that he would wait for a few days in the matter of filling up the vacancies in the National Defence Council to enable the latter to finally make up his mind. When Sikander said that he would discuss the matter with his Governor and if in the light of that discussion it seemed undesirable that he should resign from the Punjab Premiership, he would try to work out some common line with Huq and Sadullah (Assam) regarding dealing with Jinnah. The Viceroy's comment on hearing this was that these were private matters with which he had nothing to do, but that he must repeat that he could not wait long for clearing up the situation regarding the filling up of any vacancies.[133] Subsequently, Sikander saw the Punjab Governor who advised him against giving up the Premiership, but he said so on his own volition and not at the prompting of the Viceroy. When the Governor told the Viceroy that if the latter agreed that it was better for Sikander to continue as Premier he should ask Huq and Sadullah to come to Simla, the Viceroy made it clear that he could not do that. A meeting of the three Prime Ministers, convened by the Viceroy or with his encouragement, as a result of which they resigned from the Muslim League, he explained, would be open to very serious misinterpretation. They must make up their own minds and if Sikander wanted such a meeting he should convene it on his own responsibility. If they in consequence of such a meeting or otherwise resigned from the National Defence Council, the Viceroy would take counsel with the Governors concerned regarding the filling up of the vacancies. Understandably, Sikander was reported to be 'very moody and dejected' till as late as the end of September.[134] Whatever that may have been, left to their own devices, the Premiers realized that the best course for them was to maintain the solidarity of the Muslim League and resign from the National Defence Council, thereby giving a further boost to Jinnah's leadership and presenting a vivid demonstration of his extraordinary hold on the Indian Muslims.

The key to Linlithgow's behaviour during this episode is provided by his continuing conviction that however absurd or uncooperative Jinnah's stand might be towards the British, it was, even if the British were able to do so, undesirable to break up the League, 'the one genuine and effective mouthpiece of organised Muslim opinion'. And so far as that organization was concerned, there was no blinking the fact that Jinnah was in complete control and, little as the British might like it, he was a factor that they had to reckon with.[135] Besides, there were several other considerations that indicated the need for caution in dealing with Jinnah, who was then 'mad with rage'.[136] There was always the risk of an alliance between an infuriated Jinnah and the Ahrars or some other left-wing Muslim organizations. Although the Viceroy did not take that too seriously, he felt that it was one of the factors that the British had to watch out for. He attached much greater importance to the need to ensure that no responsible person in a high position on the British side should with any degree of plausibility be liable to be accused of interfering with the affairs of political parties or engaged in manoeuvres designed to split the League. The greatest difficulty was that the British really had no effective person in view who could stand up to Jinnah. So far as the British were concerned, their 'key piece' in many ways was Sikander, but the Viceroy was convinced that he had a tendency to exhibit a certain weakness of character on critical occasions and was really no match for Jinnah.[137] In such a situation, the Viceroy thought that the best course for him to follow was to take 'special pains' in any conversations that he had with his visitors to avoid any criticism either of Jinnah or of Sikander, but to continue to emphasize the importance he attached to 'the Muslim community having an effective organisation of its own to put its point of view'.[138] This was not merely a matter of keeping up appearances, but the result of Linlithgow's deep conviction that it was important, irritating as the Muslim League and its leaders might be, to keep in being an organization of standing which could speak with some degree of authority on behalf of the Muslim community in India. Indeed, he had worked so assiduously to inculcate this view among all concerned that he even thought that he could claim 'to have suffered in no mild degree in the interest . . . of humouring Jinnah and the League'.[139]

VII

In spite of arduous efforts on Jinnah's part seeking the legitimation of the Pakistan demand since its adoption by the Lahore session of the League in March 1940, and the tremendous boost to his own as also the League's popularity and prestige, the situation on the ground was that till the end of 1941 few even among his followers and admirers genuinely believed in Pakistan in its full form. For emotional as well as tactical reasons they all swore by the Pakistan idea, but they did not think that a complete separation of the Muslim-majority areas from India was feasible or even desirable. This comes out clearly from the report of the then Reforms Commissioner of the Government of India, H.V. Hodson, on his visit to Madras, Orissa, Assam, Bengal, and Bihar from 8 November to 7 December 1941. As he put it:

> The Pakistan theory itself was supported with strict orthodoxy by every Muslim League politician with whom I spoke (except Mr Fazlul Huq, who was then still nominally a leading member of the League). . . . The most interesting point was that every Muslim Leaguer, with but one exception interpreted Pakistan as consistent with a confederation of India for common purposes like defence, provided the Hindu and Muslim elements therein stood on equal terms. . . .
>
> My impression was that among the Muslim Leaguers in the provinces

visited there was no genuine enthusiasm for Pakistan. At the same time, none of them will repudiate it, not only for fear of incurring Jinnah's wrath or impairing the Muslim solidarity which they feel to be vitally necessary at the present time, but also, I thought, because the policy itself, extreme and unpalatable as it may seem to them, expresses however crudely some inarticulate but vital theme in the Muslim mind. Even Muslim critics of the League, like Sir Mahomed Usman, told me that outside Bengal it would be hopeless for anyone to try to capture a Muslim constituency on anything but the League ticket. . . .[140]

The Cripps Mission (22 March–11 April 1942) brought about a radical change in the situation depicted in the lines cited above so far as it concerned the popular perception of the viability or feasibility of the Pakistan idea in its entirety, i.e. the complete separation of the Muslim-majority areas from the rest of India without any kind of central government or agency having jurisdiction over all the parts of the country. It is beyond the scope of the present study to examine in detail the background and purpose of that mission. It will suffice here to point out that the situation created by the advance of Japan in India's neighbourhood as also the pressures from Stafford Cripps, who had recently joined the War Cabinet, the British Labour leaders who were already partners in it, and the US President, Franklin D. Roosevelt, whose support was vital to the British war effort, combined to create a situation in which Churchill felt compelled to agree to apparently make another effort to break the political deadlock in India, with a view to galvanizing the war effort. It was also decided to despatch Cripps there with proposals for that purpose, hammered by the War Cabinet. These became famous as the Cripps Plan, published in India on 29 March. Apart from inviting Indian leaders to actively participate in the governance of their country in the immediate present, it for the first time explicitly recognized the right of the Indian people, after the end of the war, to make their own constitution, through an elected Constitution-making body, on the basis of full Dominion Status, with the right to secede from the British Commonwealth if they so desired. The British Government, it was further stated, would accept and implement such a constitution subject to two conditions. One of them was the signing of a treaty with the British Government covering all matters arising out of the transfer of power from British to Indian hands. The other, mentioned first, and most important for our purpose here, was the right of any province to decide to opt out of the Indian Union to be formed after the war. The exact words used in the Cripps Plan were:

The right of any Province of British India that is not prepared to accept the new constitution to retain its present constitutional position, provision being made for its subsequent accession, should it so decide. With such non-acceding Provinces, should they so desire, His Majesty's Government will be prepared to agree upon a new constitution, giving them the same full status as Indian Union, and arrived at by a procedure analogous to that here laid down.[141]

At his press conference held on the same date after the Plan was made public, Cripps clarified that if the accession or non-accession to the proposed Indian Union was decided upon by any provincial legislature with 80 per cent voting in favour, that would be accepted. If, however, only 60 per cent voted in favour the minority could ask for a plebiscite, which would be decided on the basis of a simple majority.[142]

Although Cripps fully supported the non-accession clause, just as other clauses in the plan which went by his name, its original author or initiator had been Amery, who held that it was the natural follow-up to the assurance given to Muslims in the declaration of British policy, of which, too, he had been the author, on 8 August 1940. 'After all,' he wrote to Churchill in the first week of March 1942, when the text of the Cripps Plan was being finalized, 'except for the particular composition of the Constitution-making body, there is very little in it that I did not suggest in July 1940 [in connection with the drafting of the August Offer], and the main addition, namely provincial option in order to solve the deadlock, is for that matter mine as well. . . .'[143] A perusal of the documents included in the first volume of the *Transfer of Power* shows that Amery was not wrong in making that claim. Thus as soon as the members of the War Cabinet began their efforts to draft a declaration announcing the setting up of a Defence of India Council with wide powers to be broadcast by Churchill (which preceded the consideration of a more wide-ranging declaration to be carried to India by a Cabinet Minister), Amery had taken the opportunity to point out that it was essential 'to make it clear from the outset that our 1940 pledge stands and that we should not consider any constitution arrived at otherwise than by agreement'.[144] In the beginning there was resistance to this proposal from the Labour members of the War Cabinet. 'Insistence on the 1940 pledge at this stage,' observed Attlee, the leader of the Labour Party and Deputy Prime Minister, 'will kill the scheme dead. Far better to say nothing at this stage but allow the new body to work as a National Council. There is no need to bid the devil good morning.'[145] This failed to deter Amery from pursuing his point. 'As for bidding the devil good morning,' he immediately wrote back to Attlee, 'I know my devil sufficiently to be certain that he will want to have an answer to his questions at once and will refuse to play unless he gets it.'[146]

The idea of Churchill's broadcast regarding the Defence of India Council was soon given up, but Amery again took up his point at the time of settling the terms of the Draft Declaration, which later became famous as the Cripps Plan. The clause on provincial option to stay out of the Union arose as a natural corollary to it. After first taking Linlithgow into confidence on his thinking,[147] Amery wrote to Churchill explaining his views in detail:

> Any declaration of Indian policy for the future must make it clear, unequivocally, that we stand by our pledge of 1940, to the Muslims and the Princes, that they are not to be coerced into any system of Indian Government of which they disapprove. This is in any case vital at present, in view of possible effects upon the Muslim elements in the Indian Army.
>
> On the other hand, our insistence on agreement has been widely taken as giving Mr Jinnah a veto on all constitutional progress in India, and as a mere excuse on our part for doing nothing. This has peculiarly infuriated Hindu leaders. . . .
>
> There is only one way of meeting this criticism, and that is to couple with a reaffirmation of our pledge to the minorities the positive affirmation that the majority can go ahead of itself if it wants to.
>
> Happily, the distribution of Muslims and Hindus is such that this can be done on a purely provincial basis, by declaring that if a majority of provinces agree upon a constitution, we will accept it so far as they are concerned, leaving dissident provinces to stay out for the time being or even altogether.
>
> This is indeed the logical consequence of the whole attitude we have taken up once we have left it to Indians to frame their own constitution. That has in fact meant treating them like the Dominions, in whose case federation or union has invariably come by agreement and with freedom to stay out on the part of any particular unit.[148]

When the India Committee of the War Cabinet held its first meeting on 26 February, it considered Amery's letter to Churchill and also a suggestion to incorporate a clause relating to the provincial option in any declaration on the Indian problem. This suggestion was recorded, but no decision was arrived at.[149] Such a decision clearly accepting the suggestion was made when the Committee held its second meeting on the following day and settled the terms of the proposed declaration.[150] Some drafting amendments or improvements were made later. But the principle of provincial option, now accepted by the India Committee, was never challenged by any member of this committee or of the War Cabinet. If any member of either body ever spoke or submitted a minute against it, that has apparently gone unrecorded, at any rate in the official papers; the volume on the Cripps Mission in the *Transfer of Power* series does not contain any document mentioning such a thing.[151]

The Viceroy, after his initial approval, did raise rather serious objections on the basis of comments received from the Commander-in-Chief and the Governors. His main argument was that the provincial option would by itself be no substitute for a firm British guarantee to the minorities contained in the August (1940) offer and further that it was likely to accentuate communal bitterness in the Punjab and thus have an unsettling effect on the Indian Army, 50 per cent of whose recruits came from that province. Linlithgow went on to suggest an alternative draft that sought to substitute the clause on the provincial option by a paragraph expressing the hope that the constitution-making body would so perform its task as to ensure for its product 'the loyalty of the people of India in their different groups, communities and areas', and to see to it that its authority was not denied by 'large and powerful elements in India's national life'. If it failed to produce such a constitutional structure within two years after the cessation of hostilities and the leaders of India's principal parties and communities invited the British Government to frame a new constitutional structure for India or to entrust this task to some other appropriate authority, the said Government would accept that responsibility.[152]

Sir David Monteath, Permanent Under-Secretary of State for India, raised equally serious objections on more fundamental grounds. He pointed out that the right of provincial option without any conditions as to size, financial stability, or other necessary qualifications meant that the British Government was 'committed in advance to the possible Partition of India into uncertain number of Dominions'. He, therefore, suggested an alternative draft which expressed the hope that the constitution framed after the war would be one embracing the whole country and would be accepted by every substantial element in it. If this hope did not materialize and some units or their combinations, 'capable of undertaking the responsibilities of complete self-government', were formed outside the Indian Union, they might also be recognized as Dominions. This was, however, to be subject to the condition that 'the authority of the system of government so set up in any separate unit or group of units must not be directly denied by any important element in it'. It finally stipulated that if India was Partitioned, 'arrangements must be made in respect of matters of common concern to the resultant political units, such as defence, communications, currency, etc., either by mutual engagements or by the establishment, by agreement, of some common co-ordinating authority'.[153]

Seven out of eight Advisers to the Secretary of State for India, including two Indians and five Britons, held a meeting and recorded their conclusion that the Draft Declaration lent itself to the interpretation that if Indians failed to put forward an agreed solution after the war, the British Government would adopt measures 'which may result in India being disintegrated'. They also felt that the announcement might easily be represented as a direct threat to one of the opposing parties in India or at least as an indication that the British were losing patience at a time when the situation demanded a more sympathetic attitude than ever before. Finally, they asked the Government not to associate itself with a proposal that appeared 'to open un-necessarily wide the door leading to the disintegration of India'.[154]

R.A. Butler, at that time Minister for Education, commented that the impression created by the Draft Declaration was that 'the unity of India—the goal of British policy hitherto—must be set aside'. He did not object to the clause regarding the provincial option, but suggested that there should be a provision for some kind of central union or nexus, bringing together the three main constituents—Pakistan, Hindu India, and the confederation of Indian States—for all-India purposes. He also thought that this would require the continuance of the British connection. As he put it: 'One cannot avoid the conclusion that Indian unity is still worth aiming for, and that the British connection is indispensable for India.'[155]

The strongest objection was raised by Field Marshal J.C. Smuts, Prime Minister of South Africa. Although he, along with other Dominion Prime Ministers, had only been informed of the text of the Draft Declaration and no one had sought his advice, he felt constrained to remark:

> Express opening left for Partition may be taken as a British invitation or incitement to Partition and may lead to most unfavourable reaction in India as a whole or among majority of its people. It may be argued that Irish tactics of Partition is once more followed and India may decline to accept free constitution on such terms not without much public sympathy. Unless Indian opinion has been prepared for an announcement of such a character it may come as a great shock and do more harm than good.[156]

These criticisms, however weighty they might have looked, failed to move the War Cabinet from the decision it had already taken. Actually, the ground for it had already been prepared by the declaration of British policy as announced on 8 August 1940. As mentioned earlier, the British Government had made clear therein that it could not think of transferring its responsibilities for the peace and welfare of India to any system of government whose authority was directly denied by large and powerful elements in India's national life. As Amery explained again, the provision of the provincial option was the logical outcome of that commitment. For if certain provinces where Muslims were in a majority did not accept a constitution made for the whole of India, and coercion was ruled out, the only option before the British Government was either to refuse to grant self-government to India or to allow the provinces not willing to go with the rest of the country the freedom of remaining out of the Indian Union and framing their own constitution.[157]

The provincial option to keep out of the proposed Indian Union and to join with other provinces to form a union of their own failed to fully satisfy the Muslim League. Its Working Committee, while expressing its 'gratification that the possibility of Pakistan is recognised by implication by providing for the establishment of two or more independent Unions in India', found the detailed provisions in this regard defective and rejected the scheme. Its main objection was that the procedures laid down for opting out of the Union did not suit the Muslims, who had only thin majorities in the Punjab and Bengal and might find it difficult to secure enough votes in the legislatures (80 per cent) in their favour or even a simple majority in a plebiscite of the whole population as suggested by Cripps.[158] On the other hand, the Congress rejected the Cripps Plan on the ground mainly that it contained the provision for non-accession of a province to the Indian Union, which it described as a severe blow to the concept of Indian unity.[159] However, these objections were with regard to the future. Both the Congress and the League were willing to put these objections aside and cooperate in the immediate present if the terms of such cooperation were settled to their satisfaction. The negotiations in this regard between Cripps and the Congress leaders were carried on for several days, but failed to result in any agreement as the latter wanted the reconstituted Executive Council of the Viceroy to function as a Cabinet, as Cripps had hinted in the beginning, but the British side rejected this suggestion.[160] The Congress Working Committee thereupon published its resolution, rejecting the Cripps Plan (adopted as early as 2 April) on 11 April. The League followed suit giving its own reasons for rejection.

Even though not implemented, the Cripps Plan must be considered as an important landmark on the pathway to both Independence and Partition. For the principles and promises contained therein on both the points continued to work as guidelines to British policy in India in the coming years. With regard to Partition, in particular, its significance cannot be overestimated. Freedom in some form or the other had been promised on several occasions since 1929, if not 1917, but the British readiness to accept Partition under certain conditions was affirmed for the first time through the clause on provincial option in the Cripps Plan. Thus a commitment had been made in a State Paper in the drawing up of which the bigwigs of both the Conservative Party and the Labour Party, besides Cripps, had a hand. While the clause on the provincial option was the handiwork of the Secretary of State for India, Amery, and had the backing of Prime Minister Churchill, both Clement Attlee, the leader of the Labour Party and Deputy Prime Minister, who was Chairman of the India Committee of the War Cabinet, and Cripps, who carried the plan to India, were clearly committed to the acceptance of Partition if the League remained firm on its demand and was able to muster sufficient support for it among the Indian Muslims. This was a commitment from which no succeeding government in Britain, whether Conservative or Labour, could resile. As mentioned earlier, Cripps had also devised a formula to enable the League to surmount the difficulty in the path of Partition through the provision for the provincial option because of the Muslims having only a thin majority in the population in both the Punjab and Bengal. Before he departed he made another valuable contribution to the legitimation of the demand for Partition by using the communal divisions in India as the main ground for rejecting the Congress demand that the proposed Executive Council of the Viceroy, to be reconstituted under the Cripps Plan, should function as a national government on the basis of the principle of cabinet government. When the Congress President, Abul Kalam Azad, emphasized that this could be arranged by convention, without any statutory change,[161] Cripps replied:

> This suggestion would be rejected by all minorities in India, since it would subject all of them to a permanent and autocratic majority in the cabinet. Nor would it be consistent with the pledges already given by His Majesty's Government to protect the rights of those minorities.
>
> In a country such as India where communal divisions are still so deep an irresponsible majority government of this kind is not possible.[162]

This must have come as music to Jinnah's ears. For it was one of the major bases of the demand for Pakistan. In any system of responsible government on the basis of democratic principles there could be no escape from a Hindu-majority dominating the central government. The demand for Pakistan had been raised primarily to free as large a section of the Muslim population in India as possible from being ruled over or dominated by such a majority. In various other ways, too, the Cripps Plan and other related pronouncements in connection with it had provided a powerful rationale and justification for that demand. V.P. Menon is not wrong in underlining the significance of the latter in paving the way for Partition. As he puts it: 'This was really the death-blow to Indian unity, and subsequent assertion of their preference for a united India by British authorities carried no weight.'[163]

Ironically, the Congress too accepted Partition in principle in its response to the Cripps Plan. Before we come to discuss that response, it may not be inappropriate to point out that the Congress response to the Pakistan resolution had been ambivalent from the very beginning. Although, Nehru had publicly condemned the Lahore resolution as embodying a mad scheme, having been a close student of history as well as contemporary politics, he must have been well aware that that 'mad' scheme reflected the inner urges of a large number of politically conscious Muslims and that it was likely to gather more and more support among them in the coming years. He was equally aware of the fact that the British, in view of their traditional way of looking at India as a medley of several diverse communities and interests and their past commitments to Muslims, were not likely to part with power in India on the basis of a constitution that might not be acceptable to the latter. His attitude to the demand for Partition was conditioned by these variables. This can be the only meaning of a remark made by him on 24 April 1940 to a retiring British civilian in India, Malcolm Darling, in the course of an hour-long conversation on the political situation in India at a mutual friend's house in Bombay. According to Darling's summary, while Nehru was 'entirely opposed' to the Pakistan idea and felt that 'the Muslims would themselves in time come to rue it', he observed that 'if India could not achieve freedom otherwise, he would accept it rather than not have freedom'.[164]

It can be safely assumed that it was not Nehru's personal opinion but rather reflected the attitude of the Congress High Command as a whole. Otherwise, he would have qualified his remark accordingly. Gandhi's somewhat contradictory reactions to the Lahore Resolution, as expressed in his writings in the *Harijan* also lend themselves to the same conclusion.

Thus while recording his strong abhorrence to the idea of Partition based on the two-nation theory, Gandhi did not rule out its acceptance under all circumstances. In his comments in *Harijan*, dated 30 March 1940, he observed: 'If the vast majority of Indian Muslims feel that they are not one nation with their Hindu and other brethren, who will be able to resist them?'[165] A week later he went further (in the course of an article in *Harijan*, dated 6 April) and, albeit indirectly, lent legitimacy to the League's demand for Partition by remarking: 'The Muslims must have the same right of self-determination as the rest of India has. We are at present a joint family. Any member may claim a division.' In the same article, however, he also observed: 'The two-nation theory is an untruth. The vast majority of Muslims of India are converts to Islam or are the descendants of converts. They did not become a separate nation as soon as they became converts.'[166] Writing in the next issue of *Harijan* (dated 13 April), he made an effort to synthesize the two positions: 'As a man of non-violence I cannot forcibly resist the proposed Partition if the Muslims of India really insist upon it. But I can never be a willing party to the vivisection. I would employ every non-violent means to prevent it.'[167] On the other hand, four weeks later he observed, while referring to the proposal for Partition: 'I have called it an untruth. There can be no compromise with it. At the same time I have said that, if the eight crores of Muslims desire it, no power on earth can prevent it, notwithstanding opposition, violent or non-violent. It can not come by honourable agreement.'[168] However, while speaking at a meeting of the AICC on 16 September 1940, he addressed these words to his Muslim brethren in the country:

> It is worse than anarchy to Partition a poor country like India whose every corner is populated by Hindus and Muslims living side by side. It is like cutting a living body into pieces. No one will be able to tolerate this plain murder. I do not say this as a Hindu. I say this as a representative of Hindus, Muslims, Parsis and all. I would say to Muslim brethren, 'Cut me to pieces first and then divide India. You are trying to do something which was not attempted even during the Muslim rule of two hundred years. We will not allow you to do it.'[169]

The apparent contradictions in Gandhi's as well as Nehru's comments on the demand for Pakistan were the result, on the one hand, of their passionate attachment to the concept of a united India and, on the other, their awareness of the hard reality that all their efforts till then to bring Hindus and Muslims on a common political platform had miserably failed and that the gap between the two communities had gone on ever widening with the passage of time. This was true of the Working Committee of the Congress as a whole. Thus we find that that committee, in its resolution on the Cripps Plan, on the one hand, described the provision of the option to a province to keep out of the proposed Union of India as 'a severe blow to Indian unity' and, on the other, affirmed that it could not 'think in terms of compelling the people in any territorial unit to remain in the Indian Union against their declared and established will'. The only safeguard it asked for was that no compulsion might be exercised 'on other substantial groups within that area'.[170] It is significant that it was by referring to this clause, to which he affirmed he had been a party, that Gandhi justified his move to hold talks with Jinnah in 1944 on the basis of the Rajaji formula conceding Pakistan to a substantial extent.[171] Again, when the AICC finally accepted Partition on 15 June 1947 on the basis of the Mountbatten Plan, it justified that decision by reference to the same clause.[172]

B.R. Ambedkar's views on Partition must have also helped to some extent in according legitimacy to the Pakistan demand. Belonging to a Scheduled Caste (Mahar) family of poor means in the Maharashtra region of the Bombay Presidency, he was endowed with an indomitable courage and an extremely powerful intellect. With tremendous odds against him, but with the support of his father and timely help from the then Maharaja of Baroda, he had managed to equip himself with the highest academic degrees in both the USA and Britain, and, instead of settling in a cushy job, had chosen to concentrate on the work for the uplift of the people belonging to the Scheduled Castes. He soon acquired great prestige not merely as a scholar and author of several books but also as a spokesman for the rights of the people belonging to the Scheduled Castes through his role during the Round Table Conference on Indian constitutional reforms in London in 1931, followed by his equally prominent part in the negotiations leading to the signing of the Poona Pact and the ending of Gandhi's fast unto death in 1932, on the issue of the method of representation of the people belonging to the Scheduled Castes in the Central and Provincial Legislatures in India. Within five months of the adoption of the Pakistan Resolution by the Muslim League at Lahore, he prepared a treatise on the demand for Pakistan, which was published in early 1941 under the title *Thoughts on Pakistan*, running into nearly 400 pages, divided into four sections, and backed by a vast amount of data. It presented a history of Hindu–Muslim relations in India and discussed the demand for Pakistan from both the Hindu and the Muslim points of view, but addressed his arguments mainly to the Hindus, and these arguments were, on the whole, highly supportive of the Pakistan demand. Because of his bitter stand against Gandhi and the Congress whom he constantly accused of working against the interests of the Scheduled Castes, the Congress leaders were normally not expected to pay much attention to his writings, but Pakistan being the most burning topic of the day and Ambedkar's fame as a scholar and leader of the depressed classes firmly established, this book by him must have been noticed by at least some among the top leaders of the Congress. And as Ambedkar expressed his views most cogently and forcefully, a few among them might have even been also influenced by his arguments. The same applies to British statesmen. Even if this did not happen, we must take note of them here. For the treatise presented a most formidable case for Hindus agreeing to Partition and undoubtedly played a role in legitimizing the demand for it.

Analysing the failure of all efforts to bridge the gulf between Hindus and Muslims, Ambedkar pointed out that this was because what stood between Hindus and Muslims was not a mere matter of difference, but of mutual antagonism. And this antagonism was not caused by material causes. The antagonism was 'spiritual' in its character and was formed by causes that had their origins in historical, religious, cultural, and social antipathy, of which political antipathy was only a reflection. These formed one deep river of discontent which, being regularly fed by these sources, kept on mounting to a head and overflowing its ordinary channels.[173] As for the recent transformation in the ideology of the League leaders, symbolized by the adoption of the Pakistan Resolution, Ambedkar attributed it not to 'any dishonest drift in their opinion', but to 'the dawn of a new vision pointing to a new destiny'. The magnetism of the new destiny was irresistible for Muslims, and the new idea was bound to catch on. This was mainly because it had opened up the possibilities of realizing the Muslim idea of the linking up of all the Muslims under one Islamic State. 'A Muslim,' wrote Ambedkar, 'must be really very stupid if he is not attracted by the glamour of this new destiny and be completely transformed in his view of the place of Muslims in the Indian cosmos.' Indeed, according to him, the destiny was so obvious that it was 'somewhat surprising that the Muslims should have taken so long to own it up'.[174] Finally, he advised the Hindus that it was clearly in their interest to accept the demand for Partition without any effort at resistance. As he put it:

It is a question to be considered whether integral India is an ideal worth fighting for. In the first place even if India remained as one integral whole, India may in name be continued to be known as one country, but in reality it will be two separate countries—Pakistan and Hindustan—joined together by a forced and artificial union. This will be specially so under the stress of the two-nation theory. . . . The spread of that virus of dualism in the body politic must someday create a mentality which is sure to call for a life and death struggle for the dissolution of this forced union. If by reason of some superior force the dissolution does not take place, one thing is sure to happen to India—namely that this continued union will go on sapping her vitality, lessening its cohesion, weakening its hold on the love and faith of her people and preventing the use, if not retarding the growth, of its moral and material resources. India will be an anaemic and sickly State ineffective, a living corpse, dead though not buried.[175]

All this was based on the assumption that Hindus and Muslims did indeed constitute two separate nations. Expounding the two-nation theory in a language reminiscent of Rahmat Ali's and Jinnah's, and going into greater details than them, Ambedkar thus elucidated—regretfully though—the differences between Hindus and Muslims:

It cannot but be a matter of the deepest regret to every Indian that there is no social tie to draw them together. There is no interdining and no intermarriage between the two. . . . Their festivals are different. . . . Their religious notions are not only divergent but repugnant to each other so that on a religious platform the entry of the one means the exit of the other. Their cultures are different; their literatures and their histories are different. Not only different, they are so distasteful to each other, that they are sure to cause aversion and nausea. . . . No common meeting ground exists. None can be cultivated. There is not even sufficient physical contact, let alone their sharing a common cultural and emotional life. They do not even live together. Hindus and Muslims live in a separate world of their own. Hindus live in villages and Muslims in towns in those provinces where the Hindus are in a majority. Muslims live in villages and Hindus in towns in those provinces where the Muslims are in a majority. Wherever they live they live apart. Every town, every village has its Hindu quarters, and Muslim quarters, which are quite separate from each other. There is no common continuous cycle of participation. They meet to trade or they meet to murder. They do not meet to befriend one another. When there is no call to trade or when there is no call to murder, they cease to meet. When there is peace, the Hindu quarters and the Muslim quarters appear like two alien settlements.

The moment war is declared, the settlements become war camps. The periods of peace and the periods of war are brief. But the interval is one of continuous tension. What can mass contact do against such barriers? It cannot even get over on the other side of the barrier, much less can it produce organic unity.[176]

In an epilogue, Ambedkar summed up the main issues that according to him, had to be considered dispassionately by the Hindus in order to arrive at a correct conclusion whether they should continue to harbour the dream of one united India or accept Partition. These were:

1. Is Hindu–Muslim unity necessary for India's political advancement? If necessary, is it still possible of realization notwithstanding the new ideology of Hindus and Muslims being two different nations?
2. If Hindu–Muslim unity is possible should it be reached by appeasement or by settlement?
3. If it is to be achieved by appeasement, what are the new concessions that can be offered to the Muslims to obtain their willing cooperation, without prejudice to other interests?
4. If it is to be achieved by a settlement, what are the terms of that settlement? If there are only two alternatives: (i) Division of India into Pakistan and Hindustan or (ii) Fifty-fifty share in Legislature, Executive and the Services, which alternative is preferable?
5. Whether India, if she remained one integral whole, can rely upon both Hindus and Musalmans to defend her independence, assuming it is won from the British?
6. Having regard to the prevailing antagonism between Hindus and Musalmans and having regard to the new ideology demarcating them as two distinct nations and postulating an opposition in their ultimate destinies, whether a single constitution for these two nations can be built in the hope that they will show an intention to work it and not to stop it?
7. On the assumption that the two-nation theory has come to stay, does not India become an incoherent body without organic unity, incapable of developing into a strong united nation, bound by a common faith in a common destiny and

therefore likely to remain as a feeble and a sickly country, easy to be kept in perpetual subjection either of the British or of any other foreign power?

8. If India cannot be one united country, is it not better that Indians should help India in the peaceful dissolution of this incoherent whole into its natural parts, namely Pakistan and Hindustan?
9. Whether it is not better to provide for the growth of two independent and separate nations . . . rather than pursue the vain attempt of keeping India as one undivided country in the vain hope that Hindus and Muslims will some day be one and occupy it as the members of one nation and sons of one motherland?[177]

At the end Ambedkar explained that a large part of his argument had been addressed to Hindus not merely because they were in a majority in India, but also because their leaders seemed to him to have lost 'the Seeing Eye' (a phrase borrowed from Carlyle) and seemed to be 'walking in the glamour of certain vain illusions, the consequences of which must . . . be terrible for the Hindus'. This was, according to him, borne out by the fact that the Hindus and Muslims were 'neither one in temperament, nor in spiritual experience, nor in the desire for political union' and even on the few occasions when they approached some kind of cordiality their relations were marked by uneasiness. The Hindus continued to harbour the illusion that in spite of past experience there was still left 'a sufficient stock of broad and real community of aim, sentiments and policy to enable Hindus and Muslims to come together'. Further, they had failed to realize that Jinnah had engaged himself in 'mobilising all his forces for battle'. He had never been a man of the masses and indeed distrusted them. He was also not known before as a very devout, pious, or a professing Muslim. It was doubtful if he frequented any mosque. However, he had now undergone a complete change and had become a man of the masses. He had not only become a believer in Islam, but was also prepared to die for it and frequently joined Muslim meetings in Bombay, which began or ended with the slogans 'Allah-o-Akbar' and 'Long Live Quaid-i-Azam'. In spite of all this, bemoaned Ambedkar, the Hindus were not willing to shed the illusion that Pakistan was only Jinnah's fancy and had no support from the Muslim masses and other Muslim leaders. They were hugging that illusion because Sikander Hyat Khan and Fazlul Huq were not openly supporting Jinnah. They failed to see how in the provincial elections of 1937 both Sikander and Huq were opposed to the League, but how both had felt compelled to join it after the election. The Hindus even did not even ask themselves why if Sikander and Huq were really opposed to Partition did they not openly denounce it. Ambedkar was at a loss to understand what had made the Hindu intellect 'so weak and so dull' that it could not see the obvious and surmised that 'false sentiments and false illusions' cherished by the Hindus mainly came in the way of their understanding of the nature of the communal problem. It was this state of affairs in the Hindu camp, remarked Ambedkar, which had led him to address a large part of his argument to the Hindus.[178]

VIII

Needless to say, in expressing the views that they did on Partition the authors of the Cripps Plan, the members of the Congress Working Committee, Gandhi, and Ambedkar, were not trying to appease Jinnah or the Muslim League, but only seeking in different ways to come to terms with the existing political reality in India in the early 1940s. That reality was that the demands for Independence and Partition spearheaded respectively by the Congress and the League were both gaining momentum in India and that it was becoming clearer day by day that the one would not be possible without the other. The British were keen to absolve themselves of the charge that they were trying to use the differences between the Congress and the League as a pretext for not agreeing to hand over power to Indian hands. The provision of the provincial option in the Cripps Plan was included with that aim in view by making it possible for the Congress to move towards its goal without being bogged down by the League's demand for self-determination for Muslims in areas where they constituted a majority. The Congress Working Committee realized the force of this argument and was also conscious of the fact that the League's popularity among the Muslims was growing day by day, especially since the adoption by it of the demand for Pakistan, and that it was futile to strike their heads against that hard fact. This was also the main factor shaping the reactions of Gandhi. Though neither the Congress nor Gandhi believed in the two-nation theory on which the demand for Partition was based, they realized that if the Muslims unitedly backed that demand, there was no way in which they could move towards Independence without conceding it, at any rate so long as the British were determined not to ignore the Muslim point of view while considering any scheme for India's political advance. Ambedkar, not being associated with the Congress, was perhaps able to see that reality even more clearly. Of course, he was extremely hostile to the Congress, but it would be too far-fetched to imagine that his strong championing of the Pakistan demand was the result of his hostility to the Congress and did not represent his own objective understanding of the situation. The tone of his presentation clearly shows that he was writing out of conviction.

All the views, cited above, must have been conditioned to a large extent by the success of the League's nominees in 46 of 56 by-elections held since January 1938. While Independents won in seven, the Congress could secure victory in only three constituencies. The following table may be seen in this connection:

RESULTS OF THE BY-ELECTIONS IN MUSLIM CONSTITUENCIES FOR THE CENTRAL AND PROVINCIAL LEGISLATURES BETWEEN 1 JANUARY 1938 AND 12 SEPTEMBER 1942[179]

		Number of by-elections	Candidates elected		
			Muslim League	Congress	Independents, etc.
Central Legislature	Upper House	1	–	–	1
	Lower House	5	4	1	–
Madras	Upper House	–	–	–	–
	Lower House	1	1	–	–
Bombay	Upper House	1	1	–	–
	Lower House	3	2	–	1
Bengal	Upper House	6	5	–	1
	Lower House	7	7	–	–
United Provinces	Upper House	5	3	–	2
	Lower House	2	1	–	1
Punjab	...	12	12	(Won by the Unionist Party in alliance with the League)	

Bihar	Upper House	1	1	–	–
	Lower House	3	3	–	–
Central Provinces	...	2	2	–	–
Assam	Upper House	1	–	–	1
	Lower House	–	–	–	–
NWFP	...	4	3	1	–
Orissa	...	–	–	–	–
Sind	2	1	1	–	–
Total	...	56	46	3	7

It is clear from this table that the constituencies from which the League won were spread all over the country. The wide popular support among Muslims that the League under Jinnah's able and charismatic leadership commanded all over the country was the greatest source of legitimacy for the demand for Partition with which he was so closely identified. Other sources of legitimacy also played an important role in raising Jinnah's stature in Indian public life and pushing forward the League's demand for Pakistan, as a serious issue for consideration in connection with India's political future, but they really originated from that basic source.

NOTES

1. Penderal Moon, *Divide and Quit* (London, 1962), p. 21.
2. See Tej Bahadur Sapru to Girija Shankar Bajpai, 2 November 1940, Sapru Papers, National Archives of India, Series II.
3. Tej Bahadur Sapru to Sultan Ahmad, 11 December 1940, ibid.
4. *Quarterly Survey*, no. 11 (1 February–30 April 1940), F125/143, Linlithgow Collection (hereafter L.C.).
5. Sir Henry Craik to Linlithgow, 1 April 1940, F125/89, L.C.
6. *Selected Works of Jawaharlal Nehru* (hereafter *SWJN*), S. Gopal, ed., vol. XI (New Delhi, 1978), p. 17.
7. Ibid.
8. *Quarterly Survey*, n. 4.
9. Governor of Bihar to Governor General, Telegram, 1 April 1940, F125/108, L.C.
10. Governor General to Governors of all Provinces, 29 March 1940, F125/108, L.C.

11. Governor General to Secretary of State for India, 6 April 1940, l/P&J/8/506B, India Office Library and Records.
12. Sir Roger Lumley to Linlithgow, 30 March 1940, F125/54, L.C.
13. Note by Chief Secretary, UP, Enclosure 2 to H.S. Stephenson, Secretary to Governor, UP to J.G. Laithwaite, Secretary to Viceroy, 31 March 1940, F125/108, L.C.
14. Craik to Linlithgow, 1 April 1940, F125/89, L.C.
15. Malcolm Darling to Laithwaite, 25 April 1940, Enclosure, Private Secretary to Viceroy to Private Secretary to the Secretary of State, 4 May 1940, L/P&J/8/506B.
16. *Quarterly Survey*, no. 12, n. 4.
17. Ibid., no. 16, n. 4.
18. Governor General to Secretary of State, 18 May 1940, F125/28, L.C.
19. *Quarterly Survey*, no. 11, n. 4.
20. Quaid-i-Azam Mohammad Ali Jinnah, *The Nation's Voice, II, Annotated Speeches and Statements, April 1940–April 1942*, Waheed Ahmad, ed. (Karachi, 1996), pp. 1–7 (hereinafter *Jinnah: Speeches and Statements, II*).
21. Ibid., p. 21.
22. Ibid., p. 87.
23. Ibid., p. 90.
24. Ibid., p. 101.
25. Ibid., pp. 115–16.
26. Ibid., pp. 118–19.
27. Ibid., pp. 145–6.
28. Ibid., p. 153.
29. Ibid., pp. 169, 171.
30. Ibid., pp. 183–8.
31. Syed Sharifuddin Pirzada, ed., *Foundations of Pakistan: All-India Muslim League Documents: 1906–1947*, vol. II (hereafter *Muslim League Documents*) (Karachi, 1970), pp. 360–2.
32. Ibid., pp. 183–8.
33. *Jinnah: Speeches and Statements*, n. 21, p. 229.
34. Ibid., pp. 257–8.
35. Ibid., pp. 259-60.
36. Ibid., pp. 322-3.
37. Ibid., p. 264.
38. Ibid., pp. 301–2.
39. Ibid., pp. 303–4.
40. Ibid., p. 305.
41. Ibid., p. 340.
42. Ibid., p. 381.
43. Enclosure to Bajpai to Laithwaite, 25 April 1940, F128/135, Laithwaite's Correspondence, India Office Library and Records.

44. Enclosure to Jinnah to Gardiner, 25 December 1940, F125/136, ibid.
45. See Secretary of State for India to Viceroy, Telegram, 11 January 1940, F125/20, L.C.
46. Jinnah to Jamsaheb of Nawanagar, 21 March 1941, copy in F128/136, Laithwaite's Correspondence.
47. Sir Arthur Hope to Linlithgow, 1 June 1941, F125/69, L.C.
48. Wrench to Laithwaite, 4 December 1941, L/P&J/8/509, India Office Library and Records.
49. *Jinnah: Speeches and Statements*, n. 21, p. 387.
50. Lumley to Linlithgow, 7 May 1940, F125/54, L.C.
51. Lumley to Linlithgow, 3 January 1941, F125/55, L.C.
52. Viceroy to Secretary of State, Telegram, 28 June 1940, F125/19, L.C.
53. Viceroy to Secretary of State, 12 August 1940, F125/19, L.C.
54. Linlithgow to Lumley, 17 January 1941, F125/55, L.C.
55. *Times of India*, 26 March 1940, cited in K.K. Aziz, *A History of the Idea of Pakistan*, III (Lahore, 1987), p. 656.
56. *Civil and Military Gazette*, 30 March 1940, ibid.
57. *Times*, 27 March 1940, ibid., p. 657.
58. *Manchester Guardian*, 2 April 1940, ibid.
59. *New Statesman*, 30 March 1940, ibid.
60. *Economist*, 30 March 1940, ibid.
61. Linlithgow to Zetland, 6 April 1940, F125/19, L.C.
62. Zetland to Linlithgow, 4 April 1940, ibid.
63. Linlithgow to Zetland, 6 April 1940.
64. Jinnah to Linlithgow, 8 April 1940, F125/122, L.C.
65. Linlithgow to Zetland, 13 April 1940, F125/19, L.C.
66. Public Record Office (London), CAB 65(6), War Cabinet 89(40) 10 (12 April 1940).
67. *House of Lords Debates*, 18 April 1940, cited in notes in *Jinnah: Speeches and Statements*, vol. II, n. 21, p. 19.
68. *House of Commons Debates*, 18 April 1940, cited in ibid., p. 18.
69. Winston Churchill to Linlithgow, 3 November 1937, F125/154, L.C.
70. Public Records Office, CAB 65(5), War Cabinet 30(40), 4 (2 February 1940).
71. Ibid., n. 53.
72. Viceroy to Secretary of State, 10 June 1940, F125/19, L.C.
73. Ibid.
74. Linlithgow to His Majesty the King-Emperor, 13 June 1940, F125/1, L.C.
75. Jinnah to Linlithgow, 8 April 1940, F125/122, L.C.
76. For the text of the resolution, see *Jinnah: Speeches and Statements*, vol. II, n. 21, pp. 488–9.
77. Note of an Interview between Linlithgow and Jinnah on 27 June 1940, F128/135, Laithwaite's Correspondence.

78. Memorandum from Jinnah, dated 1 July 1940, F125/108, L.C.
79. Full text of the Declaration in K. Sarwar Hasan, ed., *The Transfer of Power* (Karachi, 1966), pp. 28–31.
80. War Cabinet, 67(7), 8 July 1940, Public Records Office.
81. Ibid., 67(8). See also John Glendevon, *The Viceroy at Bay: Lord Linlithgow in India, 1936–1943* (London, 1971), pp. 180–2.
82. *Gwyer and Appadorai*, n. 79.
83. *Jinnah: Speeches and Statements*, II, n. 21, pp. 26–9.
84. Ibid., Appendix III, pp. 487–9.
85. Note of an Interview between Private Secretary to the Viceroy and Sir Sikander Hyat Khan at Simla on 26 June 1940, F128/135, Laithwaite's Correspondence.
86. Note of an Interview between Linlithgow and Jinnah at Simla, 27 June 1940, ibid.
87. Viceroy to Secretary of State, 28 June 1940, F125/19, L.C.
88. Memorandum from Jinnah, 1 July 1940, n. 79.
89. Viceroy to Secretary of State, 1 July 1940, F125/19, L.C.
90. Viceroy to Secretary of State, 4 July 1940, ibid.
91. Linlithgow to Amery, 4 July 1940, F125/9, L.C.
92. Linlithgow to Jinnah, 6 July 1940, F125/108, L.C.
93. Jinnah to Linlithgow, 17 July 1940, ibid.
94. Viceroy to Secretary of State, 12 August 1940, F125/19, L.C.
95. Linlithgow to Jinnah, 14 August 1940, F125/108, L.C.
96. See Huq to Laithwaite, 10 August 1940, F128/135, *Laithwaite's Correspondence.*
97. Viceroy to Secretary of State, 16 August 1940, F125/19, L.C.
98. Linlithgow to Amery, 22 August 1940, F125/9, L.C.
99. Linlithgow to Amery, 26 August 1940, ibid.
100. Governor of Bombay to the Viceroy, 31 August 1940, F125/54, L.C
101. *Jinnah: Speeches and Statements*, II, n. 21, Appendix III, pp. 496–7.
102. *Quarterly Survey*, no. 13 (August 1940–31 October 1940), F125/43, L.C.
103. Ibid. This was also conveyed to the Viceroy by Sikander himself. See Linlithgow's summary of his conversation with Sikander on 9 September 1940 in Viceroy to Secretary of State, 10 September 1940, F125/19, L.C.
104. *Quarterly Survey*, no. 13, n. 90.
105. Linlithgow to Amery, 5 September 1940, F125/9, L.C.
106. Ibid., 19 September 1940.
107. Ibid., 25 September 1940. The Viceroy had also sent a letter to Jinnah on 25 September 1940, reiterating his assurance regarding the panel of names and the value he attached to the League's representatives joining his Executive Council as also the War Advisory Council which was soon going to be set up. Text in ibid.

108. Viceroy to Secretary of State, 30 September 1940, F125/19, L.C.
109. *Jinnah: Speeches and Statements*, vol. II, n. 21, Appendix II, pp. 470–1 and Appendix III, pp. 500–1.
110. Linlithgow to Amery, 2 October 1940, F125/9, L.C.
111. *Quarterly Survey*, no. 13, n. 90.
112. Amery to Linlithgow, 30 September 1940, F125/9, L.C
113. Viceroy to Secretary of State, 8 October 1940, F125/19, L.C.
114. Enclosure to Major W.H.P. Gardiner to John Parker, M.P., 28 December 1940, F128/136, Laithwaite's Correspondence.
115. Viceroy to Secretary of State, 24 February 1941, F125/20.
116. Linlithgow to Amery, 18 January 1941, F125/10, L.C.
117. Craik to Linlithgow, 4 March 1941, L/P&J/8/690.
118. Viceroy to the Governor of the Punjab, 1 March 1941, ibid.
119. Linlithgow to Amery, 1 March 1941, ibid.
120. Viceroy to Punjab Governor, 1 March 1941, n. 107.
121. Text in K.K. Azíz, ed., *Prelude to Pakistan, 1930–1940: Documents and Readings illustrating the Growth of the Idea of Pakistan*, vol. II (Lahore, 1992), pp. 937–40.
122. Linlithgow to Amery, 15 May 1941, F125/10, L.C.
123. Viceroy to Secretary of State, 22 July 1941, F125/20, L.C.
124. Linlithgow to Amery, 17 June 1941, F125/10, L.C.
125. Linlithgow to Amery, 9 July 1941, F125/10, L.C.
126. For Linlithgow's detailed instructions on the basis of which Lumley's letter to Jinnah had been drafted, see Linlithgow to Lumley, 11 July 1941, F125/55, L.C.
127. Viceroy to Secretary of State, 27 August 1941, F125/20, L.C.
128. Linlithgow to Governor of Assam, Bengal, Punjab and Sind, 17 August 1941, F125/41, L.C.
129. For the text of Sikander's letter to the Punjab Governor explaining what happened at the Bombay meeting, see Viceroy to Secretary of State, 27 August 1941, F125/21, L.C.; also enclosure to E.P. Moon (Secretary to the Punjab Governor) to Laithwaite, 26 August 1941, F125/90.
130. Viceroy to Secretary of State, 27 August 1941.
131. Viceroy to Governor of Bengal, 1 August 1941, F125/41.
132. Viceroy to Governor of Bengal, 1 September 1941, F125/41. It may be worthwhile to note here that in spite of the lack of encouragement from the Viceroy, Fazlul Huq, after some dily-dallying, did revolt against Jinnah's leadership, resulting in a split in the League in Bengal, the formation of a new Ministry by Huq in December 1941 in the name of the Progressive Coalition Party by roping in members from the Hindu Mahasabha and a section of the Congress headed by Sarat Chandra Bose, and his expulsion from the League. See Shila Sen, *Muslim Politics in Bengal, 1937–47* (New Delhi, 1976), pp. 128–34.

133. Viceroy to Secretary of State, 29 August 1941, F125/21. See also Linlithgow to Sir Bertrand Glancy (Governor of Punjab), 29 August 1941, F125/90, L.C.
134. Viceroy to Secretary of State, 25 September 1941, ibid.
135. Linlithgow to Amery, 25 August 1941, F125/10, L.C.
136. Ibid.
137. Linlithgow to Amery, 1 September 1941, F125/10, L.C.
138. Linlithgow to Lumley, 27 September 1941, F125/55, L.C.
139. Linlithgow to Twynam (Governor of CP), 25 September 1941, F125/62, L.C.
140. Nicholas Mansergh, *Constitutional Relations between Britain and India: The Transfer of Power, 1942–47* (hereafter *T.P*), I: *The Cripps Mission* (London 1970), pp. 65–6.
141. Ibid., p. 537.
142. Ibid., pp. 539, 541.
143. Amery to Churchill, 4 March 1942, ibid., pp. 316–17.
144. Enclosure to Amery to Churchill, 9 February 1942, ibid., p. 141.
145. Attlee to Amery, 10 February 1942, ibid., p. 142.
146. Amery to Attlee, 10 February 1942, ibid., p. 146.
147. Amery to Linlithgow, 21 February 1942, ibid., p. 218.
148. Amery to Churchill, 25 February 1942, ibid., p. 240.
149. War Cabinet: Committee on India I (42), 1st meeting, ibid., pp. 251–2.
150. Ibid., pp. 261–2. See also John Barnes and David Nicholson, eds., *The Empire at Bay: The Leo Amery Diaries, 1929–1945* (London, 1988), II, p. 780.
151. The existence of differences on this point, however, cannot be ruled out. H.V. Hodson, then Reforms Commissioner of the Government of India, has described the Cripps Plan as a 'package deal' representing 'armistice terms in a fierce Ministerial dispute, which had threatened to split the War Cabinet'. See his *The Great Divide* (London, 1969), p. 91.
152. Linlithgow to Amery, 8 March 1942, *T.P.*, I, n. 1, pp. 367–70.
153. Memorandum by Sir David Monteath, 6 March 1942, ibid, pp. 334–40.
154. Note by Advisers to the Secretary of State, 6 March 1942, ibid., pp. 341–3.
155. Butler to Amery, 6 March 1942, ibid., pp. 343–4.
156. Smuts to Churchill, 5 March 1942, ibid., p. 327.
157. See enclosure, Amery to Radcliffe, 28 March 1942, ibid., p. 518.
158. For the text of the League's Working Committee's resolution on the Cripps Plan, see Appendix III, *Jinnah: Speeches and Statements*, n. 21, pp. 529–33.

159. For the text of the Congress Working Committee's resolution on the Cripps Plan see A.M. Zaidi and S.G. Zaidi, eds., *The Encyclopedia of the Indian National Congress*, vol. XII (New Delhi, 1981), pp. 458–61.
160. For a detailed view of the causes of the non-implementation of the Cripps Plan, see R.J. Moore, *Churchill, Cripps and India, 1939–1945* (Oxford, 1979), pp. 122–20; also Bimal Prasad, 'The Cripps Mission', *International Studies*, January–March 1976, pp. 143–54.
161. Azad to Cripps, 10 April 1942, *TP*, vol. I, p. 729.
162. Cripps to Azad, 10 April 1942, ibid., p.733.
163. V.P. Menon, *Transfer of Power in India* (Bombay, 1968), p. 466.
164. Malcolm Darling to Gilbert Laithwaite, 25 April 1940, copy enclosed with Laithwaite to M.J. Clauson MSS Eur. F125/35, L.C.
165. *Collected Works of Mahatma Gandhi*, LXXI (New Delhi, 1978), p. 372.
166. Ibid., p. 388.
167. Ibid., p. 412.
168. Ibid., LXXI (New Delhi, 1978), p. 27
169. Ibid., LXXIII (New Delhi, 1978), p. 25. For an overview of Gandhi's role in events leading to Partition, see Bimal Prasad, 'Gandhi and India's Partition', in Amit Kumar Gupta, ed., *Myth and Reality: The Struggle for Freedom in India, 1945–47* (New Delhi, 1987), pp. 99–115.
170. The *Encyclopaedia of the Indian National Congress*, vol. XII, n. 159. The resolution had been drafted by Nehru. See *SWJN*, n. 6, vol. XII, p. 188, n. 1.
171. *Collected Works of Mahatma Gandhi*, LXXIII (New Delhi 1979), p. 141.
172. *The Encyclopaedia of the Indian National Congress*, n. 159, XIII, p. 111.
173. B.R. Ambedkar, *Thoughts on Pakistan* (Bombay, 1941), p. 331.
174. Ibid., pp. 333–4.
175. Ibid., p. 342.
176. Ibid., pp. 354–6.
177. Ibid., pp. 347–8.
178. Ibid., pp. 348–52.
179. R. Coupland, *Indian Politics, 1936–42* (London, 1943), Appendix VI, p. 333.

CHAPTER V

Growth of the Pakistan Movement and Massive Electoral Mandate 1942–1946 (1)

AS SEEN IN THE previous chapter, Jinnah had gained considerable success by April 1942 in his campaign for the legitimation of the Pakistan demand. However, he must have been fully aware of the long haul ahead before that demand acquired sufficient sanction behind it, particularly in the Muslim majority provinces. As noted by Reginald Coupland, on a mission to India in 1941–2, on behalf of Nuffield College, Oxford, in order to prepare a report on the constitutional problem in India, the Pakistan demand was quite popular in Muslim political circles in the provinces where the Muslims were in a minority, but the same could not be said about the provinces where they were in a majority. This was primarily because of the difference in their status. The 'seductiveness' of the two-nation theory, on which the Pakistan demand was based, lay mainly in the escape it provided to Muslims from the 'humiliating fact' that they were and must permanently remain a minority in India. It was, therefore, found instantly attractive by Muslims in minority provinces such as UP and Bihar, smarting as a minority and very conscious of their position of superiority during the Mughal period. Although their urge for Pakistan appeared 'paradoxical' as UP and Bihar could not be included in it, Khaliquzzaman, the UP League leader, had an explanation for it. As reported by Coupland, he argued that 'the existence of an independent "homeland" would give Muslim minorities outside it the moral and spiritual backing they needed to keep their end up against Hinduism'. The appeal of the Pakistan idea in the Muslim-majority provinces, on the other hand, was weaker as the Muslims therein were 'not conscious day by day of their minority status in India as a whole'. As the Pakistan demand had been formally adopted by the League, its members professed adherence to it, 'but not always with conviction'.[1] Besides, the League was hardly in control, on the basis of its own strength, in any of the Muslim-majority provinces. Unless this position was radically rectified in favour of the League and its demand for Pakistan, the realization of that objective was bound to remain merely a dream.

This was indeed a difficult situation and posed a serious challenge to the League leadership. Jinnah fully rose to the occasion and, in spite of his recurring ill health, utilized every available opportunity to advance the cause of Pakistan. He was aware that, while the majority of the established leaders of the League in the Muslim-majority provinces were primarily interested in advancing their own political careers and could offer only lip sympathy for the Pakistan demand, if at all, the educated youth and intelligentsia potentially constituted his real support-base and his hopes were centred on them.[2] Once they became fully imbued with enthusiasm for the Pakistan demand, the established leaders were bound to feel compelled to proclaim their full-throated allegiance to Pakistan regardless of whether they genuinely believed in it or not. The same factor would also help in augmenting the ranks of the League, turning it into a much bigger organization.

In carrying out his campaign in favour of Pakistan, Jinnah's greatest asset was that by 1942 he had emerged as a charismatic leader in the eyes of the Muslims in all parts of India, hailed everywhere as the Quaid-i-Azam or the Great Leader. The force of his personality, and his long innings in Indian politics during which, whatever strategies he might have followed at different times, he had always remained a steadfast champion of what was assumed to be the Muslim cause, partly contributed to it. However, the main factor behind his charisma was his ardent espousal of the demand for Pakistan, which touched the inner recesses of the hearts of most of the politically conscious Muslims. There were, of course, exceptions here and there, including those Muslims belonging to the Congress, but they were really like drops in the ocean. This is amply testified to by the results of the by-elections from the Muslim constituencies between 1938 and 1942, given in the earlier chapter. Another telling testimony is provided by the Muslim public's response from all parts of the country to

Jinnah's appeal for contributions to the Muslim National Fund. By the middle of May 1942, in less than eight weeks since the appeal was issued, they totalled Rs 1,75,000 and more were to follow. What is particularly remarkable, as Jinnah explained through a press statement, issued on 18 May, is that he had received 'unexpected support from poor and middle class Muslims'.[3] Even more remarkable is the fact that those who sent their contributions included small children studying in schools. The following letters addressed to Jinnah from a few of them vividly illustrate the type of charisma surrounding him in 1942 and the way in which the Pakistan demand had touched the hearts of Indian Muslims. Thus Hanifa Adam, a girl from Poona describing herself as 'your sister-in-Islam', wrote on 16 April 1942:

> I am a student studying in the seventh std. I get five rupees from my father for my pocket expense out of which I shall send you one rupee every month for the League Fund. I am enclosing one rupee in stamps for this month. I am sure you will accept this meagre amount and oblige.[4]

Md Mohfooz Alam, a student of Class XI at the Muslim H.E. School, Bankipur (Patna) wrote on 22 April 1942:

> I am a school student of extremely scanty means. But I shall not allow my limited means to come between [*sic*] my duty that I owe to the Muslims and obedience due to you. I have decided to go without breakfast for seven days every month and send the amount thus saved to you. Kindly pray God to give me the strength to stand the trial.[5]

Mikutti Hasa, 'a poor student' of the IV form in the Government Muslim High School at Aalapuram and resident of a nearby town named Ponani (at that time part of Malabar in the Madras Presidency, now a part of Malappuram district in Kerala) wrote on 18 May 1942:

> It will be the greatest crime I commit to my community if I do not contribute anything I can towards the Muslim League Fund, regardless of the appeal made by you recently. So I humbly request you to accept these two anna stamps as my humble contribution; for I am a man of poor means.
>
> I request you to enroll me as a soldier when the time will come for Muslims to fight under your command for the noble cause of Pakistan.[6]

II

Certain political developments in India during 1942–5 provided Jinnah ample opportunities to further strengthen Muslim national consciousness and sharpen the campaign for Pakistan. In this connection mention may first be made of Gandhi's demand to the British in 1942, in the wake of the abrupt termination of the Cripps Mission, to Quit India, the adoption of that demand by the Congress, the arrest of Gandhi and other leaders, and the unprecedented mass upsurge that swept many parts of the country as a result thereof. Jinnah saw in it a splendid opportunity to further strengthen Muslim national consciousness and made full use of it by raising the sceptre of the immediate establishment of Hindu Raj, which in his view was the real motivation behind the Congress demand. Whether addressing a public meeting or talking to the press, he never missed emphasizing this point, and went to the extent of describing the Quit India movement as tantamount to a declaration of civil war between Hindus and Muslims. The virulence of his campaign in this regard indeed reminds one of the similar campaign he had unleashed against the Congress ministries in the Muslim-minority provinces during 1937–9.

Thus, for instance, in the course of a statement issued to the foreign press on 31 July 1942, Jinnah observed:

> The decision of the Congress Working Committee to launch a mass movement if the British do not immediately withdraw from India is the culminating point in the policy and programme of Mr Gandhi and his Hindu Congress of blackmailing the British and coercing them to concede a system of government and transfer of power to that government which would establish a Hindu Raj immediately under the aegis of the British bayonet, thereby placing the Muslims and other minorities and interests at the mercy of the Congress raj.[7]

Through another press statement issued on 10 August two days after the AICC had formally adopted the Quit India Resolution, Jinnah deeply regretted that the Congress had 'finally declared war and . . . launched a most dangerous mass movement' and appealed to the Hindus to stop the 'internecine civil war' to which they had been called by the Congress before it was too late.[8] In the course of an interview to the *Daily Herald* (London) on 15 August, Jinnah remarked that the whole policy of the

Congress had been to ensure that power be transferred from the British to Hindu Raj and asserted that Muslims were determined to see that they were not ruled over by Hindus.[9]

The League's Working Committee at its meeting in Bombay on 16–20 August 1942 deplored the decision of the AICC on 8 August 'to launch an open rebellion' and declared that its objective was to establish 'Congress Hindu domination' in India. Reiterating its conviction that Pakistan was the only solution to the Indian constitutional problem, it emphasized that if the Congress demand was conceded by the Government, 'it would bring the 100 millions of Muslims under the yoke of a Hindu raj which must inevitably result either in anarchy and chaos or complete strangulation and annihilation of Muslim India and all that Islam stands for'. Finally, it called upon the Muslims to avoid any participation in the Quit India movement and to continue with their normal, peaceful life. At the same time, it warned all concerned that if any attempt was made by anyone to intimidate, coerce, molest, or interfere in any manner with the normal life of Muslims, the latter would be compelled to offer resistance and adopt all such measures as they might consider necessary for the protection of their life, honour, and property.[10] Through a statement to the press issued on 6 September 1942, Jinnah expressed satisfaction at the reports received by him from all parts of the country and congratulated the Muslims for keeping away as a body from the Quit India movement as advised by him as also the League's Working Committee. He also took the opportunity to ask the provincial governments with jurisdictions over areas where serious disturbances had occurred and the people living there were going to be asked to pay a collective fine to exempt Muslims from it.[11]

Jinnah amplified the League's position further at a press conference in New Delhi on 13 September 1942. He explained that the League was not opposed to the transfer of power to Indian hands, but that this was subject to one condition. That condition was that all parties must agree to and guarantee the right of the Musalmans to self-determination and that they must pledge themselves to give effect to the verdict of a Muslim plebiscite and carry out the partition of India accordingly. In answer to a question, he again emphasized that the Congress demand—that the British quit India—was not merely a declaration of war against the latter, but was also a war against the Muslim

League, which meant Muslim India and other non-Congress organizations. That demand, he further stressed, was tantamount to a demand to hand over power to the Congress 'to establish Hindudum in the country' in the garb of nationalism. Putting forward a new rationale of the demand for Partition, Jinnah observed that under the League's proposal in this regard 'Hindu India had got three-fourths of India in its pocket', but was bargaining to get the remaining one-fourth also for itself. This he implied was not reasonable, asserting that there could be 'no compromise on the question of the right to self-determination of a nation'. It was their inherent birthright' and to deny that was to deny their very existence. Finally, in a not so veiled threat to both the Government and the Congress, Jinnah remarked that if he were to ask Muslims to embarrass and non-cooperate with the Government, it would create 'at least five hundred times more trouble' than was being experienced at that time. This was because the Muslims had 'five hundred times more guts' than the Hindus. In reply to further questions he remarked: 'Any intelligent person in India will tell you. I do not want to cast any reflection on the Hindus. It is temperament and the way in which the Musalman is brought up.'[12]

Jinnah did not allow the opportunity presented by the celebration of the popular Muslim festival of Id-ul-Fitr on 13 October 1942 to go unutilized to whip up Muslim enthusiasm for Pakistan. 'Let us on this great and auspicious day,' he observed on that occasion in course of a message addressed to the Muslims, 'take a solemn vow for establishing our rightful place in the present and also in the future new order of the world according to the light of the Islamic heritage.' Reminding the Muslims that their forefathers had come to India as conquerors, traders, preachers, and teachers, with their own distinct culture and civilization, and had founded great empires and built up great civilizations, and also that at that time the 100 million Muslims of India represented the largest body of Muslims in any part of the world, he appealed to them to stand solidly behind the goal of Pakistan. It was a matter of life and death for them: 'Either we achieve Pakistan or we perish.'[13]

In the course of a long speech surveying recent political developments, delivered at Aligarh under the auspices of the Muslim University Union on 2 November 1942, Jinnah referred to the small contributions to the Muslim League Fund received from the poor, with offers of their lives if needed and asserted that that showed that the League at that time represented 'not hundreds and thousands but millions of Muslims'. He further pointed to the fact that the Muslims by keeping themselves completely aloof from the Congress during the Quit India movement had shown beyond doubt that they obeyed the mandate of the League. It had become clear that, contrary to the boasts of the Congress leaders, the Muslim masses were not with the Congress but with the League. In such a situation there was no need even for a plebiscite among Muslims to determine the fate of the Pakistan demand. Jinnah did not go back on his earlier offer of a plebiscite among Muslims on the Pakistan issue, but instead warned that the Indian constitutional problem could be solved only by treating the Muslims in the subcontinent as a nation, recognizing their right to self-determination, and abiding by their verdict given through a plebiscite among themselves. 'We cannot,' he thundered, 'compromise on this issue. It would be compromising our very existence.'[14] Addressing the League's Council exactly a week later, Jinnah succinctly summed up the basis and nature of the demand for Pakistan:

> There is no doubt whatsoever that Muslims are a nation. As a national group in their homelands in the north-western and eastern zones they are no less than 70 million in number. Our proposal is that in those zones we want our independent States and we cannot agree to any constitution on the basis of [a] democratic central government for India [as a whole]. We say we have a right to self-determination and in the zones where we are in majority those regions should be carved out as independent States. That is our inherent birthright.[15]

Needless to say, Jinnah paid special attention to the spread of the League's message in the Punjab, the most crucial province in its scheme for Pakistan. Addressing a series of meetings in the Punjab—at Jullundur, Amritsar, Lyallpur, and Lahore—between 15 and 22 November 1942, he reiterated the League's demand for Pakistan, expounding it, as usual, in simple, clear, and forceful language, leaving no room for ambiguity on any point and at the same time emphasizing again and again that the Quit India campaign represented not merely a rebellion against the British but also an internecine war against the Muslims. For if the

Congress demand was accepted by the British, it would mean the end of all the dreams of the Muslims and their total subjection to the Congress (Hindu) rule.[16]

By the time of his sixty-sixth birthday, which fell on 25 December 1942, Jinnah was quite satisfied with the Muslim response to his campaign for Pakistan. Referring to the warm felicitations showered on him on that occasion at a largely attended meeting of Muslims in New Delhi, particularly to a poem in Urdu recited there that described him as growing younger day by day, he remarked that he himself believed he was getting younger and that this was due to the tonic administered to him in the shape of happiness at the changed state of Indian Muslims during the last five years. As he put it:

> The position of Muslim India during the last two hundred years has been that of a ship without a rudder and without a captain, floating on the high seas full of rocks. . . . In 1936 with the cooperation of many others we salvaged the ship. Today the ship has a wonderful rudder and a captain who is willing to serve and always to serve. Its engines are in perfect working order and it has got its loyal crew and officers. In the course of the last five years it has turned into a battleship.
>
> . . . Pakistan is there. We have only to take it. We have to prepare ourselves for every sacrifice. We have worked only for five years. If we work with the same spirit I have no doubt that Pakistan will be achieved sooner than we may have anticipated.

Although containing some exaggeration and, by implication, also a bit of self-praise, the statement made here by Jinnah was substantially true. And nothing could be truer than what followed, showing an understanding of historical forces, which is the hallmark of a really great leader. Explaining the mystery behind the fact that he was showered with so much affection and regard by Muslims wherever he went in spite of the fact that he had only been calling for hard work on their part without offering them any material reward in the shape of a post or a title, he remarked that this was obviously because he had spoken boldly 'what was in the hearts of millions of Muslims'.[17]

The same mood of elation at the success achieved in getting more and more Muslims, particularly the youth and the intelligentsia, committed to the cause of Pakistan was reflected in Jinnah's message to Muslims in connection with the celebration of Pakistan Day on 23 March 1943. Describing the progress made by the Muslims 'as a nation' since the adoption of the Pakistan Resolution three years ago as 'a remarkable fact', Jinnah observed:

> Never before in the history of the world has a nation rallied round a common platform and a common ideal in such a short time as the Muslims have done in this vast subcontinent. Never before has a nation, miscalled a minority, asserted itself so quickly and so effectively. Never before has the mental outlook of a nation been unified so suddenly. Never before has the solidarity of millions of people been established and demonstrated in so limited a time and under such peculiar circumstances as are prevalent in India. Three years ago Pakistan was a resolution. Today it is an article of faith, a matter of life and death with Muslim India.[18]

In his presidential address to the thirtieth annual session of the Muslim League (New Delhi, 24 April 1943), Jinnah again referred with pride and elation to the phoenix-like rise and regeneration of Muslim India from 'the very ashes of its ruination'. This was borne out by the fact that during the previous seven years (1936–43) the Muslims had become, 'after the British, socially the most solid, militarily the most virile and politically the most decisive factor in modern India'. Jinnah's New Delhi address is significant not merely for such words of cheer and self-congratulation, but also for a clear and lucid exposition of the League's new objective enshrined in the Pakistan Resolution. Asserting that the goal of Muslim India was clear, he pointed out that what they wanted was to establish 'independent States' in those zones which were their homelands and where they were in a majority. Further, they did not want to have a union with those zones where the Hindus were in a majority. In this connection, Jinnah mentioned that people, including some constitutional experts, continued to ask why could there not be 'some sort of loose federation or confederation'. Others talked of giving the widest freedom to the federating units and vesting the residuary powers in them. Such people, Jinnah pointed out, tended to forget the history of federations in various parts of the world. Citing the examples of the United States and Canada, he pointed out that a federation, whatever its form and howsoever it may be described, has a tendency to deprive the federating units of their power in all vital matters and that this happens with the consent of the federating units themselves, who feel compelled to transfer their power to the federal government. Jinnah, therefore, was absolutely clear that any constitutional scheme, by whatever name it was called, on the basis of a united India would not suit the Muslims. As he put it:

> We are opposed to any scheme nor can we agree to any proposal which has for its basis any conception or idea of a central government—federal or confederal—for it is bound to lead in the long run to the emasculation of the entire Muslim nation, socially, educationally, culturally, economically or politically and to the establishment of the Hindu majority raj in this subcontinent. Therefore remove from your mind any idea of some form of such loose federation. There is no such thing as loose federation. Where there is a central government and provincial governments they will go on tightening, tightening and tightening until you are pulverized with regard to your powers as units.[19]

While stressing the point that Muslim interests could only be served by the creation of Pakistan, comprising the Muslim-majority provinces, Jinnah made it clear that he was not oblivious of the fact that Muslims living in the minority provinces would have to continue living in India as a minority. Unlike in the recent past when the hostage theory had been peddled in order to assure them against the possibility of persecution at the hands of the majority, Jinnah in his address, at the New Delhi session tackled the issue in a different way. Right in the beginning of his address he surveyed the then existing position of the League in the Muslim-majority provinces and then asked his audience not to forget the minority provinces. It was they, he emphasized, who had 'spread the light when there was darkness in the Majority Provinces' and working as 'spearheads' had suffered, during the rule by the Congress ministries, for the sake of Muslims in the majority provinces. Identifying himself with the Muslims in the minority provinces (perhaps because of his base in Bombay) and appealing to the sentiment of Islamic solidarity, he remarked: 'But never mind, it is all in the role of a minority to suffer. We of the minority [provinces] have suffered and are ready to face any consequences if we can liberate the 75 million of our brethren in the northern, western and eastern zones.'[20]

In this address Jinnah also advanced the argument that if the Congress leaders agreed to the demand for Pakistan, this could facilitate the freedom of Hindus as well as Muslims. For it was not possible for the British to devise a constitutional structure on the basis of one, united, democratic India. He did not attach any importance to Gandhi's recent letter to Linlithgow sent on 29 January, 1943 that in asking the British to quit India through the August resolution the Congress was not insisting on power being transferred to itself but to all Indians and would indeed be willing to accept if the Viceroy invited Jinnah to form a national government responsible to a duly elected body. Describing this proviso as the crux of Gandhi's proposal, Jinnah remarked that nothing was left after that. For the Viceroy together with the Secretary of State would lose all power and this would require the framing of a new constitution providing for the installation of a Government of India responsible to an elected legislature. The League's acceptance of such a proposition would not merely mean a postponement of the Pakistan demand, but actually its torpedoing and that, too, with the League's consent. Therefore, argued Jinnah, the position of the Congress had not changed but was only expressed in a different language. In effect, it meant 'Hindu raj [on the] *Akhand Hindustan* basis'; a position that the League could never accept. If, Jinnah added, there was any change in Gandhi's position and he was willing to settle with the League on the basis of Pakistan, he could write to Jinnah and could rest assured of a positive response. 'He was,' remarked Jinnah, 'writing letters to the Viceroy. Why does he not write to me direct?'[21]

After going through Jinnah's speech as produced in the *Dawn*, a daily started by him and published from New Delhi, Gandhi responded through a letter addressed to the former and sent through the Government of India on 4 May 1943. Here he evaded the issue of a change of heart but expressed a desire to meet Jinnah for finding a solution of the communal problem and hoped that if the latter was interested in doing so, the Government would not come in the way.[22] After consultations between the Viceroy and his superiors in London, extending over several weeks, it was finally decided against forwarding Gandhi's letter to Jinnah, or making public its full contents, but merely issuing a communiqué, on 27 May 1943, mentioning that Gandhi had in his letter desired to meet Jinnah and mentioning the Government's decision not to forward it to the addressee.[23] This was done on 27 May 1943.[24] Jinnah had already been officially informed of all this three days earlier.[25] He issued a statement on 28 May 1943, observing that Gandhi's letter could only be construed as a move on his part to embroil the Muslim League in a clash with the British Government with the purpose of helping his release so that he would be free to say what he liked thereafter. Even though the Government had not conveyed the contents of Gandhi's letter, apart from his desire to meet Jinnah, the latter went on to explain that really there was no change in Gandhi's position, which, as indicated by his recent correspondence with the Viceroy, remained the same as on 8 August 1942.[26]

By adopting such a stance Jinnah confounded his admirers as well as critics, who had imagined that he would take it as a serious affront if Gandhi's letter was not forwarded to him.[27] However, he followed such a course obviously in order to extricate himself from a potentially tricky situation and cement further the League's traditional relationship with the Government—in spite of occasional differences—based on common opposition to the Congress. That he admirably succeeded in achieving this comes out clearly in the following comment of the Viceroy on Jinnah's press statement of 28 May 1943, conveyed to Amery the next day:

> It is wholly satisfactory from our point of view and does much credit to Jinnah's political capacity. I am the more relieved by it since Nazimuddin [Jinnah's close associate and then head of the League Ministry in Bengal], who has just been here, had taken very seriously our refusal to forward Gandhi's letter and had been suggesting that all Muslim League Ministries might have to come out on the issue. . . .
>
> Jinnah's reply is the more satisfactory in that he now definitely places himself in the position that he as well as Government require that Gandhi and the Congress shall come off their policy of last August before there can be any dealings between Gandhi and the Muslim League. . . .[28]

In a detailed letter sent to Amery on 1 June 1943, Linlithgow again returned to this topic and remarked: 'The Gandhi–Jinnah business has gone off very well indeed. After describing the reactions of both Jinnah's friends and foes to the refusal of the Government to forward Gandhi's letter to him, the Viceroy further remarked:

> I am bound to say that while I have little personal affection for Jinnah and while as a politician I think he can on an occasion be disastrous, he has, in my judgement, on this occasion shown statesmanship and balance, and emerges as a much bigger man than one would have been prepared to anticipate.[29]

Amery fully shared such a view. In his letter to Linlithgow sent on 2 June 1943 he observed:

> It looks as if we had come very well out of the Gandhi–Jinnah correspondence. I confess I admire the skill with which Jinnah has taken advantage of your deflation of Gandhi over this business by deflating him one further, while at the same time adroitly saving his own face by making it clear that the only letter which would have satisfied him . . . was one abandoning the whole Congress policy . . . and also accepting Pakistan.[30]

Regardless of what the British thought of him on various occasions, Jinnah was always on his guard against anyone in India or abroad imagining that his strategy was based mainly on reliance on British support. Though always eager to utilize British support, when available, Jinnah had enough maturity as a politician to realize that such support could not be counted upon in all circumstances, but would be available only when there was a convergence of interests between Britain and the League. He, therefore, took care to emphasize again and again that the achievement of Pakistan depended solely upon the efforts of the Muslims and on nothing else. Thus in his presidential address to the thirty-first session of the League held at Karachi, on 24 December 1943, he emphatically asserted that the League could not depend, and did not depend, on anyone to help it in securing Pakistan. 'It is only by our own inherent strength,' he added, 'by our work, by our service, by our sacrifice that we shall achieve this goal of ours—Pakistan.' The Hindus, he explained, could not give Pakistan; all that they could do was to stop obstructing it once they realized that they could not achieve freedom for themselves—unless Pakistan was conceded. The British could give it, because it was in their possession, but it was not clear whether they would actually do so or go on 'camouflaging, evading, putting forward plausible excuses'. Regardless, however, of what they did, they could not prevent the Muslims from 'seizing Pakistan'.[31]

Some people continued to ask Jinnah again and again as to what exactly he meant by Pakistan or Partition and Jinnah always obliged, showing how baseless has been the charge that he did not explain in clear terms what exactly he meant by Partition or Pakistan. Thus, in a press interview at Karachi on 5 January 1944, he observed:

I mean a Partition in terms of the Lahore resolution of 1940, that the provinces in which the Musalmans are in a majority and the rest of India—which is three-fourth Hindustan—the provinces would be at liberty to form themselves into independent states, Pakistan and Hindustan. Naturally Pakistan will have its units as determined upon by the Musalmans and Hindustan will have its units as determined upon by the Hindus.[32]

Jinnah also effectively answered those of his critics who pointed out that he had been avoiding giving details regarding various aspects of the proposed State of Pakistan, such as defence, economy, minorities, etc. When asked to comment on such accusations, on 11 January 1944, by a British author, Beverley Nichols, who was then touring India to collect materials for his proposed book on the country, Jinnah replied that the question was neither just nor intelligent, particularly as it had been put by an Englishman. Reminding Nichols of the history of his own country, Jinnah pointed out that when Ireland was separated from Britain, the document containing the terms of separation consisted of approximately ten lines, leaving all the details to the future. Asserting that he had already given the world 'a good deal more than ten lines to indicate the principles and practices of Pakistan', he observed that it was 'beyond the power of any man to provide, in advance, a blueprint in which every detail is settled'. Examples of separation in recent Indian history, he added, also showed that such a blueprint was not at all necessary. Thus, when a decision was taken to separate Burma from India, or Sind from Bombay, this was done without calling for a blueprint, nor was there any need for it: 'The vital point was that the principle of separation was accepted, the rest followed automatically.'

After Jinnah had elucidated the two-nation theory on the usual lines as the main basis for the demand for Pakistan, he had to answer the question whether the Muslims would be richer or poorer within Pakistan. This he did by putting a counter question: 'Suppose you were asked which you would prefer, a rich England under Germany or a poor England free, what would your answer be?' After Nichols answered that it was hardly necessary to say, Jinnah appreciated that and then went on to remark: 'This great idea [i.e. Pakistan] rises far above mere questions of personal comfort or temporary inconvenience.' He further explained that the Muslims were 'a tough people, lean and hardy'. If Pakistan meant that they would have to be a little tougher, they would not complain. However, there was no reason to believe that it was going to be like that. There was no conceivable reason to suppose that 'the gift of nationality' was going to be 'an economic liability'. When the question turned to defence, Jinnah affirmed that what he had said about the economy in Pakistan also applied to its defence. Just as Afghanistan, for example, was defended by the Afghans, Pakistan would be defended by the Pakistanis. Why should there be a difference? Besides, the League was not asking the British to quit India immediately, implying that there might be a period of transition, which would enable the new nation to straighten out matters relating to defence.[33]

Jinnah clarified his thinking on defence from another angle in his interview with Stewart Emeny, representative of *News Chronicle* (London) on 29 February 1944. When the latter observed that it was not desirable to weaken India and lay her open to aggression in the future by dividing her into two countries, Jinnah remarked that he did not agree with the proposition that India would be any safer 'under a forced unity'. In fact, she might become more vulnerable to foreign attack because Hindus and Muslims would never be reconciled to each other: 'Any agreement between Muslims and Hindus to work together as a single unit even in a federation is an impossibility.' Jinnah also argued that Pakistan would be in the interest of Hindus as well as Muslims as the former would get three-fourths of India—'a territory larger and [a] population greater than any sovereign State with the exception of [the] Soviet Union and China'. When Emeny persisted with his view that Hindus would never accept Pakistan and that India might be engulfed by a civil war on the issue of Pakistan, Jinnah did not agree but pointed out that under the new constitution framed on the basis of Partition, there would be a transitional period for settlement and adjustment. During that period the British authority in defence and foreign affairs would remain intact. 'The length of the transitional period,' Jinnah further clarified, 'would depend on the speed with which the two peoples and Great Britain adjusted themselves to the new constitution.' Even while envisaging a transitional period during which Britain would continue to remain the paramount power with control over the army and foreign affairs, Jinnah was keen that there should be no delay in Partition between Hindu India and Muslim Pakistan. He again and again made it clear that on that issue there could be no compromise. 'I will believe that Britain is sincere', he finally told the *News Chronicle*' representative, 'when she divides India and gives both Hindus and Muslims freedom.'[34] In a message issued on the occasion of the annual Pakistan Day celebrations on 23 March 1944, he declared:

For us Pakistan means our defence, our deliverance and our destiny. It is the only way which will ensure to us our freedom and the maintenance of our freedom and the glory of Islam. We have to mould our people into a well organized and solid nation. The speed of the final victory depends upon the proportion of labour that we put forth and it is within our grasp.[35]

III

All this undoubtedly went on adding to Jinnah's charisma as well as credibility to the League's demand for Partition. The Gandhi–Jinnah talks in September 1944, with a view to finding out a solution of the Hindu–Muslim conflict on the basis of what became famous as the C.R. formula, contributed significantly to that process. The formula had been in the making for quite some time. C.R. had been one of Gandhi's closest colleagues as well as a member of the Congress High Command since 1920–1 and Premier of the Madras Presidency from 1937 to 1939. Ever since the outbreak of the World War II he had been working for the adoption of a moderate line on the part of the Congress so as to facilitate the establishment of a national government at the Centre and the Indian people's active participation in the war effort on the side of the Allied powers as well as the achievement of freedom at the end of the war. While recognizing the need for an understanding with the Muslim League for the success of this strategy, he had in the beginning strongly criticized the adoption of the Pakistan Resolution. Thus, in a press interview published on 27 March 1940, he described it as 'a sign of diseased mentality', which would result in the Balkanization of India without providing any lasting solution to the minority problem.[36] A little later, in the course of a speech at Salem (Tamil Nadu) reported in the press on 7 April, C.R. observed: 'Mr. Jinnah's move for the Partition of India was like two brothers cutting their own cow into two because they quarreled over its possession.'[37] When, however, reasoned pleas as well as the withdrawal of the Congress ministries in the provinces, followed by the resort to individual civil disobedience under Gandhi's leadership, failed to produce any significant change in British policy, C.R. realized that such a change could not be brought about without a Congress–League understanding. He considered such a change more urgently required than ever in the context of the contemporaneous Japanese military advances in India's immediate neighbourhood and the need for the Indian people to play their due role in the country's defence, not possible without the establishment of a national government at the Centre and the restoration of popular governments in the erstwhile Congress-ruled provinces. Even if others in the Congress leadership were not prepared to move forward with him in this direction, he felt so deeply concerned over the developing war situation that he was prepared to walk alone and resume the headship of a popular government in Madras if given a chance.[38]

Preferring, in the first instance, to take along with him the rest of the Congress leadership, C.R. made a bid to force their hands by calling a meeting of the members of the Congress Legislature Party in Madras, of which he continued to be leader, and persuading it to adopt two resolutions. The first resolution recommended that the AICC should remove the biggest hurdle in the way of the establishment of a national government at the Centre 'at this hour of peril' by accepting the Muslim League's demand for the separation of 'certain areas'. The second asked for AICC's permission to the Madras Congress Legislature Party to invite the League's support for the setting up of a popular government in Madras in order to motivate and organize the people to unitedly face the danger of a Japanese attack, considered imminent by many in view of the recent bombardment of Madras by the Japanese air force.[39]

The meeting of the Madras Congress Legislature Party, which adopted the two resolutions just mentioned, had been held on 23 April 1942, barely a week before the next meeting of the AICC (29 April–2 May 1940) at Allahabad. At that meeting C.R. moved a non-official resolution according to which the AICC was to note the failure of all efforts till then to form a national government at the Centre, which was necessary for mobilizing the Indian people for the defence of their country against foreign invasion, and show its preparedness to remove any hurdle in its way. Keeping in view the demand of the League for the separation of certain areas from United India, the AICC was to show its readiness for such separation, subject to the ascertainment of the wishes of the people inhabiting those areas, and to invite the League for cooperation in the formation of a national government. This was to be done on the basis of the argument that 'to sacrifice the chances for the formation of a national government at this grave crisis for the doubtful advantage of maintaining a controversy over the unity of India' was a most unwise policy. When put to vote, this resolution was negatived by 120 votes to 15. At the same time another non-official resolution, moved by Jagat Narain Lal (Bihar), affirmed that in the AICC's opinion the Congress could not agree to any proposal involving India's disintegration by permitting any part of its territory to secede from the Indian Union. This was adopted by 92 votes to 17. Maulana Azad, the Congress President, however, gave the ruling that the adoption of Lal's resolution would not nullify the resolution adopted by the Congress Working Committee on the Cripps Plan in April 1942, accepting the right of a province to stay outside the Indian Union.[40] The resolution regarding the formation of a Congress–League Coalition ministry in Madras could not be taken up for lack of time. As a result of the lack of Congress support for the two resolutions, C.R. had to resign his membership of the Working Committee. In view of the stern attitude of the latter, support for C.R. dwindled also in the Congress Legislature Party in Madras and soon only seven of its members remained with him. C.R. resigned his membership of the Congress as well as of the Madras Legislature Assembly, but continued his vigorous propaganda in support of his line, arguing that this was not at variance with the line adopted by the Congress in its resolution on the Cripps Plan. He later opposed the 'Quit India' call, initiated by Gandhi and adopted by the AICC at Bombay on 8 August 1942.[41]

All this while C.R.'s friendship with Gandhi had continued and they had several opportunities to meet during the latter's fast as a detenu in the Aga Khan's palace in Poona in February 1943. As a result of these meetings, C.R. was able to secure Gandhi's concurrence with his plan for ending the political deadlock by bringing the Congress and the League together, which later became famous as the C.R. Formula.[42] Perhaps waiting for a suitable opportunity to make it public, he kept it a closely guarded secret for more than a year and for the first time disclosed it to Jinnah at a meeting with him in New Delhi on 7 April 1944 and also left with him a letter enclosing the formula. Entitled 'Basis for terms of settlement between the Indian National Congress and the All-India Muslim League to which Gandhiji and Mr Jinnah agree and which they will undertake respectively to get the Congress and the League to approve', the formula contained the following clauses:

1. Subject to the terms set out below as regards the constitution for free India, the Muslim League endorses the Indian demand for Independence and will cooperate with the Congress in the formation of a provisional interim government for the transitional period.
2. After the termination of the war a commission shall be appointed for demarcating contiguous districts in the North-West and East of India, wherein the Muslim population is in absolute majority. In the areas thus demarcated, a plebiscite of all the inhabitants held on the basis of adult suffrage or other practicable franchise shall ultimately decide the issue of separation from Hindustan. If the majority decide in favour of forming a sovereign State separate from Hindustan such decision shall be given effect to, without prejudice to the right of districts on the border to choose to join either State.
3. It will be open to all parties to advocate their points of view before the plebiscite is held.
4. In the event of separation, mutual agreements shall be entered into for safeguarding defence and commerce and communication.
5. Any transfer of population shall only be on an absolutely voluntary basis.
6. These terms shall be binding only in case of transfer by Britain of full power and responsibility for the governance of India.[43]

This formula, it may be noted, conceded the principle of Partition, but this was subject to certain conditions. Jinnah's initial reaction to the formula as conveyed to C.R. during their meeting on 7 April was not at all favourable. C.R. wrote to him again on 17 April soliciting reconsideration. When this, too, did not elicit any reply for more than two months, C.R. sent a telegram to Jinnah on 30 June, conveying his wish to publish the formula as also its rejection by the latter. This elicited a reply from Jinnah in the shape of a telegram on 2 July denying that he had rejected the formula and asserting that, in spite of its not being open to any modification, he had offered to place it before the League's Working Committee; C.R. had not agreed to this and Jinnah had not, therefore, taken any further step in the matter. His position was that he could not personally take responsibility for accepting or rejecting the formula and that position still remained. Jinnah further added that if Gandhi sent 'his proposal direct' to him, he was willing to place it before the League's Working Committee.[44]

Gandhi, recently released on ground of ill-health and keenly exploring possible avenues for breaking the political deadlock, took the bait offered by Jinnah and wrote to him on 17 July, conveying his desire to see him. Recalling his earlier suggestion of a meeting with Jinnah sent in his 'invitation' from the detention camp in Poona, Gandhi wrote to Jinnah: 'Let us meet whenever you wish. Do not regard me as an enemy of Islam or of Indian Muslims. I have always been a servant and friend to you and to mankind. Do not disappoint me.'[45] To this Jinnah replied on 24 July from Srinagar, wishing Gandhi a speedy recuperation of his health and remarking: 'I shall be glad to receive you at my house in Bombay on my return, which will probably be about the middle of August . . . I would like to say nothing till we meet.'[46]

If Gandhi had hoped that he might succeed where C.R. had failed, Jinnah soon provided him sufficient grounds to think over the matter again by strongly denouncing the C.R. Formula, as well as the procedure adopted by C.R. in pushing it, in his address to the meeting of the League's Council held at Lahore on 30 July 1944. Even while acknowledging that it was conducive to further progress, from the point of view of the Muslim League, that Gandhi had 'accepted the principle of Partition or division of India' and that what remained was the question of how and when that had got to be carried out, Jinnah devoted most of his address to pointing out the shortcomings of the C.R. Formula in both procedure and substance. He finally observed:

I hope I have made it clear that the procedure and method adopted is hardly conducive to friendly negotiations; and the form is pure dictation, as it is not open to any modification This is not calculated to lead to fruitful results or solution and settlement of the problem which concerns the destiny of a nation of 100 million Muslims and their posterity. As regards the merits of the proposal, Mr Gandhi is offering a shadow and a husk—a maimed, mutilated and moth-eaten Pakistan, and thus trying to pass off having met our Pakistan scheme and Muslim demand.[47]

These remarks, however, did not deter Gandhi—who was at that time trying desperately to start a dialogue with the Viceroy—from himself seeking talks with Jinnah on the basis of the same C.R. Formula which Jinnah had denounced so strongly. Nor did Jinnah ever show any doubt or hesitation about the utility of such a meeting in spite of his serious reservations about the terms of the C.R. Formula. The old warriors had met so many times in the past under somewhat similar circumstances, without much hope of an agreement, that perhaps the unlikelihood of an agreement as a result of their meeting did not bother them so much. Or perhaps both of them saw some advantage in such a meeting at least for having a better understanding of each other's position and perhaps also for creating a favourable impression on their respective constituencies by showing their willingness to work for a settlement of the most intractable problem in Indian politics and the strongest hurdle in the way of securing freedom from foreign rule. Whatever that may have been, after a slight postponement due to Jinnah's ill health the Gandhi–Jinnah talks started in all seriousness at Jinnah's residence (10 Mount Pleasant Road) in Bombay on 7 September 1944 and continued, with brief intervals, till September 26 at the same place, Gandhi visiting it as many as fourteen times and at the same time exchanging letters with him, which, taken together, ran into more than 15,000 words.[48] Although both sides maintained strict secrecy about the nature and contents of their talks and correspondence, the fact that they continued for so long and, in addition, the two leaders' photographs, both smiling and cordially greeting each other, which the newspapers carried from day to day, created a wave of hope among the general public who felt that at long last perhaps a settlement was a round the corner. Nothing like this, however, happened. When early in the talks Jinnah expressed his strong dislike for the C.R. Formula, Gandhi said that he was shunting it out and framed a formula of his own, slightly different from the former in form, but not so in substance. The talks just dragged on and ended on 26 September, but as some time was required to prepare the text of the correspondence for the press, the announcement of their conclusion was made on the next day. Thus on the evening of 27 September, the whole world knew that the marathon Gandhi–Jinnah talks had failed to produce any mutually acceptable formula for a settlement of the Hindu–Muslim problem.

While releasing their correspondence to the press on 27 September the two leaders jointly expressed the hope that the public would not feel embittered and affirmed their trust that that was 'not the final end of their effort'.[49] That it certainly was not, but embitterment among the public could not be prevented, especially as the two leaders had felt free to explain their respective positions to the public and each took the stand that he had gone to the maximum extent possible to accommodate the other. Such a stance naturally implied that the other side had not been equally accommodating, making mutual recrimination and consequent bitterness unavoidable among the general public as well as the active workers in both the camps. The fact was that the clash between Indian nationalism and Muslim nationalism was then moving towards a climax and the leadership on neither side was at that stage prepared to lower its guard or to compromise on fundamentals. They might, of course, do so when dealing with a final British decision, as the Congress had done while dealing with the Cripps Plan in April 1942 or the League was to do later while dealing with the Mountbatten Plan (June 1947), but not when talking or negotiating among themselves. Gandhi put the whole matter succinctly when he remarked in his address to his prayer meeting on the evening of the same day (27 September), that the failure of his talks with Jinnah had been made public:

> If either of them had been weak, they would have possibly come to some sort of agreement but as responsible men they could not afford to be weak. A helmsman had to be firm and unwavering or else the ship would founder upon the rocks. Each one of them had tried to convince the other. It was possible that both of them might be in the wrong. But so long as each felt himself to be in the right he could not let go his hold.[50]

What exactly were the main points on which the two leaders

remained stuck to their respective positions? In the first place, Jinnah firmly held to the two-nation theory and wanted Gandhi to recognize the Muslims as constituting a nation by themselves, separate from the Hindus and the rest of the Indian population. Gandhi equally firmly refused to recognize Muslims as a separate nation. 'I find no parallel in history,' he wrote to Jinnah on 15 September, 'for a body of converts and their descendants claiming to be a nation apart from the parent stock. If India was one-nation before the advent of Islam, it must remain one in spite of the change of faith of a very large body of her children.'[51] To this Jinnah replied on 17 September, adumbrating the main bases of the claim for separate Muslim nationhood:

> We are a nation of a hundred million, and, what is more, we are a nation with our own distinctive culture and civilization, language and literature, art and architecture, names and nomenclature, sense of values and proportion, legal laws and moral codes, customs and calendar, history and traditions, aptitudes and ambitions—in short, we have our own distinctive outlook on life and of life. By all canons of international law we are a nation.[52]

Jinnah also strongly objected to Gandhi's assertion that he aspired to represent all the inhabitants of India and remarked:

> It is quite clear that you represent nobody else but the Hindus and as long as you do not realise your true position and the realities, it is very difficult for me to argue with you, and it becomes still more difficult to persuade you and to convert you to the realities and the actual conditions prevailing in India today.[53]

Objecting equally strongly to Gandhi's contention in his letter of 15 September that as he imagined the working of the Lahore Resolution he saw 'nothing but ruin for the whole of India', Jinnah observed that he was convinced that the true welfare not only of the Muslims but also of the rest of India lay in 'the division of India as proposed by the Lahore resolution'. He further added that it was for Gandhi to consider whether it was not his policy and programme, in which he had persisted, which had been the principal factor behind the 'ruin for the whole of India and of the misery and degradation of the people of India'.[54]

When, after putting on record their diametrically opposite perspectives on the fundamental bases of the problem of Hindu–Muslim discord, the two leaders proceeded to tackle matters of detail, they again found themselves at loggerheads. They were, of course, agreed that the problem could be solved on the basis of the principle of self-determination, but they held divergent perspectives on when and how that principle was to be applied. In the first place, the C.R. Formula had provided that whatever terms were settled between the Congress and the League, they would be implemented only after the achievement of independence and the transfer of full power and responsibility for the governance of India from the British to Indian hands. Explaining the thinking behind these stipulations, Gandhi wrote to Jinnah on 11 September:

> My life mission has been Hindu–Muslim unity which I want for its own sake but which is not to be achieved without the foreign ruling power being ousted. Hence the first condition of the exercise of the right of self-determination is achieving independence by the joint action of all parties and groups composing India. If such joint action is unfortunately impossible, then too I must fight with the assistance of such elements as can be brought together.[55]

Jinnah did not agree with this approach at all. He wanted a Congress–League settlement on the basis of Partition not after, but before the British withdrawal from India. As he wrote back to Gandhi on the same day that he received the latter's exposition:

> This in my opinion is, as I have repeatedly said, putting the cart before the horse and is generally opposed to the policy and declarations of the All India Muslim League, and you are only holding on firmly to the August Resolution of 1942. In order to achieve the freedom and independence of the people of India, it is essential, in the first instance, that there should be a Hindu–Muslim settlement.[56]

Again in his letter of 24 September Gandhi suggested that if separation was eventually decided upon, the areas demarcated for separation would form a separate State as soon as possible after India became free from foreign domination.[57] Jinnah, on the other hand, asserted in his letter sent the next day that the League proposed that 'we should come to a complete settlement of our own immediately, and by our united front and efforts do everything in our power to secure the freedom and independence of the peoples of India on the basis of Pakistan and Hindustan'.[58]

Second, while Gandhi, vide his letter dated 24 September, was prepared to concede the right of separation from India to those areas in the Muslim-majority provinces in the north-west and the north-east where the Muslims constituted a clear majority, (such areas to be demarcated by a commission approved by the Congress and the League), provided it was established through popular vote that the majority of the inhabitants of those areas (including non-Muslims as well as Muslims) wanted separation, Jinnah, vide his letter dated 25 September, seriously objected to this proposition. He asserted that if that condition was accepted, the then existing boundaries of those provinces 'would be maimed and mutilated beyond redemption and leave us only with the husk'. He further added that it would be opposed to the Lahore Resolution. Besides, he opposed the idea of the vote on separation being given to all inhabitants of even 'those mutilated areas' and not being confined to just Muslims and asserted that this again was opposed to 'the fundamentals of the Lahore Resolution'.[59] He had already expressed himself most forcefully in his letter to Gandhi dated 21 September:

> It seems to me that you are labouring under some misconception of the real meaning of the word 'self-determination'. . . . Ours is a case of division and carving out of two independent sovereign States by way of settlement between two major nations, Hindus and Muslims, and not of severance or secession *from any existing union*, which is *non-existing* in India. The right of self-determination, which we claim, postulates that we are a nation, and as such it would be the self-determination of the Muslims, and they alone are entitled to exercise that right.[60]

As mentioned earlier, the C.R. Formula had also stipulated that if separation of certain areas from the rest of India was decided upon, mutual agreements would be entered into for 'safeguarding defence, and commerce and communications and for other essential purposes'. This was not at all acceptable to Jinnah, for he saw it as a device for creating some sort of central authority which would have control in vital matters over the whole of India as it then existed and he was quite clear in his mind that Pakistan must emerge as a fully sovereign State. 'There cannot be,' he wrote to Gandhi on 21 September, 'defence and similar matters of "common concern", when it is accepted that Pakistan and Hindustan will be two separate, independent, sovereign States.'[61] Gandhi, on the other hand, was equally determined to ensure that even if Partition became unavoidable, some authority to look after matters of common concern to India and Pakistan must be created. He wrote to Jinnah on 22 September: 'I can be no willing party to a division which does not provide for the simultaneous safeguarding of common interests such as defence, foreign affairs and the like.'[62] However, Jinnah remained unmoved. 'According to the Lahore Resolution . . . ,' he clarified to Gandhi on 24 September, 'all these matters, which are the lifeblood of any State, cannot be delegated to any Central Authority or Government'.[63]

Faced with continuing divergences, Gandhi suggested help from a third party either through mediation or arbitration. He wrote to Jinnah on 22 September: 'We seem to be moving in a circle. I have made a suggestion. If we are bent on agreeing, as I hope we are, let us call in a third party or parties to guide or even arbitrate between us.'[64] Jinnah refused to accept this idea and wrote to Gandhi the next day: 'May I point out that you have repeatedly made clear to me that you are having these talks as an individual seeker? How can any question of a third party or parties to guide or arbitrate between us arise?'[65] When Gandhi persisted with his proposal and suggested that it was being rejected by Jinnah on a purely technical ground, the latter affirmed on 23 September that it was 'not merely [a] technicality, but a matter of substance'.[66]

As the talks were reaching the breaking point, Jinnah again and again turned back to his initial point that it was difficult to come to any agreement with Gandhi as he was not talking in any representative capacity, but merely as an individual. At the same time, he also pointed out that the solution suggested by Gandhi as well as the C.R. Formula was not in keeping with the terms of the Lahore Resolution. Gandhi did not agree. In his letter to Jinnah on 26 September he asserted: 'If you break [the talks], it cannot be because I have no representative capacity or because I have been unwilling to give you satisfaction in regard to the claim embodied in the Lahore resolution.'[67] In his reply on the same date Jinnah asserted: 'No responsible organization can entertain any proposal from any individual, however great he may be, unless it is backed up with the authority of a recognized organization and comes from its fully accredited representative.' However, he chose not to be labour this point as he had dwelt on it on several occasions in the past. Instead, he put his finger on a more substantive reason. 'If a break comes,' he wrote in the same letter, 'it will because you have not satisfied me in regard to the essence of the claim embodied in the Lahore resolution.'[68] These were the last letters of the series exchanged between Gandhi and Jinnah. The break had indeed come about and was made public the next day.

Although a lot of common people had developed high hopes from the Gandhi–Jinnah talks, their breakdown was quite natural. As Nehru recorded in his prison diary in the Ahmadnagar Fort after learning from the newspapers about the breakdown of the talks: 'Perhaps it was inevitable that the talks should fail.'[69] Indeed, in view of the historical background of Congress–League relations, what is surprising is not that the talks broke down, but that they were held at all. This does not, however, negate their significance as an important landmark in the League's march to its goal. Although Gandhi made the agreement on the agency to administer matters of common concern an essential condition of his acceptance of Partition, the very fact that he accepted it in principle and showed a practical way of achieving it—through the ascertainment of the wishes of the people in Muslim-majority districts in the provinces claimed for Pakistan—added further legitimacy to the League's demand for it. At the same time, it further boosted Jinnah's position at the centre stage of Indian politics, particularly valuable to him in the context of his recent failure to establish the League's supremacy over the Unionist ministry in the Punjab because of the resistance of the Premier, Khizr Hayat Khan, who had succeeded Sikander in 1942. The fact that Gandhi personally sought talks with Jinnah even after his strong public denunciation of the C.R. Formula, which carried Gandhi's blessings, and that the talks had continued for three weeks with Gandhi travelling to Bombay, shortly after his convalescence, in order to meet Jinnah, reporting to the latter's residence as many as fourteen times, without a single return visit by Jinnah, in spite of the fact that the place where Gandhi was staying—Birla House—was located on the same Mount Pleasant Road (in Malabar Hill) where Jinnah resided—all this added tremendously to the latter's prestige among his constituents and advertised his crucial position in Indian politics. Besides, the fact that Jinnah stood firmly by the letter and spirit of the Lahore Resolution, against all of Gandhi's entreaties, and insisted on the latter's acceptance of a fully sovereign Pakistan consisting of all the Muslim-majority provinces in full and in addition Assam, which was not by any means a Muslim-majority province, immensely strengthened his hold over his colleagues as well as his followers and admirers and thereby added tremendously to the growth of the Pakistan movement. The confidential official survey of political events in India recorded:

> The more orthodox Leaguers reflect that Jinnah had won an advantage over Gandhi by standing fast on the Lahore resolution; and it is felt, quite rightly, that by being approached by Gandhi so shortly after his failure to bring the Punjab Ministry to heel and by having occupied in the talks the dominating position of one who spurns what is offered him and of whom favours are to be sought, Jinnah has recovered his position at the centre of the stage.[70]

Wavell's comments on the breakdown of the Gandhi–Jinnah talks lead to a somewhat similar conclusion, though he was critical of both the leaders. Thus, he noted in his diary on 30 September 1944:

> The Gandhi–Jinnah talks ended on a note of complete futility. I must say I expected something better. . . . Anything so barren as their exchange of letters is a deplorable exposure of Indian leadership. The two great mountains have met and not even a ridiculous mouse has emerged. This surely must blast Gandhi's reputation as a leader. Jinnah had an easy task, he merely had to keep on telling Gandhi he was talking nonsense, which was true, and he did so rather rudely, without having to disclose any of the weaknesses of his own position, or define his Pakistan in any way. I suppose it may increase his prestige with his followers, but it cannot add to his reputation with reasonable men.[71]

For Jinnah, as for any leader trying to mobilize the masses, the important thing was the gain he made in the eyes of his followers regardless of the reaction of 'reasonable men', who hardly matter in the arena of mass politics. The Gandhi–Jinnah talks helped in the growth of the Pakistan movement in another way—by creating bitterness between the leaders of the Congress and the League as also generally between Hindus and Muslims, making a compromise on any basis short of Pakistan much more difficult than ever before. As the Viceroy telegraphed to the Secretary of State for India on 2 October 1944, regarding the political situation in India in the immediate aftermath of the breakdown of the Gandhi–Jinnah talks: 'Breakdown makes settlement between the parties even more difficult than before. Public reactions are so far on party lines and in spite of protestations of friendship there is undercurrent of bitterness between Gandhi and Jinnah.'[72] Also illuminating is a letter Wavell received from Sir H. Twynam, Governor of the Central Provinces and Berar, sent on 9 October 1944:

> One result [of the breakdown of the Gandhi–Jinnah talks], I fear, will be that the cleavage between the two communities will be sharper than ever and, although the mass of the people are incapable of understanding the issues involved, the cleavage among the leaders will percolate down through local leaders and will probably be translated into communal tension whenever occasions arise. . . .[73]

A few months after the breakdown of the Gandhi–Jinnah talks, another effort was made, with somewhat similar results, from the Congress side, again with Gandhi's blessings, to come to an agreement with the Muslim League. This time agreement was sought for the limited purpose of setting up a national government at the Centre, skirting the issue of Pakistan. Where C.R. had failed, Bhulabhai Desai, an eminent lawyer from Bombay and leader of the Congress party in the Central Legislative Assembly for the past so many years, hoped to succeed. After talks with Liaquat Ali Khan, General Secretary of the Muslim League and Deputy Leader of the Muslim League Party in the Central Legislative Assembly, the two jointly devised a formula for this purpose, which became popularly known as the Desai–Liaquat Pact, in January 1945. The effort proved to be stillborn. Desai had obtained Gandhi's blessings and claimed that Khan had secured similar blessings from Jinnah. However, the latter disclaimed any knowledge of it and when he reiterated that stand again and again Khan also washed his hands of it and denied that he had ever signed any document in this regard as claimed by Desai. This was, of course, not true. There was an agreement signed by the two leaders though it had not been officially published.[74] Desai lobbied hard for it with the Viceroy and the latter was interested in its terms and affirmed that they were in line with his own thinking on ways to break the political deadlock in India. Without committing himself he talked to Desai and was looking forward to seeing Jinnah in March but the meeting could not take place due to the latter's ill health. In the meanwhile, Wavell had sought clearance from London also for his calling

Desai and Jinnah together for a discussion, but that was not forthcoming as the Cabinet wanted to be satisfied on several points, including the Viceroy's power to appoint his Executive Councillors and the effect that such a change would have on the war effort. After the public disclaimer by both Jinnah and Khan of any interest in the matter on their part, it naturally faded out of official discourse.[75]

However, it will not be appropriate to brush aside the Desai–Liaquat Pact as something without any significance. For it again underlined Jinnah's crucial position in Indian politics by showing him as being repeatedly pursued by Congress leaders for an agreement, but taking no interest in it, thereby strengthening his image among his admirers and followers as a devoted Muslim leader who was only interested in the goal (Pakistan) which he had set before himself and the League and not in any short-term gains. The terms of the Desai–Liaquat Pact also underlined the much enhanced stature of both Jinnah and the League. For they provided that the Viceroy's Executive Council, which was to be reconstituted on the lines of a national government, would consist of equal numbers of representatives from the Congress and the League (40 per cent each), the rest of the seats (20 per cent) going to the representatives of the Scheduled Castes, Sikhs, and other minorities. There was also provision for the restoration of constitutional governments in the erstwhile Congress-ruled provinces with the addition of League representatives to the ministries. Such provisions naturally further strengthened the prestige of the League as well as of its leaders in the eyes of the public, for they had been agreed to by an important Congress leader, and that, too, with Gandhi's blessings. The most important gain for the League was the provision that the Congress and the League would have parity in the Viceroy's Executive Council—something which the League had been demanding since 1940—in a way exemplifying the practical application of the two-nation theory, but not till then conceded by the British Government. The League was also given satisfaction on its old demand for its representatives being taken into the ministries in the Congress-ruled provinces.[76] All this lent further legitimacy to both Jinnah's leadership and the demand for Pakistan and significantly contributed to the growth of the Pakistan movement.

IV

Much greater help in that respect came from the Simla Conference convened by the Viceroy, Lord Wavell, in order to consider the British plan—famous in history as the Wavell Plan—for resolving the Indian political deadlock. That plan owed much to the initiative taken by Wavell, who spent about two and a half months in London to give shape to it with the active participation and approval of the War Cabinet and its India Committee. As announced by him after his return to India through his broadcast on 14 June 1945, the plan did not represent an attempt to obtain or impose a constitutional settlement, but to secure the participation of the leaders of the Indian parties in tackling some of the urgent tasks facing the country. With this purpose in view, the Viceroy proposed to invite selected Indian leaders both at the central and provincial levels to take counsel with him regarding the formation of a new Executive Council 'more representative of organized political opinion'. This was to consist of representatives of the main communities in India and would have equal proportions of caste Hindus and Muslims. However, it would be an Indian Council, except for the Viceroy and the Commander-in-Chief, who would continue to function as War member. It was further proposed that the portfolio of External Affairs, which had till then been held by the Viceroy, would be placed in charge of an Indian member. It was also proposed to create a new office, that of the British High Commissioner in India, who would, like his counterparts in the Dominions, look after Britain's commercial and other such interests in India. The Council was to work under the then existing Constitution (Act of 1935) and the Governor-General would continue to exercise his special powers, but they would 'not be exercised unreasonably'. The formation of the new Council, which would in effect work as an interim Government, would not in any way prejudice the final constitutional settlement.

The main tasks before the new Executive Council would be to prosecute the war against Japan (the war against Germany had already ended with the latter's surrender on 7 May 1945) with the utmost vigour; to carry on the Government of British India and deal with all the problems of post-war development until a new permanent constitution was agreed upon and came into force; and to work for such an agreement at the opportune time. The third task, the Viceroy emphasized, was the most important. 'I want to make it quite clear,' he added, 'that neither I nor His Majesty's Government have lost sight of the need for a long-term solution, and the present proposals are intended to make a long-term solution easier.'

The Viceroy also announced in the same broadcast that he had decided to call a conference of prominent Indian political leaders in order to advise him on the formation of the new Council. The conference was to meet on 25 June at the Viceregal Lodge at Simla. Those being invited to this conference were persons holding office as premiers of provinces or those who had held office earlier as premiers of provinces then under Governor's rule under Section 93 of the Act of 1935; the leader of the Congress party and the deputy leader of the Muslim League party in the central Assembly; the leaders of the Congress and the League parties in the Council of State; the leaders of the Nationalist Party and the European Group in the Assembly; Gandhi and Jinnah as 'the recognized leaders of the two main political parties', N. Siva Raj to represent the Scheduled Castes and Master Tara Singh to represent the Sikhs. Orders had been issued for the release of those members of the Congress Working Committee who were still in prison. The question of releasing other political prisoners was being left to the new Executive Council and to the provincial governments.

If the meeting was successful, the Viceroy hoped that it would agree on the formation of a new Executive Council at the Centre. It was also his hope that it would be possible for ministries to reassume their offices in those provinces that were then under the rule of the Governors, and that those ministries would be formed on the basis of coalitions. 'If the meeting should unfortunately fail,' Wavell significantly added, 'we must carry on as at present until the parties are ready to come together.'[77]

On the same day, the Secretary of State for India issued a statement in London of behalf of His Majesty's Government. Therein he observed that, as made clear under the Cripps Plan (March 1942), the working out of India's new constitutional system was a task that could only be carried through by the 'Indian peoples' themselves. It was with a view to breaking the political deadlock and creating suitable conditions for the successful performance of such a task as well as for securing better management of the numerous problems being faced by the Indian administration that the British Government had devised the plan carried by Wavell to India, which he would place before the Indian leaders. The success of such a plan depended upon its acceptance in India and the preparedness of the Indian leaders to cooperate in making it work. 'In the absence of such general acceptance existing arrangements must necessarily continue.'[78]

This is exactly what happened. The preliminary objections or problems raised by Gandhi and Jinnah prior to the meeting of the Simla Conference were, of course, satisfactorily tackled by Wavell. Thus, Gandhi objected to his being invited as a representative of the Congress and pointed out that that position belonged to the then President of the Congress, Maulana Abul Kalam Azad. The matter was settled through correspondence between Gandhi and Wavell. The latter agreed to invite Azad to represent the Congress just as Jinnah, as President, had been invited to represent the Muslim League. Gandhi on his part agreed to remain at Simla during the period the conference of leaders was in session in order to be available for consultation by the Viceroy whenever required. Gandhi also expressed his objection to the use of the term 'caste Hindus', but was mollified by Wavell's clarification that he did not mean any offence and that his idea was merely to indicate that there must be parity of representation in the Executive Council between Hindus, minus the Scheduled Castes, and Muslims. Similarly, Jinnah wanted the conference postponed by a fortnight in order to enable him to seek certain clarifications from the Viceroy and consult his Working Committee. However, on Wavell's insistence he agreed to go to Simla to talk to the former on 24 June and after that decided to participate in the conference, which began as scheduled on 25 June.[79] After preliminary discussions till 29 June, it was adjourned to meet again on 14 July. This was done to enable the political parties to hold consultations among themselves in order to come to an agreed formula for the reconstitution of the Executive Council. As all efforts to do so failed, the Viceroy felt that he had no option but to announce the failure of the conference. This he did on 14 July.

The main issue because of which Wavell was forced to admit failure was Jinnah's claim that all the Muslim nominees for appointment to the Executive Council must belong to the League, a claim he put forward right from 24 June when he met Wavell for a private discussion. Although the League at that time neither occupied a dominant position in the legislatures of the Muslim-majority provinces nor did it control the ministries in a majority of them, Jinnah remained firm on his claim, basing it on the fact that the League had come out victorious in all the by-elections from Muslim constituencies all over India in the previous two years. The Viceroy found himself unable to accept this claim and had to consider also the claims of Congress and Unionist Muslims (Punjab) for inclusion in the Executive Council, but Jinnah never wavered from this claim.[80] On 27 June, Wavell telegraphed to Amery: 'We have arrived at the critical point of the Conference and the main stumbling-block is the attitude of Jinnah, i.e. his claim to nominate all Muslim members.'[81] Private discussions between the Congress and the League also failed to resolve this issue. The Congress remained insistent that it must have at least one if not two out of five Muslim seats. The Viceroy, too, felt that in view of the existence at that time of a Unionist ministry in the Punjab and a Congress ministry in the NWFP, Jinnah's claim was unreasonable. In order to meet Jinnah halfway, he was prepared to ignore the Congress, but in view of the Unionist ministry's role in mobilizing for the war effort in the Punjab, which sent the largest contingent of recruits to the Indian Army, he was not prepared to ignore its claim for representation in the new Executive Council.[82] The League, on the other hand, remained firm on its demand. Its Working Committee adopted a resolution on 7 July, putting the League's claim to all the Muslim seats in the Executive Council as 'one of the fundamental principles'. While all the other parties concerned submitted lists of their nominees for the Executive Council, the League refused to do so.[83]

During his interview with Jinnah on 11 July, Wavell conveyed to the former the names of four Muslim members from the League and one from the Unionist Party—provisionally selected by him. This was not acceptable to Jinnah and he refused to cooperate unless all Muslim members of the new Executive Council were taken from the League. In addition, he put forward another condition for the League's cooperation, which he had vaguely mentioned earlier. This was to the effect that in order to safeguard Muslim interests, in addition to the Governor-General's power of veto, there must also be a provision that any measure to which the Muslim members objected could be carried only by a clear two-thirds majority of the Council. Jinnah insisted on this safeguard on the ground that even if all the Muslim members of the Executive Council belonged to the League, they would barely constitute one-third of that body, as apart from the members belonging to the Congress, there would also be members representing other minorities and they were likely to side with the former. The Viceroy refused to accept either of these conditions whereupon Jinnah refused to cooperate.[84] On learning of this situation, the British War Cabinet decided at its meeting on 12 July that 'there was no alternative but to recognize that the Viceroy's strenuous efforts to reach a settlement had failed, and that the break down must be acknowledged publicly though without recrimination.[85] Wavell strictly followed this instruction. When the conference reassembled on 14 July, he announced the failure of his efforts to persuade Jinnah either to submit a panel of names, just like the other parties concerned, for consideration by him for inclusion in the Executive Council or to agree to the names of Muslim members whom the Viceroy had provisionally selected for that purpose. Since Jinnah was 'so decided', the Viceroy observed that he did not see any purpose in continuing the discussion further. Announcing the failure of the conference and asserting that no one could regret it more than he himself, he affirmed that the responsibility for the failure was his alone and that he could not put the blame on anyone else. He also appealed to all the leaders assembled there to accept that view and to see that there was no recrimination.[86] A few weeks after the break-up of the Simla Conference it was announced that general elections would be held all over India in the winter months of 1945–6. While transmitting to Wavell the British Cabinet's decision on 12 July, on the basis of which the former made the statement just referred to on 14 July, Amery recorded that the British plans behind holding the Simla Conference had broken down 'in the face of Jinnah's intransigence', but added with unconcealed glee:

> It is at any rate something to have further confirmation of the fact that the difficulty does not lie as between India and His Majesty's Government, but within India itself.... Nor will it be altogether to the bad that the Congress leaders have been in personal touch with you and brought right up against the fact that it is the Muslim League and not you or I who stand in the way of their aspirations. They have, after all, by

coming into the conference, abandoned their claim that they are the only people to take over from us. They must now either acquiesce in Pakistan, or realise that they have somehow or other to win over Muslim support against Jinnah, and that a mere façade of tame Congress Muslims does not help them.[87]

This was not an unrealistic picture of the political situation in India in the immediate aftermath of the Simla Conference. For the Congress it had already become well nigh impossible to win over sufficient Muslim support against the League. There was also no doubt by 1945 that the League held complete sway over the Muslims in the Hindu-majority provinces. However, the situation was still to some extent fluid in the Muslim-majority provinces. For many Muslim political groups in those provinces had till then refused to acknowledge Jinnah's leadership and merge their separate identities in the Muslim League. This was particularly true of the Punjab, where the majority of the Muslim members of the ruling Unionist Party had till then refused to shift their loyalty to the League in spite of persistent efforts by Jinnah to establish its supremacy in the most crucial province from the point of view of its demand for Partition. Because of the avowed pro-British proclivities of the Unionist leaders and the value of a politically stable Punjab, which supplied the bulk of recruits to the Indian Army, Wavell, just as Linlithgow before him, had been patronizing the Unionist Party though at the all-India level both of them realized the value of the Muslim League as a counter to the Congress, which had been pressing the demand for independence. About a week before the Wavell Plan was publicly announced, Wavell had conveyed a firm assurance of support to Khizr Hyat Khan Tiwana, the Unionist Premier of the Punjab, through the Governor, Sir Bertrand Glancy, and indeed hoped to blunt the appeal of the demand for Pakistan among Muslims. Referring to Khizr's anxieties regarding the likely outcome of the proposed parleys aimed primarily at conciliating the Congress and the League, leaving in the lurch a purely regional grouping like the Unionist Party, Wavell had written to Glancy on 8 June 1945:

Please explain my proposals to him in confidence and tell him I have no (repeat no) intention of handing over Central Government to any one party. If the Conference comes off I shall hope for Khizr's advice and help. An interim Government of the kind proposed might prove a useful step towards inducing Muslims to abandon the Pakistan objective.[88]

This indeed could have been the result if the Simla Conference had succeeded in installing an interim Government of Wavell's conception in which a Unionist nominee from the Punjab was to occupy one of the five seats allotted to Muslims, the rest going to the League's nominees, but thanks to Jinnah's mastery over the nuances of the then existing political situation and his firm determination, Wavell's scheme did not get through and he felt compelled to announce the failure of the Simla Conference. As a result of it, instead of helping the Unionists to successfully resist the League's onslaughts against it, the Simla Conference became instrumental in significantly contributing to the success of those onslaughts. Something similar happened in Bengal and in other Muslim-majority provinces. For once it became known that the Simla Conference, in spite of all the Viceroy's efforts, could not succeed primarily because of Jinnah's refusal to agree to any non-League Muslim being appointed to a Muslim seat in the reconstituted Executive Council, most of the politically ambitious Muslims everywhere concluded that no Muslim could safeguard his political future without bearing the stamp of the League. Such politicians, regardless of their old political labels, now began to queue up for admittance into the League's membership. This could not but doom the future of non-League formations in Muslim-majority provinces. It is in apparent recognition of this fact that both V.P. Menon, Reforms Commissioner of the Government of India at that time, and H.V. Hodson, Constitutional Advisor to the Viceroy in 1941–2, have stressed the crucial importance of the failure of the Simla Conference in India's march towards Partition. 'The Simla Conference,' observes Menon, 'afforded a last opportunity to the forces of nationalism to fight a rear-guard action to preserve the integrity of the country, and when the battle was lost the waves of communalism quickly engulfed it.'[89] Hodson similarly remarks: 'Mr. Jinnah's demonstration of imperious strength at the Simla Conference was a shot in the arm of the League and a serious blow for its Muslim opponents, especially in the Punjab. Some observers thought that Lord Wavell's sudden abandonment of his plan was the decisive move that made the Partition of India inevitable.'[90]

Blaming Wavell for having 'in effect capitulated' to Jinnah,

Hodson also argues that the Viceroy's proposal for giving one of the Muslim seats in the Executive Council to a Unionist Muslim was quite reasonable and even the Congress, which had been insisting on the inclusion of its own Muslim nominee(s), might have accepted it. The Unionist Party was still strong and not all the League leaders were in favour of Jinnah's tactics at that time. If Wavell had been 'as adamant' as Jinnah, 'the latter would have been obliged himself to give in'. This might have averted the destruction of the Unionist Party, which paved the way for the Partition of the Punjab (and, one may add, also the Partition of India).[91]

Both Menon and Hodson have, of course, assessed correctly the impact of the failure of the Simla Conference on the movement for the creation of Pakistan. The latter, however, has gone wrong in blaming Wavell for it. The responsibility for the failure lay in the then existing political situation and the background of the convening of the Simla Conference. As Hodson himself admits, Wavell had really no practicable alternative before him except to announce the failure of the conference. The only alternative available was to have an Executive Council wholly dominated by the Congress without it being balanced by the presence of the League's nominees. This was an alternative that could not be accepted by a British Cabinet headed by Churchill and that, too, at a time when the war against Japan was still going on.[92] Penderal Moon has further elucidated this point.[93] Both have produced excellent arguments in their submissions. This is, however, no longer a matter for arguments. The publication of the British documents on the transfer of power in India has conclusively proved the validity of the arguments adduced in defence of Wavell. As shown earlier in this section, on the basis of those documents, the War Cabinet had sanctioned Wavell's initiative, after considerable reluctance, on the express understanding that Wavell would secure the cooperation of all major parties, including, of course, both the Congress and the League, for the formation of a new Executive Council. The Cabinet had also been closely monitoring the progress of the Simla Conference and sending instructions to Wavell at every step. As soon as Wavell reported the final stand of Jinnah on 11 July, the former was explicitly told the next day that he had no option but to announce the failure of his effort, without blaming anyone.[94] He, of course, on his own part, also deeply abhorred the prospect of an Executive Council wholly dominated by the Congress.

V

Whatever the causes of the failure of the Simla Conference, there is no doubt that that failure contributed significantly to the growth of the Pakistan movement by underlining that no constitutional advance was possible in India without the cooperation of the Muslim League. Equally significant was the recognition of the principle that no Muslim leader could aspire to hold a high position in government without belonging to the League. This was bound to have, as in fact it did have, a tremendous positive impact on the League's campaign to establish its ascendancy in the key Muslim-majority provinces of the Punjab and Bengal, which occupied the highest priority in Jinnah's strategy since the adoption of the Pakistan Resolution in 1940. For he realized that the creation of Pakistan would merely remain a dream without it. Punjab attracted his greatest attention. However, so long as Sikander Hyat Khan lived Jinnah could not make much headway in making the League ascendant there. For though Sikander accepted Jinnah's leadership in all-India matters, however reluctantly, and sat on the central executive committee of the League, his relations with Jinnah were seldom cordial. Besides, he was not at all enthusiastic about the demand for Partition. Indeed, his opponents alleged, not without justification, that he was using his so-called pact with Jinnah (1937) not to strengthen the League in the Punjab, but to keep it subservient to himself and to the Unionist Party—consisting of Sikhs, Hindus, as well as Muslim members of the legislature—on whose behalf he ruled over the province. As mentioned in the previous chapter, he had clearly explained his reservations regarding Partition in his statement in the Punjab Legislative Assembly in March 1941. Although, because of the requirements of political expediency, especially in view of the rapid spread of the Pakistan ideology among the students and the urban intelligentsia in Punjab, he later on began to pay lip service to the demand for Partition, his heart and mind belonged elsewhere. He was basically a Punjabi patriot and believed that Partition would inevitably lead to its dismemberment. He also believed that because of the configuration of the population and the slender majority enjoyed in it by Muslims, the only way to provide a stable government to the province and safeguard its interests was to continue to strengthen the Unionist Party based on an alliance of agriculturists and rural magnates, regardless of their religious affiliations and not to overplay the League's existence in the province and certainly not its demand for Partition, which was being bitterly opposed by Hindus and Sikhs in the Punjab as also by the Muslim gentry and clerics (popularly known as *pirs*) living in the rural areas, who provided the mainstay of the Unionist Party. It had, of course, caught the imagination of Muslims in the urban areas, but many of the latter, too, were likely to recoil from it once they realized that, whatever might be said in public speeches by the protagonists of Pakistan, its creation, under any reasonable formula, was bound to involve the Partition of the Punjab. In order to bring home the realization of that truth to the latter, Sikander drafted a 'tentative formula' for the solution of the communal problem. In essence, it provided that if less than 75 per cent of the members of the Punjab Legislative Assembly voted for either accession or non-accession to the Indian Federation, an opportunity may be given to the Muslim community to decide their future through a referendum. If they decided to keep out of the Indian Federation, the non-Muslims of the province must also be given a similar chance to decide their future through a referendum. If they decided to cut themselves adrift from the Muslims, the areas of the province having a non-Muslim-majority would have to be detached from the province. While transmitting the text of Sikander's scheme as also its summary to the Viceroy, the Punjab Governor pointed out that its underlying idea was 'to bring it home to all reasonably-minded men that Pakistan, should it ever eventuate, would smash the Province as it now exists'. This estimate was based on the conversation that the Governor had with Sikander when the latter called on him to hand over its text. In the course of that conversation the latter had mentioned that his formula had 'a good chance of relegating the Pakistan issue to the background' until the end of the war and expressed the hope that during the next few years it would have the effect of 'laying the Pakistan controversy to rest'.[95]

Regardless of his political convictions, however, Sikander, for tactical reasons, could not go beyond a point in opposing Jinnah's stand on Partition, which was winning more and more adherents among Muslims, at any rate in the urban areas. During Jinnah's tour of the Punjab in November 1942, Sikander, who had skipped a Muslim students' conference addressed by Jinnah in Jullundur a few days earlier, found it expedient to attend the provincial Muslim League Conference at Lyallpur (17–18 November) and to make his obeisance to Jinnah.[96] In his speech there on 18 November, he warmly welcomed Jinnah on behalf of the people of the Punjab, affirmed that he fully subscribed to the Lahore Resolution (1940) of the League, which provided for 'territorial adjustments' and asserted that his new formula did not conflict in any way with that resolution.[97] This, to some extent, compromised his position with his Sikh and Hindu supporters in the Assembly. On the other hand, Jinnah was apparently not fully satisfied with Sikander's qualified support for the Lahore Resolution. For in the course of a speech at another meeting held at the same place the next day he issued a not so veiled warning to Sikander, without, of course, naming him. 'Ministers,' he observed, 'must understand that they cannot remain in office without our consent.'[98]

With the sudden passing away of Sikander on the night of 6 December 1942, and the appointment in his place of Malik Khizr Hyat Khan Tiwana as Premier, Jinnah's campaign to bring the Punjab ministry under the League's control acquired a new momentum. The new Premier belonged to one of the leading landowning families of the Punjab and as such commanded considerable respect in the rural areas. He had also been a member of the previous cabinet headed by Sikander and his appointment, although made initially by the Governor without reference to any party, had been later unanimously approved by the members of the Muslim League Party in the Assembly. In order to consolidate his position he also got appointed Sikander's son, Shaukat Hyat Khan, as a minister. However, with several other members of large landowing families having influence in the Assembly as well as in the countryside aspiring for the Premiership, Khizr's position was not as strong as his predecessor's. This encouraged Jinnah in his drive for control over the Punjab ministry. In the beginning, of course, he moved cautiously. At the meeting of the League's Council held in New Delhi on 7 March 1943, after Khizr's clarification, Jinnah got withdrawn a resolution moved by Maulana Abdul Hamid Badayani to the effect that the Muslim members of the Unionist Party in the Punjab should form a Muslim League Party as soon as practicable and act in accordance with the policy of the League. Khizr's submission was that the League Party already existed in the Punjab under the terms of the Sikander–Jinnah Pact (1937) and that efforts would be made to improve its functioning and to put a new life into it in the future. At the same time, he avowed his strong loyalty to the League. 'You will never find me and my Muslim colleagues,' he observed, 'failing in our loyalty to the cause of Musalmans and their sole representative body—the All-India Muslim League.'[99] However, this was not the end of the matter. 'The Premier,' reported the Governor to the Viceroy, 'has succeeded for the present in blocking the attack, but it seems evident that there are rocks ahead.'[100] In the middle of April 1943, he again reported to the Viceroy: 'The main threat to our political tranquility comes from Jinnah and the Muslim League.'[101] This was obviously said in the context of increased activity on the part of Jinnah and the League generally for spreading their influence in the Punjab and bringing the Ministry under their direct control.

It is significant that without naming the Punjab ministry, Jinnah administered a severe warning to it in the course of his presidential address to the annual session of the All-India Muslim League held on 24 April 1943 in New Delhi. After referring proudly to the functioning of the League ministries in the Muslim-majority provinces of Assam, Bengal, Sind, and Punjab, he remarked: 'It is not that we are ready and willing to make all sacrifices for the Ministries, we expect the Ministries to make all the sacrifices for us.' Referring subsequently to the Punjab, Jinnah described it as 'the corner-stone of Pakistan' and regretted the fact that it had not till then played the part that it should have played and was entitled to play. Addressing the delegates from the Punjab who had assembled for the League's session, Jinnah told them that when they returned to their land they should 'substitute love for Islam and your nation, in place of sectional interests, tribal notions and jealousies'.[102]

Although in his New Delhi address Jinnah had mentioned that there was a League ministry also in the Punjab, actually it was a Unionist ministry. All that had happened under the Sikander–Jinnah Pact (1937) was that the Muslim members of the Unionist

Party, while retaining their affiliation with that party, had also become members of the League. The Unionist Party, based on coöperation between Muslim, Hindu, and Sikh agriculturalists, continued to flourish and everyone knew that Khizr, just as Sikander before him, was Premier in his capacity as leader of the Unionist Party. The campaign for Pakistan and the pressure to convert the Unionist ministry in the Punjab into a League ministry became more intensified about this time. In April 1943, the Punjab Provincial League issued instructions to its branches to expand the Muslim National Guard (a volunteer corps of the League) to absorb smaller Muslim organizations within the League, to pay more attention to religious propaganda, and to arrange to have the idea of Muslim solidarity inculcated among the Friday congregations in mosques.[103] In May 1943, the Nawab of Mamdot, President of the Muslim League in the Punjab, issued a statement to the press that the Sikander–Jinnah Pact had come to an end, thereby implying that people could expect a more active role in Punjab politics by the League. Though the Nawab explained that he had issued that statement on his own, without consulting Jinnah, the Governor doubted the veracity of his claim. The Governor also reported that the Pakistan slogan was gaining momentum and that there was 'a general feeling of uneasiness abroad'.[104] In the first week of July, he mentioned that there was a 'considerable amount of uneasiness in political circles about the intentions of [the] Muslim League'. Jinnah's heightened interest in the Punjab was also revealed by the news that his lieutenants were trying to acquire a house for him in Lahore.[105] The Governor again wrote on 21 July 1943: 'In Muslim circles, both inside and outside the Punjab, the slogan of Pakistan has been gradually gaining ground. Jinnah is more anxious than ever to dominate the politics of the Punjab and is constantly on the watch for a chance to disrupt the Unionist Ministry. . . .' The Governor had no doubt that Jinnah was not likely to find it easy to accomplish that task as Khizr was determined to resist him, sticking firmly to the Sikander–Jinnah Pact, which was designed to prevent Jinnah from interfering in provincial politics while ensuring the supremacy of the League in all-India affairs. 'There is no denying,' added the Governor, 'that Khizr lacks the experience and political agility of his predecessor, but he is in many respects a firmer character.'[106]

In order to clarify the situation, Khizr visited Bombay incognito early in September 1943 and had a 'protracted but inconclusive' discussion with Jinnah. Jinnah talked about Pakistan, the Khaksars, and his own services to the Muslim community. When, thanks to Khizr's repeated urging, Jinnah came to the actual subject of their meeting, he asserted that his interpretation was that the Unionist Party had ceased to exist when the Sikander–Jinnah Pact had been drawn up. Khizr, on the other hand, argued that he himself had been elected to the Assembly as a Unionist and must remain loyal to that label. According to his interpretation, the Unionist Party continued to exist and its Muslim members owed dual allegiance to both the Muslim League and the Unionist Party. This incensed Jinnah and the discussion came to an abrupt end, but the two managed somehow to part on outwardly friendly terms. One point that emerged from their discussion was that Jinnah was not perturbed by the possibility of the Punjab being placed under the Governor's administration under Section 93 of the Act of 1935. Indeed, he expressed the view that, as had recently happened in the North-West Frontier Province, such a development might help to rally the Muslims around the League. Khizr left Bombay with the feeling that he had not been able to achieve more than a 'Munich'.[107]

The 'Munich' gave Khizr a breather for about six months. The confidential official survey of political developments in India for the period November 1943 to January 1944 reported that the stability of the Unionist ministry was unshaken. It went on to comment that Khizr was proving himself 'a fit successor' to Sikander in preserving his independence of the League's leadership while not giving Jinnah an opportunity to start a successful quarrel with him.[108] The logical outcome of 'Munich', however, soon materialized. Deciding to end the stalemate, Jinnah arrived in Lahore in the middle of March 1944, left for a short while on 14 April, and returned again four days later to finally settle the issue of the status of the Punjab ministry. From the beginning he adopted a hard line, reiterating his position that the Unionist Party had ceased to exist as far back as 1937 with the signing of the Sikander–Jinnah agreement and ruling out double loyalty to the Unionist Party and the League on the part of the Muslim members of the Punjab legislature. 'You cannot owe allegiance,' he declared in the course of a press statement issued on 4 April

1944, 'to two political parties. There can be no divided loyalty so far as the Muslim League is concerned.'[109] Protracted negotiations between Jinnah and Khizr produced no result as each stuck firmly to his own position. Interrupted briefly due to the passing away of Khizr's father, the talks were resumed after Jinnah's return to Lahore on 18 April, but the situation remained exactly where it had been left before the resumption of the talks—Jinnah insisting on the removal of the Unionist label and the Punjab ministry being described as a League coalition ministry and Khizr remaining firm on retaining the Unionist label. On 28 April 1944, Jinnah finally declared that the talks had failed and that it was for the League to decide the next course of action.[110] Khizr also issued a statement on the same date defending his stand in his talks with Jinnah, at the same time reaffirming his allegiance to both the League and its Lahore Resolution, describing the latter as 'the sheet anchor of the Muslims in the Punjab as elsewhere'.[111] The Committee of Action of the League thereupon served a show-cause notice on Khizr, and, finding his reply unsatisfactory, expelled him from the membership of the League in May 1944.[112] This was duly endorsed by the League's Council at its meeting in Lahore on 31 July 1944.[113] This did not, however, bring about any major change in the status of the Punjab ministry, which continued to function as a Unionist ministry under the leadership of Khizr, enjoying the support of the bulk of the Muslim members in the Provincial Assembly along with an assortment of Sikh and Hindu members. This certainly represented a severe setback to Jinnah in his efforts to strengthen the League's hold over the Punjab, the future heartland of Pakistan. 'The League has beyond all question,' recorded the confidential official survey of political developments in India, 'suffered a serious reverse by the rupture of the tie that gave it a claim to the allegiance of the most successful and powerful of the Provincial Ministries, administering a Province which must be a keystone of any Pakistan of the future.'[114]

There is no doubt, however, that, thanks to its inherent appeal to the Muslim mind and heart as well as to Jinnah's exertions on its behalf, the Pakistan idea was gaining ground day by day, particularly among the youth and the intelligentsia in the urban areas of the Punjab. Indeed, this trend had already become so strong that at least one young but thoughtful member of the

Indian Civil Service belonging to the Sikh community, Tarlok Singh, not at all happy with the prospect of Partition, had noted in one of his papers, written for his own record as early as in November 1943, that there was going to be no escape from it in some form or the other. He, of course, conceded that every Muslim did not belong to the League, but emphasized that the League had captured the imagination of the Muslim intelligentsia and while its doctrine had barely touched the masses, they could, when the occasion arose, easily be 'infected' with it. Recalling that educated Indians had till then fondly hoped and dreamed of a united India, he sadly noted:

We are now on the brink of a different situation. Those who once bethought themselves to be a minority, albeit numerous and powerful, have now come to regard themselves as a nation, an independent entity, which must carve out for itself a separate habitation, an Islamic State. Not all Muslims have gone thus far, but the vision intoxicates, the ideal appears to be worthy of every sacrifice, in accord with the highest spirit of so binding a faith as Islam, and perhaps in itself the fulfilment of a destiny. There is no doubt that the objective of Pakistan, feeding as it does upon elemental emotions, will continue to gather support.[115]

It is also significant that Jayaprakash Narayan, then an eminent Congress Socialist leader lodged as a security prisoner in the Lahore Fort and a strong critic of the League, recorded in his prison notebook on 30 April 1944, three days after the breakdown of the Jinnah-Khizr talks had been made public, that the support of the British officials in the province, headed by the Governor, was a major factor behind Khizr's victory:

Earlier this month when Mr Jinnah had come to Lahore some writer in the local press had said that the League Fuehrer was likely to meet his Stalingrad in this, the heart city of Pakistan. This eventually has proved to be so. Mr Jinnah has been defeated, but it may be interesting to ask whose has been the victory. Is it the Unionist Party which has been victorious? As I have watched this controversy from the seclusion of my cell, it has been made increasingly clear to me that the laurels of victory should really go to the British—the British steel-frame of the Province with the Governor at its head. When Mr Jinnah left Lahore after his first visit at the beginning of the month, the issue had been left undecided. Undoubtedly those who were pulling wires behind the scenes knew what the ultimate issue was to be. But the public was in no way certain. Whatever the wishes of the Muslim members of the Punjab Assembly, vocal Muslim opinion seemed to be behind Mr Jinnah. Then the Governor spoke at the opening of the War Exhibition, and twice during his speech he made it clear to the people of this Province and to all others concerned that the British Power was solidly lined up behind Lt. Col. Malik Khizr Hayat Khan and the Unionist Ministry. The issue of Mr Jinnah's endeavours, when he returned again to resume them, was no longer in doubt.[116]

The record of Khizr's confabulations with the Governor while the former's conversations with Jinnah were going on, contained in the Glancy–Wavell correspondence, lends credence to Narayan's assessment. The Governor had been told by Khizr in a succession of interviews in the recent past that he was seriously thinking of giving way to Jinnah's demand. For, according to him, the Unionist Party existed only in name. Although he himself did not believe in Pakistan, he thought that the Pakistan slogan was bound to gather momentum and that it would emerge as a decisive factor in the next elections. This was bound to affect the attitude of his Muslim supporters. In April 1944, the number of such persons among the Muslim members of the Punjab Assembly who would be ready to swing to Jinnah's side might not exceed 32, but later on this position might change. At that stage, however, their value to Jinnah might decline. Khizr stressed that he did not want to do anything that might compromise the interests of his followers. He also made it clear that he believed that in the near future there would be only two parties of any importance in India—the Congress and the Muslim League. He was also not sure what the British policy would be after the end of the war. In such a situation, the landlords or loyalists, might suffer if he remained firm in his stand against Jinnah, thereby forcing them also to do the same. His problem could be solved if the Governor could order that 'he should stand up to Jinnah in the interest of the war effort'.[117]

This was obviously a device on Khizr's part to ensure that in case he continued his fight to the finish against Jinnah, he should have a firm commitment of support from the Governor. The latter's response must have satisfied him that he had that commitment. The Governor, of course, expressed his inability to issue any order to Khizr on the lines suggested by the latter, but added that he could tell Khizr 'as a friend' what he would do if he were in Khizr's position. It was the Governor's 'considered position' that Khizr 'would have no peace hereafter, nor will he be serving the interest of the province or of India or of Muslims or of the Empire if he gives way to Jinnah and places himself in his power'; the disruption of the Unionist Party even in name was bound 'to weaken the solidarity of the Punjab and to weaken the war effort'. The Governor went on to elaborate that in the wake of the disruption of the Unionist Party, the various communities in the Punjab were likely to concentrate more and more on arraying themselves against each other rather than on the war effort. Leaders like Chhotu Ram (representing the Jat peasantry) and Baldev Singh (representing the Sikhs), who were then serving in the Unionist ministry, would refuse to serve in a Muslim League Government. As for Khizr, he would become a slave to Jinnah's caprices and would lose faith even with his own community.[118] The Viceroy heartily approved the stand of the Governor and this was duly communicated by the latter to Khizr[119], who, we can rest assured, must have communicated it to his close associates, the leading landlords of the Punjab.

There is no doubt that the awareness among the leading Muslim landlords of the Punjab that Khizr enjoyed the strong backing of the Governor was a tremendous help to Khizr in stemming the challenge posed by Jinnah and in surviving as the head of the Unionist Party and Premier of the Punjab. Popular support in the rural areas for that Party was, of course, no longer as overwhelming as it had been before as the League had entered the fray there too. The League's propaganda had begun receiving a response not merely because of its appeal more and more in the name of Islam, but also because, after the initial boom in the early years of the war, people in the rural areas had become victims of price controls of agricultural products and shortages of certain essential goods like cloth and kerosen.[120] The Gandhi–Jinnah talks in September 1944 helped boost Jinnah's reputation in the eyes of Muslims in the Punjab as elsewhere in India. 'Whatever Gandhi's intentions may have been,' wrote the Governor to the Viceroy in the fourth week of August 1944, even before the talks began, 'his advance to Jinnah has certainly come at a most inopportune time so far as the Unionist Party is concerned. Jinnah's shares in the political market had begun to deteriorate. Thanks to Mr Gandhi, Jinnah's importance has now revived. . . .'[121]

The failure of the Simla Conference due to Jinnah's opposition to the appointment of any Muslim not belonging to the League as a member of the Viceroy's proposed Executive Council, and the latter's decision not to go ahead ignoring that opposition even though he himself considered it unreasonable, but to wind up the conference itself, had an even greater impact on Punjab politics than the Gandhi–Jinnah talks. It now became clear to the landed magnates in the Punjab, the mainstay so far of the Unionist Party, that they would remain completely barred from government patronage and office unless they belonged to the League. 'It was this fear,' aptly observes Ian Talbot, a well-known authority on the political history of the Punjab in the twentieth century, 'rather than the Muslim League's depiction of Khizr and his supporters as traitors to Islam and their *millat* which sparked off the rural elite's large-scale exodus from the Unionist Party's ranks in the weeks which followed the Simla Conference.'[122] In doing so, they were following the examples set by some prominent non-League Muslim leaders holding high positions in public life. Mention may particularly be made of Abdul Qaiyum (NWFP), deputy leader of the Congress party in the Central Assembly; Sir Firoz Khan Noon (Punjab), a member of the Viceroy's Executive Council; and Mian Iftikharuddin, President of the Punjab Provincial Congress Committee. Jinnah welcomed all such new-comers who joined the League at that stage, declaring that 'the Muslim League has no malice'.[123]

NOTES

1. See Memorandum C, Reginald Coupland's Memoranda, A-D, 19–21 March 1942, unpublished 'Couplands's Dairy of his Indian visit and Back', MSS. Brit. Emp. 5.15., Rhodes House Library, Oxford University, Appendix IV, pp. 256–73; reproduced in *Quaid-i-Azam Mohammad Ali Jinnah: The Nation's Voice* (hereafter *Jinnah: Speeches and Statements*), ed. Wahead Ahmad, vol. II (Karachi, 1996), Appendix XXI, pp. 759–73. The paragraphs summarized and cited here occur on pp. 765–6.
2. Here it may be worthwhile to mention a remark made by Jinnah to a young League worker who, along with several others like himself, had climbed to the rostrum after the Pakistan resolution was adopted by the Lahore session on 24 March 1940, in order to have a closer view of their great leader: 'You wanted Pakistan; you have it now.' This was mentioned to me about three years back by Dr Mubashir Hasan, a

former Finance Minister of Pakistan, now working for India–Pakistan Friendship, who (then a young man of eighteen) had also climbed to the rostrum along with others and had heard Jinnah's remark.

3. See *Jinnah: Speeches and Statements*, n. 1, pp. 1, 3. For further details, see Qaid-i-Azam Papers, Reel 6, Files 54–8, Qaid-i-Azam Academy (Karachi).
4. Qaid-i-Azam Papers, Reel 6, File 52.
5. Ibid.
6. Ibid.
7. *Jinnah: Speeches and Statements*, vol. III (Karachi, 1997), p. 28.
8. Ibid., p. 37.
9. Ibid., p. 39.
10. Ibid., Appendix III, pp. 702–5.
11. Ibid., pp. 46–7.
12. Ibid., pp. 49–57.
13. Ibid., p. 63.
14. Ibid., pp. 69–76.
15. Ibid., pp. 96–131.
16. Ibid., pp. 135–6. It is pertinent to mention here what Jinnah said at a meeting at Quetta on 9 July 1943. Recalling that when he visited Rohilkhand (UP) after the adoption of the Lahore Resolution in 1940 a young lady had presented him with a map of Pakistan embroidered with her own hand, he remarked that it showed that Muslims had been nourishing the idea of Pakistan since long and that the League only gave it a definite shape. See ibid., p. 27.
17. Ibid., p. 170.
18. Syed Sharifuddin Pirzada, ed., *Foundations of Pakistan: All India Muslim League Documents: 1906–1947* (hereafter *League Documents*), vol. II, p. 248.
19. Ibid., pp. 426–7.
20. Ibid., p. 407.
21. The reference here is to Gandhi's letter from his detention camp to Linlithgow dated 29 January 1943. For the text, see *Transfer of Power*, 1942–7 (hereafter *TP*), Nicholas Mansergh, ed., vol. III (London, 1971), pp. 554–9.
22. For the text of Gandhi's letter to Jinnah, 4 May 1943, see ibid., pp. 953–4.
23. For details, see ibid., pp. 950–5, 967–9, 970–7, 978–83, 991, 994–1005, 1013–50.
24. Ibid., p. 1005.
25. *Jinnah: Speeches and Statements*, vol. III, n. 7, p. 218.
26. Ibid., pp. 217–18.
27. See, for instance, Jamiluddin Ahmad's letter to Jinnah from Aligarh dated 6 June 1942, in which the former wrote: 'I was astonished to see

many otherwise intelligent Muslim Leaguers shaking their heads and looking askance at your statement on the Government communiqué stopping Gandhi's letters.' He, however, added that such persons had not dared to express a contrary view in public as Muslim public opinion was solidly behind Jinnah. Ahmad further remarked: 'Thank God our masses are firmer and clearer in their thinking than some of our muddle-headed intelligentsia.' Shamsul Hasan Collection (Karachi).

28. *TP*, vol. III, n. 22, p. 1002.
29. Ibid., p. 1034.
30. Ibid., p. 1038.
31. *League Documents*, n. 18, pp. 460–1.
32. *Jinnah: Speeches and Statements*, vol. III, n. 7, p. 367.
33. Ibid., pp. 369–70. The whole interview containing Jinnah's elucidation of the rationale behind the demand for Partition, particularly the two-nation theory, was published by Beverley Nichols in a chapter entitled 'Dialogue with a giant' in his *Verdict on India* (London, 1944), pp. 189–94.
34. *Speeches and Writing of Mr Jinnah*, Jamiluddin Ahmad, ed. (Lahore, 1968), vol. I, p. 605.
35. *Jinnah: Speeches and Statements,* vol. III, n. 7, p. 433.
36. Ibid., pp. 5–6 footnote. Cited by Jinnah in his press statement issued on 11 April 1940.
37. Ibid., p. 10.
38. See Rajmohan Gandhi, *The Rajaji Story, 1937–1972* (Bombay, 1984), pp. 75–84.
39. Ibid., p. 84.
40. *Indian Annual Register*, 1942, vol. I, pp. 294–5.
41. Rajmohan Gandhi, *Rajaji: A Life* (New Delhi, 1997), pp. 234–40.
42. Rajmohan Gandhi, n. 38, pp. 85–91.
43. Enclosure, C.R. to Jinnah, 8 April 1944, Quaid-i-Azam Papers, Reel 9, File 98; published widely in the Indian Press in July 1944 and reproduced in *Gandhi–Jinnah Talk: Text of Correspondence and other Relevant Matter*, with a Preface by C. Rajagopalachari (New Delhi, 1944), p. 36; also in *Gandhi–Jinnah Talks: Text of Correspondence and other Relevant Documents etc.*, with a foreword by Nawabzada Liaquat Ali Khan (Lahore, 1993), pp. 102–3.
44. *Gandhi–Jinnah Talks*, n. 43, pp. 73–5.
45. Ibid., p. 76.
46. Ibid.
47. *League Documents*, vol. II, n. 18, p. 495.
48. Rajmohan Gandhi, n. 38, p. 102.
49. *Gandhi–Jinnah Talks*, n. 43, p. 40.
50. Ibid., p. 41.
51. Ibid., p. 12.

52. Ibid., p. 16.
53. Ibid., p. 18.
54. Ibid.
55. Ibid., p. 15.
56. Ibid., p. 5.
57. Ibid., p. 7.
58. Ibid., pp. 26, 29.
59. Ibid.
60. Ibid., p. 21.
61. Ibid.
62. Ibid., p. 22.
63. Ibid., p. 31.
64. Ibid., p. 22.
65. Ibid., p. 25.
66. Ibid., p. 33.
67. Ibid., p. 34.
68. Ibid., p. 35.
69. *Selected Works of Jawaharlal Nehru*, S. Gopal, ed., vol. XIII (New Delhi, 1980), p. 486.
70. *Quarterly Survey*, no. 29 (1 August–31 October, 1944).
71. *Wavell: The Viceroy's Journal*, Penderal Moon, ed. (London, 1973), p. 91.
72. *TP*, n. 23, vol. V (London, 1974), p. 63.
73. Ibid., p. 94.
74. A typed copy of Desai–Liaquat Pact, initialed by both on 11 January 1945, is available in the Desai Papers (National Archives of India, New Delhi). The other copy can be expected to be in the Khan papers, wherever they may be located, if extant.
75. For details of the Desai–Liaquat Pact and exchanges regarding it between the Viceroy and the British authorities in London as well as between Desai and the Viceroy and his staff and Governors, see *TP*, vol. V, n. 72, pp. 400–25, 443–5, 453–61, 464–5, 472–3, 475–97, 520–4, 540–3, 593–6, 607–8, 616–17, 632, 697, 739. See also M.C. Setalvad, Bhulabhai Desai (New Delhi, 1968), pp. 242–59, 361–7.
76. *TP*, vol. V, pp. 1122–4.
77. Ibid., pp. 1118–21.
78. Ibid., pp. 1125–36, 1139–40, 1151–5.
79. Ibid., pp. 1153–4.
80. Ibid., p. 1166.
81. Ibid., p. 1170.
82. Ibid., p. 1175.
83. Ibid., p. 1106, 1213.
84. Ibid., p. 1225.
85. Ibid., p. 1234.

86. Ibid.
87. Ibid., pp. 1236–7.
88. Ibid., p. 1104.
89. V.P. Menon, *The Transfer of Power in India* (Bombay, 1957), p. 217.
90. H.V. Hodson, *The Great Divide: Britain–India–Pakistan* (Lahore 1969), p. 127.
91. Ibid., pp. 121–5.
92. Ibid., pp. 127–8.
93. Moon, n. 72, Editorial note, pp. 157–8.
94. Ibid., p. 156.
95. Glancy to Linlithgow, 10 July 1942 (including the text of Sikander's formula as an enclosure), MSS. Eur. F125/91, Linlithgow Collection.
96. Glancy to Linlithgow, 20 November 1942, ibid.
97. *Jinnah: Speeches and Statements,* vol. III, n. 7, pp. 117–18.
98. Ibid., pp. 119–20.
99. Ibid., pp. 162–5.
101. Glancy to Linlithgow, 15 March 1943, F125/92, Linlithgow Collection.
100. Glancy to Linlithgow, 17 April 1943, ibid.
102. *Jinnah: Speeches and Statements,* III, n. 7, pp. 180.
103. *Constitutional Survey,* no. 23 (1 February to 30 April 1943).
104. Glancy to Linlithgow, 29 May 1943, F125/92, Linlithgow Collection.
105. Glancy to Linlithgow, 21 July 1943, ibid.
106. See Glancy to Linlithgow, 6 August 1943, and 7 September 1943, ibid.
107. See Glancy to Linlithgow, 16 September 1945, ibid; also *Constitutional Survey*, no. 25 (1 August–31 October 1943).
108. *Constitutional Survey*, no. 26 (1 November 1943 to 31 January 1944).
109. *Jinnah: Speeches and Statements*, vol. III, n. 7, p. 457.
110. For the text of Jinnah's statement on 28 April 1944, see ibid., pp. 472–5.
111. For the text of Khizr's statement dated 28 April 1944, see ibid., pp. 798–804.
112. For the relevant correspondence between the League's Committee of Action and Khizr, see ibid., pp. 808–16. The text of the latter's statement after his expulsion from the League is reproduced on pp. 817–26.
113. The text of the League's Council's resolution endorsing Khizr's expulsion from the League may be seen in ibid., p. 552.
114. *Constitutional Survey*, no. 28 (1 May to 31 July 1944).
115. For the text of this paper, see 'Three Windows for the Partition of India: I what if India comes to be Divided', *Iassi Quarterly* (New Delhi), vol. 9, no. 3, 1991, Its author, Tarlok Singh (born 1913), one

of the most distinguished citizens of India, had written it as a personal record in November 1943, when he was serving as a Colonization Officer, Nile Bar Colony (now in Punjab, Pakistan) with headquarters at Pakpattan. He discovered this hand-written and forgotten note accidentally among his old papers while looking for something else, in 1989.

116. *Jayaprakash Narayan: Selected Works*, ed. Bimal Prasad, vol. III (New Delhi, 2003), pp. 174–5.
117. Glancy to Wavell, 14 April 1944, L/P&J/8/662. Private Office Papers, India Office Library.
118. Ibid.
119. Wavell to Glancy, 15 April 1944, ibid.
120. Glancy to Wavell, 21 April 1944, ibid.
121. Glancy to Wavell, 23 August 1944, L/P&J/5/247, ibid.
122. Ian Talbot, *Punjab and the Raj, 1849–1947* (New Delhi, 1988), p. 199.
123. *Quarterly Survey*, no. 34. (1 August 1945–31 October 1945).

CHAPTER VI

Growth of the Pakistan Movement and Massive Electoral Mandate 1942–1946 (2)

AS THE ONLY PROVINCE in north-eastern India with a Muslim-majority and as home to the largest number of Muslims in the whole country, Bengal was second only to the Punjab as a key province for the Muslim League in the context of the Pakistan movement. To start with, here the League's position was much better than in the Punjab. While in the elections of 1937 the League had been able to secure only one Muslim seat in the Punjab Assembly, in Bengal its tally had been thirty-nine. However, this was only three more than the seats won by the Krishak Proja Party led by A.K. Fazlul Huq, who had also defeated, by a large margin, the tallest leader of the League in Bengal—Khwaja Nazimuddin—in a direct contest. The largest tally of Muslim seats had gone to Independents. Huq was inclined to explore the possibility of securing the position of Premier of the province through forming a coalition with the Congress, which had secured fifty-four seats in the Assembly. However, the Congress was not yet clear whether it was going to participate in ministry making due to its reservations regarding the special powers of the Viceroy and the Governor under the Act of 1935. The League leadership made good use of this situation and agreed to enter into a coalition headed by Huq. The latter thus became the Premier of Bengal with the help of the League and, just like Sikander, joined the League at its Lucknow session.

As has been mentioned in the previous chapter, neither accepted Jinnah's leadership except as a formality, under certain political compulsions. Also, neither had any inner enthusiasm for the demand for Pakistan, although Huq had in fact, formally moved the resolution embodying that demand at the Lahore session of the League in March 1940. Again, as noted in the previous chapter, both initially accepted the membership of the National Defence Council, being set up by the Government of India, without obtaining Jinnah's permission. After that their tactical positions diverged. When Jinnah cracked the whip with the full backing of the League's Working Committee, Sikander, as a realist, taking all the relevant factors into account, immediately backed out. On the other hand, Huq, with his volatile temperament, initially decided to defy Jinnah, only to feel compelled a little later to follow in the footsteps of Sikander, in the process offering an unqualified apology to the central leadership of the League and lowering his prestige in the eyes of his supporters much more than was the case with Sikander.

After turning the matter over in his mind for some time, Huq, much against his own judgement, decided to resign from the National Defence Council as directed by the League's Working Committee. However, as a protest against the Working Committee's decision asking him to do so, he also resigned his membership of both the Working Committee and the Council of the League. Conveying these decisions to Liaquat Ali Khan, General Secretary of the League, on 8 September 1942, Huq lodged a spirited protest against leaders from Muslim-minority provinces taking decisions without taking into consideration the wishes of the Muslim-majority provinces. Underlining the fact that the recent events in the history of Muslim politics had shown that the principles of democracy and autonomy in the League were being subordinated to 'the arbitrary wishes of a single individual', he wrote:

> I protest against the manner in which Bengal and Punjab Muslim interests are being imperilled by Muslim leaders of 'Minority Provinces'. . . . They neither realize the responsibilities of Muslim Premiers of those Provinces nor care for the repercussions on politics of Bengal and Punjab Muslims of their decisions for Muslim India as a whole. They should not meddle too much with the politics of the majority provinces. . . . I confidently hope that political dictators in future will act with greater foresight so as to prevent creation of a situation from which escape can be affected only by a course of action which is revolting to sound sense or even conscience.[1]

As Huq had resigned from the National Defence Council within the period stipulated in Liaquat's letter (ten days from the receipt of the letter, which was to end on 10 September 1941), Jinnah announced that no disciplinary action was required to be taken. However, he minced no words in expressing his displeasure over the tone as well as the substance of Huq's letter and made it clear that these would be considered by the Working Committee of the League in due course.[2] The latter, at its meeting in Delhi on 26–27 October, took a serious note of the allegations contained in Huq's letter, describing them as 'untrue and offensive' and, reserving further action, asked him to withdraw them within ten days of the receipt of the aforesaid resolution.[3] This really implied a threat of disciplinary action and Huq, after considerable deliberation, despatched a letter of regret or apology to the General Secretary of the League though slightly later than the stipulated time, pleading ill health. In that letter, dated 14 November 1941, the former reaffirmed his loyalty to the League, and conveyed his assurance that nothing was further from his intention than 'to hurt feelings of or cast aspersions on any one' and hoped that these would be 'accepted and [the] matter considered closed'. The League's Working Committee at its meeting two days later took cognizance of the letter, excused Huq for the delay in submitting his explanation, and decided not to take any further action in the matter.[4]

This was, however, not the end of the Huq–Jinnah confrontation. The former had not actually decided to end his defiance of Jinnah and sent his regrets to the central leadership of the League merely in order to gain time to regroup his forces. He used the breather thus obtained to secure the support of the League's opponents in the Assembly and mount an offensive against the leading figures of the League, loyal to Jinnah, like Khwaja Nazimuddin and H.S. Suhrawardy, who were made to face no-confidence motions in the Assembly on 27 November 1941. Rather than face these motions in the Assembly, and court defeat, the majority of the League members under the leadership of Nazimuddin chose to resign from the Cabinet. They calculated that this would force Huq to resign, thereby paving the way for Nazimuddin being given a chance to form a new ministry. Huq did resign, but after forming a new party—the Progressive Coalition Party—on 3 December 1941. Nazimuddin thereupon became the leader of the Muslim League Party in the Assembly. The Governor had no reason to be happy at this development and would have liked to administer the oath of office to Nazimuddin, but Huq was able to secure the support of a clear majority of members of the Assembly. These consisted of his own supporters in the ministerial coalition as also members of the Forward Bloc under the leadership of Sarat Chandra Bose, the Hindu Mahasabha (under the leadership of Syama Prasad Mookerjee), remnants of the Krishak Proja Party and the Independent Scheduled Caste Group, besides some other small parties and independents. Besides, the official Congress party, under the leadership of Kiran Shankar Roy, consisting of twenty-five members, also offered responsive cooperation. The Governor had, therefore, no option but to call upon Huq to form the ministry. However, he did so after considerable deliberation, only on 11 December and also after putting Sarat Bose in prison.[5] The Governor suspected the latter of being sympathetic to Japan and also in a position to dominate the new ministry. 'A Government virtually controlled by Sarat Bose,' the former wrote to the Viceroy on 5 December 1941, 'would be disastrous. . . .'[6] The Government of India had already mooted the idea of arresting Bose and the matter had been under discussion between the two Governments. As the arrest was to be made in the name of the Government of India, the Governor had to wait for the warrant of arrest to arrive, and this happened only on the afternoon of 11 December. The arrest of Bose and the swearing in of the new ministry, in that order, followed in quick succession.[7] Out of the nine ministers, five, including the Premier, Fazlul Huq, were Muslims, three were caste Hindus (two from the Forward Bloc and one from the Hindu Mahasabha, Syama Prasad Mookerjee) and one from the scheduled castes. The Muslim League party, under the leadership of Nazimuddin, formed after the break-up of the old coalition, was left with some 40 members. While in some sections of the general public the new ministry was hailed as marking the beginning of a period of communal harmony and peace, it was not clear how long it was likely to last, as there were certain fundamental political differences among its constituents. 'The driving force and the brains,' reported the Governor, 'will come from the Caste Hindus, and it will be interesting to see how far they have to give way to the Muslim Progressive Party in order to retain their support, and prevent them from rejoining the League.'[8]

II

The League's offensive had, of course, already begun. As soon as news broke out about the formation of the Progressive Coalition Party under Huq's leadership, Jinnah issued a statement on 5 December 1941, noting that the former had been 'for some considerable time trying to stab the Muslim League' and hoping that his departure from the League would enable the party in Bengal to work on a sound and healthy lines.[9] Again, when asking Huq to explain why disciplinary action should not be taken against him, Jinnah asserted that the former's conduct amounted to treachery and betrayal.[10] After Jinnah expelled him from the League, its Working Committee at its meeting at Nagpur on 26–27 December noted that action 'with great satisfaction' and accused Huq of 'treacherous betrayal of the Muslim League organization and the Musalmans generally'.[11] This set the pattern of the vigorous propaganda campaign against Huq launched by the League in Bengal. 'The Muslim League,' the Governor reported to the Viceroy in the second week of February 1942, 'continues its propaganda against the Ministry, concentrating on Huq and accusing him of being a traitor to Islam.'[12] The arrival of Jinnah in Bengal in the middle of February in order to preside over the provincial conference of the League held at Serajganj immensely helped the League in its campaign. Shortly after reaching Calcutta on 13 February Jinnah issued a message for the Muslims of Bengal in which he asked them not to trust 'traitors, quislings and fifth columnists'.[13] Even though Huq's name was not mentioned, the reference to him and his Muslim colleagues could be easily imagined. In his presidential address to the Serajganj Conference on 15 February, Jinnah devoted a good bit of his time to an attack on Huq, tracing the landmarks in the latter's political career since 1937 and after, referring to the latest episode in which Huq acted the way he did, even while occupying so many high positions in the League not only in Bengal—where he was the head of a League-dominated ministry and President of the provincial organization—but also in the All-India Muslim League, where he was a member of its Working Committee, Jinnah observed: 'I ask you for your verdict. Is this not the greatest betrayal of not only the Muslim League but [also of] the Muslims of Bengal and of the whole of India? Is this not a case of betrayal and treachery to the coalition party of which he was the leader for over four and [a] half years? Yes, it was.'[14]

Huq had really no answer to such criticisms although he went on answering them to the best of his ability and affirming his loyalty to the cause of the Muslim community. By that time, thanks to the growing appeal among the Muslims of the League's demand for Pakistan and of Jinnah's personality, more and more being considered as the authentic embodiment of the hopes and aspirations of Indian Muslims, the future of any Muslim seen working against them was doomed. The problem of Huq was that though he had built up his popularity among the Muslims, since he had first become Premier of Bengal, on the basis of his loyalty to the League and his tirade against the sceptre of Hindu domination, he was forced in his new incarnation to depend upon the support of the Hindu leaders, divided among several parties, but all working in his Progressive coalition. The most dominant among the latter was, of course, Syama Prasad Mookerjee, one of the top leaders of the Hindu Mahasabha, not only in Bengal but also in the whole of India—something unavoidable because of the imprisonment of Sarat Bose. Hence, so far as support among the mass of Muslim voters was concerned, the ground from under the feet of Huq went on slipping, as indeed it was bound to in the then existing political situation in Bengal.

Being a shrewd and experienced politician, if also volatile and mercurial, Huq seems to have become aware of that reality within less than six months of his second innings as Premier, if not right from the beginning. The Governor reported to the Viceroy as early as 23 April 1942 that Huq was shaken by the League's opposition to him personally and by the result of the by-election to the Assembly in Najore, where his candidate had forfeited the deposit.[15] So he began to explore the possibilities of a rapprochement with Jinnah. On 6 June, the Governor informed Linlithgow that the Progressive Muslims had begun feeling uncomfortable about their position among the members of their own community.[16] On 7 July, he again wrote to Linlithgow on that topic and mentioned that there was some evidence to suggest that some recent meetings that had taken place between the Progressive Muslims and the orthodox Leaguers in the Assembly constituted 'the beginning of a rapprochement between the two sections'. 'Huq is well aware of the position,' wrote the Governor, 'and, with his usual political acumen, is taking steps to safeguard his position.' At the moment he seemed to have had two irons in the fire. He was seriously thinking of going to Bombay in order to settle his differences with Jinnah. If he succeeded in achieving this, he would disband the Progressive Muslim Party in the Assembly and rejoin the Muslim League Party, retaining most, if not all, of his Hindu colleagues in the ministry. At the same time, in order to safeguard his position in case of a possible breakdown of his talks with Jinnah, Huq was also engaged in making overtures to Suhrawardy, with a view to bringing him back into the Cabinet, thereby further splitting the League in Bengal.[17]

On the same day (7 July 1942) that Herbert sent the letter, mentioned above, to Linlithgow, Huq wrote to the latter's secretary, Gilbert Laithwaite, telling him that there was a move by some of Jinnah's most trusted lieutenants in Bengal to bring about an understanding between Jinnah and himself and that there were very good prospects of a settlement. He further mentioned that he was soon going to Bombay in connection with some official business and that it was quite possible that he and Jinnah might be brought together. He felt certain that if such a meeting actually materialized, the result would be very satisfactory. While expressing his inability to say anything definite at that stage, he stated that he hoped for the best result. Jinnah might permit the League members to support the Huq ministry and waive his objection to their joining it. This, Huq thought, would be 'eminently satisfactory'.[18] Nothing of the sort, however, happened. Apparently Huq's hopes had been based on the assurances of one or more of his well-wishers with access to Jinnah, with a liberal dose of his own imagining. There was no Huq–Jinnah meeting and no settlement.

The Huq–Jinnah meeting materialized only in the middle of November 1942 after the former, during one of his visits to Delhi, wrote to the latter on 13 November mentioning their long association, lasting over a quarter of a century, pleading forgetting of all that had happened in the recent past, and seeking facilitation of his follower's re-entry into the League fold. Huq also assured Jinnah that once he re-entered the League he would strictly abide by its discipline and the instructions of its president. 'I need hardly emphasise the fact,' added Huq, 'that in the interest of

Islam and Muslim solidarity I am prepared to make any sacrifice and to subordinate my personal interests and inclinations to the supreme demand of the Muslim nation.' Huq followed this avowal of loyalty with a request for 'a few minutes' time' so he could explain everything personally, adding that he was leaving the interests of the Bengal Muslims in Jinnah's hands.[19] His interview with Jinnah followed on the same day that the latter received his letter in New Delhi. This, however, produced no positive result. After about three months, when Huq again raised this matter (on 5 February 1943), affirming that he was prepared to sacrifice everything that he had, including the office of Premier of Bengal, for the sake of his country and the solidarity of his community, and praying for the removal of the ban on his re-entry into the League,[20] he was curtly reminded by Jinnah (through his letter dated 10 February 1943) of what had transpired at that interview and the conditions laid down by the latter for the former's re-entry into the League. These included expression of regret by Huq at his past conduct and action leading to his expulsion from the League, his resignation from the office of Premier, and the dissolution of the Progressive Coalition Party. Huq was also reminded that he had then promised to fulfil these conditions within a fortnight, but that Jinnah had heard nothing from him till then.[21] As Huq's reply was a bit delayed in spite of Jinnah's telegram asking for an immediate reply,[22] Jinnah published his exchange of correspondence with Huq on 16 February in view of 'the various developments taking place in Bengal politics'.[23] These developments culminated in the forced resignation from the office of Premier by Huq and the installation of a League-dominated ministry headed by Nazimuddin, and will be noted in due course. Here it may suffice to mention that the text of the correspondence duly published on 17 February 1943 by *Star of India* and *Morning News*, both issued from Calcutta, could have done no good to Huq's image. He tried to clarify his position by issuing a press statement together with his draft letter dated 17 February 1943, which he had prepared to send to Jinnah, explaining his conduct since his meeting with the latter in November last, on the same date that the text of his correspondence with Jinnah was published.[24] However, the damage had been done.

The same factor—realization of his declining support among the Muslim public, particularly the youth—which led Huq to try to mend fences with Jinnah with a view to re-entering the League, also led him to seek from the Viceroy some position at the all-India level which would free him from the hassles of Bengal politics. This effort had begun much earlier than his knocking at Jinnah's door. Indeed, it had begun within a few months of Huq taking over as Premier of Bengal for the second time. When Sir Akbar Hydari, Member in charge of Information and Broadcasting in the Viceroy's Executive Council, passed away on 8 January 1942, Huq communicated to both the Viceroy and the Bengal Governor his desire to succeed him. Indirectly supporting his candidature, the latter wrote to the former that after a strenuous political career devoted to championing the Muslim cause, which saw him rising from the position of a Deputy Magistrate in the provincial service to that of the Premier of Bengal, Huq would like to achieve the distinction of being a member of the Viceroy's Executive Council.[25] He, of course, was not able to fulfil this ambition, but that was not due to any lack of effort on his part. Indeed, he was so serious about it that, realising that he could not secure any position at the Centre until the Government was certain that he would not work in opposition to Jinnah, he made it clear to Cripps on 29 March 1942, during a discussion on the latter's plan for resolving the Indian deadlock, that 'he had no intention of opposing Jinnah in any way either now or in the future and that if it came to a showdown he would follow Jinnah's leadership,[26] Huq, of course, could not get an opportunity to succeed Hydari in the Viceroy's Executive Council. This, however, did not deter him from trying again after some time to secure some other central assignment commensurate with his status. He, for instance, wrote to the Viceroy in the middle of February 1943—just three days after seeking a rapprochement with Jinnah—expressing his earnest wish for 'an opportunity to serve in the Middle East in a manner suited to my personal inclinations and the needs of the Empire'. Affirming that time was 'the essence of the whole scheme', as he was quite keen to set about 'working in right earnest in order to prepare in the Muslim States of the Middle East a solid ground for the establishment of British control and a bulwark for the defence of the Indian Empire'. This, he added, was among his 'fondest dreams'.[27] This, too, not succeeding, Huq made another effort about three months later, this time again for membership of the Viceroy's Executive Council.

The vacancy caused by Hydari's death had not till then been filled. Besides, three Hindu members had resigned because of the Government's refusal to order the release of Gandhi from detention in spite of his fast in February 1943. Utilizing that occasion, Huq wrote to Linlithgow on 19 February 1943, offering himself for one of the vacancies. 'May I respectfully point out to your Excellency' said Huq in support of his candidacy, 'that there is now no member representing Bengal, and that upto now no Bengali Muslim has been appointed by the Government of India.'[28] On both the occasions the Governor strongly recommended Huq's case for sympathetic consideration—not out of any liking or regard for Huq, but out of a desire to get him removed from Bengal politics.

III

The fact was that while, having no other option, in the light of a clear majority support for Huq in the Assembly, the Governor had decided to form a ministry headed by him for the second time, without the participation of the League members loyal to Jinnah, he had not been happy to do so. What was more pertinent, he was not at all satisfied with the performance of the new Huq ministry, with its large component of Forward Bloc and Hindu Mahasabha members, either in the vigorous support of the war effort or in the suppression of the Quit India movement, which spontaneously emerged in all parts of the country in the wake of the arrest of the top Congress leaders, including Gandhi, in August 1942. The ministers were also reluctant to own responsibility for stringent measures taken in these matters by the permanent officials working under the guidance of the Governor, and Huq, because of his dependence on the Hindu members of the Cabinet, was not in a position to rectify the situation. The Governor's feelings about Huq because of this were forcefully expressed in his letter to the Viceroy on 9 March 1942. According to it, while there was a general tendency to criticize ministers on the ground that they were mere ciphers and that the Governor and the permanent officials were really running the Government, the fact was that it was really Huq who was completely under the domination of his Hindu colleagues and was incapable of taking decisions without them even on matters pertaining to the Home

Department which was supposed to function under his own purview. Apparently the main purpose behind such tactics on the part of Huq was to save himself as well as his ministers from taking responsibility for unpopular actions of the Government while at the same time continuing to remain a part of it.[29] The Viceroy felt so strongly on this matter that he informed the Secretary of State through a telegram as early as 28 March 1942 that the situation was deteriorating and that a stage might arrive when the Governor should 'force the issue' even to the point of Huq's resignation.[30]

The situation, as anticipated, did go on deteriorating, at any rate from the British point of view, and the Governor kept on conveying it to the Viceroy again and again. Thus, he wrote on 21 April 1942: 'I must confess to a feeling of increasing disappointment at the failure of my Ministry to take any active interest in the war effort or to make any real endeavour to strengthen public morale.' He proceeded to point out that all his efforts to galvanize the ministers in this regard had failed. Huq was so shaken by the result of the Najore by-election to the Assembly in which his candidate polled less than 10 per cent of the votes cast that even if he went on tour ostensibly to put vigour into the war effort his real interest would be in engineering a split in the Muslim League in the districts where support for Huq was no longer what it used to be. His other partners in the ministry were also not really interested in pushing the war effort. The League leaders might be able to rally the Muslims in eastern Bengal, but they had made it clear that they would not cooperate so long as Huq remained Premier. In view of such an attitude it was also not possible to form a coalition government. Nor was it desirable to impose the direct rule of the Governor under Section 93 of the Government of India Act of 1935, without losing a considerable amount of goodwill among the Hindus. In such a situation the Governor felt that the only solution was Huq's retirement from Bengal politics and he was sure this could be secured 'if he were offered a post which would save his face and be reasonably remunerative'.[31] Writing to the Viceroy a month later, the Governor mentioned that Huq was quite keen to go to the Middle East and hoped that it might be possible for the Viceroy 'to make some proposal which would prove acceptable to his *amour propre*'.[32] When after the Congress Working

Committee's endorsement on 14 July 1942 of Gandhi's demand to the British to quit India, the British began bracing themselves for facing a civil disobedience campaign, the Governor was not satisfied with Huq's attitude. Reporting on his meeting with the latter on 22 July the Governor wrote to the Viceroy the next day that Huq was inclined to dismiss the threat of such a movement as not likely to attain any success in Bengal and had remarked that the League and the Mahasabha would be enough to deal with it. The Governor also reported that Huq seemed reluctant to issue any statement or carry out any counter-propaganda against the impending Congress movement. This on the ground that it would land him in a position identical with Jinnah's, who had already joined the fray against it; and in view of the nature of his relations with the latter, he wanted to avoid it.[33]

After the arrest of Gandhi and other Congress leaders in August 1942 and the widespread uprising of the people all over the country in its wake, the gulf between the Governor and Huq further widened. The main reason for this was the ministers' shirking of responsibility for the stern measures taken to suppress the people's movement that the permanent officials under the guidance of the Governor had resorted to. The Governor was particularly incensed by Huq's performance in this regard. 'Huq has now,' he wrote to the Viceroy, 'developed this technique at party meetings and in the Legislature to an extent which I feel may soon call for direct attention on my part.' He went on to underline that the latter had become 'the main obstacle to any general reunion of the Muslims here—let alone a coalition of united Muslims with influential Hindu elements'. Finally, the Governor expressed the view that while there were risks in any changeover, the then existing state of affairs was so undesirable that if Huq could be 'planted' somewhere outside India and the resultant situation left to find its own equilibrium, things could not be worse off so far as the British interests were concerned.[34]

The Governor's patience with Huq soon began to wear thin. On 6 October 1942, he informed the Viceroy by telegram that he had found it necessary to overrule Huq's advice for suspension of collective fines already imposed and for instituting procedures which would drastically delay their imposition in the future. Apprehending that the latter might make a public issue of it, the Governor informed the Viceroy that if that actually happened he would really take a most serious view of it. 'I feel I must tell him,' observed the Governor, 'that in present circumstances, especially in view of the seriousnes of the Midnapore situation, I should regard such action as making his position impossible and that he should resign failing which I should have to dismiss him.'[35] Two days later, he again informed the Viceroy that as the ministers were refusing to take a strong public stand against the pro-Congress movement this was creating a situation in which local officers were being deterred from exercising firmness and initiative in dealing with popular movements led by Congress sympathizers. At the same time, the ministers wanted to be allowed to offer a public explanation for the actions taken by the Governor against their wishes while showing no inclination to resign. The alternative, the Governor thought, was their dismissal, which was 'increasingly calling for consideration'.[36]

On the other hand, Huq accused the Governor of unconstitutional behaviour. His main charge, as he explained in his letter to the latter dated 2 August 1942, was that the Governor dealt directly with the permanent officials, acting as if the ministers did not exist and interfered in administrative details even relating to matters which lay clearly within the domain of ministerial responsibility. Huq ended that letter begging the Governor to act in a constitutional manner and not as a mouthpiece of permanent officials or of any political party, and to allow provincial autonomy to function in an honest way and not as 'a cloak for the exercise of autocratic powers'. During his visit to Delhi early in October he distributed printed copies of this letter to some press correspondents, at the same time telling them that it was for their personal information and not for publication.[37] On 10 October he wrote to the Viceroy forcefully complaining against the behaviour of the Governor in keeping pending the expansion of the ministry, a matter in which the wishes of the Premier could not be disregarded.[38]

At the same time, the differences between the Governor and the Premier over the handling of the popular movement in the wake of the Quit India call by the Congress continued unabated. Matters came to a head when Huq affirmed in the Assembly in February 1943 that the ministry was in favour of an impartial enquiry by persons of the status of High Court judges into the alleged excesses by officials in Midnapore. The Governor was shocked as he had not been consulted. However, when asked to explain, Huq replied that he had only expressed the views of the ministry. While reporting this incident to the Viceroy on 22 February 1943, the Governor again mentioned that in the then existing conditions Huq would welcome any assignment abroad in order to extricate himself from being 'buffeted between Gandhi and his Hindu colleagues on the one side and Jinnah and the Muslim League on the other'.[39]

The Governor, however, stayed his hand for some time more. He must have taken into account the fact that Huq had been able to form a coalition which continued to command a majority and in that situation his dismissal was most likely to result in the imposition of direct rule by the Governor under Section 93 of the Act of 1935. This the Governor was naturally keen to avoid, especially in view of the prevalence of widespread unrest in the wake of the Quit India movement and the obvious political advantage being derived from having a popular ministry in office. Mookerjee's resignation from the ministry on 20 November 1942 further complicated the situation, particularly as he justified his resignation on the ground that ministers were allowed to exercise very little power, especially where the liberties of the people were concerned, and that the Governor usually acted in disregard of their wishes, on the advice of a section of permanent officials. It became now of even greater importance than before to maintain the façade of constitutional government in Bengal.[40]

On the other hand, although Mookerjee's resignation was a blow to the ministry, the latter did not lose its majority in the Assembly. This was illustrated by the defeat of a motion of censure against the latter on the ground of its failure to satisfactorily tackle the food problem, moved by a League member on 10 March 1943. Another motion, moved by the same member from the League (Tamizuddin Khan) on 23 March, seeking to censure the ministry for its failure to assume responsibility for the actions of government officials met the same fate. A third motion of censure moved by a member belonging to the European group on 27 March, this time on the ground of the ministry's failure to deal effectively with black-marketeering and hoarding of food grains, did not fare any better.[41]

These repeated failures of the move to dislodge Huq from Premiership constitutionally spurred the Governor to come into the open and finally take the step he had been contemplating for so long. While coming to the conclusion that the only way he could end Huq's tenure as Premier was through dismissal, the Governor thought that such action on any ground related to the popular movement in Midnapore or elsewhere would 'only open the way to even more difficult problems'.[42] Fortunately for him, Huq himself, with a desire to prove his sincerity and lack of interest in clinging on to power, had on more than one occasion offered to resign in order to facilitate the formation of a broader coalition, of the nature of a national government, including representatives from all parties in the Assembly in order to pursue the war effort more vigorously. In one of such letters sent as early as 8 May 1942 he had also suggested an alternative position for himself—speakership of the Legislative Assembly with, of course, 'special allowances'.[43] He had renewed such an offer to the Governor as late as 21 March and again on 26 March 1943. The Governor used this offer to virtually force Huq to resign on 28 March. Huq underlined that offer in the course of his statement before the Assembly. Affirming that nothing was dearer to him than the formation of a national government in Bengal, he had gone on to declare that he would resign if it was found that his continuance as Premier was a hurdle in its way.[44] This was again confirmed by Huq on 29 March in answer to a question whether he had indeed resigned as per rumours floating in Calcutta since that morning.

> Sir, it is true that last night I was sent for by the Governor and I was with him from 7.30 to over 9 p.m. A long discussion took place about the formation of a national Cabinet and various proposals were put forward, some of which I could accept consistent with self-respect. His Excellency the Governor suggested to me that I should formally tender my resignation. I said I could not do so unless I had time to consult my party and my colleagues. To this the Governor did not agree and I had to sign a letter of resignation.[45]

The draft of that letter, addressed to the Governor, had already been prepared and kept ready with the Governor's Secretary. It ran as follows:

> Understanding that there is a probability of the formation of a Ministry representative of most of the parties in the event of my resignation, I hereby tender my resignation of my office as Minister in the sincere

hope that this will prove to be in the best interests of the people of Bengal.[46]

As Huq informed the Viceroy later, he 'most vehemently' protested against signing such a letter, pointing out that he was the head of a stable ministry and enjoyed the confidence of the majority in the Assembly and saw no reason why he should resign. A long discussion followed in which the Governor told Huq that he must have the latter's resignation in his hand in order to negotiate with the party leaders about the formation of an all-parties government. He then sought the Governor's leave to go and meet his colleagues and his party, but the latter asked Huq to sign his letter of resignation then and there. What followed is best described in Huq's own words:

> I pleaded with His Excellency but in vain. His Excellency was adamant and insisted on my signing the letter. I found any resistance was useless and I agreed to sign the letter and keep it with His Excellency with only the sole purpose of enabling His Excellency to negotiate with party leaders and on the clear understanding that no effect should be given to the letter unless my being in office was the only obstacle to the formation of an all-parties Government. . . . I returned home and within half an hour I received an acceptance of my resignation. . . .[47]

The Governor, on his part, explained to the Viceroy that Huq had repeatedly expressed his desire to resign office in order to facilitate the formation of an all-parties government and that these offers had recently acquired a plausibility because of his dwindling position to the point where his party had lost elections to all the six vacant seats in the Legislative Council and only ten official Congress votes in the Assembly had enabled him to continue as Premier. The Governor had, therefore, decided to clear up through an interview whether Huq was sincere in his undertaking to resign in case that was found necessary in the interest of the formation of an all-parties government. The Governor admitted that he had pointed out to Huq 'the palpable fact' that the latter's presence did stand in the way of the formation of a coalition government, but had not threatened to dismiss him if he did not resign.[48] In a further communication to the Viceroy sent the next day, the Governor denied that he had prevented Huq from consulting his party, but merely told him that his party would only make him change his mind and that 'if he really meant what he had promised, he would do it and not find excuses for avoiding it'. Asserting that Huq was free to go from the Governor's mansion at any time, the Governor remarked, 'He is neither a child nor a fool and it passes my understanding how any unprejudiced outsider could believe that he had to be compelled to do what he had openly undertaken to do the day before in the Legislative Assembly.' The Governor also denied that Huq was forced to sign a letter of resignation as already drafted by the former's secretary. Admitting that a draft letter had been prepared in advance by his secretary and approved by him, the Governor submitted that it had been shown to Huq only after the latter had agreed to resign. Besides, that was done not with a view to compelling him to sign it, but merely as an 'indication of how he might make his gesture with credit'. Indeed, the draft had been prepared on common draft paper and the services of a stenographer were offered to Huq to dictate his letter as per his liking. However, Huq chose to sign the 'rough draft' and left the Governor on 'perfectly good terms reiterating his usual request that I would try to get him some fat job'.[49]

The Viceroy, of course, was not satisfied with the Governor's explanation. He made it clear to the Governor that, while he had every sympathy with the latter's difficulties, it was not a fact that he was at all happy at the way that matters relating to Huq's resignation had been handled.[50] The grounds of the Viceroy's unhappiness were summed up in the course of his letter to Amery, the Secretary of State for India, sent on the same day:

> I am very disturbed about this business of Herbert and his Ministry . . . I cannot imagine greater folly than to present someone of the type of Huq with a draft letter of resignation, head him off from consulting his colleagues and his party on the ground that they will be certain to dissuade him from signing it; make him sign it as a result of an hour and a half's conversation, and all this with the Budget not yet through, and with full knowledge of the instability of Huq, and the risk that even if he had been a willing signatory of the letter of resignation he might well have changed his mind overnight.[51]

Whatever the Viceroy might feel, the Governor had already acted and the former naturally felt compelled to support him. As Huq had announced his resignation on the morning of 29 March and the Speaker had consequently adjourned the Assembly, without the adoption of the annual budget, it had to be passed by the Governor through certification. Further, as no alternative ministry with majority support in the Assembly seemed immediately feasible, Bengal passed under the direct rule of the Governor under Section 93 of the Government of India Act (1935). However, the Governor as well as the Viceroy wanted that arrangement ended and a ministry with majority support in the Assembly installed as soon as possible. For this the Governor turned immediately to Nazimuddin, leader of the Muslim League Party (as also of the opposition as a whole). In the beginning of April, he asked the latter to investigate the possibility of forming a broad-based ministry representing as many parties as possible and on 13 April formally commissioned him to do so. With this show of Governor's preference, Nazimuddin succeeded in securing support from a majority of members in the Assembly and was sworn in as Premier on 24 April. The Governor himself recognized that the new ministry was 'admittedly unimpressive as a whole'. Apart from its leading Muslim members such as Nazimuddin, his brother Shahabuddin, and Suhrawardy, the others were 'of the ordinary type found in East Bengal'. The ministers belonging to Scheduled Castes were 'better than one could expect'. As for the Hindus, they were 'admittedly not fully representative'.[52] The official confidential report prepared for the Viceroy went further and characterized the caste Hindu support secured for the ministry as 'poor' and described the two ministers belonging to that group as 'men of dubious personal morals as well as being turncoats' of the rebel Congress or Forward Bloc group headed by Sarat Bose,[53] who continued to languish in prison.

IV

The most significant result of the formation of the Nazimuddin Ministry was the rapid spread of the Pakistan movement all over Bengal. Indeed, the process had already begun with the formation of the second Huq Ministry, without the participation of the Muslim League, in December 1942. The latter took it as a challenge to its very survival and launched a tearing campaign against the ministry, describing Huq as a traitor to the Muslim cause and exhorting Muslims to work for the establishment of Pakistan to which the League was dedicated. For the first time, all the top leaders of the League—Nazimuddin, Suhrawardy, and

Tamizuddin Khan—who had also been powerful ministers in Huq's first ministry toured the countryside together with this message. The revitalization of the League's organization under the leadership of Maulana Akram Khan, a veteran of the Khilafat movement, who now replaced Huq as President of the Bengal Provincial Muslim League, contributed significantly to the success of this campaign. The active participation of the Muslim students in the campaign became a source of great strength. Jinnah's visit to Bengal in February 1942 with a view to presiding over the provincial conference of the League at Sirajganj provided a further boost and helped to inject a new life and vigour into the League's organization. How widely the League's message with its new goal—Pakistan—had already reached the Muslims of Bengal is borne out by the fact that when Jinnah arrived in Calcutta, about 40,000 Muslims were present at the Howrah railway station to receive him. After his visit, involving several public appearances and speeches, his and the League's appeal naturally became stronger. Muslim students in Bengal became ardent champions of the demand for Pakistan. A conference of the All-Bengal Muslim Students League held at Chinsura in the second week of September 1942 adopted a resolution calling upon the British Government to make a declaration that it would abide by 'the verdict of the national plebiscite of Muslims after the war on the Pakistan issue'. While the war was going on, the Congress being on the other side, the students urged the British to call upon Jinnah 'to form a war-time popular government in cooperation with other parties'.[54]

The growth of the Pakistan movement in Bengal, already under way, was further facilitated by the installation of the Nazimuddin ministry (1943). The League's leadership in the province naturally received a great boost to its morale and acquired much greater confidence than before in the leadership of Jinnah and in the soundness and ultimate success of his mission. The task of transmitting this new mood to the Muslim masses living in the countryside was very much facilitated by a contemporaneous change in the organizational leadership of the Bengal Provincial Muslim League. This was symbolised by the election of Abul Hashim (then 38) as the new General Secretary, replacing Suhrawardy, who had been appointed a member of the Nazimuddin Cabinet and hence could not continue as General

Secretary under a new dispensation made by the central League leadership. Well educated, young, and energetic, Hashim was full of enthusiasm for the goal of Pakistan and endowed with great organizational ability as well as a progressive social outlook. He made it his mission to strengthen and revitalize the League's organization not merely at the provincial level, but also at the district headquarters and in rural as well as urban areas in the remotest corners of Bengal, particularly in its eastern and northern parts where Muslims predominated in the population. He personally visited those areas for the fulfilment of his mission. Everywhere his effort was directed towards recruiting young workers for the League, giving them responsible positions in the League's organization, and turning them into enthusiastic missionaries for the Pakistan demand, linking that demand with the economic and social upliftment of the Muslim masses. This earned him the wrath of the old established aristocratic leaders of the League, who had till then maintained their stranglehold on the League's organization and had no interest in its expansion or revitalization on account of the fear of losing their control over it. As they saw that control now slipping out of their hands, they ganged up against Hashim and dubbed him a communist, but Hashim proved equal to the challenge posed by his opponents and with the enthusiastic support of his new recruits and his own organizational skill he decisively worsted them and further strengthened his position. Initially owing his rise to leadership in the provincial organization to the backing extended by Suhrawardy, he soon consolidated his position and emerged as an important player in the organizational power game by himself, the other two players being, of course, Nazimuddin and Suhrawardy.[55] The result achieved by the younger group under the leadership of Hashim was well summed up by the latter in his report for the year 1943–4, presented before the annual meeting of the Bengal Provincial Muslim League. According to it, the League had been able to enrol more than 500,000 members, thus achieving 'the proud record of being the biggest political body' that Bengal had ever seen till then. With this expansion of membership had also come an enlargement of the cadre of workers fully devoted to the League. As Hashim put it:

> As the League has gone out among the people, it has simultaneously found the means to develop itself. Once we have taken the League out

of the fold of the *few* into the broad world of the *many*, cadres of workers have come forward to serve the League. It is heartening to find even in some of the remotest corners of the province, young Muslims, filled with all the noble idealism and unbounded enthusiasm of the youth, offering themselves for service to the League.[56]

This streamlining and expansion of the League's organization, the large influx of young blood into it, and the spread of the message of Pakistan to the remotest corner of Bengal were, however, of no avail in saving the League's ministry in Bengal, which fell at the end of March 1945. The chief reason for the fall was the growing dissatisfaction of its Hindu supporters who thought that it was ignoring the interests of the members of their community and trying to pander only to the wishes of its Muslim supporters. Twenty-one of them crossed over to the opposition led by Fazlul Huq, who was also supported by the MLAs belonging to the Congress and the Forward Bloc. The issue was settled in the Assembly on 28 March 1945, when the demand for the grant for agriculture was outvoted by 106 to 97 votes. The next day, the Speaker gave his ruling that the Government headed by Nazimuddin had ceased to exist.[57]

It may be worth noting here that according to established parliamentary convention expected to be followed in the provinces where popular governments were functioning under the Act of 1935, the leader of the combined opposition, Fazlul Huq, should have been called upon to form a new government. However, the Governor did not follow this convention and took direct charge of the administration of Bengal under Section 93 of the Act of 1935. In his communication to the Viceroy, he justified this action on the ground that although if given a chance Huq would be able to produce a majority to back him, such a majority 'must inevitably be built on corrupt foundations and corrupt expectations'.[58] This was perhaps based on the suspicion that the Hindu members supporting Nazimuddin had deserted him as a result of being bribed by the Marwari cloth merchants in Calcutta whose premises had been recently raided by the police as part of a campaign against hoarding and black-marketeering.[59] There can be no doubt, however, that political considerations had determined the nature of the Governor's action. One week before the vote of censure in the Assembly, Nazimuddin had been sounded by Kiran Shankar Roy, leader of the Congress party in the Assembly, on the possibility of installing a Government in Bengal on the basis of a coalition. As Roy was at that time also holding discussions with the leader of the Forward Bloc, the probability was that the latter's members also might be included in the ministry. Nazimuddin, being a loyalist and keen to remain on the right side of the Governor, thought it prudent to consult the latter on the desirability of setting up such a coalition government and, on the latter's advice, gave 'a discouraging reply' to Roy.[60] The working of the mind of British officialdom was revealed by the Secretary of State for India when he wrote to the Acting Governor-General on the receipt of that news. 'I think it is just as well,' he remarked, 'that Nazimuddin was not prepared to try with the idea of a Congress Coalition in Bengal at this moment.' Explaining the cause of his feeling of relief, he added: 'Letting Congressmen loose in Assam and allowing processions, speeches, etc., may be tiresome. In Bengal, with the terrorist element, it might be really dangerous.'[61] Some such thought must have also passed through the Bengal Governor's mind when he refused to follow convention and clamped Section 93 in the province.

The Governor's partiality for Nazimuddin and his aversion to seeing a non-League ministry in office are revealed by the advice he had given Nazimuddin a few months earlier on the best way to ensure the stability of his ministry. One of the developments that had severely irked the Hindu members of the Assembly was the ministry's introduction of the Secondary Education Bill in 1944, which provided for the setting up of a Secondary Education Board with a constitution which was likely to result in a more or less permanent Muslim majority. With the opponents of the ministry extending their support to the agitated Hindu members, the debates in the Assembly became more and more unruly. There was an impression that the opponents of the ministry were aided by the attitude of the Speaker, Syed Nausher Ali, a former minister and an old supporter of Fazlul Huq. In such a situation, the Governor, leaving aside the supposed norms for the functioning of an occupant of that office, 'pointed out to the Chief Minister that the Speaker's conduct must have a serious effect on the stability of the Ministry, and *urged* him to take action for the Speaker's removal'.[62] This advice, of course, could not be followed as Nazimuddin did not feel sure of securing an absolute majority of 126 out of 250 members of the Assembly, as required by the

Act of 1935. The Governor's conduct in March 1945, therefore, in not giving a chance to Huq to form a ministry and to put the province under his direct rule as per Section 93 of the Act of 1935 cannot be described as a decision not influenced by partisan political considerations.

V

The fortunes of the Muslim League in the North-West Frontier Province during 1942–5 broadly corresponded to those of its counterpart in Bengal, with the Governors in both places lending a helping hand. Just as in the latter, in the former, too, the League came to power in 1943 with valuable help from the Governor, but had to leave office about two years later, in spite of continued interest in its well-being on the part of the latter. The conditions in the two provinces were, of course, not exactly identical. While in Bengal, as described earlier, the Governor had forced the Huq ministry to resign in order to make room for the installation of a League-dominated ministry under Nazimuddin, in the NWFP the Congress ministry resigned of its own volition, under a decision taken by the Congress leadership at the national level, in order to register a protest against India having been made a party to World War II, on the British side, without the consent of the Indian people.

The two branches of the League had also begun their march to power in different ways. In Bengal, the League had won a substantial number of seats in the Legislative Assembly at the time of the start of the experiment in Provincial Autonomy in 1937 had succeeded in securing an honoured place for itself in the coalition government formed by Fazlul Huq, leader of the Krishak Proja Party. In NWFP, in spite of serious efforts on Jinnah's part, the League had not been able to contest even a single seat. On the other hand, the Congress, though not in a majority, had been able to emerge as the largest single party (19 out of a total of 50 seats); the others being Independent Muslims 21, Hindu–Sikh Nationalist Party 7, Independent Party 2, Independent Hindu 1. A significant feature of the election results was that out of 19 seats won by the Congress, 15 were rural Muslim seats and 4 were general seats (1 urban and 3 rural). On the other hand, 18 rural seats had been won by Muslim independents,[63] indicating that although the Congress under the leadership of Khan Abdul Ghaffar Khan, head of the *Khudai Khidmatgar* (Servants of God) organization, had a strong rural base, its sway did not extend to the entire rural belt. In spit of it, there can be no doubt that had the Congress been inclined to form a ministry immediately after the elections, it would have had no insurmountable difficulty. For the members of the Hindu–Sikh Nationalist Party, the only other organized group of any significance, with 7 members, could have been easily won over and some independent members could have followed suit, with the prospect of sharing power opening up before them. As is well known, however, the Congress was not ready at that time to form a ministry in any province because of its objection to wide special powers vested in the Governors under the Act 1935. In such circumstances, a ministry was formed in the NWFP under the leadership of Sir Abdul Qaiyum, who was able to assemble an assortment of supporters to bolster his position. He was, however, able to retain his office primarily because of the support extended to him by the Governor, Sir George Cunningham.[64] When the broad constitutional issue was settled to the satisfaction of the Congress through a statement issued by the Viceroy on 22 June 1937 containing the assurance that the Governors would exercise their powers with great caution and avoid undue interference with the working of the ministries, the way was opened for the installation of Congress ministries in those provinces where they had a majority in the Assemblies. Although the Congress did not have a majority in the Assembly in the NWFP, it was obvious to anyone that it was in a position to form a ministry. Qaiyum wanted to resign immediately, but he was persuaded by the Governor to stick to office as long as he could and this was facilitated by putting off the Assembly session for quite a few months. When at last the Assembly met in September, it immediately adopted a motion of no confidence in the Ministry, moved by Khan Sahib, brother of Khan Abdul Ghaffar Khan and leader of the Congress Assembly Party. Qaiyum now resigned and a Congress ministry under Khan Sahib took over. The ministry functioned for over two years with reasonable success and introduced several progressive measures for the amelioration of the living conditions of people belonging to the weaker sections of society.[65] However, just as its advent had been delayed by the

Congress–British differences at the national level, so also its tenure came to an end because of the same reason. When the Congress decided in October 1939 to ask all its ministries to resign as a protest against the failure of the British Government to specify its war aims and make clear whether they included freedom for India, the Khan Sahib ministry duly resigned on 7 November 1939.

Much before that the Muslim League in the NWFP had been able to galvanize itself from the moribund state in which it had been lying since its foundation in 1912 and to register its presence in the Assembly. That had been made possible partly by the general atmosphere in the country created by Jinnah's incessant call to Muslims, in the wake of the formation of Congress ministries in several provinces, to wake up and organize themselves without any loss of time or face the prospect of being placed permanently under Hindu domination and the example set by the Punjab and Bengal Premiers (Sikander Hyat Khan and Fazlul Huq) who, although elected to the respective Assemblies on non-League tickets, had announced their allegiance to the League at its Lucknow session held in October 1937. Along with it, the social base of politics in the NWFP also significantly contributed to the revival of the League. Khan Abdul Ghaffar Khan and his *Khudai Khidmatgars*, who had merged with the Congress and constituted its main base in the NWFP, drew their support mainly from the small landlords or Khans, as they were popularly called, among the Pakhtuns, the Pushtu-speaking people in the rural areas of the NWFP. Their main objective was the uplift of the rural people who were being exploited by the bigger Khans enjoying British patronage as a price for their loyalty. The bigger Khans were, therefore, naturally hostile to the movement led by Ghaffar Khan. Many of the persons living in urban areas, too, belonged to the same category. Besides, the Pakhtuns did not form a majority in all the districts of the NWFP. While they were in a majority in the more populous districts of Peshawar, Kohat, and Bannu, they were in a minority in the less populous districts of Hazara and Dera Ismail Khan, which were dominated by non-Pakhtun Muslims.[66] With the formation of the Khan Sahib ministry, those not under the sway of the *Khudai Khidmatgars*, whether in towns or villages, became jealous of the position of power occupied by the latter. Most of the big Muslim landlords, hostile to the *Khudai Khidmatgars* as well as the Congress, which was increasingly being dubbed all over India as primarily a Hindu organization, felt the need to organize themselves into a political party in order to promote their interests. They became the nucleus of the Muslim League, which was revived in the NWFP in 1937. The emerging political scenario has been beautifully summed up by the Swedish scholar, Erland Jansson, who has made a special study of the politics in the NWFP between 1937 and 1947: 'There existed a party—the Muslim League—which needed a following, and a class—the big Khans—in need of a party.'[67] By 1938, there was a Muslim League Coalition Party in the Assembly functioning under the leadership of Aurangzeb Khan. The League was also able to win all the three by-elections held in that year.[68] So when the Congress ministry resigned in 1939, the Governor naturally turned to its leader for the formation of a non-Congress ministry. Jinnah was very keen to see a League ministry installed in the NWFP and encouraged Aurangzeb Khan to take advantage of the Governor's offer. However, Khan found it impossible to gather enough support in the Assembly to be able to form a ministry. The Governor, therefore, had no option but to place the NWFP under his direct rule under Section 93 of the Act of 1935 [69] and there it remained till 1943.[70]

In the meanwhile, with the adoption of the Quit India demand by the Congress and the active participation in that campaign by the Congress leaders in the NWFP, the Governor, with due encouragement from the Viceroy, made a fresh effort to install a League-dominated ministry. Jinnah had, of course, asked for the Viceroy's help in this regard[71] but the latter was intelligent enough to see that it was equally in British interest to install a League ministry in the NWFP at a time when the Congress was engaged in an open fight with them and the League was the one major political party which was opposing it. If nothing else, it would help the British in showing to the world that the writ of the Congress did not run everywhere in India. The fact that the NWFP had an overwhelming majority of Muslims made it especially important from this point of view. For the central point of the British propaganda campaign was that the Congress did not have the support of Muslims and that the latter owed allegiance to the Muslim League, an implacable enemy of the Congress.

The Linlithgow–Cunningham correspondence on this subject amply underlines the Viceroy's interest in the matter. Thus on 13 August 1942, even though realizing that the prospects for the installation of a League ministry were at that point of time indifferent, Linlithgow told Cunningham that 'there would be certain obvious propaganda advantages were we in a position to point to something of this nature . . .'.[72] The Viceroy repeated this suggestion in his communication to the Governor on 6 October in which he mentioned his talk with Feroz Khan Noon, a Punjabi Muslim member of his Executive Council, who had given him a favourable picture regarding the prospect of installing a League ministry in the NWFP.[73] Noon had seen the Viceroy obviously in order to prepare the ground for his visit to Lahore with a view to getting a League ministry installed there. However, Cunningham was still not convinced that a League ministry would be able to survive for any length of time. In his letter to the Viceroy dated 12 October 1942, he clearly stated that though he and Noon were agreed on the desirability of having a League ministry in the NWFP, they had not come to any definite conclusion about the feasibility of doing so.[74] On 9 November, the Governor again reported to the Viceroy after ' a good deal of talk' with Aurangzeb Khan, leader of the League Assembly Party, that their conclusion was that from the point of view of the League itself it would be better not to attempt to form a ministry at that time, as the majority commanded by Khan was quite precarious.[75] Khan's mood changed after some time and in the latter half of January 1943 the Governor informed the Viceroy that Khan was making a serious effort to win the support of the majority of the MLAs and form a ministry. The Governor, however, thought that Khan was 'somewhat over-optimistic' in this regard and not mindful of the difficulties in the way of his getting majority support in the Assembly.[76] In his next two reports to the Viceroy, the Governor reiterated the same view.[77] The Viceroy, while leaving the Governor free to deicide what was the best course to adopt in that situation, conveyed to him Noon's view that a League ministry 'could in fact be formed' and passed on to him a detailed note prepared by Noon describing the alignment of various members in the Assembly to buttress his view.[78] The Governor, however, still stuck to his view expressed in his three previous reports that it was not possible to have a stable League majority in the NWFP under the circumstances then prevailing in the Frontier Province and sent the Viceroy a detailed note of his own regarding the alignment of the members of the Assembly. He also did not forget to add that according to local gossip the chances of Khan forming a ministry appeared less than what they were about a month back.[79] The Governor held on to his position for some time, but ultimately changed his mind after Khan assured him of his being able to harness sufficient support in the Assembly.[80] So finally section 93 was revoked and a League ministry installed in the last week of May 1943.[81]

Actually, as an acknowledged authority on the NWFP politics has mentioned, 'it is doubtful if the [Aurangzeb Khan's] Ministry ever had a majority'. He further adds: 'In any case it would never have been able to stay in power without the support of the Governor, Sir George Cunningham.'[82] This is confirmed by the Governor himself in his reports to the Viceroy. Thus in his report no. 14 dated 25 July 1943, the Governor wrote: 'Most people whom I have consulted on the subject hold that the chances are now against Aurangzeb Khan winning a division [in the Assembly] on a crucial debate.'[83] In his next report dated 9 August 1943, the Governor, after mentioning the difficulties being then faced by Khan in marshalling majority support in the Assembly, wrote that in order to help the latter he was going 'to see one or two weaverers'.[84] The Governor's report no. 16 dated 24 August 1943 is even more revealing of the close collaboration between himself and the Muslim League. While mentioning the League's victory in all the four by-elections for the vacant Muslim seats in the Assembly, he wrote that while three of these were expected, the fourth (in the Mardan district, a known Congress stronghold) would not have been possible 'had not the ground been prepared by the propaganda which we have been doing almost since the war started, most of it on Islamic lines'. He was indeed happy to note that there was a general impression in the political circles in the NWFP that the League's victory in the by-elections really represented a victory for the British Government. 'It is satisfactory to note,' he wrote in that report, 'that the Muslim League successes in these by-elections are generally accepted as being a victory for the British Government over the subversive elements in the country.'[85] The Viceroy's comment on this shows that, although slightly worried about the possibility of such an impression causing some embarrassment to the British in future, he fully shared the Governor's satisfaction. For he remarked: 'We can meet such difficulties when we come to them.'[86]

The continued detention of ten Congress members of the Assembly was a major factor in saving the League ministry. That detention went on even after so many other political prisoners associated with the Congress had been released. When the Frontier Congress leaders brought this to the notice of the Governor, the latter pointed out that on such matters he had to go by the advice of his ministers.[87] The fact, on the other hand, was that the ministry hardly decided anything without the advice of Governor. As the latter noted in his diary on 19 July 1943: 'Aurangzeb is extremely amenable and anxious to do as I want. He seems to have forgotten that the function of a Minister is to advise the Governor. Nearly every file comes from him with a note: "I solicit the advice of H.E. the Governor."'[88] The release of the Congress MLAs could not, however, be indefinitely postponed and once their release began in 1944 the situation for the ministry worsened. The Governor thereupon chose the device of postponing the holding of the Assembly session as long as possible. When in November 1944 Mehr Chand Khanna, leader of the opposition, implored the Governor to convene a meeting of the Assembly to discuss a no-confidence motion in the ministry, the Governor rejected that request on the ground that there was no official business for discussion in the Assembly. A little later the Governor was informed that the opposition could muster 22 votes as against 21 for the ministry, but he still refused to summon the Assembly before it was due to meet to discuss the budget in the spring of 1945.[89] Shortly after that day finally arrived (9 March 1945) and the Assembly adopted a motion of no confidence in the ministry by 24 votes to 18 (12 March 1945).[90] So when the Simla Conference met in June–July 1945, there was no League ministry in any Muslim-majority province except Sind.

VI

The Muslim League did not have a single member belonging to it in the Sind Assembly in 1937. However, just as in the other Muslim-majority provinces, the League's influence and power in Sind went on steadily increasing since then. The League profited from the fact that if it was not represented in the Assembly, the election had also not thrown up any other party in 1937 with a clear-cut ideology or a stable membership in the Assembly. Indeed, membership of parties was then not important at all. What mattered in an Assembly dominated by the rural elite consisting of large landholders, clan leaders and *pirs* was personal loyalty based on kinship and economic dependence.[91] In such a situation it was possible for a person heading a comparatively small party to form a government with the help of members of other, ostensibly larger, parties who could be easily lured by offers of office and patronage. It was through this process that the first ministry was formed under the leadership of Ghulam Hussain Hidayatullah. His Sind Muslim Political Party had been able to secure only 3 seats as against the Sind United Party's 27 seats, the largest single bloc in the Assembly (total membership 60). However, the defeat of both its president, Haji Abdullah Haroon, and its vice-president, Shah Nawaz Bhutto, left that party leaderless. Hidayatullah, with his high personal standing and long innings in Sind politics, took advantage of this situation and, with discreete help from the Governor, who picked him as the person likely to command the support of the majority in Assembly, was able to form a ministry, the first under the Act of 1935. His ministry, however, did not last long and was forced to resign in March 1938. A new ministry was then formed under the leadership of Allah Bakhsh, with support from the Congress and independent Hindu members as well as a number of Muslim members. By that time, thanks partly to the impact of the call of the Lucknow session of the Muslim League to all Muslims to rally around the banner of that organization if they wanted to save themselves from Hindu domination and to realize their destiny as a nation, and partly to the play of local politics, the League had been revived in Sind and a League Assembly Party had come into existence. Some of the Muslim politicians, out of power, saw advantage in functioning under the umbrella of an all-India organization, with a charismatic leader like Jinnah, whose prestige was rising day-by-day. Two out of them, Abdul Majid Sindhi and Haji Abdullah Haroon, had already rallied under the League. After being thrown out of office Hidayatullah joined their ranks and was soon followed by G.M. Syed. By July 1938, the League could boast of 40 branches in the province and about 15,000 members, mostly in rural areas. A growing number of *pirs* (heads of religious establishments) as also Syeds (claiming direct descent from the Prophet) in such areas now extended their support to the League, thus endowing it with a social base in the countryside.[92] Most of the leaders who proclaimed their loyalty to the League, however, did so out of consideration for personal gain and not out of political conviction or devotion to the League's ideology. Personalities still counted more than parties. In such a situation, the struggle to get the Manzilgah shrine in Sukkur district declared a Muslim shrine on the ground that it had earlier been used as a mosque came in handy to the League leadership, and its ramifications, including serious communal rioting in Sukkur district, led to the fall of the Allah Bakhsh ministry. In order to take advantage of the situation by having a League-dominated ministry, the League members joined hands with a number of independent Hindu members to form a new outfit to be known as the Nationalist Party. The League also agreed to have as Premier a non-League member, one Mir Bandeh Ali. The ministry, however, had three members belonging to the League. Jinnah was not happy with his this arrangement, but out of his keenness to see the League having a foothold in power in Sind and realizing the realities in Muslim politics therein, dominated by big landholders, who were primarily interested in power without any commitment to ideology or programme, he went along with this arrangement, in spite of the opposition of some prominent League leaders led by Abdullah Haroon, who had supported the Pakistan demand from the very beginning. [93]

Bande Ali's ministry, formed with so much labour, could not last long and was forced to resign in 1941, enabling Allah Bakhsh to return to power again, with the support of an assortment of members including those belonging to the Congress. The Quit India demand of the Congress (August 1942) and the repression that followed in its wake, however, saw his undoing. His overt sympathy for the Congress led him first to oppose the repressive measures of the Government and then to renounce the titles conferred on him by the Crown. The Viceroy treated this as an 'affront to the Crown' and this led to the dismissal of Allah Bakhsh.[94] There was now a splendid opportunity for the League, which it fully utilized. It could not, of course, do so on the basis of its own inherent strength in the Assembly, but the adhesion, with his personal followers, of the old war hose, Hidayatullah, to its fold provided he was made the head of the ministry so formed came in handy and a League ministry was formed in October 1942. This ministry continued in office till 1947.

This was, of course, a major achievement, for no other ministry in Sind had lasted that long. However, its record was not distinguished by any other constructive achievement. Indeed, just like the Aurangzeb ministry in the NWFP, the Hidayatullah ministry in Sind became 'noted for inefficiency ad corruption'.[95] Along with it went intense factionalism and a bitter struggle for power between the head of the Government, Hidayatullah, and G.M. Syed, president of the Sind Provincial Muslim League.[96] Indeed, the infighting was so bitter that the Governor had to play an active role in keeping the ministry going. 'It will be readily understood, therefore,' wrote the Governor to the Viceroy in April 1943, after describing the ongoing power struggle among the ministers, 'that a great part of my time is at present spent in smoothing out differences that arise between my Ministers and in keeping the administration ticking over with reasonable somoothness.'[97]

Whatever the performance of the ministry, the very fact that there was a League ministry in Sind acted as a great spur to the expansion of the League's organization in the districts. This was the result partly of the general impact on more and more Muslims of Jinnah's speeches, and partly of the exertions of Provincial Muslim League, which was doing 'a good deal of propaganda in the districts'.[98] The result is illustrated by the spectacular rise in the number of its members as well as its branches. Thus, by 1944 the League had 547 branches and 1,77,118 members in Sind.[99]

This was, of course, a matter of great satisfaction for Jinnah. However, he was too shrewd a leader to take these numbers seriously, although they did indicate that more and more Muslims in Sind were responding to his appeal to rally under the banner of the League. When he threatened to extend his control over the League ministries in the Muslim-majority provinces and declared that 99 per cent of the Muslims in Sind were with the League, the Governor remarked that Jinnah would be well advised not to tread on the toes of the League ministry in Sind. As he informed the Viceroy in May 1943, there had undoubtedly been a great extension of the League's membership since the discomfiture of

Allah Bakhsh. However, if Jinnah attempted to put pressure on the Sind ministry in a matter in which they wished to resist, he would find that 'his new membership in Sind would fall away as easily as it has been gathered'. He further added that it was quite possible that all the ministers would resign from the League rather than give up office.[100] Jinnah was, of course, aware of this as much as the Governor. That is why in spite of repeated complaints received by him against the functioning of Hidayatullah and his ministry,[101] he generally avoided any interference with the ministry. He had, of course, neither any reason to have any liking for Hidayatullah nor would he have been inclined to tolerate his methods and manners. But he knew the value of maintaining the façade of a League ministry in Sind and must have been impressed by Habibullah's ability in that regard. This does not mean either that he had closed his eyes firmly to the developments in Sind politics, or that he had become impotent and irrelevant in that politics, as has been assumed by some.[102] This is best illustrated by his handling of the problem created by Hidayatullah's inclusion of a non-Leaguer, Maula Bakhsh, brother of the late Allah Bakhsh, in the new ministry formed by him towards the end of February 1945, in order to be able better to deal with Syed, his chief opponent in the League. Jinnah took such a firm stand that Hidayatullah was forced to dispense with Maula Bakhsh. He told Hidayatullah that the latter could retain Maula Bakhsh in the ministry, but only on the condition that he enrolled himself as a member of the League. This, he emphasized, was a matter of principle which he could not compromise even though the result might be the end of the League ministry and the imposition of Section 93 of the Act of 1935. Observed Jinnah in his letter to Hidayatullah:

> Surely we cannot barter away our fundamental principles merely to avoid 93. The honour, prestige and status of the All-India Muslim League are involved in this course, as it destroys the very basic principle, which we have maintained at all costs, that the Muslim League is the only authoritative, representative organization of the Mussalmans of India, and we cannot recognise any Muslim individual or a Muslim Group who take up a different political policy and programme from that of the All-India Muslim League or who are opposed to our policy and programme. . . . It is far more honourable for us to have no Muslim League Ministry at all. . . .[103]

It was the same principle and similar firmness that, as noted earlier, characterised Jinnah's role at the Simla Conference convened in June–July 1945 in order to consider the Wavell Plan for breaking the political deadlock in India. Obviously, Jinnah was playing for higher stakes and did not mind giving up short-term advantages in order to ensure the fulfilment of his long-term objective, which undoubtedly was the creation of Pakistan. That objective could be achieved only if the League emerged as the dominant party in the Muslim-majority provinces. That was, of course, important and he constantly worked for it. However, he was too shrewd a politician not to realize that what mattered much more was the position of the Muslim League as a standard bearer of the fight for Pakistan among the Muslim intelligentsia, youth and masses in those provinces. While the members of the legislatures could be manipulated through the offer of ministership, the latter could be drawn towards the League only if they saw the League leadership single-mindedly pursing its goal and in the process willing to withstand the lure of office or money. He knew also that the League's message was by 1945 reaching the remote towns and villages of Sind and that the Muslims were moving everyday closer to the League. That process had to be further strengthened and forging unprincipled alliances for holding on to power would not contribute to it. This was especially important in view of the coming elections all over the country.

VII

The elections did not take long in coming. As a result of the general elections held in Britain in July 1945, shortly after the end of war in Europe, Churchill's Government left office on 26 July and Clement Attlee took over the reins of government as head of the Labour Party, which had won a clear majority in the House of Commons. On 14 August Japan surrendered, bringing the World War II finally to a close. These developments, accompanied by the general British weariness at the end of the World War, helped quicken the pace of political developments in India. In view of the failure of the Cripps Mission (1942) and the Simla Conference (1945), the new British Government was clear in its mind that temporary solutions would not succeed and that the time had come to work for a permanent solution of the

Indian problem. After long consultations in London, the Viceroy, Lord Wavell, announced on 19 September that elections for the Central and Provincial Legislatures would be held during the ensuing winter season, followed by the installation of responsible ministries in the provinces and other steps necessary to bring into being a new Executive Council having the support of the main Indian parties. Steps would also be taken to convene a Constitution-making body as soon as possible after the elections and discussions would be held with the representatives of the Provincial Assemblies with a view to ascertaining whether the proposals contained in the Cripps Plan were acceptable or whether some modified or alternative scheme might be better.[104]

Even before the announcement by Wavell, Jinnah had begun exhorting his followers to start preparing for the elections. Thus as early as 22 March 1945, while issuing his message for the celebration of Pakistan Day (23 March) he declared that elections might take place sooner than people imagined and called upon every province to begin organising for the them. In the same message he declared that Pakistan was the 'irrevocable and unalterable national demand' of Muslim and that they would not rest content until they had succeeded in achieving it.[105] After the failure of the Simla Conference, he correctly surmised that elections were around the corner and considered it his duty again to exhort his followers to be prepared for them. Thus in, the course of a statement issued in Simla on 16 July prior to his departure from there, he advised the League's workers to 'concentrate all their might and main in organizing our people and getting ready to face the elections', which he warned were 'bound to come sooner than many people think'. He further added that the verdict of the elections would be the main criterion for judging the solidarity and unity of the Muslims both in India and abroad.[106]

After the announcement of elections by Wavell, the close bearing of those elections on the Pakistan objective became Jinnah's constant refrain. Thus while addressing the Baluchistan Muslim Students' Federation in Quetta on 18 October, he declared that the first and foremost question that the Muslims were facing related to the ensuing elections and added that they would show whether the Muslims of India wanted Pakistan or *Akhand Hindustan*, which would mean living as an abject minority under Hindu Raj.[107] Inaugurating the League's first election meeting in

Bombay on 31 October, Jinnah again declared: 'The elections will give a clear verdict on the issue whether the Muslims of India stand for Pakistan, or for *Akhand Hindustan*. It is therefore a question of life and death with Muslims of India.'[108] In his address to a largely attended public meeting of Muslims in Peshawar on 24 November, Jinnah reiterated this view, at the same time playing the Islamic card. Before touching on the issue of elections he observed in the course of his introductory remarks: 'Muslims worship one God, they believe in one Book and are the followers of one Prophet. The Muslim League has been striving to organize them politically on one platform and under the green flag of Islam.' (Cheers). Coming to the elections, he declared: 'We are not fighting these elections to form Ministries. We are fighting these elections to get a verdict from Muslims on the Pakistan issue.' In this connection he warned that if the Muslims failed to do their duty, they would be reduced to the status of *Sudras* and that Islam would be 'vanquished from India'. 'Our religion, our culture and our Islamic ideals,' he further observed, 'are our driving force to achieve independence.' (Shouts of *Allah-o-Akbar*).[109]

Jinnah continued to speak in the same vein after the elections to the Central Legislative Assembly were over and the time came for holding elections to the Provincial Assemblies. Thus talking to a group of 50 Muslim student leaders from all over the Punjab in Lahore on 18 January 1946, Jinnah emphasised that the League was fighting the elections not to form ministries, but to secure a Muslim verdict on Pakistan.[110] Addressing a large number of Muslims who had gathered at the Allahabad Railway Station, he observed: 'In the coming elections you have to vote for Muslim unity, solidarity and for the demand of [a] Muslim homeland—Pakistan.' He further added that they had to vote a League candidate even if he were a lamp-post, because he stood for Pakistan and their nation's freedom.[111] Speaking at a mammoth meeting of Muslims in Calcutta on 24 February 1946, he again declared: 'The Muslim League is fighting the elections not to capture Ministries but to wreck the Government of India Act of 1935 and establish Pakistan in the country.' Explaining the meaning of Pakistan, he observed further: 'The meaning of Pakistan is clear even to a child. If you want to free yourselves from the dominations of the British and the Hindus then Pakistan is the only solution.'[112] Addressing a meeting of students in the same city two days later, Jinnah emphasized that Bengal was one of the most important provinces in the scheme of Pakistan and declared: 'We are determined to have not only our own territory, our national homeland, but our independent, sovereign State where we can live our lives in accordance with our ideals and in accordance with what Islam has taught us.'[113] In his address to Muslims of Sylhet on 3 March, he thundered: 'If you are united there is no power on earth which can prevent you from getting Pakistan.'[114] On the eve of his departure from Calcutta after a three-week tour of Bengal and Assam, he issued a message to Muslims on 9 March wherein he again declared: 'Every vote cast in favour of the Muslim League candidates is a vote for Pakistan and, conversely, every vote in favour of any of their opponents will be construed as a vote against Pakistan.'[115]

Jinnah's passionate and persistent campaign in support of the Pakistan demand, echoed by the other Muslim League leaders of varying ranks, galvanized all sections of Muslim society in the rural as well as urban areas, including even children. The gist of a conversation with Jinnah in January 1946, given by one of his valued co-workers in the cause of Pakistan at the Aligarh Muslim University and editor of the first major selection of his speeches, vividly illustrates this point:

> In the course of a conversation with the present writer in January 1946 at his New Delhi home, 10, Aurangzeb Road, Quaid-i-Azam related an incident to illustrate the point that the idea of Pakistan had gone deep into the hearts of all sections of Muslims, including children. He said that during his visit to Sind in November 1945 a ten-year-old girl came to see him and presented him with a handkerchief embroidered with the map of the sub-continent, the Pakistan areas being shown in green. Quaid-i-Azam asked the girl as to what she understood by the green areas. She replied: "Sir, these are areas where Muslims are in a majority and they should rule here. The Hindus could rule in other areas." With a feeling of pride the Quaid said: "When even little children have understood the meaning of Pakistan there can be no doubt that it is the demand of the Muslim nation and we shall have it."[116]

VIII

In the light of this incident no one need be surprised by the wild enthusiasm for the Pakistan idea among the Muslim students in universities and colleges. As noted earlier, in one of his speeches before the students of the Aligarh Muslim University Jinnah had described them as the 'arsenal of Muslim India'. That view was fully shared by other League leaders, too. Thus shortly after the announcement of the elections, Liaquat Ali Khan, General Secretary of the All-India Muslim League and generally regarded as second only to Jinnah in the League's hierarchy, issued a statement on 22 September 1945, recalling his chief's description of Muslim students as the 'arsenal of Muslim India' and calling upon them to come out of their classrooms, spread over the whole country, and work for the League's victory in the elections. 'I do not ask,' he said, 'but demand of you to come forward and help us in the elections.'[117] The Muslim students most enthusiastically responded to their leaders' call.

The students of the Aligarh Muslim University were, as expected, in the forefront of the campaign for the League's victory. Almost all of them, of course, joined the battle and spread over not only UP, where some of the top leaders of the League, including Liaquat Ali Khan, were in the fray, but almost all parts of India, particularly in the Muslim-majority provinces. What particularly distinguished them was that they had been formally trained for election work by the faculty of the university, including some very senior professors. For this purpose the Muslim University Area Muslim League set up as many as 13 training centres, all in university buildings, including one in its Girls' College. Announcing the setting up of these centres, the Muslim University Area Muslim League expressed its gratification at the response of both the staff and the students of the Aligarh Muslim University to its appeal for funds for fighting the ensuing elections and then remarked:

> But money alone is not enough. Aligarh being the Arsenal of Muslim India must also supply ammunition to ensure the victory of the Muslim League in the battle for the freedom of the Muslim nation. Our ammunition really is our youth who should be fully equipped and trained to play their part in the electioneering campaign to ensure the success of the candidates set up by our national organization, the All India Muslim League.[118]

Students selected for training were expected to be above 17, good speakers or good conversationalists or capable of being placed into either of the two categories: having contacts in areas where they wished to work and being physically and mentally alert. The training course was to comprise lectures (obviously by the faculty of the Muslim University) on such themes a the Muslim League in the light of Islam and Islamic history; religious background of the Muslim League and Pakistan; brief history of the League and its achievements; analysis of the genesis Pakistan idea; and comparative study of the policies, programmes, and attitudes of the Congress and the League since 1935. The study was also to include arguments against the League and Pakistan by their opponents and preparàtion of their answers; special conditions and features of particular areas; training in publicity work; training in speaking, each worker being required to speak for at least five minutes; group reading and discussion; techniques of fighting elections; and visits to the mohallas of the town and some neighbouring village for actual practice in public speaking and canvassing.[119]

It is an index of Jinnah's qualities of leadership as well as his single-minded pursuit of victory in the elections of 1945–6 that in spite of his continuing ill health he personally supervised the work of training and deploying student-volunteers for work in the elections and regularly supplied financial resources for it. How close this supervision was is best illustrated by his correspondence at that time with M.B. Mirza, then Dean of the Faculty of Sciences and later Acting Vice-Chancellor, Aligarh Muslim University. Thus on 26 January 1946 the latter referred to his earlier letter thanking Jinnah for the honour done to him by appointing him as chairman of the Election Fund Committee and expressing his gratitude for sending a sum of Rs. 20,000 'in the first instance', for fighting the battle for Pakistan'. Mirza also informed Jinnah that the League at Aligarh had received urgent requests from the Punjab and the NWFP for more students and that they were waiting to go there, but it had no funds to sent them. 'All the accounts,' Mirza added, 'are kept up-to-date and we have been informing you from time to time as to how we utilizing the 'silver bullets'. Our majority provinces require a major effort on our behalf. Kindly send me 10,000/- more.[120] Jinnah received this letter on 31 January through a special messenger and immediately despatched a sum of Rs. 10,000, as requested. While doing so, he observed: 'Give all help you can to the Punjab and the NWFP without any delay.'[121] Incidentally, this correspondence also shows that the students and faculty at

Aligarh were quite disenchanted with the local leaders of the League in UP and were solely inspired by Jinnah. For after acknowledging the receipt of the sum sent by Jinnah, Mirza remarked:

> We are very much against the title-holders and Nawabs. They want to have all the honour for themselves without doing any work. I personally do not mind giving such honour without work only if they abstain themselves from putting obstacles in our way. Believe me that it is only for you that we stand united and shall leave no stone unturned to give you as much help as you require form us.[122]

It should not be surmised from what has been written above that the Muslim students at Aligarh were the only students who were active in the elections of 1946 or that Jinnah paid attention only to them. The Muslim students of the Punjab, particularly those belonging to the Islamia College of Lahore, played a notable part and worked shoulder to shoulder with students from Aligarh in spreading the message of Pakistan and the League as its standard-bearer to every nook and corner of the province. In spite of heavy odds they penetrated the rural areas and explained to the voters why they should vote for the candidates set up by the League. An idea of the hard work put up by them can be had from the detailed reports regularly sent to Jinnah by the Punjab Muslim Students Federation.[123] The dedication to the Pakistan objective on the part of the Muslim students of the Punjab as also their deep feeling of attachment to Jinnah, their supreme leader, is illustrated vividly by the second report of the Punjab Muslim Students Federation, covering the period from 31 December 1945 to 10 January 1946:

> Quaid-i-Azam, the Muslim students of the Punjab lay this record as a humble offering at your feet . . . an appeal from you is a command. The army is ready, the battlefield is marked out, the stage is set. We behold in the distance the dawn of our independence, the birth of Pakistan. A sign from you and the army shall march.[124]

These words did not represent an exercise in verbosity, but had really come from the hearts of the students working under the aegis of the Punjab Muslim Students Federation. The pride of place among them belonged to the students of the Islamia College in Lahore. They had a core of 600 workers who covered 50,000 miles by trains and 16,000 miles by lorries. Just as their counterparts at Aligarh, the teachers of the Islamia College fully backed the exertions of their students and lent more than a helping hand to the organization of the election work by the latter. As a report prepared by the Punjab Islamia College had remarked, the mobilization of the students of the Islamia College in such a large number would not have been possible without the cooperation of Qasim Rizvi, director of manpower of the College, and Omar Hayat Malik, its principal.[125] The impact created by the Muslim students working in the Punjab, whether from the colleges in the Punjab or from Aligarh, has been very well summed up by Mukhtar Zaman, himself one of the prominent leaders of the All India Muslim Students Federation:

> When people living in far-flung places saw batches of young students travelling for days together on difficult terrain, sleeping on straw-covered ground under thatched roofs, sharing the frugal food with their village hosts, they were impressed. . . . People asked: why are these young men going round the villages facing difficulties of all kinds? Why have they left their comfortable homes and colleges and come to us? They are not candidates for the Assemblies and have no personal stakes in the election. Surely their cause must be really important, otherwise why should they bother to come to this godforsaken place?[126]

Muslim students enthusiastically worked for the victory of the League not only in the Punjab, but all over the country. Particular mention may be made here of the part played by them in Bengal, the second most important province for the League in the context of its demand for Pakistan. As many as 7,500 students worked for the League's victory there.[127] Among them were students from the Aligarh Muslim University, who had spread out to all parts of the country as directed by Jinnah. That was not surprising in view of the fact that Aligarh had been the cradle of Muslim nationalism. As the Aga Khan remarks in his autobiography, it could surely be claimed that 'the independent, sovereign nation of Pakistan was born in the Muslim University of Aligarh'.[128] However, the Muslim students belonging to University of Dacca also played a notable part in spreading the message of Pakistan among the Muslim masses as well as the elite in Bengal and securing the League's victory in the elections of 1946. 'The part which Aligarh played in the Pakistan movement,' aptly observes Mahmud Husain, associated with the University of Dacca from 1933 till after Partition, 'was undoubtedly conspicuous, but what

Aligarh did for the movement in the sub-continent as a whole, the University of Dacca did for it in East Bengal and Assam.'[129]

While the hard work put up by Muslim students in spreading Jinnah's message to the Muslim electorate in the remotest corners of the Muslim-majority provinces need not be minimized, what proved really decisive in turning the majority of that electorate in the League's favour was the large-scale shift in the loyalty of the traditional rural elite in those provinces in favour of the Muslim League in the summer of 1945. The failure of the Simla Conference (June–July 1945), due primarily to the British reluctance to bypass Jinnah, sent a clear signal to ambitions Muslim politicians in those provinces that none of them had any political future without being associated with the League and more and more Muslim political workers as well as leaders rallied to the League. In this respect, persons like Feroze Khan Noon, Mian Iftikharuddin, and Abdul Qaiyum had shown the way even before the announcement of the elections. After their announcement the list of such persons began to grow by leaps and bounds. Indeed, many of the League's candidates in those elections had earlier been associated with the Unionist Party in the Punjab and the Krishak Majdoor Proja Party in Bengal. The Muslim intelligentsia in the towns had already gone over to the League, particularly after its adoption of the Pakistan Resolution (1940). After the failure of the Simla Conference, the Muslim elite in the countryside followed suit, regardless of whether they were attracted by the Pakistan demand or not. This was particularly true of the rural elite in the Punjab. For they were, in the post-Simla days, afraid that the Unionist Party, shorn of British patronage, could no longer be depended upon to promote their local interests. 'It was this fear,' observes Talbot, 'rather than the Muslim League's depiction of Khizar and his supporters as traitors to Islam and their *millat* which sparked off the rural elite's large-scale exodus from the Unionist Party's ranks in the weeks which followed the Simla Conferene.'[130] This thesis, of course, need not be literally accepted. For in such matters we should not look for explanations in either or terms. The attraction for Pakistan and, therefore, for the Muslim League had been growing among the Muslim elite, even in the rural areas of the Punjab, ever since the adoption of the Pakistan Resolution at Lahore (1940). Indeed, there is reason to believe that the attraction for the League had begun as early as 1937 in the aftermath of the formation of Congress ministries and the emergence of the Congress High Command as a dominant centre of power, next only to that of the Government of India. This must have been the main reason behind Sikander Hyat Khan's decision to throw in his lot with the League at Lucknow (October 1937). However, there can be no doubt that the success of Jinnah at the Simla Conference in thwarting all moves to include a non-League Muslim in the Executive Council, leading to the collapse of the Simla Conference itself, did give a big push to the shift of the rural elite's loyalty in favour of the League. Again, that push itself was helped further by the hard work put in by Jinnah and the Muslim students in carrying the message of Pakistan to every nook and corner of the province. That task was further facilitated by the growing strength and effectiveness of the League's organization, functioning on the whole under an able and dedicated leadership. Thus, ideology as well as self-interest contributed towards swinging the rural elite in the Punjab in favour of the League in the elections of 1946. In any case, the two were not mutually exclusive.

The rural elite in the Punjab comprised not only the big landlords, divided into various clans and factions, but also the hereditary heads of religious shrines or tombs of famous Sufi saints of the past, known as *pirs* or *sajjada nashins*. The latter, too, were landlords, but they exercised much greater influence in the countryside as religious guides to the people attached to their shrines (known as *murids* or disciples). The League leaders aware of the reality of the rural hinterland of the projected Pakistani areas, were keen to secure religious support for the Pakistan movement. The Jamiat-i-Ulama-i-Hind, the leading organization of Muslim clergy, most of them trained at Deoband and at that time headed by Husain Ahmad Madani, had been traditionally supporting the composite, secular nationalism preached by the Congress. A minority section of that organization, working under the leadership of Maulana Shabbir Ahmad Usmani, had, with encouragement from the League leadership, split from the parent organization and formed a new one called the Jamiat-i-Ulama-i-Islam in late 1945. A branch of the new organization was also started in the Punjab. However, its influence was largely confined to the urban areas. In the rural areas the *pirs* constituted the dominant source of religious support. Their swing towards the

League, along with that of the landlords, added a new dimension to the Pakistan movement by underlining religious backing for the Pakistan movement in the Punjab, one of the important factors behind the League's victory in the elections of 1946. As David Gilmartin, who has made a detailed study of this subject, has remarked, although the League's growing political base was sustained largely by the support of the landed magnates and leaders of powerful rural factions, that does not reduce the significance of the support extended to the League by the *pirs*. For it resulted in 'integrating into the structure of rural politics the ideal of Islamic community that had become so central to the Pakistan movement.'[131]

The support of the *pirs* was immensely helpful to the League in the elections of 1946 not only in the Punjab, but also in other Muslim-majority provinces like the NWFP, Sind, and Bengal. In the NWFP, for instance, the *pirs* played a significant role in rallying many rural Muslims under the banner of the League. This was symbolized, more than anyone else, by the *pir* of Manki Sharif. Though only a young man of 25, he wielded great influence because of the large number of persons attached to his shrine. This was true particularly of the Pakhtun areas around Peshawar, the main support-base of the veteran Congress leader, Khan Abdul Ghaffar Khan, thereby emerging as 'a very effective counter-balance' to the latter.[132] In Sind, the *pirs* had begun backing the League as early as 1938–9, even earlier than in the Punjab and the NWFP. This explains the fact that while in the latter two provinces the League's influence was confined largely to the urban areas till the 1940s, in Sind the League had established a foothold in the rural areas even before the adoption of the Pakistan demand in 1940. That foothold, not very strong till 1943, had become much stronger since then. As Sarah Ansari has pointed out, the reappointment of Hidayatullah at the head of a League-dominated ministry in Sind, and the holding of the annual session of the All India Muslim League in Karachi in December 1943, acted as 'triggers of responsibility', leading an increasing number of *pirs*, some of whom were already sympathetic towards the League, to now openly identify themselves with the party. 'Now that the League had established itself as an integral part of the framework of Sindhi politics, they saw advantages in being openly associated with it.'[133] In Bengal, too, the *pirs*, many of whom had joined the pro-League Jamiat-ul-Ulema-i-Islam and held important positions therein, played an important part in spreading the message of Pakistan to all parts of the province. Just as in other provinces they did so by touring the countryside and issuing *fatwas* calling upon the faithful to vote for the League.[134]

Apart from the impact of the Simla Conference, Jinnah's speeches, making the achievement of Pakistan the central issue in the elections, the enthusiastic efforts of students in carrying that message to all Muslims wherever they might be living, the key role played by the landlords and *pirs*, there was one factor that was peculiar to Bengal: the progressive image in the socio-economic field imparted to the League because of the rise of a powerful left wing within its organization, led by Abul Hashim. Reference has been made in an earlier section to the part played by that factor in the growth of the Pakistan movement in Bengal between 1942 and 1945. This factor also made a significant contribution to the election campaign of the League in 1946. As a result of it, the communal or national question—the urge for a separate Muslim identity, based on Islamic heritage and Muslim power—was merged with the social question—the urge of the Muslim peasantry as also the urban Muslim middle class in Bengal to see the end of Hindu domination and exploitation. A glimpse of how the appeal to the twin urges was combined together can be had from the booklet *Let us go to War*, prepared by Hashim in the first week of September 1945 and widely distributed among the Muslims in Bengal.[135]

What has been said in this as well as the previous section should make it clear that, apart from what had been done in the recent past, just on the eve of the elections of 1945–6, the Muslim League, under the leadership of Jinnah, ably supported by several other dedicated leaders, both at the Centre and in the Muslim-majority provinces, particularly in the Punjab and Bengal, had spread their organization far and wide and mounted a really powerful campaign for the mobilization of Muslim voters, based on an appeal to religion and community, on the one hand, and to economic interests, on the other. The result of the elections showed that the campaign had, eminently succeeded.

The elections had been held in three phases. Elections to the Central Legislative Assembly were held first and their results were known by December 1945. Out of a total of 102 seats, the

Muslim League won all the 30 Muslim seats without any exception, securing 86.6 per cent of the votes cast, with the non-League candidates in many cases losing their security deposits. The Congress on its part won an overwhelming majority of the general or non-Muslim seats, 57, securing 91.3 per cent of the votes polled. Of the remaining elective seats, 5 went to Independents, 2 to Akali Sikhs, and 8 to Europeans. The League's tally in the elections to the Provincial Assemblies was only slightly less impressive. To take up the Muslim-majority provinces first, in the Punjab it won an overwhelming majority of Muslim seats—75 out of 86. A little later this figure rose to 79, with some legislators changing their party loyalties. In Bengal, the League did even better, winning 113 out 119 Muslim seats. In Sind, again the League won a majority of Muslim seats—27 out of 35. Only in the NWFP, the League narrowly failed to secure a majority of Muslim seats, its tally being 17 to 19 for the Congress. If note is taken of the fact that the NWFP, thanks to the remarkable leadership of Khan Abul Ghaffar Khan, had been a Congress stronghold in the past, the League's achievement may appear impressive enough. In the Muslim-minority provinces, the League received even greater support from Muslim voters. In Assam, it won 31 out of 34 Muslim seats, in Bombay 30 out of 30, in Madras 29 out of 29, in Orissa 4 out of 4, in CP and Bearer 13 out of 14, in Bihar 34 out of 50, and in UP 54 out of 66.[136]

No one now could question the fact that the League represented the vast majority of Muslims in India in whichever part of the country they might be residing. Further, since Jinnah had repeatedly emphasized that the League was fighting the elections not for forming ministries, but for securing Pakistan—thereby turning the elections into a referendum on the Pakistan issue—their results showed the overwhelming support which the demand for Pakistan enjoyed among the Muslims of India. Indeed, the die had been cast and the Muslim League, under Jinnah's able as well as charismatic leadership, had made history. The demand for Pakistan could no longer be ignored, much less ridiculed or reviled. If the League remained determined to press that demand, there was no way it could be prevented from securing if after receiving such a massive electoral mandate in its favour and the existence of easily demarcable Muslim majority areas in the north-west and north-east of India. All that was required to be done was for the British to devise a formula for the creation of Pakistan, in some form or the other, acceptable to both the Congress and the League. The next year and a quarter were devoted to this task amidst a lot of shadow-boxing and hypocritical posturing together with ever-increasing bitterness and violence.

NOTES

1. For the text of Huq's letter to Liaquat dated 8 September 1941, see Shila Sen, *Muslim Politics in Bengal, 1937–1947* (New Delhi, 1976), Appendix IV, pp. 264–7 (*source:* Government of India, Home Political File 17/4/41-Poll I).
2. See Jinnah's statement to the press dated 11 September 1941. *Quaid-i-Azam Mohammad Ali Jinnah: The Nation's Voice* (hereafter *Jinnah: Speeches and Statements*), vol. II, pp. 292–4.
3. Ibid., Appendix III, pp. 514–16.
4. Ibid., pp. 517–18.
5. Sen, n. 1, pp. 130–2.
6. Sir John Herbert to Linlithgow, 5 December 1941, MSS Eur. F125/41, Linlithgow Collection.
7. Herbert to Linlithgow, 20 December 1941, ibid.
8. Ibid.
9. *Jinnah: Speeches and Statements,* vol. II, n. 2, p. 326.
10. Ibid., pp. 328–9.
11. Ibid., Appendix III, p. 525.
12. Herbert to Linlithgow, 11 February 1942, MSS Eur. F125/42, Linlithgow Collection.
13. *Jinnah: Speeches and Statements,* vol. II, n. 2, p. 359.
14. Ibid., pp. 362–5.
15. Herbert to Linlithgow, 23 April 1942, F125/42, Linlithgow Collection.
16. Herbert to Linlithgow, 6 June 1942, ibid.
17. Herbert to Linlithgow, 7 July 1942, ibid.
18. Huq to Laithwaite, 7 July 1942, F125/124, Linlithgow Collection.
19. Huq to Jinnah, 13 November 1942, *Jinnah: Speeches and Statements,* vol. III, pp. 156–8.
20. Huq to Jinnah, 5 February 1943, ibid., pp. 158–9.
21. Jinnah to Huq, 10 February 1943, ibid., pp. 159–61.
22. Jinnah to Huq, Telegram, 11 February 1943, ibid., p. 161.
23. For Jinnah's statement releasing the correspondence, see ibid., p. 156.
24. Ibid., pp. 156–8, footnote.
25. Herbert to Linlithgow, 22 January 1942, F125/42, Linlithgow Collection.

26. Note by Cripps on his interview with Huq, 29 March 1942, reproduced in Jinnah: *Speeches and Statements*, vol. II, n. 2, Appendix XXI, p. 531.
27. Huq to Linlithgow, 16 November 1942, F125/124, Linlithgow Collection.
28. Huq to Linlithgow, 19 February 1943, F125/127, Linlithgow Collection.
29. Herbert to Linlithgow, 9 March 1942, F125/42, Linlithgow Collection.
30. Linlithgow to Amery, 28 March 1942, *T.P.*, n. , p. 521.
31. Herbert to Linlithgow, 21 April 1942, F125/42, Linlithgow Collection.
32. Herbert to Linlithgow, 21 May 1942, ibid.
33. Herbert to Linlithgow, 23 July 1942, ibid.
34. Herbert to Linlithgow, 27 September 1942, ibid.
35. Herbert to Linlithgow, 6 October 1942, ibid.
36. Herbert to Linlithgow, 8 October 1942, ibid.
37. *Quarterly Survey*, no. 21 (1 August to 31 October 1942), F125/145, Linlithgow Collection.
38. Huq to Linlithgow, 10 October 1942, F125/124, Linlithgow Collection.
39. Herbert to Linlithgow, 22 February 1943, F125/43, ibid.
40. See Sen, n. 1, pp. 141–2.
41. Ibid., pp. 143–7.
42. Herbert to Linlithgow, 22 February 1943, F125/43, Linlithgow Collection.
43. Herbert to Linlithgow, 8 May 1943, with enclosure, F125/42, Linlithgow Collection.
44. For the texts of Huq's letters to the Governor on 21 and 26 March 1943, as also the relevant portion of Huq's statement before the Assembly on 27 March see Governor to Viceroy, Telegram, 30 March 1943, F125/43, Linlithgow Collection.
45. See Huq's statement on 29 March 1943 on the floor of the Assembly in *Bengal Legislative Assembly Proceedings*, vol. LXIV, no. 3, p. 753; cited in Sen, n. 124, p. 147.
46. Ibid.
47. Huq to Linlithgow, 16 April 1943, F125/125, Linlithgow Collection. See also Huq's statement in the Bengal Assembly on 5 July 1943 on why he resigned, *Bengal Assembly Proceedings*, vol. LXV, p. 60 and A.K. Fazlul Huq, *Bengal Today* (Calcutta 1944), p. 37.
48. Governor to Viceroy, Telegram, 30 March 1943, F125/43, Linlithgow Collection.
49. Governor to Viceroy, Telegram, 31 March 1943, ibid.
50. Linlithgow to Herbert, 2 April 1943, ibid.
51. Linlithgow to Amery, 2 April 1943, *T.P.*, vol. III, p. 875.
52. Herbert to Linlithgow, 28 April 1943, F125/43, Linlithgow Collection.
53. *Constitutional Survey*, no. 23 (1 February to 30 April 1943), n.
54. For details, see Sen, n. 124, pp. 164–71.

55. See Abul Hashim, *In retrospection* (Dacca, 1974), pp. 30–76.
56. Bengal Provincial Muslim League, *Annual Meeting 1944, Calcutta 17th November 1944: Report Presented by Mr Abul Hashim*. A copy is available in the Freedom Movement Archives, University of Karachi. See also Abul Hashim to Liaquat Ali Khan with a copy to Jinnah, 25 November 1944, Shamsul Hasan Collection, Bengal, vol. I.
57. Ibid.
58. Sen, n. 1, pp. 193–4.
59. Casey to Colville, 30 March 1945, *T.P.*, vol. V, n. 73, p. 785.
60. *Constitutional Survey*, no. 32 (1 February to 30 April 1945).
61. Ibid.
62. Amery to Colville (Acting Viceroy), 29 March 1945, *T.P.*, vol. V, n. 73, p. 784.
63. *Constitutional Survey*, no. 28 (1 May to 31 July 1944).
64. For election results in the *NWFP* in 1937, see Erland Jansson, *India, Pakistan or Pakhtunistan* (Uppsala, 1981), p. 73.
65. See Ibid., pp. 74–6.
66. On the performance of the Congress Ministry and the problems faced by it, see ibid., pp. 76–105.
67. Stephen Alan Rittenberg, 'The Independence Movement in India's North-West Frontier Province, 1937–47', Ph.D. thesis, Columbia University, 1977, pp. 21–5.
68. Erland Jansson, n. 64, p. 109.
69. Ibid., pp. 111–12.
70. Ibid., p. 115.
71. Menon, p. 766.
72. Linlithgow to Cunningham, 13 August 1942, MSS Eur. F125/78, Linlithgow Collection
73. Ibid., 6 October 1942.
74. Cunningham to Linlithgow, 12 October 1942, MSS Eur. F125/77, Linlithgow Collection.
75. Ibid., 9 November 1942.
76. Ibid., 23 July 1943, enclosing the Governor's Report no. 2 of the same date.
77. Ibid., Governor's Report no. 3, dated 7 February 1943, and Report no. 4 dated 24 February 1943.
78. Linlithgow to Cunningham, 2 March 1943, enclosing the note prepared by Feroz Khan Noon, MSS Eur. F125/78, Linlithgow Collection.
79. Cunningham to Linlithgow, 5 March 1943, MSS Eur. F125/77, Linlithgow Collection.
80. See the Governor's Reprot no. 8, dated 23 April 1943.
81. See Cunningham to Linlithgow, 4 May 1943, 13 May 1943, 18 May 1943, 21 May 1943, ibid.
82. Erland Jansson, 'The Frontier Province: *Khudai Khidmatgars* and

the Muslim League', in D.A. Low, ed., *The Political Inheritance of Pakistan* (London, 1991), p. 205.
83. NWFP Governor's Report no. 14, dated 25 July 1943, MSS Eur. F125/78, Linlithgow Collection.
84. NWFP Governor's Report no. 15, dated 9 August 1943, ibid.
85. NWFP Governor's Report no. 16, dated 24 August 1943, ibid.
86. Linlithgow to Cunningham, 3/6 September 1943, ibid.
87. See Amit Kumar Gupta, *North West Frontier Legislature and Freedom Struggle*, 1932–47 (New Delhi, 1976), p. 148.
88. Cited in Jansson, n. 63, p. 132.
89. *Constitutional Survey*, no. 31 (November 1944 to 31 January 1945).
90. Syed Waqat Ali Shah, *Muslim League in NWFP* (Karachi, 1992), p. 70.
91. Ian Talbot, *Provincial Politics and the Pakistan Movement* (Karachi, 1988), pp. 39–40.
92. See Sarah Ansari, 'Political Legacies of Pre-1947 Sind', in D.A. Low ed., *The Political Inheritance of Pakistan* (London, 1991), pp. 178–9.
93. Ibid., pp. 179–80.
94. Talbot, n. 213, pp. 42–3.
95. See in this connection Governor of Sind to Viceroy, 1 and 28 September 1942, and Viceroy to Governor, 26 September 1942, MSS Eur. F125/98, Linlithgow Collection.
96. Talbot, n. 213, p. 44.
97. Sir Hugh Dow to Linlithgow, 20 April 1943, MSS Eur. F125/99, Linlithgow Collection.
98. Ibid.
99. Talbot, n. 213, p. 46.
100. Dow to Linlithgow, 5 May 1943, Linlithgow Collection., n. 219.
101. For the texts of some of these complaints, see Khalid Shamsul Hasan, ed., *Sind's Fight for Pakistan: Rifts, Betrayal and Triumph* (Karachi, 1992), pp. 1–92.
102. See, for instance, Ayesha Jalal, *The Sole Spokesman: Jinnah, the Muslim League and the Demand for Pakistan* (Cambridge, 1985), p. 113.
103. Jinnah to Hidayatullah, 3 March 1945, Hasan, n. 100, p. 93.
104. For the text of Wavell's broadcast on 19 September 1945, see Mansergh.
105. *Jinnah: Speeches and Statements*, vol. IV (Karachi, 2000), pp. 74–6.
106. Ibid., p. 189.
107. Ibid., p. 255.
108. Ibid., p. 284.
109. Ibid., pp. 323–6.
110. Ibid., p. 396.

111. Ibid., pp. 442–3.
112. Ibid., p. 465.
113. Ibid., p. 478.
114. Ibid., p. 488.
115. Ibid., p. 509.
116. Jamil-Uddin Ahmad, *Creation of Pakistan* (Lahore, 1976), p. 235.
117. Sarfaraz Hassain Mirza, ed., *Muslim Students and the Pakistan Movement: Selected Documents* (*1937–1947*), Introduction, p. lxvii.
118. *'Career': Fortnightly Bulletin of the Aligarh Muslim University*: Special Number, n.d., Shamshul Hasan Collection (Karachi).
119. Ibid.
120. M.B. Mirza to Jinnah, 26 January 1946, Shamshul Hasan Collection.
121. Jinnah to M.B. Mirza, 31 January 1946, ibid.
122. M.B: Mirza to Jinnah, 1 February 1946, ibid.
123. For a glimpse into these reports, see Sarfaraz Hussain Mirza, *The Punjab Muslim Students Federation (1937–1947)* (Islamabad, 1991), pp. 303–37.
124. Ibid., p. 321.
125. Ibid., p. 337.
126. Mukhtar Zaman, *Students' Role in the Pakistan Movement* (Karachi, 1978), pp. 156–7.
127. Ian Talbot, *Provincial Politics and the Pakistan Movement (*Karachi, 1988), p. 76.
128. Aga Khan, *The Memories of Aga Khan* (London, 1954), p. 36.
129. Mahmud Husain, 'Dacca University and the Pakistan Movement', *The Partition of India: Policies and Perspectives, 1935–1947*, ed. C.H. Philips and Mary Doreen Wainwright (London, 1970), p. 369.
130. Ian Talbot, *Punjab and the Raj, 1849–1947* (New Delhi, 1988), p. 199. See also the same author's 'The 1946 Punjab Elections', *Modern Asian Studies*, vol. 14, no. 1 (1980), pp. 65–91.
131. David Gilmartin, *Empire and Islam: Punjab and the Making of Pakistan* (Delhi, 1989), p. 213. See also the same author's 'Religious Leadership and the Pakistan Movement in the Punjab', *Modern Asian Studies*, vol. 13, no. 3 (1979),
132. Erland Jansson, n. 64, pp. 165–6.
133. Sarah Ansari, 'Political Legacies of Pre-1947 Sind', in D.A. Low, ed., *The Political Inheritance of Pakistan* (London, 1991), p. 181.
134. Talbot, n. 249, p. 75.
135. Hashim, n. 178, pp. 174–6.
136. For details, see Government of India, *Returns Showing the Results of Elections to the Central Legislative Assembly and Provincial Legislatures in 1946–47* (New Delhi, 1948), pp. 202–25. A good summary is available in V.P. Menon, *The Transfer of Power in India* (Bombay, 1957), pp. 228, 231–4.

CHAPTER VII

The Cabinet Mission, Direct Action and Interim Government, March to October 1946

THE LAST PHASE OF the Muslim League's march to the goal of Pakistan, along with the rest of India's march to the goal of Independence, began soon after the general elections of 1945–6. On 19 February 1946, it was announced by Lord Pethick Lawrence, Secretary of State for India, in the House of Lords, that a team of three ministers of cabinet rank—namely Lord Pethick Lawrence himself, Sir Stafford Cripps (President of the Board of Trade), and A.V. Alexander (First Lord of the Admiralty)—would visit India to confer with the Viceroy and together with him discuss with the Indian political leaders ways and means of resolving the constitutional problem.[1] The main idea behind the despatch of the Cabinet Mission was explained by Prime Minister Clement Attlee in his speech before the House of Commons on 15 March 1946. He said that the tide of nationalism was riding high in India; the temperature of 1946 was not that of 1920, or 1930, or even 1942. It was, therefore, time for decisive action. The Cabinet Mission would be going to India with a view to helping India to attain her freedom as speedily as possible, without attempting to impose any particular system of government on India. The Indian people must decide what form of government they would like to have and also whether they would like to continue to remain within the British Commonwealth or not. In a clear reference to the existence of serious differences in India on the constitutional problem and with a view to assuring all concerned that, unlike in the past, the British would not use them as a weapon to stall India's advance to freedom, he further remarked: 'We are mindful of the rights of minorities and the minorities should be able to live free from fear.

On the other hand, we cannot allow a minority to place their veto on the advance of the majority.'[2] This naturally sounded quite pleasing to the people belonging to the Congress side, but their pleasure did not last long. In order to reassure the Muslim League, Lord Pethick Lawrence clarified at a press conference in New Delhi on 25 March 1946—a couple of days after the Cabinet Mission's arrival on Indian soil—that what Attlee had said did not mean that the reasonable claims of the minorities were to be disregarded. He further added:

The result of the elections has made it clear that the voters are looking to two main parties to represent their views, the Congress Party and the Muslim League. While the Congress Party are representative of the greater numbers it would not be right to regard the Muslim League as merely a minority political party. They are, in fact, the majority representatives of the great Muslim community. Our aim is to procure an agreed method of deciding on a new constitutional structure and the setting up of a more representative transitional government at the Centre.[3]

It was the search for 'an agreed method' that led, by stages, to the decision in favour of the creation of Pakistan. However, unlike what is generally imagined in India, in spite of their long record of encouraging the Muslim League in its separatist stance as one of the most effective ways of meeting the challenge to the continuance of their rule over India, once the British decided to end that rule, they were not particularly interested in partitioning India. After a close examination of the subject, they had come to the conclusion that a united India would be more helpful to the defence of British interests in India, and indeed in the whole Indian Ocean area than a divided one. For Pakistan was expected to be a weak state militarily and, in addition, likely to remain embroiled in more or less continuous conflict with India. On the other hand, an undivided India, with suitable constitutional arrangements to make the Muslims feel secure, devised through agreements between the Congress and the League, would suit Britain. If arrangements for keeping India united could not be agreed upon by the Congress and the League, the British were willing to consider Partition, provided a formula agreed to by both parties could be devised for the creation of Pakistan. What they were not prepared for, unless forced to do so by circumstances beyond their control, was to just walk out of India leaving the two major parties or communities at loggerheads, for that, in their opinion, would lead to utter chaos and confusion and do great harm to British interests. This comes out clearly in the correspondence between the Cabinet Delegation in India and the Viceroy on the one hand and Prime Minister Attlee on the other in April 1946.

Thus in a communication dated 11 April 1946, addressed to Attlee, the Cabinet Mission and the Viceroy recalled the Cabinet's directive enjoining them to see that any scheme to which they were a party contained 'adequate provision for the Defence of India and the adjoining areas' and sought his advice on the choice between two possible schemes that seemed likely to emerge as a result of an agreement between the Indian leaders. Scheme A would envisage 'a unitary India with a loose federation at the Centre charged primarily with the control of Defence and Foreign Affairs'. Scheme B would be based upon 'a divided India', with only the Muslim-majority districts going to Pakistan. The Cabinet Mission and the Viceroy went on to point out that it should be obvious that under Scheme B Defence would not be very effective as 'the small Pakistan would itself be weak and it would be strengthened only in so far as it could rely upon its Treaty with Hindustan. There would be no common control of Foreign Policy and therefore common action might easily become difficult or impossible'. Even so, agreement on this basis would be better than having no agreement at all. Asking for the Prime Minister's approval for efforts to secure agreement on the basis of Scheme B, if no such agreement could be secured on the basis of Scheme A, the Cabinet Mission and the Viceroy remarked: 'Unless we get agreement we risk chaos in India and no scheme of Defence would then be of any value. We are convinced that the overriding necessity is some agreement if it can be attained and that this is the first requirement towards any effective Defence. . . . We should of course ourselves prefer something on lines of Scheme A but this may prove impossible of attainment'.[4]

Attlee replied to this communication on 13 April, saying that the Cabinet agreed that while Scheme A was preferable, the Cabinet Mission and the Viceroy might work for an agreement on the basis of Scheme B if it provided 'the only chance of an agreed settlement'. Attlee also forwarded the views of the British Chiefs of Staff, which tallied with those of the Cabinet. After explaining the various disadvantages of Partition, from the point of view of the defence of the subcontinent, the Chiefs of Staff observed:

To sum up, Scheme B will have to be accepted if the only alternative is complete failure to reach agreement and consequent chaos. But India will be confronted by grave dangers as a result of this Partition; and if Scheme B has to be adopted, every effort should be made to obtain agreement for some form of a central defence council to be set up which will include not only Pakistan, Hindustan and the Indian States, but also Burma and Ceylon.[5]

Scheme A was, of course, not given up immediately and, indeed, for some time it held the centre of the stage. The transition to Scheme B, however, soon became inevitable, because of the firm resolve of the Muslim League to pursue the goal of Pakistan, regardless of the price to be paid for it. On the other hand, the Congress, primarily interested in securing Independence without any further delay was prepared to accept Partition as a last resort, provided no group of people were forced to secede from India against their will, rather than accept a nominal union under a scheme that might stand in the way of the emergence of a strong Indian State. The Congress leadership was, of course, also aware that it had no other option but to accept Partition in view of the overwhelming Muslim support for it and the firm British resolve not to leave India until they had secured an agreement between the Congress and the League regarding India's constitutional future.

II

Even before the arrival of the Cabinet Mission in India, the Congress had given an indication of its approach to the settlement of the Indian constitutional problem. Thus at its meeting in September 1945, before the massive electoral verdict in favour of the Muslim League in the elections of 1945–6, signifying full support for its demand for Partition, the Congress Working Committee had adopted a resolution reiterating its old stand that it would be for 'a democratically elected Constituent Assembly to prepare a constitution for India acceptable to all sections of the Indian people' and at the same time showing its preparedness to accept Partition provided the scheme for it did not envisage coercion of any group of people not willing to secede from India.

The following extract from the Working Committee's resolution in 1945 on the issue of United India *versus* Partition clearly sums up the Congress position:

> The Congress, as the Working Committee declared in April 1942 [with reference to the Cripps Plan], has been wedded to Indian freedom and unity and any break in that unity, especially in the modern world when people's minds inevitably think in terms of ever larger federations, would be injurious to all concerned and exceedingly painful to contemplate. Nevertheless, the Committee also declared that it could not think in terms of compelling the people in any territorial unit to remain in an Indian Union against their declared and established will. While recognizing this principle, every effort should be made to create conditions which would help the different units in developing a common and cooperative national life. The acceptance of this principle inevitably involves that no changes should be made which result in fresh problems being created and compulsion being exercised on other substantial groups within that area. Each territorial unit should have the fullest possible autonomy within the Union consistently with a strong national State.[6]

The President of the Congress, Maulana Azad, made his presentation to the Cabinet Mission on 3 April 1946 on the lines of the policy contained in this resolution. He divided the problem that had to be faced by the Mission into two parts—one political and the other communal. Dealing with the political aspect first, he emphasized that the Congress would like the Mission to deal with it on 'the solid basis of India's independence'. He further pointed out that the Constitution for India on that basis should be framed by a constitution-making body, which was bound to take time. Even before such a body could be set up, there would be a need for an Interim Government, which 'must be in-charge of all the subsequent stages, including setting up the Constitution-making body as well as conducting the administration of the country'. Coming to the communal issue, Azad pointed out that the picture the Congress had of the future of India was that of 'a Federal Government with fully autonomous Provinces with residuary powers vested in the units themselves'. He went on to explain that for federal subjects there would be two lists—compulsory and optional. The compulsory list would be limited to essential subjects of all-India importance, such as, for example, Defence and Foreign Affairs. The optional list would include other subjects, which any province might not like to hand over to the Centre and instead administer it itself. It was expected that such a provision would be found particularly useful by the Muslim-majority provinces which did not like a strong Centre. Azad further pointed out that after the constitution had been framed on this basis, if some well-defined, particular areas wanted to stand out of the Indian Union they would be at liberty to do so. So a province would in effect have three choices: to stand out of the Union of India, to enter the Union by federating for the compulsory subjects only, and to federate for the compulsory subjects as also the optional ones.[7]

As far as the League was concerned, it had gone on vigorously pursuing its demand for Pakistan ever since its adoption (without of course mentioning its name) in 1940 and, had indeed, turned the elections of 1945–6 into a virtual referendum among Muslims on it. After its resounding victory in the elections, the League began to pursue its objective even more vigorously than ever before and left no one in doubt that it would not brook any compromise on it. Thus shortly after the announcement of the League's success in capturing all the Muslim seats in the Central Legislative Assembly Jinnah in the course of his message for the League's Victory Day celebrations (published in the press on 11 January 1946) thus warned all those concerned with the future of India:

> Do not think you can trifle with us or manouevre and resort to machinations in order to get the Muslims to accept anything but the establishment of Pakistan. . . . The Muslim nation has already given its verdict and it will face all consequences and obstacles and make every sacrifice that it may be called upon to do. We mean what we say and will not be deviated by any threats, manouevres and machinations on the part of the Congress or the British Government. We will face any and every opposition at all cost.[8]

Further, in an interview with Arthur Moore, then editor of the *Statesman*, on 22 January 1946, Jinnah affirmed that in the changed situation after the war, the Congress and the League could not work together in the same government so long as the issue of Pakistan divided them. Upon Moore mentioning that the Congress leaders had said on various occasions that they would be willing to work in an interim government under his leadership, Jinnah remarked that it was 'complete humbug'. For the Congress leaders had also been saying that such a government must be responsible to the legislature where the Congress (being in a majority) could drive out a government whenever it wished.[9] Again, commenting on the Viceroy's speech before the Central Assembly on 28 January 1946, in which the latter had talked of the desirability of the formation of a new Executive Council with the help of the main political parties, Jinnah said in the course of a statement issued on the same day that since the war had ended, what was needed was a permanent solution of the Indian constitutional problem and not the formation of a new Executive Council. 'Muslim India,' he added, 'has made it clear beyond any doubt that the only solution of India's political problem is the division of India into Pakistan and Hindustan and it is our grim resolve and determination to set up a free Muslim State in the Muslim-majority zones in the north-western and eastern parts of India.'[10] He reiterated this stand in his conversation with the members of the British Parliamentary Delegation, then on a visit to India, when they called on him on 4 February 1946. Hoping that the Delegation would correctly represent the position of Muslim India to all concerned, Jinnah wrote to the Secretary of State for India on 9 February 1946: 'I have left no doubt in their minds that the British Government should make an immediate declaration of their policy accepting Muslim India's demand of Pakistan which is the only solution of India's constitutional problem.'[11] Jinnah was also reported to have told the correspondent of the *New York Times* in New Delhi on 7 February 1946 that if the British did not concede Pakistan and went on to set up a single Constituent Assembly for the whole country, the only result would be a Muslim revolt throughout India.[12] In a press interview on 17 February, he reiterated the same point.[13]

Indeed, it will not be wrong to say that Jinnah did not allow a single opportunity to go by without underlining the firm resolve of the Muslim League to resist any move in the constitutional field unless it was based on the recognition of Pakistan in principle, leaving the details to be handled later. Thus commenting on the announcement in London on 19 February regarding the proposed despatch of a Cabinet Mission to India in order to sort out the constitutional problem, Jinnah recalled in the course of a press interview the next day that the League had made it repeatedly clear that it was opposed to the setting up of a single Constituent Assembly as also that of an interim government with the cooperation of the Indian political parties. He went on to stress that the major issue must be decided first and that was Muslim India's demand for Pakistan. 'There can be,' he observed, 'and there is no room for compromise on the Pakistan demand of Muslim India.'[14] In an interview to the correspondent of the United Press of America the same day, he remarked that the setting up of a single constitution-making body for all India would mean a 'flagrant breach' on the part of the British Government of their declaration of 8 August 1940, in which they had pledged themselves not to impose upon Muslims 'either the machinery of the framing of the constitution or the constitution itself'. Besides, Muslims would be in 'a hopeless minority' in a single constitution-making body and that would 'threaten the very existence of the Muslims' and would mean a question of life and death for them.[15] Referring to the British Prime Minister's speech in the House of Commons on 15 March, in which he had said that while the British were mindful of the rights of a minority, they could not allow a minority to veto the advance of a majority, Jinnah in a press interview the next day asserted that Muslims in India were not a minority but a nation and that self-determination was their birthright.[16] In his Pakistan Day message, issued on 22 March, Jinnah observed: 'Let me state in unequivocal terms that we are determined to establish Pakistan by negotiations, peacefully if possible, but, if necessary, we are prepared to shed our blood if that is going to be the test and fire through which we are required to go.'[17] On 30 March, a week after the arrival of the Cabinet Mission in India, he told the Reuters' political correspondent in New Delhi: 'One thing certain is that there will be no compromise on the subject of Pakistan, because that means our very existence is at stake.'[18] On 3 April, he observed in the course of an interview with the BBC correspondent in New Delhi that Pakistan must be a fully sovereign State with complete control over defence and foreign policy. In a federation, he pointed out, member states were compelled to grant more and more power to the central authority and lost their 'independence' little by little. This, he said further, might have been all right in such federations as the USA, but in an Indian federation, the central authority would 'inevitably be Hindu'. Asked how he was going to deal with the difficulty posed by the two parts of the proposed State of Pakistan being divided by about 1,000 miles of Indian territory, Jinnah replied that he did not foresee any difficulty and remarked: 'We travel from the Muslim areas of the north-east to the Muslim areas of the north-west across this so-called Hindu corridor without any difficulty today. Why should that arrangement not continue?'[19]

Jinnah adopted the same line in his parleys with the members of the Cabinet Mission. Cripps in his note on his hour-long conversation with Jinnah on 30 March reported: 'He was calm and reasonable but completely firm on Pakistan.'[20] The same can be said about his detailed discussion with all the members of the Cabinet Mission and the Viceroy on 4 April. After elucidating at length the two-nation theory and dilating upon the differences between Hindus and Muslims, Jinnah remarked: 'How are you to put 100 millions of Muslims together with 250 millions whose way of life is so different. No government can ever work on such a basis and if this is forced upon India it must lead us to disaster.' There was, according to him, 'no other solution than the division of India'. Asked about the boundaries of Pakistan, as envisaged by him, he observed that he 'wanted a viable Pakistan which would not be carved out or mutilated' and added that while he was willing to consider mutual adjustments, 'Pakistan must be a live state economically'. He also observed that he was not insisting on including a large number of Hindus in Pakistan, 'but if it were said that only the number of heads could be considered, he could not agree to that'.[21] About the same time Jinnah told the foreign editor of *News Chronicle* that there was no room for compromise on the issue of Pakistan as it was a question of the very existence of Muslims. Asked if that implied loyalty to the community before loyalty to the country, Jinnah replied: 'There is no country in that sense. I don't regard myself as an Indian. India is a State of nationalities including two major nations, and all we claim is a distinct sovereign State for our nation, Pakistan.'[22]

On 7 April began the All-India Muslim League Legislature's Convention in New Delhi (7 to 9 April 1946). Delivering his inaugural address as Chairman of the Convention, Jinnah observed amidst prolonged cheers: '. . . we stand for Pakistan, and we shall not falter or hesitate to fight for it, to die for it if necessary—and achieve it we must, or else we perish'. After referring to 'the fundamental and vital differences' between Hindus and Muslims and asserting that the acceptance of 'the fundamental principle of Pakistan' was a sine qua non of the League's cooperation in the formation of an Interim Central Government', he declared:

It follows that the idea of a single constitution-making body has then no place, and we shall not accept it, for it means our consent to proceed on the basis of a united India, which is impossible, and we cannot give consent to such a course. Apart from many other objections, one is quite clear: that a single 'constitution-making body will only register the decree of the Congress as it is a foregone conclusion that Muslims will be in a hopeless minority there.

On the other hand, according to our formula there would be two sovereign constitution-making bodies, one for Hindustan and the other for Pakistan, and it is the Pakistan constitution-making body which will be in a position to deal with defence and such other matters as may require adjustment, by virtue of contiguity, which will naturally arise. But all this can only be done by means of treaties and agreements between Pakistan and Hindustan.

We cannot accept any proposal, which would be, in any way, derogatory to the full sovereignty of Pakistan.[23]

The ideas contained in these passages were incorporated in the resolution adopted by the Convention. The most important section of its resolution was the one that called for the constitution of 'a sovereign independent State comprising Bengal and Assam in the north-east zone and the Punjab, North-West Frontier Province, Sind and Baluchistan in the north-west zone'.[24] This significantly modified the League's objective adopted under the Lahore Resolution (1940), which had called for the formation of 'Independent States' in the north-western and north-eastern Muslim-majority zones of India.[25] This change meant that the eastern and western Muslim-majority zones were to form one single State instead of two, as assumed earlier, giving a sharper edge to the movement for Pakistan.

Armed with this resolution, Jinnah had a detailed discussion with the members of the Cabinet Mission and the Viceroy on 16 April. Pethick Lawrence explained to Jinnah that while the Mission recognized the importance of the case put up to them about the claims of the Muslims, the Congress had an entirely different perspective regarding the future of India and the Cabinet Mission was trying to find a via media so that the gap between the two organizations could be bridged. This they were trying to do by devising a formula that did not require either party to make all the sacrifices necessary for an agreement. While trying to do so, the Delegation had come to the conclusion that 'the full and complete demand for Pakistan' in the form proposed by Jinnah had little chance of acceptance. In its view, Jinnah 'could not reasonably hope to receive both the whole of the territory, much of it inhabited by non-Muslims, which he claimed, and the full measure of sovereignty which he said was essential'. If he wanted all the territories, he would have to relinquish some element of sovereignty. On the other hand, if he desired full sovereignty, his claim to non-Muslim territories could not be conceded. Amidst a good deal of arguments and questioning Jinnah stood his ground. When it was suggested by Cripps that if Jinnah had any other alternative for an agreement with the Congress, he could mention it so that the Delegation could convey it to the Congress and see its reaction, Jinnah replied that the Congress must say first what it wanted.[26] One of the members of the Cabinet Delegation, A.V. Alexander, noted in his diary that evening that Jinnah's tactics was based on 'first making large demands and secondly insisting that he should make no offer reducing that demand but should wait for the other side always to say how much they would advance towards granting that demand'. Alexander further added: 'He of course was under a pretty severe cross-examination from Sir Stafford Cripps who, however, failed to move him.' The efforts by the Secretary of State for India and Alexander also failed to move Jinnah. 'The official note of the meeting,' observes Alexander, 'will reveal how great were the efforts made to get Mr Jinnah to move, but upto this moment I feel that we have not shaken him.'[27]

On the following day Cripps saw Jinnah. As the former reported to the other members of the Cabinet Mission and the Viceroy, at their meeting on 18 April, he had got 'nothing much' out of Jinnah. However, Cripps had returned from the talk with the impression that Jinnah realized that he could not get all that he wanted, but would prefer that to happen through an award given by the British rather than through discussion with the Congress leaders. Though he was prepared to have conversations with the Congress leaders, if the Cabinet Mission so wished, he did not think any useful purpose would be served by such conversations. For the rest, Jinnah stood as firm as ever on the demand for Pakistan, with control over all subjects, including foreign policy and defence. The official report of the Cabinet Mission's deliberations on 18 April, thus records Cripps's report on his conversation with Jinnah on the previous day:

He was quite immovable in regard to the policy on Pakistan and would do nothing as regards the Centre except through a Treaty. He would be prepared to discuss the way in which a Treaty would provide for arrangements between Hindustan and Pakistan in regard to defence, foreign affairs, customs and communications, provided that the basis of discussion was that there should be no Legislature or Executive. Mr Jinnah agreed that there would have to be a common foreign policy and defence policy and said that force of events would lead to it in any case. He was, however, firmly opposed to any Legislature or Executive even on the basis of equal representation.

When Cripps asked what Jinnah thought the Cabinet Mission should do under the circumstances, Jinnah replied that whatever the Mission did was likely to lead to loud cries of opposition, but he was quite sure that if it gave 'a firm and just decision', it would be able to put it through. At the same time, he added, rather as an afterthought, that 'of course the Muslims would fight any unjust decision'.[28]

III

Jinnah seemed to relent a bit when Cripps saw him on 24 April with a new plan for settlement on the basis of a three-tier constitution of the Indian Union providing for the grouping of Hindu and Muslim provinces in between the provinces and the Centre. In the beginning he was totally unresponsive and indeed said that there was no use discussing the matter further and that progress was possible only if the Cabinet Mission itself took the decision. Towards the end of their conversation, however, although Jinnah reiterated his strong objection to the proposal for the setting up of an Interim Government, he took down the main points of the three-tier scheme and said that if the Congress accepted it, he would be prepared to place it before his Working Committee.[29] The Congress leaders had, however, already rejected the idea of a three-tier constitution.[30]

In view of the wide divergence of views between the Congress and the League, the Cabinet Mission tried the expedient of a conference of four leaders from each of the two parties together meeting with the three members of the Cabinet Mission and the Viceroy. The conference met at Simla from 5 to 12 May and came to be known as the second Simla Conference. The basis for discussion had been set out in the identical letters of invitation sent, on 27 April, by Lord Pethick Lawrence to Azad and Jinnah as presidents of the two organizations. According to it, the future constitution of India would be a three-tier structure. At the Centre there would be a Union Government dealing only with Foreign Affairs, Defence, and Communications. The second tier would consist of two groups of provinces, the one 'predominantly Hindu' and the other 'predominantly Muslim', dealing with all other subjects which the provinces in the respective groups desired to be dealt with in common. The third tier would be formed by provincial governments, which would deal with all other subjects and would have the residuary 'sovereign rights'. The Indian States were expected to take their appropriate place in that structure on terms to be negotiated with them.[31] Discussions continued through seven sessions in all, but the Congress and the League remained poles apart. Jinnah was prepared to accept a Union executive formed on the basis of parity between Hindus and Muslims, functioning without a legislature and not having even the power to raise money through taxation for the limited functions to be assigned to it, but to depend upon the voluntary contributions made to it from time to time by the legislatures of the two federations formed after the grouping of provinces. On the other hand, the Congress wanted a central executive without parity, with a full-fledged legislature, and dealing also with subjects like customs and currency, having the power to raise funds for meeting its expenses through taxation—in short, a strong and organic Centre. Similarly, while the League showed its readiness to accept a Central Government, however weak, mainly because it was pleased with the grouping of provinces, which would virtually give it an expanded Pakistan, in substance if not immediately in form, the Congress did not like grouping at all, describing it as a federation within a federation and that too formed on a communal basis. Besides, Jinnah's demand for a review of the provisions of the constitution within five years and his proposal that the Union should be initially for a period not exceeding five years (in the fourth session of the Conference, 6 May) raised serious misgivings in the minds of the Congress leaders' regarding his real motive in laying so much emphasis on an extremely weak Centre and strong groups of provinces. They naturally began to wonder whether Jinnah was planning to utilize the opportunity provided by the Cabinet Mission for preparing the ground for the eventual creation of an expanded Pakistan after entrenching itself in the groups of Muslim provinces. Indeed, Patel remarked then and there that Jinnah's suggestion about limiting the Union to five years only in the first instance 'clearly indicated' the reality behind the grouping proposal. In such a situation the second Simla Conference was bound to fail to secure an agreement between the Congress and the League and this failure was duly acknowledged before it was wound up on 12 May.[32]

It may be worthwhile here to record the final positions of the Muslim League and the Congress on the various points under dispute as indicated by their presidents in letters addressed to the Secretary of State for India on 12 May 1946. The League's position as defined by Jinnah was as follows:

1. The six Muslim provinces (Punjab, NWFP, Baluchistan, Sind, Bengal and Assam) should be grouped together as one Group. They would deal with all those subjects except Foreign Affairs, Defence and Communications necessary for Defence, which might be dealt with by the constitution-making bodies of the two Groups of provinces—Muslim provinces (hereinafter named the Pakistan Group) and Hindu provinces—sitting together.
2. There should be a separate constitution-making body for the six Muslim provinces named above, which would frame constitutions for the Group and the Provinces in the Group and the provinces and will determine the list of subjects that should be provincial and Central (of the Pakistan Federation) with the residuary sovereign powers vesting in the provinces.
3. The method of election of the representatives to the constitution-making body would be such as would secure proper representation to the various communities in proportion to their population in each province of the Pakistan group.
4. After the constitutions of the Pakistan Federal Government

and the provinces were finally settled, it would be open to any province of the Group to decide to opt out of its Group, provided the wishes of the people of that province were ascertained by a referendum to opt out or not.

5. It must be open to discussion in the joint constitution-making body as to whether the Union would have a Legislature or not. The method of providing the Union with finance should also be left for decision of the joint meeting of the two constitution-making bodies, but in no event should it be by means of taxation.
6. There should be parity of representation between the two Groups of provinces in the Union Executive and the Legislature, if there is any.
7. No major point in the Union constitution that affected the communal issue should be deemed to be passed in the joint constitution-making body unless the majority of the members of the constitution-making body of the Pakistan Group, present and voting, were separately in its favour.
8. No decision, legislative, executive, or administrative, should be taken by the Union in regard to any matter of a controversial nature, except by a majority of three-fourths.
9. In Group and provincial constitutions, fundamental rights and safeguards concerning religion, culture, and other matters affecting the different communities would be provided for.
10. The constitution of the Union should contain a provision whereby any province could, by a majority vote of its Legislative Assembly, call for reconsideration of the terms of the constitution, and would have the liberty to secede from the Union at any time after an initial period of ten years.[33]

The final position of the Congress, as conveyed by Azad on the same date, contained the following points:

1. The Constituent Assembly should consist of representatives from the Provinces of British India and from the Indian States. The former would be elected by each Provincial Assembly through proportional representation (single transferable vote). The number so elected should be one-fifth of the number of members of the Assembly. The method

of selection of representatives from the States was to be decided later.

2. The Constituent Assembly would draw up a constitution for the Federal Union. This would consist of an All-India Federal Government and Legislature dealing with Foreign Affairs, Defence, Communications, Fundamental Rights, Currency, Customs and Planning, as well as such other subjects as, on closer scrutiny, might be found to be intimately allied to them. The Federal Union would have the necessary powers to obtain for itself the finances it might require for these subjects and the power to raise revenues in its own right. The Union must also have the power to take remedial action in cases of breakdown of the constitution and in grave public emergencies.
3. All the remaining powers should vest in the Provinces or Units.
4. Groups of provinces might be formed and such groups might determine the provincial subjects that they desired to take in common.
5. After the Constituent Assembly had framed the Constitution for the All-India Federal Union, the representatives of the Provinces might form Groups to frame the provincial constitutions for their Group and, if they so wished, a Group constitution.
6. No major point in the All-India Federal Constitution that affected the communal issue would be deemed to have been adopted by the Constituent Assembly unless a majority of the members of the community or communities concerned, present in the Assembly and voting, were separately in its favour. Provided that in case there was no agreement on any such issue, it would be referred to arbitration. In case of doubt as to whether any point constituted a major communal issue, the Speaker would decide, or, if so desired, it may be referred to the Federal Court.
7. In the event of a dispute arising in the process of constitution-making, the specific issue would be referred to arbitration.
8. The constitution should provide machinery for its revision at any time subject to such checks as might be desired. If so desired, it might be specifically stated that this whole constitution could be reconsidered after ten years.[34]

Azad also submitted a note to the Cabinet Mission elucidating the divergence of the Congress from the views of the League as expressed in Jinnah's note to the Cabinet Mission. This divergence should be obvious to all those who go through the two notes submitted respectively by Jinnah and Azad and need not be dilated upon here in detail. It will suffice to point out that the starting point for the League was the setting up of two federations, one for Pakistan and the other for Hindustan, to be followed by the setting up of a confederal agency at the Centre, with extremely limited powers, which would not have a legislature of its own and no powers to levy taxes to meet its expenses and whose executive would be constituted on the basis of parity between the two federations. The starting point for the Congress, on the other hand, was the framing of a constitution for India as a whole providing for the setting up of an All-India Federal Government, endowed with both an executive and a legislature, and having much wider powers than just Defence, Foreign Affairs and Communications and these were to include also the power to raise money through taxation for meeting its expenses. Provinces were to have full autonomy and would be at liberty to form Groups and to frame Group Constitutions if they so wished, but there could be no compulsion in this matter. There was one significant matter on which the points of view of the League and the Congress converged. While Jinnah had asked in his note for a provision for a review of the Constitution after ten years including the option for a province to secede from the Union, Azad too had suggested a similar provision. Though he initially mentioned only reconsideration and not secession, his supplementary note to the Cabinet Mission, commenting on the various points of Jinnah's note, however, shows that this represented merely a semantic difference and no difference in substance. As Azad explained the Congress viewpoint on this issue:

> The Constitution of the Union will inevitably contain provisions for its revision. It may also contain a provision for its full reconsideration at the end of ten years. The matter will be open then for a complete reconsideration. Though it is implied, we would avoid reference to secession, as we do not wish to encourage this idea.[35]

This shows that in order to provide a basis for a negotiated settlement with the League, the Congress was prepared to concede the right of secession from the Union to a Province. It remained, however, firmly opposed to any proposal to make the Centre almost totally powerless and dependent on Groups of Provinces for its revenue as well as to compulsion being imposed on any Province, regardless of its wish or that of any large section of the non-Muslim population of a Province, however large, to join a Group.

IV

While carrying on discussions with the Congress and the Muslim League leaders during the second Simla Conference, the members of the Cabinet Delegation and the Viceroy had also been seriously working on the draft of a statement they planned to issue, with the approval of the British Cabinet, after the failure of that conference. This statement was issued on 16 May 1946. Here they put forward what they considered as 'the best arrangements possible' to ensure a speedy setting up of a new constitution based on independence and of an Interim Government consisting of the representatives of the major political parties to carry out the tasks of administration while the constitution was being finalized. The statement went on to note that the Cabinet Mission and the Viceroy had applied their minds most seriously to 'the fundamental issue of the unity or division of India' and had held discussions with leaders of public opinion of all shades regarding it. It noted that these discussions had shown 'an almost universal desire, outside the supporters of the Muslim League, for the unity of India'. At the same time, the members of the Cabinet Mission were 'greatly impressed by the very genuine anxiety of the Muslims lest they should find themselves subjected to a perpetual Hindu-majority rule'. The members of the Mission, therefore, examined in the first instance the question of a fully independent Pakistan comprising six provinces in the north-west and the north-east of India as demanded by the League. As this area contained a large non-Muslim population, its creation, in their opinion, would not resolve the minority problem in India. Nor could they see any justification for including in a sovereign Pakistan those areas of the Punjab and of Bengal and Assam where the non-Muslims were in a majority. The Mission thereupon examined whether it would be possible to form a smaller Pakistan consisting only of the Muslim-majority areas in the north-west and the north-east. However, the League considered such a

Pakistan as 'quite impractical' because it would entail the exclusion of large areas from Pakistan. The Mission also did not favour the Partition of the Punjab and Bengal as each of them had its own distinctive culture and tradition. The division of the Punjab would be hurtful also to the interests of the Sikhs as they would be divided into two by the border. 'We have, therefore,' declared the Mission's statement, 'been forced to the conclusion that neither a larger nor a smaller sovereign State of Pakistan would provide an acceptable solution for the communal problem.' The statement further cited various administrative, economic, and strategic considerations that stood in the way of the creation of Pakistan and expressed the inability of the Mission to recommend to the British Government that it hand over power to two entirely separate sovereign States.

This decision of the Mission did not, however, blind it to 'the very real Muslim apprehensions that their culture and political and social life might become submerged in a purely unitary India, in which the Hindus with their greatly superior numbers must be a dominant element'. The Mission also did not consider as practical or adequate the Congress proposal of having compulsory and optional lists of subjects at the Centre in order to enable any province, if it so wished, to enjoy a greater sphere of autonomy than other provinces by opting to be under the writ of the Centre only for the compulsory subjects. It, therefore, proceeded to offer its own solution to the problem, which, in its view, 'would be just to the essential views of all parties and would at the same time be most likely to bring about a stable and practicable form of constitution for All-India'. With this end in view, it recommended the following points as constituting the basic form of the Constitution:

1. There should be a Union of India embracing both British India and the States, which should deal with the following subjects: Foreign Affairs, Defence and Communications, and should have the powers necessary to raise the finances required for the above subjects.
2. The Union should have an Executive and a Legislature constituted from British Indian and States representatives. Any question raising a major communal issue in the Legislature should require for its decision a majority of the representatives present and the voting of each of the two

major communities as well as a majority of all the members present and voting.

3. All subjects other than the Union subjects and all residuary powers should vest in the provinces.
4. The States will retain all subjects and powers other than those ceded to the Union.
5. Provinces should be free to form Groups with Executives and Legislatures, and each Group could determine the Provincial subjects to be taken in common.
6. The constitutions of the Union and of Groups should contain a provision whereby any province could, by a majority vote of its Legislative Assembly, call for a reconsideration of the terms of the constitution after an initial period of ten years and at ten-yearly intervals thereafter.

After thus laying down the broad basis of the future constitution, the Mission's statement proceeded to propose the constitution-making machinery that was to be brought into being forthwith in order to enable the constitution to be worked out. The ideal method of constituting such a machinery, it observed, would be the holding of elections on the basis of adult franchise, but if this method was to be adopted, it would take too much time and the situation in India called for speedy action. It, therefore, thought that the practical method was to utilize the recently elected Provincial Assemblies as the elective bodies under a formula that would ensure that each member of the constitution-making body represented roughly one million people in a Province and that in each province the number of such members from each community in a province corresponded to the proportion of the members of the community to the total population. In this way there would be a total of 292 members from the provinces. The number of members from the States would also be fixed according to the same formula and was expected to exceed 93. The method of selection of members from the States would, however, have to be settled by consultation. In the preliminary stage the States would be represented by a Negotiating Committee.

The Mission's Statement also suggested the procedure to be followed by the constitution-making body. The elected members would first assemble in New Delhi as soon as possible for a preliminary meeting. At this meeting they would decide the general order of business, elect a Chairman and other officers, and constitute an Advisory Committee on the rights of citizens, minorities, and people belonging to tribal and excluded areas. Thereafter the provincial representatives would divide up into three sections: A (consisting of Madras, Bombay, United Provinces, Bihar, Central Provinces, and Orissa); B (consisting of Punjab, North-West Frontier Province, and Sind, with the addition of a representative of British Baluchistan); and C (Bengal and Assam). These sections would proceed to settle the provincial constitutions for the provinces included in each section and also decide whether any Group constitutions should be framed for these provinces and, if so, with what provincial subjects the Groups should deal. provinces would have the power to opt out of the Groups after the first elections held under the new constitution.

After the Group constitutions had been framed, the representatives of the provinces and also those of the States would reassemble for the purpose of settling the Union constitution. In the Union Constituent Assembly any resolution seeking to change any one or more of the points suggested as parts of the basic form of the constitution (given in paragraph 15 of the Mission's Statement) or raising any major communal issue would require a majority of the representatives present and voting of each of the two major communities. The Chairman of the Assembly was to decide which resolution raised a major communal issue. However, if so requested by a majority of the members of either of the major communities, he would consult the Federal Court before giving his decision.

The Viceroy would forthwith request the Provincial Assemblies to proceed with the election of their representatives to the Constituent Assembly and the States to set up a Negotiating Committee. The Mission hoped that the process of constitution-making would proceed as rapidly as the complexities of the task permitted so that the interim period might be as short as possible. It would be necessary to negotiate a treaty between the Union Constituent Assembly and the United Kingdom to provide for certain matters arising out of the transfer of power.

While the task of constitution-making proceeded, the administration of India had to be carried on. The Mission's statement emphasized that it attached the greatest importance to the setting up at once of an Interim Government having the support of the major political parties and noted that the Viceroy had already begun discussions in this regard. All the portfolios in the Interim Government, including that of the War Member, would be held by Indian leaders enjoying the confidence of the people. The British Government would extend the fullest possible cooperation to such a Government.

Finally, the statement expressed the Cabinet Mission's hope that the new, independent India might choose to be a member of the British Commonwealth. Even if it did not do so, the Mission looked forward to close and friendly relations between the British people and the Indian people. These, it affirmed, were matters for India's free choice.[36]

This statement was followed by Pethick Lawrence's broadcast, Cripps's press conference, and another broadcast by Wavell, all of whom elucidated its provisions further and stressed the urgent necessity of the Congress and the League accepting its contents and agreeing to cooperate in the formation of an Interim Government so as to provide effective administration of the country and make possible the speedy drafting of the Indian constitution.[37] Neither the Congress nor the League, however, was fully satisfied with the Cabinet Mission's statement and there followed a series of correspondence and interviews between the members of the Cabinet Mission and the Viceroy on the one hand, and the leaders of the two parties, on the other, both regarding the provisions relating to constitution-making and the powers and composition of the Interim Government. Without dealing with these exchanges here in detail, it may be enough to point out that as far as the method of functioning of the Constituent Assembly was concerned, while the League attached the greatest importance to the early formation of Groups of provinces on the basis of communal majorities,[38] the Congress saw a clear contradiction in the position of the Cabinet Mission with regard to their formation. For in the beginning it said that the provinces should be free to form Groups, but later on it provided that after the preliminary meeting of the Constituent Assembly the provincial representatives would assemble in three sections and proceed to form the constitution of the three Groups; a province could opt out of a Group, but only after the elections under the new constitution. This, according to the Congress, was a flagrant violation of the principle of Provincial Autonomy, which was supposed to be the basis of the Cabinet Mission's

Plan. At the same time, the Congress was keen that the Interim Government should function as a Cabinet, *de facto* if not *de jure*, and that the Viceroy should have no control over it.[39]

In order to deal with this situation the Cabinet Mission and the Viceroy issued another statement on 25 May 1946, clarifying their stand on some of the major controversial issues centred on their statement of 16 May. It was clearly stated therein that the Congress interpretation of paragraph 15 of the earlier statement (dealing with the formation of Groups) did not 'accord with the Delegation's intentions'. While the Congress laid stress on the freedom of a province to decide whether to belong to a Group right at the beginning, the statement of 25 May pointed out that the formation of Groups was 'an essential feature of the scheme' and could only be altered through agreement between the parties. The statement pointed out that the right to opt out of a Group could be exercised by a province only after the formation of the Groups and the holding of the first elections under the new constitution. Regarding the nature of the Interim Government proposed to be set up at the Centre, the statement pointed out that while all portfolios, including that of the War Member, would be held by representative Indians, selected on the basis of consultations with the main political parties, and that the Interim Government would be given 'the greatest possible freedom in the exercise of the day-to-day administration of India', it could not be made legally responsible to the Central Legislature.[40]

In the meanwhile, efforts had begun on the part of the Cabinet Delegation and the Viceroy to deal with the task of formulating a plan, acceptable to both the Congress and the League, for the formation of an Interim Government, as envisaged in their statement of 16 May. This task became more and more difficult with each passing day. The Congress firmly opposed any kind of parity in the composition of the Interim Government, either between the Hindus and the Muslims or between itself and the League. At the same time it insisted on including a Muslim within the quota of seats allotted to it. The League, on the other hand, was equally determined upon parity between itself and the Congress, and at the same time insisted that no Muslim not belonging to the League could be appointed as a member of the Interim Government, in effect equating the Congress–League parity with Hindu–Muslim parity. After all efforts to arrive at a compromise between these conflicting views had failed, the Cabinet Mission and the Viceroy came out with their own plan for the formation of an Interim Government on 16 June 1946. According to it, the Interim Government was to consist of fourteen members (all mentioned by name), with six from the Congress (all Hindus, including a representative from the Scheduled Castes), five from the League, and three others—one Sikh, one Indian Christian, and one Parsee.[41]

The Congress, after prolonged discussions, decided to reject the plan concerning the formation of an Interim Government as it was not prepared to compromise its position as a national organization representing all sections of the Indian people. However, largely for tactical reasons, it decided to accept the long-term plan (16 May) regarding the setting up of a Constituent Assembly, of course, with its own reservations and interpretations. Both the decisions, contained in a single resolution, were made by the Working Committee on 25 June, and communicated to the Viceroy the same evening.[42] The League, on the other hand, had already decided upon its acceptance of the Cabinet Mission's long-term plan on 6 June, of course with its own interpretation of its meaning and purpose.[43] After learning about the Congress decision to reject the short-term plan on 25 June from the Viceroy, it immediately conveyed its acceptance of that plan late that very night.[44]

Even before securing the acceptance of the Cabinet Mission's long-term Plan—on 6 June by the Working Committee of the League and on the following day by its Council—Jinnah, aware of the reservations and hesitations on the Congress side, had obtained an assurance from Wavell that if one party accepted the Cabinet Mission Plan of 16 May, and the other did not, the Mission would proceed with its Plan in cooperation with the party accepting it though it hoped that both would accept.[45] This assurance had been duly utilized by Jinnah in persuading the League bodies to accept the Cabinet Mission's long-term Plan of 16 May. This was reaffirmed by the Cabinet Mission and the Viceroy in paragraph 8 of their statement announcing the proposed membership of the Interim Government on 16 June:

> In the event of the two major parties or either of them proving unwilling to join the setting up of a coalition Government on the above lines, it is the intention of the Viceroy to proceed with the formation of an Interim

Government which will be as representative as possible of those willing to accept the statement of 16 May.[46]

The interpretation of this paragraph at once became a bone of contention between the League, on the one hand, and the Cabinet Mission and the Viceroy, on the other. After the rejection of the scheme of Interim Government proposed in the Mission's statement on 16 June by the Congress on 25 June, Jinnah contended that as the Congress had rejected the Mission's scheme of Interim Government, which was an integral part of the Cabinet Mission Plan, it should be treated as having rejected that Plan as a whole. Contrary to this, the Mission and the Viceroy held that as the Congress had accepted their statement of 16 May, it could not be considered as having rejected it, and, as per the terms of paragraph 8 of the statement of 16 June, efforts would continue to form an Interim Government with the help of both the Congress and the League. While this controversy was going on an event took place that is supposed by many, no doubt wrongly, as having brought about the League's rejection of the Cabinet Mission Plan and the recourse to Direct Action with a view to achieving Pakistan, thereby shattering all hopes of preventing Partition. To this we must now turn.

V

The All-India Congress Committee met in Bombay on 6–7 July to ratify the decision of the Working Committee taken on 25 June to accept the Cabinet Mission Plan of 16 May. Winding up the discussion on this subject on 7 July, Nehru, who had taken over as the new Congress President on the previous day, made certain observations regarding the Congress attitude towards the Cabinet Mission Plan and reiterated them with much greater force at a press conference in Bombay on 10 July. This supposedly led Jinnah and other leaders of the League to decide to secure the reversal of the League's earlier decision by convening another meeting of its Council at Bombay on 27 July. This, it is further held by many scholars and publicists, caused a severe setback to the ongoing efforts for the preservation of Indian unity, assured by the League's acceptance of the Cabinet Mission Plan, and led straight to Partition. Ironically, this view has been presented most eloquently by none other than a long-time member of The

Congress High Command and Nehru's close friend and comrade, Azad, who had handed over charge to the former as Congress President on 6 July. Claiming that the Cabinet Mission Plan of 16 May 1946, was basically the same as the scheme he had formulated,[47] he observes in his supposed memoir:

> The acceptance of the Cabinet Mission Plan by both the Congress and the Muslim League was a glorious event in the history of the freedom movement in India. It meant that the difficult question of Indian freedom had been settled by negotiation and agreement and not by methods of violence and conflict. It also seemed that the communal difficulties had been finally left behind. Throughout the country there was a sense of jubilation and all the people were united in their demand for freedom. We rejoiced but we did not then know that our joy was premature and bitter disappointment awaited us.[48]

The 'bitter disappointment', Azad proceeds to tell us, was caused by Nehru's performance at his press conference in Bombay on 10 July 1946. Although Nehru had said something identical three days earlier at the meeting of the AICC while explaining the meaning of the Working Committee's resolution accepting the Cabinet Mission Plan of 16 May for some reason Azad chose to touch upon his remarks at the press conference to show that Nehru was the wrecker of the Cabinet Mission Plan of 16 May and, by implication, of India's unity. Says Azad after underlining the significance of both the Congress and the League having accepted that Plan:

> Now happened one of those unfortunate events which changed the course of history. On 10 July, Jawaharlal held a press conference in Bombay in which he made an astonishing statement. Some press representatives asked him whether, with the passing of the Resolution by the AICC, the Congress had accepted the Plan *in toto*, including the composition of the Interim Government.
>
> Jawaharlal in reply stated that Congress would enter the Constituent Assembly 'completely unfettered by agreements and free to meet all situations as they arise'.
>
> Press representatives further asked if this meant that the Cabinet Mission Plan could be modified.
>
> Jawaharlal replied emphatically that the Congress had agreed only to participate in the Constituent Assembly and regarded itself free to change or modify the Cabinet Mission Plan as it thought best.

Nehru's observations, adds Azad, came to Jinnah 'as a bombshell' and he immediately ordered the summoning of the League's Council in order to review its earlier decision to accept the Cabinet Mission Plan of 16 May. Here it may be added that just in the paragraph preceding the one which contains a severe indictment of Nehru for giving Jinnah a chance to reverse the League's earlier acceptance of the Cabinet Mission's Plan, Azad presents quite a different background of the change in Jinnah's stance: Jinnah's own ambivalent attitude towards that Plan and the adverse reactions among a section of the League's leadership to the acceptance of the Cabinet Mission's Plan. As Azad puts it:

> The Muslim League had accepted the Cabinet Mission Plan only under duress. Naturally, Mr Jinnah was not very happy about it. In his speech to the League Council, he had clearly stated that he recommended acceptance only because nothing better could be obtained. His political advisers started to criticize him by saying that he had failed to deliver the goods. They accused him that he had given up the idea of an independent Islamic State. They also taunted him that if the League was willing to accept the Cabinet Mission Plan—which denied the right of the Muslims to form a separate State—why had Mr Jinnah made so much fuss about an independent Islamic State?[49]

Whatever that may have been, all those who share Azad's view—and their number is by no means insignificant—base their theory—about Nehru's responsibility for scuttling the Cabinet Mission Plan and thereby making Partition inevitable—on two assumptions. One of them is that by accepting the Cabinet Mission Plan the Muslim League had jettisoned its demand for Partition. The other assumption is that Nehru's observations at the AICC meeting on 7 July, and at the press conference three days later, constituted the primary factor behind the League's decision to reverse its earlier decision regarding the Cabinet Mission Plan. Neither of the two assumptions is based on facts.

A perusal of the text of the resolution adopted by the Muslim League's Council on 6 June 1946, under the guidance of Jinnah, will show that by agreeing to cooperate in constitution-making under the terms of the Cabinet Mission's statement of 16 May, the League had not at all jettisoned its cherished objective of establishing a sovereign Pakistan. After recording its strong objection to some of the initial paragraphs of the Cabinet Mission's statement which had declared that the establishment of Pakistan was not a practicable or desirable objective, the resolution declared:

In order that there may be no manner of doubt in any quarter, the Council of the All-India Muslim League reiterates that the attainment of the goal of a complete sovereign Pakistan still remains the unalterable objective of the Muslims in India, for the achievement of which they will, if necessary, employ every means in their power, and consider no sacrifice or suffering too great.

Explaining why, in view of its continuing to hold on to the objective of a sovereign Pakistan, the League was being advised to accept the Cabinet Mission Plan of 16 May, which had not hidden its dislike for that objective, the League's Council went on to observe why it was doing so:

Having regard to the grave issues involved, and prompted by its earnest desire for a peaceful solution, if possible, of the Indian constitutional problem, and *inasmuch as the basis and foundation of Pakistan are inherent in the Mission's Plan by virtue of the compulsory grouping of the six Muslim Provinces in Sections B and C*, is willing to cooperate with the constitution-making machinery proposed in the scheme outlined by the Mission, *in the hope that it would ultimately result in the establishment of complete, sovereign Pakistan* and in the consummation of the goal of independence for the major nations, Muslims and Hindus, and all the other people inhabiting the vast subcontinent.

It is for these reasons that the Muslim League is accepting the scheme, and will join the constitution-making body, and *it will keep in view the opportunity and right of secession of Provinces or Groups from the Union, which have been provided in the Mission's Plan by implication.*

The resolution went on to point out the reservations and conditions under which the League was accepting the Cabinet Mission Plan. It declared that the ultimate attitude of the Muslim League was going to depend on the final outcome of the labours of the constitution-making body, and on the final shape of the 'constitutions' that might emerge from the deliberations of that body jointly and separately in its three sections. The League also reserved the right to revise and modify the policy and attitude set forth in the Council's resolution at any time during the deliberations of the constitution-making body or thereafter, if the course of events so required. While taking any decision on this matter the League would bear in mind '*the fundamental principles and ideals here before adumbrated, to which the Muslim League is irrevocably committed*'.[50]

The irrevocable commitment of the League to its 'fundamental principles and ideals' was further underlined by Jinnah in his presidential remarks at the time the resolution was adopted. For he declared amidst loud cheers: 'Let me tell you that Muslim India will not rest content until we have established a full, complete and sovereign Pakistan.' He further added:

> The Lahore Resolution [1940] did not mean that when Muslims put forward their demand, it must be accepted at once. It is a big struggle and a continuing struggle. . . . Acceptance of the Mission's proposal was not the end of their struggle for Pakistan. They should continue their struggle till Pakistan is achieved.[51]

Both the text of the League Council's resolution as also that of Jinnah's observations on it make it clear that the League had decided to participate in the work of the constitution-making body, under the framework provided in the Cabinet Mission Plan of 16 May 1946, but under certain conditions and reservations, and had certainly not given up its objective of establishing a sovereign Pakistan. Indeed, the decision to continue to work for that objective was the most important among the reservations attached to the acceptance of the Cabinet Mission Plan.

Nor is there any evidence to suggest that the League's back-tracking on its decision to join the Constituent Assembly was prompted solely by Nehru's utterances in Bombay on 7 and 10 July. Even the resolution adopted by the League's Council on this subject at its meeting in Bombay (27–29 July) did not say so. Indeed, Nehru, though speaking forcefully, as he often did, uttered those words by which the League claimed to have been offended not in reply to anything which the League had said or done, but in reply to the criticism of the Congress Working Committee's decision to participate in the work of the Constituent Assembly, by the leaders of the socialist wing of the Congress, headed by Jayaprakash Narayan, who preferred the path of struggle to that of negotiation and compromise for achieving the goal of independence. Even so, Nehru did not say anything which the then Congress President (Azad) or the Working Committee had not said before 25 June, when the League had decided to agree to cooperate in implementing the short-term plan of the Cabinet

Mission and to join the Interim Government, under the scheme of the Cabinet Mission announced on 16 June, thereby taking a major step forward after announcing its decision to participate in the work of the Constituent Assembly though with certain reservations and conditions on 6 June. Since so much has been made of Nehru's remarks, it may be worthwhile here to go into them in detail and compare them with the stand already adopted by the then Congress President and the Congress Working Committee. Thus Nehru had said at the meeting of the AICC on 7 July:

> There is a good deal of talk of the Cabinet Mission's long-term plan and short-term plan. So far as I can see, it is not a question of our accepting any plan—long or short. It is only a question of our agreeing to go into the Constituent Assembly. That is all, and there is nothing more than that. We will remain in the Assembly so long as we think it is good for India, and we will come out when we think it is endangering our cause, and then offer our battle.[52]

At his press conference in Bombay on 10 July, Nehru thus amplified these remarks on being requested to do so by the press:

> As a matter of fact, if you read the correspondence that has passed between the Congress President and [the] Cabinet Mission and the Viceroy, you will see in what conditions and circumstances we agreed to go into this Constituent Assembly. The first thing is that we have agreed to nothing else. It is true that in going into the Constituent Assembly we have inevitably to agree to a certain procedure in advance, that is, the election of candidates to the Constituent Assembly. What we do there, we are entirely and absolutely free to determine. We have not committed ourselves on any single matter to any body. Naturally, even though one might not agree to commit oneself, there is a certain compulsion of facts which makes one accept this thing or that thing. I do not know what that might be in this particular context. But the nature of compulsion of the facts would be not of the British Government's desires or intents, but how to make the Assembly a success, and how to avoid its breaking up. That will certainly be a very important consideration.

Nehru proceeded to inform the press that when the Congress took the stand that the Constituent Assembly would be a sovereign body, the Cabinet Mission did not contradict it. All that it said was that this would be subject to two considerations: first, proper arrangements regarding the protection of the right of minorities and, second, the negotiation of a treaty between India and Britain. Both these things, according to Nehru, were non-controversial. For the minorities question had to be settled satisfactorily and, if there was to be a peaceful transfer of power, some kind of a treaty with Britain might become necessary.

Another important question raised at the press conference related to the provision for the grouping of provinces as provided for in the Cabinet Mission Plan. Nehru gave his assessment that no such grouping was likely to take effect. As he put it:

> The big probability is that, from any approach to the grouping question, there will be no grouping. Obviously Section A [consisting of Hindu-majority provinces] will decide against grouping. Speaking in betting language, there is a four-to-one chance of the North-West Frontier Province deciding against grouping. The Group B collapses. It is highly likely that Assam will decide against grouping with Bengal, although I would not like to say what the initial decision may be, since it is evenly balanced. But I can say, with every assurance and conviction, that there is going to be, finally, no grouping there, because Assam will not tolerate it under any circumstances whatever. Thus you see this grouping business, approached from any point of view, does not get on at all.

Nehru was equally forthright and frank when a question was raised about the powers of the Centre. Although the Cabinet Mission's statement had assigned only three or four subjects to the Centre—Defence, Foreign Affairs, and Communications and the power to raise finances for them—he pointed out that a large number of industries came under Defence and Communications, and they were likely to grow. These industries were bound to be under the Centre. Similarly, the sphere of activities under Defence was bound to expand and that, too, would be under the Centre. Besides, External Affairs would have to include policy regarding Foreign Trade. The Centre also would have to come in if there was trouble between Provinces or States or if there was an economic breakdown. In conclusion, Nehru emphasized that however limited the Centre might be, one could not help it having wide powers.[53]

It is time now to turn to the official Congress position, already on record, on some of the important matters touched upon by Nehru on both the occasions and to examine whether Nehru had only reiterated the official Congress position, as he claimed, or if he had gone beyond it, and added something new as held by his critics. The first detailed statement of the Congress Working Committee on the Cabinet Mission Plan is to be found in the resolution adopted by it on 24 May 1946. Affirming therein that the Congress was moved by a desire to find a way for a peaceful transfer of power and the establishment of a free and independent India, it added: 'Such an India must have a strong central authority capable of representing the nation with power and dignity in the councils of the world.' Enumerating its objectives, it gave the first place to the independence of India but immediately after that put 'a strong, though limited, central authority.' It then went on to stress that the Constituent Assembly must function as a sovereign body while framing the Constitution and the recommendations made by the Cabinet Mission and the Viceroy should not be considered binding on it in any way. 'In their view,' said the Working Committee, 'it will be open to the Constituent Assembly itself at any stage to make changes and variations, with the proviso that in regard to certain major communal matters a majority decision of both the major communities will be necessary.' Coming to the provisions in the Cabinet Mission Plan regarding the grouping of provinces, the Committee pointed out that while in the beginning the former had observed that the provinces would be 'free' to form groups, it later suggested a procedure for the formation of groups which made grouping compulsory for the provinces whether any of them liked it or not. This violated the principle of provincial autonomy. The discrepancy between the two parts of the Cabinet Mission's statement of 16 May, the Committee urged, must be removed and the provinces left free to decide whether they wanted to join groups or not. At the same time it again stressed that 'the Constituent Assembly must be considered a sovereign body with final authority for the purpose of drawing up a constitution and giving effect to it'.[54]

Basically reiterating the stand taken by it on 24 May, the resolution adopted by the Congress Working Committee on 25 June observed:

> The kind of independence which the Congress has aimed at is the establishment of a united democratic Indian Federation with a Central authority which would command respect from the nations of the world, maximum provincial autonomy and equal rights for all men and women of the country. The limitation of the Central authority, as contained in

the proposals, as well as the system of grouping of Provinces, weakened the whole structure and was unfair to some Provinces, such as the North-West Frontier Province and Assam, and to some of the minorities, notably the Sikhs.

The Committee disapproved of this. They felt, however, taking the proposals as a whole, that there was sufficient scope for enlarging and strengthening the Central authority and for fully ensuring the right of a Province to act according to its choice in regard to grouping, and to give protection to such minorities as might otherwise be placed at a disadvantage. . . .

Proceeding to deal with the proposal for the formation of the Interim Government in the statement issued by the Cabinet Mission, the Committee described it as defective on many counts, including the lack of provision for its functioning, 'in fact if not in law as a *de facto* independent Government', responsible to the Indian people and not to any external authority, the provision of parity among its members and the non-inclusion among them of any nationalist Muslim. Rejecting the plan regarding the formation of the Interim Government as contained in the Cabinet Mission's statement of 16 June, it added: 'The Committee have, however, decided that the Congress should join the proposed Constituent Assembly with a view to framing the Constitution of a free, united and democratic India.'[55] The clear implication of this resolution was that the Congress was agreeing to participate in the work of the Constituent Assembly with reservations and with its own interpretation of the disputed clauses of the Cabinet Mission statement of 16 May. This is fully confirmed by the concluding paragraph of Azad's letter to Wavell dated 25 June, while forwarding to him the resolution adopted by the Working Committee on the same day:

With regard to the proposals made in the statement of 16th May, 1946, relating to the formation and functioning of the constitution-making body, the Working Committee of the Congress passed a resolution on the 24th May, 1946, and conversations and correspondence have taken place between Your Excellency and the Cabinet Mission on the one hand and myself and some of my colleagues on the other. In these we have pointed out what in our opinion were the defects in the proposals. We also gave our interpretation of some of the provisions of the statement. While adhering to our views, we accept your proposals and are prepared to work them with a view to achieving our objective. We would add, however, that the successful working of the Constituent

Assembly will largely depend on the formation of a satisfactory Provisional Government.[56]

All this conclusively shows that Nehru had said nothing new either in his address to the AICC or in his interview to the press in the second week of July 1946, but had merely reiterated the known and widely publicized Congress position with regard to the Cabinet Mission's statement of 16 May. Azad was apparently suffering from amnesia when he said that Nehru's performance at his press conference changed the course of history. As for the scholars and journalists who have expressed a similar view in a milder language, one can only wonder whether they had taken the trouble of going through the texts of the relevant resolutions adopted by the Congress Working Committee and the correspondence between the Congress President and other Congress leaders, on the one hand, and the members of the Cabinet Mission and the Viceroy, on the other. These make it abundantly clear that if Nehru's remarks in Bombay led the League to retract from its earlier position to join the Constituent Assembly, it would have done so on 25 June itself after seeing the texts of the Working Committee's resolution on the Cabinet Mission Plan and Azad's letter to Wavell on the same date. For they said substantially the same thing that Nehru said on 7 or 10 July. Indeed, it could have done so even earlier after going through the text of the Congress Working Committee's resolution (on the Cabinet Mission Plan) adopted on 24 May. On the contrary, what it did was to decide on 6 June to participate in the Constituent Assembly. Similarly, even after learning about the rejection by the Congress, on 25 June, of the Mission's scheme for the formation of the Interim Government, it conveyed to Wavell, that very night, its consent to work that scheme. This appears really strange in view of the League's strong objections to the Cabinet Mission Plan as well as to its elucidation of the rationale behind the Plan.

Apparently the League imagined that if it could somehow get into the Interim Government without the Congress being there, it would function therein as the dominant group and utilize the opportunity to shape the future developments as far as possible according to its wishes and mould them in the direction of the realization of the goal to which it remained as committed as ever—the establishment of a sovereign Pakistan. Only on this assumption can one get to any possible rationale behind the

League's decision both on 6 June and on 25 June. It was the failure of this strategy that led Jinnah to advise the League to reverse its earlier decision regarding the Cabinet Mission Plan and to resort to Direct Action. Nehru's utterances on 7 and 10 July were just used as an excuse.

This is confirmed by Jinnah's interactions with the Cabinet Mission and the Viceroy and also by the statements issued by him and his chief deputy and spokesman, Liaquat Ali Khan between 25 June and 6 July. Jinnah's discussion with the Cabinet Delegation and the Viceroy on the evening of the 25 June, prior to which the former had been given a copy of Azad's letter of the same date to Wavell, rejecting the scheme of the Interim Government contained in the Viceroy's statement of 16 June, but agreeing to join the Constituent Assembly, though with certain reservations, shows how determined Jinnah was to prove that the Congress acceptance of the Mission's long-term plan was really no acceptance, with a view to buttressing the League's claim to be invited to join the Interim Government, leaving the Congress out. According to the official record, when Pethick Lawrence pointed to the contents of Azad's letter. Jinnah observed that the acceptance of the Mission's Plan by the Congress was subject to a particular interpretation regarding the functioning of the Constituent Assembly. Pethick Lawrence, however, pointed out that the Cabinet Mission was satisfied that Azad's letter constituted an acceptance. He further added that the Muslim League in accepting the Mission's statement had also adhered to its own point of view and talked about maintaining its goal of a 'complete sovereign Pakistan', which along with other statements 'went quite as far as any reservations made by the Congress'. Jinnah countered this by saying that while the League had indeed 'reiterated that sovereign Pakistan was their goal', it had accepted the Mission's Plan and put no interpretation on its provisions. Pethick Lawrence thereupon pointed out that the League's resolution of 6 June referred to the right of secession being implied in the Mission's statement and that was 'definitely an interpretation'. While not agreeing with this view, Jinnah went on to argue that the reservations held by the Congress, particularly regarding grouping, were different in kind; they were 'most vital and broke the whole thing'. Pethick Lawrence rebutted Jinnah's argument and pointed out that the League's reservations were 'quite as fundamental', for it held itself free to withdraw from the Constituent Assembly at any stage or reject the Constitution framed by that Assembly if it was not to the liking of the League. A.V. Alexander intervened to clarify that the provision in the Mission's statement about the revision of the Constitution did not mean that there was a right of secession. It only meant that any party to the Constitution could after ten years have an amendment moved to it. However, the amendment had to be agreed to before it had effect. Alexander also gave his view that Azad's letter was 'an acceptance even more than the Muslim League's resolution'. Such repeated rebuffs at the hands of the members of the Cabinet Delegation did not prevent Jinnah from coming to the main point, the urgent need for the establishment of the Interim Government with the League's cooperation, and he continued to persist with his demand even though he was rebuffed more than once, thereby showing most vividly his determined pursuit of his objective. Says the official record of that interview:

> Mr Jinnah said he disliked the suggestion for a postponement of the question of the Interim Government. He thought it was bad for the prestige of the Delegation and also for his own prestige. It would destroy both but the Delegation could, of course, do as they pleased. His view was that they should proceed now to form an Interim Government on the basis of the statement of 16 June with those who were prepared to accept it. Sir S. Cripps said that it was clear from paragraph 8 of the statement of the 16 June that the fresh negotiations for an Interim Government must be on a new basis. Mr Jinnah said that the point was, the Congress having rejected the statement of 16 June, the Delegation felt they could not adhere to it. In his opinion it would be wrong and misguided to depart from that statement. The Secretary of State said that the Delegation were not asking for Mr Jinnah's opinion of their conduct.[57]

Jinnah argued that day so tenaciously, in spite of repeated rebuffs from the members of the Cabinet Mission, because his whole short-term strategy of establishing the League's dominance over the Central Government lay in a shambles once the Congress, however belatedly and with whatever reservations, decided to accept the long-term plan of the Cabinet Mission even while rejecting the scheme regarding the Interim Government. Alexander, who had a soft corner for Jinnah, though, of course, not for his objective of establishing a sovereign Pakistan, has accurately sized up Jinnah's mood as well as summed up the proceedings of that day lasting about two hours:

Mr Jinnah was quite evidently feeling a severe setback as a result of the Congress decision and claimed indeed that the acceptance in the last paragraph of Azad's letter was not really unqualified acceptance. Unfortunately there developed a long argument about this in which, whilst we all engaged in trying to persuade Mr Jinnah of the mistakenness of his view of the situation, the Secretary of State and Sir Stafford Cripps interrupted him so sharply at times as to create an atmosphere very little short of acrimonious. . . . When he had left I expressed the view that I thought he had been much too manhandled.[58]

Jinnah, however, was not a leader to be deflected from his chosen path by rebuff, acrimony, or even verbal manhandling. Within hours of his return from the marathon and frustrating discussion with the Cabinet Mission and the Viceroy on 25 June, he secured the adoption by the League's Working Committee of a resolution accepting the scheme of Interim Government as per the Viceroy's statement of 16 June and sent it to the Viceroy before going to bed.[59] He must have thought that although the Cabinet Mission was at that time not helpful to the League in fulfilling its immediate objective of entering the Interim Government without the Congress, it might be persuaded to change its line after some time through effective propaganda and public pressure. It is to this that Jinnah now applied himself. While engaged in this task he and his chief lieutenant, Liaquat Ali Khan, spoke in a vein that clearly showed that their main attack was directed against the Cabinet Mission and the Viceroy for keeping both the Congress and the League at par so far as accepting the long-term plan was concerned and not allowing the League to enter the Interim Government without the Congress. However, they did not spare the Congress and continued to attack it on various grounds, including its opposition to the grouping of provinces, largely with a view to showing that it had not really accepted the long-term plan.

Thus in his long statement issued on 27 June 1946, Jinnah, after giving his version of what had happened in the negotiations for the formation of the Interim Government, expressed regret at the decision of the Cabinet Delegation and the Viceroy to indefinitely postpone the formation of the Interim Government, wondering what 'mysterious reasons and causes' were behind that 'sudden departure'. In his opinion, all contingencies, including rejection by the Congress, had been provided for in the Viceroy's statement of 16 June; clause 8 of that statement 'taken along with the context' was quite clear and the Cabinet Delegation and the Viceroy 'were in honour bound to go ahead with the formation of the Interim Government immediately with those who were willing to come into the Interim Government on the basis and principles set out in their statement of 16 June'. Jinnah was equally critical in that statement of the Congress attitude towards grouping. This, according to him, was 'a clear indication' that the Congress was not accepting the long-term proposal of the Cabinet Mission in a sincere and honest spirit of cooperation and peaceful settlement. If it persisted with that attitude, warned Jinnah, the whole plan would be 'wrecked at its very inception'.[60] This proves conclusively that what Nehru had said in the first-half of July was nothing new, but a reaffirmation of the well-established policy of the Congress, first articulated in its Working Committee's resolution of 24 May and later reiterated in a resolution by the same body adopted on 25 June. It, of course, suited Jinnah to pinpoint that hole in Nehru's remarks in July because of their sharpness, but there was nothing more to it than that. They were not the reason behind the League's change of strategy towards the end of July. The reason was the refusal of the Cabinet Mission and the Viceroy to invite the League's representatives to join the Interim Government while the Congress stayed away.

VI

This is further confirmed by some other significant statements that followed from the League's side even before 7 July, when Nehru, for the first time, made those remarks of which so much was made by Jinnah then and by scholars and publicists later on. Thus on 1 July, Liaquat Ali Khan issued a strong statement attacking the Cabinet Mission and the Viceroy for not honouring their word by inviting the League representatives to take their seats in the Interim Government without the Congress and also the Congress for having not budged an inch from the position that it took up from the very beginning, especially regarding the grouping of provinces. In the end it warned the Government in words foreshadowing the language used by the League leaders at the meeting of their Council on 27–29 July, at the time of withdrawing its acceptance of the Cabinet Mission Plan and announcing the launching of Direct Action to achieve the goal of Pakistan. Said Liaquat Ali Khan:

> In view of the betrayal of the Muslims by the Cabinet Delegation and the Viceroy, I wish to give a timely warning to His Majesty's Government not to be under the delusion that the reasonableness shown by the Muslim League during these negotiations is to be taken as a sign of its weakness. . . . We have tried our best to avoid a struggle but if it is thrust on us, we shall face it with courage and determination. If it is only the shedding of blood which convinces the British Government the Mussalmans will not hesitate to resort to that course, if forced into it, to protect their honour and save themselves from annihilation. We shall not go to a shambles like tame sheep.[61]

It is obvious that such a statement could not have been issued by the General Secretary of the Muslim League except at the instance of its President. Any one who has an idea of the Jinnah–Liaquat equation will agree to it. In any case, Jinnah soon followed suit through his letter on 6 July, to the British Prime Minister, Clement Attlee. After roundly attacking the Cabinet Delegation and the Viceroy for their handling of the negotiations regarding the formation of the Interim Government, he warned Attlee in words broadly similar to those used by his chief deputy in his press statement less than a week ago:

> I therefore trust that the British Government will still avoid compelling the Mussalmans to shed their blood, for, their surrender to the Congress at the sacrifice of the Muslims can only result in that direction. If power politics are going to be the deciding factor in total disregard for fair play and justice, we shall have no other course open to us except to forge our sanction and meet the situation which, in that case, is bound to arise. Its consequences, I need not say, will be most disastrous and a peaceful settlement will then become impossible.[62]

On the same day Jinnah sent an identical letter to Winston Churchill, Leader of the Opposition in the House of Commons, accusing the Cabinet Mission of injustice to Muslims and warning of serious consequences to follow.[63]

The proceedings of the meeting of the Council of the Muslim League in Bombay on 27–29 July also show that the main reason given for the decision to withdraw the League's acceptance of the Cabinet Mission Plan was the decision of the latter not to go ahead with the formation of the Interim Government without the Congress, based on its rejection of the League's contention that the Congress acceptance of the long-term plan of the Cabinet Mission was really no acceptance, as it was full of reservations and interpretations of its own. The Congress stand also came in for a good deal of criticism, but that stand was declared to have been continuing since the beginning of negotiations with the Cabinet Mission and was not related exclusively to Nehru's remarks at the AICC and the press conference in Bombay respectively on 7 and 10 July 1946. Reference was made to the latter not for raising any new point of grievance, but only to buttress the League's old argument that the Congress had not really accepted the long-term plan of the Cabinet Mission.

Thus in his opening address before the Council on 27 July, Jinnah contended that the Congress had never sincerely accepted the Cabinet Mission Plan sincerely, but always put forward its own reservations and interventions and blamed the Cabinet Mission for playing into its hands. The Cabinet Mission, he affirmed had 'played a game of its own'. According to him, the Cabinet Mission 'like a drowning man ready to catch hold of a straw, treated this conditional acceptance of the Congress as genuine acceptance'. Jinnah referred to Nehru's press conference in this context:

> The Congress Working Committee's resolution was bad enough, but Pandit Jawaharlal Nehru, as the elected President having taken charge of his office, at a press conference in Bombay, on July 10, made the policy and attitude of the Congress towards the long-term proposal clear. In that interview the Pandit made it quite clear that the Congress was committed to nothing, and they were not bound by either Para 15 or Para 19 of the State Paper [dealing with the grouping of Provinces].

These paras, he emphasized, constituted the essential part of the scheme from the League's point of view. In this connection he further referred to Nehru's speech at a mass meeting in Delhi on 23 July, in which the latter had been reported as having declared that if the Congress could not mend the Constituent Assembly, it could end it. But having said all this Jinnah again turned to the Cabinet Mission and observed: 'The Mission went back on its words with regard to the Interim Government. The Mission today is cowed down and paralysed.' Reference to the Congress followed. The Congress, he declared, had resorted to methods that even an ordinary individual would be ashamed of. It did not have the decency and the sense of honour and courage to say that it could not accept the Cabinet Mission's proposals because they were opposed to its fundamental principles and objectives. His conclusion was that the only solution to India's problem was Pakistan.[64]

The resolution adopted by the League's Council on 29 July, withdrawing its acceptance of the Cabinet Mission Plan recounted in detail the repeated breach of faith allegedly committed by the Cabinet Delegation and the Viceroy on several occasions in the course of negotiations for the formation of the Interim Government and asserted that the Congress acceptance of the Mission's Plan, with its own reservations and interpretations, was no acceptance at all. That, it contended, had been 'made further clear and beyond any doubt' by Nehru's utterances in Bombay on 7 and 10 June and again in Delhi on 23 July. The final paragraph summing up the League's ground for reversing its earlier decision accepting the Cabinet Mission's Plan reads as follows and shows that the main ground given was dissatisfaction with British policy as not being steadfast in defence of Muslim interests in the face of the supposed opposition of the Congress towards them:

> The Cabinet Delegation and the Viceroy, collectively and individually, have stated on more than one occasion that the basic principles [of the Cabinet Mission Plan] were laid down to enable the major parties to join the Constituent Assembly, and that the Scheme cannot succeed unless it is worked in a spirit of cooperation. The attitude of the Congress clearly shows that these conditions, precedent for the successful working of the Constitution-making body, do no exist. This fact, taken together with the policy of the British Government of sacrificing the interests of the Muslim nation and some other weaker sections of the peoples of India, particularly the Scheduled Castes, to appease the Congress, and the way they have been going back on their oral and written solemn pledges and assurances given from time to time to the Muslims, leaves no doubt that in these circumstances the participation of the Muslims in

the proposed Constitution-making machinery is fraught with danger; and the Council, therefore, hereby withdraws its acceptance of the Cabinet Mission's proposals. . . .[65]

By another resolution the League's Council affirmed its conviction that the time had come for the Muslim nation 'to resort to Direct Action to achieve Pakistan, to assort their just rights, to vindicate their honour and to get rid of the present British slavery and the contemplated future Caste-Hindu domination'. Further, it called upon the League Working Committee to prepare forthwith a programme for Direct Action. At the same time it also called upon Muslims to renounce all titles conferred upon them by an alien Government 'as a mark of protest against and in token of their deep resentment of the attitude of the British'.[66]

The significance of the two resolutions was underlined by Jinnah in his concluding remarks from the chair after their adoption:

We have taken a most historic decision. Never before in the whole life history of the Muslim League did we do anything except by constitutional methods and constitutional talks. We are today forced into this position by a move in which both the Congress and Britain have participated. We have been attacked on two fronts—the British front and the Hindu front. Today we have said good-bye to constitutions and constitutional methods. Throughout the painful negotiations, the two parties with whom we bargained held a pistol at us; one with power and machine-guns behind it, and the other with non-cooperation and the threat to launch mass civil disobedience. This situation must be met. We also have a pistol.[67]

While Jinnah blamed both the Congress and the British for forcing the League to take that decision, the recollection of its background by Choudhry Khaliquzzaman, who was at that time one of the most prominent members of the League's Working Committee—a position he had held for many years—shows that what really moved the League leaders to decide to withdraw their acceptance of the long-term plan of the Cabinet Mission was the Viceroy's refusal to go ahead with the formation of the Interim Government with the cooperation of the League, leaving the Congress out. As Khaliquzzaman puts it:

Mr Jinnah insisted on the Viceroy's proceeding with the formation of a National Government as stated by him on 16 June. The Viceroy took shelter behind the fact that, as the Congress had not rejected the long-term plan, he would continue to negotiate with the parties and in the meanwhile appoint a non-party Interim Government. Clearly it was reversal of a policy which the Viceroy had given the Muslim League to understand would be followed by him. A meeting of the Muslim League was, therefore, held on 27 July 1946, at Bombay, at which a resolution was passed fully explaining the circumstances which led to the League's withdrawal of its acceptance of the Cabinet Missions' proposals of 6 June 1946. A direct action resolution was also passed with great enthusiasm.[68]

Indeed, even Azad, who has made so much of Nehru's remarks in Bombay in July 1946, as the cause of the League's withdrawal of its acceptance of the Cabinet Mission Plan, implies at another place in his supposed memoirs that the main cause of the League's reversal of its earlier decision was its not having been asked to join the Interim Government, without the Congress, and that it merely used Nehru's utterances as an 'opportunity' to announce a shift in its policy. Says Azad:

The Muslim League had accepted the Cabinet Mission Plan regarding both its long-term and short-term arrangements. In fact Mr Jinnah had perhaps thought that since the Congress rejected the proposals of [for] the Interim Government, while the League had accepted both, he would be invited to form the Government. He was, therefore, furious when the Viceroy made a statement that since the negotiations for forming a representative Interim Government had failed, he would set up a temporary caretaker Government of officials and resume negotiations for forming the Interim Government after the election of the Constituent Assembly. The Viceroy also expressed his pleasure that constitution making could proceed with the cooperation of the two major parties and the States. Readers will remember how, soon after this, Jawaharlal made a statement in Bombay which gave Jinnah an opportunity of rejecting the Cabinet Mission Plan in toto.[69]

Somewhat similar was the reaction of Pethick Lawrence. After hearing about the League's decision to withdraw its acceptance of the Cabinet Mission Plan, he told Sudhir Ghose, an emissary of Gandhi, in London: 'Now you see what Nehru has done. By his irresponsible statement at a Press Conference in Bombay he has given Jinnah precisely the excuse he was looking for to get out of his commitment.'[70] Whatever that might have been, Azad felt that if the Congress clarified its stand on the Cabinet Mission Plan, in a conciliatory tone, the League might revert to its earlier position. At his instance, the Congress Working Committee adopted a resolution on 10 August 1946 with this object in view. The resolution expressed regret at the League's withdrawal of its acceptance of the Cabinet Mission Plan and emphasized the need for 'the largest measure of agreement among the people of India and their representatives'. Even while recognizing the existence of differences in the outlook and objective of the Congress and the League it made a direct appeal to the League to cooperate with the Congress with a view to facilitating the early achievement of India's independence and the solution of many of India's problems. Without announcing any change in the basic Congress policy towards the long-term plan, particularly with reference to the problem of the grouping of provinces and the powers of the Constituent Assembly, the resolution went on to observe:

> The Committee further noted that criticisms have been advanced on behalf of the Muslim League to the effect that the Congress acceptance of the proposals contained in the Statement of 16 May was conditional. The Committee wish to make it clear that while they did not approve of all the proposals contained in this statement, they accepted the scheme in its entirety. They interpreted it so as to resolve the inconsistencies contained in it and fill the omissions in accordance with the principles laid down in that Statement. They hold that provincial autonomy is a basic provision and each province has the right to decide whether to form or join a group or not. Questions of interpretation will be decided by the procedure laid down in the Statement itself, and the Congress will advise its representatives in the Constituent Assembly to function accordingly.
>
> The Committee have emphasized the sovereign character of the Constituent Assembly, that is, its right to function and draw up a constitution for India without the interference of any external power or authority. But the Assembly will naturally function within the internal limitations which are inherent in its task, and will therefore seek the largest measure of cooperation in drawing up a constitution of free India allowing the greatest measure of freedom and protection for all just claims and interests. It was with this object and the desire to function in the Constituent Assembly and make it a success that the Working Committee passed their resolution on 26 June 1946, which was subsequently ratified by the All India Congress Committee on 7 July 1946. By that decision of the AICC they must stand, and they propose to proceed accordingly with their work in the Constituent Assembly.

The Committee hope that the Muslim League and all other concerned, in the wider interests of the nation as well as of their own, will join in this great task.[71]

This resolution failed to evoke any positive response from the League. On 12 August, Jinnah issued a long statement in which he quoted extensively from the earlier resolutions of the Congress Working Committee and remarked with reference to its latest resolution adopted on 10 August that it did not carry them anywhere because it was 'only a repetition of the Congress stand taken by them from the very beginning but only put in a different language and phraseology'. He further remarked: 'I am afraid the situation remains as it was and we are where we were.'[72] It should be obvious from this statement that the basic objection of the League was to the stand adopted by the Congress towards the Cabinet Mission Plan, particularly the provision for the compulsory grouping of provinces. However, since that seemed to foreshadow the rejection of the plan by the Congress, which would have paved the way for the League joining the Interim Government without the Congress, thereby establishing itself in a dominant position therein and utilizing it to mould future developments in its interest, it went on to accept the short-term Plan of the Cabinet Mission (14 June 1946). Once the Congress outmanouvred the League by accepting the long-term Plan (16 May 1946) while rejecting the scheme of Interim Government contained in the statement of 14 June 1946, the situation changed drastically, putting a serious question mark on the soundness of the League's strategy. In such a situation, the statements of Nehru in Bombay in July came as a godsend to the League and the latter partly used it as an alibi for rescinding its earlier decision regarding the Cabinet Mission Plan, of course, without hiding its grievance against the British Government for treating the Congress stand as communicated in Azad's letter of 25 June as a genuine acceptance of the long-term Plan and, on that ground, rejecting the League's claim for joining the Interim Government without the Congress. While this was the position adopted by the League in the resolution adopted by its Council at Bombay on 29 July 1946, in subsequent propaganda it suited the League leaders as well as British officials to trace the change in the League's stand regarding the Cabinet Mission Plan (long term) entirely to the utterances of the Congress leaders, particularly Nehru, and to the Congress stand on the compulsory grouping of provinces. This has since been the line also adopted generally by the scholars writing on this topic.

Thus Wavell, ignoring the League's grievance on account of the former's refusal to ask the League to join the Interim Government without the Congress, clearly mentioned—and mentioned first—in the League's Council's resolution of 29 July, imagined that the League's changed stance was caused by the intemperate language used by the Congress leaders since the Bombay meeting of the AICC in July 1946, in particular Nehru, and that it was, therefore, for the Congress to try to persuade the League to again agree to join the Constituent Assembly by extending to it the required assurances.[73] Members of the British Cabinet, as also the senior British officials in India, readily lapped up this view. There was, however, one notable exception among the latter, Sir John Colville, Governor of Bombay. In a communication to Wavell in the first week of August 1946, he pointed out that the League's changed stance was not the result of a fit of pique, but of a well-thought-out strategy for a rapid push towards its goal—Pakistan—by delaying a political settlement and then taking advantage of the disturbances and turmoil expected to emerge as a result, particularly in view of the sharpening differences between the Government and the Congress, increasingly under pressure from its left-wing, demanding the termination of the ongoing negotiations with the British and taking recourse to the path of struggle for achieving independence. As Colville put it:

I feel that the [League's] decision cannot be due to pique on the part of Jinnah, or he would have shown his hand sooner, but is more likely to be due to deeply laid strategy, the intention being to embroil Government and Congress in a first-class row and then to pick up some kind of Pakistan out of the resulting disturbance. Jinnah probably reckons that Congress with its insistent Left Wing cannot brook indefinite delay, and that if he succeeds in holding up progress long enough there will be a widespread outbreak of violence with which we should have to cope. He may then calculate that if we succeed in putting out Congress we will give him Pakistan, while if on the other hand chaotic conditions result for a considerable period the Muslims in majority areas may be able to help themselves to some sort of *de facto* Pakistan. I am doubtful if the League has as yet any plans for effective action but I think that Jinnah counts on trouble to break out in order to give him his chance.[74]

The guess presented here regarding the real reason behind the League's decision to withdraw its acceptance of the Cabinet Mission's long-term plan (16 May 1947) may or may not be accurate. This much, however, is absolutely certain. The change in the League's attitude was not the result of pique. As Colville has pointed out, if pique was the reason, the League's rejection would have come much earlier, regardless of whether the pique was caused by the British refusal to form an Interim Government with the cooperation of the League, without the Congress, or by the Congress stand on the issue of the formation of Groups of provinces. To turn first to the latter, as shown earlier, Nehru, in his supposedly objectionable statements, had not said anything that the Congress Working Committee had not said before 6 June 1946, when the League decided to accept the Cabinet Mission's long-term plan in the first instance or even later but before 25 June 1946, when the League decided to accept also the short-term plan of the Mission relating to the formation of the Interim Government. There was also no valid ground for the League to claim that the British had gone back on their commitment to go ahead with the formation of the Interim Government without the Congress. The Viceroy had made it clear to Jinnah as early as 25 June 1946, after receiving Azad's letter of that date to the effect that the Congress, although rejecting the plan about the formation of the Interim Government contained in the Cabinet Mission's short-term plan announced on 16 June 1946, had accepted the Cabinet Mission's long-term plan (16 May 1946). It was the latter which torpedoed the League's game plan of entering the Interim Government without the Congress, in the process turning the very paragraph formulated to help the League into an obstacle in its path. Jinnah must have realized this, but apparently thought that the best bet for the League was to refuse to admit it and to go on persisting with its own interpretation of the Congress stand, and using it to pressure the Viceroy into inviting the League to join the Interim Government without the Congress. In spite of his known sympathy with Jinnah, however, Wavell refused to oblige. He underlined the absurdity of the League's stand in his letter to Sir F. Burrows, Governor of Bengal, on 19 July 1946, at the same time mentioning the fact that he had informed Jinnah on the evening of 25 June itself (before the latter got his Working Committee to accept the short-term plan) of the change in the situation as a result of the unexpected Congress stand:

Paragraph 8 of the Statement of the 16th June was put in deliberately to safeguard the Muslim League since Congress had stated in writing that they considered the two plans (the short-term one and the long-term one) to hang together and that they would either accept or reject both. When the Congress turned round and accepted the long-term scheme of May 16th while rejecting the proposals for the Interim Government in the Statement of June 16th, we found ourselves compelled by paragraph 8 of the Statement of June 16th to make a fresh attempt to negotiate an agreement with both major parties about an Interim Government. I do not think there can be two opinions about the meaning of paragraph 8 of the 16th June, and that it compelled us to consult both main parties in any fresh attempt when both had accepted the Statement of May 16th.[75]

If in spite of all this if Jinnah went on accusing both the Viceroy and the Congress leadership of bad faith and on that basis advising a drastic change in the League's strategy, he must have had some weighty reason for doing so and not just pique. In any case, as befits a great leader, Jinnah never adopted a political line out of pique; his whole political life bears testimony to this. Every move in that career was well-calculated and the prevailing situation at any given time and the likely outcome of a fresh move from the point of view of the League's interests were fully taken into account before a decision was made or recommended. Colville has made one guess regarding the cause of the change in the League's strategy in the last week of July 1946. Most of the historians and journalists who have so far written on this topic have repeated the cause publicly aired by the senior British officials as well as the League leaders, namely the attitude of the Congress towards the compulsory grouping of provinces, which, for the League, was the most prized element in the Cabinet Mission Plan (16 May 1946) and the intemperate utterances of the Congress leadership, particularly those of Nehru, on that subject. Colville's estimate, which has so far escaped all attention, provides a fresh avenue for exploring the real cause for the change in the League's strategy in the last week of July 1946. To the present writer it seems that while it may be going too far to say that the motivation of the League behind the change in its strategy was 'to embroil

Government and Congress in a first-class row', the rest of Colville's conjecture is based on a correct analysis of the developing political situation in India at that time and not on pure imagination. The exchanges between the Viceroy and the Secretary of State during the second half of 1946, extensively covered in vol. 8 of the *Transfer of Power*, leave no doubt about the ever-present possibility of a conflict between the British authorities and the Congress, increasingly under pressure from its left wing, headed by Jayaprakash Narayan, released from a long spell in prison in the middle of April 1946 and being hailed everywhere in India as a national hero. He was going around the country passionately pleading for the termination of all negotiations with the Government and advocating a recourse to a struggle for the achievement of independence. There were also signs of growing tension among industrial workers. Indeed, at one time the political situation appeared so serious to Wavell that he decided to push forward his favourite 'Breakdown Plan', which provided for the immediate withdrawal of British forces from Congress provinces and their stationing for the time being in the Muslim provinces, both in the west and in the east. In such a situation, especially after the disappearance of the prospect of the League entering the Interim Government without the Congress, it might not have been unnatural for a leader in Jinnah's position to think of advising the League to revise its stand on the Cabinet Mission Plan (16 May) and prepare for Direct Action at a suitable moment in order to achieve its goal.

We must also remember that, just like Gandhi, Jinnah, too, always had his fingers firmly on the pulse of his flock, and he must have had the feeling that his thinking at that moment was in line with the wishes of most of the other leading figures of the League, including the members of its Working Committee and Council. Contemporary evidence suggests that this had indeed been the case both when the League had decided in favour of accepting the Cabinet Mission Plan and when it decided to withdraw its acceptance. Thus, on the earlier occasion, the *Times of India* (Bombay), in its issue of 5 June 1996 flashed the news regarding the mood of the League's Working Committee as assessed on 4 June, under banner headlines: 'League Reactions Favourable. Proposals said to contain germs of Pakistan'. The next day (6 June 1946) its headlines were: 'League May Accept

Cabinet Scheme. Reported Support at Council Meeting'. Identical reports were published by the *Pioneer* (Lucknow) on the same dates. On the later occasion, the mood both in the Working Committee and the Council, because, of the reasons explained earlier, had evidently changed and, as on the previous occasion, this had become evident before the resolution of the rejection of the Cabinet Mission Plan had been adopted or even moved for consideration. Thus, while the resolution was adopted on 29 July 1946, the *Times of India* reported on the same date the substance of the proceedings of the League's Council on the previous day under the headlines: 'League may reject long-term Plan. Majority view favours 'Back to Pakistan'. Plea for Direct Action and Title Renunciation. Mr Jinnah Bitter against Mission and Congress'. A similar report was published by the *Pioneer* on the same date under the headlines: 'League Working Committee Drafting 'Rejection' Resolution. Text based on Council Speeches against Cabinet Mission Proposals'.

Whatever the cause, the significance of the League's decision to free itself from the commitment to join the Constituent Assembly as per the Cabinet Mission Plan of 16 May, and to resort to Direct Action for achieving Pakistan cannot be over-estimated. For it meant that the League had decided not to remain content with 'the substance and foundation of Pakistan', which it had justifiedly seen in the Cabinet Mission Plan of 16 May, with the hope of manipulating future developments to its advantage by establishing itself as the dominant party in the Interim Government, but to resort to Direct Action for speeding up the establishment of Pakistan. In spite of the ensuing twists and turns, depending on the exigencies of the situation, and the calculation of the League's interests, Jinnah firmly adhered to that decision and never wavered in his determination to ensure the formation of Pakistan as expeditiously as possible. This is fully substantiated by his role in the political developments that followed.

VII

While the League was considering a change in its strategy for expediting the creation of Pakistan, the British were engaged in reformulating their plan for the setting up of the Interim

Government. After the failure of the first such plan at the end of June 1946, a caretaker Interim Government had been set up consisting purely of officials. It was soon realized in British decision-making circles that in view of the growing political and communal tension in India, such a government must be replaced as soon as possible by an Interim Government consisting fully of leaders representing the various shades of political opinion in India, particularly those from the Congress and the League. After a good deal of exchanges between New Delhi and London (where the members of the Cabinet Mission had returned on 29 June 1946, but continued to play an important role in the Cabinet consultations on India policy), it was decided to approach the Presidents of both the Congress and the League for their co-operation for the formation of an Interim Government on a new basis. That basis was spelled out by the Viceroy's identical, confidential letters to Nehru and Jinnah on 22 July. The new Interim Government was to consist of 14 members. Out of them six (including one Scheduled Caste representative) were to be nominated by the Congress, five by the League, and three were to be representatives of minorities, out of which one would be a Sikh, by the Viceroy. The Viceroy's letter went on to make it clear that it would not be open either to the Congress or the League to object to the names submitted by the other party, provided they were accepted by the Viceroy. As for the distribution of portfolios, that was to be decided by the Viceroy after the parties had agreed to enter the Government and submitted the lists of their nominees. The Congress and the League would each have 'an equitable share' of the most important portfolios. The Viceroy would welcome a convention, as freely offered by the Congress, that major communal issues could only be decided by the assent of both the major parties, but he took care to point out that he had never thought that it was essential to make this a formal condition, since in fact a coalition government could function on no other basis. As for the status of the Interim Government, the Viceroy just mentioned that the assurances that he had given to Azad on 30 May 1946 would stand.[76]

In this letter the Viceroy had made it clear that the Interim Government would not have the same powers as a Dominion Government, as the constitutional position in the two cases was very different, but had gone on to affirm that it would be his endeavour to ensure that it should have the greatest possible freedom in dealing with the day-to-day administration of the country and be able to prepare for complete freedom after the framing of the new Constitution.[77]

The initial response from both Nehru and Jinnah was quite negative. Nehru's main concern was the question of the status and powers of the Interim Government. He was not at all satisfied with the terms of the Viceroy's letter to Azad on 30 May. The Congress, Nehru wrote to Wavell on 23 July 1946, had always attached the greatest importance to the 'independence in action' of any Provisional Government to be formed at the Centre, meaning thereby that the Government should have perfect freedom and that the Viceroy should function only as a constitutional head. Once that matter was settled, 'other relatively minor issues' would not offer much difficulty. The question of the status and powers of the Interim Government had, therefore, to be decided first in unambiguous language and only after that would it be appropriate to take up other questions for consideration. On these grounds Nehru declined to cooperate in any way in the formation of the Interim Government under the conditions suggested by the Viceroy.[78] Wavell was quite enraged by Nehru's reply, which he considered as symbolic of the Congress determination to emerge as 'the only effective power in India'. Indeed, he considered it a challenge to British authority which, in his opinion, had to be met. For, he reminded the authorities in London, the British had 'obligations in honour not to hand over the Muslims and other minorities to the unchecked domination of Congress and our interests demand that we should not surrender tamely'. As far as Wavell was concerned, he was thinking of giving a piece of his mind to Nehru during their next meeting fixed for 29 July.[79] The authorities in London, however, took a different view and advised him to deal with Nehru in a friendly way, though without conceding his demand on the question of the status and powers of the Interim Government. According to them, it was customary for Indian leaders to make tall demands, while negotiating with the British in order to 'squeeze some further concessions' from the latter.[80] Wavell's talk with Nehru, therefore, passed off without any fireworks, with both sides only ventilating their known positions.[81]

Jinnah replied to Wavell's invitation on 31 July 1946, two days after the League Council had reversed its earlier decision to join the Constituent Assembly and decided instead to resort to Direct Action for achieving its goal. He pointed out several defects in Wavell's new scheme for an Interim Government from the League's point of view, in particular the removal of parity between Hindus and Muslims as also between the League and the Congress and the opening up of the possibility of the Congress nominating a Muslim member from its own quota and the nomination of the representatives of the other minorities by the Viceroy without any consultation with the League. On these grounds, Jinnah conveyed to the Viceroy, there was no chance of the League's Working Committee accepting the latter's proposals.[82]

Even before Wavell could convey to London the gist of Jinnah's response to his letter of 22 July, the British Prime Minister, taking account of the League's Council's decision of 29 July, had concluded that the League was not likely to agree to join the Interim Government. He, therefore, thought that Wavell should see Jinnah once more and try to persuade him to agree to join the Interim Government, but if he did not succeed in his endeavour he should go ahead with the formation of both the Interim Government and the Constituent Assembly with the cooperation of the Congress alone.[83] Wavell, however, was of the opinion that it would not be advisable for him to send for Jinnah immediately and that in the then existing situation it was better from the British point of view to place responsibility on the Congress for satisfying the League. 'If I send for Jinnah at once,' he wrote further, 'it will be regarded as a panicky reaction to a threat and will put up Jinnah's stock and increase his intransigence.'[84] The authorities in London, therefore, decided not to press the Viceroy to see Jinnah and advised him to go ahead with the formation of the Interim Government with the cooperation of the Congress.[85] The upshot of all this was Wavell's letter to Nehru dated 6 August 1946, inviting him, as President of the Congress, to submit to the former 'proposals for the formation of an Interim Government'. Wavell made it clear that the status of the Interim Government would remain the same as indicated to Nehru earlier, that is, as per the assurance contained in Wavell's letter to the then Congress President, Azad, on 30 May 1946. Wavell also mentioned that it was for Nehru to decide whether he should discuss with Jinnah the question of the League joining the Interim Government before making his proposals for the formation of the Interim Government. Wavell further added that if the two were able to reach an agreement, he would naturally be delighted; for a coalition government could 'best direct effectively the destinies of India at this critical juncture'.[86]

Nehru now conveniently forgot what he had written earlier (on 23 July 1946) to Wavell regarding the inability of the Congress to agree to cooperate in the formation of an Interim Government if its status and powers were to be as per Wavell's letter to Azad on 30 May. Perhaps, this was because earlier, he had conveyed only his own estimate of the likely reaction of the Congress to the Viceroy's proposal, as the latter had asked him to keep the proposal completely confidential. Discussion with Gandhi and the Working Committee, however, led to the adoption of a different approach. It is, of course, quite possible that a positive approach now was the result of the changed context created by the League's resolutions and the new procedure that was being followed by inviting Nehru to make proposals for the formation of the Interim Government, foreshadowing the dominant position of the Congress in the Interim Government.

Whatever that may have been, after the Viceroy made his offer to Nehru public, the latter immediately got in touch with Jinnah in order to seek his cooperation, first through correspondence (13 to 15 August) and then through a face-to-face meeting (15 August), but neither produced any positive result. Jinnah's attitude was made clear in his reply dated 15 August to Nehru's dated 13 August. Referring to the Viceroy's invitation to Nehru to make proposals for the formation of the Interim Government, Jinnah wrote: 'If this means that the Viceroy has commissioned you to form an Executive Council of the Governor-General, and has already agreed to accept and act upon your advice, and proceed to constitute his Executive accordingly, it is not possible for me to accept such a position on that basis.'[87] On Nehru assuring Jinnah that he had not yet had a detailed discussion with Wavell and was very keen to secure the League's cooperation before making any proposals to the Viceroy and to see Jinnah with this purpose in mind, the latter agreed to meet him. The meeting between the two was held in Bombay on 15 August. As Nehru informed Wavell three days later, he had conveyed to Jinnah assurances about the Congress attitude towards the functioning of the Constituent Assembly. He particularly mentioned that no major communal issue would be settled without the agreement between the main political parties. He also clarified that the Congress was not opposed to the grouping of provinces, but only wanted that no province should be made a member of a Group without its consent. As for the composition of the Interim Government, he mentioned the Viceroy's formula according to which the League would have five members and assured Jinnah that whatever names were suggested by the League would be accepted by the Congress. Upon Jinnah raising the point about the inclusion of a Nationalist Muslim in the Interim Government, Nehru remarked that he did not see how the League could object to it if the seat came from the Congress quota. However, in spite of these clarifications and assurances Jinnah remained firm on the League's decision not to cooperate with the formation of the Interim Government and suggested that it might be better to hold up all action in this regard for six months. Nehru conveyed to Wavell that his impression was that Jinnah had gone further than he had intended and was now at a loss how to get out.[88]

While, because of a wholly non-cooperative response from Jinnah and the desire of the British Cabinet to install an Interim Government as soon as possible in view of the political situation then prevailing in India, Nehru had been formally asked to submit proposals in this regard, Wavell was not at all happy with the prospect of having to deal with a purely Congress-dominated Government. Indeed, ever since the idea of the formation of an Interim Government was mooted in the Cabinet Mission Plan of 16 May, he had been dreading such a prospect. In a confidential note addressed to Pethick Lawrence, who was going to address a press conference on 17 May, Wavell stressed that the former must remain 'entirely firm and definite' on two points: one, that the Interim Government must function within the parameters of the Constitution (Act of 1935) then in force till a new one was framed, and, two, that there must be 'the strongest possible Muslim representation in the Interim Government', so that it could not be entirely controlled by the Congress. Stressing the latter point, Wavell wrote further: 'I am sorry for being so persistent about this, but from my point of view it is absolutely vital. I am going to have an almost impossible task anyhow during the Interim period, but if the Central Government is going to be controlled by one party, with no check on it, the situation will be impossible indeed'.[89]

Under pressure of circumstances and the Cabinet's insistence the Viceroy had reluctantly agreed in August 1946 to ask Nehru to submit proposals for the formation of the Interim Government, but he kept on urging him on every possible occasion to somehow persuade the League also to come in. The happenings on 16 August, the day observed by the Muslim League all over India as the Direct Action Day, provided him with a special opportunity for stressing this point. While the celebration of the day passed of peacefully in most parts of India (including Sind, which had a League Ministry in office and had, like the Bengal Ministry, declared 16 August as a public holiday), Calcutta burst out in flames. As is well known, Hindu–Muslim clashes began on that day on an unprecedented scale and continued for about five days, resulting, according to a conservative official estimate, in 4,400 dead, 16,000 injured and 100,000 homeless. Not surprisingly, they coined the name of the 'Great Calcutta Killings', a phrase coined by the *Statesman* (Calcutta), then owned by the British. The League leadership in Bengal, particularly Husain Shaheed Suhrawardy, the head of the League ministry there, had contributed significantly towards them by fomenting communal hatred against the Congress and the Hindus for quite some time before it and encouraging anti-social Muslim groups in the Calcutta underworld, of which he had long since been a patron. However, sensing that trouble was in the offering, the Hindus, too, had prepared themselves fairly well for retaliation, and the Muslims being in a minority in Calcutta, they suffered larger casualties than Hindus.[90]

Now Wavell began to pursue his main objective of not letting the Congress alone dominate the Interim Government by somehow also bringing in the Muslim League. The greater part of his interview with Nehru on 18 August, was taken up with the discussion on this point, with the two interlocuters taking opposite sides. Pleading for a further approach to Jinnah, Wavell pointed out that it was just possible that Jinnah might feel more inclined to agreeing to the League joining the Interim Government in view of the latest happenings. He further argued that a very grave responsibility would lie on the British and the Congress if they did not make every possible effort to secure Jinnah's cooperation and reminded Nehru of the latter's own recent assessment that Jinnah was looking for a way out. Nehru, however, remained unmoved by these arguments and pointed out that the events of the past forty-eight hours (i.e. the Calcutta killings) had made it even more difficult for him to approach Jinnah. On the other hand, in Nehru's view there was no chance of Jinnah agreeing and he also stated that the Congress would certainly not agree to give up the nomination of a non-League Muslim. An approach to Jinnah under these circumstances would mean further delay. The discussion ended with the agreement that Nehru would consult his Working Committee and inform Wavell the next day.[91] Nehru wrote to the latter on 19 August that he had consulted his Working Committee and that their reaction to the proposal about making a fresh approach to Jinnah was identical with his own. Recalling the circumstances under which he had agreed to shoulder the responsibility of making proposals for the formation of the Interim Government, Nehru remarked that the Viceroy's new proposal would change the whole approach to the problem and put an end to the responsibility that the Congress had undertaken at the latter's instance. He also pointed out that in view of the recent happenings, such a step 'far from leading to harmony, will be misconstrued and lead to a contrary result'.[92] In spite of this, Wavell again began his discussion with Nehru on 22 August—held mainly for considering the Congress proposals for the membership of the Interim Government, particularly relating to the Muslim seats—by saying that 'our whole object must be directed towards an eventual coalition with the Muslim League, and that in considering the present proposals we must bear that in mind'.[93] He also conveyed to Nehru Azad's view that he (Wavell) should make an indirect approach to Jinnah on this point. Nehru's comment on this was that the Congress was always in touch with the League through mutual friends and that he did not think it would be suitable for the Viceroy to make an indirect approach at that point of time.[94] Nehru followed this up with a letter to Wavell on the same day, reiterating the Congress position more strongly than ever before on the issue of a coalition with the League. 'We have been anxious,' said Nehru, 'to have a coalition with the Muslim League and we shall continue to work to that end. But I want to make it clear that our idea of a coalition does not mean a submission to the demands or the peculiar ways which the League has adopted.' A coalition, he further explained, could only come into existence when the League accepted the position that it could nominate five persons to fill up the seats allotted to it in the Interim Government, but could not interfere with the names suggested by the Congress, including that of a nationalist Muslim, for filling up the seats allotted to it.[95] Nevertheless, when Wavell had another interview with Nehru the next day he began the discussion by remarking, among other things, that he was 'quite convinced that without the cooperation of the Muslim League there would be no chance of a united India or of a peaceful transfer of power. Nor would the States be likely to negotiate freely with a one-party Government.'[96]

Apart from the problem of making a fresh approach to Jinnah, there were certain differences between Wavell and Nehru regarding particular persons to be appointed to the Interim Government, particularly for seats earmarked for the Muslim League. Wavell would have preferred all those seats to be left vacant, to be filled up when the League agreed to come in, but Nehru was strongly opposed to it. According to him, while the country required the installation of a strong and effective government, the implementation of Wavell's suggestion would weaken the Interim Government at the very start and create an atmosphere of instability around it. Finally, Nehru had his way although he had in the process to accept Wavell's advice regarding one or two names. An announcement was made on 24 August that an Interim Government was going to be set up soon with the following members: Jawaharlal Nehru, Sardar Vallabhbhai Patel, Rajendra Prasad, M. Asaf Ali, C. Rajagopalachari, Sarat Chandra Bose, Jagjivan Ram, John Matthai, Sardar Baldev Singh, Shafaat Ahmad Khan, Syed Ali Zaheer, and C.H. Bhabha. The names of two more Muslim members were to be announced later. In his broadcast on the same day Wavell underlined the fact that with the decision to shortly install an Interim Government, a very momentous step forward had been taken on India's road to freedom. Addressing those who might not be happy with the way in which that Government was proposed to be formed, he said that no one could be sorrier than himself for the failure to secure a coalition government because of the League's decision not to join it in spite of the assurances given to it. He, however, continued to be as convinced as ever that such a government, having in it the representatives of both the Congress and the League, was the need of the hour. Adding that this view was also shared by Nehru and his colleagues, he affirmed that both of them would continue with the efforts to persuade the League to join the Interim Government.[97]

It is not known what effort, if any, Nehru made in that direction. However, so far as Wavell was concerned it became his chief preoccupation till his objective of bringing the League representatives into the Interim Government was fulfilled. The very next day after his broadcast he left for Calcutta and came back to Delhi after a whirlwind tour of the city on 26 August. As he mentioned in a telegram sent to Pethick Lawrence the same evening, he returned from Calcutta fully convinced that there was 'no hope at all of avoiding further and more serious rioting in Calcutta and elsewhere in India' unless there was some settlement at the Centre. According to him, there were certain leaders in the League who wanted to come to a settlement if possible but Jinnah appeared to be 'still quite intransigent'. Wavell was particularly impressed by the view of Nazimuddin, the former head of the League ministry in Bengal and who still enjoyed Jinnah's trust, namely, that the League might consider rescinding the last Bombay resolution of its Council if either the Congress or the British Government could unequivocally confirm that provinces could not opt out of a Group except under the provision made for it in the Cabinet Delegation's statement of 16 May.[98] Next day, Wavell had an interview with Gandhi and Nehru and urged upon them the urgency of satisfying the League on the issue of the grouping of provinces, thereby ensuring its joining the Interim Government. He also went on to say that until they did so he could not undertake the responsibility of calling together the Constituent Assembly and handed over to them a draft statement which he wanted the Congress to make in this regard:

> The Congress are prepared in the interest of communal harmony to accept the intention of the Statement of May 16th that Provinces cannot exercise any option affecting their membership of the Section or of the Groups if formed until the decision contemplated in paragraph 19 (VIII) of the Statement of the 16th May is taken by the new Legislature after the new constitutional arrangements have come into operation and the first general elections have been held.

This was followed by a heated discussion between Wavell, on

the one side, and Gandhi and Nehru, on the other. Nehru described all the build up of expected communal trouble by Wavell as just bullying on the part of the Muslim League. Wavell must have mentioned the danger of a lot of bloodshed if the Congress and the League did not come to a settlement, but that did not unnerve Gandhi. For Wavell recorded Gandhi as having said that 'if a blood-bath was necessary, it would come about in spite of non-violence'. Wavell was apparently shocked at such words coming from Gandhi,[99] but Gandhi, as he said in his letter to Wavell dated 28 August 1946, only wanted to convey to the latter that the Congress could neither impose its will on the warring elements in India through the use of British arms nor could it be expected to bend itself and adopt what it considered a wrong course because of 'the brutal exhibition recently witnessed in Bengal'. 'Such submissions,' he added, 'would lead to an encouragement and repetition of such tragedies.' In conclusion, he wanted Wavell either to trust the Congress Government which he had already announced or reconsider his decision as Gandhi had already suggested during his last interview.[100] Nehru sent Wavell a similar reply on the same date after consulting the Working Committee, at the latter's insistence: 'To change our declared policy, which is generally acknowledged to be fair, because of intimidation, is surely not the way to peace but is an encouragement for further intimidation and violence.'[101]

Wavell was quite perturbed by the prospect of having a Congress Government at the Centre and went on wishing for the League, too, to join it. As he wrote to Pethick Lawrence on 28 August:

> I must . . . tell you frankly that I fear that the actions of this new Government may frequently infringe my sense of fairness and justice; and I shall therefore have either to consent to something which my conscience will not approve; or by refusing consent, to bring about a crisis with the Congress party, which the H.M.G. is not likely to desire. . . .
>
> If the new Government had been a coalition of the League and Congress these difficulties might not have arisen so acutely, and I shall continue to do my very best to secure such a coalition. . . .[102]

Indeed, Wavell was so keen to bring the League into the Interim Government that he was preparing to talk tough with the Congress leaders so as to persuade them to accept the compulsory grouping of the provinces, as demanded by the League, and, if the Congress did not fall in line, to even indefinitely postpone the installation of the Interim Government. He was, however, helpless in the face of the British Cabinet's clear disapproval of such a course. The latter, of course, sympathized with Wavell's apprehension about the danger of intensified communal trouble unless the Congress and the League came to a settlement and the need, therefore, to do one's best to bring about such a settlement, but they refused to countenance the measures that Wavell was thinking about. After discussing the Indian political situation with Attlee, Pethick Lawrence wrote to Wavell on 28 August, asking him 'not to take any steps which are likely to result in a breach with the Congress without prior consultation with us, as the consequences of such a step would also be very grave'.[103] Two days later he again wrote to Wavell after discussion with Attlee, imploring him to keep in mind 'the paramount necessity of securing that the Interim Government does now take office'. In support of this view, he mentioned that the formation of the Interim Government having been already announced, any further delay in its installation would not only cause an offence in India, but also damage the image of Britain in the eyes of the world at large and would indeed be treated as a breach of faith.[104] Wavell had no choice but to order the installation of the Interim Government on 2 September 1946, with the same members as announced on 24 August and with Nehru as its Vice-President and the Viceroy as President.

VIII

The question of the League's participation in that Government still remained wide open. It continued to be on the top of Wavell's agenda, but Nehru, too, was in a cooperative frame of mind on this issue provided, of course, there was no interference with the right of the Congress to select its own nominees, including a nationalist Muslim. In his letter to Wavell dated 1 September, suggesting the allocation of various portfolios to the members of the Interim Government, he wrote:

> As we have made it clear, we shall welcome the cooperation of the Muslim League in the provisional Governments. If they so choose they can nominate five members of the Government. When they decide to do so five of our members will retire in their favour, and a reshuffling of

the portfolios will take place so as to give them an equitable share in them.[105]

In his broadcast as Vice-President of the Interim Government on 7 September, Nehru made it a point to adopt a conciliatory attitude on the part of the Congress towards some of the matters of serious concern to the Muslim League regarding the formation of sections and groups in the Constituent Assembly and the method of the latter's functioning in general. As he put it:

There has been much heated argument about sections and groupings in the Constituent Assembly. We are perfectly prepared for, and have accepted, the position of sitting in sections, which will consider the question of formation of groups. I should like to make it clear, on behalf of my colleagues and myself, that we do not look upon the Constituent Assembly as an arena for conflict or for the forcible imposition of one viewpoint over another. That would not be the way to build up a contented and united India. We seek agreed and integrated solutions with the largest measure of goodwill behind them.[106]

However, Nehru was not prepared to go to the extent of accepting the compulsory grouping of provinces as demanded by the League and strongly supported by Wavell. Indeed, the latter got the impression after an interview with Nehru at that time that the latter did not want to secure the League's cooperation.[107] However, that did not deter Wavell from pursuing his objective of getting the League into the Interim Government as soon as possible. Encouraged by Jinnah's statement during an interview with a representative of the *Daily Mail*, that if he were invited by the British Government to London to start a new series of conferences on an equal footing with others, he would accept, and Suhrawardy's statement in London that if Jinnah felt assured that there was a spirit of cooperation on the part of the Congress side he might agree to accept less than his demands at that time, Wavell thought that it was time to renew his efforts for a Congress–League settlement. 'I am sure,' he telegraphed to Pethick Lawrence on 10 September, 'that now is the time to send for Jinnah and try to get a settlement especially as the Congress seem to aim at consolidating their power and disregarding the League altogether. The longer we wait the more difficult a settlement is likely to be.'[108] In his letter to Pethick Lawrence sent on the same day, he further elucidated the main source of his concern, namely the Congress determination to utilize the League's absence from the

Interim Government to consolidate its power, something which he thoroughly disliked:

I am afraid the Congress policy is to consolidate itself in power, to use British assistance in putting down riots from day-to-day, and perhaps if necessary to buy off the Muslims at a lower price when we finally go. I am quite clear that we must not allow the Congress virtually to monopolise power under the protection of the British regime, and we must continue our efforts to get a coalition.[109]

Wavell had obviously made up his mind to send for Jinnah and impress upon him the desirability of the League joining the Interim Government, but he thought it proper to sound Nehru about it before actually doing so. This he did on 11 September, immediately after a meeting of the Cabinet, telling Nehru that he wished to send for Jinnah and make another attempt to get him both into the Constituent Assembly and the Interim Government and went on to add that Jinnah was likely to ask for certain assurances regarding the working of the Constituent Assembly, particularly relating to sections. Nehru, however, expressed the inability of the Congress to provide any such assurance, and in that connection mentioned that the Congress was bound by its assurances to the provinces, particularly Assam. He also minimized the problem of communal trouble and asserted that the police could easily suppress it. When, however, Wavell differed from Nehru on this and continued to stress the danger on that account, Nehru, perhaps out of exasperation, remarked: 'If you want to see Jinnah, I can't prevent you.'[110]

The Viceroy immediately approached Jinnah, and their meeting took place on 16 September. Both exchanged their views on what had happened recently, without any commitment for the future, but it is clear that Jinnah was happy at this initiative by Wavell in restarting the conversation with him. 'Jinnah,' recorded Wavell, 'was quite friendly throughout, was polite and much less discursive than he often is. In fact he was at his best, as I have known him on one or two occasions before.'[111] This was followed by a series of talks, Wavell always trying to impress upon Jinnah that in its own interests the League would be well advised to join the Interim Government. Jinnah, being an astute politician, of course realized this himself, but he did not show his hand to Wavell in order to let Wavell have the satisfaction of feeling that Jinnah was yielding to his persuasion; this was similar to what he had done in his talks with Linlithgow—when the latter had repeatedly advised him to come forward with his own 'constructive' plan instead of standing on a purely negative platform—before the adoption of the Pakistan Resolution by the League in March 1940. The record of all their talks, as prepared by Wavell, is available and shows how persistently Wavell sought to put before Jinnah the advisability of the League joining the Interim Government in its own interest.[112] Jinnah mentioned several points on which he would like to be satisfied before going before his Working Committee with a proposal in favour of the League joining the Interim Government, at Wavell's suggestion and submitted a list of nine such points in writing. They included such demands as the Congress not including a Muslim in its quota of six members; setting up of a convention that on major communal issues no decision should be arrived at if the majority of Hindu or Muslim members were not in its favour; the position of the Vice-President of the Interim Government to be made rotational; the League to be consulted in future on all appointments of the representatives of minorities in the Interim Government; the most important portfolios should be equally distributed between the Congress and the League; none of the arrangements mentioned above should be changed or modified unless both the major parties—the League and the Congress—agreed; and last, but not the least, the problem of the settlement of the long-term Plan should stand over until a better and more conducive atmosphere was created and an agreement had been reached on the points stated earlier and after the Interim Government had been reformed and finally set up.[113] On some of these points Wavell expressed his inability to agree. For instance, he pointed out in his reply to Jinnah that each party must be free to nominate its own representatives, thus turning down Jinnah's demand against the inclusion of a Muslim in the Congress quota. Regarding Jinnah's demand for a convention on the procedure to be followed in dealing with major communal issues, the Viceroy pointed out that in a coalition government such matters should not be decided by vote but by general consensus. He also rejected the demand for a rotational Vice-President and suggested instead that a League representative could be appointed as Vice-Chairman of the Coordination Committee of the Cabinet. On the other hand, he agreed that in filling up future vacancies of members from the minority communities, both the Congress and the League would be consulted and that all the arrangements listed earlier would not be changed or modified without the agreement of both the parties. He also assured Jinnah that the most important portfolios would be equally distributed between the Congress and the League. Wavell's answer to the last point raised by Jinnah was most significant for the future: 'Since the basis for participation in the Cabinet is of course acceptance of the Statement of the 16 May, I assume that the League Council will meet at a very early date to reconsider its Bombay resolution [withdrawing its earlier acceptance of that Statement].'[114] This meant that Wavell was not making a reconsideration of the Bombay resolution a pre-condition for the League joining the Interim Government. This was an important strategic victory for Jinnah, who was obviously interested in securing a foothold in the Interim Government without making any commitment regarding the future which might in any way come in the way of the early achievement of his cherished goal: Pakistan.

It is really surprising that the significance of the last point in the exchange of letters between Wavell and Jinnah completely escaped Nehru whom the former had consulted before sending his reply to Jinnah. As Wavell informed Pethick Lawrence on 4 October, the only point about which Nehru was really bothered was the suggestion for making the Vice-Presidentship of the Interim Government alternative or rotational. Wavell had actually anticipated this and accepted Nehru's view on that point without any difficulty.[115] After receiving the text of the Wavell–Jinnah correspondence on the nine points raised by the latter, Nehru did write to Wavell mentioning his thoughts on some of the questions dealt with, but did not mention at all either the ninth point raised by Jinnah or Wavell's reply to it.[116] The only other contentious point was about the Congress not being allowed to nominate a Muslim out of its quota but, although Wavell had more than once pressed the Congress to concede this point, if not in theory, at any rate in practice, he had finally accepted the view that each party must remain free to nominate whomsoever it wished to do out of its quota. As Wavell recorded after his interview with Jinnah on 2 October, he had told the latter that he had failed to secure any concession from the Congress over the nationalist Muslim issue and that he could not press it further on this matter.

In spite of this, however, Wavell strongly urged Jinnah to decide in favour of the League joining the Interim Government in its own interest, showing how keenly he was pursuing this point. As Wavell himself recorded:

I said that it was in the obvious interest of the Muslim League to come into the Government at once and unconditionally. If the Congress has, as Mr Jinnah seems to suspect, the object of disrupting the Muslim League, this is the most effective way to defeat it and to protect Muslim interests. The Muslim League, with the prestige and influence of being in the Central Government, will be in a far stronger position than they are now; if Congress do nominate a nationalist Muslim, the League will be not merely on a parity with the caste Hindus in the Congress, but will [also] out-number them.[117]

About this time the Nawab of Bhopal, at the instance of Gandhi,[118] arranged a meeting between Jinnah and Nehru in order to thrash out the terms of a Congress–League settlement. For that purpose he sent to Jinnah a formula signed by Gandhi that might work as a basis for such a settlement.[119] A meeting between Jinnah and Nehru did take place on 5 October, but there was no success in bringing about a settlement. According to the formula, the Congress was prepared to accept the Muslim League at that time as 'the authoritative representative of the overwhelming majority of the Muslims of India'. Gandhi's formula was as follows:

Congress does not challenge, and accepts that the Muslim League now is the authoritative representative of the overwhelming majority of the Muslims of India. As such, and according to democratic principles, they alone have today the unquestionable right to represent the Muslims of India. But the Congress cannot agree that any restriction or limitation should be put upon Congress to choose such representatives as they think proper, from amongst the members of Congress as their representatives.[120]

While talking to Jinnah the next day Nehru agreed with the substance of the idea contained in this draft, but put it in a slightly different way, adding these words to Gandhi's formula: 'provided that for identical reasons, the League recognizes Congress as the authoritative organization representing all non-Muslims and all such Muslims as have thrown in their lot with Congress'. Further, he put forward the view that all this was so self-evident that no agreement was required for this. Nehru also dealt with various other points raised by Jinnah at their meeting on the previous day. These points were almost identical with the nine points submitted by Jinnah to Wavell earlier and Nehru's comments on them, too, were the same as Wavell's, except in one respect. Unlike Wavell, Nehru expressed the hope that while deciding to join the Interim Government, the League's Working Committee would also decide 'simultaneously' to join the Constituent Assembly, or recommend to its Council to do so.[121] Apparently Nehru had by that time realized the importance of this point—something which he had missed while writing to Wavell after going through the texts of Jinnah's nine points and Wavell's reply.

In his reply to this letter from Nehru, Jinnah quoted the text of the formula signed by Gandhi, mentioned earlier, and refused to countenance any change or amendment and strongly objected to Nehru's remark that Gandhi's formula contained something which was so obvious that it need not require any agreement. 'I regret,' said Jinnah, 'that I cannot agree to any change, in language or otherwise, as it was the agreed basis of our discussion on other points: nor can I agree with you that no formula is necessary. It was signed by Mr Gandhi and accepted by me.'[122] When they had met on 5 October Nehru had told Jinnah that he and his colleagues (presumably members of the Congress Working Committee) had not accepted the formula signed by Gandhi. Nor had the meeting between Nehru and Jinnah been organized on that basis. Nehru added that he and his colleagues had been aware of the formula and, as conveyed to Jinnah during their meeting on 5 October, the Congress side was prepared to accept its substance. However, Gandhi's formula contained a further paragraph which Jinnah had not quoted in his letter. This additional paragraph, according to Nehru, ran as follows:

> It is understood that all ministers of the Interim Government will work as a team for the good of the whole of India and will never invoke the intervention of the Governor-General in any case.[123]

Jinnah in his rejoinder to Nehru dated 12 October flatly refused to accept this paragraph and argued that it was not a part of the original formula as drafted by Gandhi. The same, according to him, was also true of the Congress claim to represent all minorities. After dealing with some other points in dispute between him and Nehru, he closed their discussion with this remark at the end of his long letter: 'I deeply regret that we have failed to come to ar honourable agreement of our own, satisfactory to both parties.'[124]

It may not be out of place to mention here that Wavell, who was keeping a close tab over the Nehru–Jinnah negotiations, had been informed of their failure by the Nawab of Bhopal, a day earlier than Jinnah's final letter to Nehru closing the talks. Wavell's estimate was that the talks had failed because of differences between the Congress and the League mainly on two points. The first was the insistence of Nehru that Jinnah must accept the second paragraph of Gandhi's draft which Jinnah had excluded and which the Nawab of Bhopal told Wavell had been added by Gandhi at the instance of the Patel group in the Congress Working Committee. The next major difficulty was about the procedure to be followed in filling up any vacancy in the seats allotted to the minorities other than the Scheduled Castes. Wavell's undertaking was to consult both the main parties, but the Congress wanted the whole cabinet to be consulted. 'Jinnah,' wrote Wavell, 'naturally preferred my formula.' He further added: 'The division on this point as on the other was due to Congress determination to eliminate the Governor-General and to Jinnah's refusal to acquiesce in a position which would have meant the capture of complete power by the Congress.'[125]

Whatever that might have been, the failure of the Nehru–Jinnah talks opened the way for the League's entry into the Interim Government solely on the basis of an understanding with the Viceroy. A discussion between Jinnah and Wavell took place on 12 October on such issues as the distribution of portfolios between the Congress and the League, the right of the latter to include a member from the scheduled castes in the League's quota of seats in the Interim Government, and the nature of the letter to be sent by Jinnah to the Viceroy conveying the League's agreement to join the Interim Government.[126] This was followed the next day by the letter itself. Here Jinnah, as indicated by him to Wavell a day earlier, first conveyed to the latter, on behalf of the League's Working Committee, its disapproval of the basis and scheme of setting up the Interim Government as also of the decision in this regard and the arrangements thereof already made by the Viceroy, and then added that in spite of all that it had decided to join the Interim Government. Jinnah's explanation for that decision given in his letter leaves no doubt that it had been taken purely for tactical reasons, in the interests of the League, and not with a view to contributing in any way towards the implementation of the Cabinet Mission Plan of 16 May or in furthering Hindu–Muslim unity and facilitating India's advance towards complete independence on a united basis. Said Jinnah:

> . . . my Committee have, for various reasons, come to the conclusion that in the interests of Mussulmans and other communities it will be fatal to leave the entire field of administration of the Central Government in the hands of the Congress. Besides, you may be forced to have in your Interim Government Muslims who would not command the respect and confidence of Muslim India which would lead to very serious consequences; and, lastly, for other very weighty grounds and reasons, which are obvious and need not be mentioned, we have decided to nominate five [members] on behalf of the Muslim League in terms of your broadcast dated 24 August 1946 and your two letters to me dated 4 October 1946 and 12 October 1946, respectively, embodying clarifications and assurances.[127]

It, however, took another two weeks for the League representatives to be sworn in as members of the Interim Government. Jinnah forwarded the names of the League representatives soon enough, on 14 October—they being Liaquat Ali Khan (UP), I.I. Chundrigar (Bombay), Abdur Rah Nishtar (NWFP), Ghaznafar Ali Khan (Punjab), and Jogendra Nath Mandal (Bengal). The last one, belonging to a non-Muslim Scheduled Caste, had been nominated as a reply to the Congress, which had insisted on having a nationalist Muslim among its nominees. There was, however, one significant difference. While the nationalist Muslim nominated by the Congress was a member of that organization, Mandal did not belong to the League. During his meeting with Jinnah and Liaquat Ali Khan on the 13, Wavell had strongly advised the latter against nominating a non-Muslim member belonging to the Scheduled Caste, going to the extent of saying that it would be an embarrassment to him 'because it was obviously intended as a challenge to Congress, and would mean that the two parties entered the Coalition Government in a mood of antagonism', whereas he wished them to work together as a team in as much harmony as possible. But Jinnah had remained unmoved and told Wavell that while the League was anxious to cooperate with Wavell to the extent possible, it had its own interests to consider.[128] As, however, the Congress did not strongly oppose it, it did not become a cause for delay in swearing in the League members.

The chief causes of delay were the question of the distribution of portfolios among the Congress and League nominees and the ambiguity about the League's commitment regarding the future and its refusal to take immediate steps to ensure a review of its Council's decision in that regard taken in Bombay on 29 July 1946. On the latter issue, Wavell informed Nehru at their meeting on 14 October that he had explained to Jinnah that the League's entry into the Interim Government must be considered as conditional on its acceptance of the long-term plan of the Cabinet Mission. To that, Wavell added, Jinnah had replied that he was prepared to call a meeting of the League's Council in order to reverse its Bombay decision of 29 July 1946 as soon as he was fully satisfied that the Cabinet Mission's statement of 16 May 1946 was going to be observed.[129] As Nehru did not say anything further on that point, it did not become an insurmountable hurdle in the way of Wavell's plan to somehow ensure the League's entry into the Interim Government.

The question of the distribution of portfolios between the Congress and the League became more difficult. At their meeting on 14 October, Wavell raised that issue with Nehru. The former's view was that out of the four major portfolios, always in the past kept in charge of the British members of the Executive Council in the past—Defence, External Affairs, Home, and Finance—the League must be allotted one. As it was generally agreed that John Mathai should continue to be in-charge of Finance, the League must be given one of the remaining three portfolios. However, Wavell would have liked Baldev Singh to continue to be in-charge of Defence and assumed that Nehru would not like to be shifted from External Affairs. Nehru agreed with both the propositions, but pointed out that it would be very difficult to shift Patel from Home.[130] Nehru followed this up with a letter to Wavell on 15 October, expressing the view that at that moment 'to ask Sardar Patel to leave his portfolio would be an act of extreme discourtesy to him'. This would be particularly so in view of the fact that the official organ of the League had at that time made him a special target of attack. Nehru also mentioned that if Patel was asked to give up the Home portfolio he might not care to remain in the Government.[131] This was confirmed by Patel himself in the course of his conversation with Wavell on 16 October 1946. Upon Wavell mentioning to him that the League must be allotted one of the four major portfolios, Patel said immediately that he was quite prepared to give up the Home portfolio and leave the Government altogether.[132] Upon Wavell insisting upon a change in the Home portfolio from the hands of the Congress to the League, Nehru had warned him that if this did indeed take place Patel would leave the Government and that the rest of the Congressmen 'could not continue in the Government without him'.[133] Nehru had already suggested to Wavell that the portfolios of Finance and Commerce might be offered to the League.[134] In view of Nehru's stiff attitude on 24 October and the British Cabinet's determination to avoid a break with the Congress, Wavell had no option left but to accept Nehru's proposal. Jinnah was hesitant and felt very strongly that the League should get either Defence or Home. At that stage Choudhary Muhammad Ali, then a senior official in the Ministry of Finance, strongly advised Jinnah to settle for Finance, by arguing that it was the most important portfolio as its holder would have influence over every department of the Government.[135] So Jinnah accepted Wavell's offer and the League joined the Interim Government with Finance and Commerce among the important portfolios, and three other portfolios earmarked for it. So the crisis over portfolios passed over and the League members of the Interim Government were sworn in on 26 October 1946. It had been announced earlier that, in order to create vacancies for them, Sarat Chandra Bose, Shafaat Ahmad Khan, and Syed Ali Zaheer had resigned. Two seats were already vacant.

This was a great strategic victory for the League. For it had been able to get a foothold in the Interim Government without having had to rescind its Council's resolution of 29 July. This meant that it could continue to carry on its campaign for Direct Action, particularly in the Punjab and the NWFP, with even greater vigour than before, and indeed transform the Interim Government itself into a new arena for it. Under these circumstances the advent of Pakistan naturally seemed quite close at hand. And so indeed it actually proved to be.

NOTES

1. *Indian Annual Register*, 1946, I, p. 38.
2. Ibid., p. 43.
3. Nicholas Mansergh, ed., *The Transfer of Power, 1942–47* (hereafter referred to as *TP*), vol. VII (London, 1977), p. 6.
4. Ibid., pp. 220–1.

5. Ibid., pp. 260–1.
6. A.M. Zaidi and S.G. Zaidi, eds., *the Encyclopedia of the Indian National Congress*, vol. XII (New Delhi, 1958), pp. 481–2.
7. *TP*, vol. VII, n. 3, pp. 110–12.
8. Waheed Ahmad, ed., *Quaid-i-Azam Mohammad Ali Jinnah: The Nation's Voice: Annotated Speeches, Statements and Interviews*, (hereinafter referred to as *Jinnah: Speeches and Statements*), vol. IV (Karachi, 2000), pp. 380–1.
9. See *TP*, vol. VI (London, 1976), pp. 874–8.
10. *Jinnah: Speeches and Statements*, n. 8, pp. 419–20.
11. *TP*, vol. VI, n. 9.
12. *Jinnah: Speeches and Statements*, n. 7, p. 439.
13. Ibid., p. 449.
14. Ibid., pp. 453–4.
15. Ibid., pp. 455–6.
16. Ibid., pp. 518–20.
17. Ibid., pp. 538–9.
18. Ibid., p. 561.
19. Ibid., pp. 571–2.
20. *TP*, vol. VIII, p. 59.
21. Ibid., pp. 118–24.
22. *Jinnah: Speeches and Statements*, n. 8, pp. 623–4.
23. Syed Sharifuddin Pirzada, ed., *Foundations of Pakistan, All-India Muslim League Documents: 1906–1947* (hereinafter referred to as *Muslim League Documents*), vol. II (Karachi, 1970), pp. 508–9.
24. Ibid., pp. 512–13.
25. Ibid., pp. 340–1.
26. *TP*, vol. VII, pp. 280–5.
27. *A.V. Alexander Papers, 6/2, Diaries: Mission to India* (Churchill College, Cambridge), Entry on 16 April 1946.
28. *TP*, vol. VII, pp. 310–11.
29. Ibid., p. 330.
30. Ibid., p. 323.
31. Ibid., p. 352.
32. For details of the proceedings of the Second Simla Conference (5–12 May 1946), along with other related documents), see ibid., pp. 425–526. See also entries on 5–12 May 1946 in *Alexander's Diaries*, n. 27, particularly for talks and moves outside the Conference for a settlement between the Congress and the League.
33. *TP*, vol. VII, pp. 516–17.
34. Ibid., pp. 518–19.
35. Ibid., pp. 520–1.
36. Ibid., pp. 582–91.
37. Ibid., pp. 592–9, 611–13.

38. See the text of the statement issued by Jinnah on 22 May 1946, ibid., pp. 663–9.
39. See the text of the resolution adopted by the Congress Working Committee on 24 May 1946, in ibid., pp. 679–82.
40. For the text of the Cabinet Mission's Statement of 25 May 1946, see ibid., pp. 688–9.
41. Ibid., pp. 954–5.
42. For the text of the Congress Working Committee's Resolution dated 25 June 1946 see ibid., pp. 1036–8. See also Azad to Wavell, on the same date, ibid., pp. 1032–6.
43. Text of the resolution adopted by the League's Council on 6 June 1946, in ibid., pp. 836–8.
44. Text in ibid., pp. 1049–50.
45. Ibid., pp. 785–99.
46. Ibid., pp. 955.
47. Maulana Abul Kalam Azad, *India Wins Freedom: The Complete Version* (Hyderabad, 1988), p. 153. The first edition of this book, some passages omitted, was published in 1989 and was reprinted several times during the following three decades).
48. Ibid., p. 158.
49. Ibid., p. 165.
50. *TP*, vol. VII, pp. 836–8; italics added.
51. *Indian Annual Register*, 1946, I, pp. 181–2. This is further confirmed by the note of Major Woodrow Wyatt, M.P. and Personal Assistant to Cripps while a member of the Cabinet Mission, on his conversation with Jinnah on 8 June. According to Wyatt, Jinnah told him that 'he had not given up the idea of Pakistan'. See *TP*, vol. VII, p. 866. Interestingly, Syed Sharifuddin Pirzada, editor of the *League Documents* in two volumes has not included among them the proceedings of the meeting of the League's Council on 6 June 1946, though he has included the proceedings of several other meetings of the League's Working Committee and Council.
52. *Selected Works of Jawaharlal Nehru* (hereinafter referred to as *SWJN*), ed. S. Gopal, vol. XV (New Delhi, 1982), p. 237.
53. Ibid., pp. 241–5.
54. *TP*, vol. VII, pp. 679–82.
55. Ibid., pp. 1036–7.
56. Ibid., p. 1036.
57. Ibid., pp. 1044–7.
58. Alexander, n. 27.
59. See *TP*, vol. VII, p. 1049.
60. Ibid., pp. 1069–73.
61. *Amrit Bazar Patrika*, 2 July 1946.
62. For the text, see *TP*, vol. VIII (London, 1979), pp. 106–7.

63. Quaid-i-Azam Papers, Reel 3, File 74.
64. *Muslim League Documents*, n. 23, pp. 544–9.
65. Ibid., pp. 554–7.
66. Ibid., pp. 537–8.
67. Ibid., p. 560.
68. Choudhary Khaliquzzaman, *Pathway to Pakistan* (Lahore, 1961), p. 362.
69. Azad, n. 44, pp. 183–4.
70. Sudhir Ghose, *Gandhi's Emissary* (London, 1967), p. 180.
71. Azad, n. 44, pp. 166–7.
72. *Dawn*, 13 August 1946; also *Hindustan Times*, 14 August 1946.
73. See notes of Wavell's interview with Nehru on 30 July 1946, *TP*, vol. VIII, pp. 144–5.
74. Colville to Wavell, 4 August 1946, ibid., p. 189.
75. Wavell to Burrows, 19 July 1946, ibid., pp. 86–7.
76. For text, see ibid., pp. 98–9.
77. *TP*, vol. VII, p. 472.
78. For text see *TP*, vol. VIII, pp. 112–13.
79. Wavell to Pethick Lawrence, 24 July 1946, ibid., pp. 114–15.
80. Pethick Lawrence to Wavell, 26 July 1946, ibid., pp. 123–6.
81. See ibid., pp. 144–6.
82. Ibid., pp. 156–7.
83. Ibid., pp. 163–4.
84. Ibid., p. 168.
85. Ibid., pp. 177–8.
86. Ibid., p. 188.
87. For the text of the Nehru–Jinnah correspondence before they met on 15 August, see ibid., pp. 237–9.
88. Ibid., p. 248.
89. Ibid., vol. VII, p. 600.
90. For details, see Bengal Governor to Viceroy, 22 August 1946, ibid., pp. 293–304; Wavell to Pethick Lawrence, 28 August 1946, ibid., p. 323; Francis Tuker, *While Memory Serves* (London, 1950), pp. 156–8; Stanley Wolpert, *Jinnah of Pakistan* (Delhi, 1985), pp. 284–7; and Anita Inder Singh, *The Origins of the Partition of India* (Bombay, 1987), pp. 181–7.
91. *TP*, vol. VIII, 253–4.
92. Ibid., pp. 258–9. At the time, Azad was pursuing an approach to the problem of persuading Jinnah to reconsider his attitude to the League joining the Interim Government which was quite contrary to that outlined by Nehru in his letter to Wavell dated 18 August. While, according to Nehru, the Working Committee was not at all in favour of making a fresh effort to persuade Jinnah, Azad during his interview with Wavell on the next day favoured such a course. According to the

'top secret' note of the interview kept by Wavell, Azad said to him that though it would be inadvisable for him to approach Jinnah direct, 'would it be possible by indirect contact to give Jinnah some reassurance and persuade him to come in', ibid., pp. 261–2.

93. Ibid., pp. 281–2
94. Ibid., pp. 283–4.
95. Ibid., p. 285.
96. Ibid., pp. 290–1.
97. Ibid., p. 306.
98. Ibid., p. 311.
99. Ibid., pp. 312–13. See also Penderal Moon, ed., *Wavell: The Viceroy's Journal* (London, 1973), p. 341. According to Moon, Wavell used to say that on that occasion Gandhi thumped the table and said: 'If India wants her blood bath, she shall have it.' Several British and Pakistani scholars have jumped upon Gandhi's remark to question his commitment to non-violence. However, this is based on fallacious thinking. All that Gandhi was trying to do was to convey to Wavell that the Congress would not submit to any blackmail through emphasis on the danger of intensified communal violence if it did not accept the League's stand on the grouping of provinces.
100. *TP*, vol. VIII, pp. 322–3.
101. Ibid., pp. 326–7.
102. Ibid., p. 328.
103. See Pethick Lawrence to Wavell, 28 August 1946, ibid., p. 332.
104. Pethick Lawrence to Wavell, 30 August 1946, ibid., pp. 352–3.
105. Nehru to Wavell, 1 September 1946, ibid., p. 380.
106. *Jawaharlal Nehru's Speeches*, vol. I (New Delhi, 1983), pp. 4–5.
107. See Wavell to Pethick Lawrence, 9 September 1946, *TP*, vol. VIII, p. 474.
108. Wavell to Pethick Lawrence (Telegram), 10 September 1946, ibid., pp. 476–7. For a somewhat detailed version of Jinnah's interview with the representative of the *Daily Mail*, see ibid., p. 478.
109. Wavell to Pethick Lawrence, 10 September 1946, ibid., p. 482.
110. *Wavell: The Viceroy's Journal*, n. 99, p. 149. Sudhir Ghosh, who was quite close to Gandhi and frequently saw Cripps and Pethick Lawrence, records Nehru as having thus explained to him, on 2 October 1946, his agreement to Wavell starting his talks with Jinnah regarding the League's lateral entry into the Interim Government: the Viceroy had been pestering Nehru to take in the Muslim League, and he had said to the Viceroy 'in sheer exasperation' that he was not going to talk to Jinnah; if Lord Wavell was so keen, he could talk to Jinnah himself, see Sudhir Ghosh, *Gandhi's Emissary* (London, 1967), pp. 25–6; also J.B. Kripalani, *My Times: An Autobiography* (New Delhi, 2004), p. 605.

111. *TP*, vol. VIII, p. 527.
112. See ibid., pp. 524–7, 534, 587–8, 625–6, 643–50.
113. Ibid., pp. 650–1.
114. Ibid., pp. 654–5.
115. Ibid., p. 656.
116. Ibid., pp. 657–9
117. Ibid., pp. 643–4.
118. See Wavell to Pethick Lawrence, 11 October 1946, ibid., p. 694.
119. See Nawab of Bhopal to Jinnah, 4 October 1946, Quaid-i-Azam Papers, Reel 16, File 238.
120. Reproduced in Jinnah to Nehru, 7 October 1946, *TP*, vol. VIII, 673.
121. Nehru to Jinnah, 6 October 1946, ibid., pp. 671–2
122. Jinnah to Nehru, 7 October 1946, ibid., p. 673.
123. Nehru to Jinnah, 8 October 1946, ibid., pp. 676–7
124. Jinnah to Nehru, 12 October 1946, ibid., p. 701–3.
125. Wavell to Pethick Lawrence, 11 October 1946, ibid., p. 694
126. See Wavell's note on his talks with Jinnah, 12 October 1946, ibid., pp. 703–5.
127. Jinnah to Wavell, 13 October 1946, ibid., pp. 709–10.
128. See Wavell's note on his interview with Jinnah and Liaquat Ali Khan, 13 October 1946, ibid., p. 712.
129. Wavell's note on his interview with Nehru, 14 October 1946, ibid, p. 721.
130. Ibid., pp. 721–2.
131. Nehru to Wavell, 15 October 1946, ibid., p. 734.
132. Note of Wavell's interview with Patel, 16 October 1946, ibid., p. 742.
133. Nehru to Wavell, 24 October 1946, ibid., p. 801.
134. Nehru to Wavell, 23 October 1946, ibid., p. 784.
135. See Choudhary Muhammad Ali, *The Emergence of Pakistan* (Lahore, 1979; first published in 1967), p. 84.

CHAPTER VIII

Interim Government to the Mountbatten Plan and Partition, October 1946–August 1947

ON RECEIVING CONFIRMATION from Wavell that the decks had at last been cleared for the League's entry into the Interim Government, Pethick Lawrence warmly congratulated him by telegram on 16 October and followed it up by a letter sent two days later, in which he wrote:

You have now achieved what I know you have been aiming at ever since you first took office. In recent weeks we have obviously been on the edge of a volcano and, while one cannot be too confident that the Interim Government will endure, we can at least hope for a relaxation of communal tension for a time. It will not be an easy team but I hope they shake down and that the effect of working together on practical affairs will be to remove, or at any rate reduce, their suspicions of one another.[1]

Actually what happened was just the opposite. The Congress leaders resented the fact that the League had preferred to join the Interim Government via an understanding with the Viceroy rather than with the Congress. They were particularly upset by the fact that the League had been brought into the Interim Government without any commitment on its part to the long-term plan of the Cabinet Mission, which would involve participation in the Constituent Assembly set up under that Plan—stipulated as an essential condition for being inducted into the Interim Government. The League leaders on their part gave no indication of their intention to convene a meeting of their Council in order to rescind its decision of 29 July to withdraw its acceptance of the long-term plan of the Cabinet Mission. As if adding salt to injury, they refused point-blank to treat the Interim Government as a virtual Cabinet under a parliamentary system, with Nehru as its leader and boycotted the informal meetings—generally called Cabinet meetings—in Nehru's office and under his Chairmanship. This had the full backing of Wavell, who all along thought that the Interim Government was not a Cabinet, but only a reconstituted Executive Council of the Viceroy and that that position would continue till the framing of a new constitution with the cooperation of both the major political parties in the Constituent Assembly and its acceptance by the British Government.[2]

The attitude of the League members of the Interim Government towards cooperation with the Congress members was not surprising. For some of the League leaders had made it clear even while the way was being paved for their joining that Government that it should not imply that the League was abandoning the path of struggle based on Direct Action as provided for in its Council's resolution on 29 July 1946. Thus Ghaznafar Ali Khan, one of the League leaders designated to join the Interim Government, observed while addressing the students of Islamia College, Lahore, on 19 October 1946:

> We are going into the Interim Government to get a foothold to fight for our cherished goal of Pakistan and I assure you that we shall achieve Pakistan. The disturbances that have occurred in many parts of the country after the installation of the purely Congress Government at the Centre have established the fact beyond a shadow of a doubt that the ten crores of Indian Muslims will not submit to any Government which does not include their true representatives. The earlier the Congress realizes this the better that no power can suppress the freedom upsurge among the Muslim nation. . . . The Interim Government is one of the fronts of the Direct Action campaign and we shall most scrupulously carry out the orders of Mr Jinnah on any front he orders us.[3]

Liaquat Ali Khan, another member designate of the Interim Government and a prominent leader of the League, next only to Jinnah, was reported to have expressed similar thoughts at Karachi on 20 October 1946. According to him, joining the Interim Government was in no way inconsistent with the League's Bombay resolution on Direct Action (29 July 1946) and that Muslims must not relent, even to the smallest extent, their preparation for the final struggle, because that ultimate fight was inevitable for the winning of their goal—Pakistan.[4]

In such a situation it was futile to hope that there was going to be cooperation between the Congress and the League in the Interim Government, and there was none.

This naturally had an adverse impact on the general communal situation in the country, which was already grave. While stray incidents continued to occur in Calcutta, serious trouble erupted in the second week of October 1946 in Noakhali and Tippera districts in Eastern Bengal. The situation was not one of rioting, but of mass attacks by Muslims, who were in an overwhelming majority, on Hindus. According to the Governor of Bengal, the situation by 16 October was that 'large bands of Muslim hooligans' were moving about 'terrorizing Hindus and committing acts of arson, loot and murder, kidnapping and forcibly converting Hindus'. Villages had been cordoned off and booty and money extracted under threats. The gangs appeared to have been organized. Roads had been cut off at certain places, making communication more difficult than ever.[5] In the Congress circles it was generally believed that the attacks on Hindus in Eastern Bengal had really been organized by the Muslim League. In a report prepared by K.C. Neogi, a prominent Congress leader of East Bengal enjoying Nehru's confidence, it was mentioned that the lawlessness had been given the colour of pure goondaism, but it was not really so. It was an organized attack engineered by the Muslim League and carried out with the active connivance of the administrative officials.[6] While the Chief Minister of Bengal, H.S. Suhrawardy, had declared at a press conference that the League condemned all such disturbances,[7] Ghaznafar Ali Khan, as per a report received by Nehru, had remarked in the course of a statement issued from Lahore on 19 October that the East Bengal happenings were a part of the all-India battle for Pakistan.[8] When during his meeting with Jinnah on 22 October, Wavell emphasized the need to ease communal tension and referred to the recent utterances of Ghaznafar Ali Khan and Liaquat Ali Khan, Jinnah, in the words of Wavell, 'became rather communal' and spoke of Gandhi's 'continuous outpouring of poison'. On Wavell remarking that he was 'very disappointed' that neither Jinnah nor the League had issued an unequivocal statement condemning the happenings in Eastern Bengal, Jinnah said that he had thought of issuing a statement, but referred to what was happening in other parts of India.[9]

The situation in other parts of India, of course, went on deteriorating day-by-day as a chain reaction to the happenings in East Bengal. The lurid details of those happenings carried in newspapers and narrated in person by Hindu refugees from East

Bengal inflamed communal passions among large sections of Hindus. Calcutta which had seen a major bout of communal riots in August 1946 witnessed a recrudescence of riots again towards the end of October and early November. Those riots, though not as extensive as the earlier ones, were serious enough to cause the Viceroy and four members of the Interim Government, Nehru, Patel, Liaquat Ali Khan, and Abdur Rab Nishtar, to visit Calcutta along with East Bengal in the first week of November 1946. The four members also issued a joint statement on 4 November, declaring that much had happened in the recent past which had 'degraded Indian humanity and shamed us before others' and earnestly appealed to people not merely in Calcutta and Bengal, but also all over India for the cessation of violence and a return to the methods of peace.[10] When, however, the Governor suggested that it would improve the communal situation if the leaders of both the communities also issued a statement condemning mass or large-scale conversions in Noakhali and Tippera, and specifically asked Liaquat Ali Khan whether he could help in this matter, the latter observed that it would be better to have such a statement issued by prominent Muslim religious leaders. When after appreciating that point, the Governor insisted that a statement by political leaders would also be of immense advantage, Patel immediately agreed but Nishtar remained silent.[11] The end result was that there was no statement by the members of the Interim Government condemning mass or forced conversions.

As a result partly of the visit of the four members of the Interim Government to Bengal and partly the sojourn of Gandhi in Noakhali, where he was moving from village to village with his message of peace and goodwill, the situation in Bengal gradually improved. However, the same could not be said about other areas where Hindus had launched mass attacks on Muslim localities in retaliation for what had happened in Noakhali and Tippera. The situation was particularly deplorable in Bihar, where such attacks took place over a vast area, including the districts of Saran, Patna, Gaya, Monghyr, and Bhagalpur. As the Governor of Bihar, Sir Hugh Dow, reported to Wavell on 9 November 1946, roving Hindu mobs had sought to 'exterminate the Muslim population wherever they could find them'. Almost all casualties had been Muslim and it was estimated that of those 75 per cent had been women and children.[12] Nehru's report on the communal situation in Bihar in the first week of November was somewhat similar:

> In the affected areas . . . there has been a definite attempt on the part of Hindu mobs to exterminate the Muslims. They have killed indiscriminately, men, women and children *en masse*. Some stories are incredibly brutal and inhuman. Indeed, one can only explain all this by saying that a madness had seized the people.[13]

Even while Nehru, along with other leaders, was busy dealing with the disturbances in Bihar, Garhmukteshwar, a Hindu pilgrimage centre in the Meerut district of UP, witnessed the outbreak of somewhat similar disturbances, on 6 November, triggered by a small incident during the Hindu fair on the bank of the Ganga River.[14] As the Governor of UP reported, entire families had in some cases been wiped out and all this had been done with the most hideous cruelty. The whole town was just stunned. A considerable number of people were still left there, but there was no sound of life and an awful stillness had settled over the place.[15]

Indeed, as far as the number of casualties was concerned, many more people died in disturbances or riots in different parts of India that occurred as a reaction to the events in Noakhali and Tippera than in those districts themselves. The latter acquired notoriety and created an outcry all over northern India chiefly because of wide publicity given to atrocities against women such as rape, conversion, and forced marriages. Thus between 2 September and 18 November 1946, only 133 persons were reported to have lost their lives in Noakhali and Tippera, but roughly 5,000 persons were reported killed in Bihar and 445 in UP.[16] While the victims in these places in most cases belonged to one community (Hindu or Muslim), in Bombay, which had 622 casualties, the number was evenly balanced between the two communities,[17] just as had been the case during the August disturbances in Calcutta.

II

The widespread riots and killings, even though stopped by force, were bound to aggravate the ever-present distrust and tension among the leaders of both the Congress and the League and so they did, in ample measure, each side blaming the other for encouraging the rioters or at least not doing enough to suppress them. In the meanwhile, the contentious issue created by the League's induction into the Interim Government without rescinding its Bombay decision not to join the Constituent Assembly and to resort to Direct Action for the achievement of Pakistan remained unresolved. While the Congress leaders were determined to commence the meetings of the Constituent Assembly on 9 December and were pressing the Viceroy to ensure the League's participation in it if it wanted to remain in the Interim Government, Jinnah was not prepared to call a meeting of his Council in order to consider this. Indeed, he was reported to have declared at a press conference in New Delhi on 14 November 1946 that in his view 'the only solution' of India's communal problem was a Partition of the country into Pakistan and Hindustan. He further added that by Pakistan he meant 'Absolute Pakistan—anything else would be artificial and unnatural'. He went on to add that after Partition the two States, Pakistan and Hindustan, would be friends in the subcontinent, would go to each other's rescue in case of danger, and would be able to say 'hands off' to other nations. They would then have a Monroe Doctrine more solid than in America. Asked what would happen if the Congress and the League did not come to an agreement regarding Partition, Jinnah replied: 'What happens is what you see, you have been witnessing what is happening.'[18]

On 17 November, Jinnah addressed a letter to Wavell in reply to the latter's of 5 November. There he cited several documents to prove that the Congress had never accepted in full the Cabinet Mission's Statement of 16 May, implying those sections of the Statement that dealt with the formation of Groups. Nor did Jinnah see any merit in the Congress stand that any dispute between the Congress and the League with regard to the interpretation of any section of the Cabinet Mission's Statement could be referred to the Supreme Court. For, argued Jinnah, there was no provision for it in the Cabinet Mission's Statement. 'Besides', he added, 'the basic and fundamental principle underlying that document is not, and cannot be made, a justiciable issue.' He also referred to the mass Hindu attacks on Muslims in Bihar and communal riots of varying intensity taking place in various other parts of India and remarked: 'In this highly surcharged and explosive atmosphere even to think of the proposed Constituent Assembly or any talk about it, when we are faced with two hostile camps, with the result that killing, murder and destruction of property are going on apace, is neither advisable nor possible. It will only exacerbate the present situation'.[19] He reiterated this point in his interview with Wavell two days later, on 19 November, and warned that if the Viceroy went ahead with the plan to summon the Constituent Assembly, he and the British Government would be responsible for the disasters that would follow.[20]

Some of Jinnah's comments during this interview with regard to the League's demand for Pakistan show his deep commitment to it and his preparedness to accept even a truncated Pakistan provided, of course, it was a sovereign Pakistan. Thus, as per Wavell's record of that interview, Jinnah asserted at one moment that 'he had never rejected the smaller Pakistan suggested by the [Cabinet] Mission, though he had insisted on Calcutta'. Asserting that agreement between the Congress and the League was quite impossible, he asked the British Government to give the Muslims 'their own bit of country'. It could be as small as the British liked, 'but it must be their own and they would live on one meal a day. . . . '[21]

On the other hand, Nehru in his interview with the Viceroy on the same day insisted on the Constituent Assembly being called on 9 December as already suggested by him and again referred to the League's membership in the Interim Government being dependent on its acceptance of the long-term plan of the Cabinet Mission.[22] In his letter to Wavell on 21 November, Nehru drew his attention to the editorial in *Dawn* that day declaring that the League's participation in the Interim Government was not made conditional on a rescinding of the Bombay decision (29 July). The editorial went on to remark that if the League adhered to its decision to stay out of the Constituent Assembly while sharing power in the Interim Government, there was no authority that could prevent it from doing so. Nehru then went on to ask the Viceroy to clarify the British position on that issue, using rather strong language:

. . . We had been repeatedly told that acceptance of the so-called short-term plan, that is entry into the Interim Government, was dependent on an acceptance of the long-term plan, that is the Cabinet Mission's

Statement of 16 May. If the Muslim League refuse to accept the long-term plan, it is not at all clear to me how they can function in the Interim Government.

It seems to me clear, and it is stated on behalf of the Muslim League, that they have deliberately avoided committing themselves to anything at all in regard to any matter. While we were assured by you that they were committed, in fact it was not so. It is for you to consider whether you were misled or not. We were certainly misled by what you assured us.[23]

Addressing the Subjects Committee of the Meerut session of the Congress on 21 November 1946, Nehru went a step further and indicated that if things did not improve the Congress might feel forced to launch a mass struggle again. Revealing for the first time that he had been feeling so unhappy at the recent trend of developments in connection with the working of the Interim Government, with the League members functioning as a king's party and at the same time not showing any inclination to accept the long-term plan of the Cabinet Mission, Nehru observed:

I do not know what will happen in future, but this much I want to tell you that if the present state of affairs continues a struggle is imminent whether we are in the Interim Government or outside it. There is a conflict of ideologies. I want to say that our patience is strained to the breaking point and if these things continue, they will lead to a big struggle.

Observing that the main cause of resentment in the Congress circles was the League's continuance in the Interim Government in spite of its refusal to accept the long-term plan of the Cabinet Mission, Nehru added:

It was clear from Mr Jinnah's statements that the League entered the Government not to work it but because they feared they would be weakened if they kept out. It was also clear from Mr Jinnah's letters to the Viceroy that the League did not accept the Statement of May 16. If so, how could they continue in the Interim Government?[24]

On the same day that Nehru made these observations Jinnah issued a statement to the press expressing his resentment at the decision of the British Government to summon the Constituent Assembly on 9 December and describing it as 'one more blunder of a very grave and serious character'. He also declared that the resolution adopted by the League Council at Bombay on 29 July continued to remain in force and that no League member was expected to participate in the Constituent Assembly.[25]

Seeing this statement Wavell sent for Liaquat Ali Khan on 23 November and told the latter that he could not agree to the League staying in the Interim Government without accepting the long-term plan. Khan replied that the League members of the Government would be willing to resign the moment they were asked to do so by the Viceroy, but so long as they were not assured of the working of the sections according to their wishes they would not accept the long-term plan. The main issue, according to him, was that the League could accept the long-term plan only if it became certain that the sections would decide about the provincial as well as group constitutions through vote by a majority of its members and not by voting province-wise. This was a point that the Congress was not expected to concede as it had from the beginning made it clear that every province must be free to decide about its constitution as well as its position in a group, if formed. The Congress was, of course, prepared to agree to the reference of this point to the Supreme Court and to abide by the latter's verdict, but this was not acceptable to the League.

III

The British Government, realizing that the situation could no longer be allowed to drift, decided to summon to London for discussion the Viceroy and two representatives each from the Congress and the Muslim League and one representative of the Sikh community (suggested by the Viceroy). The invitation to the leaders concerned was extended by the Viceroy on behalf of the British Government on 26 November. However, because of the tense situation then prevailing in Indian political circles, the British Prime Minister had to personally intervene before Nehru and Jinnah could be persuaded to leave for London. Patel, who had been invited as the second person on behalf of the Congress, refused to go right at the beginning. Nehru wrote to Wavell on the same day that he had been conveyed the British Government's invitation, but after consultations with his colleagues he felt that it was not possible for him at that stage to go to London. The Congress, he added, would be agreeable to holding discussions with the British Governments' representatives in India. He further remarked: 'The invitation to us to go to London appears to us to reopen the whole problem which was settled to a large extent by the Cabinet Mission's statement and the formation of the Interim Government.' This reopening, Nehru thought, was being undertaken in order to placate the League. 'It would,' he added, 'mean giving in to the League's intransigence and incitement to violence and this would have disastrous consequences.'[26] Nehru changed his mind only after receiving Attlee's message the next day assuring him that nothing like that was going to happen. 'The object of our talks', he observed, 'would be to try and ensure a successful meeting of the Constituent Assembly on 9th December.' He further added: 'There is no intention of abandoning either the decision of the Assembly to meet or the plan put forward by the Cabinet Delegation. It is our desire to see that this is implemented in the full and not any desire to abandon or alter it that has prompted us to ask you and your colleagues to come to London.'[27] Sardar Baldev Singh, the leader of the Sikhs and Defence Member in the Interim Government, too, followed Nehru, both in declining to go to London in the beginning and later agreeing to do so.[28] When Jinnah came to know about it, he wanted to know what had led Nehru to change his earlier decision not to go. Upon his being supplied with a copy of Attlee's letter to Nehru, Jinnah immediately sent a telegram saying that no such thing as said in that letter had ever been conveyed to Liaquat Ali Khan when the League leaders had been invited to go to London and announcing that he would not be able to go to London unless it was made clear that 'all aspects [of the] present situation in light of all that has happened will be open for consideration.[29] It was now Attlee's turn to reassure Jinnah: 'Your refusal must be based on a misunderstanding of my telegram to Nehru. There is nothing in it to prejudice a full consideration of all points of view.'[30] Abell, Wavell's private secretary, sent an apt note to his boss on the same day that Attlee's message to Jinnah was received: 'The messages that have been sent will mean to the Congress that there can be no *de novo* discussion and to the League that there can: and I expect this chicken will come home to roost in London, if not earlier.'[31]

Actually, not one, but several chickens could come home to roost in London. For the British authorities, including Cabinet ministers as well as the Viceroy, had made contrary statements to the Congress and the League leaders ever since the arrival of the Cabinet Mission in India. Instead of discussing these statements, the attention of the conference of Indian and British leaders in London was, of course, focused on bridging the gulf between the Congress and the League so that they could work in cooperation with each other and jointly frame a constitution for a united India. It was, however, too late to attempt this. The leaders on both sides remained as firmly committed to their mutually contradictory positions as ever. Nehru was not prepared to accept the compulsory grouping of provinces, claimed by the League as part of their scheme of Pakistan, which alone could satisfy the League, and insisted on the freedom of a province to decide whether to join a group or not. Jinnah, from the moment he landed in London, asserted that it was no longer possible to forge any understanding between the Congress and the League. Indeed, even while taking part in the discussions regarding the grouping of provinces, he made it clear on more than one occasion that in his opinion the creation of Pakistan was the only solution of the Indian problem, and he was fully determined to secure it.

Jinnah's first public engagement in London, was a lunch hosted by Major Woodrow Wyatt, who had served as private secretary to Stafford Cripps during the visit of the Cabinet Mission to India and had established a good rapport with Jinnah. According to notes made by Wyatt of Jinnah's utterances at that lunch, the latter had 'returned to the proposition that only the creation of Pakistan can deal with the situation'. Wyatt further noted:

> I asked him the direct question: 'If Congress were now to say without equivocation that they accepted the Cabinet Mission Plan, together with the grouping system in its entirety, would you feel that there were still some possibilities in the Constituent Assembly and the Cabinet Mission Plan?' His answer was most decisively No, that it was not even worth discussing the proposition.[32]

Jinnah adopted an equally determined and uncompromising stand in his conversation with Pethick-Lawrence on the same day and clearly stated that no compromise solution was possible on the Constituent Assembly because of the stand of the Congress. When the latter mentioned that if the League did not agree to participate in the Constituent Assembly, world opinion, having considerable value in such matters, would turn against them,

Jinnah said that he realized the value of world opinion, but he had also his own supporters in India to think of and they were determined not to be submerged in the Hindu nation. Pethick-Lawrence, while presenting the gist of this conversation to the Prime Minister and other concerned members of the Cabinet, thus summed it up: 'I could not shake Jinnah in his standpoint. I felt that he was very bitter and determined.'[33]

Jinnah appeared equally determined during his conversations with Attlee on 4 December. As the latter reported to the concerned ministers assembled at his residence immediately after his encounter with Jinnah, the burden of the latter's discourse had been that 'it was a mistake to have tried to introduce self-government into India. . . . Mr Jinnah seemed convinced that the Congress did not mean business in regard to the Constituent Assembly; his own aim was simply that of Pakistan, within the British Commonwealth. He held out no prospect of an arrangement with the Congress as regards procedure in the Constituent Assembly.'[34]

Jinnah remained firm on the League's interpretation of the meaning of the provisions of the Cabinet Mission Plan dealing with the procedure to be followed by the sections, into which the Constituent Assembly was to be divided, for the purpose of deciding about the desirability of forming groups consisting of provinces included in particular sections and settling the terms of the groups' constitutions. The League's contention always had been that the decisions in the sections on such issues would be made by a majority of their members. The British Government agreed with this interpretation. The Congress, on the other hand, had always contended that decisions in the sections should be made on the basis of majority support in every province included in the section. However, it had shown its preparedness earlier to have this point settled by a reference to the Supreme Court of India and Nehru repeated this offer in discussions with British Cabinet ministers.[35] The latter conveyed to Jinnah that the verdict of the Supreme Court was likely to be in favour of the League's standpoint, which was also their own standpoint, and asked him whether he could assure the League's participation in the Constituent Assembly if such a verdict was given. All that Jinnah said in response to this question was that he would place this matter before his Council and explain all the pros and cons, but would not make any recommendation to it and leave it free to decide as it pleased.[36]

Thus the position in the meetings in London was that both Nehru and Jinnah were firm on the positions adopted earlier by their respective parties. And both seemed equally determined to reach their goals—independence for Nehru and Pakistan for Jinnah. While the latter refused to enter the Constituent Assembly unless it could be ensured to its satisfaction that the Congress would agree to the League's interpretation of the provision in the Cabinet Mission's Statement of 16 May, which it claimed with full justification tallied with the Mission's own intentions. In any case, it considered the then existing situation in India most inopportune for holding the session of the Constituent Assembly and wanted it to be postponed indefinitely. Nehru, on the other hand, was determined that the Constituent Assembly should meet on 9 December, as scheduled, even though initially only for a short session, whether the League agreed to participate in it or not. His attitude seemed to be that the Constituent Assembly must meet as scheduled, with the League members present if possible, or without them if they wished to stay out. He must have been aware of the ultimate result of the latter—Partition. However, although deeply pained by the prospect, he was prepared to accept it, as he knew the Congress leadership as a whole was prepared, so long as the League was not allowed to manoeuvre itself into a position that might enable it to include in Pakistan those areas the overwhelming majority of whose inhabitants were not willing to belong to Pakistan. If the League's view of the functioning of sections in the Constituent Assembly was accepted that might enable it to achieve its ultimate objective of 'Full Pakistan', which Jinnah underlined in several of his interviews and discussions in London. Thus the stakes were high for both sides and it is not surprising that they both adopted an uncompromising attitude at the London Conference.

Whatever that might have been, the British Government, in its wisdom, thought of making one more effort to bring the Congress and the League together in the Constituent Assembly, while at the same time underlining what the failure of that effort might lead to. This was done through a statement by His Majesty's Government, issued on 6 December 1946. It supported the Muslim League's interpretation of paragraphs 19(V) and (VIII) of the

Cabinet Mission's Statement of 16 May 1946 and wanted all concerned to accept that:

> The Cabinet Mission have throughout maintained the view that the decisions of the Sections should, in the absence of agreement to the contrary, be taken by simple majority vote of the representatives in the Sections. This view has been accepted by the Muslim League, but the Congress have put forward a different view. They have asserted that the true meaning of the Statement, read as a whole, is that the Provinces have a right to decide both as to grouping and as to their own constitutions.
>
> His Majesty's Government have had legal advice which confirms that the Statement of 16 May means what the Cabinet Mission have always stated was their intentions. This part of the Statement as so interpreted must therefore be considered an essential part of the scheme of May 16th, for enabling the Indian people to frame a constitution which His Majesty's Government would be prepared to present to Parliament. It should, therefore, be accepted by all parties in the Constituent Assembly.

The statement issued by the British Government went on to observe that other questions of interpretation of the Cabinet Mission's Statement of 16 May might arise. It expressed the hope that if the Council of the Muslim League decided to participate in the Constituent Assembly, they would also agree, as had the Congress, that the Federal Court should be asked to decide matters of interpretation that may be referred to them by either side and would accept such decisions. On the matter immediately in dispute, however, the British Government's statement urged the Congress to accept the view of the Cabinet Mission so that the way might be opened for the League to reconsider its attitude towards the Constituent Assembly. If in spite of this re-affirmation of the view of the Cabinet Mission, the Constituent Assembly desired that this 'fundamental point' should be referred to the Federal Court for its decision, such reference should be made at a very early date and the meetings of the Sections of the Constituent Assembly be postponed until the decision of the Supreme Court became available. Then followed the warning as to what would happen if the efforts to persuade the League to participate in the Constituent Assembly failed, thus opening a wide door to Partition. This was contained in the last paragraph of the Statement:

There has never been any prospect of success for the Constituent Assembly, except upon the basis of an agreed procedure. Should a Constitution come to be framed by a Constituent Assembly in which a large section of the Indian population had not been represented, His Majesty's Government could not of course contemplate—as the Congress have stated they would not contemplate—forcing such a Constitution upon any unwilling parts of the country.[37]

Jinnah had every reason to be pleased with the outcome of the London Conference. For one thing the Muslim League's interpretation of the disputed points in the Cabinet Mission's statement of 16 May had been fully upheld and declared to be in line with the Mission's own interpretation and an appeal had been made to the Congress to accept that interpretation, without insisting on a reference to the Supreme Court. Even if such a reference was to be made, the League was assured that it was obliged to follow the verdict of the court only if it upheld its own interpretation. Above all, a warning had been given to the Congress that if it failed to persuade the League to participate in the Constituent Assembly, a Constitution prepared by that Assembly would apply only to those areas whose representatives had participated in it. That clearly meant that either the Congress had to satisfy the League or be prepared for the creation of Pakistan.

It is not surprising, therefore, that Jinnah now saw Pakistan coming sooner rather than later. This is borne out by what he told Sardar Baldev Singh, the Sikh representative at the London Conference, seeking the support of his community for Pakistan:

Baldev Singh, you see this matchbox. Even if Pakistan of this size is offered to me I will gladly accept it, but it is here that I need your collaboration. If you persuade the Sikhs to join hands with the Muslim League, we will have a glorious Pakistan, the gates of which will be near about Delhi if not Delhi itself.[38]

Unlike Nehru and Baldev Singh, Jinnah and Liaquat Ali Khan did not return immediately after the end of the London Conference to India, but stayed on in London for a few days more. Calling on him on the morrow of the end of the Conference, his old friend Kanji Dwarkadas surprisingly found him 'sick and depressed', and, what is more significant, wanting 'no settlement except on the basis of Pakistan'.[39] On the other hand, talking to Jinnah on 9 December, Woodrow Wyatt formed the impression that he was 'generally very pleased' with the British Government's statement of 6 December and expressed happiness that the Government had been 'honest' about the interpretation of the disputed clauses of the Cabinet Mission's statement of 16 May. However, although he was inclined to give it a trial, he thought that, because of the Congress attitude, 'the Constituent Assembly would not function properly, and the only solution was, as ever, Pakistan'.[40]

Jinnah found another source of happiness after the end of the Conference in the speech in the course of the debate on India policy in the House of Commons by Winston Churchill, leader of the Opposition, on 13 December, signifying an assurance that the Conservative Party was continuing its traditional policy of support to the Muslim League and opposition to the Congress. Said Churchill:

> I must record my own belief . . . that any attempt to establish the reign of a Hindu numerical majority in India will never be achieved without a civil war, proceeding, not perhaps at first on the fronts of armies or organized forces, but in thousands of separate and isolated places. The war will, before it is decided, lead through unaccountable agonies to an unlawful abridgement of the Indian population. . . . The Muslims, numbering 90 million, . . . comprise the majority of the fighting elements in India . . . the word 'minority' has no relevance or sense when applied to masses of human beings numbered in many scores of millions.[41]

Jinnah, along with Liaquat Ali Khan, was sitting in the Dominion Gallery when Churchill spoke. Earlier he had met the latter and had briefed him on the Indian situation.[42] Apparently they had got along quite well and Churchill had promised Jinnah all possible help in his drive for Pakistan. The level of rapport established between them before Churchill made his speech in the House of Commons comes out clearly in the following letter from Churchill to Jinnah sent on 11 December:

> I should greatly like to accept your kind invitation to luncheon on December 12. I feel, however, that it would perhaps be wiser for us not to be associated publicly at this juncture.
>
> I greatly valued our talk the other day and I now enclose the address to which any telegram you may wish to send me can be sent without attracting attention in India. I will always sign myself 'Gilliatt'! Perhaps you will let me know to what address I should telegram to you and how you will sign yourself.[43]

The happenings in London in the early part of December 1946 must have strengthened Jinnah's conviction that the creation of Pakistan was not far off, if only the Muslim League remained firmly glued to that objective. Regardless of what other League leaders might or might not do and regardless, too, of the British Government's Statement of 6 December 1946, which Jinnah had promised to place before his Council for consideration after the attitude of the Congress became clear, he remained as firmly attached as ever to that objective. En route to India he spent a few days at Cairo, where he continued his campaign for Pakistan and indeed added a new international dimension to the rationale for it. While talking to the Prime Minister of Egypt, Nokrashy Pasha, on 17 December, he observed: 'It is only when Pakistan is established that Indian and Egyptian Muslims will be really free. Otherwise there will be the menace of a Hindu Imperialist Raj spreading its tentacles right across the Middle East.' At a press conference in Cairo on 20 December, he observed that if India came to be ruled by 'Hindu imperialist power', it would be as great a menace, if not greater, to the future of the Islamic countries of the Middle East as the British imperialistic power had been and the whole of the Middle East would fall 'from the frying pan into the fire'.[44]

While the Muslim League, or at any rate its top leader, was busy with the campaign for Pakistan, the Congress, with Gandhi's absence from Delhi due to his visit first to Noakhali and then to Bihar, under the joint leadership of Nehru and Patel was busy speeding up the march to independence. In spite of the League's opposition, the British leaders' advice, and Gandhi's forebodings, the Constituent Assembly met as scheduled on 9 December and went ahead with settling its organizational structure with Rajendra Prasad, one of the foremost Congress leaders, as its President and laying down rules for its functioning. Various committees were also formed, though certain seats were left vacant for the League members in case they decided to join the Constituent Assembly later. Not confining itself to procedural matters, the Constituent Assembly proceeded to deal also with matters of substance. On 13 December, Nehru moved the famous 'Objectives Resolution' setting forth the aims and objects of the Constituent Assembly. Through it the Assembly, among other things, declared 'its firm and solemn resolve to proclaim India as an Independent Sovereign

Republic and to draw up for her future governance a Constitution', providing for a Union of India with autonomous units having residuary powers and guaranteeing to all its citizens justice, equality and freedom, including freedom of thought, expression, belief, faith, worship, association and action, and ensuring adequate safeguards for minorities, backward and tribal areas, and depressed and other backward classes. While moving this resolution, Nehru at the outset expressed regret at the absence of the League members and stressed that the Assembly should be careful to ensure that nothing was done which was not acceptable to all sections of the Indian people. Further, he expressed the hope that the members who were absent would soon join the Constituent Assembly, but made it clear that the Constituent Assembly would go on with its work regardless of whether they did so or not. As Nehru put it:

> It has ever been and shall always be our ardent desire to see the people of India united together so that we may frame a constitution, which will be acceptable to the masses of the Indian people. It is, at the same time, manifest that when a great country starts to advance, no party or group can stop it. This House, although it has met in the absence of some of its members, will continue functioning and try to carry out its work at all costs.[45]

Even so, after a number of speeches had been delivered on the resolution, further consideration was deferred in deference to the view of some members of the Constituent Assembly, notably M.R. Jayakar, that a resolution such as the one moved by Nehru, setting forth the fundamentals of the Constitution, should not be adopted in the absence of the representatives of the Muslim League as also of the Indian states, and the House adjourned to meet again on 22 January 1947.

This was obviously done in the hope that it would give sufficient time to the League to finally make up its mind about joining the Constituent Assembly. The League was, of course, waiting for the Congress decision on the British Government's statement. That came finally in the shape of a resolution adopted by the All India Congress Committee on 6 January 1947. That resolution, affirming keenness to ensure that the work of the Constituent Assembly should proceed with the goodwill of all the parties concerned and to remove the hurdles in the way, agreed 'to advise action in accordance with the interpretation of the British

Government with regard to the procedure to be followed in Sections'. This was, however, accompanied by the old Congress reservations with regard to the Cabinet Mission's Statement of 16 May. For the AICC's resolution proceeded to explain that the decision to work in accordance with the British statement of 6 December 1946 must not involve any compulsion for a province, and that the rights of the Sikhs in the Punjab should not be jeopardised. It further added that in the event of any attempt at such compulsion, 'the province or part of a province has the right to take such action as may be deemed necessary in order to give effect to the wishes of the people concerned'. In view of recent observations made by the British and League leaders to the effect that the latter would be obliged to accept the verdict of the Supreme Court on the disputed points in the Cabinet Mission's statement of 16 May, only if it went in favour of the League, the AICC also declared that a reference to the Supreme Court had become purposeless and undesirable. All this was said after endorsing the resolution adopted earlier by the Working Committee (on 22 December 1946), which had described the British Government's statement of 6 December as also other statements pertaining to it made by the members of that Government in the Parliament as 'clearly additions to, and variations of' the Cabinet Mission's statement of 16 May and gone on to refer at length to that document as well as the earlier, off-repeated stand of the Congress relating to it.[46]

In the meanwhile, the Constituent Assembly resumed its session on 22 January, as decided earlier, and began further consideration of the 'Objectives Resolution' moved by Nehru six weeks earlier. Obviously the dominant view in the Assembly was that there was no use waiting any further for the League representatives to arrive in that body. This mood was reflected in Nehru's speech on that occasion:

> It was right, . . . if I may say so with all respect, that this House decided to adjourn consideration of this motion and thus not only demonstrated before the world our earnest desire to have all those people here who have not so far come in here, but also to assure the country and everyone else, how anxious we were to have the cooperation of all. Since then six weeks have passed, and during these weeks there has been plenty of opportunity for those who wanted to come. Unfortunately, they have not yet decided to come and they still hover in this state of indecision. I

regret that, and all I can say is this, that we shall welcome them at any future time when they may wish to come. But it should be made clear without any possibility of misunderstanding that no work will be held up in future whether anyone comes or not. There has been waiting enough.[47]

Nine days after Nehru made this speech signifying that the Congress would welcome the cooperation of the League, but was prepared to push ahead towards its goal—independence—even without such cooperation, the League stated its position regarding the British statement of 6 December 1946 and the Congress stand thereon through a resolution adopted by its Working Committee, sitting under Jinnah's presidentship, on 31 January 1947. After a detailed exposition of its stand and that of the Congress on the Cabinet Mission's proposal of 16 May 1946, and taking into account the stand of the Congress on the British Government's statement of 6 December 1946, and its role in the Constituent Assembly, the Working Committee gave its definite opinion that the Congress had 'destroyed all fundamentals of the statement of the 16 May and every possibility of compromise on the basis of the Cabinet Mission's Constitutional Plan'. It accordingly called upon the British Government to declare that the constitutional plan formulated by the Cabinet Mission had failed because 'the Congress after all these months of efforts have not accepted the statement of 16 May 1946, nor have the Sikhs, nor the Scheduled Castes'. The Working Committee further asserted that the elections to and thereafter the summoning of the Constituent Assembly, in spite of the protests and objections of the League 'was . . . void, invalid and illegal as not only the major parties had not accepted the statement but even the Sikhs and the Scheduled Castes had also not done so; and that the continuation of the Constituent Assembly and its proceedings and decisions are *ultra vires*, invalid and illegal, and it should be forthwith dissolved'. In the light of all this, the Working Committee resolved that no useful purpose would be served by summoning a meeting of the Council of the League.[48]

The adoption of this resolution set the Congress leaders thinking about their next course of action. During his meeting with Wavell on 1 February, Nehru discussed with the latter—who, too, expressed regret at the way things had developed—the probable repercussions of the League's latest resolution in a general way without making any definite demand. He did, however, remark that the effect of the League's resolution on the working of the Interim Government required careful consideration: 'It was not merely that the League had refused to join the Constituent Assembly, but that until the Bombay resolution was withdrawn, they were committed to a policy of direct action, i.e. of active opposition to the Government of which they at present formed part.' Fully realizing the seriousness of the situation, Wavell asked Nehru to submit his considered view as early as possible.[49]

Wavell did not have to wait long. He received a letter on 5 February signed by all the non-League members of the Interim Government observing that they were clearly of the opinion that in view of the League's Working Committee's resolution, it was no longer possible for the members of the League to continue in the Interim Government. They recalled that prior to the inclusion of the latter in the Interim Government, it had been repeatedly emphasized that they must accept the long-term plan of the Cabinet Mission and that the Viceroy's reply had been that that was indeed a prerequisite to their joining the Interim Government.[50]

When consulted by Wavell on a suitable reply to the non-League members of the Council, Pethick Lawrence recognized that the Congress had agreed to the League members entering the Interim Government on the understanding that the League would reconsider its Bombay resolution and the Viceroy had given assurances to Nehru about it, but had insisted that the British Government could not take any precipitate action and would require reasonable time to consider such an important matter.[51] Liaquat Ali Khan, however, adopted a different stand and wrote to Wavell on 8 February that the non-League members of the Interim Government had no right to ask for the resignation of the League members. For while the League had accepted the Cabinet Mission's statement of 16 May right from the beginning, the Congress, according to him, had never done so. He, therefore, contended that the question of the reconsideration by the League of its Bombay resolution did not arise so long as the Congress did not 'unequivocally' accept the British Government's statement of 6 December 1946.[52] Thus both the Congress and the League stuck to their old positions, clearly ruling out any settlement between them, except on the basis of Partition.

IV

It seems that the British authorities, too, had come to this conclusion after observing the mood of the Indian leaders and realizing the significance of the issues dividing them during discussions with them at the London Conference in the first week of December 1946. The last paragraph in the statement of 6 December, clearly foreshadowing Partition, indicates that the British were getting tired of the endless negotiations, especially in the context of their own compulsion to finally quit India as soon as possible and to do so not in the midst of turmoil and anarchy, but with a legitimate government or governments in position. This explains why shortly after issuing the statement of 6 December 1946, the Cabinet began consideration of the terms of another statement in case the former failed to work, even before the Congress and the League had come out with their final stands towards the statement of 6 December. The following extract from the Confidential Annexures to the minutes of the Cabinet meeting as early as 10 December 1946 shows how the minds of the leading members of the Government, particularly the Prime Minister, were working at that time:

> In the course of the Cabinet's discussion on the results of the recent visit of Indian leaders to this country, the Prime Minister said that it was impossible to be confident that the main political Parties in India had any real will to reach agreement between themselves. Pandit Nehru's present policy seemed to be to secure complete domination by Congress throughout the Government of India. If a Constitution was framed which had this effect, there would certainly be strong reactions from the Muslims. Provinces with a Muslim majority might refuse to join a Central Government on such terms at all, and the ultimate result of Congress policy might be the establishment of that Pakistan which they so much disliked. The Prime Minister warned the Cabinet that the situation might so develop as to result in civil war in India, with all the bloodshed which that would entail.[53]

While we need not take seriously Attlee's estimate of the Congress attitude being the sole cause of the likely failure of the British Government's statement of 6 December 1946, which followed the traditional British estimate of the cause of every single step leading to Partition since 1937, if not earlier, his realization, within less than a week of the issue of the statement of 6 December, that that statement was not likely to succeed in solving the Indian constitutional problem is noteworthy. The developments that followed the publication of that statement not only confirmed the soundness of Attlee's prognosis, but also made the British Government seriously consider the outlines of another statement of British policy.

Things indeed moved quickly in that direction. Attlee's pronouncement just mentioned had been made on 10 December 1946. The India and Burma Committee of the Cabinet headed, by Attlee himself and constituting the main decision-making body on Indian affairs, met the very next day to have a more detailed discussion of the Indian situation and the possible British policy to meet it. It was agreed at that meeting that if it became certain that either of the two communities would refuse to cooperate in carrying out the Cabinet Mission's Plan, 'then a situation would have arisen which justified and necessitated a fresh statement of policy by His Majesty's Government'. How close the Committee was to a decision in favour of the creation of Pakistan is indicated by this sentence from the minutes of this meeting of the India and Burma Committee: 'It was agreed that, if Congress persisted in an intransigent attitude, the logical consequence would be the establishment of the Pakistan which they so much disliked.' Another matter discussed at length on this occasion—which, too, foreshadowed the nature of future developments in other respects—was the oft-repeated suggestion by Wavell that an early announcement should be made of the British intention to leave India by a certain date. No decision was taken, but Attlee invited both the Secretary of State for India and the Viceroy to prepare a first draft as the basis of discussions in the Committee for a further statement of British policy to be issued if it became obvious that the Cabinet Mission's Plan would not work as was intended owing to the intransigence of either or both parties.[54]

The draft by the senior members in the office of the Secretary of State for India was circulated among the members of the India and Burma Committee on 15 December and that by the Viceroy, who was continuing to linger on in London in order to be available for discussions, on the next day. While there were several points of divergence between the two drafts, particularly relating to the modalities of British withdrawal, both of them favoured an announcement that the British would finally quit India at an early date, not later than 31 March 1948. And both also stipulated that power over the whole country could not be transferred to the Government of India if the Constituent Assembly continued to function without the participation of representatives of people from all parts of the country.[55] A long series of meetings of the British Cabinet as a whole as well as of its India and Burma Committee followed in quick succession and considered the draft of a new statement of British policy in India. This was officially announced on 20 February 1947 and became famous as Attlee's Declaration. It was simultaneously announced that Rear Admiral Viscount Mountbatten, Supreme Commander of the Allied Forces in South-East Asia, would soon replace Wavell as the Viceroy of India.

The new statement of British policy was a fairly long document, containing fifteen paragraphs. The most important among them were numbered seven and ten. Paragraph seven stated that the British Government wished to make it clear that it was their definite intention 'to take the necessary steps to effect the transference of power into responsible Indian hands by a date not later than June 1948'. Paragraph ten provided that if a Constitution based on agreement among all the parties could not be made by a fully representative Constituent Assembly by the date stipulated in paragraph seven, 'His Majesty's Government will have to consider to whom the powers of the Central Government in British India should be handed over, on the due date, whether as a whole to some form of Central Government for British India or in some areas to the existing Provincial Governments, or in such other way as may seem most reasonable and in the best interests of the Indian people.'[56]

V

As always in the recent past, the leading members of the British Cabinet hoped again that the new policy statement was likely to push the leaders of the Congress and the League—who seemed to have come to the breaking point—towards a compromise settlement by making them face reality and realizing that the British were determined to withdraw from India by a fixed date. As Attlee explained to Field Marshal Smuts, the Prime Minister of South Africa, on 19 February 1947:

> A fundamental element in the Indian situation has always been the attempts of the two major parties to throw responsibility upon us. If we

say that unless there is agreement on a new constitution we shall remain, parties will continue to be uncompromising. In our belief it is only when they are faced with definite date for our withdrawal that there is any prospect of their reaching an accommodation. It therefore seems to us essential to make this statement while both parties are still in Government as we hope that [the?] fact that they have only a limited period in which to settle their differences would induce a sense of sober realism and encourage compromise.[57]

Actually, the 'limited period' within which the final settlement of the Indian constitutional problem had to be settled in order to enable Britain to wind up its rule over India before the period ended had an entirely opposite impact. This was particularly because the promise of ending British rule over India was combined with a clear indication that the creation of Pakistan would not at all be a problem if only certain provinces continued to refuse to be represented in the Constituent Assembly and stuck to their desire to form a State of their own. The League leadership, which had never wavered in its determination to secure Pakistan, naturally felt elated. This mood was reflected in the League's mouthpiece, *Dawn*, of 21 February 1947:

As one reads [the] Statement issued yesterday by His Majesty's Government one cannot help feeling that it represents a new approach to the Indian problem. Mr Attlee and his colleagues appear to have realized at last what the Muslim League has repeatedly asserted that the hope of framing an agreed Constitution for a united India was an idle dream.[58]

With such an understanding of the nature and significance of the new declaration of British policy and that, too, based on fact and not on fancy, it is not surprising that instead of exploring the means for a settlement with the Congress, the League now turned its attention towards adding more vigour to its programme of Direct Action in the Punjab—already underway—in order to establish its dominance in that province. For it was the key province of the projected State of Pakistan and if it continued to be ruled by a coalition of non-League parties, headed by Khizr Hyat Khan Tiwana, the birth of Pakistan might be aborted in spite of the Statement of 20 February. It was, therefore, necessary from the League's point of view to push the movement in the Punjab as much as possible. The Governor of the Punjab, Sir E. Jenkins, aptly put it in his note recorded on 14 February after being shown the draft of the new statement of British policy:

> The document is presumably intended to bring the Congress and the Muslim League up against reality and to force them to cooperate with one another. In my judgment it will have the diametrically opposite effect. If the British, as now appears, are leaving within seventeen months and are prepared to hand over power to those exercising *de facto* authority at the Centre or in the Provinces when the time comes, what incentive is there for the contending parties to get together? Few Indian politicians want an amicable settlement, except on their own terms, and the tendency will unquestionably be for all parties to seize as much power as they can—if necessary by force.
>
> My particular concern is with the Punjab. Here the struggle for power has already begun. . . . In the Punjab the statement, as it stands, may lead to an explosion of great violence. The statement will be regarded as the prelude to the final communal show-down, and the disturbances—if any—resulting from it might be of the gravest description. . . .[59]

And so it proved to be. The provincial elections in the Punjab in 1946 had resulted in the League's emergence as the largest single party as also the party that had won the overwhelming majority of Muslim seats. However, all the non-League parties together formed a majority in the Assembly and, being opposed to the League, particularly because of its espousal of the goal of Pakistan, combined together to form a non-League ministry. The League leaders in the Punjab as well as at the all-India level were quite unhappy with this situation. The wave of bitter communal troubles in 1946 starting from Bengal and moving on to Bihar and then to UP finally touched the Punjab too, and this provided a congenial atmosphere for the League to carry on its agitation against the Tiwana ministry. Indeed, the one helped the other. While the agitation resulted in fostering communal troubles, the latter provided strength to the League's agitation and brought more and more recruits to it. By the middle of November 1946 the situation had already come to such a pass that the Governor had to promulgate the Punjab Public Safety Ordinance, with the full support of Premier Tiwana. According to the Governor, this had 'a sobering effect'. The Government, using the powers conferred by it, were able to turn back to the NWFP a group of uniformed League volunteers and to arrest some members of the RSS, which had recently become quite active in the Punjab.[60] By January, the League's agitation had gathered further momentum, particularly because of the activities of its National Guards, a semi-military organization. The same was true of the RSS. The

Governor thought that sooner or later the Government would have to deal with those bodies as their activities might create a dangerous situation. Tiwana agreed with that analysis and the Government went into action on 24 January 1947. Both the organizations were declared illegal and a number of raids were carried out on their offices. Faced with resistance at the office of the Muslim National Guards at Lahore, the police had to arrest a number of them. This led to widespread disturbances in Lahore. Fifteen members of the Assembly belonging to the League were arrested on 25 January for defying the ban on meetings and processions. About a thousand helmets were recovered from the office of the Muslim National Guards. Tiwana returned from Delhi the same day and, though not happy with the arrests, realized that order must be enforced and supported the police action.[61]

The League's agitation in the Punjab, however, showed no sign of slackening, especially as it received strong support from its all-India leadership. The League's Working Committee, for instance, in its resolution on the Punjab situation adopted at Karachi on 1 February 1947, strongly condemned the Punjab Government's order banning the Muslim National Guards and stressed the 'fundamentally unrepresentative and unpopular character' of that Government.[62] Several leaders of the League, including members of the Interim Government, openly supported the League's agitation in the Punjab and described it as a precursor of the shape of things to come in India as a whole.[63] Even so, the League's agitation in the Punjab had till then been following the pattern of the civil disobedience movement launched by the Congress in the past, based on hartals, meetings and processions, criticism of police actions and eulogization of the heroism of demonstrators, and just like them was drawing less attention from the people as time went on.[64] On 19 February 1947, Wavell reported to Pethick Lawrence: 'The trouble in the Punjab continues, but both sides seem to be ready to consider terms for a compromise'.[65]

The political situation in the Punjab, including the character of the League's agitation, underwent a drastic change after the announcement of the new British policy on 20 February. 'During the past few days,' reported Jenkins to Pethick-Lawrence, 'demonstrators have been increasingly mischievous and violent, invading courts and private houses and endeavouring to hoist Muslim League flag in place of Union Jack.' Equally significant was the change in the attitude of the Premier, Tiwana. He was no longer prepared to continue with the policy of repression. The attitude of senior British members of the civil and police services also changed and their main thought now was when they would return home. The Governor himself became conscious of the fact that in the new situation his position in the exercise of his special responsibilities was no longer the same. The most significant result of the announcement of 20 February was that Tiwana was no longer interested in fighting with the League. Indeed, he immediately decided to settle with it as soon as possible. His thinking was that in the changed situation his ministry could not last for long, and that if chaos and civil war had to be avoided there must be a ministry representing the bulk of Muslims and Sikhs. Jenkins fully supported this line and was indeed holding discussions with one of the prominent leaders of the League in Bengal, Nazimuddin, in the hope of persuading the League to come to terms with the Tiwana Ministry.[66] Wavell was also sympathetic to this move.[67]

However, nothing came out of that move. In the meanwhile, Tiwana, who had been increasingly gloomy since Attlee's Declaration of 20 February, suddenly resigned on 2 March 1947, though he had promised the Governor that he would not do so until the budget session of the Assembly (which was to begin the next day) was over.[68] 'Khizr evidently made up his mind,' commented Wavell, 'with a minimum of consultation and a maximum of speed which has markedly been absent from other Indian political decisions in my time'[69] Khizr, however, had his reasons. He must have realized that Muslims by and large were opposed to him and in such a situation he could not deal effectively with the developing situation in the Punjab, especially after 20 February. Whatever his reasons, his resignation brought to the fore the Pakistan issue in the Punjab, with Muslims clearly for it and Sikhs and Hindus equally clearly opposed. In such a situation, the Nawab of Mamdot, the top League leader as also leader of the Opposition in the Assembly, who was charged by the Governor with forming a ministry, failed to satisfy the Governor about his having the support of the majority in the Assembly, and the Punjab had to be placed under Governor's rule under Section 93 of the Government of India Act of 1935. The basic cause of Mamdot's failure to marshal majority support in the Assembly was the strong opposition of Hindus and Sikhs to the League's demand for Pakistan and their refusal to serve in a League ministry, which they thought would amount to an undiluted Muslim rule, which they could never tolerate. In the meanwhile, largely due to the deep Hindu and Sikh resentment at all this, the communal situation in the Punjab worsened further and serious riots broke out in Lahore, Amritsar, Multan, and Rawalpindi. Indeed, the situation appeared so serious that the British Cabinet began considering the Partition of the Punjab, and the Secretary of State for India asked the Viceroy for his suggestions in that regard after consulting the Governor.[70] The Governor even prepared a note examining the pros and cons of Partition, even though his own inclination was to go on trying to keep the Punjab united, if at all possible.[71] This was now a vain hope, based on an underestimate of the depth of resentment among Sikhs and Hindus in the Punjab over what appeared to them as the forcible overthrow of a duly constituted coalition ministry and the effort being made to install a League-dominated ministry with a view to taking the whole of the Punjab into Pakistan. The Governor's note had been finalized on 7 March. On 8 March, the Congress Working Committee adopted a resolution referring to the unconstitutional and violent means adopted for the overthrow of the Punjab ministry, showing concern at the continuing violence and suggesting the Partition of the Punjab into two provinces, one with Muslim-majority areas and the other with non-Muslim-majority areas.[72]

In the meanwhile, the League had also launched its Direct Action programme in the NWFP with a view to overthrowing the Congress ministry in office there, based on the support, among others, of the majority of the Muslim members in the Assembly. The overthrow of this ministry was as important for the League as was the overthrow of the Punjab ministry. For the scheme of Pakistan, on which the League leadership had set their heart, could not be complete without NWFP, with an overwhelming Muslim majority, being included in it. The by-election to the Assembly at Mardan held in the middle of February 1947 had gone in the League's favour. This was a great source of encouragement to the League. And so were the happenings in the Punjab, so close to the NWFP.

The widespread Muslim resentment over the Government's handling of the case of a Sikh widow in Hazara, who had been forcibly converted and married to a Muslim, but allowed by

Premier Khan Sahib, after she had stayed in his house for a few days, to return to her Sikh relatives as per her choice, provided the League with a splendid opportunity, which it fully utilized. The cry of 'Islam in danger' went up and the League decided to take advantage of it in order to whip up Muslim feelings against the Congress ministry. A large meeting was organized in Peshawar on 21 February 1947 and that developed into a procession 5,000 strong. The processionists, armed with spears and daggers, entered the garden of Khan Sahib's residence and, besieging it from all sides, broke all the windows and threw stones into the rooms. When the Governor visited the house he found it 'a shambles of broken glass'. The senior executive and police officers somehow succeeded in dispersing the crowd. Tear-gas shells were used, but the police, without, of course, staging a mutiny, quietly refused to carry out the order to fire and confined themselves to just loading their guns. In the Governor's opinion, Khan Sahib was 'brave as a lion', and refused to give way on any point and went out on top of the porch to tell the crowd what he thought of them. He was, however, 'lucky to get away with his life'. As trouble was apprehended the next day also, a flag march by troops was organized around the city and troops were placed at strategic points with instructions to fire if found necessary. So 22 February passed off peacefully. 'So far,' wrote the Governor, 'this show of force has succeeded in preserving any repetition of yesterday's incidents, but what is worrying is the proof of police demoralization.'[73]

Among the various factors that could have been responsible for this demoralization, one certainly was the gathering momentum of the League's agitation and the growing Muslim support for it. And this despite, or perhaps because of, most of the League MLAs being in prison as a result of their involvement in the agitation, which often took a violent turn.[74] 'League Direct Action Campaign,' observed the Governor, 'is growing in volume, and I do not feel that my Ministry realize that the flood may quite conceivably sweep them away.'[75] Pethick Lawrence's comment on going through the detailed report of the Governor was that the Muslim League in the NWFP seemed poised to attempt 'a repetition of the recent events in the Punjab'.[76]

It is clear that the Muslim League, under Jinnah's leadership, was firmly determined to secure Pakistan and had demonstrated tremendous support for it among Muslims, not only in the Muslim-minority provinces but, what was really important, also in the Muslim-majority provinces, as per the results of the elections of 1946. Its Direct Action programme in Bengal, Punjab, and the NWFP was clearly geared towards the speedy achievement of that goal. Indeed, Jinnah was so determined on it that even while the Direct Action campaign was in full swing in the NWFP, he was secretly preparing to launch a special programme based on *jihad* in the tribal areas of the NWFP in case it became necessary in order to dislodge the Congress ministry in the NWFP and secure that province for Pakistan. He entrusted this task to Iskander Mirza (later to become President of Pakistan for a short time), belonging to the Indian Political Service and at that time working in the Ministry of Defence, Government of India, as Joint Secretary. This has been recently revealed by the latter's son, Humayun Mirza, in his book on his father. Not being a historian, and besides writing perhaps from memory on the basis of the version of events given by his father, he has made a serious error in mentioning February as the month of the conversation between Jinnah and his father. As Mountbatten was mentioned by Jinnah in connection with his doubt whether Pakistan would be conceded or not, the month was most probably April (first half), when Jinnah had his preliminary talks with Mountbatten. With this introduction, we can now turn to Humayun Mirza himself:

> Muslim pressure for the creation of Pakistan began to increase as talks for independence of India progressed. But Mountbatten showed no sign of giving way on this issue. Thus it was that, in February [*sic*] 1947, Jinnah again sent for Iskander Mirza and told him that the prospects of getting Pakistan did not look good. He felt that Muslim anger had to be properly demonstrated, otherwise the British would hand the country over to the Congress. He declared that if Pakistan could not be won by negotiation then it would have to be won by the will of the Muslims. While he intended to continue his negotiations with vigour, he felt it prudent to be prepared for the worst. He, therefore, decided that should negotiations fail by the middle of May, a dramatic statement must be made by the Muslims. He asked Iskander Mirza to be prepared to resign from the Government of India, and return to the tribal territory that he knew so well. There he was to start a *jihad* (holy war) against the British. . . .

Jinnah's request, continues Humayun Mirza, stunned his father. He had served the British for long and had developed a good deal of respect for them. He also thought of the bloodshed that would result from a *jihad* by the tribesmen. 'Yet he could not refuse Jinnah.' So he agreed to undertake the task, but pointed out that money would be needed, particularly if it involved inviting the tribesmen in Waziristan, Tirah, and the Mohammad country to rebel against the British. When asked how much, he estimated would be the cost, Mirza mentioned about a crore of rupees (£750,000 at the rate of exchange at that time). Mirza also said that some cover story would have to be manufactured before he resigned from the Government and disappeared into the tribal territory. 'Jinnah had already anticipated these requirements: he had the money and the cover ready.' Iskander Mirza received Rs. 20,000 for his immediate expenses, with the assurance that the Nawab of Bhopal would provide the rest. As for the cover, Iskander Mirza was to be told 'at the right time'. Jinnah further assured him that if anything should happen to him, the former would take care of his family. Iskander Mirza immediately began to draw up a plan of action. As he prepared to see Jinnah with his plan, however, he was informed that there was no longer any need for *jihad*. As pointed out by Humayun Mirza, this incident shows, that Jinnah 'was prepared to go to any length to achieve Pakistan'.[77]

On the other hand, the Congress had made its stand on Partition clear about 5 years ago in the course of its resolution on the Cripps Plan (1942). That stand implied that while the Congress was opposed to Partition, it could not think of any compulsion on any group of people to belong to the Indian Union against their wishes. However, by the same logic, those who stood for Partition could not carry with them large groups of people in any area who were not willing to go along with them and wanted to remain in India. The Congress Working Committee's resolution of 8 March 1947, demanding the Partition of the Punjab, was a clear indication of the fact that its members had realized that Partition had by that time become inevitable and further that they were prepared to accept it, provided the Hindu and Sikh majority areas in the Punjab and the Hindu majority areas in Bengal were not allowed to be made parts of Pakistan, as would happen if the League's demand for a province-wise decision regarding Pakistan was accepted. Explaining the difference between province-wise Pakistan and area-wise Pakistan, Nehru conveyed to Wavell:

The distinction is important as both in Bengal and Punjab there are very large non-Muslim minorities. In the event of Bengal or Punjab, as Provinces, deciding by a bare majority, not to adhere to a Union [of India], the question immediately arises about Western Bengal and Eastern Punjab which are predominantly non-Muslim areas and which have no intention whatever of separating themselves from the Indian Union.

It is in order to get over all these difficulties that we have suggested a Partition of the Punjab and the same principle applies to Bengal. If the Muslim League accepts the Cabinet Mission's scheme of May 16th and cooperates in the Constituent Assembly, then this question does not arise in this form. . . . In the event of the Muslim League not accepting the Cabinet Delegation's scheme and not coming to the Constituent Assembly, the division of Bengal and Punjab becomes inevitable.[78]

Thus by the time Mountbatten arrived in India, the situation on the ground in India had moved quite close to Partition. The question really was no longer whether India would be partitioned or not, but partitioned on what terms or under what modalities. Attlee's Declaration of 20 February had also clearly indicated that the decision makers on the British side had finally veered round to the same view. Though, just like the leaders of the Congress, they continued to refer to the Cabinet Mission's long-term proposal, which might still become a basis for the settlement of the Indian problem, that was merely a formality.

VI

Mountbatten arrived in India on 22 March 1947 and was sworn in as Viceroy and Governor-General of India two days later. Before leaving Britain he had received his formal instructions for guidance in the discharge of his duties in India in the form of a letter addressed to him by Attlee on 18 March. Here, among other things, the Prime Minister told Mountbatten that he had to do his best to persuade all political parties in India to work together in the Constituent Assembly on the basis of the Cabinet Mission's Plan in order to draw up a constitution for a united India, preferably within the British Commonwealth. This was, of course, a proforma directive. Attlee by that time knew as well as

Mountbatten that a united India was no longer in the realm of possibility. If it had been, there would have been no need for a new statement of policy and indeed for a new Viceroy. So the really important directive was contained in these words which followed:

Since, however, this plan can only become operative in respect of British India by agreement between the major Parties, there can be no question of compelling either major Party to accept it.

If by October, you consider that there can be no prospect of reaching a settlement on the basis of a unitary government for British India, either with or without the cooperation of the Indian States, you should report to His Majesty's Government on the steps which you consider should be taken for the handing over of power on the due date.

Attlee also told Mountbatten that it was essential that there should be the fullest cooperation with the Indian leaders in all steps that were taken regarding the withdrawal of British power so that the process might go forward as smoothly as possible.[79]

Mountbatten dutifully followed these instructions. He did not take much time to realize that speed was the essence of the matter as the political situation in India was fast deteriorating. As he mentioned in his first personal report to the higher authorities in London on 2 April 1947:

The scene here is one of unrelieved gloom. . . . At this early stage, I can see little common ground on which to build any agreed solution for the future of India. The Cabinet is fiercely divided on communal lines; each party has its own solution and does not at present show any sign of being prepared to consider any other.

In addition, the whole country is in a most unsettled state. There are communal riots and troubles in the Punjab, NWFP, Bihar, Calcutta, Bombay, UP and even here in Delhi. In the Punjab all parties are seriously preparing for civil war. . . .[80]

Mountbatten, however, refused to be affected by the surrounding gloom. It speaks volumes of his understanding of the Indian political situation as well as his sense of urgency for the completion of the task assigned to him that he started his series of interviews with the Indian leaders right on 24 March, the day of his swearing in as Viceroy, with a view to finding out whether a settlement of the Indian problem was to be based on a united or a divided India.

Talking to Gandhi first among the top Indian leaders, Mountbatten was 'staggered' by the former's suggestion during their meeting on 1 April that the best course under the then existing circumstances was to forthwith ask Jinnah to head the Interim Government as Prime Minister with full freedom to choose his colleagues.[81] Gandhi elaborated his plan at his next meeting with Mountbatten on 2 April. As the latter recorded:

He wants me to invite Mr Jinnah to form a new Central Government for India, which will be the Government to which I have to turn over power. He suggests I should leave it to Mr Jinnah to select the Ministers, if necessary, entirely from the Muslim League, but if he feels so inclined he can of course make it a coalition Government by including Nehru and other Congress Ministers as well as representatives of Minorities. In fact he suggests that Jinnah would be well-advised to try and get the highest class team together and one likely to enjoy the greatest confidence of the Assembly.

Gandhi wanted that Mountbatten should guide such a Government in order to ensure fair play. Apparently Gandhi had it also in his mind that the reconstituted Government should continue way beyond June 1948, a date by when the British would have withdrawn from India and Mountbatten, too, would have been gone—thereby postponing, if not altogether avoiding, Partition and ensuring that if it came, it should be as a result of a decision arrived at by the Indians themselves, without the presence of the British. This is borne out by the following extract from Mountbatten's record of his interview with Gandhi on 2 April:

The essence of the scheme was that it should be put through quickly in order that I might have as many months as possible as Viceroy and President of the Cabinet, and, by retaining the right of veto, continue to exercise complete control in the interests of fair play. The fact that I should be there to see fair play for the first few months would ensure Mr Jinnah's Government no[t] doing anything foolish which would prejudice its reputation in the Assembly or in the country; and he felt that I could guide them along in a manner which would ensure their continuing along the straight and narrow path after I left in June 1948.

Gandhi also added that if Jinnah refused this offer, the same should be made to the Congress, as the only other major party in India.[82]

It is extremely doubtful if Jinnah, with his strong determination to achieve Pakistan as soon as possible, would have been lured by the offer of prime ministership into accepting Gandhi's plan.

For one of its essential features was that the Interim Government would continue well beyond June 1948, implying an indefinite postponement of Partition and the final decision on it without the presence of the British power. Besides, another feature of the Gandhi Plan that would make it useless to Jinnah was that the Government headed by him was expected to function with the support of the Central Assembly, in which the Congress enjoyed an overwhelming majority. On the other hand, if he did accept the Gandhi Plan, without giving up the objective of having a full Pakistan, carrying with it also areas with non-Muslim majority—and it would be absurd to imagine that he could do otherwise just because he had become Prime Minister—he would naturally use his new position to facilitate his objective, just as had happened after the League's entry into the Interim Government, with the acquiescence, if not support, of the Congress. That would surely land India and the Congress into a fierce civil war, after the exit of the British power, the Prime Minister himself leading the other side. It is, therefore, not surprising that Gandhi failed to persuade the Congress leaders, with the sole exception of Khan Abdul Ghaffar Khan, to accept his plan and duly conveyed this to Mountbatten.[83] So the stage did not arrive when Mountbatten could have made the offer of Prime Ministership to Jinnah. It may be added that one cannot be sure what Mountbatten—in spite of being sympathetic to Gandhi's plan and quite enthusiastic about the prospect of having a genuine coalition Government at the Centre—would have actually done if that stage had arrived. For almost all his senior advisers considered the Gandhi Plan as 'not workable'.[84]

In any case, Jinnah, in his discussions with Mountbatten, stood firm as a rock on the demand for Partition. Mountbatten mentioned in his third personal report, dated 17 April 1947, to the authorities in London:

> I have had six meetings during the past week with Jinnah, averaging between two to three hours each, and the conversations continued on the same lines which I reported last week. He has made it abundantly clear that the League will not in any circumstances reconsider the Cabinet Mission Plan, and he is intent on having Pakistan. . . . When pressed for details of his scheme and how it was to be carried out, he said "you must carry out a surgical operation; cut India and its army firmly into half and give me the half that belongs to the Muslim League". I told him

that if I accepted his arguments on the need for Partition of India, then I could not resist the arguments that Congress were putting forward for the Partition of the Punjab and Bengal. He was quite horrified and argued at great length on the need to preserve the unity of the Punjab and Bengal, pointing out that the Punjabis and Bengalis regarded their provinces as unified territories which they would hate to see split up.

I told him that I had been so impressed by his arguments that I was prepared to accept them. He was delighted, but only until I pointed out that his arguments had also convinced me that the Partition of India itself would be criminal. Then we started going round the Mulberry bush again.

When, on another occasion, Mountbatten persisted with his argument that if India was divided, by the same logic Punjab and Bengal, too, would have to be divided, Jinnah told him: 'If you persist in chasing me with your ruthless logic we shall get nowhere.' Finally, Mountbatten told Jinnah that the latter had a choice between two options: (1) the Cabinet Mission Plan which gave him all five Provinces of Pakistan with complete autonomy within India and only a very weak Centre; and (2) 'a very moth-eaten Pakistan'. Jinnah replied: 'I do not care how little you give me as long as you give it to me completely.'[85]

While Jinnah remained firm like a rock on the demand for Partition, Nehru conveyed no objection to it as such, but only insisted on the Partition of the Punjab and Bengal if India was going to be divided. This is borne out by Mountbatten's record of his interview with Nehru on 8 April 1947:

We then discussed with Pandit Nehru what his solution would be for the transfer of power. He thought that it would not be right to impose any form of constitution on any community that had a majority in any specific area. Thus if we were to demit Province by Province, he felt they should have the right to decide whether to join a Hindustan Group, a Pakistan Group, or possibly even remain completely independent. He added that of course before such a thing were done the Punjab and Bengal would have to be split into separate Provinces.[86]

Partly in answer to certain questions raised by Mountbatten and partly by way of elucidating his own stand, Nehru went into the mechanics of Partition, and made observations, which taken together with his observations noted earlier, virtually presented some of the core elements, in spirit though not in letter, of what was to become famous later as the Mountbatten Plan and accepted by the leaders of the Congress and the League on 3 June 1947. To turn again to Mountbatten's record:

In reply to a question about how to obtain the real views of the people of the NWFP, on which group they wished to join he suggested that a fresh election should be held after a statement had been made.

The whole thing revolved round having a strong Centre, certainly to begin with, and for that reason Pandit Nehru would favour making a statement soon and transferring power to Provinces while there was still time for me to be in charge at the Centre to help in the early stages of negotiations at the Centre.[87]

Rajendra Prasad, then President of the Constituent Assembly and generally regarded as a most devoted follower, indeed a yes-man of Gandhi, also did not mention to Mountbatten one word against Partition if the latter found that that was the only way to avoid a civil war. As per Mountbatten's record of his interview with Prasad on 10 April 1947:

I said that I still had a completely open mind, but that it had become clear to me that Mr Jinnah was thinking only along the line of Partition.

Dr Rajendra Prasad enlarged on the disastrous consequences of the break-up of Indian unity; and I expressed agreement with his sentiments and his reasoning. I then asked him whether he considered that those reasons were strong enough to override the objection that there would certainly be a civil war if I were to enforce it against the wishes of the Muslim League.

He agreed that the position now reached made civil war very likely if I were to try and enforce a decision against the wishes of any large section of the people.[88]

Mountbatten's interview with C. Rajagopalachari in April also went along the same lines. To cite from Mountbatten's record again:

I told Rajagopalachari in strict confidence the general drift of my conversations with Mr Jinnah, and he admitted with great expression of regret that the ideal of a unified India could not be imposed by force, and if in fact the decision to hand over to a unified India were to lead to civil war that would indeed be a tragic paradox. He accepted entirely that I must be guided by what was practicable and what would produce a peaceful solution; but begged me not to make such binding decisions that the Indian people could not work out their own salvation as time went on.[89]

Sardar Patel was interviewed by Mountbatten on 12 April. When asked by the latter whether he felt that the Congress could be made to accept the Cabinet Mission Plan without any reservations, Patel replied that it was he who had persuaded the Congress to accept that plan and promised his full support in persuading it again after Jinnah was made to feel compelled to accept it. At the same time, he suggested to Mountbatten a way of bringing about a change in Jinnah's attitude: offering him option of the Partition of India along with the Partition of the Punjab and Bengal. Such a suggestion could not have come from a person totally opposed Partition. As Mountbatten put it:

Sardar Patel told me that the mistake that all the British had permanently made with Mr Jinnah was always to give way to him, as a means of saving his face. He said that Mr Jinnah would only accept the Cabinet Mission Plan when the force of circumstances gave him no alternative. He told me that as soon as I announced the Partition of Bengal, the Muslims of Bengal would secede from the League in order to preserve the unity of Bengal. He thought that this might possibly follow in the Punjab, and it would not be unlikely that there would be a revolt of the League against Mr Jinnah if he had nothing better than Sind, and possibly half of the Punjab to offer them for Pakistan, if Congress still retained their hold on the NWFP.[90]

Maulana Azad was the next Congress leader to be interviewed by Mountbatten on the same day. Azad, viewing the issue as between Partition and the Cabinet Mission Plan, in the context of the interests of Indian Muslims as he perceived them, made no secret of his strong dislike for Partition and his equally strong liking for the Cabinet Mission Plan. This was based on his assumption that while the Cabinet Mission Plan gave the Muslims a full Pakistan with provision for seceding from India after ten years, immediate Partition was likely to be based only on a truncated Pakistan. Mountbatten recorded:

I gave Maulana Azad the broad outline of my conversations with Mr Jinnah. In conclusion he told me that whereas the full Pakistan, such as proposed by the Cabinet Mission, could be made to work, a truncated Pakistan would spell disaster for the Musalmans, and that if Mr Jinnah were now prepared to accept such a decision, he would be committing suicide.

He failed to see why Mr Jinnah could not accept the Cabinet Mission

Plan, since after all it gave them the right to secede from the rest of India at the end of ten years if they wished.[91]

For the rest, Azad, too, like Sardar Patel, indulged in wishful thinking and thought that Jinnah was likely to lose his commanding position if it became known that he had agreed to the Partition of Bengal and the Punjab. Further, he offered to do his best to persuade both the Congress and the League to accept the Cabinet Mission Plan. In any case, just like Patel, he was quite convinced that 'if Mr Jinnah really accepted the Cabinet Mission Plan, at almost any stage within the next few months, the chances of Congress cooperating were really very fair.[92]

By that time it had become quite clear to all concerned, including Mountbatten, that the League was not going to agree to go back to the Cabinet Mission Plan and was determined upon full Partition without any further delay. It was also not a secret that even if the League agreed to go back to the Cabinet Mission Plan, the Congress would not at that stage agree to Assam and the non-Muslim areas of the Punjab and Bengal becoming part of a bigger Pakistan within the Indian Union, with a strong possibility of its getting out of the Union at the next available opportunity. So Azad's conviction as well as Patel's promise to rally around the Congress if the League unreservedly accepted the Cabinet Mission Plan amounted virtually to the acceptance of the inevitability of Partition.

Indeed, Azad had already signified his support for Partition, while also expressing his support for the Gandhi Plan and the Cabinet Mission Plan, in the course of his conversation with Mountbatten as early as 2 April. As the latter points out in his record of that interview, Azad 'staggered' him by mentioning that in his opinion, the Cabinet Mission Plan was 'perfectly feasible of being carried out'. When asked to express his preference between Gandhi's Plan and the Cabinet Mission Plan, he said that if all concerned parties fully accepted the latter, this would be preferable to the Gandhi plan. Questioned further, Azad affirmed that Partition (of Mountbatten's conception at that time, involving the division of India into several parts, not just two, with a very weak Central authority) might also be a good alternative. As this completely negates the impression sought to be created by Azad's supposed memoir,[93] which has become the basis of the contention by some that Azad continued to work for saving India's unity even after Gandhi had given way, it seems appropriate to present here the exact words used in Mountbatten's record of this part of his interview with Azad on 2 April:

I mentioned the other alternative [Partition] which I had put to Mr Gandhi an hour before, and he thought this also a very good alternative.

In fact Maulana Azad said that the sooner a decision could be taken and implemented, and the longer I could remain at the Centre to get things straightened out and running smoothly before I left the better for the future of Inda.[94]

Even Gandhi, while engaged in promoting his plan, did not, at the beginning directly oppose Partition in his conversation with Mountbatten. When on 2 April, for instance, after listening to his exposition of his plan, Mountbatten raised the issue of Partition, Gandhi did not react forcefully against it, perhaps because he was at that stage quite optimistic about his plan being implemented, which would in any case have postponed that issue beyond June 1948 when the British would have left India. As Mountbatten records:

We discussed alternatives, and I told him I favoured the Cabinet Mission Plan most of all and he replied that he too would be in favour of it if it could be revived.

Finally I discussed the possibility of turning over power to the areas of India in accordance with the wishes of the majority of the residents in those areas. Broadly speaking this would make a Hindu India with a Congress Government in Delhi, a truncated Pakistan, and the large States like Mysore, Tranvancore, Hyderabad, Kashmir, and groups of States, each having separate power turned over to them, owing allegiance to a Central authority for Defence, External Affairs, Communications, and possibly food.

He agreed that whatever the decision, it should be taken soon and implemented as early as possible, and that meanwhile it would be an excellent thing if I remained in charge of the Central Government with the power of veto until June 1948.[95]

At his next meeting with Mountbatten on 3 April, Gandhi strongly pleaded for his plan as providing the best solution, but at the same time affirmed that if Mountbatten was not able to decide in its favour, he would support the latter 'in any other solution' which he could put as being 'in the best interests of the Indian people'. As per Mountbatten's record, Gandhi agreed that if the Muslim League remained completely intransigent, 'Partition might have to come though he was anxious to retain as strong a Centre as possible' in that case.[96] The mention of a strong Centre by Gandhi was clearly made with reference to Mountbatten's idea of a weak Central authority which might function after Partition.

It was much later, after it had become known that Partition was going to take place on the basis of a truncated Pakistan, but without any Central authority, that Gandhi, during his meeting with Mountbatten on 4 May, forcefully opposed Partition. His view was that if Partition had to take place it must do so after the complete withdrawal of British power from India. He refused to agree with Mountbatten that whatever was being planned was on the basis of the wishes of the Indians themselves and asserted that the British were practically 'imposing Partition'. When asked for an alternative, Gandhi again mentioned his original plan and advised Mountbatten to transfer power either to the Muslim League or to the Congress, grant India Dominion Status, and remain in India as Governor-General till June 1948. Upon Mountbatten's pointing out that the implementation of such a plan might lead to a civil war, Gandhi countered him by pointing to the joint appeal to the Indian people abjuring the use of force for the settlement of political differences signed by him and Jinnah on 15 April. Mountbatten refused to accept that argument and contended that Jinnah had signed that appeal when he thought that the Viceroy was going to give a fair decision. Mountbatten proceeded to affirm that he 'did not for one moment believe that the Muslims would not immediately go to war', if he went on to betray them by accepting Gandhi's suggestion. Mountbatten added further that in any case the British Government would never allow him to 'hand over such a colossal minority like the Muslims into the power of the Congress'.[97]

Gandhi did not give up and followed up his oral presentation by a written communication reiterating his viewpoint even more forcibly and adding some new points. In a letter sent to Mountbatten from inside a train carrying him from New Delhi to Patna on 8 May, he observed:

> Whatever may be said to the contrary, it would be a blunder of the first magnitude for the British to be party in any way whatsoever to the division of India. If it has to come, let it come after the British withdrawal, as a result of understanding between the parties or an armed conflict which according to Quaid-i-Azam Jinnah is a taboo.

Proceeding, further Gandhi clarified that he was equally opposed to the Partition of the Punjab and Bengal. He observed: 'I feel that Partition of the Punjab and Bengal is wrong in every case and a needless irritant to the League. This as well as all innovations can come after the British withdrawal not before, except always for mutual consent.' Gandhi further added:

> If you are not to leave a legacy of chaos behind, you have to make your choice and leave the Government of the whole of India, including the States, to one party. The constituent Assembly has to provide for the governance even of that part of India which is not represented [in the Constituent Assembly] by the Muslim League or some States.[98]

However, Gandhi's exertions, coming almost at the last moment, were in vain. The main decision regarding Partition had already been taken and approved in principle by the Congress Working Committee at its meeting in New Delhi on 1 May, at which Gandhi, too, had been present and found no one except Khan Abdul Ghaffar Khan supporting his point of view. This was by no means a lone occurrence. Gandhi's role in decision-making by the Congress Working Committee was no longer what it had been in the past (since 1920) and had considerably dwindled during the last one year. While he continued to be deeply revered by the bulk of the Hindu masses and other non-Muslim groups, with some Muslims, too, thrown in here and there, the leadership inside the Working Committee had slipped from his hands into those of is chief political disciples, Nehru and Patel.[99] Mountbatten had been well aware of this since the first week of April, when Gandhi's plan about offering Prime Ministership to Jinnah had been found unacceptable by the top Congress leaders. This was most poignantly reflected by the fact that while Gandhi was still thinking of a way to avoid Partition, the Working Committee on 1 May, in spite of Gandhi's presence on it, had accepted Partition in principle, without, of course, going into the details of the proposed mechanism for it and this had been communicated on the same day to Mountbatten by Nehru.[100] In view of all this, it is not surprising that Gandhi's letter to Mountbatten written on 8 May proved as unfruitful as his oral presentation to the latter had been. Indeed, as perhaps during their last meeting Mountbatten had already dealt with Gandhi's basic point about the British agreeing to the decision about Partition being taken by the Indians after the termination of British power in India, all that his letter of 8 May achieved was a curt, if also polite, acknowledgement from Mountbatten: 'Thank you for your letter of the 8th and for the advice you were kind enough to send me, which I appreciated receiving.'[101] The move towards Partition had actually advanced too for by then to be reversed and that, too, by the intervention of a forlorn and lonely pilgrim, revered by the masses but no longer in command of the Congress, with which he had been identified since 1920.

VII

As already indicated, the fact was that although Mountbatten often talked about his predilection for a united India and had also been asked by Attlee to first try to see whether the Cabinet Mission Plan could be revived, neither Attlee or Mountbatten really believed that that was possible at that stage. That is why even while the latter had still to interview the really top leaders of the country, like Gandhi, Jinnah, and Nehru, he was ready by 31 March—exactly a week after having been sworn in as Viceroy—with a tentative Partition Plan, which he presented at his sixth staff meeting held on that date. It is remarkable that although it passed through innumerable revisions, both in New Delhi and London, that plan had several features that found a place in the final Partition Plan, which became ready by the end of May. The main features of the Partition Plan of 31 March were as follows:

1. The essence of the plan would be a form of Partition with a Central authority for reserved subjects; this to be an experimental arrangement and to come into being in the near future.
2. The three units which would be the result of this Partition would be:
   a. Hindustan, to include the predominantly Hindu provinces,
   b. Pakistan, to include the predominantly Muslim provinces,
   c. The States.
3. Each of these units would be offered a form of Dominion Status. In the case of the States, the larger ones would be offered this status; the smaller ones would have to combine into units of suitable size.
4. In view of the grant of Pakistan, and on the same principles

which justified that grant, there would be Partition of the Punjab and Bengal.

5. The plan would be brought into force in about May 1947, and would run experimentally until June 1948.
6. The Central authority, which might be called 'Central Government' or 'Central Council', would deal only with the reserved subjects of Defence; Foreign Affairs; Food; and Finance to cover these.
7. The Central Authority as well as the Hindustan Government would be situated in Delhi.
8. Each of the reserved subjects would be dealt with by a Council or Board, containing representatives from Hindustan, Pakistan, and the States.
9. The Viceroy would continue to have the right of veto on these reserved subjects.
10. About three months before June 1948, a decision would be made as to whether or not the Central authority would remain in being after that date.[102]

After discussions with the top Indian leaders as well as at his successive staff meetings, Mountbatten reported to the staff meeting on 11 April that of the many possible plans that were being considered, the two receiving the most serious thought were Plan 'Union' and Plan 'Balkan'. While the former was the Cabinet Mission's Plan with possible modifications in certain respects, the latter was based on the principle of 'leaving to each Province the choice of its own future' and would almost certainly result in a form of truncated Pakistan and the eventual abolition of Centre.[103] A slightly revised version of this plan, providing for the Partition of the Punjab and Bengal and elections in the NWFP, was placed before the Governor's Conference on 14–15 April.[104] At the end of this conference, Mountbatten's mind was finally made up as between a united or a divided India. Although all the details regarding the mechanism for Partition and the process of revising the Partition Plan were continuing, Mountbatten had become convinced by that time that Partition might to be 'the only possible alternative'.[105]

In his report to his superiors in London dated 17 April, where he expressed this view, Mountbatten also underlined the gravity of the political situation in India and emphasized that the British had to make up their minds one way or the other 'in the very near future', if they were to avert civil war and the risk of a complete breakdown of the administration. He further added: 'On this, there is complete unanimity of opinion, both European and Indian in this country.'[106]

With this assumption in his mind, Mountbatten applied himself immediately to the finalization of the Partition Plan. The Plan presented to the Governors' Conference on 14–15 December was revised more than once in consultation with the Viceroy's, senior staff members and important political leaders. By 30 April, it was ready in more or less final form[107] (although minor amendments here and there continued to be made even after that day).[108] On the same day, the Viceroy's Principal Secretary, Sir Eric Mieville (in the unavoidable absence of the Viceroy's Chief of Staff, Lord Ismay), took the Plan to Jinnah (forenoon) and Nehru (afternoon). Both made some adverse comments here and there, but said nothing about its basic structure or essential features.[109] Ismay left for London with the same Plan on 2 May for securing the Cabinet's approval and returned after eight days with some changes made by the India and Burma Committee of the Cabinet chaired by the Prime Minister himself. While the process of scrutiny and modification, where considered desirable, was still going on, Ismay sent a telegram to Mountbatten saying, 'We have spent whole morning re-drafting announcement and are having another go at it in the afternoon. Substance remains same but we think you will find presentation considerably improved in the light of very helpful comments of Cabinet Committee.'[110] It is this supposed improvement that caused quite a crisis in Mountbatten's apparently smooth negotiations with the Congress and led to a revision of the Partition Plan in some important respects. This necessitated a postponement of the meeting of top Indian leaders for a final consideration of the Mountbatten Plan from 17 May to 3 June.

It so happened that on 10 May, while Nehru was having a short holiday at Simla as a guest of Mountbatten, the latter received by telegram the text of the revised plan (with only a few minor gaps still to be filled up) for the transfer of power.[111] Although the original idea was that it would be shown to the five leaders representing the Congress (2), Muslim League (2), and Sikhs (1) at the same time at their meeting with Mountbatten on 17 May, and the senior members of his staff had advised him not to depart from it in order to show the revised plan to Nehru alone, Mountbatten had a distinct 'hunch' that he should take advantage of his 'new-found friendship with Nehru to ask his personal opinion of the new draft', a draft which had, just as in the case of Ismay, appeared better to Mountbatten than the one earlier sent out to London. So on 10 May, after dinner was over and Nehru was going to retire to his room, Mountbatten gave him a copy of the new draft to take along with him to read and advise him 'merely as a friend' of the likely reception it would have at his scheduled meeting with the leaders on 17 May. Next day when Mountbatten was in the middle of a meeting with the Governor of the Punjab, he received a response from Nehru in the form of a letter, which he described as 'a bombshell'.[112]

Nehru had indeed felt so agitated and depressed after going through the new draft during the night of 10 May that he immediately sent his reaction to Mountbatten the next morning through a handwritten letter, without waiting for the typist and without even retaining a copy for his own files—indicating his strong feelings and his sense of urgency in communicating his views to Mountbatten. For he saw in the document passed on to him by Mountbatten a neat blueprint for the Balkanization of India into endless units and did not want to lose any time in lodging his protest. As he put it in his letter to Mountbatten:

> I read the draft proposals you gave me with the care they deserved and with every desire to absorb them and accept them in so far as I could. But with all the goodwill in the world I reacted to them very strongly. Indeed they produced a devastating effect upon me. The relatively simple proposals that we had previously discussed now appeared, in the garb that HMG had provided for them, in an entirely new context which gave them an ominous meaning. The whole approach was completely different from what ours had been and the picture of India that emerged frightened me.

That picture, Nehru added, was 'a picture of fragmentation, and conflict and disorder, and, unhappily also, of a worsening of relations between India and Britain'.[113] Nehru followed this up on the same day with a fairly detailed note on the new plan. Though this, too, had been drafted hurriedly, Nehru here proceeded to elucidate the bases of his objections to the various features of the new plan and, what was more important, pinpoint, with great clarity, the key factor behind his disappointment. That factor was the threat of the dismantling of the Indian Union and bringing about the endless Balkanization, going much beyond just the creation of Pakistan, to which the Congress had long since reconciled itself. As Nehru put it:

In our consultations we had proceeded on the present basis of the Cabinet Mission's Plan and the Statement of February 20th. Owing to the stress of circumstances we had agreed to vary this basis to a certain extent, but the general approach continued to be the same. This variation consisted in the acceptance of the fact that certain Muslim majority areas might go out of the Union, if they so willed. The Union was still the basic factor. In the new proposals the whole approach has been changed completely and is at total variance with our own approach in the course of recent talks. The proposals start with the rejection of an Indian Union as the successor to power and invite the claims of large numbers of succession [successor?] states who are permitted to unite if they so wish in two or more states.[114]

In view of this clear exposition by Nehru of the background of his dismay and unhappiness after seeing the draft received from London on 10 May, it is indeed surprising that his outburst has given rise to so much speculation as to its probable cause. Indeed, with the sole exception of R.J. Moore, who has, while presenting a mastery analysis of all the relevant factors, come to the conclusion that Nehru's reaction was 'appropriate to the circumstances',[115] all others who have written on this subject have gone astray. This is largely because of their assumption that there was hardly any significant difference between the draft shown to Nehru by Mieville on 30 April before it was taken to London by Ismay, and the one received from London on 10 May after being revised by the British Cabinet. This has led to various contradictory surmises. On one extreme is that by Mountbatten, who held that the very fact that the draft taken to London had been revised by the British Cabinet had led Nehru to suspect its bona fides. He told his staff meeting on 12 May that while all the Indian leaders seemed to have reasonable faith in his 'honesty and straightforwardness', they appeared to suffer from a 'unanimous phobia amongst them about any document issuing from London, in which they expected and looked for crookedness and catches'.[116] According to Hugh Tinker, the 'drama' that Nehru enacted at Simla was the result of his amnesia or emotional crisis produced by the realization that Partition, which he detested so much, was soon going to become a fact—and apparently he required some time to reconcile himself to it.[117] H.V. Hodson holds a somewhat similar view and remarks that so far as the mode of Partition was concerned, there was hardly any difference 'except in details and nuances', between the three versions of the Mountbatten Plan: the one taken to London by Ismay on 2 May, the revised version received in India on 10 May, and the final version, which was prepared in consultation with Nehru and approved by the leaders of the Congress, the Muslim League, and the Sikhs on 3 June 1947. Apparently, however, Hodson does not feel sure of his ground. For after proceeding to cite Tinker's views approvingly, he almost turns around full circle and observes that there was more behind Nehru's outburst than just his 'complex and emotional personality'. Besides, he says further, if the changes made in London were mere nuances, that does not reduce their importance and Nehru was not altogether wrong in detecting in the 'London plan' a tendency to accept fission into not merely two but probably several parts as inevitable.[118] Even Mountbatten, who had waxed so eloquent in the beginning about his puzzlement at Nehru's reaction, insisting that the revised plan was substantially the same as the original one, later admitted that while the new plan (as revised in London) did not seem to alter the essentials, it perhaps put slightly more stress on the independence option, both for the Provinces and the States.[119] Actually, even this was an under-statement. For the stress was not merely slightly more, but of a nature which had brought about a basic change in the structure of the Partition Plan as carried to London by Ismay.

This was the main reason why Nehru had felt so upset after going through the revised plan at Simla. In such a situation, it is futile to point out, as C.H. Philips and S. Gopal have done, that Nehru had not seen the Partition Plan in full before it was sent to London.[120] It is true that, as pointed out by Gopal, while conveying to Mountbatten on 1 May, the Congress Working Committee's decision in principle to accept Partition, Nehru had mentioned that neither he nor any other member of the Interim Government present at the meeting of the Working Committee knew 'the full extent' of the proposals that Ismay was taking to London.[121] Obviously, however, Nehru was fully aware of the essential features, even though not of the details, of the Partition Plan sent to London. Otherwise, he would not have been able to delineate with full accuracy, as he did in his note dated 11 May (cited earlier) the major difference between the text of the plan sent to London and the one received from there by Mountbatten.

Whatever the background of Nehru's bombshell, there can be no doubt about the significance of its impact on the making of the final version of the Mountbatten Plan. Indeed, the whole plan was now recast in consultation with Nehru, and with the help of V.P. Menon, Constitutional Adviser to the Viceroy. In the absence of Ismay (still in London), the latter now emerged from the shadows and performed the role truly belonging to his office. The fact that he had a good rapport with the top Congress leaders, especially Patel, made him particularly useful to the Viceroy at this stage. As Mountbatten mentions in his final report on his Viceroyalty, the changes now made in the earlier draft were 'designed to meet, so far as possible, Pandit Nehru's objections, and at the same time maintaining the greatest possible degree of likelihood that it would remain acceptable to the Muslim League'.[122] The most important of these changes were the following:

Unlike in the previous drafts, the Introduction did not mention that arrangements must be made to transfer power to more than one authority. On the other hand, it was clearly recognized that the representatives of the majority of the people of Assam, Bihar, Bombay, Central Provinces and Berar, North-West Frontier Province, Orissa and Madras, together with Delhi, Ajmer—Merwara and Coorg, were already participating in the work of preparing a constitution for India, and hence no choice was offered to them regarding the future. The only exception was made in the case of the NWFP, where, for certain special reasons, a referendum was to be held to ascertain the wishes of its people. As for the Provinces of Sind, Punjab, and Bengal which had a Muslim-majority, a choice was to be given to the members of their Legislatures to decide whether they wished to join the then existing Constituent Assembly or form a new one. For this purpose the Legislators of the Punjab and Bengal were to be divided into two parts on the basis of their representing the Muslim-majority areas of their provinces or the non-Muslim-majority areas. The wishes of the people of the Sylhet district of Assam, which had an overwhelming Muslim majority and lay adjacent to Eastern Bengal, was to be ascertained, just as in the NWFP, through a referendum.[123] The choice of independence for any province or area was not mentioned at all. This was to affect the future of the NWFP and to some extent also of Bengal.

VIII

To turn to Bengal first, the Muslim League had repeatedly expressed its strong opposition to the Partition of Bengal as well as Punjab and wanted both the provinces, without any reduction in their size or population, for Pakistan on the ground that they were parts of the homeland of the Muslim nation. This remained their stand even after Attlee's Declaration of 20 February 1947, envisaging the possibility of such a Partition and the Congress Working Committee's resolution of 5 March suggesting the Partition of the Punjab into Muslim-majority areas and non-Muslim-majority areas, which it was clarified later would by implication apply also to Bengal. So far as Bengal was concerned, the League was particularly keen not to lose Calcutta, the largest city of India, a thriving port and the hub of the economic life of Bengal. They thought that if Bengal was divided, Calcutta, because of its demographic composition, was bound to belong to West Bengal and that might reduce East Bengal to a rural slum. Besides, some sections of the League's leadership in Bengal were also apprehensive about the fate of Eastern Bengal if it was separated from Western Bengal and made a part of Pakistan. In this connection they vividly remembered the treatment meted out to Fazlul Huq by the League's central leadership. S.H. Suhrawardy, the head of the Muslim League's Government of Bengal, was also aware of the fact that he was not really trusted by Jinnah and that his political future was likely to be bleak in Eastern Bengal.

Besides, some of the League leaders in Bengal had worked enthusiastically for Pakistan on the assumption that the Lahore Resolution of 1940 envisaged the creation of an independent Muslim-dominated State in Bengal. This situation had changed only in 1946, when the word 'States' in the Lahore Resolution was changed to just 'State', implying the creation of one single Pakistan. The older objective, they thought, could still be achieved through united Bengal. On the other hand, as a result of their experience in the recent past of dealing with the Congress High Command, particularly on the part of Subhas Chandra Bose,

Bengal's most popular leader, as also one of India's greatest leaders, they were attracted by the prospect of remaining in united Bengal independent of both India and Pakistan. The elder brother of Subhas, Sarat Chandra Bose, was the most prominent among them. He had fully sided with his brother in his battle with the Congress High Command (1939–40). Though temporarily elevated to the membership of the Interim Government as a Congress nominee, he had to lose that position in order to make room for the nominees of the League in October 1946 when the latter decided to join that Government. After that his alienation from the Congress High Command had deepened further, leading to his resignation from the Congress Working Committee in January 1947. He failed, however, to persuade most of the other Congress leaders except Kiran Shankar Roy, a former loyalist of the Congress High Command, to join him in supporting his movement. That movement had really been initiated by Abul Hashim, the dynamic General Secretary of the Bengal Muslim League, who had done a lot to spread the Pakistan idea among Muslims in Eastern Bengal with the full backing of Suhrawardy. The leaders of the two sides were also able to draw up an agreement among themselves regarding the terms for the formation of united Bengal, including such items, quite attractive for Hindus, like joint electorates, a coalition government, and 50 per cent reservation for Hindus in the services.[124]

Even Jinnah, though not openly supporting the united Bengal movement, found the idea quite acceptable. In his conversation with Mountbatten on 26 April 1947, when asked by the latter for his opinion on Suhrawardy's proposal for united and independent Bengal, Jinnah answered: 'I should be delighted. What is the use of Bengal without Calcutta? They had much better remain united and independent; I am sure that they would be on friendly terms with us.'[125] This apparently remained Jinnah's position for quite some time. This is not surprising. For he knew well that a united Bengal would be a Muslim-dominated State and could, therefore, be expected to be closely associated with Pakistan, if not finally merging with it at some later stage. Mountbatten explained Jinnah's thinking to the members of the India and Burma Committee of the British Cabinet at its meeting on 19 May 1947. 'Mr Jinnah,' he said, 'considered that, with its Muslim-majority, an independent Bengal would be a sort of subsidiary

Pakistan and was, therefore, prepared to agree to Mr Suhrawardy's plan.'[126] This was an accurate interpretation of Jinnah's position.

The same cannot, however, be said about Mountbatten's interpretation of the Congress position on the idea of united Bengal. Indeed, that interpretation was quite confused. For on the one hand, Mountbatten asserted that the Congress might also agree to that plan, but then added that it would be on the condition not only that it would not form part of Pakistan, which Suhrawardy's plan had already provided for, but also that 'special arrangements, which were unlikely to be acceptable to the Muslims, were made with the Central Government of Hindustan' Mountbatten further added that the Congress was also opposed to Calcutta being made a free city as Jinnah had decided, for it 'believed that, without Calcutta, Eastern Bengal might well, within two or three years, rejoin the western part of the Province'.[127]

Actually, Nehru had clearly told Mountbatten as early as 11 May at the 14th Miscellaneous Meeting convened by the latter that the Congress was not at all in favour of a united and independent Bengal. He, of course, admitted that the Partition of Bengal was harmful from many points of view, but added that exactly the same argument applied to the cutting off of Bengal from India. He also pointed out that 'Calcutta was the port for the whole of Northern India; if Bengal was independent, Calcutta would wither away.' Nehru made several other points. To quote the official record of what further Nehru said on 11 May:

> Pandit Nehru went on to say that he considered that there had been quite enough rioting in Bengal without the suggestion that the Province should be Partitioned; however Congress had been forced to recommend Partition. He personally hoped that the conception of Partition would recede. He would be prepared to consider special arrangements with Bengal and the Punjab but the feeling of the people of Western Bengal was an important factor. The situation in Bengal had become intolerable for them. There was not likely to be more than one per cent of non-Muslims who would agree to independence. . . .[128]

Nehru stuck to this view right till the end. When Mieville asked him on 27 May how he viewed the discussions then going on about an independent Bengal, Nehru 'reacted strongly and said there was no chance of the Hindus there agreeing to put themselves under permanent Muslim domination which was what the proposed agreement really amounted to. He did not, however, rule out the possibility of the whole of Bengal joining up with Hindustan.'[129] In an interview to the *News Chronicle* on 27 May, Nehru again observed:

The independence of Bengal really means in present circumstances the dominance of the Muslim League in Bengal. It means practically the whole of Bengal going into the Pakistan area, although those interested may not say so.

We can agree to Bengal remaining united only if it remains in the Union. As a matter of fact, there is an overwhelming feeling [among Hindus] in Western Bengal and in Eastern Punjab to separate from Eastern Bengal and Western Punjab.[130]

The policy of the Congress leadership towards the move for a united and independent Bengal was not improvised on the spur of the moment, but was in tune with the policy laid down by the Congress Working Committee in its resolution on the Cripps Plan in March 1942. It had been made clear then that although devoted to the ideal of Indian unity, the Congress would be prepared to allow certain well-marked areas to secede from the Indian Union and form a State or States of their own if the majority of the people living therein so wanted, but the latter could not be allowed to take with them certain other people, again living in well-marked areas, who did not want to go along. Besides, the assumption of the Congress leadership in 1947 that the overwhelming majority of the people in West Bengal were bitterly opposed to joining their counterparts in forming a united State even if that State would be independent and not a part of Pakistan also cannot be faulted. Indeed, not a single historian, however nostalgic or sympathetic to the move for an independent Bengal, has tried to do so. Even while differing in their appreciation of the nature and cause of the strong Hindu opposition in West Bengal to join hands with the Muslims in the movement for a united and independent Bengal, they all accept the strength of that opposition.[131]

Indeed, it will not be wrong to say that in spite of Sarat Bose's exertions, the Hindus as a whole, whether belonging to the Congress or the Hindu Mahasabha (which had done miserably in the elections of 1946, but was rallying some support on the basis of strong opposition to the move for United Bengal), or whether to upper castes or Scheduled Castes, there was little support for United Bengal, which was bound to have a Muslim majority and dominance regardless of the nature of the agreement arrived at between Suhrawardy and Bose. As Suhrawardy wrote to Liaquat Ali Khan in the last week of May 1947:

There is not the ghost of a chance of winning in any fight once the Partition is announced. Even before the Partition is announced, it is impossible to arouse Hindu public opinion against it. . . . We have not been able to touch a single Scheduled Caste member yet and not one of them has come forward to say that he is in sympathy with the non-Partition movement.

Even the Hindus of East Bengal, who do not count in the voting, are supporting the Partition with death staring them in the face.[132]

A slightly earlier letter by Suhrawardy to Khan confirms that regardless of what Jinnah had conveyed to Mountbatten regarding his attitude towards united and independent Bengal, he was not really interested in the movement for it, either because he knew that it could not succeed or because he did not relish the prospect of Bengal, whether united or not, opting out of Pakistan, even though at the same time opting out of India, too. For the whole purpose of Suhrawardy's letter to Khan (running into closely-typed four and a half pages) was to persuade the latter to realize the nature of the advantages likely to accrue to the Muslims of Bengal by its remaining undivided, and persuade Jinnah to put in a word on that time to Akram Khan, Jinnah's trusted lieutenant in Bengal and President of the provincial Muslim League.[133]

It is not known what the reactions of Khan were and whether he interceded with Jinnah in favour of Suhrawardy's stand. In any case, it was too late by then to steer the course of the fateful developments then taking place in India in the direction of a united and independent Bengal. It is not, therefore, surprising that Jinnah did not break his silence on that issue. It is also possible that he had become wiser after his initial reaction and remembered the old adage that a bird in hand is worth more than two in the bush. The same was true of Gandhi whose initial sympathetic attitude to the movement for united Bengal gradually disappeared and who was beset with various doubts regarding its desirability, particularly in the context of the rest of India being divided.[134]

The upshot of all this was that the option of independence for any province did not find any place in the revised draft of the Mountbatten Plan. It was provided that the members of the

Bengal Legislature, just as those of the Punjab Legislature, would be given only two options between which to choose—joining India or joining Pakistan. However, as he wrote in the consolidated personal report of his Viceroyalty, although the option of provinces to stand out independently was omitted as it was realized that if such a choice was given to one province it could not be denied to others, if all parties in one province, 'notably Bengal', desired to stand alone, 'it did not seem that His Majesty's Government would be able to prevent them from so doing'.[135] He also conveyed this understanding of the likely attitude of the British Cabinet to Suhrawardy. While in London for securing the British Cabinet's approval for the revised draft of his Plan, he got news of talks about the likelihood of the installation of a League–Congress coalition government in Bengal in order to facilitate the creation of united Bengal. He immediately communicated this to the British Cabinet, which authorized him to use his discretion if that materialized. But nothing of the sort happened as Kiran Shankar Roy failed to persuade the Congress High Command to support such a move. As a last-ditch effort to retain a foothold in Bengal, Suhrawardy pleaded with Mountbatten to place Calcutta, on an experimental basis, under the joint control of the Congress and the League. This, he said, would ease communal tension in Calcutta while Partition was taking place and its successful working for some time might create a favourable situation for the agreement of the Congress to continue the arrangement on a permanent basis. Mountbatten immediately sent V.P. Menon to Patel to secure his agreement for such an arrangement for six months. Patel sent a firm reply: 'Not even for six hours.'[136]

IX

The principle of no third option to provinces—apart from joining India or Pakistan—which Nehru, on behalf of the Congress, had done so much to get incorporated in the Mountbatten Plan, undoubtedly served India's interests—long-term as well as short-term. However, it dealt a lethal blow to the aspirations of the Khan Brothers and their followers in the NWFP, who had stood with the Congress through thick and thin since 1930 and had indeed become a valued part of the saga of the Indian struggle for freedom. Under their leadership the Congress in the NWFP had secured power through the process of elections (1937 and 1946) and won more seats (including Muslim seats) than the League in a province with an overwhelming Muslim majority. However, as noted earlier in this chapter, with severe communal riots sweeping a good part of northern India from Bengal to the Punjab, the NWFP also became a scene of growing communal conflict and became a fertile ground for the growth of the Muslim League with its slogan of Pakistan. The Congress ministry, of course, held its ground, but there is no doubt that its position was becoming shakier day by day because of the growth of the Pakistan Movement in that province accompanied by the growth of violent activities on the part of the League's supporters, particularly the students and members of the Muslim National Guards. The situation obtaining in the NWFP was well described by the official Fortnightly Report of the Chief Secretary of the province dated 11 April 1947:

> The general picture has been one of processions, picketing and interference with the running of trains, accompanied by lathi-charges, the use of tear-gas, and the arrest of a substantial number of people. Occasional murders of Hindus and Sikhs, . . . bomb explosions by night in and around Peshawar City, cutting of telegraph lines and sabotage on a small scale of road-bridges and railways have all contributed to maintain an atmosphere of uneasiness everywhere and fear in the case of the minorities.[137]

The developing situation in the NWFP convinced the British authorities in India that the Congress ministry, though still enjoying the support of the majority of members in the legislature, no longer enjoyed the support of the majority of Muslims in the province. They had long since believed that the Muslim League represented the overwhelming majority of Muslims in India. It, therefore, appeared incongruous to them that the Frontier Province, with a large Muslim majority, was ruled over by a Congress ministry. Besides, as the emergence of Pakistan appeared more and more likely, they considered it to be a geographical monstrosity that a Muslim dominated province like the NWFP, surrounded on the east by Muslim-dominated Western Punjab and on the west by the Frontier Tribes owing allegiance to Islam, should not belong to the new State going to be created. They, therefore, thought that the Congress domination of the province was soon going to be a thing of the past. Sir Olaf Caroe, Governor of the province, with his pronounced pro-League sympathies, went on hammering this to Mountbatten from the day he landed on Indian soil. Thus he wrote to the latter on 22 March 1947:

> Here are we between storm-ridden Punjab on one side and the tribes on the other, and in the strange position of having a Congress Government which has—or had—a considerable Muslim backing. But the influence of the North-Western Punjab to the East and the tribes to the West—all declaiming against Hindu–Sikh domination—is, I think, certain to squeeze Congress out before long, for Congress is not natural here.[138]

The Viceroy's Chief of Staff and closest adviser, Lord Ismay, was also of the same view. Speaking at the eighth staff meeting of the Viceroy on 4 April, he stressed the 'unnaturalness' of the then existing situation in the NWFP and warned that 'the tribes were most unlikely to tolerate it indefinitely'.[139] According to him, the existence of a Congress ministry in a province with 97 per cent Muslims in the population was a 'bastard situation'.[140]

Caroe's remedy for that was to hold a general election in the NWFP as soon as possible to determine who really represented the majority of the people there. For he was convinced that the ground was slipping from under the feet of the Congress ministry and that more and more Muslims were turning to the League. When Ismay visited the province in the first week of April, Caroe suggested 'forcing a general election on the Government' on the ground that it was necessary to ascertain, beyond any shadow of a doubt, to whom the British would transfer power before they left India. According to him, the best way of doing that was 'to dismiss the Ministry, dissolve the House, and for the Governor to take power under Section 93'. According to Caroe, this alone could assure a clean election. It is remarkable that Mountbatten did not mention any objection on his part to a fresh election but only to its being held under Governor's rule after the dismissal of the Ministry, and remarked that it would be 'clearly a big and difficult move which might infuriate Congress'.[141]

On the other hand, the position of the Congress the NWFP was ambivalent from the start. As Mountbatten's record of his interviews with the Congress leaders shows, while Gandhi, Nehru, Ghaffar Khan, and Azad had all opposed a fresh election and complained against Caroe and described him as violently anti-Congress and pro-League, Nehru had, from the beginning of his talks with Mountbatten, showed no opposition to election as such but only insisted that it could only be held at the proper time. Thus, as mentioned earlier in this chapter, as early as 8 April, when asked by Mountbatten as to how to obtain the real views of the people of the NWFP on which Group they wished to join, Nehru suggested that 'a fresh election should be held after a statement had been made'.[142] It seems that, as communicated to Azad by Mountbatten, on 12 April, Nehru had even told the former that in an election Congress might not be re-elected, since the frontier people were always 'against the Government'.[143]

Azad's interview with Mountbatten also makes it clear that the latter, regardless of what Nehru or anyone else said, was determined on a fresh chance being given to the Muslims of the NWFP, to finally indicate where their loyalties really lay. In this he was undoubtedly influenced by the unanimous view of the Governor and his own senior advisers headed by Ismay as well as his own judgement and instinct. To quote Mountbatten:

> Maulana Azad asked me whether I would be prepared to hold elections in other Provinces, and I replied 'No, not unless it could be proved to me that they were necessary.' He then asked me why I considered an election necessary in the NWFP, and I replied that in all other Provinces the separate electorates enable one to forecast, with considerable accuracy, the results of elections as between the League and Congress, since all Muslims voted for the League. In the NWFP, however, the election was largely between the Congress Muslims and the League Muslims, and of course there was no separate electorate in this case. I said that the results would clearly show whether the inhabitants wanted a League or a Congress Government.[144]

With Partition imminent, Mountbatten began to think of referendum rather than election, but his basic position about the necessity of giving the Frontier Muslims another chance to choose between the Congress and the League, or between India and Pakistan, remained as strong as ever. In such a situation, Nehru thought it prudent not to oppose the proposed referendum but to confine himself to asserting that such a referendum ought to be made only when the violent agitation then being carried out by the League stopped. This is the stand that he consistently adopted in his talks with Mountbatten and his advisers. When it became clear that a referendum could no longer be postponed for any length of time due to the decision to expedite the whole process of the grant of both Independence and Partition, Nehru could no longer sustain his old stand in favour of postponing referendum till normal conditions were restored in the Province. He also must have realized that he could not, as desired by the Khan brothers, plead on behalf of the NWFP for the option of independence to be added to the two options given to the other provinces, whose views were to be ascertained, namely opting for India or opting for Pakistan. For such a plea could be used against the fundamental principle on the basis of which the original Mountbatten Plan had been revised in accordance with Nehru's wishes.

X

An important addition to the revised version of the Mountbatten Plan was the provision for immediate transfer of power to the Governments of both India and Pakistan (still to be created) on the basis of Dominion Status. In bringing about this addition V.P. Menon played a key role. Even before Mountbatten arrived in India, Menon had come to the conclusion that negotiations on the basis of the Cabinet Mission Plan would lead nowhere. According to him, the only viable solution of the Indian constitutional problem was for all the parties concerned to agree to Partition, with provision for immediate transfer of power to both India and Pakistan on the basis of Dominion Status. He prepared a plan embodying this solution and discussed it with Patel. The latter, a great realist, had also by that time realized—on the basis of his experience both of the protracted tripartite negotiations relating to the Cabinet Mission Plan and of working with Muslim League colleagues in the Interim Government—that Partition was unavoidable. He had, therefore, no difficulty in seeing the merit in the Menon Plan, which, though involving the creation of a truncated Pakistan, would ensure the emergence of a strong India, even though minus the areas included in Pakistan, and the immediate transfer of power to the central government on the basis of Dominion Status, which was really independence in all but name. He told Menon frankly that if the latter's plan was adopted by the British Government, he would do his best to secure its acceptance by the Congress. That plan had been seen by Wavell and, with his permission, sent to the office of the Secretary of State for India in London. However, it could not at that time secure any serious attention either in New Delhi or London. While in Simla, along with Mountbatten and Nehru in the second week of May 1947, Menon had discussed his plan with both of them separately as well as together. He had come to the conclusion that Nehru, too, might accept his plan. Menon was, of course, keeping Patel (in New Delhi) duly informed of all the goings-on through long-distance telephone, and there was no ground to imagine any dissent on the latter's part.

In the beginning Nehru, who had long been campaigning for complete Independence in preference to Dominion Status as the ideal objective for India and cherishing the dream of having a republican constitution here, was hesitant in opting for Dominion Status. However, being a leader endowed with practical insight as well as idealistic vision, he did not take much time in realizing that opting for Dominion Status at that point of time would be on the whole quite advantageous to India. In the first place, it would hasten the march to independence instead of having to wait for it till June 1948, as envisaged in the Attlee Declaration of 20 February 1947. Secondly, it would prevent Pakistan from gaining special advantage at the cost of India by forging a special relationship with Britain and acquiring membership of a prestigious international organisation without the presence therein of India.[145]

The fear about Pakistan trying to steal a march over India so far as the membership of the British Commonwealth was concerned was not unfounded. As early as 9 April 1947, Jinnah had conveyed to Mountbatten 'with a smile on his face' that 'the first act of the Pakistan Government would probably be to apply for admission to the British Commonwealth on [the basis of] Dominion Status'. However, he did not receive much encouragement from Mountbatten as the latter was then at a preliminary stage of his negotiations with Indian leaders and was keen to have either a united India or—if India was divided—both India and Pakistan within the British Commonwealth.[146] Indeed, this was one of the most cherished goals he had set for achievement during his Indian mission. In the meanwhile, not at all discouraged by Mountbatten's cold reception to his proposal regarding getting Pakistan into the Commonwealth, Jinnah had come into the open by the end of April instead of just hinting about it. He told Mountbatten in no uncertain terms that it was not a question of Pakistan applying for admission into the Commonwealth but of whether the latter could expel Pakistan against its wish; according to Mountbatten, Jinnah adopted the following position:

All the Muslims have been loyal to the British from the beginning. We supplied a high proportion of the army which fought in both wars. None of our leaders have ever had to go to prison for disloyalty. Not one member of the Muslim League was present in the Constituent Assembly when the Congress passed the resolution for an Independent, Sovereign Republic of India. In fact not one of us has done anything to deserve expulsion from the Empire. And what about the other Dominions—Australia and New Zealand—will they accept our being expelled against our will? Is there anything in the Statute of Westminster that allows you to kick out parts of the Commonwealth because a neighbouring State that used to be a member wishes to leave?[147]

All this pleading was based on the assumption that the Congress with its old apathy to Dominion Status and commitment to republicanism was most unlikely to seek membership of the British Commonwealth. This was also the apprehension of Mountbatten who was most keen to have India inside the British Commonwealth. With the Change in Congress strategy just when the final version of the Mountbatten Plan for the transfer of power of India was being finalized, neither the League's assumption nor Mountbatten's apprehension proved true. India, according to that Plan, was going to be Partitioned, but both the nations would be ensconced in the British Commonwealth on the basis of Dominion Status.

XI

V.P. Menon's ideas formed the basis of the final version of the Plan which Mountbatten sent to London for the consideration of the British Cabinet and later went there himself to successfully plead for it. Before doing so, he had taken the precaution of sending its copies to Nehru, Jinnah, and Baldev Singh so as to secure its acceptability by them. Nehru's reply on behalf of the Congress was on the whole positive, though he expressed some dissatisfaction on some minor points. Jinnah, on behalf of the League, expressed his strong opposition to the Partition of Bengal and Punjab. If Bengal was indeed partitioned, he demanded that Calcutta should be made a free port. Similarly, if Punjab had to be partitioned, he wanted the matter to be settled by a referendum. This reply, according to Mountbatten, was 'the best that one could expect from Mr Jinnah'. However, on reading and re-reading his comments, Mountbatten felt that he could go ahead on the assumption of Jinnah's eventual acceptance of the Partition of Bengal and Punjab. That assumption was based on what Liaquat Ali Khan had told him a couple of days ago: 'We shall never agree to it, but you may make us bow to the inevitable.'[148] Baldev Singh, on behalf of the Sikhs, neither accepted nor rejected the revised plan. He suggested that the Boundary Commission intended to be set up to demarcate the boundary between East and West Punjab should be instructed to include as many Sikhs as possible in East Punjab and to take into account not only the size of the population, but also the property held by non-Muslims and the land revenue paid by them to the Government. At the same time, he wanted an extra paragraph added to the revised plan including his suggestions and referring to the position of the Sikhs in general. Mountbatten felt that he could not accept Singh's suggestions. All that he did was to see the latter and explain to him that while all concerned—Governor of the Punjab, Nehru, and Mountbatten himself—had full sympathy with the predicament of the Sikhs in the then existing situation, they could not depart from the fundamental basis of Partition—whether the majority in an area was constituted by Muslims or non-Muslims.[149]

While seeking the opinions of the key players in the political field on the revised draft, Mountbatten also sounded them on the plan formulated at Simla for the immediate transfer of power on the basis of dominion status by suitably amending the Act of 1935. Another major issue for discussion was that in the event of Partition taking place as per the provisions of the revised plan, whether there should be a common Governor-General for both the proposed dominions of India and Pakistan or each was to have a separate Governor-General. It was an open secret that Mountbatten himself preferred the former and indeed looked upon himself as occupying that office. Nehru's reaction was quite positive. He not only liked the idea of a common Governor-General for the two dominions, but also conveyed on behalf of the Congress that it would be happy if Mountbatten became the first incumbent of that office. Jinnah took some time to reply and when he did so, his reply appeared to Mountbatten as 'un-cooperative'. In the first place, he was 'not willing to accept Dominion Status out of hand'. He also raised objections to the idea of a common Governor-General for the two dominions and thought that discussion on that matter might be postponed till after the British Government's statement. Later he made a suggestion that while each Dominion should have its own Governor-General, Mountbatten should be an 'Overall Governor-General', to act as Supreme Arbitrator for the division of assets between the two. Mountbatten did not consider this a practical proposition.[150] Jinnah's attitude at that time was a cause for concern on Mountbatten's part also on another account. While he was in London in the latter half of May for explaining his revised plan to the British cabinet and securing its approval Jinnah had given notice that he would make a fresh demand in connection with Partition, namely, the creation of 'a corridor' through India to connect the two groups of Pakistan provinces in north-western and north-eastern India. At the same time, he reiterated that the League would 'fight every inch' against the Partition of the Punjab and Bengal.[151]

Undeterred by such statements which, of course, he did not consider as serious, Mountbatten continued his able advocacy before the British cabinet and soon secured its approval for his revised plan without any substantial change. He also, with due encouragement from Attlee, called on the prominent leaders of the opposition, including Winston Churchill, and secured their backing for the plan. His meeting with Churchill was particularly useful to him in dealing with Jinnah. For after listening to Mountbatten's difficulty in making Jinnah finally accept his plan without any conditions, Churchill authorized him to convey on his behalf this message to Jinnah: 'This is a matter of life and death for Pakistan, if you do not accept this offer with both hands.'[152]

After securing the approval for his plan by the leaders of the opposition as well as of the Government in London, Mountbatten returned to New Delhi on 30 May and immediately applied himself to securing the approval of the Congress, the Muslim League, and the Sikhs. The formal meeting with their leaders had already been scheduled for 3 June. Mountbatten, however, decided to have an informal meeting with them a day earlier on 2 June, so that there might not be any hitch at the formal meeting. Nehru, Patel, and J.B. Kripalani (Congress President) represented the Congress. The League was represented by Jinnah, Liaquat Ali Khan, and Abdur Rab Nishtar. Baldev Singh was the sole representative of the Sikh community. Their reactions to the revised plan were on the whole favourable though each side advocated a different line here and there. Before midnight all of them, in different ways—Kripalani and Singh in writing and Jinnah orally—assured Mountbatten that the plan would go through at the formal meeting the next day subject to subsequent endorsement by their central representative bodies—the All India Congress Committee and the Council of the All-India Muslim League. So the formal meeting of the Viceroy with the leaders on 3 June was indeed formal and nothing more. The revised Mountbatten Plan was duly approved without much discussion. Jinnah did not utter a word but, as earlier agreed between him and Mountbatten, conveyed his approval by just a nod of his head.

That marked the successful end of the struggles both for the independence of India and the creation of Pakistan, with both nations being assured of their positions as independent members of the British Commonwealth of Nations, with the right to secede from it whenever they wished. The meeting was followed by the broadcasts over the All India Radio, first by Mountbatten explaining the rationale as well as the key provisions of the Plan just approved by the leaders and then by Nehru, Jinnah, and Singh explaining the rationale of their decisions to accept the plan, subject to approval by their representative bodies. Attlee's broadcast, covering more or less the ground already done by Mountbatten, explained how the British had tried hard to maintain the unity of India, but had finally agreed to Partition and creation of Pakistan as there was no other viable alternative for the settlement of the Indian problem. He also assured his listeners that the British Government would do its best to expedite the legislative changes in the Act of 1935 in order to provide for both the independence of India and the creation of Pakistan. That process was indeed expedited and India and Pakistan finally emerged as independent countries with dominion status by 15 August 1947.

XII

The period between 3 June and 15 August was devoted to working out the details of the division of the British Indian Army into two parts and settling the assets and liabilities of the two emerging countries. A Partition Council consisting of the top leaders of the two sides, assisted by a group of able and senior civil servants, handled this task fairly satisfactorily, but not without some help from Mountbatten. For being able to play a similar role even after 15 August 1947, Mountbatten had shown his readiness to continue as Governor-General of both India and Pakistan for a short period between August 1947 and June 1948, the time earlier set for the final transfer of power as per Attlee's declaration of 20 February 1947. As mentioned earlier, the leaders of the Congress had readily agreed, but those of the League, for their own reasons, into which we need not go here, decided that it would be best for them to have Jinnah instead of Mountbatten as their Governor-General. Mountbatten was quite upset by that decision and was for some time in two minds whether to continue in India as its Governor-General alone or not. However, under the advice of senior British leaders, he finally decided to stay on and continued to work with the same dynamism and drive as he had shown before. This certainly proved useful to the leaders of both India and Pakistan in settling some of the problems between 3 June and 15 August 1947. One of the most difficult problems related to the future of the Indian States, but this was somehow resolved. Here the guidelines provided by the Cabinet Mission's Plan proved quite helpful. Although that plan had declared that the British would not transfer their paramountcy over the States to any successor government, it had added that the rulers of the States were expected to work out cooperative arrangements with the central authorities in their proximity. Mountbatten, too, played quite a helpful role by making it clear that the British Government would not agree to having any direct relations with the Indian States and that it was advisable for them to seek to associate themselves with either of the two emerging Governments (India and Pakistan), depending on their proximity. A few of them acceded to Pakistan, but the overwhelming majority acceded to India, with only three still remaining undecided, namely, Junagadh, Jammu and Kashmir, and Hyderabad.

The one problem that completely escaped the attention of the leaders of both India and Pakistan as also Mountbatten was the likely occurence of large-scale massacres and migrations across the borders between India and Pakistan. These borders were settled through an award by Sir Cyril Radcliffe, a senior British jurist, who had been appointed Head of the Boundary Commission consisting of the representatives of both India and Pakistan, published on 17 August 1947. While in Bengal the situation was kept under control mainly because of the exertions of Gandhi, who decided at that time to camp in Calcutta, the situation went totally out of control across the border between the two countries in the Punjab. A Boundary Force, 50,000 strong, especially constituted to deal with the problem utterly failed to stem the powerful tide of migrations and massacres. Some twelve million refugees were on the move and about half a million persons of all ages lost their lives.[153] The refugees carried to both India and Pakistan the most horrid tales about their experiences. Some had also experienced compassion and generosity from the people of the opposite side, but such experiences were rare. These unprecedented migrations and killings created a very difficult situation for the new governments and while they did their very best, suffering persons failed to get timely or adequate relief. The long-term impact of such unfortunate incidents on such a vast scale in shaping the attitudes of the peoples of the emerging nations towards each other was not at all favourable to the establishment of friendly relations between them. That was in any case difficult in view of the bitterness created on both sides of the divide in the wake of the rise and growth of the Pakistan movement and the strong opposition to it by the Hindus and Sikhs. The interactions between the Congress and the League leaders between 3 June and 15 August 1947 did not, to say the least, do anything to reduce that bitterness. The violent eruptions at the time of Partition on both sides of the border and the unspeakable horrors committed indiscriminately against men, women, and children in their wake could only add further to the already present legacy of mutual hostility in a large measure. Indeed, it will not be inappropriate to say that 15 August 1947 marked not only the end of one conflict—between Hindus and Muslims—but also the beginning of another—between India and Pakistan—which has been continuing ever since in some form or other.

NOTES

1. Pethick-Lawrence to Wavell, 18 October 1946, *TP*, vol. VIII, p. 746.
2. Wavell to Pethick Lawrence, 15 October 1946, ibid., p. 738.
3. Enclosure to Patel to Wavell, 20 October 1946, ibid., p. 756.

4. Footnote 4 to Nehru to Wavell, 23 October 1946, ibid., p. 779.
5. F. Burrows to Pethick-Lawrence, Telegram, 16 October 1946, ibid., p. 743.
6. Cited by Nehru in his letter to Wavell, on 23 October 1946, ibid., p. 782.
7. Burrows to Pethick-Lawrence, 16 October, ibid., p. 745.
8. Nehru to Wavell, 23 October 1946, ibid., p. 782.
9. Record of Wavell's discussion with Jinnah on 22 October 1946, ibid., p. 762. During his next meeting with Wavell on 23 October Jinnah seems to have been in a conciliatory mood. Although no record of this meeting is available, Wavell informed Nehru that Jinnah had assured him that the League would join the Interim Government with the intention of cooperating and that he regretted and condemned as deeply as Nehru did the recent disturbances in Bengal, Wavell to Nehru, 23 October 1946, ibid., p. 780.
10. *TP*, vol. IX, p. 7.
11. Ibid.
12. Ibid., p. 39.
13. Nehru to Patel, 5 November 1946, *Selected Works of Jawaharlal Nehru*, Second Series, no. I (New Delhi, 1984), p. 63. For detailed notes by Nehru on the situation in Bihar as also his speeches and his experiences in the area of disturbances in Bihar, which he, along with Prasad, Azad, and Jayaprakash Narayan, toured extensively from 4 to 9 November 1946, see ibid., pp. 55–87.
14. Sir F. Wylie to Pethick Lawrence, 8 November 1946, *TP*, vol. IX, p. 30.
15. Wylie to Wavell, 21 November 1946, ibid., p. 127.
16. See the statement by Pethick Lawrence made in the House of Lords on 27 November 1946 regarding casualties in communal disturbances in India between 2 September and 18 November 1946, ibid., p. 188.
17. See Sir A. Clow to Wavell, 4 November 1946, ibid., p. 3. This report dealt only with the period till the end of October 1946: out of 480 persons killed till then, 230 were Hindus, 240 Muslims, and 10 others. It may not be too much to say that broadly the same pattern continued till a few weeks later.
18. Ibid., pp. 73–5.
19. Ibid., pp. 92–4.
20. Ibid., p. 110.
21. Ibid., p. 109.
22. Ibid., pp. 110–11.
23. Ibid., pp. 124–5.
24. *Selected Works of Jawaharlal Nehru*, Second Series, no. I, p. 18.
25. *TP*, vol. IX, p. 135.
26. Ibid., pp. 184–5.
27. Ibid., pp. 186–7.

28. Ibid., p. 217.
29. Ibid., p. 226.
30. Ibid., p. 227.
31. Ibid.
32. Ibid., p. 246.
33. Ibid., p. 248.
34. Ibid., p. 253.
35. Ibid., pp. 260–1.
36. Ibid., pp. 262–5.
37. Ibid., pp. 295–6.
38. As recalled by Baldev Singh to Nehru, 18 September 1955, cited in S. Gopal, *Jawaharlal Nehru: A Biography*, vol. I (London, 1975), p. 338.
39. Kanji Dwarkadas, *Ten Years to Freedom* (Bombay, 1968), p. 190.
40. *TP*, vol. IX, pp. 312–13.
41. *Parliamentary Debates*, House of Commons, Fifth Series, vol. 431, pp. 1360–7.
42. Dwarkadas, n. 39, pp. 193, 196.
43. Churchill to Jinnah, 11 December 1946, Reel 3, File 21, Quaid-i-Azam Papers. Elizabeth Gilliett was Churchill's Private Secretary.
44. Atique Z. Sheikh and M.R. Malik, eds, *Quaid-i-Azam and the Muslim World: Selected Documents* (Karachi, 1978), pp. 166–8.
45. For the text of Nehru's speech, see *Constituent Assembly Debates, Official Report*, I, 9 to 23 December 1946, pp. 55–62.
46. *TP*, vol. IX, pp. 462–3. This resolution had been drafted by Nehru and approved by Gandhi during the former's visit to Noakhali where Gandhi had at that time stationed himself. See secret report of Patel's talk with some Congressmen from Bengal on 4 January 1947, ibid., p. 509.
47. For the text, see *Constituent Assembly Debates*, II, 20 to 25 January 1947, pp. 296–303.
48. *TP*, vol. IX, pp. 586–93.
49. Ibid., pp. 594–5.
50. Ibid., pp. 622–3.
51. Ibid., p. 646.
52. Ibid., pp. 647–51.
53. Ibid., p. 319.
54. Ibid., pp. 332–7.
55. Ibid., pp. 351–5.
56. Full text in ibid., pp. 773–5.
57. Ibid., p. 761.
58. Ibid., p. 777.
59. Ibid., pp. 728–31.
60. Ibid., p. 229.
61. Ibid., pp. 556–7.
62. Ibid., p. 609.

63. See Patel's letters to Wavell, dated 26 January 1947 and 14 February 1947, ibid., pp. 561, 710–1.
64. See Jenkins to Pethick Lawrence, 8 February 1947, ibid., p. 654.
65. Wavell to Pethick Lawrence, 19 February 1947, ibid., p. 768.
66. Jenkins to Pethick Lawrence, 25 February 1947, ibid., pp. 814–16.
67. Wavell to Pethick Lawrence, 26 February 1947, ibid., p. 819.
68. For the Governor's report on Tiwana's resignation, see Jenkins to Wavell, 3 March 1947, pp. 829–34.
69. See Wavell to Pethick Lawrence, 5 March 1947, ibid., p. 870.
70. See Pethick Lawrence to Wavell, 5 February 1947, ibid., p. 872.
71. See enclosure to Jenkins to Wavell, 7 March 1947, ibid., pp. 879–84.
72. For the text of the Congress Working Committee's resolution on the Punjab, see ibid., pp. 900–1.
73. Caroe to Wavell, 22, February 1947, ibid., pp. 787–9.
74. Caroe to Wavell, 8 March 1947, ibid., p. 896.
75. Caroe to Wavell, 13 March 1947, ibid., pp. 930–1.
76. Pethick Lawrence to Wavell, 14 March 1947, ibid., p. 954.
77. Humayun Mirza, *From Plassey to Pakistan: The Family History of Iskander Mirza, the First President of Pakistan* (New York, 1999), pp. 151–2.
78. Nehru to Wavell, 9 March 1947, *TP*, vol. IX, pp. 898–9.
79. Attlee to Mountbatten, 18 March 1947, ibid., pp. 972–3.
80. Mountbatten's first Personal Report, 2 April 1947; *TP*, vol. X, p. 90.
81. Ibid., p. 69.
82. Ibid., pp. 83–4; also pp. 140–1.
83. See Gandhi to Mountbatten, 11 April 1947, ibid., p. 197.
84. See the record of the Viceroy's Staff Meeting, 5 April 1947, ibid., pp. 125–7.
85. Mountbatten's Personal Report no. 3, ibid., pp. 298–300.
86. Record of Mountbatten's interview with Nehru, 8 April 1947, ibid., p. 154.
87. Ibid.
88. Record of Mountbatten's interview with Rajendra Prasad, 10 April Ibid., pp. 179–80.
89. Record of Mountbatten's interview with C. Rajagopalachari, 11 April 1947, ibid., p. 194.
90. Record of Mountbatten's interview with Sardar Patel, 12 April 1947, ibid., pp. 213–14.
91. Record of Mountbatten's interview with Maulana Azad, 12 April 1947, ibid., p. 215.
92. Ibid., p. 216.
93. Abul Kalam Azad, *India Wins Freedom* (New York, 1960), pp. 216–21.

94. Record of Mountbatten's interview with Maulana Azad on 2 April 1947, *TP*, vol. X, p. 86.
95. Record of Mountbatten's interview with Gandhi, 2 April 1947, ibid., p. 84.
96. Ibid., 3 April 1947, p. 103.
97. Ibid., 4 May 1947, p. 611.
98. Gandhi to Mountbatten, 8 May 1947, ibid., pp. 667–8.
99. For more details about Gandhi's dwindling role in decision-making in the Congress during 1946–7 as well as an overview of his handling of the Hindu–Muslim problem in India since 1920, see Bimal Prasad, 'Gandhi and India's Partition', in Amit Kumar Gupta, ed., *Myth and Reality: The Struggle for Freedom in India*, 1945–7 (New Delhi, 1987), pp. 99–115.
100. See Nehru to Mountbatten, 1 May 1947, *TP*, vol. X, pp. 517–19.
101. Mountbatten to Gandhi, 1 May 1947, ibid., p. 669.
102. Ibid., pp. 49–51.
103. Ibid., p. 207.
104. Ibid., pp. 230–1.
105. See Mountbatten's Personal Report, no. 3, 17 April 1947, ibid., p. 301.
106. Ibid.
107. Ibid., pp. 496–9.
108. See ibid., pp. 550–3.
109. See ibid., pp. 487–9.
110. Ibid., p. 636.
111. For text see ibid., pp. 723–8.
112. Viceroy's Personal Report no. 7, 15 May 1947, ibid., p. 836. In his final report on his Viceroyalty Mountbatten went even further and described Nehru's letter as 'a bombshell of the first order'; Lionel Carter, ed., *Mountbatten's Report on the Last Viceroyalty* (New Delhi, 2003), p. 140.
113. Nehru to Mountbatten, 11 May 1947, *TP*, vol. X, pp. 756–7.
114. Note by Nehru, 11 May 1947, ibid., pp. 766–71. The lines cited occur on p. 767.
115. R.J. Moore, *Escape from Empire* (London 1983), p. 273.
116. Minutes of the Viceroy's Thirty-First Staff Meeting, 12 May 1947, ibid., pp. 780–1. Lord Ismay, the Viceroy's Chief of Staff, was also of the same view. See Ismay, *Memoires* (London, 1960), p. 421.
117. H.R. Tinker, *Experiment with Freedom* (London, 1967); see also the same author's 'Jawaharlal Nehru at Simla, May 1947'; *Modern Asian Studies*, vol. 4, no. 4, 1970, pp. 349–58.
118. H.V. Hodson, *The Great Divide* (London, 1969), pp. 297–8.
119. Carter, n. 112, p. 130.

120. C.H. Philips in Philips and Wainwright eds., *The Partition of India* (London, 1970), p. 20 and S. Gopal, *Jawaharlal Nehru: A Biography*, vol. I (Delhi, 1975), p. 346.
121. For the full text of Nehru's letter to Mountbatten, 1 May 1947, see *TP*, vol. X, pp. 514–17.
122. Carter, n. 112, p. 141.
123. *TP*, vol. X, pp. 883–6.
124. For details, see Abul Hashim, *In Retrospection* (Dacca, n.d.), pp. 134–64.
125. *TP*, vol. X, p. 452.
126. Ibid., p. 899.
127. Ibid.
128. Ibid., p. 764.
129. Ibid., p. 1013.
130. Ibid., p. 1040.
131. See Shila Sen, *Muslim Politics in Bengal* (New Delhi, 1976), pp. 203–45; Joya Chatterji, *Bengal Divided: Hindu Communalism and Partition, 1932–1947* (Cambridge, 1996), pp. 220–65; Partha Chatterjee, *The Present History of West Bengal: Essays in Political Criticism* (Delhi, 1997), pp. 30–40; and Bidyut Chakrabarty, *Politics of Accommodation and Confrontation: The Second Partition of Bengal* (New Delhi, 2003), p. 1–59.
132. H.S. Suhrawardy to Liaquat Ali Khan, 23 May 1947, Reel 16, 7238, Jinnah Papers, Quaid-i-Azam Academy, Karachi.
133. Suhrawardy to Khan, 21 May 1947, ibid.
134. See Abul Hashim, n. 256.
135. Carter, n. 112, p. 144.
136. Ibid., p. 145.
137. *Fortnightly Report of the Chief Secretary of NWFP*, 11 April 1947, cited in Erland Jansson, *India, Pakistan or Pakhtunistan: The Nationalist Movements in the North-West Frontier Province*, 1937–47 (Uppsala, 1981), p. 194.
138. *TP*, vol. X, p. 1.
139. Ibid., p. 116.
140. Alan Campbell Johnson, *Mission with Mountbatten* (London, 1951), p. 54.
141. Viceroy's Personal Report, no. 2, dated 9 April 1947, *TP*, vol. X, p. 168.
142. Record of Interview between Mountbatten and Nehru, 8 April 1947, ibid., p. 154.
143. Record of Interview between Mountbatten and Azad, 12 April 1947, ibid., p. 217.
144. Ibid.

145. See V.P. Menon, *The Transfer of Power in India* (paperback; Madras, 1968), pp. 371–6; also S. Gopal, n. 120, pp. 352–3; and Moore, n. 115, pp. 280–4.
146. Mountbatten's observation at the Viceroy's Staff Meeting, 11 April 1947, *TP*, vol. X, p. 191.
147. Ibid., p. 541.
148. Carter, n. 112, p. 147.
149. Ibid., pp. 148.
150. Ibid., pp. 148–9.
151. *TP*, vol. X, p. 929.
152. Ibid., pp. 945–6.
153. For details, see *TP*, vol. XI; Menon, n. 145, pp. 394–410; Hodson, n. 118, pp. 322–400; Moore, n. 115, pp. 290–356; and Avtar Singh Bhasin, *Some Called it Partition Some Freedom: Last 75 Days of the Raj*, pp. 1–376.

Epilogue

THE DETAILED ACCOUNT OF the march to Pakistan between 1937 to 1947, presented in this volume, illustrates the pivotal role in it of Mohammed Ali Jinnah, as the top leader of the Muslim League. This has led many contemporaries as well as historians to conclude that Pakistan owes its creation primarily to Jinnah and that there would have been no Pakistan, at any rate at the time it was created, if the League did not have the advantage of his leadership. The verdict of contemporaries is very well reflected in the remarks of one of the most perceptive among them, the veteran Indian journalist and author, Frank Moraes, who wrote soon after Jinnah's passing away:

> The Quaid-i-Azam is assured of a place among the Great Muslims of our time. Kemal Ataturk revived the ramshacle State which was Turkey. But Jinnah's achievement was in a sense more considerable. Out of next to nothing he willed a State into being. . . . The ifs of history are fascinating and if Mohammed Ali Jinnah had not taken upon himself to lead a crusade for an Islamic Land of the Pure, it is problematical whether Pakistan would ever have been established.[1]

H.V. Hodson, the author of the most authoritative work on the intricate, tripartite negotiations leading to Partition, does not basically differ from this view. Writing about the main actors in the drama leading to Partition, he observes:

> Of all the personalities in the last act of India's rebirth to independence Mohammed Ali Jinnah is at once the most enigmatic and the most important. One can imagine any of the other principal actors. . . . replaced by a substitute in the same role. . . . a different representative of this or that interest or community, even a different Viceroy, without thereby implying any radical change in the final denouement. But it is barely conceivable that events could have taken the same course, that the last struggle would have been a struggle of three, not two, well balanced adversaries, and that a new nation state of Pakistan would have been created, but for the personality and leadership of one man, Mr. Jinnah. The irresistible demand for Pakistan and the solidarity of the Indian

Muslims behind that demand were creations of the decade (1937-47) alone, and supremely the creation of one man.[2]

Ishtiaq Hussain Qureshi, one of the senior-most historians of Pakistan, and indeed of the whole subcontinent, in modern times, takes a broader view about the creation of Pakistan, but that does not lead him to underestimate in any way the role of Jinnah in it. He remarks:

It is true that the destinies of nations are moulded by their innermost urges and their determination to achieve their purpose, but if they fail to produce a leader of the necessary ability and stature at the crucial moment, their urges may be frustrated and their determination may prove to be of little avail. Even without Jinnah Pakistan would have come, but it would have been delayed for decades and would have entailed much greater conflict and travail. It was he who guided people right at every single step, saved them from many a pitfall, and, through his single-minded devotion to the cause of the freedom of his people, led them to victory within the incredible period of seven years.[3]

Sharif Al Mujahid, who has presented the most comprehensive interpretation of Jinnah's leadership from various angles, comes to a somewhat similar conclusion. While recognizing that both Jinnah and the Muslim League were 'indeed a product of the whole past of Muslim India', he asserts: 'Pakistan was not so much a product of that past as the product of one of the most event-making figures in modern history. Thus Jinnah's presence was necessary, at least as far as the calendar date of Pakistan's emergence was concerned.'[4]

However, to ascribe the creation of Pakistan primarily to one individual, however capable or devoted to its cause, goes against the well-known axiom of historical research now, namely that events like the partition of a country or the creation of a new State result primarily from a certain constellation of forces and their conjunction with other favourable factors. Leaders do play an important role in this process, but only if their leadership is in tune with the aspirations of the dominant social forces surrounding them. Those working against those forces, however talented or devoted, are compelled to court defeat. It is the harmonious working of the social forces and their leaders that makes history. The latter indeed are usually thrown up by the former, though the latter too, in their turn, significantly contribute to the further evolution of the former. The traditionalist view regarding the role of Jinnah in the creation of Pakistan is thus no longer tenable.

II

Equally untenable, however, is the view of the members of the revisionist school on this subject, pioneered by Ayesha Jalal. The holders of this view differ among themselves on several minor points, but they are all united on one basic point, namely, that Jinnah, in spite of appearing to work for Partition did not really want it and indeed sought to preserve the political unity of the Indian subcontinent till the very end. If Partition nevertheless became a fact, the attitudes and policies of the top Congress leaders like Gandhi, Nehru and Patel were responsible for it. Surprisingly such a view has become acceptable to some Indian scholars also since the publication in 1985 of Jalal's book on Jinnah's leadership and the creation of Pakistan. A Pakistani scholar, her main problem was the realization that 'the most striking fact about Pakistan is how it failed to satisfy the interests of the very Muslims who are supposed to have demanded its creation'. Obviously endowed with a modernist outlook and being an admirer of Jinnah she does not like to argue that it was a mistake on Jinnah's part to have worked for Pakistan. Instead she asserts that he neither wanted Partition nor worked for it, but used the demand for it actually as a device to establish his control over the politics of the Muslim majority provinces and to use it as a bargaining counter to secure the best possible terms for Muslims at the time of the final settlement of the Indian problem. Jinnah had, of course, personally, with the support of the majority in the League Working Committee, deleted the clause relating to an all-India agency with limited powers in the draft resolution proposed to be placed before the Lahore session of the League (1940), prepared by Sikander Hyat Khan. The motivation behind that deletion has so far been almost universally regarded as the desire to provide for the establishment of independent Muslim majority States in the north-west and north-east of India. According to Jalal, however, Jinnah's real purpose in getting removed the clause relating to a weak centre was to facilitate the emergence of a powerful central government for the whole of

India, in which he was keen to play an important part. According to her, Jinnah was well aware that the Muslims of India were not alone going to be the arbiters of their destiny and that the British and the Congress would certainly play important roles in determining it. The latter two, he calculated, would never agree to the emergence of a situation in which there would be no central government or a very weak central government for the whole of India. So the ultimate result of the Lahore resolution would be the establishment of a strong central government for the whole of India which Jinnah really wanted in spite of so much insistence by him on the right of self-determination of Muslims in those areas of India in which they were in a majority. Several others have argued that the Lahore resolution did not define the political objective of the Indian Muslims, but was merely a bargaining counter for Jinnah and the League. The originality of Jalal lies in her assertion that the real objective behind Jinnah's sponsorship of the Lahore resolution, with its vague and ambiguous paragraphs, was that it would lead ultimately to the establishment of a powerful all-India Centre. She writes:

> The Lahore resolution should . . . be seen as a bargaining counter which had the merit of being acceptable (on the face of it) to the majority-province Muslims, and of being totally unacceptable to the Congress and in the last resort to the British also. This in turn provided the best assurance that the League would not be given what it now apparently was asking for, but which Jinnah in fact did not really want.[5]

This is an original, but absurd formulation, without any supporting evidence. All available evidence on Jinnah's attitude towards a central government for India, since the adoption of the resolution on India's constitutional future by the League's annual session at Lahore in 1924, underlines the fact that Jinnah had been an ardent advocate of a weak Centre, as demanded by the Punjab leadership of the League, and had included it in all his subsequent formulations of Muslim demands. Disregarding all that evidence, however, Jalal holds the view that Jinnah always wanted a strong central government for the whole of India. It is not surprising, therefore, that she interprets every significant move by Jinnah between 1937 and 1947 as motivated primarily by his desire to preserve India's unity and not by that of securing Pakistan, the declared objective of the Muslim League, adopted under his own leadership, since 1940. According to her so-called revisionist thesis on the background of Partition, when the final hour struck, 'It was the Congress that insisted on Partition. It was Jinnah who was against Partition.'[6] This is nothing but imagination run riot.

III

It is no doubt true that Jinnah's early political career was that of an Indian nationalist leader. He had not associated himself with either the Simla Deputation or the foundation of the All-India Muslim League in 1906. Indeed, while the League was being founded at Decca in December that year, Jinnah was busy attending the annual session of the Indian National Congress and working as Secretary to its President, Dadabhai Naoroji. He joined the League in 1913, but continued with his membership of the Congress for some time and played a key role, along with Bal Gangadhar Tilak, the veteran Congress leader, in the formulation of the well-known Congress–League Agreement on constitutional reforms in 1916. It is not surprising, therefore, that he was around that time widely acclaimed in Congress circles as an Ambassador of Hindu–Muslim unity. His association with the Congress ended in 1920. This, however, did not take place on account of any difference between him and other Congress leaders on the communal issue, but purely on that of the new technique of struggle adopted by the Congress under Gandhi's leadership. The latter was based on a recourse to non-violent mass action like non-cooperation and civil disobedience. Jinnah, believing at that time in the efficacy of constitutional agitation, like other Congress leaders of the pre-Gandhi era belonging to the moderate school, did not like it. Even after the end of his association with the Congress and his continuous leadership of the Muslim League, Jinnah, while no doubt trying to advance the supposed Muslim interests in politics—which he had indeed been doing ever since 1910, when he was elected to the Central Legislative Assembly from the Bombay Muslim constituency—continued to work for an understanding between the League and the Congress. Unlike Choudhary Rahmat Ali, Jinnah had had nothing to do with either the emergence of the Pakistan idea or its development during the decade before he himself accepted it around 1937. The same applies to the Two Nation theory, which became the mainstay of the Pakistan idea. That theory, having been propounded first by Syed Ahmad Khan in the second half of the nineteenth century, was as old as the beginning of political awakening among Indian Muslims and drew great strength from the utterances of Muhammad Iqbal in the twentieth century. However, Jinnah did not subscribe to it till 1937.

Once, however, he became convinced that Partition was the only solution of the intractable Hindu–Muslim problem, as well as the only objective capable of bringing almost all Muslims—who would never agree to live under Hindu domination—on one political platform, he became fully devoted to it and worked tirelessly for its achievement. He first prepared the ground for its adoption by the Muslim League as its goal at Lahore in March 1940 and then applied all his energy to lead his people to that goal, in spite of his advanced age and ill health. Whether addressing a public meeting or participating in a conference with British and/or Congress representatives or having one to one talks with any of the Viceroys—Linlithgow, Wavell or Mountbatten—or with any of the Congress leaders—Gandhi, Nehru, Bose or Prasad—or with other important persons like Sir Girija Shankar Vajpayi and the representatives of important newspapers in India or abroad, he never lost sight of his objective. He was an extremely shrewd leader, but not a dishonest or deceitful one, who might declare that he was pursuing one objective, but really be working for something else, indeed its opposite, as Jalal's thesis, in effect though certainly not in intent, makes him out to have been. He had no interest in fighting against the Partition of India and never did so since March 1940, but he did fight, to the best of his ability, against the partition of the Punjab and Bengal. For, as a devoted Pakistani patriot, his objective was to take them whole, undivided, into Pakistan, regardless of the wishes of the large non-Muslim populations inhabiting them, who were strongly opposed to the League's demand. As Sharif Al Mujahid aptly observes in his book cited earlier:

> The historical situation during the 1937–47 decade presented and permitted . . . two major alternative paths of development for Muslim politics: (I) going along with the Congress viewpoint, if not actually merging the League into it or accepting for it a satellite status; and (II) striking out an independent line. These alternative paths were present at least on seven different but specific occasions (1937, 1939, 1940, 1942, 1944, 1945 and 1946). But on no occasion did Jinnah waver, and each

time he chose for himself and for Muslim India the path towards establishing Muslim religio-political identity on a constitutional plane—the path concretized since 1940 in the Pakistan platform. And this he did whatever the toils and tribulations, whatever the circumstances and consequences.[7]

Those who hold that Jinnah neither wanted Pakistan nor worked for it, but was forced to do so by the Congress leadership, do scant justice to his qualities of leadership and his persistent application of them to the objective he had set before himself by 1937 and had been mainly instrumental in persuading the Muslim League to adopt as its goal in 1940. It goes without saying that Jinnah was a great leader, indeed one of the greatest produced by the India-Pakistan subcontinent in the twentieth century. Like other great leaders, including Gandhi, he had the knack of understanding what was going on in the minds and hearts of the youth and intelligentsia among his people at a given time, even though the latter might not themselves be able to give expression to that in clear terms. The widespread enthusiasm created among the Muslim youth and intelligentsia, though not in the beginning among the Muslim leadership in various fields, including the teachers of the Aligarh Muslim University, after the call for the creation of Pakistan at Lahore confirmed this and further encouraged Jinnah in pursuing his chosen path. His speeches and actions from 1939–40 onwards fully illustrate his single-minded devotion to the cause of creating Pakistan. They clearly bring out the fact that he was not a reluctant, but a devoted and determined champion of Pakistan, and left no stone unturned in ensuring its creation. . . . It is not without reason that the people of Pakistan remember him as Father of the Nation.

IV

Those who argue that Jinnah was not keen on Pakistan and had actually been forced to reluctantly work for it because of Congress attitudes and policies concentrate mainly on two points—its failure to play ball with him in the formation of Congress–League coalition ministries in the provinces in 1937 and its opposition to the compulsory groupings of provinces according to communal majorities, in a three-tier constitution, under the Cabinet Mission Plan in 1946 and Nehru's use of strong language in expressing that opposition and stressing the inevitability of the ultimate emergence of a strong centre in a federal system. Both these points are based not on facts, but on wishful thinking and imagination.

To take up first the charge regarding the failure of the move to form Congress–League coalition ministries in the provinces in 1937, even though the Muslim League was interested in it. In this connection it is argued by the critics of the Congress, that there had been a prior understanding between the Congress and League leaderships, in UP, to the effect that they would form a coalition ministry after the elections. However, as the Congress secured a majority of seats by itself in UP, it went back on the pre-election understanding. It is further argued that this for the first time turned the mind of the League leadership towards Partition. Nehru is made particularly responsible for the failure of the coalition talks in UP, because of his supposed insistence on including in the ministry only one member from the League instead of two as demanded by the latter. As explained by the present author in detail, with full documentation, in the last chapter of volume 2 of this series, these assumptions have no foundation in fact. There had been, for instance, no pre-election understanding between the Congress and the League in UP regarding the formation of a coalition ministry. It is also not a fact that the Congress leadership in UP, particularly Nehru, had refused to take in two ministers from the League in the proposed coalition ministry. Further, as Iqbal's letters to Jinnah in 1937, quoted at length in volume 2 clearly show, both of them had already begun thinking about demanding self-determination for the Muslim majority provinces of India (an emphemism for demanding Pakistan) even before the negotiations for the formation of a Congress–League coalition ministry in UP had entered a serious phase. To say this, however, is not to assert that the failure of the coalition talks between the Congress and the League had no significance so far as the spread of the Pakistan movement is concerned. Though the Pakistan idea had already been born and been slowly spreading, the failure of the Congress–League coalition talks certainly contributed a good deal to the further spread of the idea in all parts of the country by accentuating among the Muslim *elite* the feeling of alienation from the Congress and providing Jinnah with a splendid opportunity to fan the embers of discontent among them and turning their minds more and more towards the goal of Pakistan.

Again, as shown in the present volume, those who accuse the Congress leaders of sabotaging the Cabinet Mission Plan (May 1946) and, therefore, of the supposedly last bid to prevent Partition base themselves not on facts, but on wishful thinking. Unlike what is generally assumed by them, the League, by agreeing to go into the Constituent Assembly, had not given up its goal of Pakistan. If one just takes the trouble of going through, even cursorily, the text of the resolution adopted by the League's Council in this regard on 6 June 1946, it will become quite clear that the decision to enter the Constituent Assembly, and that too under certain conditions, had been taken primarily because the Council saw in the Cabinet Mission Plan of 16 May 1946, 'the basis and substance' of Pakistan. Besides, the Council had in the same resolution reiterated its firm determination to go on working for the creation of full Pakistan with the same vigour as before. The same applies to the contention that Nehru's utterances in Bombay between 7 and 10 July sabotaged the League's plan to work out the Cabinet Mission Plan on the basis of united India. Nehru, of course, had spoken in Bombay quite forcefully, as he generally used to do, but he had directed his words primarily to the socialist leaders, headed by Jayaprakash Narayan, who had strongly opposed the Working Committee's decision to accept the Cabinet Mission Plan. In any case, Nehru had not said anything of substance in Bombay which had not been said earlier in more than one resolution on the Cabinet Mission Plan adopted by the Congress Working Committee. If the League wanted to refuse to participate in the work of the Constituent Assembly on the ground of the Congress opposition to the compulsory grouping of provinces on the basis of communal majorities, it could have certainly done so much earlier. The real reason for the change in the League's policy regarding joining the Constituent Assembly was the refusal of the Viceroy (Wavell) to invite the League to cooperate in the formation of the Interim Government, thereby conceding to it the leading position in the latter, in the absence of the Congress. The League had accepted the long-term as also the short-term plan of the Cabinet Mission, though with certain reservations, on the assumption that the Congress would never accept the Cabinet Mission Plan, whether short-term or long-term, thereby leaving the field open to the League to emerge as the sole claimant to man the Interim Government. However, the Congress put a spanner in the works by deciding at the last moment, on the night of June 25, to accept the long-term plan of the Cabinet Mission even though rejecting its short-term plan, dealing with the formation of the Interim Government. This did not deter the League from pressing its claim to be called upon to form the Interim Government on the ground that the acceptance of the long-term plan of the Mission by the Congress was hedged by serious reservations and therefore not genuine. The Cabinet Mission and the Viceroy, however, rejected its argument by contending that the League too had hedged its acceptance of the Cabinet Mission Plan by its own reservations. The League's strategy of entering the Interim Government without the Congress and using that position to hasten its march to Pakistan thus failed and it thereupon decided to change its strategy and to rescind its earlier decision to join the Constituent Assembly in order to achieve Pakistan as soon as possible.

A perusal of the texts of the resolutions adopted by the League's Council on 29 July 1946, embodying these decisions, should make clear the real reason behind them. The first resolution mentioned the Viceroy's refusal to invite the League to cooperate in the formation of the Interim Government, which it considered its due. It is only the second resolution that referred to the attitude of the Congress and particularly of Nehru, accusing them of their determination to foist the caste Hindus' rule over all other communities in India as a cause for changing its decision. The working of the mind of the League leadership should also become clear from a perusal of Jinnah's identical, confidential letters to Prime Minister Attlee and leader of the Opposition, Churchill, protesting against the British decision disallowing the formation of an Interim Government under the League's dominance and containing the same assertion regarding the readiness of Muslims to shed blood if required, which was made later while adopting the plan of recourse to Direct Action. Here, it is significant that both the letters were despatched on 6 July 1946, a day before Nehru's supposedly provocative speech to the All India Congress Committee at Bombay.

V

To say all this, however, is not to assert that Pakistan owed its birth solely to Jinnah's leadership, or that he must be held primarily responsible for Partition, as many in India continue to believe. Pakistan represented a victory for Muslim nationalism, which had had deep religious and historical roots and had been developing over a period of time. Several leaders, writers and poets had played their part in that development. This has been discussed in detail in the earlier two volumes of this trilogy and need not be elaborated here. It must, however, be reiterated that those who want to have a full understanding of the genesis of Partition or Pakistan will have to carefully go into the foundations and early evolution of that nationalism. Every leader, however forceful his personality or however great his contribution to a historical event at a particular point of time, plays his part in the context of the historical and social forces of which he is himself a product and which condition his role at every stage in the further evolution of those forces. A leader becomes great and finds a place in history only if he fully understands the nature of his historical heritage and carries it forward, bringing out and fully developing the potentialities inherent in it. That was the role of Jinnah.

As shown in all the three volumes of this trilogy, Muslim nationalism was helped substantially at every stage of its development by British policy, which almost always supported the Muslim demands. The demands themselves, however, were genuine Muslim demands and not artificially created by the British. This applies to the entire spectrum of Muslim demands, from separate electorates and weightage to Partition. To say this is not to underestimate the value of British support, but to underline the basically indigenous nature of the birth and growth of Muslim nationalism, from the time of Syed Ahmad Khan right up to that of Jinnah.

Surprising though it may seem, from the beginning to the end, Muslim nationalism also received considerable, though indirect, support from Hindu nationalism, which always emphasized the differences between Hindus and Muslims—the mainstay also of Muslim nationalism. The climax was reached in the late-1930s when V.D. Savarkar, famous for his revolutionary exploits involving the risk of life before 1914, used the platform of the Hindu Mahasabha, of which he had become president after being released from the Andamans prison, to openly preach the two-nation theory, emphasizing that the Hindus constituted a nation by themselves and they must prepare to fight for India's Independence on their own without wasting much time in seeking the cooperation of Muslims, which was not likely to be available to them in any case.

The Rashtriya Swayamsevak Sangh or RSS, as it is popularly called, founded in 1926, stressed that since their religion was born abroad Muslims could not be trusted to be loyal to India. Neither the Hindu Mahasabha not the RSS had much following among Hindus in the late 1930s and 1940s of the twentieth century when Muslim nationalism reached its climax. However, the leaders of the Muslim League generally believed that they and not the Congress really represented the true sentiments of the Hindus and this further strengthened their resolve to create a separate sovereign state for themselves where the Muslims could live without any fear of Hindu domination.

VI

If Jinnah cannot be held responsible for Partition, it is even more absurd to foist the responsibility for Partition on the Congress leadership, particularly Gandhi, Nehru and Patel. In this connection, it may be mentioned that it continues to be argued by some people in India as well as Pakistan that Partition could have been avoided if the Congress leadership had accepted compulsory grouping of provinces in both East and West as, according to British and the Muslim League's interpretation, provided for in the Cabinet Mission Plan of 16 May 1946. It is forgotten by the advocates of this theory that compulsory grouping would involve the merger in the groups of areas both in the Punjab and Bengal of people who were strongly opposed to it. The unfairness of compulsory grouping reached its climax in relation to Assam, where only one district (Sylhet) had a Muslim majority, which might be reasonably expected to support merger with the eastern group. It is not surprising that both Gandhi and Nehru, indeed the entire Congress leadership, opposed compulsory grouping. It can, of course, he argued that compulsory grouping, with all its inequities, was not too high a price for preserving India's unity. However, as the Cabinet Mission Plan provided for a review of the entire constitutional structure after ten years of the making of the Constitution and the Muslim League, even while agreeing to join the Constituent Assembly, adhered as firmly as ever to the goal of what it described as a complete Pakistan, no one could be sure whether the provision for compulsory grouping was meant for helping the preservation of Indian unity, as claimed by the British officials, or for enabling the ultimate emergence of a complete Pakistan, dragging with it areas inhabited by non-Muslim majorities. The Congress leadership obviously realized that it was no longer possible to prevent Partition and the struggle had to be directed towards the prevention of the forcible dragging of non-Muslim populations, both in the east and the west, into Pakistan and retaining within India all those people who were keen to belong to it. It has been held by many historians and journalists that the Cabinet Mission Plan provided the last chance for preserving the unity of India. Seen in the context of the provisions of compulsory grouping and ten-yearly review of the entire constitutional structure, it can well be surmised that the Cabinet Mission Plan actually made Partition inevitable. Prime Minister Attlee's declaration of 20 February 1947, facilitated the early completion of the process initiated by the Cabinet Mission Plan. Partition had to come immediately without waiting for ten years, but with the provision that no area populated by people opposed to Pakistan could be forced to belong to it. This represented a success for the strategy adopted by the Congress leadership.

On the other hand, some continue to hold the Congress leadership, particularly Gandhi, as responsible for Partition, because of the so-called Congress policy of appeasement of the Muslim League and its failure to effectively resist the latter and the British and accepting Partition. They fail to realize that the Congress leadership had no other choice in 1947 in the face of almost unanimous support of the League's demand for Partition on the part of Muslims, whether belonging to Muslim majority provinces or minority provinces, except the North West Frontier Province, with a few honourable exceptions associated with the Congress and the socialist and Communist parties. A virtual civil war between Hindus and Muslims was raging in various parts of the country and a stage had arrived where there was no solution available of the Indian problem except Partition or continuation of British rule, for which neither the Congress nor the Muslim

League was prepared. Readers may ask whether Partition was unavoidable. The answer, according to the present author, is that at the stage at which the final decision in this regard was taken, Partition was indeed unavoidable and it was beyond the capacity of anyone to prevent it.

This applied also to Gandhi, justly acclaimed in India as also elsewhere as Father of the Nation and indeed the greatest political leader produced by the Indian subcontinent in modem times. Despite all facts to the contrary, it is felt in some quarters that if Gandhi had used his powerful weapons like civil disobedience and fast unto death, Partition could have been prevented. This indicates an utter lack of understanding of the political situation in India in 1946–7. It was a situation in which a call to civil disobedience, would only have resulted in further intensification of the Hindu–Muslim riots which had already spread to far-flung areas of India. Nor could a fast unto death by Gandhi in that situation have produced any positive result apart from further deepening the acrimony and bitterness between Hindus and Muslims. Gandhi understood fully the dynamics of the situation prevailing in the country in 1946–7. He was also aware of the fact that a political leader, however popular, was not a magician who could conjure up a movement whenever he wished regardless of the direction which the social forces around him were taking. When in August 1947, one of his close associates, Nirmal Kumar Bose, asked him to explain his action in supporting the Working Committee's decision to accept Partition in spite of his strong opposition to it, he pointed out that as a result of one year of communal riots the situation was surcharged with communalism and not at all favourable for a struggle. When asked further whether he could not have by his efforts created a situation, as he had apparently done on many occasions in the past, Gandhi replied, in words which show his deep understanding of the dynamics of relationship between a leader and the masses apparently being led by him:

> I have never created a situation in my life. I have one qualification which many of you do not possess. I can almost instinctively feel what is stirring in the hearts of the masses. And when I feel that the forces of good are dimly stirring within, I seize upon them and build up a programme. And they respond. People say that I had created a situation;

but I had done nothing except giving a shape to what was already there. Today I see no sign of such a healthy feeling. And therefore I shall have to wait until the time comes.[8]

It might, of course, be true that Gandhi had on some occasions in the past had remarked that Partition could come only over his dead body. Here we may remind ourselves that in his whole life he had never claimed to be consistent with what he had said on earlier occasions. Whenever he was criticized for being inconsistent with his past stand on any issue, he replied that he always tried to be consistent not with what he had said before, but with truth as he saw it on any particular occasion. It should be obvious that he saw the truth in 1947 and realized that Partition was unavoidable in the circumstances then prevailing.

VII

Sixty years after Partition, it is now time for all concerned to accept the truth which Gandhi, with undeniable anguish and torment, accepted in 1947, namely, that Partition was unavoidable under the circumstances then prevailing. There have been all varieties of nationalism in history and the emergence and growth of Muslim nationalism in British India was a part of history which we must come to terms with, treat Pakistan as its legitimate offspring and stop searching for scapegoats in the shape of this or that leader to explain its birth. The leaders on both sides functioned honourably and did their best to protect the interests of their constituents as per their perceptions. Gandhi could not prevent Partition, but was steadfast in his determination to stop the continuance of ill-will and antagonism between the two new nations. Unfortunately, the bullets fired by a Hindu fanatic on 30 January 1948 did not give him a chance. Sane persons in both India and Pakistan have realized by now that the need of the hour is to forget the past bitterness and work for the establishment of harmony between the two nations. While the objective is clearly visible, the path to it is still full of difficulties of all kinds. Let the peoples in both countries try unitedly to overcome these difficulties and herald a new era in the history of our relations. That will be the best way of celebrating the diamond jubilee year of both Independence and Partition.

NOTES

1. Jamil-ud-din Ahmad, comp., *Quaid-i-Azam as Seen by His Contemporaries* (Lahore, 1966), p. 231.
2. H.V. Hodson, *The Great Divide* (London, 1969), pp. 37–8.
3. Ishtiaq Hussain Qureshi, *The Struggle for Pakistan* (Karachi, 1979; first published 1965).
4. Sharif Al Mujahid, *Quaid-i-Azam Jinnah: Studies in Interpretation* (Karachi, 1981), p. 411.
5. Ayesha Jalal, *The Sole Spokesman: Jinnah, the Muslim League and the Demand for Pakistan* (Cambridge, 1985), p. 57.
6. Ibid., p. 262.
7. Mujahid, n. 4, pp. 411–12.
8. Nirmal Kumar Bose, 'My Experiences as a Gandhian', in M.P. Sinha, ed., *Contemporary Relevance of Gandhi* (Bombay, 1970).

APPENDICES

APPENDIX I

Note of an Interview between Linlithgow and Jinnah, New Delhi 4 November 1939

AFTER CONCLUDING MY conversation with Mr. Gandhi on the morning of Saturday, 4th November, I invited Mr. Jinnah to come to see me that afternoon.

2. He started off by describing at great length how Mr. Gandhi had approached him before the Conference with me on 1st November, a move of which Mr. Jinnah was disposed to complain and had enquired of him as to whether it was not possible for Congress and Muslims to get together and to present a joint claim for the declaration that Congress wanted. They had pressed him on this line for two or three days, and he had had a most exhausting time and been placed in most difficult position, since they had made particular use of the argument that unless he was prepared to meet them, he and his friends would be clearly exposed before the public as the one real obstacle to home rule for India. No effort had been spared by the Congress spokesmen to get him to adopt their point of view.

3. I said that as Mr. Jinnah was aware, I had avoided the idea of an All-Parties Conference partly with a view to preventing that line of argument from being fully developed against him, and I had hoped that the specific remit which I had embodied in my letter to him, Gandhi and Rajendra Prasad of 1st November with reference to joint representation, would not arouse the same risk of a concentrated attack upon him on the ground he mentioned.

4. Mr. Jinnah replied that the plain fact was that he had been quite unable to get anyone on the Congress side to take any interest in the proposal for the expansion of the Executive Council. They kept hammering away at the declaration, and incidentally, at the question of his own position. Not only had there been preliminary questioning, most strongly urged, of the right of Muslims to speak for themselves through the Muslim League. Congress had not hesitated to carry the matter a point further and to

*Mss Eur. F125/8. Linlithgow Collection, India Office Library and Records (London).

question Mr. Jinnah's own right to speak on behalf of the Muslims. In three days' discussion it had proved quite impossible to get even these preliminary matters disposed of. He had urged the Congress not to worry too much about the declaration until the Congress and the Muslims had got together generally. They could then see to what extent it would be possible to formulate a scheme. But Congress were not satisfied, and had refused to accept that proposition. The fundamental issue was, in fact, that the Muslims were determined to settle their own main grievances with the Hindus before there could be any question of further constitutional advances. The Hindus on the other hand were insistent on securing constitutional pledges first and leaving a settlement with the Muslims until later.

5. Passing from this aspect of the matter, I said to Mr. Jinnah that I hoped he would not think me impertinent if I talked for a moment of his own position and of that of the Muslim League as developed by him. He had given me very valuable help by standing firm against Congress claims and I was duly grateful. It was clear that if he, Mr. Jinnah, had supported the Congress in their demand for a declaration and confronted me with a joint demand, the strain upon me and upon His Majesty's Government would have been very great indeed. I thought, therefore, I could claim to have a vested interest in his position, and I had been asking myself how far that position was intrinsically sound. But I was bound to confess that I did not like it. His constituents, as I saw it, had been so thoroughly soured by the experiences of democratic institutions in the Provinces for 2½ years from April 1937, that he and they had now turned their back on everything that had been said by them and by their representatives at the Round Table Conferences and the Joint Select Committee, and were prepared publicly to repudiate the idea of democracy, self-Government and Federation, because of the risk involved in them of Hindu domination at the Centre. But was there not the risk that, while he was at the moment out of his immediate difficulties, he and his friends might find that they were in something like a dead end? Where did the future lie? The Muslims now had the appearance of being anti-national and anti-democratic. What outlet did he foresee for his young men, and what method of dealing with the demands for a stronger policy of nationalism which his younger generation would certainly advocate? Moreover, I did not believe that he could escape from this dilemma by the idea which had been so widely ventilated of having two Indias; or that any real solution was to be found in transferring populations from the humid South to the cold and barren North and by parcelling out the Princes. In short, he was, if I might so describe it, "sitting pretty" now, but I was apprehensive that he was laying up stores of trouble for himself before very long, and that the eroding effect of nationalism on the foundations of his platform was likely to be swift and serious.

6. Mr. Jinnah said that he did not in the least resent what I had been saying and, indeed, felt the force of my argument. He realized that His

Majesty's Government and I were still attracted by the dream of Federation. He called it a dream because in his view it definitely was a dream. The principle that a government resting solely on indigenous support should be able to compel obedience, did not run true to India's history, and it was in these circumstances that he had reluctantly found himself driven to set aside as practical politics the idea of Federation. Equally, he was extremely doubtful as to the capacity of India and Indians to look after themselves. When Mr. Gandhi had asked him a couple of days earlier why he had promised support to His Majesty's Government, he had replied "Because of India". If the British should by any chance be beaten in the war and driven out of India, India would break into a hundred pieces in three months and lie open, in addition, to external invasion. It was because he knew that we were really clinging still to Federation, that he had pressed me in connection with the clarification of my declaration as to how far the review, which His Majesty's Government had expressed their willingness to undertake at the end of the war, was on the scheme as a whole and not merely on "details".

7. I said at once that he was quite right in thinking that we did still adhere to Federation as the best practical solution of this extremely difficult problem. As for his second point, the promise was in terms to review the whole position.

8. Mr. Jinnah replied that he had felt certain that the first was the case and that he appreciated the frankness of my reply, which again was what he had expected, and which he respected. He thought himself that we would have to abandon Federation and he repeated that he thought Federation was a dream. He knew that we were a very persistent people and most reluctant to give up anything to which we had put our hand more particularly when, as in the present case, our project had taken statutory form after a long period of preliminary investigation. But reluctant as we might be to give up Federation, he thought himself that we should find that it would be Federation that would give us up and that it was no more than a fantasy.

9. I said to Mr. Jinnah that I of course accepted the sincerity of his view, but that my own feeling was that his "dream" was very much a reality. I proceeded to develop the urge for unification as the only route to enhanced status, and the strength of that urge; and I added that to the extent that he was in fact on a bad wicket in opposing unification, I wished I could convince him that our dream might move into a new phase of evolution and have to be tried out. He said he quite understood my point of view but felt bound still to disagree.

10. Mr. Jinnah having secured from me an assurance that we would be concerned with the whole scheme of the Act in these post-war conversations and not merely with "details", and having thus established his point on that matter, dismissed it as of relatively little value; and went on to say that the really important thing was the securing of an undertaking that the Muslim community would not be compelled by His Majesty's Government

to accept something they did not want. I asked him in reply how long it would be, if we were to give any community or party the right of veto such as he clearly desired, before the next claimant with similar rights would come along? How were we to reconcile these vetos? No government, in my judgement, responsible as the Paramount Authority for a country such as India could have its freedom of action fettered by a majority, much less by a minority, however important. Perhaps he would tell me who was to decide where in such an event "the interests" of Muslims would end. He would realize at once that we might find ourselves inhibited from action in almost any direction because of the possibility of a claim in connection with any matter, however remotely it reacted on Muslim interests.

11. Mr. Jinnah said that I was going too far in putting the case as I had put it. There was in fact substance and reason in his point and he wished to make an appeal to me about it. After the war, in his judgement, we were almost certain to have a radical government in Great Britain and he had been greatly struck by the Lords' debate of a couple of days previously in the course of which prominent personages who were quite likely to be in the Cabinet after the war had frankly urged that in India the majority must rule and the minority take their medicine. That seemed to him a complete fallacy, based on a misunderstanding of the closeness of the analogy between conditions in the United Kingdom and conditions here. Where there was, broadly speaking, a common blood and a homogeneous people, that proposition might work, but we could not come to India, with its immense variety of differences—cultural, religious, geographical, historical, and the depth of the cleavages as between great communities—and endeavour to apply a wholesale and rough and ready solution of difficulties such as could be expected and such as we could agree to make work at Home. What he was apprehensive of was that the type of outlook represented by the opposition at Home at the present day would, when it came into power, force democratic government on India and anaesthetise the Muslims. He had not the least doubt that that was a real and serious risk. What he wanted in these circumstances was a guarantee against the next government, or against at any rate a government of the type he had mentioned. I admitted that there was some substance in his point. I asked Mr. Jinnah whether he suggested that if he had adopted the line he was taking today in regard to Federation and democracy at the three Round Table Conferences and the Joint Select Committee, the scheme of the Act would have been written in its present form. He and his friends had, after all, supported the general concept of the Act. He replied that he took the point but that at that time he had not had the bitter experience that he had since had of life under a Hindu communal government. He did not anticipate that His Majesty's present government would be false to the pledges that had been given, or would endeavour to coerce the minorities. But a government of the type which we might expect post-war might well lose patience with the

representations of the minorities and try to drive those minorities to accept an unacceptable scheme. I told him that I understood his point even if I did not altogether agree with it.

12. Mr. Jinnah then said that he thought the best thing would be that he should send me a letter, with a request for an answer, putting the point on which he had just touched. I warned him that neither he nor any other party would persuade His Majesty's Government to give him a veto such as he clearly wanted on constitutional reform, but that I would myself readily submit his views to the Secretary of State for the decision of His Majesty's Government. Mr. Jinnah expressed his appreciation and left me with the impression that he would be quite prepared to accept a refusal.

L.,—4-11-39

APPENDIX II

Linlithgow to Zetland, 28 November 1939

I SENT YOU ON 6th November copy of a letter dated the 5th November from Mr. Jinnah indicating certain matters affecting the Muslim community in respect of which he desired a clarification of the position. I enclose with this letter a copy of the acknowledgement which I have sent to him, in which I promised to let him have an answer as soon as practicable. Mr. Jinnah has since raised the question of publishing his letter of 5th November, and my reply; and that matter has been under discussion between us. In the same connection I would refer to the note of my interview with Mr. Jinnah on 4th November last, a copy of which you have already received, and out of which to some extent his present letter has emerged.

2. The points raised in Mr. Jinnah's letter are of great general importance, and I have been in consultation with my Advisers as to the line which could best be taken in dealing with them, as to the degree of detail into which it would be appropriate to enter, and finally as to the channel through which, and the manner in which, a reply to them could most appropriately be given. I cannot do better in this connection than to send you the copy I enclose of a letter from my Home Member, dated 20th November which, in addition to examining the questions to which I have just alluded, touches in general terms on certain of the wider considerations of importance which arise in the present connection.

3. In inviting my Home Member and the other officers to whom reference is made in his letter dated the 20th November to assist me with their advice on the points raised in Mr. Jinnah's letter, I indicated that there were two further points which were present to my mind in considering this whole matter. The first the extent to which the principle that majority rule must prevail is really sound in Indian conditions: the second, the apprehensions which Mr. Jinnah had expressed in his conversation with me on 4th November (apprehensions which in my judgement continue to underlie certain at any rate of the assurances which his letter of 5th November shows him as anxious to secure) as to the possible attitude of future governments at Home to constitutional advance in India in its effect on the

*Mss Eur. F125/13, India Office Library & Records (London).

position of the Indian minorities. Sir Reginald Maxwell's letter of 20th November touches on those issues, and I deal with them at greater length below.

4. Before proceeding to examine the specific points raised by Mr. Jinnah in any detail, I would take the preliminary point of the method in which any reply on the issues referred to by him had best be conveyed, and the extent to which it is appropriate that in a reply to an individual political leader the Governor-General, on behalf of His Majesty's Government, should precisely define the attitude of His Majesty's Government in relation to issues of such very wide extent. I agree entirely with the view expressed by my Reforms Commissioner, and by my Home Member in his letter of 20th November, that other communities are directly interested in any proposition of broad general importance affecting the constitutional position; and that there are sound arguments, if it is proposed to make a pronouncement of the first importance, against conveying it in the form of a personal letter from the Governor-General to the leader of any particular political party. For the reasons which I give later in this letter I have, however, reached the conclusion that, while it is desirable that I should in my present letter set out in some detail my own views on certain aspects of the general political position in this country, particularly in relation to the Muslims, the balance of argument is as yet against any radical change; and that so far as Mr. Jinnah is concerned the wise course will be to send him a guarded and concise reply. I am clear in particular that major constitutional changes can neither be worked out nor applied in detail at a time when the attention of His Majesty's Government and of Parliament, and the energies of the government in India as well as in Great Britain are concentrated primarily on the prosecution of the war; and that argument applies with even greater force to any radical readjustment of policy such as might be involved in the acceptance for example of Mr. Jinnah's thesis that democracy in India is a failure, and that a complete abandonment of that solution of the constitutional problems of this country must be contemplated.

5. I am, subject to your better judgement, of opinion in those circumstances that the reply to Mr. Jinnah can appropriately go in the form of a letter from myself, so long as that reply is carefully worded, limited in scope, and guarded in its language. Were it a question of announcing major changes of policy, I should regard it as more appropriate that they should be announced either in Parliament, or in a statement made with the approval of His Majesty's Government by the Governor-General; and that the reply to the leader of the Muslim League should be merely to the effect that, given the importance of the issues raised, it was proposed to take an early opportunity of indicating that they have been raised and of expressing the view upon them of His Majesty's Government. But, if you accept the suggestions I make below, that will not be the case, and a reply can, I think, appropriately issue as a letter from the Governor-General to Mr. Jinnah.

6. I think it will be desirable, given the nature of the matters under discussion, that before I proceed to put forward my suggestions as to the line to be taken with Mr. Jinnah I should as briefly as practicable comment on the background of his questions, and on certain of the wider issues implicit in them. I would propose in the first place briefly to review the position of the various political interests in India as I see it today, and I would formulate my conclusions in the light not only of the discussions which I have now been having for some considerable time with prominent leaders of political thought in this country, but of the resolution which has emerged from the discussions of the Working Committee of the Congress at Allahabad from the 19th to the 23rd November, of Mr. Gandhi's article in the *Harijan* of 25th November, and of the statement issued on 24th November by the General Secretary of the Muslim League, which latter statement we may I think, assume to embody a policy which has received the approval of Mr. Jinnah. For convenience of reference, I enclose copies of all those documents.

THE CONGRESS POSITION

7. As between the Congress and the Muslim community, the position is briefly as indicated by Mr. Jinnah in his interview with me on 4th November, viz., that Congress are anxious to secure a settlement of the constitutional issue, and of India's goal, before taking any steps to deal with the difficulties which arise from the existence of minorities in this country, difficulties which they assert will admit of being disposed of without trouble once the constitutional issue is cleared. The Muslim community, on the other hand, as represented by the Muslim League, are strongly averse from any constitutional advance or move (save of course such advance as might meet with their explicit approval) until a satisfactory settlement has been reached of the problem of Muslim grievances in the Provinces. In general, Congress have made swift progress in the constitutional field since the outbreak of war. Federation (though there is reason to think that the Right Wing element in Congress appreciate its value, and would even now in certain circumstances consider reversion to it) has been relegated to the background: the reopening at the end of the war of the Act of 1935, and its modification in the light of Indian opinion, have been conceded; the principle of the association of Indian opinion with the conduct of the war, through a consultative group, has been admitted: the expansion of the Governor-General's Council to include as a war measure leaders of political parties has been offered and rejected.

8. Congress, encouraged no doubt by the success they have so far had, and susceptible to the pressure of their Left Wing elements, continue in these circumstances insistently to urge their claim to speak with authority on behalf of India as a whole. They press their demand, which they have

backed by the withdrawal of Congress governments, for a declaration of British constitutional aims which will represent a recognition of the freedom and the independence of India, and of the right of India and her peoples (whether in British India or, it would appear, the Indian States) to settle the problem of her future constitution on the basis and the advice of a Constituent Assembly based on the widest possible franchise and, as I see it, without weightage for individual communities or interests. The Constituent Assembly is to frame a constitution in which the rights of all "*accepted* minorities" (a term not defined, but according to Press comment likely in the first instance to cover Muslims and Sikhs) "could be protected to their satisfaction"; and separate electorates will be retained in the election to the Assembly for such minorities as desire them, "the number of those members in the Assembly to reflect numerical strength". Mr. Gandhi has indicated (*Harijan* of 4th November 1939, page 328) that "a free India will claim to examine every European interest on its merit, and that which conflicts with the national interest will go by the board", and he has repeated, in the *Harijan* of 25th November (page 353), that "European interests are absolutely safe so long as they are not in conflict with the interests of India", a phrase not precisely defined. No special provision is made for what I might describe as the minor minorities; and the Congress resolution referred to in paragraph 6 suggests that they are equally not prepared to make special provision for special interests of any kind. In a different field, the Congress press has touched on the need for an arrangement between His Majesty's Government and India in regard to the Indian national debt. The problem of defence, vital not only in its general importance, but in its reactions on the Muslim community and the States, has attracted little attention, and the underlying assumption would appear to be that His Majesty's Government will continue to play their part in the defence of India, and that no insuperable difficulty need arise over the recruitment and control of the Indian Army.

9. As regards the Princely Order, the claim of Congress, even though it may not be stated specifically in those terms, is clearly to be allowed to take over the functions of Paramountcy; and the suggestion has been advanced that what really matters in this connection is the problem of the peoples of the Indian States rather than the Rulers of those States (cf. Working Committee Resolution of 23rd November 1939) (I may remark incidentally that the question of communal electorates with or without weightage in the States for the representation of States peoples in the Constituent Assembly is going to be no easy one, if they ever reach that stage!). Mr Gandhi (*Harijan* of 25th November, page 351) has in the same connection remarked, commending solution by means of a Constituent Assembly, "To raise the question of the Princes is still more untenable. They are part of the Paramount Power. It is painful to think that British statesmen do not so much as mention the millions of people of the States. Have they no voice in their own government?"

10. The Congress claim is, in effect, one for a predominant Congress control, reflecting a Hindu population majority, over India as a whole, and for an acceptance on trust by all other elements in this country of Congress capacity and willingness adequately to safeguard all communities and interests. As a corollary of that claim, they deny that they are as a body communal in character (and it is the case that Congress contains non-Hindu elements, and that the strictly communal Hindu organisations, such as the Mahasabha, repudiate its claim to speak for Hinduism). For all that, Congress as a body is essentially Hindu in character, and, whatever criticism Hindu bodies may make of it, there is little likelihood in the last resort of Hinduism generally in British India, with the possible exception of the Scheduled Castes and a very small conservative element, failing to make a solid front with it against either Muslim or European opposition.

THE MUSLIM POSITION

11. So far as the Muslims are concerned, one of the most significant features of the last two or three years has in my judgement been the emergence of the Muslim League, from a position of relatively secondary importance, as an All-India political organisation which, whatever internal dissensions may from time to time reveal themselves, is second only in importance to the Congress; and in certain respects second not even to that body. The second significant feature in this connection has been the extent to which Muslim demands have expanded and have crystallised during the same period. Those demands in their latest form are well represented by the statement by the Secretary of the Muslim League referred to in paragraph 6 above read with Mr. Jinnah's letter to me of 5th November. They now represent (so far as British India is concerned) neither more nor less than a claim to be treated on a position of "absolute equality" (in the words used by Mr. Jinnah in a speech at Bombay on 7th November) with the Hindu community, despite the fact that the Muslims are in a numerical minority; a demand for the full safeguarding of Muslim interests in the Provinces; a claim that the prior consent of the Muslim community shall be secured to any further constitutional advance; and an emphatic repudiation of the idea of a Constituent Assembly in which the vote should go by heads. It would appear to have been over this issue of whether or not His Majesty's Government should be invited to make a statement in regard to constitutional advance *before* any settlement was reached between the Muslim League and the Hindu community as represented predominantly by the Congress, that the discussion between Mr. Jinnah, Mr. Gandhi, and Pandit Nehru which took place in Delhi at the beginning of this month broke down.

12. I myself feel no doubt that the Muslims are profoundly embittered by 2½ years' experience of Congress rule in the Hindu majority Provinces: that they are determined if they can to secure some strengthening of their

position and their safeguards in those Provinces: and that recognising as they do that what really matters in the future is the control of the Centre, they are deeply apprehensive that by legislative enactment, or by an agreement to which they have not been a party, they may be handed over at the Centre to the control, or the predominant influence of the major community. It is, I think, at the same time fair to say that as I write the Muslims feel for the moment a greater confidence, though it would, I suspect, take very little to shake that confidence, both in themselves and in the probability that His Majesty's Government will not without their full concurrence conclude a bargain with parties or interests which the Muslims regard as opposed to themselves. I would trace that greater confidence, for what it is worth, not only to the unbending rigidity of the position which Mr. Jinnah has for some time past maintained, but to the fact that the Congress and the Muslim League were treated on an equal footing for the purpose of my recent conversations with political leaders; and that Mr. Jinnah took the opportunity to make it very clear to the public that he expected Congress to come to him rather than that he should go to the Congress. Moreover, the declaration which I issued with the approval of His Majesty's Government on 18th October contained a specific assurance that the scheme of the Act of 1935 will be regarded as open to modification in the light of Indian opinion at the end of the war, and that in planning afresh, or modifying in any respect, any important part of India's future constitution His Majesty's Government will again take counsel with the minorities. The Muslims can therefore point to a definite commitment by His Majesty's Government to consider their views; and Congress insistence on the reconsideration of the scheme of the Act has played into their hands by securing the reopening of the whole scheme of the Act, and so of the provincial sections which the Muslims wish amended.

13. I would only add that, while Muslim grievances in respect of Hindu administration of the Congress-governed Provinces are intangible to a degree, (as has I think been shown by the correspondence noted in the margin), and while they have either rarely admitted of specific proof [the incident quoted by Mr. Jinnah in his interview with me on 4th October (paragraph 10) is an example of the contrary] or have proved to be of somewhat subordinate importance, there is no question whatever as to the existence of a very definite feeling of inferiority on the part of the Muslim community in Provinces in which they are not in a majority, a feeling which I would judge to be in no sense comparable to the feeling of Hindu minorities in comparable

1. Letter to Governors of the United Provinces, Central Provinces and Berar, and Bihar, dated 13th April 1939
2. Letter from Governor of the United Provinces, dated 10th May 1939.
3. Letter from Governor of the Central Provinces, dated 18th April 1939.
4. Letter from Governor of Bihar, dated 8th May 1939.

circumstances. Unsubstantial as Muslim complaints in such conditions may frequently be, the existence of the atmosphere is the thing that matters and the thing to which we have to give weight in formulating our policy and reaching our conclusions.

ACUTENESS OF DIVERGENCE BETWEEN CONGRESS AND MUSLIM POSITIONS

14. We find ourselves in these circumstances faced by Congress claims of a sweeping character which are opposed by a Muslim minority, stronger and more self-assertive than in the past, and convinced that if it is to avoid absorption by the Congress, it must be prepared to contest every inch of the ground. But that minority, despite its substantial numbers, its virility, its martial tradition, its geographical position, the capacity, and the readiness, which it has shown in two major Provinces, to work the Provincial scheme of the Act of 1935, and its affiliations with Islam in the international field, is, broadly speaking, less intelligent, less highly cultured and less wealthy than the majority community. It lacks a press, and a publicity organisation; and it has taken no active steps to interest individuals in Parliament in its case. And it is open to the criticism that its present policy makes it the sole, or the most important, obstacle to the achievement of Indian independence, and of Indian national ambitions. That is a point likely to increase in importance as time goes on, and as a younger generation more susceptible to nationalist pressure comes to the fore. There are dangers, in such circumstances, in leaning too heavily on the Muslim community or attaching undue weight to their more exaggerated claims, though it would be as foolish to underrate the importance of their support to us, whatever its motives, as it would be shortsighted and unfair to fail to give the fullest consideration to its legitimate claims.

POSITION OF OTHER MINORITIES IN BRITISH INDIA

15. Save for the Europeans, with whose case I deal in the following paragraph, I do not think that I need devote any special attention in this review to the position of the remaining minorities. The Sikhs culturally and geographically are strong and united; they have the advantage of being strongly represented in Army recruitment, and they will require careful consideration in any constitutional settlement. But they are not in themselves of decisive importance. The Parsees are of great commercial significance, but not by themselves of sufficient consequence to turn the scale. The Anglo–Indians equally, though Parliament has always taken a very close interest in their fate and though it must naturally be a source of concern to us, are not of sufficient weight to turn the scale. Nor are the Indian Christians. The one exception I would make in my present survey is in respect of the

Scheduled Castes. Strictly speaking they form part of the great Hindu community. But the special arrangements' that are embodied in the present constitution to secure their representation have marked them out as a body requiring safeguards of their own; and the number of seats which they enjoy in the Provincial and the Central Legislatures entitles them to full consideration. They again would stand, it may be remarked, to be swamped in a Constituent Assembly where voting was by heads and where weightage or special protection was not given, for there would be very little chance of maintaining the arrangements which Parliament was at such pains to devise in 1932–35 for ensuring that the Scheduled Castes were represented, and their point of view put forward, only by persons genuinely competent to put forward that point of view with detachment and with sincerity; or of avoiding less worthy motives from influencing the vote of individuals. Their apprehension of being dominated by Congress has been well brought out in connection with the statements which I have made since the war began.

THE EUROPEANS

16. I turn now to the position of the Europeans. We can, I think, agree that Europeans are not a minority in the same sense as other indigenous minorities. For all that, they are in practice a minority and a very important one, if only because of the magnitude of the commercial intersects which they represent, of the contribution, cultural and political, which the European community has made to India, and of the extreme sensitiveness of Parliament in regard either to discrimination against the European community as such, or to unjustifiable attacks whether by tariff legislation or otherwise on legitimate European interests. I do not, however, think that I need discuss their position and their attitude, with which you are fully familiar, in my present letter, save to say that I am increasingly impressed by the desirability of keeping the problem which it represents prominently before the public, and by the importance of ensuring that their case does not in any way go by default, and that the essential necessity for securing their position is borne in mine in any proposals that may fall to us to consider.

THE POSITION OF THE INDIAN STATES

17. I will finally say a word about the position of the Indian States. We are both agreed that the level of administration in the States varies greatly. There are many things which we might desire to see done otherwise: and His Majesty's Government, the Secretary of State, and the Crown Representative have spared no pains in their endeavour to secure the introduction of liberal administration, and the achievement of standards of performance in the Indian States which would enable them to play their

part in a unified and federated India. The difficulties implicit in a Constituent Assembly based on the widest possible franchise, substantial as they are in British India, would clearly be even greater in the case of the Indian States. The position of the Indian States differs from that of British India, in that the relations of their Rulers with the Paramount Power are governed by Treaty engagements of varying degrees of complexity, which date over the period of British connection with India, which impose definite obligations on His Majesty's Government as well as on the Rulers, but which are in few, if any, instances of such a nature as to admit of any unilateral denunciation. The communal issue is less acute as an internal question in the case of most States; nor is it of importance in determining the attitude of States towards constitutional change, the general attitude of the Rulers being one of aversion from any such change, and certainly of aversion, from any change, or any promise of change, which would appear likely prejudicially to affect their own position or to bring them under the control of British India. That fact is of importance, because, on the general political platform it tends to align them with the Muslims and with those minorities who are not in favour of accepting the lead of Congress. Mr. Gandhi has indicated that Congress would not recognise the States as a minority, and it would indeed be unreasonable to use that term in respect to them. They are in no sense a minority, but they represent in the general Indian picture an area so wide and on the whole so homogeneous as to admit more fairly of being described as a separate element which must be brought into relation with the remaining elements and harmonised with them if there is ever to be any question of unity of India or of a Dominion of India as distinct from a Dominion of British India. And the obligations which His Majesty's Government have undertaken towards the States are of direct and immediate relevance in relation to the vital problem of Defence.

THE GENERAL BACKGROUND OF THE INDIAN POLITICAL SCENE

18. It is against the background which I have just endeavoured to describe that the present Muslim demands must be considered. On the one hand we have a political organisation which, while it does not represent the Hindu community as such, may properly be regarded as speaking for that community, in a substantial majority in numbers, and in many respects in the intellectual and cultural field in a position far ahead of that of other communities in this country. That community, which contains also the most important indigenous trading and commercial interests, and which is solidly established in the political life of British India, in which up to a few days ago it provided Ministries in eight Provinces, is naturally anxious to establish its predominance throughout the country as a whole, a predominance which can be established only in ratio to the degree of the

relinquishment of its present position by His Majesty's Government; and which could be maintained only by the assistance of His Majesty's Government in the field of internal and external security.

19. But while it is of such immense importance in numbers, in wealth and in education, the minorities with which it has to deal are equally not to be ignored. The Muslim community, consisting of some 80 or 90 million people, divided by a profound gulf culturally, religiously, and in general outlook, holding the Frontier (I do not attach overmuch importance to the fact that there has been a Congress Ministry in the North-West Frontier Province), the Punjab, Sind and Bengal; making a contribution of the first importance to the defence of India; and above all geographically linked with the Muslim States of Western Central Asia and culturally and religiously linked with Islam wherever it may stand, is deeply apprehensive that Congress may with the assistance of His Majesty's Government succeed in producing a constitutional scheme of such a character as severely to hamper the Muslims in their aim of independence as a community and in the safeguarding of their interests. Those doubts in various ways are shared by minorities such as the Scheduled Castes, the Sikhs, the non-Congress Hindus, for whom the non-Brahmin element in southern India speaks; by the small minorities such as the Indian Christians, Parsees, etc., and, I suspect, by the Princes. But the Muslims, and those who find themselves thus temporarily associated with them in a community of interest are at the disadvantage that, save so far as the Europeans are concerned, they have not the same organisation as the Congress; that they lack a press; and that they admit of being pilloried as the obstacle to the achievement by India of the natural desire of any country for complete independence.

20. In this last regard the Princely Order, whose relations with the Crown are of a different nature, and to whom the Crown has undertaken specific and detailed obligations of a different character, can afford to regard their position with greater equanimity. But they are well aware that a Congress government at the Centre, more particularly a government exercising any sort of paramountcy, would not long allow their continued independence. The struggle in this analysis is thus rather one between Congress on the one hand and the remainder of the country on the other. And of the remainder of the country the Muslims are of greater *immediate* importance, since the first stage of this struggle must be a British Indian state.

IS A DEMOCRATIC SYSTEM, BASED ON THE RULE OF MAJORITY, SOUND AND WORKABLE IN INDIAN CONDITIONS?

21. Our ambition has in the past been to introduce into India that system of democratic working which has on the whole been so successful in our own country, and which in the Dominions again has on the whole worked

reasonably successfully. We have accepted throughout that the problem of India is different in character from our own problem or that of the Dominions, thanks to the existence in India of minorities substantial in cultural difference, in religious difference, and in numbers, in no way comparable with minorities elsewhere. The problem of Northern Ireland, though acute, is relatively a small one. The problem of Quebec again is relatively small, and Quebec admits of being isolated. The application of democratic principles in a country such as India, where minorities may run into tens of millions, where they are scattered over the whole of a sub-continent, and where allegations of maltreatment or injustice in one Province have an immediate reaction in another, is by no means so simple; and that fact is reflected in the endeavours which have been made in the Government of India Act to secure the position of minorities by inserting safeguards, by the Communal Award and the distribution of seats based upon it, and the like.

22. I cannot but feel that Sir Reginald Maxwell's analysis identifies the weaknesses which have so often been suspected, and which experience has now more clearly revealed, in the application of the Western democratic system to British India. It would be cowardly, if we were satisfied that the great experiment on which His Majesty's Government have been engaged now for so many years has been a failure, and that the problems of this country cannot be solved on the basis of ordinary majority–minority rule, or of the democratic systems of the West, that we should not frankly admit that that is the case and endeavour, with the assistance of political parties in this country, to find an alternative solution. The frank and public claim of the Muslim League that democracy has broken down in operation is admittedly in this connection a most important and a most significant feature.

23. But, grave as may be the doubts which I myself begin to feel in this regard, I am nevertheless after the most careful consideration of the opinion that the stage has not yet been reached at which we can feel satisfied that the democratic experiment has failed, and that there is no way in which the specific difficulties that its working has revealed can be overcome; or that the long process of 30 years of constitutional endeavour, by successive governments of all political complexions at Home, which culminated for the time being in the Act of 1935, has been misconceived, and that we must now go back upon it. I have not failed in reaching that conclusion to give weight to the fact that for so radical a change of policy as would be involved in the acceptance of the proposition that the democratic experiment has broken down, we should need to be in possession of immediate and convincing evidence to satisfy the public mind not only in Parliament, and at Home generally, but in the international sphere, that our conclusion is incontestable or almost incontestable. And I do not myself feel, grave as

may be the doubts we have entertained from time to time about the adequacy and soundness of the existing constitutional scheme or of certain aspects of our constitutional intentions for the future, that any such convincing case, convincing, that is, to a degree which would satisfy Parliament and the public, could easily be established, even though we could point to differences between the communities; to administrative weaknesses or failures, or to the incompatibility of an elaborate system of safeguards with the existence of democratic government in the western sense.

24. It is not irrelevant, too, that we could certainly anticipate vigorous opposition from Congress and from their sympathisers and supporters, whether here or at Home, to any suggestion on our part that the democratic system had broken down; and I feel a good deal of doubt as to whether the Muslims, when faced with the alternative of a complete abandonment of the principle of a democratic constitution in favour of something which could not at the outset be at all precisely defined, and which would have to take shape after lengthy discussion and consultation, might not be likely to take a somewhat different view from that represented by Mr. Jinnah's recent condemnations of democracy in Indian conditions. Nor finally even if the case was more patently convincing than, I think, it is, do I conceive that there would be any likelihood of our being able to consider the problem of alternatives in war time.

25. My own judgement in these circumstances is that, with a full recognition of the defects and the possible dangers, even, of the application of the democratic principle in India, and, too, of the responsibility which we assume in proceeding to apply it in some still more advanced form, the practical course as well as the course of political wisdom is for all that to go ahead, and not yet to abandon our endeavour to make the democratic system His Majesty's Government have for so many years had in mind to work. How precisely to dispose of the difficulties that experience has revealed, particularly as affecting the Muslims, does not fall to be answered in this letter. It may well be that we should be able to devise legal safeguards still more extensive, or of a different character from those which already exist; for Muslim interests in minority Provinces (safeguards which would of course have to be balanced by some corresponding safeguards for Hindu minorities in Muslim majority Provinces): and that Congress on the one hand and the Muslims on the other might be prepared in the interests of general constitutional advance to acquiesce in some such arrangement. The Muslim claim to equality is a far more difficult problem. The numerically major community cannot be turned into a minority: nor has the minority community, important as it may be, itself really faced the difficulty involved in a right of veto which would turn the majority into a minority. But unless these two communities can reach some accommodation there can be no hope (any question of the association of Princely India apart) of their

collaborating to work any form of central responsibility in a country in which there are no party divisions, and in which community is the essential basis of separation; or of any stable constitutional advance; and realisation of that may contribute to a more accommodating attitude on the part of political leaders and to the reaching of a compromise. While, therefore, I am by no means confident of the outcome of the present position in terms of relations between the two major communities, and so of our capacity, however willing we may be, to further the cause of constitutional advance, we must, as I see it, continue in present circumstances with the democratic experiment, and make the best of the situation that confronts us.

MUSLIM STATUS IN INDIA: INTERNATIONAL AFFILIATIONS OF THE MUSLIM COMMUNITY

26. There is one further point on which it would be well that I should touch before I turn to answer Mr. Jinnah's specific questions. It is the question of Muslim status in India to which Sir Reginald Maxwell refers in paragraph 5 of his letter of 20th November. As I have elsewhere recorded in this letter, the claim of the Muslim League appears now to be that the Muslim community shall be treated on a basis of equality for constitutional purposes with the majority community, and the note by Sir John Ewart, which my Home Member quotes, emphasises the possibility that the Indian Muslim problem, given the fact that the Muslim community are part of the international Muslim community and very conscious of their extra-Indian Islamic ties, may well become a matter of international concern in a degree unlikely in the case of the Hindu community, which is after all essentially an Indian community with few if any ramifications outside. I do not myself think that (even if we were to leave out of consideration the obligations falling on His Majesty's Government, to which you referred in your speech in the House of Lords on 7th November) we can accept the principle that any one community, whether majority or minority, shall have the last word in questions of constitutional advance; and I would note that the Muslim community does not itself appear at any stage to have produced any concrete suggestion for working a system under which they, though a minority in numbers, should be regarded as on an equality for purposes of business with the majority. The objections to turning a majority into a minority, and the risk that might result from the acceptance of the Muslim proposition are patent. But the point taken by Sir John Ewart and Sir R. Maxwell is of real importance; and I agree that we must take particular care to endeavour to avoid so handling our policy in this country as to risk the Indian Muslim question becoming a general Islamic question, of deep concern to the other Islamic countries. But I think it only proper to utter a word of caution in that connection. Great as may be the force of the argument, and great as

must be the importance which His Majesty's Government must at all times attach to Muslim opinion, Pan-Islamism has grave potential dangers from our own point of view; and I should hesitate to subscribe without much further and closer consideration to any proposition the effect of which would appear to be likely to increase the risk of encouraging Pan-Islamism, or of recognising the existence of the Pan-Islamic factor as a consideration, of decisive weight when dealing with the Indian Muslim problem. The difficulties of accepting the principle of equality between these two Communities are very present to me—much more present indeed than any solution of them: and while I hesitate as I have said to accept in its completeness the Pan-Islamic argument, I have always felt that it would be essential in any major constitutional advance that might be contemplated that His Majesty's Government should take the Muslim community with them. I would add only that if a particular type of constitutional change or a particular degree of advance could be secured only at the cost, to take perhaps an extreme example, of an armed resistance on the part of the Muslims, or a complete refusal to cooperate, it seems to me difficult to imagine that Parliament would not wish to reconsider the position; and I am convinced that in such circumstances the greatest attention must be paid to Muslim apprehensions and Muslim demands, and that even if the position of equality for which they ask cannot be conceded to them, it would be an error of the first magnitude to fail to give the greatest possible weight to their representations, feelings, and suggestions. Beyond that I do not at the moment feel disposed to go in this matter of the status of the Muslims in India.

MR. JINNAH'S QUESTIONS

27. The argument contained in the earlier part of this letter has largely covered much of the ground of the specific questions raised by Mr. Jinnah: but I now turn to consider those questions *seriatim*.

POINT (I). RECONSIDERATION OF THE ACT OF 1935

28. As regards Mr. Jinnah's first point, I would invite attention to paragraph 7 of Sir Reginald Maxwell's letter of 20th November. I agree with his argument, and I would recommend that the reply to be given should be as suggested by him, viz., that His Majesty's Government's declaration does not exclude any part of the Constitution Act from the reconsideration promised at the end of the war; and that the extent to which the whole or part of the scheme of the Act then comes under revision will be determined only by the wishes of representatives of the various interests to be taken into consultation with His Majesty's Government.

POINT (II). NO CONSTITUTIONAL DECLARATION WITHOUT MUSLIM (AND HINDU) CONCURRENCE

29. As regards Mr. Jinnah's second point, I agree with Sir Reginald Maxwell's view, as stated in paragraph 8 of his letter, that the question of ascertaining the existence or extent of agreement to any constitutional proposals is of the first importance in connection with the very difficult problem which we have under our consideration at the moment. I do not, however, propose to enter into any detailed discussion of that issue here; and I have dealt elsewhere with the question of the status of Muslims in India. So far as the answer to Mr. Jinnah is concerned I would agree with Sir R. Maxwell both that the less surface we expose the better; and that it is desirable to be as positive and as encouraging as is safely practicable. I suggest that the answer might be that His Majesty's Government fully appreciate the great importance and the scope of the issues raised by this question. They are issues which directly affect other communities, and which cannot therefore be exhaustively dealt with in the scope of the present reply. His Majesty's Government, however, while retaining their own responsibility, recognise that no constitution can be workable which is not acceptable to the two major communities of India, and the Muslims may rest assured that His Majesty's Government in any constitutional proposals which they may frame will give the opinion of the Muslims the full weight to which their importance as a community entitles them.

POINT (III). PALESTINE

30. On the Palestine issue, subject to your views, I think it would suffice to reply that His Majesty's Government have at all times been anxious to meet all reasonable national demands of the Arabs in Palestine, and that they continue to be fully alive to the importance of that issue. If you think it safe and desirable, I should he very ready, as suggested by Sir John Ewart (paragraph 10 of Sir Reginald Maxwell's letter of 20th November) to make a reference to the fact that the peaceful situation at present existing in Palestine is evidence of the extent to which the demands of the Arabs have been satisfied. But you are in a better position than I am to judge how far the facts justify us in going in that matter, and if you see advantage in such a reference I should be grateful if you would suggest a form of words which I could use.

POINT (IV). EMPLOYMENT AGAINST MUSLIMS OF INDIAN MUSLIM TROOPS

31. I entirely agree with Sir Reginald Maxwell that Mr. Jinnah cannot have thought out the implications of the demand contained in his fourth point. Which cannot possibly commit ourselves to a pledge which could be used to prevent our employing Muslim troops not only in areas remote

from India, but possibly on the North-West Frontier, and which might well expose the Muslims to the argument that the existence of such a pledge must necessarily react on the strength of Muslim representation in our Defence Forces. You will remember the pains which we have, in fact, taken in connection with the Indian troops sent to Egypt, not only to ensure that they should not be used in Palestine, but to make it perfectly clear to the political leaders who were confidentially informed of the dispatch of the force and to the Muslim public in this country that that was the case. On the whole, I suggest that the reply proposed by my Home Member, with the concurrence of the Commander-in-Chief as set out in paragraph 11 of Sir R. Maxwell's letter would best meet the case; and that I might accordingly say that the question raised is hypothetical since His Majesty's Government are at present at peace with all Muslim powers; that Mr. Jinnah will appreciate that it is impossible to give a guarantee in terms so wide as those suggested, which would have the effect of limiting India's right of using its own army in its own defence in circumstances which cannot now be foreseen; but that in the present situation every precaution has been taken by His Majesty's Government at the instance of the Government of India to avoid any risk of such a contingency arising.

POINT (V). GRIEVANCES OF MUSLIMS IN CONGRESS PROVINCES

32. On the matter of Muslim minorities in Congress Provinces to which Mr. Jinnah refers in general terms in the penultimate paragraph of his letter, I am myself disposed to agree with Sir Reginald Maxwell's advice that we should tacitly acquiesce in Mr. Jinnah's suggestion that it could be shelved so long as Congress Ministries remained out of office.

33. So much for Mr. Jinnah's specific demands. There are in conclusion two matters on which I would like to touch:

(*a*) The apprehensions entertained by Mr. Jinnah that some future government at Home might endeavour irrespective of the feeling of the Muslims to apply a constitutional policy which the Muslims regarded as wholly detrimental to their interests in face of their protests;

(*b*) The necessity for increasing attention on our part to their importance as a community.

QUESTION OF A GUARANTEE FOR THE MUSLIMS AGAINST DECISIONS PREJUDICIAL TO THEM BY FUTURE GOVERNMENTS AT HOME

34. As regards the first of these matters you will recollect that in the note of my conversation with Mr. Jinnah on 4th November I placed on record the anxiety which he told me he and certain of his friends felt lest at some time

in the future, when they are differently constituted, His Majesty's Government should themselves feel so convinced of the case for a much more extensive, or a different, type of constitutional advance in India as to give effect to such advance irrespective of the feelings of the minorities, and particularly of the Muslims. This, it goes without saying, is a matter of no little delicacy. No government can bind its successors, and it is, in my judgement, out of the question to give Mr. Jinnah or his friends the assurance in terms or the guarantee which clearly they are anxious to secure on the subject. All, as I see it, we could do is to bear in mind the existence of these apprehensions, and to endeavour as suitable occasions offer, in Parliament or elsewhere, to assure the Muslims that they need not fear that merely because they are in a numerical minority their interests are likely to be lightly regarded or prejudiced by His Majesty's Government. Neither you nor I, working as we do with a very different background from Mr. Jinnah, and with a greater familiarity with the tradition of government which has been inherited at Home, are likely to share his fears that a great minority such as that which we are discussing would be cavalierly treated, or its interests lightly disregarded, by any future government such as we can envisage. There are indeed obvious arguments which no government, whatever its political complexion, would be likely to overlook, of interest as well as of principle against action on such lines. If Mr. Jinnah should revert to this matter, I would propose therefore, if you agree, to tell him that I have given full weight to the importance of the point which he had taken with me on 4th November; that I have taken such steps to confirm my own judgement of the position in regard to it as I could; that in the outcome all I would say to him was that as he was well aware it was well settled that no government could bind its successor; but that the attitude of a community so large and so important as the Muslim community must clearly at all times be a matter of deep concern to those on whom there falls the responsibility for handling the affairs of India, and in particular for framing its future constitution; and that I could not myself envisage any circumstances in which that great community need anticipate that full weight would not be given to its views or that the fullest attention would not be given to representations from it in connection with any constitutional changes likely in its own judgement prejudicially to affect it. If you think that I could safely go any further, I shall, I need not say, welcome any suggestion that you can let me have.

NECESSITY FOR INCREASING ATTENTION ON OUR PART TO THE MUSLIM PROBLEM

35. I turn now to the second point referred to in paragraph 33 above. I feel myself that there is force in the suggestion made by Mr. Jinnah in his conversation with me on 4th November that there is perhaps a certain

tendency in the freedom of parliamentary debate to think in terms merely of numerical majorities and minorities; and that, if the suggestion is at all well founded, does injustice to the special position of the Muslim minority and the difference existing between it and other minorities in Empire countries. If I develop this point further, it is only because it is in my judgement of great importance in considering future constitutional development, and in particular the position of the minorities, to give full weight to the fact that the Muslim minority is no ordinary minority, but one of 90 million people, occupying in relation to India as a whole strategic positions of great importance, separated by profound differences, religious, historical, and, cultural, from the majority community, and strongly represented in the Defence Forces. The argument of the solidarity of Islam on which I have touched in paragraph 26 above is one which, for the reasons given in that paragraph, I would desire to approach with care. But it is one of substantial importance, and one which in our confidential correspondence and in our deliberations on policy must clearly be given its full weight. I am certain that matters have now reached a point at which it will be necessary to pay increasing attention to the Muslims and to their importance as a community; and that it is desirable that we should in Parliament and elsewhere endeavour to bring out our sense of their significance, and our anxiety to give the weight properly attaching to their views. Of the sensitiveness of this community, all the greater because it lacks an effective press, and in particular of the sensitiveness of individual leaders such as Mr. Jinnah, you are well aware. And here as elsewhere in the Indian political field, even if we regard that sensitiveness as unjustified or exaggerated, it constitutes a political point which you will, I am sure, agree with me in thinking well worth watching.

36. The specific questions put to me by Mr. Jinnah do not I am conscious bulk very large in this letter. But I have thought it desirable to take the opportunity to present them to you with the background, as I see it, against which they fall appropriately to be considered even at the cost of a material expansion of the scope of my reference to you. We are both agreed as to the desirability of the earliest possible reply to Mr. Jinnah's questions; and I would suggest therefore that once you have received this letter and have been able to consider it, we might settle by telegram the terms of the reply to be given to him in the light of the suggestions which I have made above.

Yours sincerely,
LINLITHGOW

To
The Most Honourable the Marquess of Zetland,

P.C., G.C.S.I., G.C.I.E.,
His Majesty's Secretary of State for India.

APPENDIX III

Jinnah's Presidential Address to the All-India Muslim League Session, Lahore, 22 March 1940

WE ARE MEETING TODAY in our session after fifteen months. The last session of the All-India Muslim League took place at Patna in December 1938. Since then many developments have taken place. I shall first tell you briefly what the All-India Muslim League has had to face since the Patna session of 1938. You remember that one of the tasks, which was imposed on us and which is far from completed yet, was to organise Muslim Leagues all over India. We have made enormous progress during the last fifteen months in this direction. I am glad to inform you that we have established provincial Leagues in every province. The next point is that in every by-election to the Legislative Assemblies we had to fight powerful opponents. I congratulate the Muslims for having shown enormous grit and spirit throughout their trials. There was not a single by-election in which our opponents won against Muslim League candidates. In the last election to the U.P. Council, that is the Upper Chamber, the Muslim League's success was cent per cent. I do not want to weary you with details of what we have been able to do in the way of forging ahead in the direction of organising the Muslim League. But I may tell you that it is going up by leaps and bounds.

Next, you might remember that we appointed a central committee of ladies at the Patna session. It is of very great importance to us, because I believe that it is absolutely essential for us to give every opportunity to our women to participate in this, our struggle of life and death. Women can do a great deal within their homes, even in *purdah*. We appointed this committee with a view to enabling them to participate in the work of the League. The objects of this committee were: (1) to organise provincial and district Muslim Leagues; (2) to enlist a larger number of women to the membership of the Muslim League; (3) to carry on intensive propaganda amongst Muslim women throughout India in order to create in them a sense of greater political consciousness—because if political consciousness is awakened

*Jamil-ud-din Ahmad, *Some Recent Speeches and Writings of Mr. Jinnah*, vol. I, pp. 159–81.

amongst our women, remember, our children will not have much to worry about; (4) to advise and guide them in all such matters as mainly rest on them for the uplift of Muslim society. This central committee, I am glad to say, started seriously and earnestly. It has done a great deal of useful work. I have no doubt that when we come to deal with its report of work done we shall really feel grateful to it for all the services that it has rendered to the Muslim League.

From January 1939, right up to the declaration of the war, we had to face many difficulties. We had to face the Vidya Mandir in Nagpur. We had to face the Wardha Scheme all over India. We had to face ill-treatment and oppression of Muslims in the Congress-governed provinces, and some of the Indian States such as Jaipur and Bhavnagar. We had to face a vital issue that arose in the small State of Rajkot. Rajkot was made the acid test of its strength by the Congress and this would have affected one-third of India. Thus the Muslim League had all along to face various issues from January 1939 up to the time of the declaration of the war. Before the war was declared, the greatest danger to the Muslims of India was the possible inauguration of the federal scheme for the Central Government. We knew what machinations were going on. But the Muslim League was stoutly resisting them in every direction. We felt that we could never accept the dangerous scheme for a Federal Central Government embodied in the Government of India Act, 1935. I am sure that we have made no small contribution towards persuading the British Government to abandon that scheme of Federal Government. You know that the British are a very obdurate people. They are also very conservative; and although they are very clever, they are slow in understanding. After the war was declared, the Viceroy naturally wanted help from the Muslim League. It was only then that he realised that the Muslim League was a power, for it will be remembered that up to the time of the declaration of the war, the Viceroy never thought of me but of Gandhi and Gandhi alone. I have been the leader of an important party in the Central Legislature for a considerable time, larger than the one I have the honour to lead at present, the Muslim League Party. Yet the Viceroy never thought of me before. Therefore, when I got this invitation from the Viceroy, along with Mr. Gandhi, I wondered within myself why I had so suddenly been promoted. Then I concluded that the answer was the 'All-India Muslim League' whose President I happen to be. I believe that was the worst shock that the Congress High Command has ever received, because it challenged their sole authority to speak on behalf of India. And it is quite clear from the attitude of Mr. Gandhi and his High Command that they have not yet recovered from that shock. My point is that I want you to realise the value, the importance, and the significance of organising yourselves. I will not say anything more on the subject.

A great deal yet remains to be done. I am sure from what I can see and hear that Muslim India is now conscious and awake, and the Muslim League has grown into such a strong institution that it cannot be destroyed by anybody, whoever he might be. Men may come and men may go, but the League will live for ever.

Now, coming to the period after the declaration of the war, our position was that we were between the devil and the deep sea. But I do not think that the devil or the deep sea is going to get away with it. We stand unequivocally for the freedom of India. But it must be freedom for all India and not freedom for one section or, worse still, for the Congress caucus and slavery for the Muslims and other minorities.

Situated as we are in India, we naturally have learnt from our past experience. Particularly from the experiences of the last two and a half years in the Congress-governed provinces, we have learnt many lessons. We are, therefore, now, very apprehensive and can trust nobody. I think it is a wise rule for everyone not to trust anybody too much. Sometimes we are led to trust people but when we find in actual experience that our trust has been betrayed, surely that ought to be sufficient lesson for any man not to continue to trust those who have betrayed him. Ladies and gentlemen, we never thought that the Congress High Command would act in the manner in which they actually did in the Congress-governed provinces. I never dreamt that they would ever come down so low as that. I never could believe that there would be a "gentlemen's agreement" between the Congress and the Britishers. Although we cried hoarse, week in and week out, the British Governors were supine and the Governor-General was helpless. We reminded them of their special responsibilities to us and to the other minorities and the solemn pledges they had given to us. But all that was a dead letter. Fortunately, Providence came to our help and that "gentlemen's agreement" was broken and the Congress, thank Heavens, went out of office. I think they are regretting their resignations very much. The bluff has been called. So far so good. I appeal to you, with all the earnestness that I can command, to organise yourselves in such a way that you should depend upon none, only on your own inherent Strength. That is your best safeguard, your only safeguard. Depend upon yourselves. That does not mean that you should have ill-will or malice towards others. In order to safeguard your rights and interests you must create strength in yourselves so that you may be able to defend yourselves. That is all that I wish to urge.

Now, what is our position with regard to the future constitution? It is that as soon as circumstances permit, or immediately after the war at the latest, the whole problem of India's constitution must be examined *de novo* and the Act of 1935 must go once and for all. We do not believe in asking the British Government to make declarations. These declarations are really of no use. You cannot possibly succeed in getting the British Government out of this land by asking them to make declarations. However, the Congress asked the Viceroy to make a declaration. The Viceroy said, "I have made the declaration." The Congress said, "No, no; we want another kind of declaration. You must declare and at once that India is free and independent with the right to frame its own constitution through a Constituent Assembly to be elected on the basis of adult franchise or as low a franchise as possible. This Assembly will, of course, satisfy the minorities' legitimate interests." Mr. Gandhi says that if the minorities are not satisfied, then he would be willing that some tribunal of the highest and most impartial character should decide the dispute. Now, apart from the impracticable nature of this proposal—being historically and constitutionally absurd to ask the ruling power to abdicate in favour of a Constituent Assembly—apart from all that, suppose we do not agree to the franchise according to which the Assembly is to be elected, or suppose we, the solid body of Muslim representatives, do not agree with the non-Muslim majority in the Assembly, what will happen? It is said that we have no right to disagree with anything that this Assembly may do in framing a national constitution for this huge subcontinent, except in those matters which may be germane to safeguards for the minorities. So we are given the privilege to disagree only with regard to, what may strictly be called, safeguards of the rights and interests of minorities. We are also given the privilege to choose our own representatives by separate electorates. Now this proposal is based on the assumption that as soon as this constitution comes into operation the British hand will disappear. Otherwise there will be no meaning in it. Of course, Mr. Gandhi says that the constitution will decide whether the British will disappear and, if so, to what extent. In other words, his proposal comes to this: first, give me the declaration that we are a free and independent nation, then I will decide what I should give you back! Does Mr. Gandhi really want complete independence for India when he talks like this? But whether the British disappear or not, it follows that extensive powers must be transferred to the people. In the event of there being a disagreement in the Constituent Assembly between the majority and the Muslims, in the first instance, who will appoint the tribunal? And suppose an agreed tribunal is possible and it gives a decision, who will, may I ask, be there to see that it is implemented and carried out in accordance with the terms of the award ? And who will see that it is honoured in practice, for, we are told, the British will have parted with their power, completely or mainly? What then will be the sanction for the enforcement of the award? We come back to the same answer: the Hindu majority will do it—and will it be with the help of British bayonets or Mr. Gandhi's *Ahimsa*? Can we trust either any more? Besides, ladies and gentlemen, can you imagine that a question of this character involving a contract, upon which the future constitution of India would be based and affecting 90 million Muslims, can be decided by means of a judicial tribunal? Still that is the proposal of the Congress.

Before I deal with what Mr. Gandhi said a few days ago, I shall refer to the pronouncements of some of the other Congress leaders, each one speaking with a different voice. Mr. Rajagopalachariar, the ex-Prime Minister of Madras, says that the only panacea for Hindu–Muslim unity is joint electorates. This is his prescription as one of the great doctors of the Congress organisation! Babu Rajendra Prasad, on the other hand, only a few days ago said, "Oh, what more do the Muslims want?" I will read out to you his words. Referring to the minority question he says: "If Britain would concede our right of self-determination, surely all these differences would disappear." How will our differences disappear? He does not enlighten us about it. But he continues: "But so long as Britain remained and held power, the differences would continue to exist. The Congress has made it clear that the future constitution will be framed not by the Congress alone but by the representatives of all political parties and religious groups. The Congress has gone further and declared that the minorities can have their representatives elected for this purpose by separate electorates, though the Congress regards separate electorates as an evil. It will be representatives of all the peoples of this country, irrespective of their religions and political affiliations, who will be deciding the future constitution of India and not this or that party. What better guarantee can the minorities have?" So, according to Babu Rajendra Prasad, the moment we enter the Assembly, we shall shed all our political affiliations, and religions and everything else. This is what Babu Rajendra Prasad said as late as 18th March, 1940.

This is what Mr. Gandhi said on 20th March, 1940: "To me Hindus, Muslims, Parsis, *Harijans* are all alike, I cannot be frivolous"—but I think he is frivolous—"I cannot be frivolous when I talk of Quaid-i-Azam Jinnah. He is my brother." The Only difference is this, that brother Gandhi has three votes and I have only one vote! "I would be happy indeed if he could keep me in his pocket." I do not know really what to say to this latest offer of his. "There was a time when I could say that there was no Muslim whose confidence I did not enjoy. It is my misfortune that it is not so today." Why has he lost the confidence of the Muslims today, may I ask, ladies and gentlemen?

"I do not read all that appears in the Urdu press, but perhaps I get a lot of abuse there. I am not sorry for it. I still believe that without a Hindu–Muslim settlement there can be no *Swaraj*." Mr. Gandhi has been saying this now for the last 20 years. "You will perhaps ask in that case why do I talk of a fight? I do so because it is to be a fight for a Constituent Assembly."

He is fighting the British. But may I point out to Mr. Gandhi and the Congress that they are fighting for a Constituent Assembly which the Muslims cannot accept, in which the Muslims will be one against three. In that way, by the counting of heads, the Muslims say that they will never be able to come to an agreement with the Hindus, which will be a real agreement from the heart, which will enable them to work as friends. Therefore, this idea of a Constituent Assembly is objectionable. Mr. Gandhi says that he is fighting for a Constituent Assembly, and not fighting the Muslims at all. He says, "I do so because it is to be a fight for a Constituent Assembly. If Muslims who come to the Constituent Assembly"—mark the words, "who come to the Constituent Assembly through Muslim votes"—he is first forcing us to come to that Assembly—and then says, "declare that there is nothing common between Hindus and Muslims then alone would I give up all hope, but even then I would agree with them because they read the *Koran* and I have also studied something of that Holy Book."

So he wants the Constituent Assembly for the purpose of ascertaining the views of the Muslims and if they do not agree with him then he will give up all hope, but even then he will agree with us! Well, I ask you, ladies and gentlemen, is this the way to show real, genuine desire, if there exists any, to come to a settlement with the Muslims? Why does not Mr. Gandhi, as I have suggested to him more than once, and I repeat it again from this platform, why does not Mr. Gandhi honestly acknowledge now that the Congress is a Hindu Congress, that he does not represent anybody except the solid body of Hindu people? Why should not Mr. Gandhi be proud to say, "I am a Hindu, the Congress has solid Hindu backing." I am not ashamed of saying that I am a Muslim. I am right and I hope and believe, even a blind man must have been convinced by now, that the Muslim League has the solid backing of the Muslims of India. Why then all this camouflage? Why all these machinations? Why all these methods to coerce the British to overthrow the Muslims? Why this declaration of non-cooperation? Why this threat of civil disobedience? And why fight for a Constituent Assembly for the sake of ascertaining whether the Muslims agree or do not? Why not come as a Hindu leader, proudly representing your people, and let me meet you proudly representing the Muslims? This is all that I have to say so far as the Congress is concerned.

So far as the British Government is concerned, our negotiations with it are, as you know, not yet concluded. We had asked for assurances on several points. We have made some advance, at any rate, with regard to one point, which is this. You remember our demand was that the entire problem of the future constitution of India should be examined *de novo,* and apart from the Government of India Act of 1935. To that the Viceroy's reply, with the authority of His Majesty's Government, was sent to us on 23rd December. I had better quote it and not put it in my own words:

"My answer to your first question is that the declaration 1 made with the approval of His Majesty's Government on October the 13th last does not exclude"—mark the words "does not exclude"—"examination of any part either of Act of 1935 or of the policy and plans on which it is based."

As regards other matters, we are still negotiating. The most important points are that no declaration should be made by His Majesty's Government with regard to the future constitution of India without our approval and consent, and that no settlement of any question should be made with any party behind our back. Well, ladies and gentlemen, whether the British Government in their wisdom agree to give us that assurance or not, I trust that they will still see that it is a fair and just demand. We say that we cannot leave the future fate of 90 millions of people in the hands of anybody else. We, and we alone, must be the final arbiters of our destiny. Surely that is a just claim. We do not want that the British Government should thrust upon the Muslims a constitution which they do not approve of and to which they do not agree. Therefore the British Government will be well advised to give that assurance and give the Muslims complete peace and confidence in this matter and win their friendship. But whether they do that or not, after all, as I have told you before, we must depend upon our own inherent strength. I make it plain from this platform that if any declaration is made, if any interim settlement is arrived at, without our approval and without our consent, the Muslims of India will resist it. And no mistake should be made on that score.

The next point is with regard to Palestine. We are told that "endeavours, earnest endeavours, are being made to meet the reasonable national demands of the Arabs". Well, we cannot be satisfied by earnest endeavours, sincere endeavours, best endeavours. We want that the British Government should in fact and actually meet the demands of the Arabs in Palestine.

Another point is with regard to the sending of the troops abroad. Here there is some misunderstanding. But anyhow we have made clear our position that we did not demand that Indian troops should not be used to the fullest for the defence of our country. Hence if there are any misapprehensions on this score they are not justified. We simply wanted the British Government to give us assurance that Indian troops would not be sent against any Muslim country or any Muslim Power. Let us hope that we may yet be able to get the British Government to clarify the situation further.

This, then, is the position with regard to the British Government. The last meeting of the Working Committee had asked the Viceroy to reconsider his letter of 23rd December, having regard to what had been explained to him in pursuance of the resolution of the Working Committee passed on 3rd February. We are informed that the matter is receiving his careful consideration.

Ladies and gentlemen, that is where we have stood since the outbreak of the war and up to 3rd February. As far as our internal position is concerned, we have been examining it. As you know, there are several schemes which have been proposed by various well-informed constitutionalists and others who take interest in the problem of India's future constitution. We have also appointed a sub-committee to examine the details of the schemes that have come in so far. But one thing is quite clear. It has always been taken for granted mistakenly that the Muslims are a minority and, of course, we ourselves have got used to it for such a long time. Settled notions such as this one sometimes are very difficult to remove. The Muslims are not a minority. The Muslims are a nation by any definition. The British and, particularly, the Congress proceed on the basis, "Well, you are a minority after all, what do you want?" "What else do the minorities want?", as Babu Rajendra Prasad said. But surely the Muslims are not a minority. We find that even according to the British map of India, we occupy large parts of this country, where the Muslims are in a majority, such as Bengal, Punjab, NWFP, Sind and Baluchistan.

Now the question is, what is the best solution of this problem between the Hindus and the Muslims? We have been considering, and as I have already said, a committee has been appointed to consider the various proposals. But whatever the final scheme of constitution, I will present to you my views and in confirmation of what I am going to put before you, I will just read to you a letter from Lala Lajpat Rai to Mr. C.R. Das. It was written, I believe, about fourteen or fifteen years ago and that letter has been reproduced in a recently published book by one Indra Prakash, and that is how this letter has come to light. Lala Lajpat Rai was a very astute politician and a staunch Hindu Mahasabhite. But before I read this letter let me say that it is plain from it that you cannot get away from being a Hindu if you are a Hindu! The word 'nationalist' has now become the plaything of conjurers in politics. This is what he says:

"There is one point more which has been troubling me very much of late and one which I want you to think about carefully and that is the question of Hindu–Mohammedan unity. I have devoted most of my time during the last six months to the study of Muslim history and Muslim law and I am inclined to think it is neither *possible nor practicable.* Assuming and admitting the sincerity of Mohammedan leaders in the non-cooperation movement, I think their religion provides an effective bar to anything of the kind.

'You remember the conversation I reported to you in Calcutta which I had with Hakim Ajmal Khan and Dr. Kitchlew. There is no finer Mohammedan in Hindustan than Hakim Ajmal Khan, but can any Muslim leader override the *Koran*? I can only hope that my reading of the Islamic law is incorrect.' I think his reading is quite correct. 'And nothing would relieve me more than to be convinced that it is so. But if it is right then it comes to this that although we can unite against the British we cannot do so to rule Hindustan on British lines. We cannot do so to rule Hindustan *on democratic lines.*' "

Ladies and gentlemen, when Lala Lajpat Rai said that we cannot rule this country on democratic lines it was all right but when I had the temerity to speak the same truth about eighteen months ago there was a shower of attacks and criticism. But Lala Lajpat Rai said fifteen years ago that we cannot do so, viz., to rule Hindustan on democratic lines. What is the remedy? The remedy according to the Congress is to keep us in the minority and under their majority rule. Lala Lajpat Rai proceeds further:

"What is then the remedy? I am not afraid of the seven crores of Muslims. But I think the seven crores in Hindustan plus the armed hosts of Afghanistan, Central Asia, Arabia, Mesopotamia and Turkey, will be irresistible.

I do honestly and sincerely believe in the necessity or desirability of Hindu–Muslim unity. I am also fully prepared to trust the Muslim leaders. But what about the injunctions of the *Koran* and *Hadis*? The leaders cannot override them. Are we then doomed? I hope your learned mind and wise head will find some way out of this difficulty."

Now, ladies and gentlemen, that is merely a letter written by one great Hindu leader to another great Hindu leader fifteen years ago. Now, I should like to put before you my views on the subject taking everything into consideration as it strikes me at the present moment. The British Government and Parliament, and indeed the British nation, have for many decades past been brought up and nurtured on settled notions about India's future. These notions are based on developments in their own country, which have resulted in the British constitution, functioning through the Houses of Parliament and the cabinet system. Their concept of government by parties, functioning on the political plane, has become the ideal with them. They regard it as the best form of government for every country. The powerful one-sided propaganda of the Congress party, which naturally appeals to the British, has led them into a serious blunder—that of producing the constitution envisaged in the Government of India Act of 1935. We find that most leading statesmen of Great Britain, saturated with these notions, have in their pronouncements, seriously asserted and expressed the hope that the passage of time will harmonise inconsistent elements in India.

A leading journal like the *London Times*, commenting on the Government of India Act of 1935, wrote, "Undoubtedly the differences between the Hindus and Muslims are not of religion in the strict sense of the word but also of law and culture, that they may be said, indeed, to represent two entirely distinct and separate civilizations. However, in the course of time, the superstition will die out and India will be moulded into a single nation." So, according to the *London Times*, the only difficulties are the superstitions. These fundamental and deep-rooted differences in the spiritual, economic, social and political spheres have been euphemised as mere 'superstitions'. But surely it is a flagrant disregard of the past history of the subcontinent of India, as well as of the fundamental Islamic conception of society *vis-a-vis* that of Hinduism, to characterise these differences as mere 'superstitions'.

Notwithstanding a thousand years of close contact, nationalities, which are as divergent today as ever, cannot at any time be expected to be transformed into one nation merely by the method of subjecting them to a democratic constitution and holding them forcibly together by the unnatural and artificial means of a British Parliamentary statute. What the unitary government of India had failed to achieve in 150 years cannot be realised by the imposition of a central federal government. It is inconceivable that the fiat or the writ of a government so constituted can ever command willing and loyal obedience throughout the subcontinent by various nationalities, except by means of the armed force behind it.

The problem in India is not that of an inter-communal character but manifestly of an international one, and it must be treated as such. So long as this basic and fundamental truth is not realised, any constitution that may be built will result in disaster and will prove destructive and harmful not only to the Muslims but also to the British and Hindus. If the British Government are really in earnest and sincere to secure peace and happiness for the people of this subcontinent, the only course open to them is to allow the major nations to have separate homelands by dividing India into autonomous national states. There is no reason why these states should be antagonistic to each other. On the contrary, the rivalry between them and the desire and effort on the part of one to dominate the social order and establish political supremacy over the other in the government of the country will disappear. It will lead more towards natural goodwill and, by international pacts between them, they can live in complete harmony as neighbours. This will lead further to a friendly settlement, all the more easily, with regard to minorities by reciprocal arrangements and adjustments between Muslim India and Hindu India, which will far more adequately and effectively safeguard the rights and interests of Muslims and various other minorities.

It is extremely difficult to appreciate why our Hindu friends fail to understand the real nature of Islam and Hinduism. They are not religions in the strict sense of the word, but are, in fact, different and distinct social orders. It is a dream that the Hindus and Muslims can ever evolve a common nationality. This notion of one Indian nation has gone far beyond the limits and is the cause of most of our troubles and will lead India to destruction if we fail to revise this misconception in time. The Hindus and Muslims have different religious philosophies, social customs and literatures. They neither intermarry nor interdine and, indeed, they belong to two different civilisations which are based mainly on conflicting ideas and conceptions. Their views on life and of life are different. It is also quite clear that Hindus and Muslims derive their inspiration from different sources of history. They have different epics, different heroes in different episodes. Very often the hero of one is a foe of the other and, likewise, their victories and defeats overlap. To yoke together two such nations under a single state, one a numerical minority and the other a majority, must lead to growing discontent and the final destruction of any fabric that may be so built-up for the government of such a state.

History has presented to us many similar examples, such as the union of Great Britain and Ireland, of Czechoslovakia and Poland with Austria. History has also shown that many geographical tracts, much smaller than the subcontinent of India, which might otherwise have been called one country, have been divided into as many states as there are nations inhabiting them. The Balkan Peninsula comprises as many as seven or eight sovereign states. Likewise, the Portuguese and the Spanish stand divided in the Iberian Peninsula. Whereas under the plea of the unity of India and one nation, which does not exist, it is sought to pursue the line of one central government. We know that the history of the last twelve hundred years has failed to achieve unity, and have witnessed, during the ages, India always divided into Hindu India and Muslim India. The present artificial unity of India dates back only to the British conquest and is maintained by British bayonets. The termination of the British regime, which is implicit in the recent declaration of His Majesty's Government, will be the herald of an entire break-up, and a worse disaster for the Muslims than has ever taken place during the last one thousand years. Surely that is not the legacy which Britain would bequeath to India after 150 years of her rule, nor would Hindu and Muslim India risk such a sure catastrophe.

Muslim India cannot accept any constitution which must necessarily result in a Hindu majority government. If Hindus and Muslims are brought together under a democratic system, forced upon the minorities, it can only mean Hindu raj. Democracy of the kind with which the Congress High Command is enamoured would mean the complete destruction of what is most precious in Islam. We have had ample experience of the working of the provincial constitutions during the last two and a half years. Any repetition of such government must lead to civil war and the raising of private armies, as was recommended by Mr. Gandhi to the Hindus of Sukkur. He told them that they must defend themselves non-violently or violently, giving blow for blow, and if they could not, they must emigrate.

Muslims are not a minority as it is commonly known and understood. One has only to look around. Even today, according to the British map of India, in four out of eleven provinces, the Muslims predominate more or less. Here governments are functioning notwithstanding the decision of the Hindu Congress High Command to non-cooperate and prepare for civil disobedience. Muslims are a nation according to any definition of a nation, and they must have their homelands, their territory and their state. We wish to live in peace and harmony with our neighbours as a free and independent people. We wish to develop to the fullest our spiritual, cultural, economic, social and political life in a way that we think best and in consonance with our own ideal and according to the genius of our people. Honesty demands and the vital interest of millions of our people impose a sacred duty upon us to find an honourable and peaceful solution, which would be just and fair to all. But at the same time, we cannot be moved or diverted from our purpose and objective by threats or intimidation. We must be prepared to face all difficulties and make all the sacrifices that may be required of us to achieve the goal we have set in front of us.

Ladies and gentlemen, that is the task before us. I fear I have gone beyond my time limit. Still there are many other things that I should like to tell you, but I have already published a little pamphlet containing most of what I have to say. You could easily get that publication both in English and in Urdu from the League office. It might give you a clearer idea of our aims. It contains some very important resolutions of the Muslim League and various other statements. Anyhow, I have placed before you the task that lies ahead of us. Do you realise how big and stupendous it is? Do you realise that you cannot get freedom or independence by mere arguments? I want to appeal to the intelligentsia. The intelligentsia in all countries of the world has been the pioneer of movements for freedom. What does the Muslim intelligentsia propose to do? I tell you that unless you get this into your blood, unless you are prepared to take off your coats and are willing to make sacrifices and work selflessly, earnestly and sincerely for your people, you will never realise your aim. Friends, I therefore want you to make up your mind definitely and then think of devices to strengthen your organisation and consolidate the Muslims all over India. I think that the masses are wide-awake. They only want your guidance and your lead. Come forward as servants of Islam, organise the people economically, socially, educationally and politically and I am sure that you will be a power that will be recognized by everybody.

APPENDIX IV

Resolution of the All-India Muslim League Council on the Cabinet Mission Plan, 6 June 1946

THIS MEETING OF THE Council of the All-India Muslim League, after having carefully considered the statement issued by the Cabinet Mission and the Viceroy on 16th May and other relevant statements and documents officially issued in connection therewith, and after having examined the proposals set forth in the said statement in all their bearings and implication, places on record the following views for the guidance of the nation and direction to the Working Committee:

That the references made and the conclusions recorded in paragraphs 6, 7, 8, 9, 10 and 11 of the statement concerning the Muslim demand for the establishment of a full sovereign Pakistan as the only solution of the Indian constitutional problem are unwarranted, unjustified and unconvincing and should not, therefore, have found place in a State document issued on behalf and with the authority of the British Government.

These paragraphs are couched in such language and contain such mutilation of established facts, that the Cabinet Mission have clearly been prompted to include them in their statement solely with the object of appeasing the Hindus in utter disregard of Muslim sentiments. Furthermore, the contents of the aforesaid paragraphs are in conflict and inconsistent with the admissions made by the members of the Mission themselves in paragraphs 5 and 12 of their statement, which are to the following effect:

First, the Mission "were greatly impressed by the very genuine and acute anxiety of the Muslims, lest they should find themselves subject to a perpetual Hindu majority rule;"

Secondly, "this feeling has become so strong and widespread amongst the Muslims that it cannot be allayed by mere paper safeguards;"

Thirdly, "If there is to be internal peace in India, it must be secured by measures, which will assure to the Muslims control in all matters vital to their culture religion economic or other interests;" and

Fourthly, very real Muslim apprehensions exist that "their culture and political and social life might become submerged in a purely unitary India in which Hindus, with their greatly superior numbers, must be a dominating element."

In order that there may be no manner of doubt in any quarter, the Council of the All-India Muslim League reiterates that the attainment of the goal of complete sovereign Pakistan still remains the unalterable objective of the Muslims of India, for the achievement of which they will, if necessary, employ every means in their power and consider no sacrifice or suffering too great.

That notwithstanding the affront offered to Muslim sentiments by a choice of injudicious words in the preamble of the statement of the Cabinet Mission, the Muslim League, having regard to the grave issues involved, and prompted by its earnest desire for a peaceful solution, if possible, of the Indian constitutional problem, and inasmuch as the basis and the foundation of Pakistan are inherent in the Mission's plan by virtue of the compulsory grouping of the six Muslim provinces in sections B and C, is willing to co-operate with the constitution-making machinery proposed in the scheme outlined by the Mission, in the hope that it would ultimately result in the establishment of a complete sovereign Pakistan and in the consummation of the goal of independence for the major nations, and all the other peoples inhabiting this vast subcontinent.

It is for these reasons that the Muslim League is accepting the scheme and will join the constitution-making body and will keep in view the opportunity and the right of secession of provinces or groups from the Union, which have been provided in the Mission's plan by implication.

The ultimate attitude of the Muslim League will depend on the final outcome of the labours of the constitution-making body and on the final shape of the constitutions which may emerge from the deliberations of that body jointly and separately in its three sections.

The Muslim League also reserves the right to modify and revise the policy and attitude set forth in this resolution at any time during the progress of deliberations of the constitution-making body or the Constituent Assembly or, thereafter, if the course of events so require, bearing in mind the fundamental principles and ideals hereinbefore adumbrated to which the Muslim League is irrevocably committed.

That with regard to the arrangements for the proposed Interim Government at the Centre, this Council authorises its President to negotiate with the Viceroy and to take such decisions and actions as he deems fit and proper.

APPENDIX V

Jinnah to Attlee, 6 July 1946

DEAR MR. ATTLEE,

It is not without deep regret that I have to say that the Cabinet Delegation and the Viceroy have, by handling the negotiations in the manner in which they did, impaired the honour of the British Government and have shaken the confidence of Muslim India and shattered their hopes for an honourable and peaceful settlement. They allowed themselves to play in the hands of the Congress, who all along held out the threat of non-cooperation and civil disobedience, if they were not satisfied; and virtually, from the very beginning, adopted an aggressive and dictatorial attitude, pistol in their hand. They are determined to seize power and try to establish Caste-Hindu domination over Muslim India and the other communities inhabiting this vast subcontinent. I hope when you go through all the relevant correspondence and hear the Mission, you will come to the same conclusion as I have indicated above. I think you will agree with me that it is not only an obsession but has become a disease with the Congress, and it is an impossibility. Even now, having wrecked the formation of the Interim Government as proposed by the Cabinet Delegation and the Viceroy in their final Statement of 16th June, they have accepted the long-term plan, not in the spirit of cooperation and to construct but to wreck it. This will be clear to you from the reservations and interpretations that they have put upon the long-term plan and which are contrary to those embodied in the Statement of the Cabinet Delegation and the Viceroy dated 16th May and their further Statement of May 25th (particularly grouping of provinces).

I therefore trust that the British Government will still avoid compelling the Muslims to shed their blood, for, your surrender to the Congress at the sacrifice of the Muslims can only result in that direction. If power politics are going to be the deciding factor, in total disregard for fair play and justice, we shall have no other course open to us except to forge our sanctions to meet the situation which, in that case, is bound to arise. Its consequences, I need not say, will be most disastrous and a peaceful settlement will then become impossible.

* *Transfer of Power*, vol. 8, pp. 106–7.

I am writing this letter to you in confidence and to one whom I have known for a long time. Today you happen to be at the helm of the British nation as the Prime Minister and, I hope, you will give your most earnest and careful consideration to what I have urged not without painfulness, which is apparent from my letter and that you will maintain the honour of the British nation for fairplay.

I am enclosing herewith for your information and consideration my two Statements that I have issued, in case you may not have come across them; and also two editorials from the only British paper now left in India.

I am sending a similar letter to Mr. Churchill, the Leader of the Opposition.

This letter is strictly private, personal and confidential.

Hoping you are well and with kind regards,

Yours sincerely,
M.A. JINNAH.

APPENDIX VI

Text of the Two Resolutions Passed by the All-India Muslim League Council, Bombay, 29 July 1946

RESOLUTION NO. 1

ON THE 6TH OF June 1946, the Council of the All-India Muslim League accepted the Scheme embodied in the Statement of the Cabinet Delegation and the Viceroy, dated 16th May 1946, and explained by them in their statement, dated 25th May 1946. The Scheme of the Cabinet Delegation fell far short of the demand of the Muslim nation for the immediate establishment of an Independent and fully Sovereign State of Pakistan comprising the six Muslim Provinces, but the Council accepted a Union Centre for ten years strictly confined to three subjects, viz., Defence, Foreign Affairs and Communications, as the Scheme laid down certain fundamentals and safeguards and provided for the grouping separately of the six Muslim Provinces in Sections B and C for the purpose of framing their provincial and group constitutions unfettered by the Union in any way; and also with a view to end the Hindu–Muslim deadlock peacefully and accelerate the attainment of freedom of the peoples of India. In arriving at this decision, the Council was also greatly influenced by the statement of the President which he made with the authority of the Viceroy that the Interim Government, which was an integral part of the Mission's Scheme, was going to be formed on the basis of a formula, viz., 5 Muslim League, 5 Congress, 1 Sikh and 1 Indian Christian or Anglo–Indian stipulating that the most important portfolios would be distributed equally between the two major parties, the Muslim League and the Congress. The Council authorised the President to take such decision and action with regard to further details of setting up the Interim Government as he deemed fit and proper. In that very Resolution the Council also reserved the right to modify and revise this policy, if the course of events so required.

The British Government committed a breach of faith with the Muslim

**Transfer of Power*, vol. 8, pp. 135–9.

League in that the Cabinet Delegation and the Viceroy went back on the original formula of 5 : 5 : 2 for setting up of the Interim Government to placate the Congress.

Having gone back on the original formula upon the faith of which the Muslim League Council had come to their decision on the 6th of June, the Viceroy suggested a new basis of 5 : 5 : 3 and after carrying on considerable negotiations with the Congress and having failed to get the Congress to agree to it, intimated to the Parties on the 15th of June that he and the Cabinet Delegation would issue their final statement with regard to the setting up of the Interim Government.

Accordingly on the 16th of June the President of the Muslim League received a Statement embodying what was announced to be the final decision for setting up the Interim Government by the Viceroy making it clear that if either of the two major parties refused to accept the Statement of June 16th, the Viceroy would proceed to form the Interim Government with the major party accepting it and such other representatives as were willing to join. This was explicitly laid down in paragraph 8 of the Statement of June 16th.

Even this final decision of the Cabinet Mission of the 16th of June with regard to the formation of the Interim Government was rejected by the Congress, whereas the Muslim League definitely accepted it. Though this proposal was different from the original formula of 5 : 5 : 2, the Muslim League accepted it because the Viceroy had provided safeguards and given other satisfactory assurances which were contained in his letter, dated the 20th of June 1946, addressed to the President of the Muslim League.

The Viceroy, however, scrapped the proposal of the 16th of June and postponed the formation of the Interim Government on the plea concocted by the "legalistic talents" of the Cabinet Mission putting a most fantastic and dishonest construction upon paragraph 8 of the Statement to the effect that as both the major parties, i.e. the Muslim League and the Congress had accepted the statement of May 16th, the question of the Interim Government could only be taken up in consultation with the representatives of both the parties *de novo*.

Even assuming that this construction was tenable, for which there is no warrant, the Congress by their conditional acceptance with reservations and interpretations of their own, as laid down in the letter of the President of the Congress, dated the 25th of June, and the Resolution of the Working Committee of the Congress passed at Delhi on the 26th of June, repudiating the very fundamentals of the Scheme had, in fact, rejected the Statement of the 16th of May and there was therefore no justification, whatsoever, for abandoning the final proposals of the 16th of June.

As regards the proposal embodied in the Statement of the 16th and 25th of May of the Cabinet Delegation and the Viceroy, the Muslim League alone of the two major parties has accepted it.

The Congress have not accepted it because their acceptance is conditional and subject to their own interpretation which is contrary to the authoritative Statements of the Delegation and the Viceroy issued on the 16th and the 25th of May. The Congress have made it clear that they do not accept any of the terms or the fundamentals of the Scheme but that they have agreed only to go into the Constituent Assembly and to nothing else; and that the Constituent Assembly is a sovereign body and can take such decisions as it may think proper in total disregard of the terms and the basis on which it was proposed to be set up. Subsequently this was made further clear and beyond any doubt in the speeches that were made at the meeting of the All-India Congress Committee in Bombay on the 6th of July by prominent members of the Congress and in the Statement of Pandit Jawaharlal Nehru, the President of the Congress, to a Press Conference on 10th July in Bombay and then again even after the debate in the Parliament in a public speech by him at Delhi on the 22nd of July.

The result is, that of the two major parties, Muslim League alone has accepted the Statements of May 16th and 25th according to the spirit and the letter of the proposals embodied therein and in spite of the attention of the Secretary of State for India having been drawn to this situation by the statement of the President of the Muslim League of 13th July from Hyderabad Deccan, neither Sir Stafford Cripps in the House of Commons, nor Lord Pethick-Lawrence in the House of Lords, in the course of the recent debate, have provided or suggested any means or machinery to prevent the Constituent Assembly from taking decisions which would be *ultra vires* and not competent for the Assembly to do so. The only reference that the Secretary of State made to this serious situation was a mere expression of pious hope when he stated that "that would not be fair to the other parties who go in".

Once the Constituent Assembly were summoned and met there was no provision or power that could prevent any decision from being taken by the Congress with its overwhelming majority, which would not be competent for the Assembly to take or which would be *ultra vires* of it, and however repugnant it might be to the letter or the spirit of the scheme. It would rest entirely with the majority to take such decisions as they may think proper or suit them and the Congress have already secured by sheer numbers an overwhelming Hindu-Caste majority whereby they will be in a position to use the Assembly in the manner in which they have already declared, i.e. that they will wreck the basic form of the grouping of the Provinces and extend the scope, powers and subjects of the Union Centre which is confined strictly to three specific subjects as laid down in paragraph 15 and provided for in paragraph 19 of the Statement of 16th May.

The Cabinet Delegation and the Viceroy collectively and individually have stated on more than one occasion that the basic principles were laid down to enable the major parties to join the Constituent Assembly and that the Scheme cannot succeed unless it is worked in a spirit of cooperation. The attitude of the Congress clearly shows that these conditions precedent for the successful working of the constitution-making body do not exist. This fact, taken together with the policy of the British Government of sacrificing the interests of the Muslim Nation and some other weaker sections of the peoples of India particularly the Scheduled Castes to appease the Congress and the way in which they have been going back on their oral and written solemn pledges and assurances given from time to time to the Muslims, leaves no doubt that in these circumstances the participation of the Muslims in the proposed constitution-making machinery is fraught with danger and the Council, therefore, hereby withdraws its acceptance of the Cabinet Mission's proposals which was communicated to the Secretary of State for India by the President of the Muslim League on the 6th of June 1946.

RESOLUTION NO. 2

Whereas the Council of the All-India Muslim League has resolved to reject the proposals embodied in the Statement of the Cabinet Delegation and the Viceroy, dated 16th May 1946, due to the intransigence of the Congress on one hand, and the breach of faith with the Muslims by the British Government on the other; and

Whereas Muslim India has exhausted without success all efforts to find a peaceful solution of the Indian problem by compromise and constitutional means; and

Whereas the Congress is bent upon setting up Caste-Hindu Raj in India with the connivance of the British; and

Whereas recent events have shown that power politics and not justice and fairplay are the deciding factors in Indian affairs; and

Whereas it has become abundantly clear that the Muslims of India would not rest contented with anything less than the immediate establishment of Independent and fully Sovereign State of Pakistan and would resist any attempt to impose any constitution-making machinery or any constitution, long term or short term, or the setting up of any Interim Government at the Centre without the approval and consent of the Muslim League.

The Council of the All-India Muslim League is convinced that now the time has come for the Muslim Nation to resort to Direct Action to achieve Pakistan, to assert their just rights, to vindicate their honour and to get rid of the present British slavery and the contemplated future Caste-Hindu domination.

This Council calls upon the Muslim Nation to stand to a man behind their sole representative and authoritative organisation, the All-India Muslim League, and to be ready for every sacrifice.

This Council directs the Working Committee to prepare forthwith a programme of Direct Action to carry out the policy enunciated above and to organise the Muslims for the coming struggle to be launched as and when necessary.

As a protest against and in token of their deep resentment of the attitude of the British, this Council calls upon the Musalmans to renounce forthwith the titles conferred upon them by the alien Government.

Bibliography

PRIMARY SOURCES: MANUSCRIPT SOURCES

INDIAN OFFICE LIBRARY & RECORD (IOR), LONDON

MSS Eur. Fl 15/2A&2B, Haig Collection.
MSS Eur. F128, Laithwaite Correspondence.
MSS Eur. F125, Linlithgow Collection.
MSS Eur. D609, Lord Lothian Collection.
L/P&J/8/509, Private Office Papers.
L/P&J/8690, Private Office Papers.

PUBLIC RECORD OFFICE, LONDON

AB 65(6), (7) War Cabinet Papers.
AB 89 (40) War Cabinet Papers.

BROADLAND ARCHIVES

Mountbatten Papers.

CHURCHIL COLLEGE, CAMBRIDGE

A.V. Alexander Papers, 612.
Diaries: Mission to India.

NATIONAL ARCHIVES OF INDIA, NEW DELHI

Bhulabhai Desai Papers.
Rajendra Prasad Papers.

NATIONAL GANDHI MUSEUM, NEW DELHI

Mahatma Gandhi Papers.

Nehru Memorial Museum & Library, New Delhi

AICC Papers.
Jawaharlal Nehru Papers.
K.M. Munshi Papers.
T.B. Sapru Papers.

Archives of Freedom Movement, University of Karachi

Muslim League Papers.

National Archives of Pakistan (Islamabad)

Quaid-i-Azam Papers (also available at the Quaid-i-Azam Academy, Karachi, on microfilm).

Printed Sources: Official Publications

Bengal Legislative Assembly Proceedings, vols. LXIV & LXV (Calcutta).

Government of India: *Return Showing the Results of Elections to the Central Legislative Assembly and Provisional Legislatures in 1946–47* (New Delhi, 1948).

Parliamentary Debates, House of Commons, Fifth Series, vol. 431 (London).

Punjab Legislative Assembly Debates: Official Report, vol. IV, no. 12 (Lahore, 1939).

Ahmad, Jamil-ud-din, ed., *Historic Documents of the Muslim Freedom Movement* (Lahore, 1970).

Ahmed, Waheed, ed., *Letters of Mia Fazl-i-Husain* (Lahore, 1976).

———, ed., *Quaid-i-Azam Mohammad Ali Jinnah: The Nation's Voice: Speeches and Statements*, 5 vols. (Karachi, 2002).

Aziz, K.K., ed., *Muslims under Congress Rule, 1930–39: A Documentary Record I* (Delhi, 1986).

———, *Prelude to Pakistan, 1930–40: Documents and Readings Illustrating the Growth of the Idea of Pakistan*, 2 vols. (Lahore, 1992).

Barnes, John and David Nicholson, eds., *The Empire at Bay: The Leo Amery Diaries 1929–45*, vol. II (London, 1988).

Birla, Ghanshyam Das, *Bapu: A Unique Association*, 4 vols. (Bombay, 1977).

Carter, Lionel, ed., *Mountbatten's Report on the Last Viceroyalty* (New Delhi, 2003).

———, ed., *Punjab Politics, 1940–1943, Strains of War: Governor's Fortnightly Reports and Other Documents*, (New Delhi, 2005).

Collected Works of Mahatma Gandhi, vols. LXIV–LXXXIX, *1936–1947* (New Delhi, 1982–4).

Congress Bulletin, All India Congress Committee, New Delhi, 1939–47.

Gandhi-Jinnah Talks: Text of Correspondence and Relevant Matters with a Foreword by C. Rajagopalachari (New Delhi, 1944).

Gopal, S., ed., *Selected Works of Jawaharlal Nehru*, vols. 8–15 (New Delhi, 1976–81).

————, ed., *Selected Works of Jawaharlal Nehru*, Second Series, vols. 1–3 (New Delhi, 1984–5).

Gwyer, M. and A. Appadorai, eds., *Speeches and Documents on the Indian Constitution, 1921–47*, 2 vols. (Delhi, 1957).

Iqbal, Muhammad, *Letters of Iqbal to Jinnah* (Lahore, 1974, rpt.; 1st pub. 1943).

Ismay, *Memories* (London, 1960).

Jafri, Qaim Hussain, ed., *Quaid-i-Azam's Correspondence with Punjab Muslim Leaders* (Lahore, 1977).

Jinnah-Gandhi Talks: Text of Correspondence and Other Relevant Documents With a Foreword by Nawabzada Liaquat Ali Khan (New Delhi, 1944).

Mansergh, Nicholas, ed., *Constitutional Relations Between Britain and India: The Transfer of Power 1942–47*, 12 vols. (London, 1970–83).

Mirza, Sarfaraz Husain, ed., *Muslim Students and Pakistan Movement: Select Documents 1937–47*, 3 vols. (Islamabad, 1991).

————, *The Punjab Muslim Students Federation 1937–47* (Islamabad, 1991).

Moon, Penderel, Wavel, *The Viceroy's Journal* (London, 1973).

Pirzada, Sayed Sharifuddin, ed., *Leader's Correspondence with Mr. Jinnah* (Bombay, 1944).

————, ed., *Foundations of Pakistan: All India Muslim Documents, 1906–47*, 2 vols. (Karachi, 1970).

————, ed., *Mohammad Ali Jinnah: Correspondence*, 3rd edn. (Karachi, 1977).

Prasad, Bimal, ed., *Jayaprakash Narayan: Selected Works*, vol. III (New Delhi, 2003).

Rashidi, Syed Ali Muhammad H., ed., *Report of the General Secretary of the First Sind Provincial Muslim League Conference*, 8–12 October 1938.

Rizwan, Ahmad, ed., *Quaid-i-Azam Papers 1941–42* (Karachi, 1976).

SECONDARY SOURCES: BOOKS AND ARTICLES

Ahmed, Akbar S., *Jinnah, Pakistan and Islamic Identity: The Search for Saladin* (Karachi, 1997).

———, ed., *Quaid-i-Azam Jinnah and Story of Pakistan* (Karachi, 1997).
Ahmad, Jamil-ud-din, *Creation of Pakistan* (Lahore, 1976).
———, *Speeches and Writings of Mr. Jinnah* (Lahore, 1976).
Ali, Choudhary Muhammad, *The Emergence of Pakistan* (Lahore, 1979).
Ambedkar, B.R., *Thoughts on Pakistan* (Bombay, 1941).
Ansari, Sarah, 'Political Legacies of Pre-1947 Sind', in D.A. Low, ed., *The Political Inheritance of Pakistan* (London, 1991).
Aslam, Muhammad, *The Making of the Pakistan Resolution* (Karachi, 2001).
Azad, Abul Kalam, *India's Choice* (London, 1940).
———, *India Wins Freedom: The Complete Version* (Hyderabad, 1988).
Aziz, K.K., *A History of the Idea of Pakistan*, 4 vols. (Lahore, 1987).
———, *Confederacy of India* (Lahore, 1990).
Bandopadhyaya, S.K., *Quaid-i-Azam Mohammad Ali Jinnah and the Creation of Pakistan* (New Delhi, 1991).
Bhasin, Avtar Singh, *Some Called it Partition, Some Freedom: Last 75 Days of the Raj* (New Delhi, 1998).
Bolitho, H., *Jinnah, Creator of Pakistan* (Lahore, 1954).
Burke, S.M. and S. Quraishi, *Quaid-i-Azam Mohammad Ali Jinnah: His Personality and Politics* (Karachi, 1997).
Campbell-Johnson, A., *Mission with Mountbatten* (London, 1951).
Chagla, M.C., *Roses in December* (Bombay, 1973).
Chakrabarty, Bidyut, *Politics of Accommodation and Confrontation: The Second Partition of Bengal* (New Delhi, 2003).
———, *Partition of Bengal and Assam 1932–1947: Contour of Freedom* (London, 2005).
Chatterji, Joya, *Bengal Divided: Hindu Communalism and Partition, 1934–1947* (Cambridge, 1996).
Chatterjee, Partha, *The Present History of West Bengal: Essays in Political Criticism* (Delhi, 1997).
Coupland, R., *Indian Politics 1936–1942*, 3 vols. (London, 1943).
Dani, Ahmad Husain, ed., *World Scholars on Quaid-i-Azam Mohammad Ali Jinnah*, 2 vols. (Islamabad, 1979).
———, ed., *Quaid-i-Azam Jinnah and Pakistan* (Islamabad, 1981).
Das, Durga, *India from Curzon to Nehru and After* (New York, 1971).
Dwarkadas, Kanji, *Ten Years to Freedom 1938–1947* (Bombay, 1968).
Edib, Halide, *Inside India* (London, 1937).
Gandhi, Rajmohan, *The Rajaji Story*, 2 vols. (Bombay, 1984).
———, *Eight Muslim Lives: A Study of Hindu Muslim Encounter* (New Delhi, 1985).
———, *India Wins Errors* (New Delhi, 1989).
Glendevon, John, *The Viceroy at Bay: Lord Linlithgow in India, 1936–1943* (London, 1971).
Ghose, Sudhir, *Gandhi's Emissary* (London, 1967).

Gilmartin, David, *Empire and Islam: Punjab and the Making of Pakistan* (Delhi, 1989).

———, 'Religious Leadership and the Pakistan, Movement in the Punjab', *Modern Asian Studies*, 13, 3.

Gopal, S., *Jawaharlal Nehru: A Biography*, 3 vols., vol. I (London, 1975).

Gupta, Amit Kumar, *North West Frontier Legislature and Freedom Struggle, 1932–1947* (New Delhi, 1976).

———, ed., *Myth and Reality: The Struggle for Freedom in India 1945–47* (New Delhi, 1976).

Hamid, Saiyida Saiyidain, ed., *Zakir Husain: Teacher Who Became President* (New Delhi, 2000).

Hasan, K. Sarvar, ed., *The Transfer of Power: Documents on the Foreign Relations of Pakistan* (Karachi, 1966).

Hasan, Khalid Shamsul, ed., *Sindh's Fight for Pakistan: Rifts, Betrayals and Triumphs* (Karachi, 1992).

Hasan, Mushirul, *Islam in the Subcontinent: Muslims in a Plural Society* (New Delhi, 2002).

———, ed., *India's Partition: Process, Strategy and Mobilization* (Delhi, 1993).

———, 'The Muslim Mass Contact Campaign: Analysis of a Strategy of Political Mobilization', Richard Session et al., *Congress and Indian Nationalism* (Berkeley, 1988).

Hasan, Syed Shamsul, . . . *Plain Mr. Jinnah* (Karachi, 1976).

Hasan, Syed Zafarul and Mohammad Afzal Qadri, *The Problem of Indian Muslims and its Solution* (Aligarh, n.d.).

Hashim, Abul, *In Retrospection* (Dacca, 1974).

Hodson, H.V., *The Great Divide* (London, 1969).

Huq, A.K. Fazlul, *Bengal Today* (Calcutta, 1944).

Husain, Mahmud, 'Dacca University and the Pakistan Movement', in C.H. Philips and Ian Bryant Wells, *Ambassador of Hindu-Muslim Unity: Jinnah's Early Politics* (New Delhi, 2005).

Jalal, Ayesha, *The Sole Spokesman: Jinnah, the Muslim League and the Demand for Pakistan* (Cambridge, 1985).

———, *Self and Sovereignty: Individual and Community in South Asian Islam Since 1850* (London, 2000).

Jansson, Erland, *India, Pakistan or Pakhtunistan: The Nationalist Movement in North-West Frontier Province, 1937–1947* (Uppasala, 1981).

Johnson, Alan Campbell, *Mission with Mountbatten* (London, 1951).

Kaura, Uma, *Muslims and Indian Nationalism 1928–40* (New Delhi, 1977).

Khaliquzzaman, Choudhary, *Pathway to Pakistan* (London, 1961).

Khan, Aga, *The Memories of Aga Khan* (London, 1954).

Khan, Sikander Hyat, *Outlines of a Scheme of Indian Federation* (Lahore, n.d.).

Khan, Wali, *Facts are Facts: The Untold Story of Indian Partition* (New Delhi, 1987).

Khurshid, K.H., *Memories of Jinnah* (Karachi, 1990).
Latif, Syed Abdul, *The Cultural Future of India* (Bombay, 1938).
———, *The Muslim Problem in India* (Bombay, 1939).
Low, D.A., ed., *The Political Inheritance of Pakistan* (London, 1991).
Majumdar, S.K., *Jinnah and Gandhi* (Calcutta, 1966).
Malik, H., *Iqbal: Poet Philosopher of Pakistan* (New York, 1971).
Malik, Muhammad Aslam, *The Making of the Pakistan Resolution* (Karachi, 2001).
Menon, V.P., *The Transfer of Power in India* (Princeton, 1957).
Mirza, Humayun, *From Plassey to Pakistan: The Family History of Iskander Mirza, the First President of Pakistan* (New York, 1999).
Moon, Penderel, *Divide and Quit* (London, 1945).
Moore, R.J., *The Crisis of Indian Unity, 1917–1940* (Oxford, 1947).
———, *Churchil, Cripps and India, 1939–1945* (Oxford, 1979).
———, *Escape from Empire* (London, 1983).
Pal, J.J., *Jinnah and the Creation of Pakistan* (Delhi, 1983).
Panigrahi, D.N., *India's Partition: The Story of Imperialism in Retreat* (London, 2004).
Philips, C.H. and Mary Doreen Wainwright, eds., *The Partition of India: Politics and Perspectives* (London, 1970).
Prasad, Bimal, *Pathway to India's Partition*, vols. I and II (New Delhi, 1999–2000).
———, 'The Emergence of the Demand for India's Partition', *International Studies*, vol. 9, no. 3, January 1968.
———, 'M.A. Jinnah and the Making of Pakistan', A Review Article, *International Studies*, vol. 21, no. 3, 1982.
———, 'Gandhi and India's Partition', in Amit Kumar Gupta, ed., *Myth and Reality: The Struggle for Freedom in India 1945–47* (New Delhi, 1987).
———, 'Congress and Muslim League 1935–37', in Richard Sisson and Stanley Wolpert, eds., *Congress and Indian Nationalism* (Berkeley, 1988).
———, 'Jawaharlal Nehru and Partition', in Amrik Singh, ed., *The Partition in Retrospect* (New Delhi, 2000).
———, 'Zakir Husain's Correspondence with Mahatma Gandhi', in Saiyida Saiyidain Hamid, ed., *Zakir Husain: Teacher Who Became President* (New Delhi, 2000).
Prasad, Rajendra, *India Divided* (Bombay, 1946).
Pyarelal, *Mahatma Gandhi: The Last Phase*, 2 vols. (Ahmedabad, 1955).
Qureshi, I.H., *Struggle for Pakistan* (Karachi, 1962).
Qureshi, Saleem M.M., *Jinnah and Making of a Nation* (Karachi, 1969).
Raza, S. Hasim, ed., *Mountbatten and Pakistan* (Karachi, 1982).

Rittenberg, Stephen Alan, 'The Independence Movement in India's North-West Frontier Province, 1937–1947', Ph.D. thesis, Columbia University, 1977.

Rizvi, Gowher, *Linlithgow and India: A Study of British Policy and the Political Impasse in India, 1936–1943* (London, 1978).

Saiyid, M.H., ed., *India's Problem of the Future Constitution* (Bombay, n.d.).

————, *Political Study of Mohammad Ali Jinnah* (Lahore, 1945).

Sen, Shiela, *Muslim Politics in Bengal* (New Delhi, 1976).

Seervai, H.M., *Partition of India: Legend and Reality* (Bombay, 1989).

Shah, Syed Waqat Ali, *Muslim League in N.W.F.P.* (Karachi, 1992).

Sheikh, Atique Z. and M.R. Malki, eds., *Quaid-i-Azam and the Muslim World: Selected Documents* (Karachi, 1978).

Siddiqui, Muhammad Ali, ed., *Quaid-i-Azam Jinnah: A Chronology* (Karachi, 1996).

Singh, Amrik, ed., *Partition in Retrospect* (New Delhi, 2000).

Singh, Anita Inder, *The Origins of the Partition of India, 1936-1947* (Delhi, 1987).

Singh, Tarlok, 'Three Windows for the Partition of India', *IASSI Quarterly*, vol. 9, no. 3, 1991.

Suleri, Zia-ud-din Ahmad, *My Leader: Being an Estimate of Mr. Jinnah's Work for Indian Mussalmans* (Lahore, 1945).

Talbot, Ian, *Punjab and the Raj, 1849-1947* (New Delhi, 1988).

————, *Provincial Politics and the Pakistan Movement* (Karachi, 1988).

Tinker, H.R., *Experiment with Freedom* (London, 1967).

Tirmizi, S.A.I., ed., *The Paradoxes of Partition*, vol. I, *1937-1939* (New Delhi, 1998).

Tuker, Francis, *While Memory Serves* (London, 1950).

Wolpert, Stanley, *Jinnah of Pakistan* (Delhi, 1998).

Wolpert, Stanley and Richard Sission, eds., *Congress and Indian Nationalism: The Pre-Independence Phase* (Delhi, 1988).

Zaidi, A.M. and S.G. Zaidi, *The Encyclopaedia of the Indian National Congress*, vol. XII (New Delhi, 1958).

Zaidi, Z.H., ed., *M.A. Jinnah–Isphani Correspondence 1936-1948* (Karachi, 1976).

Zakaria, Rafiq, *The Man Who Divided India: An Insight into Jinnah's Leadership and its Aftermath* (Mumbai, 2001).

Zamam, Mukhtar, *Students Role in the Pakistan Movement* (Karachi

Zetland, Lord, *The Memories of Lawrence: Second Marquess of Zetland* (London, 1956).

Ziring, Lawrence, 'Jinnah: The Burden of Leadership', in Ahmad Hasan Dani, ed., *World Scholars on Quaid-i-Azam, Mohammad Ali Jinnah* (Islamabad, 1979).

NEWSPAPERS AND JOURNALS

Civil and Military Gazette
Dawn
Harijan
Hindustan Times
Modern Asian Studies
New Statesman
Statesman
Times
Times of India

Index